Lecture Notes in Artificial Int

Subseries of Lecture Notes in Compute
Edited by J. G. Carbonell and J. Siekma...

Lecture Notes in Computer Science

Edited by G. Goos, J. Hartmanis and J. van Leeuwen

Springer

Berlin
Heidelberg
New York
Barcelona
Hong Kong
London
Milan
Paris
Tokyo

Thomas Eiter   Wolfgang Faber
Miros law Truszczyński (Eds.)

Logic Programming and Nonmonotonic Reasoning

6th International Conference, LPNMR 2001
Vienna, Austria, September 17-19, 2001
Proceedings

 Springer

Series Editors

Jaime G. Carbonell,Carnegie Mellon University, Pittsburgh, PA, USA
Jörg Siekmann, University of Saarland, Saarbrücken, Germany

Volume Editors

Thomas Eiter
Wolfgang Faber
Vienna University of Technology, Institut für Informationssysteme
1040 Wien, Austria
E-mail:{eiter,faber}@kr.tuwien.ac.at

Miros law Truszczyński
University of Kentucky, Department of Computer Science
Lexington, KY 40506-0046, USA
E-mail: mirek@cs.uky.edu

Cataloging-in-Publication Data applied for

Die Deutsche Bibliothek - CIP-Einheitsaufnahme

Logic programming and nonmonotonic reasoning : 6th international conference ;
proceedings / LPNMR 2001, Vienna, Austria, September 17 - 19, 2001.
Thomas Eiter ... (ed.). - Berlin ; Heidelberg ; New York ; Barcelona ; Hong Kong ;
London ; Milan ; Paris ; Tokyo : Springer, 2001
  (Lecture notes in computer science ; Vol. 2173 : Lecture notes in
  artificial intelligence)
ISBN 3-540-42593-4

CR Subject Classification (1998): I.2.3, I.2, F.4.1, D.1.6

ISBN 3-540-42593-4 Springer-Verlag Berlin Heidelberg New York

Springer-Verlag Berlin Heidelberg New York
a member of BertelsmannSpringer Science+Business Media GmbH

http://www.springer.de

© Springer-Verlag Berlin Heidelberg 2001
Printed in Germany

Typesetting: Camera-ready by author, data conversion by DATeX Gerd Blumenstein
Printed on acid-free paper   SPIN 10840410   06/3142   5 4 3 2 1 0

Conference Organization

Program Co-chairs

Thomas Eiter (Vienna University of Technology, Austria)
Mirosław Truszczyński (University of Kentucky, USA)

Program Committee

Alexander Bochman (Holon Academic Institute of Technology, Israel)
Piero Bonatti (Università degli Studi Milano/Crema, Italy)
Gerhard Brewka (University of Leipzig, Germany)
James Delgrande (Simon Fraser University, Canada)
Marc Denecker (Katholieke Universiteit Leuven, Belgium)
Norman Foo (University of New South Wales, Australia)
Michael Gelfond (Texas Tech University, USA)
Katsumi Inoue (Kobe University, Japan)
Antonis Kakas (University of Cyprus)
Nicola Leone (Università degli Studi della Calabria, Italy)
Vladimir Lifschitz (University of Texas at Austin, USA)
Fangzhen Lin (The Hong Kong University of Science and Technology, China)
Victor Marek (University of Kentucky at Lexington, USA)
Zhang Ming-Yi (Guizhou Academy of Sciences, China)
Ilkka Niemelä (Helsinki University of Technology, Finland)
Luís Moniz Pereira (Universidade Nova de Lisboa, Portugal)
Marco Schaerf (Università di Roma "La Sapienza," Italy)
Torsten Schaub (University of Potsdam, Germany)
Francesca Toni (Imperial College, London, U.K.)
Li-Yan Yuan (University of Alberta, Canada)

Publicity Chair

Wolfgang Faber (Vienna University of Technology, Austria)

Additional Reviewers

José Alferes
Cristina Baroglio
Krysia Broda
Maurice Bruynooghe
Francesco Buccafurri
Carlos Damásio
Emmanuel De Mot
Yannis Dimopoulos
Esra Erdem
Wolfgang Faber
Daya Gaur
Jens Happe
Tomi Janhunen
Joohyung Lee
Nicola Leone
Thomas Linke
Thomas Lukasiewicz
Paolo Mancarella
Cristinel Mateis
Rob Miller

Mehmet Orgun
Maurice Pagnucco
Viviana Patti
Nikolay Pelov
Gerald Pfeifer
Fabrizio Riguzzi
Riccardo Rosati
Giuliana Sabbatini
Fariba Sadri
Chiaki Sakama
Francesco Scarcello
Tommi Syrjänen
Andrea Tettamanzi
Bert Van Nuffelen
Helmut Veith
Gerard Vreeswijk
Kewen Wang
Jia-Huai You
Dongmo Zhang

Sponsoring Institutions

We would like to acknowledge financial support for the conference from the European Office of Aerospace Research and Development (EOARD), under contract F61775-01-WF077, the Austrian Computer Society (OCG), the European Commission, the Austrian Ministry of Transport, Innovation & Technology, and Microsoft.

Preface

These are the proceedings of the *Sixth International Conference on Logic Programming and Nonmonotonic Reasoning* (LPNMR 2001). The conference was held in Vienna from 17th to 19th of September, 2001. It was collocated with the Joint German/Austrian Conference on Artificial Intelligence (24th German/9th Austrian Conference on Artificial Intelligence), KI 2001.

LPNMR conferences aim to promote research in logic-based programming languages, database systems, nonmonotonic reasoning, and knowledge representation. LPNMR 2001 was the sixth conference in the series. The previous meetings were held in Washington, DC, in 1991, in Lisbon, Portugal, in 1993, in Lexington, Kentucky, in 1995, in Dagstuhl, Germany, in 1997, and in El Paso, Texas, in 1999.

The technical program of LPNMR 2001 was comprised of five invited talks that were given by Jürgen Dix, Georg Gottlob, Phokion Kolaitis, Maurizio Lenzerini, and Chiaki Sakama. It also contained 23 technical presentations selected by the program committee during a rigorous review process. Finally, as a part of the technical program, the conference featured a special session comprised of nine presentations and demonstrations of implemented nonmonotonic reasoning systems. All these contributions are included in the proceedings.

Many individuals worked for the success of the conference. Special thanks are due to all members of the program committee and to additional reviewers for their efforts to produce fair and thorough evaluations of submitted papers. Furthermore, we would like to thank the members of the Knowledge Based Systems Group of the Vienna University of Technology, which took care of the local organization. We particularly appreciated the never tiring effort of Elfriede Nedoma, secretary to the group. We would also like to thank Gerd Brewka for his supportive role in arranging the collocation of the conference with KI 2001. Last, but not least, we thank the sponsoring institutions for their generosity.

September 2001

Thomas Eiter
Wolfgang Faber
Mirosław Truszczyński

Table of Contents

System Descriptions

A Computational Logic Approach to Heterogenous Agent Systems

Jürgen Dix *

The University of Manchester, Dept. of CS
Oxford Road, Manchester M13 9PL, UK
dix@cs.man.ac.uk
http://www.cs.man.ac.uk/~jdix

Abstract. I report about a particular approach to heterogenous agent systems, IMPACT, which is strongly related to computational logic. The underlying methods and techniques stem from both non-monotonic reasoning and logic programming. I present three recent extensions to illustrate the generality and usefulness of the approach: (1) incorporating planning, (2) uncertain (probabilistic) reasoning, and (3) reducing the load of serving multiple requests. While (1) illustrates how easy it is to incorporate *hierachical task networks* into IMPACT, (2) makes heavily use of *annotated logic programming* and (3) is strongly related to *classical first-order reasoning*. This paper is a high-level description of (1)–(3), More detailed expositions can be found in [1,2,3,4] from which most parts of this paper are taken.

1   The Basic Framework

The *IMPACT* project (http://www.cs.umd.edu/projects/impact) aims at developing a powerful multi agent system, which (1) is able to deal with heterogenous and distributed data, (2) can be realized on top of arbitrary legacy code, but yet (3) is built on a clear foundational bases and (4) scales up for realistic applications.

In this article I am pointing to some recent extensions of the basic framework (which has been implemented and is running) that show very clearly the strong links to computational logic, even though *IMPACT*'s implementation is not realized on top of a logic related procedural mechanism.

To get a bird's eye view of *IMPACT*, here are the most important features:

- Each *IMPACT* agent has certain *actions* available. Agents act in their environment according to their *agent program* and a well defined *semantics* determining which of the actions the agent should execute.
- Each agent continually undergoes the following cycle:

---

* The work I am reporting has been done with many colleagues, notably Th. Eiter, S. Kraus, K. Munoz-Avila, M. Nanni, D. Nau, F. Özcan, T.J. Rogers, R. Ross and, last but not least, V.S Subrahmanian. It resulted in a variety of papers and I gratefully acknowledge their support.

T. Eiter, W. Faber, and M. Truszczyński (Eds.): LPNMR 2001, LNAI 2173, pp. 1–21, 2001.

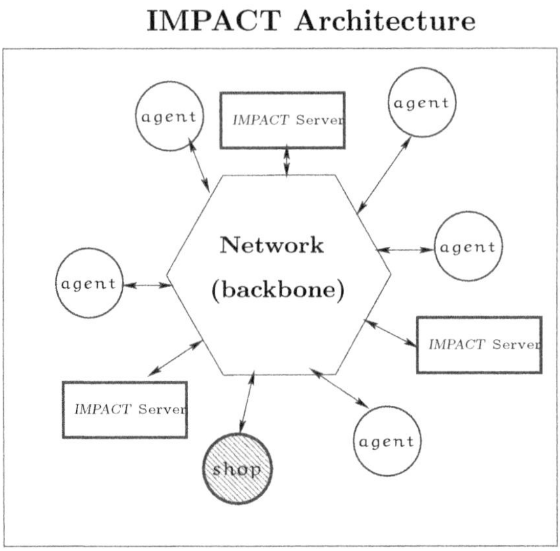

IMPACT Architecture

Fig. 1. SHOP as a planning agent in *IMPACT*

(1) Get messages by other agents. This changes the state of the agent.
(2) Determine (based on its program, its semantics and its state) for each action its *status* (permitted, obliged, forbidden, . . .). The agent ends up with a *set of status atoms*.
(3) Based on a notion of concurrency, determine the actions that can be executed and update the state accordingly.
- *IMPACT* Agents are built on top of arbitrary software code (*Legacy Data*).
- A methodology for transforming arbitrary software (legacy code) into an *agent* has been developed.

A complete description of all these notions is out of scope of this paper and we refer to [3] for a detailed presentation.

Before explaining an agent in more detail, we need to make some comments about the general architecture. In *IMPACT* agents communicate with other agents through the network. Not only can they send out (and receive) messages from other agents, they can also ask the server to find out about services that other agents offer. For example a planning agent (let us call it A-SHOP), confronted with a particular planning problem, can find out if there are agents out there with the data needed to solve the planning problem; or agents can provide A-SHOP with information about relevant legacy data.

One of the main features of *IMPACT* is to provide a method (see [3]) for *agentizing* arbitrary legacy code, i.e. to turn such legacy code into an agent. In order to do this, we need to abstract from the given code and describe its main features. Such an abstraction is given by the set of all datatypes and functions the software is managing. We call this a *body of software code* and denote it by

$\mathcal{S} = (\mathcal{T}_{\mathcal{S}}, \mathcal{F}_{\mathcal{S}})$. $\mathcal{F}_{\mathcal{S}}$ is a set of predefined functions which makes access to the data objects managed by the agent available to external processes.

For example, in many applications a statistics agent is needed. This agent keeps track of distances between two given points and the authorized range or capacity of certain vehicules. These information can be stored in several databases. Another example is the supplier agent. It determines through its databases which vehicles are accessible at a given location.

Definition 1 (State of an Agent, $\mathcal{O}_{\mathcal{S}}(t)$). *At any given point t in time, the state of an agent, denoted $\mathcal{O}_{\mathcal{S}}(t)$, is the set of all data objects that are currently stored in the relations the agent handles—the types of these objects must be in the base set of types in $\mathcal{T}_{\mathcal{S}}$.*

In the examples just mentioned, the state of the statistics agent consists of all tuples stored in the databases it handles. The state of the supplier agent is the set of all tuples describing which vehicles are accessible at a given location.

We noted that agents can send and receive messages. There is therefore a special datastructure, the *message box*, part of each agent. This message box is just one of those types. Thus a state change occurs already when a message is received.

1.1   The Code Call Machinery

To perform logical reasoning on top of third party data structures (which are part of the agent's state) and code, the agent must have a language within which it can reason about the agent state. We therefore introduce the concept of a *code call atom*, which is the basic syntactic object used to access multiple heterogeneous data sources.

Definition 2 (Code Calls (cc)). *Suppose $\mathcal{S} =_{def} (\mathcal{T}_{\mathcal{S}}, \mathcal{F}_{\mathcal{S}})$ is some software code, $f \in \mathcal{F}_{\mathcal{S}}$ is a predefined function with n arguments, and $d_1, \ldots, d_n$ are objects or variables such that each d_i respects the type requirements of the i'th argument of f. Then, $\mathcal{S}:f(d_1, \ldots, d_n)$ is a code call. A code call is ground if all the d_i's are objects.*

We often identify software code $\mathcal{S}$ with the agent that is built on top of it. This is because an agent really is uniquely determined by it.

A code call executes an *API* function and returns as output a set of objects of the appropriate output type. Going back to our two agents introduced above, statistics may be able to execute the cc statistics: *distance*(locFrom, locTo). The supplier agent may execute the following cc:
supplier: *cargoPlane*(locFrom).

What we really need to know is if the result of evaluating such code calls is contained in a certain set or not. To do this, we introduce code call atoms. These are *logical atoms* that are layered on top of code calls. They are defined through the following inductive definition.

A Single *agent*

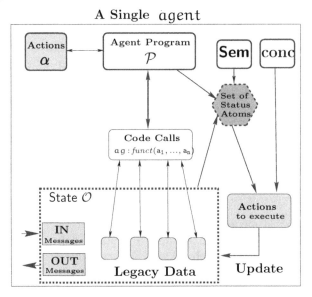

Fig. 2. An Agent in *IMPACT*

Definition 3 (Code Call Atoms (in(X, cc))). *If* cc *is a code call, and* X *is either a variable symbol, or an object of the output type of* cc*, then* **in**(X, cc) *and* **not_in**(X, cc) *are code call atoms.* **not_in**(X, cc) *succeeds if X is **not** in the set of objects returned by the code call cc.*

Code call atoms, when evaluated, return boolean values, and thus may be thought of as special types of logical atoms. Intuitively, a code call atom of the form **in**(X, cc) succeeds if X can be set to a pointer to one of the objects in the set of objects returned by executing the code call.

As an example, the code call atom

in($f22$, supplier : *cargoPlane*(collegepark)) tells us that the particular plane "$f22$" is available as a cargo plane in College Park.

Often, the results of evaluating code calls give us back certain values that we can compare. Based on such comparisons, certain actions might be fired or not. To this end, we need to define *code call conditions*. Intuitively, a code call condition is a conjunction of code call atoms, equalities, and inequalities. Equalities, and inequalities can be seen as additional syntax that "links" together variables occurring in the atomic code calls.

Definition 4 (Code Call Conditions (ccc)).

1. *Every code call atom is a code call condition.*
2. *If* s, t *are either variables or objects, then* s $=$ t *is a code call condition.*
3. *If* s, t *are either integer/real valued objects, or are variables over the integers/reals, then* s $<$ t, s $>$ t, s $\geq$ t, s $\leq$ t *are code call conditions.*
4. *If* χ_1, χ_2 *are code call conditions, then* χ_1 & χ_2 *is a code call condition.*

A code call condition satisfying any of the first three criteria above is an atomic *code call condition.*

1.2 Agent Programs and Semantics

We are now coming to the very heart of the definition of an agent: its *agent program*. Such a program consists of rules of the form:

$$\mathsf{Op}\alpha(t_1, \ldots, t_m) \leftarrow \mathsf{Op}_1\beta_1(\ldots), \ldots, \mathsf{Op}_n\beta_n(\ldots),$$
$$ccc_1, \ldots, ccc_r,$$

where $\alpha, \beta_1, \ldots \beta_n$ are *actions* (the agent can execute), $\mathsf{Op}_1, \ldots, \mathsf{Op}_n$ describe the status of the action (*obliged, forbidden, waived, doable*) and ccc_i are code call conditions to be evaluated in the actual state.

Thus, Op_i are operators that take actions as arguments. They describe the status of the arguments they take. Here are some examples of actions: (1) to load some cargo from a certain location, (2) to fly a plane from a certain location to another location, (3) to unload some cargo from a certain location. The action status atom **F** *load* (resp. **Do** *fly*) means that the action *load* is forbidden (resp. *fly* should be done). Actions themselves are terms, only with an operator in front of them they become atoms.

In *IMPACT*, actions are very much like STRIPS operators: they have preconditions and add and delete-lists (see appendix). The difference to STRIPS is that these preconditions and lists consist of *arbitrary code call conditions*, not just of logical atoms.

Figure 2 illustrates that the agent program together with the chosen semantics SEM and the state of the agent determines the set of all status atoms. However, the doable actions among them might be conflicting and therefore we have to use the chosen concurrrency notion to finally determine which actions can be concurrently executed. The agent then executes these actions and changes its state.

1.3 Evaluability of ccc's

Code call conditions provide a simple, but powerful language syntax to access heterogeneous data structures and legacy software code. However, in general their use in agent programs is not limited. In particular, it is possible that a ccc can not be evaluated (and thus the status of actions can not be determined) simply because there are uninstantiated variables and thus the underlying functions can not be executed. Here is a simple example.

Example 1 (Sample ccc). The code call condition

in(FinanceRec, rel : *select*(*financeRel, date*, "=", "11/15/99")) &
FinanceRec.sales $\geq 10K$ &
in(C, excel : *chart*(*excelFile*, FinanceRec, *day*)) &
in(Slide, ppt : *include*(C, "presentation.ppt"))

is a complex condition that accesses and merges data across a relational database, an Excel file, and a PowerPoint file. It first selects all financial records associated

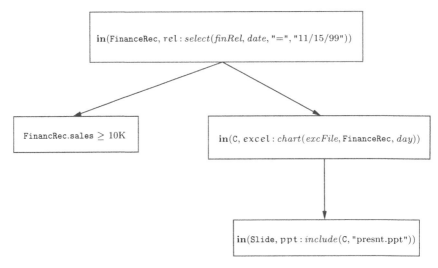

Fig. 3. A code call evaluation graph (cceg)

with "11/15/99": this is done with the variable `FinanceRec` in the first line. It then filters out those records having sales more than $10K$ (second line). Using the remaining records, an Excel chart is created with day of sale on the x-axis and the resulting chart is included in the PowerPoint file "presentation.ppt" (fourth line).

In the above example, it is very important that the first code call be evaluable. If $finance Rel$ were a variable, then $rel : select($`FinanceRel`$, date,"=","11/15/99")$ would not be evaluable, unless there were another condition instantiating this variable.

We have introduced syntactic conditions, similar to *safety* in classical databases, to ensure evaluability of ccc's. It is also quite easy to store ccc's as evaluation graphs (see Figure 3), thereby making explicit the dependency relation between its constituents (see [4]). It is, however, still perfectly possible that the execution of a code call does not terminate and we have to add another condition to ensure termination (see Subsection 2.3).

2   Planning

In this section we show how an HTN planning system, SHOP, can be integrated to the *IMPACT* multi-agent environment. We define the A-SHOP algorithm, an agentized adaptation of the original SHOP planning algorithm ([5]) that takes advantage of *IMPACT*'s capabilities for interacting with external agents, performing mixed symbolic/numeric computations, and making queries to distributed, heterogeneous information sources (such as arbitrary legacy and/or specialized data structures or external databases). We also show that A-SHOP is both sound and complete if certain conditions (related to evaluability and termination of the underlying code calls) are met.

2.1   HTN Planning

Rather than giving a detailed description of the kind of HTN planning used by SHOP ([5]), we consider the following example taken from [2].

In order to do planning in a given planning domain, SHOP needs to be given knowledge about that domain. SHOP's knowledge base contains *operators* and *methods*. Each operator is a description of what needs to be done to accomplish some primitive task, and each method is a prescription for how to decompose some complex task into a totally ordered sequence of subtasks, along with various restrictions that must be satisfied in order for the method to be applicable.

Given the next task to accomplish, SHOP chooses an applicable method, instantiates it to decompose the task into subtasks, and then chooses and instantiates other methods to decompose the subtasks even further. If the constraints on the subtasks prevent the plan from being feasible, SHOP will backtrack and try other methods.

As an example, Figure 4 shows two methods for the task of traveling from one location to another: *travelling by air*, and *travelling by taxi*. Travelling by air involves the subtasks of purchasing a plane ticket, travelling to the local airport, flying to an airport close to our destination, and travelling from there to our destination. Travelling by taxi involves the subtasks of *calling a taxi, riding in it to the final destination*, and *paying the driver*.

Note that each method's preconditions are not used to create subgoals (as would be done in action-based planning). Rather, they are used to determine whether or not the method is applicable: thus in Figure 4, the *travel by air* method is only applicable for long distances, and the *travel by taxi* method is only applicable for short distances.

Here are some of the complications that can arise during the planning process:

- The planner may need to recognize and resolve interactions among the subtasks. For example, in planning how to travel to the airport, one needs to make sure one will arrive at the airport in time to catch the plane. To make the example in Figure 4 more realistic, such information would need to be specified as part of SHOP's methods and operators.

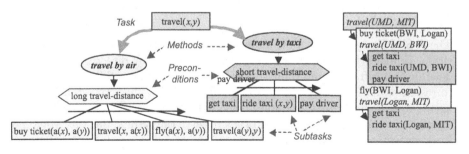

Fig. 4. Travel planning example

– In the example in Figure 4, it was always obvious which method to use. But in general, more than one method may be applicable to a task. If it is not possible to solve the subtasks produced by one method, SHOP will backtrack and try another method instead.

2.2   Agentization of SHOP

A comparison between *IMPACT*'s actions and SHOP's methods shows that *IMPACT* actions correspond to fully instantiated methods, i.e. no subtasks. While SHOP's methods and operators are based on STRIPS, the first step is to modify the atoms in SHOP's preconditions and effects, so that SHOP's preconditions will be evaluated by *IMPACT*'s code call mechanism and the effects will change the state of the *IMPACT* agents. This is a fundamental change in the representation of SHOP. In particular, it requires replacing SHOP's methods and operators with *agentized* methods and operators. These are defined as follows.

Definition 5 (Agentized Method: (AgentMeth $h \chi t$)). *An* agentized method *is an expression of the form* **(AgentMeth** $h \chi t$**)** *where* h *(the method's* head*) is a compound task,* χ *(the method's* preconditions*) is a code call condition and* t *is a totally ordered list of subtasks, called the* task list.

The primary difference between definition of an agentized method and the definition of a method in SHOP is as follows. In SHOP, preconditions were logical atoms, and SHOP would infer these preconditions from its current state of the world using Horn-clause inference. In contrast, the preconditions in an agentized method are *IMPACT*'s code call conditions rather than logical atoms, and A-SHOP (the agentized version of SHOP defined in the next section) does not use Horn-clause inference to establish these preconditions but instead simply invokes those code calls, which are calls to other agents (which may be Horn-clause theorem provers or may instead be something entirely different).

Definition 6 (Agentized Operator: (AgentOp $h \chi_{add} \chi_{del}$)). *An* agentized operator *is an expression of the form* **(AgentOp** $h \chi_{add} \chi_{del}$**)**, *where* h *(the* head*) is a primitive task and* χ_{add} *and* χ_{del} *are lists of code calls (called the* add- *and* delete-lists*). The set of variables in the tasks in* χ_{add} *and* χ_{del} *is a subset of the set of variables in* h.

The Algorithm

The A-SHOP algorithm is now an easy adaptation of the original SHOP algorithm. Unlike SHOP (which would apply an operator by directly inserting and deleting atoms from an internally-maintained state of the world), A-SHOP needs to reason about how the code calls in an operator will affect the states of other agents. One might think the simplest way to do this would be simply to tell these agents to execute the code calls and then observe the results, but this would not work correctly. Once the planning process has ended successfully, A-SHOP will

---

procedure *A-SHOP*($\mathbf{t}, \mathcal{D}$)
   1. **if** $\mathbf{t} = nil$ **then return** *nil*
   2. $t :=$ the first task in $\mathbf{t}$; $R :=$ the remaining tasks
   3. **if** t is primitive and a simple plan for t exists **then**
   4. $q := simplePlan(t)$
   5.   **return** $concatenate(q, \text{A-SHOP}(R, \mathcal{D}))$
   6. **else if** t is non-prim. $\wedge$ there is a reduction of t **then**
   7.   **nondeterministically** choose a reduction:
        Nondeterministically choose an agentized method,
        (**AgentMeth** $h \chi t$), with μ the most general
        unifier of h and t and substitution θ s.t.
        $\chi\mu\theta$ is ground and holds in *IMPACT*'s state $\mathcal{O}$.
   8.   **return** *A-SHOP*($concatenate(t\mu\theta, R), \mathcal{D}$)
   9. **else return** *FAIL*
  10. **end if**
end *A-SHOP*

procedure $simplePlan(t)$
  11. **nondeterministically** choose agent. operator
       $op = (\mathbf{AgentOp}\ h\ \chi_{add}\ \chi_{del})$ with ν the most
       general unifier of h and t s.t. h is ground
  12. monitoring : $apply(op\,\nu)$
  13. **return** $op\,\nu$
end *A-SHOP*

Fig. 5. A-SHOP, the agentized version of SHOP

return a plan whose operators can be applied to modify the states of the other *IMPACT* agents—but A-SHOP should not change the states of those agents during its planning process because this would prevent A-SHOP from backtracking and trying other operators.

Thus in Step 12, SHOP does not issue code calls to the other agents directly, but instead communicates them to a monitoring agent. The monitoring agent keeps track of all operators that are supposed to be applied, without actually modifying the states of the other *IMPACT* agents. When A-SHOP queries for a code call $cc = \mathcal{S} : f(\mathbf{d}_1, \ldots, \mathbf{d}_n)$ in χ to evaluate a method's precondition (Step 7), the monitoring agent examines if cc has been affected by the intended modifications of the operators and, if so, it evaluates cc. If cc is not affected by application of operations, *IMPACT* evaluates cc (i.e., by accessing $\mathcal{S}$). The list of operators maintained by the monitoring agent is reset everytime a planning process begins. The *apply* function applies the operators and creates copies of the state of the world. Depending on the underlying software code, these changes might be easily revertible or not. In the latter case, the monitoring agent has to keep track of the old state of the world.

2.3   Finite Evaluability of ccc's and Completeness of **A-SHOP**

An important question for any planning algorithm is whether all solution plans produced by the algorithm are correct (i.e., soundness of the algorithm) and whether the algorithm will find solutions for solvable problems (i.e., completeness of the algorithm). Soundness and completeness proofs of classical planners assume that the preconditions can be evaluated relative to the current state. In SHOP, for example, the state is accessed to test whether a method is applicable, by examining whether the method's preconditions are valid in the current state. Normally it is easy to guarantee the ability to evaluate preconditions, because the states typically are lists of predicates that are locally accessible to the planner. However, if these lists of predicates are replaced by code call conditions, this is no longer the case.

We mentioned in Subsection 1.3 the condition of safeness to ensure evaluability of a code call. We also mentioned that an evaluable cc does not need to terminate. Consider the code call

$$\mathbf{in}(X, \mathrm{math}\!:\! geq(25)) \,\&$$
$$\mathbf{in}(Y, \mathrm{math}\!:\! square(X)) \,\&\, Y \le 2000,$$

which constitutes all numbers that are less than 2000 and that are squares of an integer greater than or equal to 25.

Clearly, over the integers there are only finitely many ground substitutions that cause this code call condition to be true. Furthermore, this code call condition is safe. However, its evaluation may never terminate. The reason for this is that safety requires that we first compute the set of all integers that are greater than 25, leading to an infinite computation.

Thus in general, we must impose some restrictions on code call conditions to ensure that they are finitely evaluable. This is precisely what the condition of strongly safeness ([6,3]) does for the code-call conditions. Intuitively, by requiring that the code call condition is safe, we are ensuring that it is executable and by requiring that it is strongly safe, we are ensuring that it will only return finitely many answers.

Note that the problem of deciding whether an arbitrary code call execution terminates is undecidable (and so is the problem of deciding whether a code call condition χ holds in $\mathcal{O}$). Therefore we need some input of the agent designer (or of the person who is responsible for the legacy code the agent is built upon). The information needed is stored in a *finiteness table* (see [6,3]). This information is used in the *purely syntactic* notion of strong safeness. It is a *compile-time check*, an extension of the well-known (syntactic) safety condition in databases.

Lemma 1 (Evaluating Agentized Operators). *Let (**AgentMeth** $h\,\chi\,\mathbf{t}$) an agentized method, $\mathcal{O}$ a state, and (**AgentOp** $h'\,\chi_{add}\,\chi_{del}$) an agentized operator. If the precondition χ is strongly safe wrt. the variables in h, the problem of deciding whether χ holds in $\mathcal{O}$ can be algorithmically solved. If the add and delete-lists χ_{add} and χ_{del} are strongly safe wrt. the variables in h', the problem of applying the agentized operator to $\mathcal{O}$ can be algorithmically solved.*

Theorem 1 (Soundness, Completeness). *Let $\mathcal{O}$ be a state and $\mathcal{D}$ be a collection of agentized methods and operators. If all the preconditions in the agentized methods and add and delete-lists in the agentized operators are strongly safe wrt. the respective variables in the heads, then* A-SHOP *is correct and complete.*

3 Probabilistic Reasoning

Up to now our framework of agent programs does not allow us to reason about uncertain information. Consider a code call of the form $d : f(\text{args})$. This code call returns a set of objects. If an object o is returned by such a code call, then this means that o is *definitely* in the result of evaluating $d : f(\text{args})$.

However, there are many cases, particularly in applications involving reasoning about knowledge, where a code call may need to return an "uncertain" answer. We show in this section that our framework can be easily generalized to deal with probabilistic reasoning.

Example 2 (Surveillance Example). Consider a surveillance application where there are hundreds of (identical) surveillance agents, and a geographic agent. The data types associated with the surveillance and geographic agent include the standard `int,bool,real,string,file` data types, plus those shown below:

Surveillance Agent	Geographic Agent
image:record of	map:↑ quadtree;
imageid:file;	**quadtree:record of**
day:date;	place:string;
time:int;	xcoord:int;
location:string	ycoord:int;
imagedb: *setof* image;	pop:int
	nw,ne,sw,se:↑ quadtree

A third agent may well merge information from these two agents, tracking a sequence of surveillance events.

The surv agent may support a function surv : *identify*() which takes as input an image and returns as output the set of all identified vehicles in it. It may also support a function called surv : *turret*() that takes as input, a vehicle id, and returns as output, the type of gun-turret it has. Likewise, the geo agent may support a function geo : *getplnode*() which takes as input a map and the name of a place and returns the set of all nodes with that name as the place-field, a function geo : *getxynode*() which takes as input a map and the coordinates of a place and returns the set of all nodes with that coordinate as the node, a function called geo : *range*() that takes as input a map, an x, y coordinate pair, and a distance r and returns as output, the set of all nodes in the map (quadtree) that are within r units of location (x, y).

In this example, surv : *identify*(image1) tries to identify all objects in a given image—however, it is well–known that image identification is an uncertain task.

Some objects may be identified with 100% certainty, while in other cases, it may only be possible to say it is either a T-72 tank with 40–50% probability, or a T-80 tank with 50-60% probability.

Image processing algorithms for vehicle surveillance applications that return probabilistic identifications are readily available (e.g., see [7] and [8]).

3.1   Probabilistic Code Calls

The first step to extend our framework is to introduce the notion of a *probabilistic code call*. Its main ingredient is a random variable.

Definition 7 (Random Variable of Type τ). *A random variable of type τ is a finite set* **RV** *of objects of type τ, together with a probability distribution $\wp$ that assigns real numbers in the unit interval $[0,1]$ to members of* **RV** *such that $\Sigma_{o \in \mathbf{RV}} \wp(o) \leq 1$.*

It is important to note that in classical probability theory [9], random variables satisfy the stronger requirement that $\Sigma_{o \in \mathbf{RV}} \wp(o) = 1$. However, in many real–life situations, a probability distribution may have missing pieces, which explains why we have chosen a weaker definition.

Definition 8 (Probabilistic Code Call $\mathsf{a} :_{\mathbf{RV}} f(d_1, \ldots, d_n)$). *Suppose the code call $\mathsf{a} : f(\mathsf{d}_1, \ldots, \mathsf{d}_n)$ has output type τ. The probabilistic code call associated with $\mathsf{a} : f(\mathsf{d}_1, \ldots, \mathsf{d}_n)$, denoted $\mathsf{a} :_{\mathbf{RV}} f(d_1, \ldots, d_n)$, returns a set of random variables of type τ when executed.*

Example 3. Consider the code call $\mathsf{surv} : identify(\mathtt{image1})$. This code call may return the following two random variables.

$$\langle \{t72, t80\}, \{\langle t72, 0.5 \rangle, \langle t80, 0.4 \rangle\} \rangle \text{ and } \langle \{t60, t84\}, \{\langle t60, 0.3 \rangle, \langle t84, 0.7 \rangle\} \rangle$$

This says that the image processing algorithm has identified two objects in image1. The first object is either a T-72 or a T-80 tank with 50% and 40% probability, respectively, while the second object is either a T-60 or a T-84 tank with 30% and 70% probability respectively.

Probabilistic code calls and code call conditions look exactly like ordinary code calls and code call conditions—however, as a probabilistic code call returns a set of *random variables*, probabilistic code call atoms are true or false with some probability.

We are now ready to generalize the notion of a state of an agent to its probabilistic counterpart.

Definition 9 (Probabilistic State of an Agent). *The probabilistic state of an agent a at any given point t in time, denoted $\mathcal{O}^p(t)$, consists of the set of all instantiated data objects and random variables of types contained in $\mathcal{T}_{\mathsf{a}}$.*

3.2   Conjunction Strategy and Probabilistic Agent Programs

The next step is to define the satisfaction relation of probabilistic code call conditions. This is problematic as the following example illustrates.

Example 4. Consider the probabilistic code call condition

$$\mathbf{in}(X, \mathsf{surv} :_{\mathbf{RV}} \mathit{identify}(\mathtt{image1})) \, \& \, \mathbf{in}(a1, \mathsf{surv} :_{\mathbf{RV}} \mathit{turret}(X)).$$

This code call condition attempts to find all vehicles in "image1" with a gun turret of type a1. Let us suppose that the first code call returns just one random variable specifying that image1 contains one vehicle which is either a T-72 (probability 50%) or a T-80 tank (probability 40%). When this random variable (X) is passed to the second code call, it returns one random variable with two values— a1 with probability 30% and a2 with probability 65%. What is the probability that the code call condition above is satisfied by a particular assignment to X? The answer to this question depends very much upon the knowledge we have (if any) about the dependencies between the identification of a tank as a T-72 or a T-80, and the type of gun turret on these. For instance, if we know that all T-72's have a2 type turrets, then the probability of the conjunct being true when X is a T-72 tank is 0. On the other hand, it may be that the turret identification and the vehicle identification are independent for T-80s—hence, when X is set to T-80, the probability of the conjunct being true is $0.4 \times 0.3 = 0.12$.

Therefore the probability that a conjunction is true depends not only on the probabilities of the individual conjuncts, but also on the dependencies between the events denoted by these conjuncts.

We have solved this problem by introducing the notion of a *probabilistic conjunction strategy* $\otimes$ to capture these different ways of computing probabilities via an abstract definition. We are also using *annotations* to represent probability intervals. For instance, $[0, 0.4], [0.7, 0.9], [0.1, \frac{V}{2}], [\frac{V}{4}, \frac{V}{2}]$ are all annotations. The annotation $[0.1, \frac{V}{2}]$ denotes an interval only when a value in $[0, 1]$ is assigned to the variable V.

Definition 10 (Annotated Code Call Condition $\chi : \langle [\mathsf{ai}_1, \mathsf{ai}_2], \otimes \rangle$). *If χ is a probabilistic code call condition, $\otimes$ is a conjunction strategy, and $[\mathsf{ai}_1, \mathsf{ai}_2]$ is an annotation, then $\chi : \langle [\mathsf{ai}_1, \mathsf{ai}_2], \otimes \rangle$ is an annotated code call condition. $\chi : \langle [\mathsf{ai}_1, \mathsf{ai}_2], \otimes \rangle$ is ground if there are no variables in either χ or in $[\mathsf{ai}_1, \mathsf{ai}_2]$.*

Intuitively, the ground annotated code call condition $\chi : \langle [\mathsf{ai}_1, \mathsf{ai}_2], \otimes \rangle$ says that the probability of χ being true (under conjunction strategy $\otimes$) lies in the interval $[\mathsf{ai}_1, \mathsf{ai}_2]$. For example, when X is ground,

$$\mathbf{in}(X, \mathsf{surv} :_{\mathbf{RV}} \mathit{identify}(\mathtt{image1})) \, \& \, \mathbf{in}(\mathtt{a1}, \mathsf{surv} :_{\mathbf{RV}} \mathit{turret}(X)) : \langle [0.3, 0.5], \otimes_{ig} \rangle$$

is true *if and only if* the probability that X is identified by the surv agent and that the turret is identified as being of type a1 lies between 30 and 50% assuming that nothing is known about the dependencies between turret identifications and identifications of objects by surv.

We are now ready to define the concept of a probabilistic agent program.

Definition 11 (Probabilistic Agent Programs $\mathcal{PP}$). *Suppose Γ is an annotated code call condition, and $A, L_1, \ldots, L_n$ are status atoms. Then*

$$A \leftarrow \Gamma \& L_1 \& \ldots \& L_n \tag{1}$$

is a probabilistic agent rule. *For such a rule r, we use $B_{as}^+(r)$ to denote the positive status atoms in $\{L_1, \ldots, L_n\}$, and $B_{as}^-(r)$ to denote the set of negative status literals in $\{L_1, \ldots, L_n\}$.*

A probabilistic agent program (pap *for short) is a finite set of probabilistic agent rules.*

Consider an intelligent sensor agent that is performing surveillance tasks. The following rules specify a small pap that such an agent might use.

$$\mathbf{Do} \; send\_warn(\mathtt{X}) \leftarrow \mathbf{in}(\mathtt{F}, \mathsf{surv} : file(\mathtt{imagedb})) \; \&$$
$$\mathbf{in}(\mathtt{X}, \mathsf{surv} :_{\mathbf{RV}} identify(\mathtt{F})) \; \&$$
$$\mathbf{in}(\mathtt{a1}, \mathsf{surv} :_{\mathbf{RV}} turret(\mathtt{X}))) : \langle [0.7, 1.0], \otimes_{ig} \rangle$$
$$\neg \mathbf{F} \, send\_warn(\mathtt{X}).$$
$$\mathbf{F} \, send\_warn(\mathtt{X}) \leftarrow \mathbf{in}(\mathtt{F}, \mathsf{surv} : file(\mathtt{imagedb})) \; \&$$
$$\mathbf{in}(\mathtt{X}, \mathsf{surv} :_{\mathbf{RV}} identify(\mathtt{F})) \; \&$$
$$\mathbf{in}(\mathtt{L}, \mathsf{geo} :_{\mathbf{RV}} getplnode(\mathtt{X.location})) \; \&$$
$$\mathbf{in}(\mathtt{L}, \mathsf{geo} :_{\mathbf{RV}} range(100, 100, 20)).$$

This agent operates according to two very simple rules. The first rule says that it sends a warning whenever it identifies an enemy vehicle as having a gun turret of type a1 with over 70% probability, as long as sending such a warning is not forbidden. The second rule says that sending a warning is forbidden if the enemy vehicle is within 20 units of distance from location $(100, 100)$.

Defining the semantics for this kind of programs is out of scope of this paper and we refer to [1].

4   Serving Requests more Efficiently

With the increase in agent-based applications, there are now agent systems that support *concurrent* client accesses. The ability to process large volumes of simultaneous requests is critical in many such applications. In such a setting, the traditional approach of serving these requests one at a time via queues (e.g. FIFO queues, priority queues) is insufficient. In this section we review the approach of [4]. The overall idea is that for a given set of requests one needs to

1. identify *commonalities* among them. This information can be used to simplify the set and merge some of the requests together.
2. compute a *single* global execution plan that simultaneously optimizes the total expected cost of this set of code call conditions.

Instead of sending many individual requests one after another, sending one large merged request (the answer from which the answers to the original requests can be deduced) can already save a lot of network time.

4.1   Invariants

How can we detect commonalities? Obviously, we need input from the agent developer. In our framework, an agent developer specifies several parameters. One of these parameters must include some *domain-specific* information, explicitly laying out what inclusion and equality relations are known to hold of code calls. Such information is specified via *invariants*. An important ingredient for their definition are *invariant expressions*.

Definition 12 (Invariant Expression).

- *Every evaluable code call condition is an invariant expression. We call such expressions* atomic.
- *If ie_1 and ie_2 are invariant expressions, then $(ie_1 \cup ie_2)$ and $(ie_1 \cap ie_2)$ are invariant expressions. (We will often omit the parentheses.)*

Example 5. Two examples of invariant expressions are:

in(StudentRec, rel : *select*(*courseRel, exam,* "=", *midterm1*)) &
in(C, excel : *chart*(*excelFile,* StudentRec, *grade*))

in(X, spatial : *horizontal*(T, B, U)) $\cup$ (**in**(Y, spatial : *horizontal*(T′, B′, U′)) $\cup$
in(Z, spatial : *horizontal*(T′, B′, U))).

What is the meaning, i.e. the *denotation* of such expressions? The first invariant represents the set of all objects c such that

in(StudentRec, rel : *select*(*courseRel, exam,* "=", *midterm1*)) &
in(*c,* excel : *chart*(*excelFile,* StudentRec, *grade*))

holds: we are looking for instantiations of C. Note that under this viewpoint, the intermediate variable StudentRec which is needed in order to instantiate C to an object c does not matter. There might just as well be situations where we are interested in pairs $\langle c, studentrec \rangle$ instead of just c.

Definition 13 (Invariant Condition (ic)). *An* invariant condition atom *is a statement of the form t_1 Op t_2 where $Op \in \{\leq, \geq, <, >, =\}$ and each of t_1, t_2 is either a variable or a constant. An* invariant condition (IC) *is defined inductively as follows:*

1. *Every invariant condition atom is an ic.*
2. *If C_1 and C_2 are ic's, then $C_1 \wedge C_2$ and $C_1 \vee C_2$ are ic's.*

Definition 14 (Invariant inv, INV). *An* invariant, *denoted by inv, is a statement of the form*

$$ic \implies ie_1 \; \Re \; ie_2 \tag{2}$$

where

1. *ic is an invariant condition, all variables occuring in ic are among*
   $var_{base}(ie_1) \cup var_{base}(ie_2)$.

2. $\Re \in \{=, \subseteq\}$, *and*
3. *ie_1, ie_2 are invariant expressions.*

If ie_1 and ie_2 both contain solely atomic *code call conditions, then we say that* inv *is a simple invariant. If* ic *is a conjunction of invariant condition atoms, then we say that* inv *is an ordinary invariant. The set of all invariants is denoted by* INV.

The invariant,

$$\mathtt{Rel} = \mathtt{Rel}' \wedge \mathtt{Attr} = \mathtt{Attr}' \wedge \mathtt{Op} = \mathtt{Op}' = \texttt{"≤"} \wedge \mathtt{Val} < \mathtt{Val}'$$
$$\Longrightarrow$$
$$\mathbf{in}(\mathtt{X}, \mathtt{rel}: select(\mathtt{Rel}, \mathtt{Attr}, \mathtt{Op}, \mathtt{Val})) \subseteq \mathbf{in}(\mathtt{Y}, \mathtt{rel}: select(\mathtt{Rel}', \mathtt{Attr}', \mathtt{Op}', \mathtt{Val}'))$$

says that the code call condition $\mathbf{in}(\mathtt{X}, \mathtt{rel}: select(\mathtt{Rel}, \mathtt{Attr}, \mathtt{Op}, \mathtt{Val}))$ can be evaluated by using the results of the ccc $\mathbf{in}(\mathtt{Y}, \mathtt{rel}: select(\mathtt{Rel}', \mathtt{Attr}', \mathtt{Op}', \mathtt{Val}'))$ if the above conditions are satisfied. Note that this expresses *semantic information* that is not available on the syntactic level: the operator "≤" is related to the relation symbol "<".

4.2   Merging Requests

Let us suppose now that we have a set $\mathcal{I}$ of invariants, and a set $\mathcal{S}$ of data structures that are manipulated by the agent. How exactly should a set $\mathcal{C}$ of code call conditions be merged together? And what needs to be done to support this? Our architecture contains two parts:

(i) a *development time* phase stating what the agent developer must specify when building her agent, and what algorithms are used to operate on that specification, and
(ii) a *deployment time* phase which specifies how the above development-time specifications are used when the agent is in fact running autonomously.

Development Time Phase. When the agent developer builds her agent, the following things need to be done.

1. First, the agent developer specifies a set $\mathcal{I}$ of invariants.
2. Suppose $\mathcal{C}$ is a set of CCCs to be evaluated by the agent. Each code call condition $\chi \in \mathcal{C}$ is represented via an evaluable cceg (see Figure 3 in Subsection 1.3). Let $INS(\mathcal{C})$ represent the set of all nodes in ccegs of χs in $\mathcal{C}$:

$$INS(\mathcal{C}) = \{v_i \mid \exists \chi \in \mathcal{C} \text{ s.t. } v_i \text{ is in } \chi's \text{ cceg}\}.$$

This can be done by a topological sort of the cceg for each $\chi \in \mathcal{C}$.
3. Additional invariants can be derived from the initial set $\mathcal{I}$ of invariants. This requires the ability to check whether a set $\mathcal{I}$ of invariants implies an inclusion relationship between two invariant expressions. Although we have defined a formally precise notion of a set of invariants implying other invariants we

will provide a *generic* test called **Chk_Imp** for implication checking between invariants. There are various instances of **Chk_Imp** that are sound but not complete, thereby allowing us to specify various parameters and heuristics. Given an arbitrary (but fixed) **Chk_Imp** test, we will provide an algorithm called **Compute-Derived-Invariants** that calculates the set of derivable invariants from the initial set $\mathcal{I}$ of invariants and needs to be executed just once.

Deployment Time Phase. Once the agent has been "developed" and deployed and is running, it will need to continuously determine how to merge a set $\mathcal{C}$ of code call conditions. This will be done as follows:

1. The system identifies three types of relationships between nodes in $INS(\mathcal{C})$.

   Identical ccc's: First, we'd like to identify nodes $\chi_1, \chi_2 \in INS(\mathcal{C})$ which are "equivalent" to one another, i.e. $\chi_1 = \chi_2$ is a logical consequence of the set of invariants $\mathcal{I}$. This requires a definition of *equivalence* of two code call conditions w.r.t. a set of invariants. This strategy is useful because we can replace the two nodes χ_1, χ_2 by a single node. This avoids redundant computation of both χ_1 and χ_2.

   Implied ccc's: Second, we'd like to identify nodes $\chi_1, \chi_2 \in INS(\mathcal{C})$ which are not equivalent in the above sense, but such that either $\chi_1 \subseteq \chi_2$ or $\chi_2 \subseteq \chi_1$ hold, but not both. Suppose $\chi_1 \subseteq \chi_2$. Then we can compute χ_2 first, and then compute χ_1 from the answer returned by computing χ_2. This way of computing χ_1, χ_2 may be faster than computing them separately.

   Overlapping ccc's: Third, we'd like to identify nodes $\chi_1, \chi_2 \in INS(\mathcal{C})$ for which the preceding two conditions do not hold, but $\chi_1 \,\&\, \chi_2$ is consistent with $INS(\mathcal{C})$. In this case, we might be able to compute the answer to $\chi_1 \vee \chi_2$. From the answer to this, we may compute the answer to χ_1 and the answer to χ_2. This way of computing χ_1, χ_2 may be faster than computing them separately.

   We will provide an algorithm, namely **Improved-CSI**, which will use the set of derived invariants returned by the **Compute-Derived-Invariants** algorithm above, to detect commonalities (equivalent, implied and overlapping code call conditions) among members of $\mathcal{C}$.

Example 6. The two code call conditions **in**(X, spatial: *vertical*(T, L, R)) and **in**(Y, spatial: *vertical*(T′, L′, R′)) are equivalent to one another if their arguments are unifiable. The results of evaluating the code call condition

$$\mathbf{in}(Z, \text{spatial}: range(T, 40, 50, 25))$$

is a subset of the results of evaluating the code call condition

$$\mathbf{in}(W, \text{spatial}: range(T', 40, 50, 50))$$

if $T = T'$. Note that $\mathsf{spatial}\!:\!range(T, X, Y, Z)$ returns all points in T that are Z units away from the point $\langle X, Y \rangle$. In this case, we can compute the results of the former code call condition by executing a selection on the results of the latter rather than executing the former from scratch. Finally, consider the following two code call conditions:

$$\mathbf{in}(X, \mathsf{spatial}\!:\!horizontal(map, 100, 200)),$$
$$\mathbf{in}(Y, \mathsf{spatial}\!:\!horizontal(map, 150, 250)).$$

Here $\mathsf{spatial}\!:\!horizontal(map, \mathsf{a}, \mathsf{b})$ returns all points (X, Y) in map such that $a \leq Y \leq b$. Obviously, the results of neither of these two code call conditions are subset of the results of the other. However, the results of these two code call conditions *overlap* with one another. In this case, we can execute the code call condition $\mathbf{in}(Z, \mathsf{spatial}\!:\!horizontal(map, 100, 250))$. Then, we can compute the results of the two code call conditions by executing selections on the results of this code call condition.

2. We will then provide two procedures to merge sets of code call conditions, **BFMerge** and **DFMerge**, that take as input, *(i)* the set $\mathcal{C}$ and *(ii)* the output of the **Improved-CSI** algorithm above, and *(iii)* a cost model for agent code call condition evaluations. Both these algorithms are parameterized by heuristics and we propose three alternative heuristics. Then we evaluate our six implementations (3 heuristics times 2 algorithms) and also compare it with an A^* based approach.

For an implementation, we implemented both these algorithms on top of the *IMPACT* agent development platform, and on top of a (non-*IMPACT*) geographic database agent.

4.3   Results

Development Phase. The definition of a sound and complete instance of **Chk_Imp** is based on the definition of a certain monotone fixpoint operator, the least fixedpoint of which constitutes the set of implied invariants ([4]). Completeness is proved by reducing the problem to the completeness of a particular first-order calculus and using a Henkin-like construction.

Proposition 1 (co-NP Completeness of Checking Implication).
Suppose all datatypes have a finite domain (i.e. each datatype has only finitely many values of that datatype). Then the problem of checking whether an arbitrary invariant expression ie_1 implies another invariant expression ie_2 is co-NP complete. The same holds for the problem of checking whether an invariant is a tautology.

We have therefore studied the tradeoffs involved in using sound, but perhaps incomplete implementations of implication checking.

There are clearly many ways of implementing the algorithm **Chk_Imp** that are sound, but not complete. We considered a generic algorithm to implement **Chk_Imp**, where the complexity can be controlled by two input parameters—an *axiomatic inference system* and a *threshold*.

Deployment Phase. We developed two algorithms (and various accompanying heuristics) which allow an agent to automatically rewrite requests so as to avoid redundant work—these algorithms take invariants associated with the agent into account. Our algorithms are independent of any specific agent framework. For an implementation, we implemented both these algorithms on top of the *IM-PACT* agent development platform, and on top of a (non-*IMPACT*) geographic database agent. Based on these implementations, we conducted experiments and show that our algorithms are considerably more efficient than methods based on the well known algorithm in [10] for merging multiple *relational database only* queries using the A^* algorithm. Our experiments show that although the A^* algorithm finds better global results, the cost of obtaining those results is so prohibitively high that the A^* is often infeasible to use in practice.

Figure 6 shows, that the execution time for determining overlapping code calls still is below one second for a set of 20 ccc's. Similar times are obtained for equivalent and implied ccc's. We also noted that there are often more ccc's falling in the implied or overlapping categories, than in the equivalence category. As the methods based on the A^* algorithm only searches for the latter category, our optimizations pay off.

Although the A^* algorithm finds better global results, the cost of obtaining those results is so prohibitively high that the A^* is often infeasible to use in practice. We have also shown that our merging algorithms *(1)* can handle *more than twice* as many simultaneous code call conditions as the A^* algorithm and *(2)* run *100* to *6300* times faster than the A^* algorithm and *(3)* produce execution plans the cost of which is *at most 10%* more than the plans generated by the A^* algorithm.

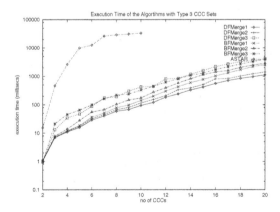

Fig. 6. Execution Time of **Merge** Algorithms with overlapping ccc Sets

5 Conclusion

We have illustrated three powerful extensions to the basic *IMPACT* framework: incorporating *planning*, incorporating *uncertain reasoning* and *optimizing queries* sent over a network. While the first extension required an *agentization procedure* to incorporate an efficient HTN planner into *IMPACT*, the second extension extended the notion of a code call to one dealing with random variables and required heavy use of annotated logic programming. The third extension required fixpoint techniques and automated reasoning mechanisms (to prove the completeness result).

The semantics of the basic framework as well as of the extensions described are based on the notion of an *agent program* and thus are very much related to nonmonotonic formalisms like the stable and wellfounded semantics. We can conclude that any formal approach to heterogenous agent systems can benefit a lot from *Computational Logic*, to which all the above techniques belong.

References

1. Dix, J., Nanni, M., Subrahmanian, V. S.: Probabilistic agent reasoning. Transactions of Computational Logic **1** (2000) 201–245 1, 14
2. Dix, J., Munoz-Avila, H., Nau, D., Zhang, L.: IMPACTing SHOP: Putting an AI planner into a Multi-Agent Environment. Annals of Mathematics and AI (2001) to appear. 1, 7
3. Subrahmanian, V., Bonatti, P., Dix, J., Eiter, T., Kraus, S., Özcan, F., Ross, R.: Heterogenous Active Agents. MIT-Press (2000) 1, 2, 10
4. Dix, J., Öczan, F., Subrahmanian., V.: Improving performance of heavily loaded agents. Technical Report CS-TR-4202, Dept. of CS, University of Maryland, College Park, MD 20752 (2000) 1, 6, 14, 18
5. Nau, D., Cao, Y., Lotem, A., Muñoz-Avila, H.: Shop: Simple hierarchical ordered planner. In: Proceedings of IJCAI-99. (1999) 6, 7
6. Eiter, T., Subrahmanian, V., Rogers, T. J.: Heterogeneous Active Agents, III: Polynomially Implementable Agents. Artificial Intelligence **117** (2000) 107–167 10
7. Friedman, N., Russell, S.: Image segmentation in video sequences: A probabilistic approach. In: Proceedings Thirteenth Conf. on Uncertainty in Artificial Intelligence. (1997) 12
8. Huang, T., Russell, S.: Object identification: A Bayesian analysis with applications to traffic surveillance. Artificial Intelligence **103(1-2)** (1998) 77–93 12
9. Ross, S.: A First Course in Probability. Prentice-Hall (1997) 12
10. Shim, K., Sellis, T. K., Nau, D.: Improvements on a heuristic algorithm for multiple-query optimization. Data and Knowledge Engineering **12** (1994) 197–222 19
11. Dix, J., Kraus, S., Subrahmanian, V.: Temporal agent reasoning. Artificial Intelligence **127** (2001) 87–135
12. Dix, J., Subrahmanian, V. S., Pick, G.: Meta Agent Programs. Journal of Logic Programming **46** (2000) 1–60
13. Eiter, T., Subrahmanian, V., Pick, G.: Heterogeneous Active Agents, I: Semantics. Artificial Intelligence **108** (1999) 179–255

14. Eiter, T., Subrahmanian, V. S.: Heterogeneous Active Agents, II: Algorithms and Complexity. Artificial Intelligence **108** (1999) 257–307

Declarative Information Extraction, Web Crawling, and Recursive Wrapping with *Lixto*[*]

Robert Baumgartner[1], Sergio Flesca[2], and Georg Gottlob[1]

[1] DBAI, TU Wien, Vienna, Austria
{baumgart,gottlob}@dbai.tuwien.ac.at
[2] DEIS, Università della Calabria, Rende (CS), Italy
flesca@si.deis.unical.it

Abstract. *Lixto* is a system and method for the visual and interactive generation of wrappers for Web pages under the supervision of a human developer, for automatically extracting information from Web pages using such wrappers, and for translating the extracted content into XML. This paper describes some advanced features of *Lixto*, such as disjunctive pattern definitions, specialization rules, and *Lixto*'s capability of collecting and aggregating information from several linked Web pages.

1 Introduction and Motivation

Extracting relevant information automatically from HTML Web pages of changing content, and converting the extracted information to a structured representation is an important problem, to which a lot of research has been dedicated [3,7,8,10,11,13,14]. XML was designed to enrich the semantics of Web information [1,6]. Even if in some respects XML may not yet fulfill this goal perfectly, XML appears to be the right representation format for the information extracted from HTML. Programs that perform such extraction and translation tasks are referred to as *wrappers*. Wrappers can be hand-coded, e.g. in specialized languages such as Jedi [9] or Florid [12], or they can be produced via *wrapper generators*. Wrapper generators are software tools that generate wrappers via induction (such as e.g. [2,10,13]) or that semi-automatically support the generation of wrappers via an interactive process supervised by a human designer ([11,14]). Wrapper generators support the task of reverse engineering, as the goal of a wrapper is to reverse the processing of dynamic Web sites that generate HTML starting from an internal structured representation (such as a relational database).

In a recent paper [5] we introduced *Lixto*, a new method and system for visually generating HTML/XML wrappers under the supervision of a human designer. *Lixto* allows a wrapper designer to interactively and visually define information extraction patterns on the base of visualized sample Web pages. These extraction patterns are collected into a hierarchical knowledge base that

---

[*] All new methods and algorithms of the *Lixto* system are covered by a pending patent. Future developments of *Lixto* will be reported at www.lixto.com.

T. Eiter, W. Faber, and M. Truszczyński (Eds.): LPNMR 2001, LNAI 2173, pp. 21–41, 2001.

constitutes a declarative wrapper program. The extraction knowledge is internally represented in a datalog like special-purpose logic programming language, called *Elog*. However, a user of *Lixto* is not concerned with the syntax of *Elog* and does not need to learn this language as she constructs an *Elog* wrapper program by purely visual and interactive primitives without ever seeing the resulting *Elog* program. Wrapper programs in *Elog* can be directly executed over input Web sites by an extractor module that interprets the *Elog* rules taking care of the evaluation of special built-in predicates. *Lixto* also allows a designer to define XML translation rules that specify how extracted content should be translated into XML, a so-called *XML translation scheme*. An XML translation scheme together with extraction pattern definitions (the *Elog* program) in addition enables the system to construct a Document Type Definition (DTD) which describes the characteristics of the output XML documents.

The advantages of the *Lixto* wrapper generator over competing approaches are mainly the following. *(1) Very high expressive power*, i.e., an unprecedented capability of defining sophisticated extraction patterns. *(2) Excellent visual support*: The wrapper designer's sole view of an example HTML document is the browser-displayed standard image of the document (no annotations, overlays, HTML-sources or DOM trees) and the wrapper designer uses directly this display for marking extraction patterns. *(3) Good learnability*, because no extraction language needs to be learned and neither HTML nor XML knowledge is necessary. *(4) Sample parsimony*, which means that very few sample pages (in most cases a single one) are needed in order to define robust wrappers for large classes of Web pages. A *(5) simple and smooth XML translation mechanism* that gives a designer several options for formatting or modifying the XML output.

Basic features of *Lixto* are described in [4,5], where also a comparison to related research is given. The main goal of the present paper is to introduce and illustrate some of the more advanced features of the *Elog* language. All the presented advanced features can be visually created by using *Lixto* without knowing *Elog*. Details of the visual interface and the way of creating patterns can be found in [4] and [5], where a precise description of the pattern generation algorithm is given. There, these details are discussed for a restricted environment w.r.t. some advanced concepts discussed in this paper, but a quite similar approach can be used for these advanced features. The present paper is self-contained at the level of general description, but not at the level of details. For the latter, we refer to [5].

Among the advanced features we discuss here are *disjunctive wrapping*, i.e., defining one pattern through several alternative definitions; *pattern specialization*, i.e., defining a new pattern by restricting another pattern; interactively defining new *document patterns*, which are patterns corresponding to entire documents that are identified via extracted URLs; *Web crawling*, which, in this context, means that a pattern hierarchy is built that aggregates information from various Web pages by starting at a given input page and automatically following URLs to other pages; and *recursive wrapping* which means that recursive pattern structures (akin to recursive data types) can be constructed that allow the system to crawl to an indefinite number of Web pages and extract information from all these pages. We will also discuss some interesting *nonmonotonic issues* such as pattern minimization principles and the semantics of range restrictions. Moreover, this paper introduces *pattern graphs* for describing the structure of the pattern hierarchy interactively defined by a designer (see Figures 3,4,6, and 7). Note that pattern graphs for simple extraction tasks are trees, which means that there is a strict pattern hierarchy. When disjunctive pattern definitions are used, then the corresponding pattern graphs are dags, while with recursive wrapping they are cyclic graphs.

The paper is structured as follows. In the next two sections we give an overview of *Lixto* and a description of the basic features of the *Elog* language. Section 4 gives a closer look on some features. In Section 5 we illustrate the power of disjunctive pattern descriptions, whereas in Section 6 some light is shed on *Elog*'s aspects concerning link crawling and recursion. These sections introduce advanced features of the internal language of *Lixto* both with an abstract description and examples from the commercial domain. Section 7 discusses various nonmonotonic aspects of *Lixto* such as minimization, range conditions, and further recursive aspects introduced by pattern references.

2   Pattern Generation with *Lixto*

Architecture. The *Lixto* prototype consists of two main blocks: The *Wrapper Generator* and the *Program Evaluator*. One module of the wrapper generator, the *Interactive Pattern Builder*, allows a wrapper designer to create and to store a wrapper in form of an extraction program (a program in the language *Elog*). Moreover, the wrapper generator contains the *XML Translation Builder* that allows a designer to specify how extracted data should be translated into XML format and to store such a specification in form of an XML translation scheme. The program evaluator automatically executes an extraction program (performed by the *Extractor* module) and a corresponding XML translation scheme (performed by the *XML translator* module) over Web pages by extracting data from them and translating the extracted data into XML format. (For details see [5].)

Extraction Patterns. A wrapper is constructed by formalizing, collecting, and storing the knowledge about desired extraction patterns. Extraction patterns describe single data items or chunks of coherent data to be extracted from Web pages by their locations and by their characteristic internal or contextual properties. Extraction patterns are generated and refined interactively and semi-automatically with help of a human wrapper designer. They are constructed in a hierarchical fashion on sample pages by marking relevant items or regions via mouse clicks or similar actions, by menu selections, and/or by simple textual inputs to the user interface. A wrapper, in our approach, is thus a knowledge base consisting of a set of extraction patterns.

While patterns are descriptions of data to be extracted, pattern instances are concrete data elements on Web pages that match such descriptions, and hence are extracted. *Lixto* distinguishes different types of patterns: Tree, string, and document patterns. Tree patterns serve to extract parts of documents corresponding to tree regions, i.e., to subtrees of their parse tree. String patterns serve to extract textual strings from visible and invisible parts of a document (an invisible part could be, e.g., an attribute value such as the name of an image). Document patterns are used for navigating to further Web pages.

Logical Organization of Patterns. The logical organization of an extraction pattern is as follows: each extraction pattern has a name and contains one or more so-called *filters*. Each filter provides an alternative definition of data to be extracted and to be associated with the pattern. The set of filters of a pattern is interpreted disjunctively (i.e., connected by logical ORs). Each filter is associated to a parent pattern from which it extracts the desired information. Tree (string) patterns are specified via tree (string) filters.

A tree filter contains a representation of a generalized parse tree path that matches a set of items on a Web page, and contains a set of conditions that these items must satisfy. All the conditions of a filter are interpreted conjunctively, i.e., an element of a Web page satisfies a filter if and only if it matches its generalized tree path and satisfies all the conditions of the filter. Similarly, a string filter specifies the characteristics of the text to be extracted (using a formal language), and possibly further conditions.

Lixto offers a wrapper designer the possibility to express various types of conditions restricting the intended pattern instances of a filter. The main types of conditions are inherent (internal) conditions, contextual (external) conditions, and range conditions. In addition to these three basic types of conditions, *Lixto* allows a designer to express auxiliary conditions like pattern reference conditions, concept conditions and comparison conditions. They are discussed as atoms of the *Elog* language in more detail in Section 3.

Visual Pattern Generation. Extraction patterns are defined by the designer in a hierarchical manner. A pattern that describes an entire document is referred to as a document pattern. In particular, the document pattern corresponding to the starting Web page, the so-called "home document pattern", is available as a preexisting pattern. Other patterns are defined interactively. Filters or patterns are usually defined in the context of other patterns (so-called parent patterns). For example, a pattern <name> may be defined first, and then patterns <firstname> and <familyname>, etc., may be defined in the context of the source pattern <name>. For the majority of common extraction tasks, defining flat patterns or a strict hierarchy of patterns will in practice be sufficient. However, *Lixto* does not limit the pattern definition to be strictly hierarchical (i.e. tree-like). Moreover, pattern definitions are allowed to be recursive (similar to recursive type definitions in programming languages). While patterns are not required to form a strict hierarchy, pattern instances do always form one and can be arranged as a tree (or forest, in case they stem from different documents, which can be the case in recursive programs as explained in Section 6).

The visual and interactive pattern definition method allows a wrapper designer to define an extraction program and an associated XML translation scheme without any programming efforts. The *Lixto* Interactive Pattern Builder allows a wrapper designer to define filters and patterns with the help of one or more characteristic example pages, and to modify and store patterns. At various intermediate steps, the designer may test a partially or fully constructed filter or pattern, both on the example pages used to construct the pattern as well as on any other Web page. The result of such a test is a set of pattern instances, which is displayed by a browser as a set of highlighted items.

The filter description procedure for tree-filters can be described as follows: The designer marks an initial element on an example Web page (for example, a table). The system associates with this element a generalized tree path of the parse tree that (possibly) corresponds to several similar items (for example, several tables). The designer then tests the filter for the first time. If more than just the intended data items are extracted (and thus highlighted) as a result of the test, then the designer adds restrictive conditions to the filter and tests the filter again. This process is repeated as long as undesired data items are extracted. At the end of the process, the filter extracts only desired items. A similar procedure is used for designing string filters. However, for creating a string rule usually no example is selected, but some characterizations are visually composed, e.g. by relying on concept conditions. A pattern is designed by initially asserting one filter for the pattern, and, in case this is not sufficient (because testing shows that not all intended extraction items on the test pages are covered), by asserting successively more filters for the pattern under construction, until each intended extraction item is covered by at least one filter associated to that pattern.

Observe that the methods of filter construction and pattern construction correspond to methods of definition-narrowing and definition-broadening that match the conjunctive and disjunctive nature of filters and patterns, respectively. It is the responsibility of the wrapper designer to perform sufficient testing, and – if required by the particular application-test filters and patterns also on Web pages different from the initially chosen example pages. Moreover, it is up to the wrapper designer to choose suitable conditions that will work not only on the test pages, but also on all other target Web pages.

The visual and interactive support for pattern building offered by *Lixto* also includes specific support for the hierarchical organization of patterns and filters. A wrapper definition process according to *Lixto* (and consequently, a *Lixto* wrapper) is not limited to a single sample Web document, and not even to sample Web pages of the same type or structure. During wrapper definition, a designer may move to other sample Web pages (i.e., load them into the browser), continuing the wrapper definition there.

XML Translation. The XML Translation Builder which constitutes another interactive module of the wrapper generator, is responsible for supporting a wrapper designer during the generation of the XML translation scheme. By default, pattern names are used as output XML tags and the hierarchy of extracted pattern instances determines the structure of the output XML document. Thus, in case no specific action is taken by the designer, the pattern instances are translated into XML in a standard way without any need of further interaction. However, *Lixto* also offers the wrapper designer the option to modify the

standard XML translation in the various ways: Renaming patterns, suppressing
auxiliary patterns, writing some HTML attributes, and deciding whether instances of document patterns are all treated at the same level, or hierarchically
ordered as defined by the extraction process. Moreover, to define a DTD based
on an output, a wrapper designer can assign a multiplicity to each pattern, i.e. if
one or several instances are required/allowed to occur within a parent pattern.

These desired modalities of the XML translation are determined during the
wrapper design process by a very simple and user-friendly graphical interface and
are stored in the form of an XML translation scheme that encodes the mapping
between extraction patterns and the XML output in a suitable form.

3   An Overview of the *Elog* Extraction Language

As mentioned in the previous sections, patterns are internally represented using the declarative extraction language *Elog*. The *Elog* language is specifically
designed for hierarchical and modular data extraction and it is ideally suited
for representing and successively incrementing the knowledge about extraction
patterns. It uses a datalog-like syntax and semantics, enriched with several predefined predicates related to information extraction. An *Elog* program is a collection of rules containing special extraction atoms in their bodies.

We illustrate the main characteristics of *Elog* using an example program
which can be applied to *eBay* pages, e.g. to the sample page in Figure 1. Figure 2
shows an *Elog* program applied to a category search result page of *eBay*. In
the following examples, we additionally use a *pattern graph* to represent a *Lixto*
wrapper. A pattern graph is a directed graph whose nodes represent patterns and
an arc from a pattern p_2 to a pattern p_1 specifies that there is a filter defining p_2
that extracts information from instances of p_1. Moreover, document, tree, and
string patterns are represented using different shapes. Finally, it is possible to
represent also information about the XML translation scheme using this graph.
In particular, we specify that a pattern is translated to an XML element by
writing a text "pattern name/elementname" into the pattern node. If the element
name is missing, then the pattern name is used as default translation. The set
of included attributes are embedded in a list, e.g. "[url, font]", and patterns
that are not translated are drawn with dashed lines. It is possible to specify a
minimum and maximum multiplicity on the arcs ("[min,max]", to specify the
information used in the construction of the DTD (see the end of this section).
When no multiplicity of a pattern is explicitly indicated in the pattern graph,
then a minimum and maximum multiplicity of 1 for that pattern are assumed.
The pattern graph of the program in Figure 2 is shown in Figure 3. In this case,
as all filters of one pattern point to the same parent, it forms a tree.

An extraction program consists of a set of patterns. In *Elog*, a pattern p is
represented by a set of rules having all the same head atom of the form $p(S, X)$.
Elog rules define elements to be extracted from Web pages. Each rule corresponds
to one filter. The head of an *Elog* rule r is always of the form $p(S, X)$ where p
is a pattern name, S is a variable which is bound in the body of the rule to the

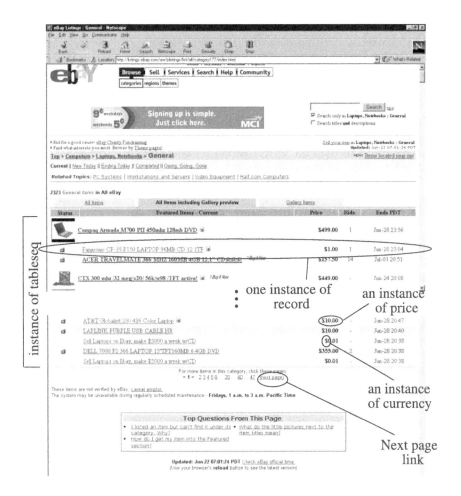

Fig. 1. Sample *eBay* page

parent-pattern instances of the filter corresponding to r, and X is the target variable which, at extraction time, is bound to some target pattern instance to be extracted (either a tree region or a textual string). The body of an *Elog* rule contains atoms that jointly restrict the intended pattern instances. For example, an *Elog* rule corresponding to a tree filter contains in its body an atom expressing that the desired pattern instances should match a certain tree path and another atom that binds the variable S to a parent-pattern instance.

In the example program, the pattern <tableseq> is used to extract a sequence of tables which represent records. Observe that in each search result page of *eBay*, a record is a whole table consisting of a single table row. This sequence of tables is required to be preceded by a table which contains the word "Current", and to be followed by an image representing a horizontal line.

```
ebaydocument(S, X) ← getDocument(S = $1, X)
   tableseq(S, X) ← ebaydocument(_, S),
                    subsq(S, (*.body. * .center, []), (.table, []), (.table, []), X),
                    before(S, X, (*.tr, [(elementtext, Current, substr)]), 0, 0, _, _),
                    after(S, X, (*.img, [(src, spacer.gif, substr)]), 0, 0, _, _)
       record(S, X) ← tableseq(_, S), subelem(S, .table, X)
     itemdes(S, X) ← record(_, S), subelem(S, (*.td. * .content, [(href, , substr)], X)
       price(S, X) ← record(_, S),
                    subelem(S, (*.td, [(elementtext, \var[Y].*, regvar)]), X),
                    isCurrency(Y)
        bids(S, X) ← record(_, S), subelem(S, *.td, X), before(S, X, .td, 0, 30, Y, _)
                    price(_, Y)
        date(S, X) ← record(_, S), subelem(S, *.td, X), notafter(S, X, .td, 100)
    currency(S, X) ← price(_, S), subtext(S, \var[Y], X), isCurrency(Y)
     pricewc(S, X) ← price(_, S), subtext(S, [0 − 9]⁺\.[0 − 9]⁺, X)
```

Fig. 2. *Elog* Extraction Program for a a single *eBay* page

The rule with head predicate *record*(S, X) in Figure 2 identifies all tables within a specific area, which is the instance of *tableseq*(_, S). For each ground atom *tableseq*(p, s) (where p and s are tree regions), this rule derives atoms of the form *record*(s, x) for each table x contained in s. Thus the variable S identifies the context of the extraction, in this case, these are the instantiations of *tableseq*. Optionally, the body of an *Elog* rule may contain further atoms expressing conditions that the pattern instances should additionally satisfy. In particular, for each type of condition, there exists a built-in predicate (see below).

The description of each item (occurring in the second column of each record) is determined by the extraction rule whose head is *itemdes*(S, X). The first atom in the rule body specifies that the context S of the extraction is a table and ensures that the variable S is instantiated with a table. The second atom in the rule body looks for subelements of the table that qualify as table columns with some specific properties, in particular requiring that they contain a link (*href*). The rule has as many matches as there are items on the given page. If the Web page is updated and two new records are inserted into the table, then the same rule will produce two more matches. Each match gives rise to a corresponding instantiation of the variable X.

Thus, the head predicates defined by an *Elog* program represent the extraction patterns defined by the wrapper program. For instance, the program in Figure 2 defines patterns such as `<record>`, `<itemdes>`. *Elog* rule bodies contain the following important ingredients. For a more detailed discussion about *Elog* predicates see Section 4.4 of [5].

Incompletely specified tree paths. These refer to the position(s) of the desired element(s) in the HTML tree. More details on the used document model are specified in [5]. There are various ways to specify a tree path pointing to

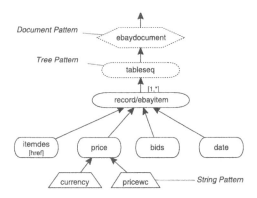

Fig. 3. Pattern Structure of Example of Figure 2

e.g. a table row in an *eBay* page. The fully specified tree path to this node is: *body.table.tr* (the elements satisfying these paths are referred to as matched pattern instances). Two incompletely specified tree paths to the same node are . ⋆ .*body*. ⋆ .*tr* and . ⋆ .*body*. ⋆ .*table*. ⋆ .*tr*, where the star signs are wildcards (the dots just act as concatenation sign). An incompletely specified tree path .⋆.*name* is an abbreviation of the skip-to sequence $(\Sigma - name)^* name$ where Σ is the alphabet of element types. The first discovered elements of the type "name" are considered in all possible paths. Observe that, interpreting the star in this way, a tree path .⋆.*table* identifies only the outermost tables in a document, and hence acts as some kind of minimization.

Attribute Conditions. An incompletely specified tree path may be too general for describing an intended extraction target. In that case, additional atoms in the rule body may express further restricting conditions. Among these are so-called *attribute conditions*. Attribute conditions impose restrictions on matched elements. For example, leaf nodes of the HTML tree representing text strings may have a *font-style* attribute which takes the value *italics* if the represented text is in italics. Moreover, we treat the contents of an element as special attribute *elementtext*. Consider the rule for *tableseq* in Figure 2: One of its predicates uses an attribute condition expressing that the elementtext needs to contain the word "Current" ("contain" due to the *substr* keyword) This attribute condition restricts the tree path . ⋆ .*table*, which identifies tables by limiting the matches to those text fields that contain the word "Current". Attribute Conditions may require exact matches or partial matches, or satisfaction of a particular regular expression possibly extended by the use of variables.

Element Characterizations. A set of elements of a subtree of an HTML tree are identified with a tree path (starting from the subtree root), where additionally a set of attribute conditions is satisfied. Such a characterization is called an *element path definition*. Equivalently, *XPath* expressions can be used instead (with some extensions, such as the possibility to express that an attribute value is a concept like "isCity"). To simplify presentation, however, we stick to our introduced notation. A set of substrings can be identified by using a *string path definition*, which can either be a regular expression, or refer to a concept, or even combine both. Consider the example of Figure 2, in which the rule defining `<currency>` refers to a variable whose instances are currencies.

Tree Extraction Definition Predicates. These predicates specify that a variable should be instantiated with a node in the HTML tree which matches an element path definition. See, for example, the *subelem* atom of the fourth rule in Figure 2, where the variable X is instantiated to all those text fields that occur within `<record>` and contain a link. The variable S in this atom denotes the super entity or, as we call it, the *parent pattern*, from which the current target should be extracted via *subelem*. This parent pattern instance is constrained to be an instance of `<record>` by the first atom of the rule. Note that the tree path specified in a tree extraction definition predicate is always relative to the parent pattern, i.e., its starting point is a node corresponding to the parent pattern (in our example rule, an instance of `<record>`). Moreover, with *subregion*, a sequence of elements can be extracted (e.g. used in *tableseq* in Figure 2).

String Extraction Definition Predicates. In the HTML parse tree, strings are represented by the text of leaves of type *content*. However, we associate a string C_n to *every* node n of the parse tree by simply concatenating (in left-to-right order) all strings corresponding to leaves of the subtree rooted in n. The string C_n associated to node n is available in the *Lixto* system as the value of an additional attribute *elementtext* of any given node n. Several special conditions that express restrictions on such elementtexts can be expressed in *Elog*. *Elog* predicates expressing such special string conditions are referred to as *string extraction definition predicates*. As an example, consider the final two rules of the program of Figure 2. The last rule uses a regular expression as string path definition, the other one a variable reference to a concept atom (explained below). Moreover, *Attribute Extraction Predicates* such as *subatt* (see examples in Section 6) allow to extract the contents of attribute values.

Contextual Conditions. Contextual conditions specify that some other elements must or must not appear either before or after some instance. These contextual elements are not limited to text elements. For example, on a page with several tables, the final table could be identified by an external condition stating that no table appears after the desired table. The rule defining a `<tableseq>` uses both an *after* and a *before* condition to express that one is interested in exactly the region between some specified elements. The definition of `<date>` uses a *notafter* condition to express that the column which contains the date is not followed by another column.

Internal Conditions. Such conditions require that some characteristic feature must or must not appear within an instance. Imagine, one wants to extract all tables containing a word typeset in italics. This could be obtained by adding an internal condition called *contains* to the body of the rule that defines the pattern `<record>`. This condition expresses that in the subtree rooted at the node representing the desired table row, a node must exist whose *font-style* attribute is defined and has the value *italics*.

Concept Conditions. These predicates define concepts of some built-in top-level ontology. For example, one may enrich the system with predicates $isEmail(X)$, $isCountry(X)$, or $isCurrency(X)$ (see Figure 2), stating that a string X represents an email address, a country, or a currency, respectively. These values of the variable X are created as output of concept attribute conditions or string path definitions (using $\backslash var[X]$). They are not required to be unary, e.g. $isDate(X, Y)$ is a binary predicate with output Y in standard date format.

Comparison Conditions. These are predefined relations for predefined ontological classes of elements. Using these conditions, one can e.g. compare two dates (binary predicate), or require that an email address exists (unary predicate).

Pattern References. Each standard filter contains a reference to its parent pattern which defines the context of a rule. For example, see the rule defining <itemdes> in Figure 2. It refers to <record> as parent. The substitution for S is the actual tree region which acts as parent instance. Moreover, additional pattern references can be used, for instance to express that an instance of some pattern always occurs after an instance of another pattern. Such additional pattern references open the way for reference recursion (see Section 7 for details).

Range Conditions. A range condition further restricts the set of pattern instances extracted by a filter by selecting only a subset of the pattern instances which satisfy the conditions in the body of the filter. Indeed the pattern instances extracted from a certain parent pattern instance are ordered according to their position in the document, and a range condition selects only those pattern instances that belong to the required range of solutions. To any rule a range condition such as "[3,7]" can be added, indicating that the solution only includes the third up to the seventh matched target. Counting can occur starting with the first or with the last instance.

Using the above predicates, a *standard extraction* rule looks as follows:

$$\text{New}(S, X) \leftarrow \text{Par}(\_, S), \text{Ex}(S, X), \text{Co}(S, X, \ldots)[a, b]$$

where S is the parent instance variable, X is the pattern instance variable, $Ex(S, X)$ is an extraction definition predicate, and the optional $Co(S, X, \ldots)$ are further imposed conditions. A tree (string) extraction rule uses a tree (string) extraction definition atom and possibly some tree (string) conditions and general conditions. The numbers a and b are optional and serve as range parameters. *New* and *Par* are pattern predicates referring to the parent pattern and defining the new pattern, respectively. This standard rule reflects the principle of aggregation.

The semantics of a rule is given as the set of matched targets x: A substitution s, x for S and X evaluates $New(s, x)$ to *true* iff all atoms of the body are true for this substitution. Only those targets are extracted for which the head of the rule resolves to true. Moreover, if the extraction definition predicate is a subsequence predicate, only minimal instances are matched (i.e. instances that do not contain any other instances). This is a nonmonotonic concept discussed in Section 7. Observe that range criteria are applied after non-minimal targets have been sorted out. Note that range conditions are well-defined only in the case of no reference recursion (cf. to Section 7).

A *pattern definition* (for short, *pattern*) is a set of extraction rules defining the same head. We distinguish document, tree and string patterns. To tree patterns, only tree extraction rules can be asserted, and to string patterns only string extraction rules. The third kind of patterns, document patterns, are discussed in the next section. A pattern acts like a disjunction of rule bodies: To be an extracted instance of a pattern, a target needs to be in the solution set of at least one rule. The set of matched target instances of a pattern additionally obeys a minimality criterion (see Section 7). In patterns, even in those consisting of a single rule, overlapping targets may occur. Observe that we do not pose the requirement that each rule belonging to a given pattern refers to the same parent pattern. This, together with the capability of document navigation, allows for recursion over patterns as explained in more detail in Section 6.

An extraction program P is a set of patterns. *Elog* program evaluation differs from Datalog evaluation in the following three aspects: The use of built-in predicates, various kinds of minimization, and the use of range conditions. Moreover, atoms are not evaluated over an extensional database of facts representing a Web page, but directly over the parse tree of the Web page.

The application of a program to an HTML page creates a set of hierarchically ordered tree regions and string sources (called a *pattern instance base*) by applying all patterns of the program to a given and possible further HTML pages (see the notion of document filters in Section 4). Each pattern produces a set of instances. Each pattern instance contains a reference to its parent instance. Observe that the pattern instance base always forms a forest, regardless of the structure of the pattern graph. We consider the instances of document filters as root node of each tree of this forest. The pattern instance base can be translated into XML as already described in Section 2.

4   A Closer Look at some *Lixto* Features

In this section, we discuss some more advanced features of *Lixto*, in particular two further kinds of rules. A standard rule reflects the principle of aggregation, however, designers of wrappers sometimes wish to express specialization. For instance, if one rule extracts a set of tables, it might be desirable to create a rule which restricts the extracted tables to those which contain some particular feature. A *specialization rule* looks as follows:

$$\text{New}(S, X) \leftarrow \text{Old}(S, X), \text{Co}(S, X, \ldots)[a, b]$$

In such a rule a pattern is specialized, i.e. some of the parent-pattern instances are returned as pattern instances of the new pattern definition. It does not contain a parent-pattern reference and an extraction definition atom; instead it only contains a pattern reference. Observe that equally to specialization rules, generalization rules can be used by simply creating multiple specialization rules for one pattern which refer to different patterns and do not contain any conditions. Another kind of rule is the *document rule*, using a *getDocument(S,X)* atom, where S is a string source representing an URL, and X the Web page the URL points to. With such rules, one can crawl to further documents.

$$\texttt{New(S,X)} \leftarrow \texttt{Par(\_,S)}, \texttt{getDocument(S,X)}$$

Each *Elog* program has an initial rule using the *getDocument* atom with user-specified input. The initial document rule is the only rule without a parent-pattern reference. Instead, it uses a variable "$1" (or a fixed URL) which is instantiated to a string source representing an URL during run time (the start document). Document filters can be applied to document patterns only. Parents of tree patterns are either tree or document patterns, parent of string patterns are tree or string patterns, and parents of document patterns are string patterns.

Figure 4 illustrates the use of document rules together with specialization rules. This example moreover illustrates the use of disjunctive pattern definitions pointing to two different parents which actually evolved in this case from two different kind of documents. Consider the root pattern `<document>` and its child patterns `<ebaydocument>` and `<yahoodocument>`. Both are specializations requiring that the document is an *eBay* page (a category search result on `www.ebay.com` such as `http://listings.ebay.com/aw/plistings/list/all/category3707/index.html`), or a *yahoo auctions* page (i.e., a search result of `auctions.yahoo.com`), respectively. Observe that the patterns `<ebaydocument>` and `<yahoodocument>` are not document patterns, but tree patterns, since they refer to instances of tree regions. The predicate *contains* is an internal condition,

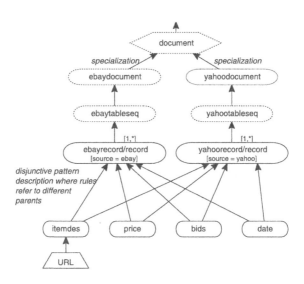

Fig. 4. Wrapper for *eBay/Yahoo* using Specialization and Disjunctive Patterns

expressing that there is an element in X which satisfies the given element path definition.

$$\text{document}(\mathtt{S}, \mathtt{X}) \leftarrow \text{getDocument}(\mathtt{S} = \$1, \mathtt{X})$$
$$\text{ebaydocument}(\mathtt{S}, \mathtt{X}) \leftarrow \text{document}(\mathtt{S}, \mathtt{X}),$$
$$\text{contains}(\mathtt{X}, (\star.\text{body}, [(\text{elementtext}, \text{eBay}, \text{substr})]), \_)$$
$$\text{yahoodocument}(\mathtt{S}, \mathtt{X}) \leftarrow \text{document}(\mathtt{S}, \mathtt{X}),$$
$$\text{contains}(\mathtt{X}, (\star.\text{body}, [(\text{elementtext}, \text{Yahoo}, \text{substr})]), \_)$$

5   Disjunctive Pattern Construction

There are several cases, where it is necessary to define more than one filter for the same pattern to express how to extract desired pieces of information from a Web page. In this section we show some real world examples where it is useful to define a pattern using a disjunction of filters. Moreover, we show that is generally possible that different filters of the same pattern can extract information from different parent patterns. Let us first consider an example where a wrapper designer wants to define a pattern consisting of filters that describe extraction targets for different page types. Assume a wrapper extracts prices from two kind of Web pages displaying books and their prices, where pages of the first kind are US pages and pages of the second kind are UK pages. The characteristic features of prices are a dollar sign on US Web pages and a pound sterling sign on UK pages. Assume, furthermore, the current sample page is a US page. A pattern named <price> should thus be defined via two filters: the first taking care of US pages and the second of UK pages. After having visually created an appropriate filter for prices in USD on an already loaded US sample page, the designer switches to a UK sample page and visually defines the second filter for the <price> pattern on that page. The wrapper then works on both types of pages.

In *Lixto* it is not only possible to create a pattern consisting of several filters, but also that filters of a particular pattern definition refer to a different parent pattern. Again, consider the example in Figure 4. For both the <ebaydocument> and the <yahoodocument> pattern we now have to extract the list of available items (records). Since records are structured differently in *eBay* and *yahoo auctions*, it is necessary to create for each kind of page a record pattern of its own, i.e. <ebayrecord> and <yahoorecord>. Once we have defined the patterns for the records, the patterns <itemdes>, <price>, <bids> and <date> can be easily defined with one filter for each kind of record. Although this wrapper works fine for both *yahoo* and *eBay* auctions, it still only returns results from one summary page as it does not follow the "next" link, and also is not capable of extracting detail information. Moreover, using the pattern <itemdes> as parent, a string pattern *URL* is defined using an attribute filter. This attribute filter extracts the value of the link to detailed information of the particular item. This attribute filter works for both sites, since both store the URL pointing to the detail page in the corresponding *href* attribute.

$$\text{URL}(\mathtt{S}, \mathtt{X}) \leftarrow \text{itemdes}(\_, \mathtt{S}), \text{subatt}(\mathtt{S}, \text{href}, \mathtt{X})$$

An attribute filter uses the extraction definition predicate *subatt* to extract an attribute value of instances of S and instantiates a string source X with it. The following additional features are currently implemented and can be added via *Lixto*'s XML Tool:

1. The pattern <ebayrecord> and <yahoorecord> can be both mapped to the XML element <record>, and an attribute *source* of <record> can be defined, which takes the constant value *eBay* or *yahoo*, respectively.
2. In case the string source of <URL> is a relative URL, a prefix variable (BASE) can be added to it, which has the value of the base URL of the document from which the information is extracted. This variable can also be used for following relative links when crawling to further pages (see next section).
3. Auxiliary patterns such as <ebaydocument> and <yahoodocument> can be decided to not being mapped to XML, and a DTD can be created by additionally assigning a multiplicity to each data type (Figure 4).

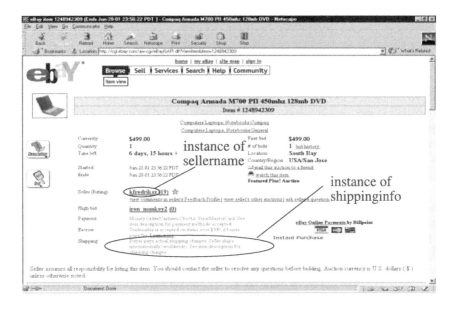

Fig. 5. Ebay item description page

6   Web Crawling and Recursive Wrapping

6.1   Following Links

For each item, *eBay* pages contain a reference to a page containing detailed information about the item itself. In the previous section, we have shown how to extract the URL pointing to detail pages, but we did not further use it. In this section we extend the wrapper program to extract also the detailed description of each item. This is an instance of a general class of applications, where a wrapper needs to collect and group together elements from several pages. The wrapper designer thus needs to "teach" the system on the base of sample pages how to follow URLs and collect the elements from the different pages. On *eBay*, each item is described by a line stating summary information for each given auction item. Each such line contains a link to a Web page with more detailed information on the respective item, such as the seller name and the shipping information (Figure 5).

The designer adds a child document pattern `<detaildocument>` to the string pattern `<URL>` which resulted from extracting the value of the *href* attribute of `<itemdes>`. For this, the designer proceeds by following one example detail document, loading the corresponding page, and defining the remaining relevant patterns (such as "sellername" and "shippinginfo") as child patterns of this new document pattern. Figure 6 illustrates an expanded *Elog* program of Figure 3, which defines an attribute filter extracting an URL (as in Figure 4), and a further document pattern consisting of one filter to extract detailed information for each item. The auxiliary patterns `<URL>` and `<detaildocument>` are not mapped to XML via the XML translation scheme. The navigation to a detail document looks as follows:

$$\mathrm{URL}(\mathrm{S}, \mathrm{X}) \leftarrow \mathtt{itemdes}(\_, \mathrm{S}), \mathtt{subatt}(\mathrm{S}, \mathtt{href}, \mathrm{X})$$
$$\mathtt{detaildocument}(\mathrm{S}, \mathrm{X}) \leftarrow \mathrm{URL}(\_, \mathrm{S}), \mathtt{getDocument}(\mathrm{S}, \mathrm{X})$$

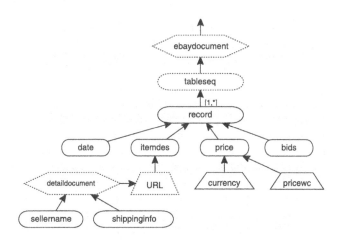

Fig. 6. Following Links

6.2 Recursive Wrapping

As we have already pointed out, each filter of a given pattern may refer to a different parent pattern. Here, we show how to apply this feature to reuse patterns. This paves the way for creating recursive programs. We call this kind of recursion *pattern recursion*. Another kind of recursion, *reference recursion*, based on pattern references is discussed in Section 7.

Let us first consider the example program below.

$$\mathtt{document(S, X) \leftarrow getDocument(\$1, X)}$$
$$\mathtt{table(S, X) \leftarrow document(\_, S), subelem(S, . \star .table, X)}$$
$$\mathtt{table(S, X) \leftarrow table(\_, S), subelem(S, . \star .table, X)}$$

It extracts all nested tables within one page, starting with the outermost, and stores them in this hierarchical order in the pattern instance base. The second rule of `<table>` is iteratively called, until no further table can be extracted.

Another possible use of recursively defined wrappers is the following real-world application. Usually a wrapper designer does not want to extract data from a single *eBay* page on notebooks, but from all pages which are connected to each other via a "next page" link. We illustrate how the *eBay* program of Figure 6 can be extended to follow the next link and can reuse the already created pattern structure. Thus, the pattern `<ebaydocument>` is a document pattern consisting of two filters with different parents. The first one refers to the specified start document, whereas the second one follows the "next" link on each page. This part of the program looks as follows:

$$\mathtt{next(S, X) \leftarrow ebaydocument(\_, S),}$$
$$\mathtt{subelem(S, (\star.content, [(href, , substr),}$$
$$\mathtt{(elementtext, (next\ page), exact)]), X)}$$
$$\mathtt{nexturl(S, X) \leftarrow next(\_, S), subatt(S, href, X)}$$
$$\mathtt{ebaydocument(S, X) \leftarrow getDocument(S = \$1, X)}$$
$$\mathtt{ebaydocument(S, X) \leftarrow nexturl(\_, S), getDocument(S, X)}$$

Recall that "$1" is interpreted as a constant whose value is the URL of the start document of a *Lixto* session. This initial filter was already present in the previous example, and is the starting point of evaluation. The second filter refers to a different parent pattern, which is `<nexturl>`. Instances of the pattern `<nexturl>` are string sources which represent an URL. The pattern `<nexturl>` is created via an attribute filter which extracts via *subatt* the value of "href" present in the element which contains the text "next page".

In the second rule defining the pattern `<ebaydocument>`, the variable S is instantiated with string sources which represent URLs. For each "next" link, a new instance of `<ebaydocument>` is created, pointing to the next page. This new page serves as parent pattern for `<tableseq>` and `<next>`. The pattern structure is hence re-used for this new page. In this example, two different document patterns are used, on the one hand `<ebaydocument>`, on the other hand `<detaildocument>`. Instances of the pattern `<ebaydocument>` are the summary pages, whereas instances of the pattern `<detaildocument>` are the detail information pages for each item. In an XML translation scheme, the wrapper designer moreover wants to state how the documents are arranged inside the XML document. Although further instances of `<ebaydocument>` are hierarchically embedded in the previous one, the wrapper designer may maintain all `<record>` instances on the same level.

In the visual interface of *Lixto*, a document pattern can be generated without the need to manually define auxiliary patterns. Instead visual guidance is offered for creating a single rule which uses a sequence of extraction definition predicates. For this example program, this single rule can be represented as follows:

$$\text{ebaydocument}(S, X) \leftarrow \text{ebaydocument}(\_, S), \text{subatt}(Y, \text{href}, Z), \text{getDocument}(Z, X)$$
$$\text{subelem}(S, (\star.\text{content}, [(\text{href}, , \text{substr}),$$
$$(\text{elementtext}, (\text{next page}), \text{exact})]), Y),$$

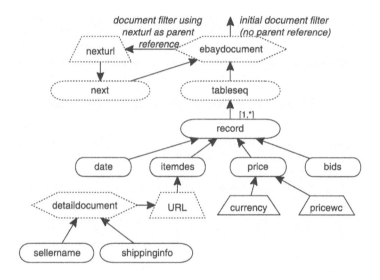

Fig. 7. Recursive Extraction

7 Nonmonotonic Issues

Minimization of pattern instances. The set of matched targets of an *Elog* pattern are minimized in the way that pattern instances which contain other instances of the same pattern w.r.t. the same parent-pattern instance, are ignored. Pattern minimization applies both to tree and string rules. If a pattern consists of a single filter, the minimized set of its matched targets equals the initial set except if the extraction definition predicate of the filter is *subregion* (which extracts a sequence of elements).

Consider the following simple example. Assume the major headlines of a particular newspaper Web page are a table consisting of various table data (the wrapper designer is interested in all the contents), and the minor headlines of the same newspaper which appear at the same page, are table columns of another table. The minor headlines are moreover characterized by a red font, and the major headlines contain a link (*href*) somewhere. However, the table containing the data of all minor headlines also contains links (i.e. the *href* attribute is a characteristic attribute occurring in these two tables only). A program for extracting all headlines can be written in the following way, where *par* is the parent pattern identifying the relevant area of the newspaper page.

$$\texttt{headline}(S, X) \leftarrow \texttt{par}(\_, S), \texttt{subelem}(S, . \star .\texttt{table}, X)$$
$$\texttt{contains}(S, (.\texttt{content}, [(\texttt{href}, , \texttt{substr})]), X)$$
$$\texttt{headline}(S, X) \leftarrow \texttt{par}(\_, S), \texttt{subelem}(S, . \star .\texttt{td}, X)$$
$$\texttt{contains}(S, (.\texttt{content}, [(\texttt{font} - \texttt{color}, \texttt{red}, \texttt{exact})]), X)$$

Hence, the first rule also matches the table which contains all minor headlines. However, since in this table, other pattern instances are matched, too, only the minimal instances are returned, which are in this case the table columns. For the major headlines, however, the table is extracted. Another example is the minimization of the set of instances generated by a single rule:

$$\texttt{tableseq}(S, X) \leftarrow \texttt{par}(\_, S), \texttt{subregion}(S, . \star .\texttt{body}. \star .\texttt{center}, .\texttt{table}, .\texttt{table}, X)$$

Such a rule (with additional conditions) is used in the *eBay* program of Figure 2. However, with no additional condition, the semantics is to extract all possible sequences of tables and to minimize the result; since the minimal sequences of tables are sequences of a single table, this rule returns such instances only. To enforce a particular longer sequence of tables, such as the sequence of tables containing the relevant data of sold items, some before and after conditions need to be added. In the case of *eBay*, immediately before and after the target instance a particular text or image shall occur, respectively. This returns a single pattern instance, the sequence of desired record tables.

Pattern minimization can be expressed in *Elog* extended with stratified negation and a suitable built-in predicate *contained_in(X, Y)* expressing offset-wise containment of X in Y. In particular, a set of filters of $p(S, X)$ defining the pattern p is rewritten in the following way. Consider the initial pattern definition:

$$p(S, X) \leftarrow \texttt{par}_1(\_, S), \texttt{Ex}_1(S, X), \texttt{Co}_1(S, X, \ldots)$$
$$p(S, X) \leftarrow \cdots$$
$$p(S, X) \leftarrow \texttt{par}_n(\_, S), \texttt{Ex}_n(S, X), \texttt{Co}_n(S, X, \ldots)$$

The pattern name is renamed to p' and additional rules are added:

$$p'(S, X) \leftarrow \texttt{par}_1(\_, S), \texttt{Ex}_1(S, X), \texttt{Co}_1(S, X, \ldots)$$
$$p'(S, X) \leftarrow \cdots$$
$$p'(S, X) \leftarrow \texttt{par}_n(\_, S), \texttt{Ex}_n(S, X), \texttt{Co}_n(S, X, \ldots)$$
$$p''(S, X) \leftarrow p'(S, X), p'(S, X_1), \texttt{contained\_in}(X_1, X)$$
$$p(S, X) \leftarrow p'(S, X), \texttt{not } p''(S, X)$$

The final rule requires that instances of X and X_1 are both from the same parent pattern instance (otherwise, if they stem from different parent-pattern instances, minimization is usually undesired). In the rewriting, p' is the pattern predicate initially being built by different filters. Each instance $p(s, x)$, which is non-minimal, i.e. for which there exists a smaller valid $p''(s, x)$, is not derived. Only minimal instances are derived.

Ranges. The semantics of range criteria $[a, b]$ of a filter rule $NewPat(S, X) \leftarrow filterbody[a, b]$ can also be expressed by a suitable rewriting of the rule. A range condition assumes that an order relation is defined among pattern instances extracted by the same parent pattern instance, thus in the rewriting we assume the presence of a predicate $greater(S, X, Y)$ which evaluates to *true* if X and Y are instances derived from S and X precedes Y (using character offsets for comparison). The first step of rewriting consists of adding a new predicate $NewPat'$ that is defined by a unique filter $NewPat'(S, X) \leftarrow filterbody$. Then, two predicates $FirstSol$ and $succ$ are defined. $FirstSol$ selects from the instances in $NewPat'$ the first instance, and $succ$ defines a successor relation among instances in $NewPat'$ (due to the lack of space we omit the formal definition). The complete rewriting is as follows:

$$\text{NewPat}(S, X) \leftarrow \text{NewPat}'(S, X), \text{Solposition}(S, X, P), a \leq P \leq b$$
$$\text{Solposition}(S, X, 1) \leftarrow \text{NewPat}'(S, X), \text{FirstSol}(S, X)$$
$$\text{Solposition}(S, X, P) \leftarrow \text{Solposition}(S, X', P'), \text{NewPat}'(S, X), \text{succ}(S, X', X), P = P' + 1.$$

In both predicates $FirstSol$ and $succ$, the predicate $NewPat'$ appears negated, hence, the predicate $NewPat$ depends on negation of all the predicates appearing in $filterbody$.

Pattern Reference Recursion and Ranges. Using ranges together with pattern references might introduce unstratified negation. Using pattern references can introduce *reference recursion*. Still, without ranges, a unique model is returned. However, additionally allowing range conditions to occur in such recursive rules requires to use a semantics akin to the stable model semantics (returning multiple models) or well-founded semantics (returning a minimal model) as this introduces unstratified negation into the program (considering the above rewriting). For the following example (possibly containing additional filters for p and q), a nonmonotonic semantics is required.

$$p(S, X) \leftarrow par(\_, S), subelem(S, epd, X), before(S, X, \ldots, Y), q(S, Y)[a, b]$$
$$q(S, X) \leftarrow par(\_, S), subelem(S, epd, X), before(S, X, \ldots, Y), p(S, Y)[c, d]$$

Observe that a program which uses range and pattern recursion, but no reference recursion, is always locally stratified, i.e. its ground instantiation is stratified. For implementation issues, we limit pattern references in the way that the program remains locally stratified. This is a subset of programs whose rewriting contains only stratified negation.

8   Current/Future Work

Further work includes to consider various extensions of *Elog* such as using stratified negation instead of special negative predicates like *notbefore*, to extend
handling of pattern references together with recursion as discussed above, to
study further possibilities of conditions such as universally quantified ones (that
require all elements to have a particular feature), and complement extraction
(e.g. to remove advertisments from Web pages). An editor of *Elog* rules will be
offered for more experienced wrapper designers who nevertheless lack programming facilities. This editor describes *Elog* patterns using a colloquial pattern
description language. A concept editor for adding syntactic and semantic concepts to the list of built-in predicates is currently under construction. Moreover,
the *Lixto* prototype is currently being re-designed as servlet version allowing
pattern generation in the user's favorite browser. Finally, an *Elog2XSLT* conversion tool is going to be developed which will transform a subset of possible
Elog programs into XSLT.

References

1. S. Abiteboul, P. Buneman, and D. Suciu. *Data on the Web - From Relations to
   Semistructured Data and XML*. Morgan Kaufmann, 2000. 21
2. B. Adelberg. NoDoSE - a tool for semi-automatically extracting semi-structured
   data from text documents. In *Proc. of SIGMOD*, 1998. 21
3. P. Atzeni and G. Mecca. Cut and paste. In *Proc. of PODS*, 1997. 21
4. R. Baumgartner, S. Flesca, and G. Gottlob. Supervised wrapper generation with
   Lixto. To appear in *Proc. of VLDB (Demonstration Session)*, 2001. 22
5. R. Baumgartner, S. Flesca, and G. Gottlob. Visual web information extraction
   with lixto. To appear in *Proc. of VLDB*, 2001. 21, 22, 23, 28
6. S. Chawathe. Describing and manipulating XML data. *Bulletin of the IEEE
   Technical Committee on Data Engineering*, 22(3):3-9, 1999. Invited paper. 21
7. H. Davulcu, G. Yang, M. Kifer, and I. V. Ramakrishnan. Computat. aspects of
   resilient data extract. from semistr. sources. In *Proc. of PODS*, 2000. 21
8. C-N. Hsu and M. T. Dung. Generating finite-state transducers for semistructured
   data extraction from the web. *Information Systems*, 23/8, 1998. 21
9. G. Huck, P. Fankhauser, K. Aberer, and E. J. Neuhold. JEDI: Extracting and
   synthesizing information from the web. In *Proc. of COOPIS*, 1998. 21
10. N. Kushmerick, D. Weld, and R. Doorenbos. Wrapper induction for information
    extraction. In *Proc. of IJCAI*, 1997. 21
11. L. Liu, C. Pu, and W. Han. XWrap: An extensible wrapper construction system
    for internet information. In *Proc. of ICDE*, 2000. 21
12. W. May, R. Himmeröder, G. Lausen, and B. Ludäscher. A unified framework for
    wrapping, mediating and restructuring information from the web. In *WWWCM*.
    Sprg. LNCS 1727, 1999. 21
13. I. Muslea, S. Minton, and C. Knoblock. A hierarchical approach to wrapper in-
    duction. In *Proc. of 3rd Intern. Conf. on Autonomous Agents*, 1999. 21
14. A. Sahuguet and F. Azavant. Building light-weight wrappers for legacy web data-
    sources using W4F. In *Proc. of VLDB*, 1999. 21

On the Complexity of Model Checking and Inference in Minimal Models

Extended Abstract

Lefteris M. Kirousis[1*] and Phokion G. Kolaitis[2**]

[1] Department of Computer Engineering and Informatics, University of Patras
GR-265 04 Patras, Greece
kirousis@ceid.upatras.gr
[2] Computer Science Department, University of California, Santa Cruz
Santa Cruz, CA 95064, USA
kolaitis@cse.ucsc.edu

Abstract. Every logical formalism gives rise to two fundamental algorithmic problems: model checking and inference. In propositional logic,
the model checking problem is polynomial-time solvable, while the inference problem is coNP-complete. In propositional circumscription, however, these problems have higher computational complexity, namely the
model checking problem is coNP-complete, while the inference problem
is Π_2^{P}-complete. In this paper, we survey recent results on the computational complexity of restricted cases of these problems in the context of
Schaefer's framework of generalized satisfiability problems. These results
establish dichotomies in the complexity of the model checking problem
and the inference problem for propositional circumscription. Specifically,
in each restricted case the model checking problem for propositional circumscription either is coNP-complete or is polynomial-time solvable.
Furthermore, in each restricted case the inference problem for propositional circumscription either is Π_2^{P}-complete or is in coNP. These dichotomy theorems yield a complete classification of the "hard" and the
"easier" cases of the model checking problem and the inference problem for propositional circumscription. Moreover, they provide efficiently
checkable criteria that tell apart the "hard" cases from the "easier" ones.

1 Introduction

Circumscription, introduced by McCarthy [McC80], is one of the most well developed and extensively studied formalisms of nonmonotonic reasoning. In circumscription, formulas of a logic are used to specify properties of objects, models
of formulas are ordered according to a suitable partial order, and preference is

---

* Part of this research was carried out while on sabbatical at the University of California, Santa Cruz. Research partially supported by the Research Commmittee of
the University of Patras and by the Computer Technology Institute.

** Research partially supported by NSF grants CCR-9610257 and CCR-9732041.

T. Eiter, W. Faber, and M. Truszczyński (Eds.): LPNMR 2001, LNAI 2173, pp. 42–53, 2001.
© Springer-Verlag Berlin Heidelberg 2001

given to models that are minimal with respect to this partial order. The key intuition behind the focus on minimal models is that they are the ones that embody common sense, because they have as few "exceptions" as possible. Consequently, circumscription can be thought of as an application of Ockham's razor principle (principle of parsimony) to the formalization of common-sense reasoning.

Propositional circumscription is the basic case of circumscription in which satisfying truth assignments of propositional formulas are partially ordered according to the *coordinatewise* partial order $\leq$ on Boolean vectors, which extends the order $0 \leq 1$ on $\{0, 1\}$. Specifically, if $\alpha = (a_1, \ldots, a_n)$ and $\beta = (b_1, \ldots, b_n)$ are two truth assignments, then $\alpha \leq \beta$ holds if $a_i \leq b_i$ for every i such that $1 \leq i \leq n$. A *minimal model* of a propositional formula φ is a truth assignment α such that the following two conditions hold: (1) $\alpha(\varphi) = 1$; (2) if β is a truth assignment such that $\beta(\varphi) = 1$ and $\beta \leq \alpha$, then $\alpha = \beta$. For example, the minimal models of the formula $(x \vee y) \wedge (\neg x \vee y) \wedge (x \vee \neg y)$ are $(0, 1)$ and $(1, 0)$.

Every logical formalism gives rise to two fundamental decision problems: *model checking* and *inference*. Intuitively, the former is the problem of deciding whether a "structure" satisfies a "formula", whereas the latter is the problem of deciding whether a "formula" can be inferred from another "formula" in the context of the formalism under consideration. In the case of propositional circumscription, these two problems take the following precise form.

Definition 1: The *model checking problem for propositional circumscription* asks: given a propositional formula φ and a truth assignment α, is α a minimal model of φ?

The *inference problem for propositional circumscription* asks: given two propositional formulas φ and ψ, is ψ true in every minimal model of φ?

We write $\varphi \models_{\text{CIRC}} \psi$ to denote that ψ is true in every minimal model of φ.

□

It has been shown that the model checking problem for propositional circumscription is coNP-complete (Cadoli [Cad92]), whereas the inference problem for propositional circumscription is Π_2^P-complete[1] (Eiter and Gottlob [EG93]). In fact, the model checking problem for propositional circumscription remains coNP-complete even when restricted to 3CNF-formulas, while the inference problem $\varphi \models_{\text{CIRC}} \psi$ for propositional circumscription remains Π_2^P-complete even when φ is a 3CNF-formula and ψ is a negative literal $\neg u$. These results quantify the increase in computational complexity that arises when making the transition from ordinary propositional logic to propositional circumscription, since in the case of ordinary propositional logic the model checking problem is solvable in linear time and the inference problem is coNP-complete (Cook [Coo71]). Moreover, these results raise the problem of identifying restricted cases in which the model checking problem and the inference problem for propositional circumscription have computational complexity lower than the general case. To this effect, Cadoli [Cad92,Cad93] found several polynomial-time solvable cases of the model

---

[1] The class Π_2^P forms the second level of the polynomial hierarchy PH, and contains both NP and coNP as subclasses (see [Pap94]).

checking problem for propositional circumscription; in a similar vein, Cadoli and Lenzerini [CL94] studied restricted cases in which the inference problem for propositional circumscription is polynomial-time solvable or is in coNP.

In studying restricted cases of an algorithmic problem, ideally one would like to have a rich conceptual framework that makes it possible to express a variety of restricted cases and analyze their complexity. For Boolean satisfiability, such a framework was introduced and investigated by Schaefer [Sch78], who succeeded in obtaining a complete classification of the complexity of Boolean satisfiability problems in this framework. Cadoli [Cad92,Cad93] proposed that the model checking problem for propositional circumscription be investigated in Schaefer's framework and raised the question of whether it is possible to obtain a complete classification of its complexity. This question was settled affirmatively in [KK01a]; moreover, in [KK01b] the complexity of the inference problem for propositional circumscription was investigated in the context of Schaefer's framework and a characterization of the Π_2^P-complete cases was obtained.

The balance of this extended abstract is organized as follows. In Section 2, we present Schaefer's framework and state his main results on the complexity of Boolean satisfiability problems. In Section 3, we describe our results on the complexity of the model checking problem and the inference problem for propositional circumscription in the context of Schaefer's framework. Finally, in Section 4 we discuss certain open problems and directions for future research.

2   Schaefer's Framework for Boolean Satisfiability

A *logical relation* R is a non-empty subset of $\{0,1\}^k$, for some $k \geq 1$. Such a logical relation can be thought of as the set of all satisfying truth assignments of a *generalized propositional connective* R'. Schaefer [Sch78] investigated Boolean satisfiability problems in which the inputs are formulas in *generalized conjunctive normal form*, that is to say, they are conjunctions of atomic formulas derived from a fixed finite set of logical relations.

Definition 2: Let $S = \{R_1, \ldots, R_m\}$ be a finite set of logical relations of various arities, let $S' = \{R_1', \ldots, R_m'\}$ be a set of relation symbols whose arities match those of the relations in S, and let V be an infinite set of variables.

– A CNF(S)-formula is a finite conjunction $C_1 \wedge \ldots \wedge C_n$ of clauses built using relation symbols from S', variables from V, and the constants **0** and **1**, that is, each C_i is an atomic formula of the form $R_j'(\xi_1, \ldots, \xi_k)$, where R_j' is a relation symbol of arity k in S', and each ξ_j is a variable in V or one of the constants **0** and **1**. The semantics of CNF(S)-formulas are defined in a standard way by assuming that variables range over the set of bits $\{0,1\}$, each relation symbol R_j' in S' is interpreted by the corresponding relation R_j in S, and the constant symbols **0** and **1** are interpreted by 0 and 1 respectively.

– SAT(S) is the following decision problem: given a CNF(S)-formula φ, is it satisfiable? (i.e., is there a truth assignment to the variables of φ that makes every clause of φ true?)   □

It is clear that, for each finite set S of logical relations, $\text{SAT}(S)$ is a problem in NP. Moreover, the family of all $\text{SAT}(S)$ problems contains several well-known variants of Boolean satisfiability, as evidenced by the following examples.

Example 3: 3-SAT, the prototypical NP-complete problem, coincides with the problem $\text{SAT}(S)$, where $S = \{R_0, R_1, R_2, R_3\}$ and

- $R_0 = \{0,1\}^3 - \{(0,0,0)\}$ (expressing the clause $(x \vee y \vee z)$);
- $R_1 = \{0,1\}^3 - \{(1,0,0)\}$ (expressing the clause $(\neg x \vee y \vee z)$);
- $R_2 = \{0,1\}^3 - \{(1,1,0)\}$ (expressing the clause $(\neg x \vee \neg y \vee z)$);
- $R_3 = \{0,1\}^3 - \{(1,1,1)\}$ (expressing the clause $(\neg x \vee \neg y \vee \neg z)$).

Similarly, but on the side of tractability, 2-SAT coincides with the problem $\text{SAT}(S)$, where $S = \{T_0, T_1, T_2\}$ and

- $T_0 = \{0,1\}^2 - \{(0,0)\}$ (expressing the clause $(x \vee y)$);
- $T_1 = \{0,1\}^2 - \{(1,0)\}$ (expressing the clause $(\neg x \vee y)$);
- $T_2 = \{0,1\}^2 - \{(1,1)\}$ (expressing the clause $(\neg x \vee \neg y)$).

POSITIVE-1-IN-3-SAT is the following decision problem: given a 3CNF-formula such that each clause is of the form $(x \vee y \vee z)$, does there exist a truth assignment that makes true exactly one variable in each clause? This problem is known to be NP-complete ([GJ79, LO4, page 259]). A moments' reflection reveals that POSITIVE-1-IN-3-SAT coincides with the problem $\text{SAT}(S)$, where S is the singleton $\{R_{1/3}\}$ consisting of the relation

$$R_{1/3} = \{(1,0,0), (0,1,0), (0,0,1)\}.$$

Furthermore, it is easy to see that several other variants of Boolean satisfiability, including 1-IN-3-SAT, NOT-ALL-EQUAL-3-SAT and HORN 3-SAT, can be cast as $\text{SAT}(S)$ problems for particular sets S of logical relations.   □

The above examples demonstrate that the family of all $\text{SAT}(S)$ problems constitutes a flexible and rich framework for expressing restricted cases of Boolean satisfiability. Schaefer [Sch78] studied the computational complexity of $\text{SAT}(S)$ problems and obtained the following remarkable classification theorem: for every finite set S of logical relations, either $\text{SAT}(S)$ is NP-complete or $\text{SAT}(S)$ is solvable in polynomial time; moreover, there is an algorithm to decide whether $\text{SAT}(S)$ is NP-complete or solvable in polynomial time. To appreciate Schaefer's result, one should recall that Ladner [Lad75] showed that if P $\neq$ NP, then there are problems in NP that are neither NP-complete nor in P, i.e., there exist problems of intermediate computational complexity between NP-complete and polynomial-time solvable. Consequently, Schaefer's result can be described as a *dichotomy theorem* asserting that no $\text{SAT}(S)$ problem is of such intermediate computational complexity. In fact, Schaefer's result was the first non-trivial dichotomy theorem for a family of NP-complete problems. Since that time, dichotomy theorems have been obtained for several other families of decision, counting, enumeration, and optimization problems (for instance, see [FHW80,HN90,Cre95,CH96,CH97,KSW97]). Overall, however, dichotomy theorems for families of algorithmic problems are rare; moreover, in view of Ladner's theorem [Lad75], their existence cannot be taken for granted.

Before stating Schaefer's dichotomy theorem in precise terms, we need to introduce several necessary concepts.

Definition 4: Let φ be a propositional formula.

- φ is *bijunctive* if it is a 2CNF-formula, i.e., it is a conjunction of clauses each of which is a disjunction of at most two literals.
- φ is *Horn* if it is the conjunction of clauses each of which is a disjunction of literals such that at most one of them is a variable.
- φ is *dual Horn* if it is the conjunction of clauses each of which is disjunction of literals such that at most one of them is a negated variable.
- φ is *affine* if it is the conjunction of subformulas each of which is an *exclusive disjunction* of literals or a negation of an exclusive disjunctions of literals (by definition, an exclusive disjunction of literals is satisfied exactly when an odd number of these literals are true; we will use $\oplus$ as the symbol of the exclusive disjunction).

Note that a formula φ is affine precisely when the set of its satisfying assignments is the set of solutions of a system of linear equations over the field $\{0, 1\}$.   □

Definition 5: Let R be a logical relation and S a finite set of logical relations.

- R is *bijunctive* (*Horn*, *dual Horn*, or *affine*, respectively) if there is a propositional formula φ which is bijunctive (Horn, dual Horn, or affine, respectively) and such that R coincides with the set of truth assignments satisfying φ.

- S is *Schaefer* if at least one of the following four conditions hold:
  • every member of S is bijunctive;
  • every member of S is Horn;
  • every member of S is dual Horn;
  • every member of S is affine.

- Otherwise, we say that S is *non-Schaefer*.   □

There are simple criteria to determine whether a logical relation is bijunctive, Horn, dual Horn, or affine. In fact, a set of such criteria was already provided by Schaefer [Sch78]; moreover, Dechter and Pearl [DP92] gave even simpler criteria for a relation to be Horn or dual Horn. Each of these criteria involves a *closure property* of the logical relations at hand under a certain function. Specifically, a relation R is bijunctive if and only if for all $t_1, t_2, t_3 \in R$, we have that $(t_1 \vee t_2) \wedge (t_2 \vee t_3) \wedge (t_1 \vee t_3) \in R$, where the operators $\vee$ and $\wedge$ are applied coordinate-wise to the bit-tuples. Note that the i-th coordinate of the tuple $(t_1 \vee t_2) \wedge (t_2 \vee t_3) \wedge (t_1 \vee t_3)$ is equal to 1 exactly when the majority of the i-th coordinates of t_1, t_2, t_3 is equal to 1. Thus, this criterion states that R is bijunctive exactly when it is closed under coordinate-wise applications of the ternary *majority* function. R is Horn (respectively, dual Horn) if and only if for all $t_1, t_2 \in R$, we have that $t_1 \wedge t_2 \in R$

(respectively, $t_1 \vee t_2 \in R$). Finally, R is affine if and only if for all $t_1, t_2, t_3 \in R$, we have that $t_1 \oplus t_2 \oplus t_3 \in R$. As an example, it is easy to apply these criteria to the ternary relation $R_{1/3} = \{(1, 0, 0), (0, 1, 0), (0, 0, 1)\}$ and verify that $R_{1/3}$ is neither bijunctive, nor Horn, nor dual Horn, nor affine.

There are well-known polynomial-time algorithms for the satisfiability problem for the class of all bijunctive formulas (2-SAT), the class of all Horn formulas, and the class of all dual Horn formulas. Moreover, if S is an affine set of logical relations, then SAT(S) is solvable in polynomial time using Gaussian elimination. Schaefer's seminal discovery was that these four cases are the *only* ones that give rise to tractable cases of SAT(S).

Theorem 6: [Schaefer's Dichotomy Theorem, [Sch78]] *Let S be a finite set of logical relations. If S is Schaefer, then* SAT(S) *is solvable in polynomial time; otherwise, it is is* NP-*complete.*

As an application, Theorem 6 immediately implies that POSITIVE-1-IN-3-SAT is NP-complete, since it coincides with SAT($R_{1/3}$), and $R_{1/3}$ is not Schaefer.

To obtain the above dichotomy theorems, Schaefer had to first establish a result concerning the expressive power of CNF(S) formulas. Informally, this result asserts that if S is a non-Schaefer set of logical relations, then CNF(S)-formulas have extremely highy expressive power, in the sense that every logical relation can be defined from a CNF(S)-formula using existential quantification.

Theorem 7: [Schaefer's Expressibility Theorem, [Sch78]] *Let S be a finite set of logical relations. If S is non-Schaefer, then for every k-ary logical relation R there is a* CNF(S)-formula $\varphi(x_1, \ldots, x_k, z_1, \ldots, z_m)$ *such that R coincides with the set of all truth assignments to the variables $x_1, \ldots, x_k$ that satisfy the formula* $(\exists z_1) \cdots (\exists z_m) \varphi(x_1, \ldots, x_k, z_1, \ldots, z_m)$.

3 Model Checking and Inference in Circumscription

Schaefer's framework makes it possible to introduce and study restricted cases of the model checking problem and the inference problem for propositional circumscription.

Definition 8: Let S be a finite set of logical relations.

– MC-CIRC(S) is the following decision problem: given a CNF(S)-formula φ and a truth assignment α, is α a minimal model of φ?

– INF-CIRC(S) is the following decision problem: given a CNF(S)-formula φ and a CNF-formula ψ, is ψ true in every minimal model of φ?   □

Using the definitions, it is easy to see that, for every finite set S of logical relations, MC-CIRC(S) is in coNP and INF-CIRC(S) is in Π_2^P. There are natural sets S of logical relations such that MC-CIRC(S) is coNP-complete and INF-CIRC(S) is Π_2^P-complete. In particular, this holds true for the set

$S = \{R_0, R_1, R_2, R_3\}$ of logical relations in Example 3 that give rise to 3-SAT (see [Cad92,Cad93,EG93]). In contrast, as pointed out in [Cad92,Cad93,CL94], if S is a bijunctive or a dual Horn set of logical relations, then MC-CIRC(S) in P and INF-CIRC(S) is in coNP. Moreover, if S is a Horn set of logical relations, then both MC-CIRC(S) and INF-CIRC(S) are in P; this is so because every satisfiable Horn formula has a *minimum* (unique minimal) satisfying truth assignment that can be found in polynomial time.

In view of Schaefer's dichotomy theorem for Boolean satisfiability problems, it is natural to ask whether similar dichotomy theorems can be obtained for the family MC-CIRC(S) of model checking problems for propositional circumscription and the family INF-CIRC(S) of inference problems for propositional circumscription, where S is a finite set of logical relations. At first, one may expect that, if such dichotomy theorems hold, then the boundary of the dichotomy will be the same as that in Schaefer's dichotomy theorem. In particular, one may expect that if S is a non-Schaefer set of logical relations, then MC-CIRC(S) should be coNP-complete and INF-CIRC(S) should be Π_2^P-complete. Nevertheless, this turns out to be a rather naive expectation. Indeed, consider the set $S = \{R_{1/3}\}$ consisting of the logical relation $R_{1/3} = \{(1,0,0),(0,1,0),(0,0,1)\}$. As seen earlier, S is non-Schaefer and so SAT(S) is NP-complete (recall that in this case SAT(S) is POSITIVE-1-IN-3-SAT). It is easy to see, however, that if φ is a CNF(S)-formula, then *every* satisfying truth assignment of φ is a minimal model of φ. Consequently, MC-CIRC(S) is in P (in fact, it is solvable in linear time) and INF-CIRC(S) is in coNP (in fact, it is coNP-complete).

In [KK01a], the following dichotomy theorem was established for the family MC-CIRC(S) of model checking problems for propositional circumscription: if S is a finite set of logical relations, then either MC-CIRC(S) is coNP-complete or MC-CIRC(S) is in P. Furthermore, in [KK01b], the following dichotomy theorem was established for the family INF-CIRC(S) of inference problems for propositional circumscription: if S is a finite set of logical relations, then either INF-CIRC(S) is Π_2^P-complete or INF-CIRC(S) is in coNP. It was also shown that the boundaries in these two dichotomies coincide, but differ from the boundary in Schaefer's dichotomy theorem for Boolean satisfiability problems. These new dichotomy theorems were proved by first establishing corresponding dichotomy theorems in a key special case and then using the results for this special case as a stepping stone towards the full dichotomy theorems.

Definition 9: A k-ary logical relation R is *1-valid* if it contains the all-ones k-tuple $(1, \ldots, 1)$. A set S of logical relations is *1-valid* if every relation in S is 1-valid. □

For example, the logical relation $K = \{(1,1,1),(0,1,0),(0,0,1)\}$ is 1-valid. Note that the set $S = \{R_0, R_1, R_2, R_3\}$ in Example 3 is not 1-valid, since the relation R_3 is not 1-valid. In contrast, the set $P = \{R_0, R_1, R_2\}$ is 1-valid.

We now have all the prerequisites to state our dichotomy theorems for the model checking problem MC-CIRC(S) and the inference problem INF-CIRC(S), when S is a 1-valid set of logical relations. In this case, the boundary of the dichotomies coincides with the boundary in Schaefer's dichotomy theorem.

Theorem 10: [KK01a,KK01b] *Let S be a 1-valid set of logical relations.*

– *If S is Schaefer, then* MC-CIRC(S) *is in* P; *otherwise, it is* coNP-*complete.*

– *If S is Schaefer, then* INF-CIRC(S) *is in* coNP; *otherwise, it is* Π_2^P-*complete. Actually, if S is non-Schaefer, then even the following case of* INF-CIRC(S) *is* Π_2^P-*complete: given a* CNF(S)-*formula φ and a negative literal $\neg u$, does $\varphi \models_{CIRC} \neg u$?*

Moreover, there is a polynomial-time algorithm to decide, given a finite 1-valid set of logical relations, whether MC-CIRC(S) *is in* P *or* coNP-*complete, and also whether* INF-CIRC(S) *is in* coNP *or* Π_2^P-*complete.*

The following examples illustrate the preceding Theorem 10 and provide new instances of restricted cases of the model checking problems and the inference problem for propositional circumscription having the same inherent complexity as the general case.

Example 11 : Consider again the logical relation $K = \{(1,1,1), (0,1,0), (0,0,1)\}$. Using the closure properties that characterize when a logical relation is bijunctive, Horn, dual Horn, or affine, it is easy to see that K is none of the above. For instance, K is not Horn because $(0,1,0) \wedge (0,0,1) = (0,0,0) \notin K$; similarly, K is not affine because $(1,1,1) \oplus (0,1,0) \oplus (0,0,1) = (1,0,0) \notin K$. Consequently, Theorem 10 implies that MC-CIRC$(\{K\})$ is coNP-complete and INF-CIRC$(\{K\})$ is Π_2^P-complete.   □

Example 12: Consider the 1-valid set $P = \{R_0, R_1, R_2\}$, where, as seen earlier, $R_0 = \{0,1\}^3 - \{(0,0,0)\}$ (expressing the clause $(x \vee y \vee z)$), $R_1 = \{0,1\}^3 - \{(1,0,0)\}$ (expressing the clause $(\neg x \vee y \vee z)$), and $R_2 = \{0,1\}^3 - \{(1,1,0)\}$ (expressing the clause $(\neg x \vee \neg y \vee z)$). Thus, the class of CNF(P)-formulas consists of all 3CNF-formulas that do not contain a clause of the form $(\neg x \vee \neg y \vee \neg z)$. Using the closure properties, it is easy to verify that R_1 is not bijunctive, Horn, or affine, and that R_2 is not dual Horn. Consequently, Theorem 10 implies that MC-CIRC(P) is coNP-complete and INF-CIRC(P) is Π_2^P-complete.   □

Theorem 10 can be used as a stepping stone to obtain dichotomy theorems for the family of all MC-CIRC(S) problems and the family of all INF-CIRC(S) problems, where S is an arbitrary set of logical relations. To this effect, we use the following crucial concept, which was first introduced in [KK01a].

Definition 13: Let R be a k-ary logical relation. We say that a logical relation T is a 0-*section* of R if either T is the relation R itself or T can be defined from the formula $R'(x_1, \ldots, x_k)$ by replacing at least one, but not all, of the variables $x_1, \ldots, x_k$ by 0.   □

To illustrate this concept, observe that the 1-valid logical relation $\{(1)\}$ is a 0-section of $R'_{1/3} = \{(1,0,0), (0,1,0), (0,0,1)\}$, since it is definable by $R_{1/3}(x_1, 0, 0)$. Note that the logical relation $\{(1,0), (0,1)\}$ is also a 0-section of $R_{1/3}$, since it is definable by the formula $R'_{1/3}(0, x_2, x_3)$, but it is not 1-valid. In fact, it is easy to verify that $\{(1)\}$ is the *only* logical relation that is both 1-valid and a 0-section of $R_{1/3}$.

Theorem 14: [KK01a,KK01b] *Let S be a set of logical relations and let S^* be the set of all logical relations T such that T is both 1-valid and a 0-section of some relation in S.*

– If S^* is Schaefer, then MC-CIRC(S) is in P; otherwise, it is coNP-complete.

– If S^* is Schaefer, then INF-CIRC(S) is in coNP; otherwise, it is Π_2^P-complete. Actually, if S^* is non-Schaefer, then even the following case of INF-CIRC(S) is Π_2^P-complete: given a CNF(S)-formula φ and a negative literal $\neg u$, does $\varphi \models_{CIRC} \neg u$?

Moreover, there is a polynomial-time algorithm to decide, given a finite 1-valid set of logical relations, whether MC-CIRC(S) is in P or coNP-complete, and also whether INF-CIRC(S) is in coNP or Π_2^P-complete.

We now present several different examples that illustrate the power of Theorem 14. The first example shows how the main result in [EG93] can be easily derived from Theorem 14.

Example 15: Let $S = \{R_0, R_1, R_2, R_3\}$ be the set of logical relations that give rise to 3-SAT. Since R_0, R_1, R_2 are 1-valid logical relations, they are members of S^*. It follows that S^* is not Schaefer, since, as seen earlier, R_1 is not bijunctive, Horn or affine, and R_2 is not dual Horn. Theorem 14 immediately implies that INF-CIRC(S) is Π_2^P-complete.   □

Example 16: Consider the set $S = \{R_0, R_3\}$, where R_0 and R_3 are as in the preceding Example 15. In this case, SAT(S) is the problem MONOTONE 3-SAT, that is to say, the restriction of 3-SAT to 3CNF-formulas in which every clause is either the disjunction of positive literals or the disjunction of negative literals. It is well known that this problem is NP-complete (this can also be derived from Schaefer's Dichotomy Theorem 6). It is not hard to verify that every relation in S^* is dual Horn (for instance, S^* contains R_0, which is dual Horn). Consequently, Theorem 14 implies that MC-CIRC(S) is in P and INF-CIRC(S) is in coNP.   □

The preceding example shows that the boundary in Schaefer's dichotomy theorem for Boolean satisfiability is different from the boundary in the dichotomy theorem for the model checking problem and the inference problem in propositional circumscription. Our final example provides several other instances of this phenomenon.

Example 17: If m and n are two positive integers with $m < n$, then $R_{m/n}$ is the n-ary logical relation consisting of all n-tuples that have m ones and $n - m$ zeros. It is easy to see that $R_{m/n}$ is not Schaefer. Consequently, if S is a set of logical relations each of which is of the form $R_{m/n}$ for some m and n with $m < n$, then SAT(S) is NP-complete. In contrast, S^* is easily seen to be Horn (and, hence, Schaefer), since every relation T in S^* is a singleton $T = \{(1, \ldots, 1)\}$ consisting of the m-ary all-ones tuple for some m. Consequently, Theorem 14 implies that MC-CIRC(S) is in P and INF-CIRC(S) is in coNP.

This family of examples contains POSITIVE-1-IN-3-SAT as the special case where $S = \{R_{1/3}\}$.   □

Remark 18: The proofs of Theorem 10 and Theorem 14 can be found in [KK01a,KK01b]. They make use of the aforementioned Schaefer's expressibility theorem (Theorem 7), additional specialized expressibility results, and a series of delicate reductions between problems.

It should be pointed out that the problem actually studied in [KK01a] is the *minimal satisfiability* problem MIN SAT(S), which is the complement of MC-CIRC(S): given a CNF(S)-formula S and a satisfying truth assignment α, is there a satisfying truth assignment β of φ such that $\beta < \alpha$? Consequently, the dichotomy obtained in [KK01a] is a dichotomy between NP-completeness vs. membership in P, and clearly implies the dichotomy for MC-CIRC(S).

Note that here the logical constants **0** and **1** were allowed in the construction of CNF(S)-formulas. Schaefer [Sch78] also obtained a dichotomy theorem for the satisfiability problem SAT(S), when restricted to CNF(S)-formulas without constants; this result requires the deployment of additional technical machinery. Dichotomy theorems for MC-CIRC(S) and INF-CIRC(S), when restricted to CNF(S) formulas without constants were also obtained in [KK01a,KK01b].   □

Remark 19: The dichotomy theorem for the family INF-CIRC(S) can be interpreted as asserting that, for every finite set S of logical relations, either INF-CIRC(S) is as hard as the full inference problem for propositional circumscription (Π_2^P-complete) or INF-CIRC(S) is no harder than the inference problem for ordinary propositional logic (since the latter is coNP-complete).

It should be noted that researchers in computational complexity have isolated and studied several interesting complexity classes between coNP and Π_2^P, each with its own distinctive complete problems, such as the class DP of problems that are conjunctions of NP and coNP predicates. In fact, an entire hierarchy of complexity classes, known as the Boolean Hierarchy BH, is sandwiched between coNP and Π_2^P (see [Joh90]). Thus, our dichotomy theorem for the family INF-CIRC(S) reveals a dramatic gap in the complexity of the inference problem for propositional circumscription between sets S of logical relations that are Schaefer and those that are non-Schaefer.   □

4 Open Problems

The dichotomy theorem for the family INF-CIRC(S), where S is a finite set of logical relations, characterizes the "truly hard" (Π_2^P-complete) cases of the inference problem for propositional circumscription in Schaefer's framework, but leaves open the possibility that further distinctions can be made between the "easier" cases of this problem. To this effect, we conjecture that a *trichotomy theorem* holds for the family INF-CIRC(S). Specifically, we conjecture that, for every finite set S of logical relations, exactly one of the following three alternatives holds:

1. INF-CIRC(S) is Π_2^P-complete;
2. INF-CIRC(S) is coNP-complete;
3. INF-CIRC(S) is in P.

In view of the results described here, it remains to show that a dichotomy theorem holds for INF-CIRC(S), when S is a Schaefer set of logical relations. Although partial results in this direction have been obtained in [CL94], much more remains to be done. In particular, the exact complexity of INF-CIRC(S) is not known, when S is an affine set of logical relations.

All dichotomy theorems described here are rather special to Boolean logic. Schaefer [Sch78] raised the problem of establishing dichotomy theorems for satisfiability problems over domains with at least three elements, i.e., dichotomy theorems for many-valued propositional logic. This problem remains open to date with no solution in sight, even for the case of 3-valued logic.

References

Cad92. M. Cadoli. The complexity of model checking for circumscriptive formulae. *Information Processing Letters*, pages 113–118, 1992. 43, 44, 48

Cad93. M. Cadoli. *Two Methods for Tractable Reasoning in Artificial Intelligence: Language Restriction and Theory Approximation*. PhD thesis, Università Degli Studi Di Roma "La Sapienza", Rome, Italy, 1993. 43, 44, 48

CH96.   N. Creignou and M. Hermann. Complexity of generalized satisfiability counting problems. *Information and Computation*, 125(1):1–12, 1996. 46

CH97.   N. Creignou and J.-J. Herbrard. On generating all solutions of generalized satisfiability problems. *Theoretical Informatics and Applications*, 31(6):499–511, 1997. 46

CL94.   M. Cadoli and M. Lenzerini. The complexity of closed world reasoning and circumscription. *Journal of Information and System Sciences*, pages 255–301, 1994. Preliminary version in *Proceedings of the 8th National Conference on Artificial Intelligence* - AAAI '90. 44, 48, 52

Coo71. S. A. Cook. The complexity of theorem proving procedures. In *Proc. 3rd ACM Symp. on Theory of Computing*, pages 151–158, 1971. 43

Cre95. N. Creignou. A dichotomy theorem for maximum generalized satisfiability problems. *Journal of Computer and System Sciences*, 51:511–522, 1995. 46

DP92.   R. Dechter and J. Pearl. Structure identification in relational data. *Artificial Intelligence*, 48:237–270, 1992. 46

EG93.   Th. Eiter and G. Gottlob. Propositional circumscription and extended closed-world reasoning are Π_2^P-complete. *Theoretical Computer Science*, 114:231–245, 1993. 43, 48, 50

FHW80. S. Fortune, J. Hopcroft, and J. Wyllie. The directed homeomorphism problem. *Theoretical Computer Science*, 10:111–121, 1980. 46

GJ79.   M. R. Garey and D. S. Johnson. *Computers and Intractability - A Guide to the Theory of NP-Completeness*. W. H. Freeman and Co., 1979. 45

HN90.   P. Hell and J. Nešetřil. On the complexity of H-coloring. *Journal of Combinatorial Theory, Series B*, 48:92–110, 1990. 46

Joh90. D. S. Johnson. A catalog of complexity classes. In J. van Leeuwen, editor, *Handbook of Theoretical Computer Science, Volume A: Algorithms and Complexity*, chapter 2, pages 67–161. North-Holland, Amsterdam, 1990. 51

KK01a. L. M. Kirousis and Ph.G. Kolaitis. The complexity of minimal satisfiability problems. In *Proc. of the 18th Annual Symposium on Theoretical Aspects of Computer Science – STACS 2001*, volume 2010 of *Lecture Notes in Computer Science*, pages 407–418. Springer, 2001. Full version at: Electronic Colloquium on Computational Complexity - (www.eccc.uni-trier.de/eccc), Report No. 82, 2000. 44, 48, 49, 50, 51

KK01b. L. M. Kirousis and Ph.G. Kolaitis. A dichotomy in the complexity of propositional circumscription. In *Proc. of the 16th Annual IEEE Symposium on Logic in Computer Science – LICS 2001*, pages 71–80, 2001. 44, 48, 49, 50, 51

KSW97. S. Khanna, M. Sudan, and D. P. Williamson. A complete classification of the approximability of maximization problems derived from boolean constraint satisfaction. In *Proceedings of the 29th Annual ACM Symposium on Theory of Computing*, pages 11–20, 1997. 46

Lad75. R. Ladner. On the structure of polynomial time reducibility. *Journal of the Association for Computing Machinery*, 22:155–171, 1975. 45, 46

McC80. J. McCarthy. Circumscription - a form of nonmonotonic reasoning. *Artificial Intelligence*, 13:27–39, 1980. 42

Pap94. C. H. Papadimitriou. *Computational Complexity*. Addison-Wesley Publishing Company, 1994. 43

Sch78. T. J. Schaefer. The complexity of satisfiability problems. In *Proc. 10th ACM Symp. on Theory of Computing*, pages 216–226, 1978. 44, 45, 46, 47, 51, 52

Data Integration Needs Reasoning

Maurizio Lenzerini

Dipartimento di Informatica e Sistemistica, Università di Roma "La Sapienza"
Via Salaria 113, 00198 Roma, Italy
lenzerini@dis.uniroma1.it
http://www.dis.uniroma1.it/~lenzerini

Abstract. Data integration is the problem of combining the data residing at different sources, and providing a unified view of these data,
called global schema, which can be queried by the user. The interest in
this kind of systems has been continuously growing in the last years.
However, the design of a data integration system is a very complex task,
and several issues remains open, including how to express the relation
between the global schema and the sources, and how to process queries
expressed on the global schema. In this paper we deal with these two
problems, by presenting a logical framework for data integration, and
by discussing the various choices for both the specification of a data
integration system, and the design of query answering methods. Also,
we elaborate on the observation that, in real world scenarios, the case
of mutually inconsistent local databases will be very common, and we
present the basic ideas in order to extend the integration framework with
suitable nonmonotonic reasoning features for dealing with this case.

1 Introduction

Data integration is the problem of combining the data residing at different
sources, and providing the user with a unified view of these data, called global
schema, or global schema. The global schema is therefore a reconciled view of
the information, which can be queried by the user. It is the task of the data
integration system to free the user from the knowledge on where data are, and
how data are structured at the sources.

The interest in this kind of systems has been continuously growing in the
last years. However, the design of a data integration system is a very complex
task, and several issues remains open. Two main problems complicate the task:

1. How to express the relation between the global schema and the sources,
2. How to process queries expressed on the global schema.

With regard to Problem (1), two basic approaches have been used to specify
the relation between the sources and the global schema. The first approach, called
global-as-view (or query-based), requires that the global schema is expressed in
terms of the data sources. More precisely, to every concept of the global schema,
a view over the data sources is associated, so that its meaning is specified in

T. Eiter, W. Faber, and M. Truszczyński (Eds.): LPNMR 2001, LNAI 2173, pp. 54–61, 2001.
© Springer-Verlag Berlin Heidelberg 2001

terms of the data residing at the sources. The second approach, called *local-as-view* (or source-based), requires the global schema to be specified independently from the sources. The relationships between the global schema and the sources are established by defining every source as a view over the global schema. Thus, in the local-as-view approach, we specify the meaning of the sources in terms of the concepts in the global schema. It is clear that the latter approach favors the extensibility of the integration system, and provides a more appropriate setting for its maintenance. For example, adding a new source to the system requires only to provide the definition of the source, and does not necessarily involve changes in the global schema. On the contrary, in the global-as-view approach, adding a new source typically requires changing the definition of the concepts in the global schema. A comparison between the two approaches is reported in [20].

Problem (2) is concerned with the choice of the method for computing the answer to queries posed in terms of the global schema. While query answering in the global-as-view approach typically reduces to unfolding, an integration system based on the local-as-view approach must resort to more sophisticated query processing techniques. The main issue is that the system should be able to reason on the mapping so as to re-express the query in terms of a suitable set of queries posed to the sources. In this reformulation process, the crucial step is deciding how to decompose the query on the global schema into a set of subqueries on the sources, based on the meaning of the sources in terms of the concepts in the global schema. The computed subqueries are then shipped to the sources, and the results are assembled into the final answer.

Independently on the method used for the specification of the mapping between the global schema and the source schemas, it is easy to see that query processing in data integration is related to query answering using views. In turn, query answering using views can be seen as a form of reasoning with incomplete information. The interested reader is referred to [21] for a survey on this subject. Query answering using views has been investigated in the last years in the context of simplified frameworks. In [16,18], the problem has been studied for the case of conjunctive queries (with or without arithmetic comparisons), in [2] for disjunctive views, in [19,10,13] for queries with aggregates, in [11] for recursive queries and nonrecursive views, and in [6,7] for several variants of regular path queries. Comprehensive frameworks for view-based query answering, as well as several interesting results for various query languages, are presented in [12,1].

Query answering using views is also tightly related to query rewriting [16,11,20]. In general, a *rewriting* of a query with respect to a set of views is a function that, given the extensions of the views, returns a set of tuples that is contained in the answer set of the query with respect to the views. Usually, one fixes a priori the language in which to express rewritings (e.g., unions of conjunctive queries), and then looks for the best possible rewriting expressible in such a language. On the other hand, we may call *perfect* a rewriting that returns exactly the answer set of the query with respect to the views, independently of the language in which it is expressed. Hence, if an algorithm for answering queries using views exists, it can be viewed as a perfect rewriting [8,9].

In this paper, we present a logical framework for data integration, and we discuss the various choices for both the specification of a data integration systems, and the design of query answering methods. Also, we elaborate on the observation that, in real world scenarios, the case of mutually inconsistent source databases will be very common, and we present the basic ideas in order to extend the integration framework with suitable nonmonotonic reasoning features for dealing with this case.

The paper is organized as follows. In the next section we set up a formal framework for data integration, based on first order logic. In Section 3, we discuss three basic means for specifying the mapping between the global schema and the source schemas. In Section 4 we extend the framework in order to cope with the problem of integrating incoherent source databases. Section 5 concludes the paper.

2   Framework

In this section we set up a formal framework for *data integration systems* (DISs). In what follows, one of the main aspects is the definition of the semantics of both the DIS, and of queries posed to the global schema. For keeping things simple, we will use in the following a unique semantic domain Δ, composed of a fixed, infinite set of symbols.

Formally, a DIS $\mathcal{D}$ is a triple $\langle \mathcal{G}, \mathcal{S}, \mathcal{M}_{\mathcal{G},\mathcal{S}} \rangle$, where $\mathcal{G}$ is the global schema, $\mathcal{S}$ is the set of source schemas, and $\mathcal{M}_{\mathcal{G},\mathcal{S}}$ is the mapping between $\mathcal{G}$ and the source schemas in $\mathcal{S}$.

We denote with $\mathcal{A}_{\mathcal{G}}$ the alphabet of terms of the *global schema*, and we assume that the global schema $\mathcal{G}$ of a DIS is expressed as a theory (named simply $\mathcal{G}$) in a logic $\mathcal{L}_G$.

We assume to have a set $\mathcal{S}$ of n *source schemas* $\mathcal{S}_1, \ldots, \mathcal{S}_n$. We denote with $\mathcal{A}_{\mathcal{S}_i}$ the alphabet of terms of the source schema $\mathcal{S}_i$. We also denote with $\mathcal{A}_{\mathcal{S}}$ the union of all the $\mathcal{A}_{\mathcal{S}_i}$'s. We assume that the various $\mathcal{A}_{\mathcal{S}_i}$'s are mutually disjoint, and each one is disjoint from the alphabet $\mathcal{A}_{\mathcal{G}}$. We assume that each source schema is expressed as a theory (named simply $\mathcal{S}_i$) in a logic $\mathcal{L}_{S_i}$, and we use $\mathcal{S}$ to denote the collection of theories $\mathcal{S}_1, \ldots, \mathcal{S}_n$.

The *mapping* $\mathcal{M}_{\mathcal{G},\mathcal{S}}$ is the heart of the DIS, in that it specifies how the concepts[1] in the global schema and in the source schemas map to each other. We discuss this aspect more deeply in the next section. Here, we simply assume that $\mathcal{M}_{\mathcal{G},\mathcal{S}}$ is an appropriate specification of how the concepts in the various schemas map to each other.

Intuitively, in specifying the *semantics* of a DIS, we have to start with a model of the source schemas, and the crucial point is to specify which are the models of the global schema. Thus, for assigning semantics to a DIS $\mathcal{I} = \langle \mathcal{G}, \mathcal{S}, \mathcal{M}_{\mathcal{G},\mathcal{S}} \rangle$, we start by considering a *source model* $\mathcal{B}$ for $\mathcal{D}$, i.e., an interpretation that is a model

---

[1] Here and below we use the term "concept" for denoting a concept of the schema, which in turn can be represented either by a class or by a relation (not necessarily atomic) in logic.

for all the theories of $\mathcal{S}$. We call *global interpretation* for $\mathcal{D}$ any interpretation for $\mathcal{G}$. A global interpretation $\mathcal{I}$ for $\mathcal{D}$ is said to be a *global model for $\mathcal{D}$ wrt $\mathcal{B}$* if:

- $\mathcal{I}$ is a model of $\mathcal{G}$,
- $\mathcal{I}$ satisfies the mapping $\mathcal{M}_{\mathcal{G},\mathcal{S}}$ wrt $\mathcal{B}$.

In the next section, we will come back to the notion of satisfying a mapping wrt a source model. The semantics of $\mathcal{D}$, denoted $sem(\mathcal{D})$, is defined as follows:

$$sem(\mathcal{D}) = \{\ \mathcal{I} \mid \text{there exists a source model } \mathcal{B} \text{ for } \mathcal{D}$$
$$\text{s.t. } \mathcal{I} \text{ is a global model for } \mathcal{D} \text{ wrt } \mathcal{B}\ \}$$

Queries posed to a DIS $\mathcal{D}$ are expressed in terms of a query language $\mathcal{Q}_{\mathcal{G}}$ over the alphabet $\mathcal{A}_{\mathcal{G}}$ and are intended to extract a set of tuples of elements of Δ. Thus, every query has an associated arity, and the semantics of a query q of arity n is defined as follows. The answer $q^{\mathcal{D}}$ of q to $\mathcal{D}$ is the set of tuples

$$q^{\mathcal{D}} = \{(c_1, \ldots, c_n) \mid \text{for all } \mathcal{I} \in sem(\mathcal{D}),\ (c_1, \ldots, c_n) \in q^{\mathcal{I}}\ \}$$

where $q^{\mathcal{I}}$ denotes the result of evaluating q in the interpretation $\mathcal{I}$.

3   Specifying the Mapping

As we said before, the mapping $\mathcal{M}_{\mathcal{G},\mathcal{S}}$ represents the heart of a DIS $\mathcal{D} = \langle \mathcal{G}, \mathcal{S}, \mathcal{M}_{\mathcal{G},\mathcal{S}} \rangle$, and allow for mapping a concept in one schema into a *view*, i.e., a query, over the other schemas. In this section we discuss the various ways that one can use for specifying the mapping. The terminology used in this section is inspired by [15,14]. In our analysis, we will concentrate on mapping with "sound" views. More general kinds of mappings are discussed in [4].

3.1   Global-Centric Approach

In the global-centric approach (aka global-as-view approach), we assume we have a query language $\mathcal{V}_{\mathcal{S}}$ over the alphabet $\mathcal{A}_{\mathcal{S}}$, and the mapping between the global and the source schemas is given by associating to each term in the global schema a *view*, i.e., a query, over the sources. The intended meaning of associating to a term C in $\mathcal{G}$ a query V_s over $\mathcal{S}$, is that such a query represents the best way to characterize the instances of C using the concepts in $\mathcal{S}$. Let $\mathcal{B}$ be a source model for $\mathcal{D}$, and $\mathcal{I}$ a global interpretation for $\mathcal{D}$. Then $\mathcal{I}$ satisfies the pair $\langle C, V_s \rangle$ in $\mathcal{M}_{\mathcal{G},\mathcal{S}}$ wrt $\mathcal{B}$, if all the tuples satisfying V_s in $\mathcal{D}$ satisfy C in $\mathcal{I}$. We say that $\mathcal{I}$ satisfies the mapping $\mathcal{M}_{\mathcal{G},\mathcal{S}}$ wrt $\mathcal{B}$, if $\mathcal{I}$ satisfies every pair in $\mathcal{M}_{\mathcal{G},\mathcal{S}}$ wrt $\mathcal{B}$.

The global-centric approach is the one adopted in most data integration systems. It is a common opinion that this mechanism allow for a simple query processing strategy, which basically reduces to unfolding the query using the definition specified in the mapping, so as to translate the query in terms of accesses to the sources [20]. Recently, we have showed that in the case where we add constraints (even of a very simple form) to the global schema, query processing becomes harder, due to the need of dealing with a form of incomplete information.

3.2 Source-Centric Approach

In the source-centric approach (aka local-as-view approach), we assume we have a query language $\mathcal{V}_{\mathcal{G}}$ over the alphabet $\mathcal{A}_{\mathcal{G}}$, and the mapping between the global and the source schemas is given by associating to each term in the source schemas a *view*, i.e. a query, over the global schema. Again, the intended meaning of associating to a term C in $\mathcal{S}$ a query V_g over $\mathcal{G}$, is that such query represents the best way to characterize the instances of C using the concepts in $\mathcal{G}$. Let $\mathcal{B}$ be a source model for $\mathcal{D}$, and $\mathcal{I}$ a global interpretation for $\mathcal{D}$. Then $\mathcal{I}$ satisfies the pair $\langle V_g, C \rangle$ in $\mathcal{M}_{\mathcal{G},\mathcal{S}}$ wrt $\mathcal{B}$, if all the tuples satisfying C in $\mathcal{D}$ satisfy V_g in $\mathcal{I}$. As in the global-centric approach, we say that $\mathcal{I}$ satisfies the mapping $\mathcal{M}_{\mathcal{G},\mathcal{S}}$ wrt $\mathcal{B}$, if $\mathcal{I}$ satisfies every pair in $\mathcal{M}_{\mathcal{G},\mathcal{S}}$ wrt $\mathcal{B}$.

Recent work on data integration follows the source-centric approach [17,5,3]. The major challenge of this approach is that in order to answer a query expressed over the global schema, one must be able to reformulate the query in terms of queries to the sources. While in the global-centric approach such a reformulation is guided by the definitions in the mapping, here the problem requires a reasoning step, so as to infer how to use the sources for answering the query [8,3]. Many authors point out that, despite its difficulty, the source-centric approach better supports a dynamic environment, where source schemas can be added to the systems without the need of restructuring the global schema.

3.3 Unrestricted Mapping

In the unrestricted approach, we have both a query language $\mathcal{V}_{\mathcal{S}}$ over the alphabet $\mathcal{A}_{\mathcal{S}}$, and a query language $\mathcal{V}_{\mathcal{G}}$ over the alphabet $\mathcal{A}_{\mathcal{G}}$, and the mapping between the global and the source schemas is given by relating views over the global schema to views over the source schemas. Again, the intended meaning of relating the view V_g over the global schema to the view V_s over the source schema is that V_s represents the best way to characterize the objects satisfying V_g in terms of the concepts in $\mathcal{S}$. In other words, in the unrestricted approach we try to combine and extend the representation power of the previous approaches. Let $\mathcal{B}$ be a source model for $\mathcal{D}$, and $\mathcal{I}$ a global interpretation for $\mathcal{D}$. Then $\mathcal{I}$ satisfies the pair $\langle V_g, V_s \rangle$ in $\mathcal{M}_{\mathcal{G},\mathcal{S}}$ wrt $\mathcal{B}$, if all the tuples satisfying satisfying V_s in $\mathcal{D}$ satisfy V_g in $\mathcal{I}$. Again, we say that $\mathcal{I}$ satisfies the mapping $\mathcal{M}_{\mathcal{G},\mathcal{S}}$ wrt $\mathcal{B}$, if $\mathcal{I}$ satisfies every pair in $\mathcal{M}_{\mathcal{G},\mathcal{S}}$ wrt $\mathcal{B}$.

This approach is largely unexplored, mainly because it combines the difficulties of the other ones. However, we argue that, in real world settings, this is the only approach that provides the appropriate expressive power.

4   Beyond First-Order Logic

According to our definition of a DIS $\mathcal{D}$, it is easy to see that it may happen that no global model for $\mathcal{D}$ exists, even when at least one source model for $\mathcal{D}$ exists. This may happen because knowledge in the various source schemas cannot be completely reconciled in the global schema. In the formalization presented in the previous sections, this situation gives rises to an inconsistent DIS $\mathcal{D}$ (i.e., $sem(\mathcal{D}) = \emptyset$), which cannot support query processing.

A more general approach would be to provide a formalization that is able to support query processing even when the source schemas to be integrated are mutually incoherent. Here, we present a preliminary proposal aiming at this goal.

The basic idea is that given a DIS $\mathcal{D} = \langle \mathcal{G}, \mathcal{S}, \mathcal{M}_{\mathcal{G},\mathcal{S}} \rangle$ and a source model $\mathcal{B}$ for $\mathcal{D}$, we would like to focus our attention on those global interpretations $\mathcal{I}$ that are models of the global schema $\mathcal{G}$ and that *approximate as much as possible* the satisfaction relation for the mapping $\mathcal{M}_{\mathcal{G},\mathcal{S}}$. One way to formalize this idea is to distinguish between *strict* mappings, as the ones considered in Section 3, and *loose* mappings. In particular, we add to every pair in $\mathcal{M}_{\mathcal{G},\mathcal{S}}$ a new item, which is either *strict*, or *loose*, and then we define an ordering wrt $\mathcal{B}$ between the models of $\mathcal{G}$. We concentrate directly on the most general case of unrestricted mapping.

If $\mathcal{I}_1$ and $\mathcal{I}_2$ are two models of $\mathcal{G}$, we say that $\mathcal{I}_1$ is better than $\mathcal{I}_2$ wrt $\mathcal{B}$, denoted as $\mathcal{I}_1 \gg_{\mathcal{B}} \mathcal{I}_2$, iff for all triples $\langle V_g, V_s, x \rangle \in \mathcal{M}_{\mathcal{G},\mathcal{S}}$, except for a distinguished one $\langle V_g', V_s', loose \rangle$, we have that $V_g^{\mathcal{I}_1} = V_g^{\mathcal{I}_2}$ and $V_s^{\mathcal{I}_1} = V_s^{\mathcal{I}_2} = V_s^{\mathcal{B}}$; while for the distinguished triple $\langle V_g', V_s', x' \rangle$ we have that $V_s'^{\mathcal{I}_1} = V_s'^{\mathcal{I}_2} = V_s'^{\mathcal{B}}$, and there exists a tuple $t \in V_s'^{\mathcal{B}}$ such that $t \in V_g'^{\mathcal{I}_1}$ and $t \notin V_g'^{\mathcal{I}_2}$. It is easy to verify that the relation $\gg_{\mathcal{B}}$ is a partial order. With this notion in place we define global models for $\mathcal{D}$ wrt $\mathcal{B}$ those models $\mathcal{I}$ of G that are maximal wrt $\gg_{\mathcal{B}}$, i.e., for no other model $\mathcal{I}'$ of G, $\mathcal{I}' \gg_{\mathcal{B}} \mathcal{I}$.

5   Conclusions

We have illustrated a logic-based framework for data integration, and we have discussed several choices for the specification of the mapping between the global schema and the source schemas. The form of such a specification greatly influences the method for query answering. As we said before, most of the research work on data integration are based on first-order logic, following either the global-centric or the local-centric approach. However, it is our opinion that, in real world settings, the case of mutually inconsistent source databases will be very common. We have presented some preliminary ideas in order to extend the integration framework with suitable nonmonotonic reasoning features for dealing with this case, and we plan to study query processing strategies based on these ideas.

Acknowledgments

Most of the ideas presented in this paper were developed jointly with Diego Calvanese and Giuseppe De Giacomo. I warmly thank both of them. The work presented here was partly supported by MURST Cofin 2000 D2I – From Data to Integration.

References

1. Serge Abiteboul and Oliver Duschka. Complexity of answering queries using materialized views. In *Proc. of the 17th ACM SIGACT SIGMOD SIGART Symp. on Principles of Database Systems (PODS'98)*, pages 254–265, 1998. 55

2. Foto N. Afrati, Manolis Gergatsoulis, and Theodoros Kavalieros. Answering queries using materialized views with disjunction. In *Proc. of the 7th Int. Conf. on Database Theory (ICDT'99)*, volume 1540 of *Lecture Notes in Computer Science*, pages 435–452. Springer-Verlag, 1999. 55

3. Diego Calvanese, Giuseppe De Giacomo, and Maurizio Lenzerini. Answering queries using views over description logics knowledge bases. In *Proc. of the 17th Nat. Conf. on Artificial Intelligence (AAAI 2000)*, pages 386–391, 2000. 58

4. Diego Calvanese, Giuseppe De Giacomo, and Maurizio Lenzerini. Ontology of integration and integration of ontologies. In *Workshop on Description Logics*, 2001. 57

5. Diego Calvanese, Giuseppe De Giacomo, Maurizio Lenzerini, Daniele Nardi, and Riccardo Rosati. Description logic framework for information integration. In *Proc. of the 6th Int. Conf. on Principles of Knowledge Representation and Reasoning (KR'98)*, pages 2–13, 1998. 58

6. Diego Calvanese, Giuseppe De Giacomo, Maurizio Lenzerini, and Moshe Y. Vardi. Answering regular path queries using views. In *Proc. of the 16th IEEE Int. Conf. on Data Engineering (ICDE 2000)*, pages 389–398, 2000. 55

7. Diego Calvanese, Giuseppe De Giacomo, Maurizio Lenzerini, and Moshe Y. Vardi. Query processing using views for regular path queries with inverse. In *Proc. of the 19th ACM SIGACT SIGMOD SIGART Symp. on Principles of Database Systems (PODS 2000)*, pages 58–66, 2000. 55

8. Diego Calvanese, Giuseppe De Giacomo, Maurizio Lenzerini, and Moshe Y. Vardi. View-based query processing and constraint satisfaction. In *Proc. of the 15th IEEE Symp. on Logic in Computer Science (LICS 2000)*, pages 361–371, 2000. 55, 58

9. Diego Calvanese, Giuseppe De Giacomo, Maurizio Lenzerini, and Moshe Y. Vardi. What is query rewriting? In *Proc. of the 7th Int. Workshop on Knowledge Representation meets Databases (KRDB 2000)*, pages 17–27. CEUR Electronic Workshop Proceedings, http://sunsite.informatik.rwth-aachen.de/Publications/CEUR-WS/Vol-29/, 2000. 55

10. Sara Cohen, Werner Nutt, and Alexander Serebrenik. Rewriting aggregate queries using views. In *Proc. of the 18th ACM SIGACT SIGMOD SIGART Symp. on Principles of Database Systems (PODS'99)*, pages 155–166, 1999. 55

11. Oliver M. Duschka and Michael R. Genesereth. Answering recursive queries using views. In *Proc. of the 16th ACM SIGACT SIGMOD SIGART Symp. on Principles of Database Systems (PODS 1997)*, pages 109–116, 1997. 55

12. Gösta Grahne and Alberto O. Mendelzon. Tableau techniques for querying information sources through global schemas. In *Proc. of the 7th Int. Conf. on Database Theory (ICDT'99)*, volume 1540 of *Lecture Notes in Computer Science*, pages 332–347. Springer-Verlag, 1999. 55

13. Stéphane Grumbach, Maurizio Rafanelli, and Leonardo Tininini. Querying aggregate data. In *Proc. of the 18th ACM SIGACT SIGMOD SIGART Symp. on Principles of Database Systems (PODS'99)*, pages 174–184, 1999. 55

14. Alon Y. Halevy. Theory of answering queries using views. *SIGMOD Record*, 29(4):40–47, 2000. 57

15. Richard Hull. Managing semantic heterogeneity in databases: A theoretical perspective. In *Proc. of the 16th ACM SIGACT SIGMOD SIGART Symp. on Principles of Database Systems (PODS 1997)*, 1997. 57

16. Alon Y. Levy, Alberto O. Mendelzon, Yehoshua Sagiv, and Divesh Srivastava. Answering queries using views. In *Proc. of the 14th ACM SIGACT SIGMOD SIGART Symp. on Principles of Database Systems (PODS'95)*, pages 95–104, 1995. 55

17. Alon Y. Levy, Divesh Srivastava, and Thomas Kirk. Data model and query evaluation in global information systems. *J. of Intelligent Information Systems*, 5:121–143, 1995. 58

18. Anand Rajaraman, Yehoshua Sagiv, and Jeffrey D. Ullman. Answering queries using templates with binding patterns. In *Proc. of the 14th ACM SIGACT SIGMOD SIGART Symp. on Principles of Database Systems (PODS'95)*, 1995. 55

19. D. Srivastava, S. Dar, H. V. Jagadish, and A. Levy. Answering queries with aggregation using views. In *Proc. of the 22nd Int. Conf. on Very Large Data Bases (VLDB'96)*, pages 318–329, 1996. 55

20. Jeffrey D. Ullman. Information integration using logical views. In *Proc. of the 6th Int. Conf. on Database Theory (ICDT'97)*, volume 1186 of *Lecture Notes in Computer Science*, pages 19–40. Springer-Verlag, 1997. 55, 57

21. Ron van der Meyden. Logical approaches to incomplete information. In Jan Chomicki and Günter Saake, editors, *Logics for Databases and Information Systems*, pages 307–356. Kluwer Academic Publisher, 1998. 55

Nonmonotonic Inductive Logic Programming

Chiaki Sakama

Department of Computer and Communication Sciences, Wakayama University
Sakaedani, Wakayama 640 8510, Japan
sakama@sys.wakayama-u.ac.jp
http://www.sys.wakayama-u.ac.jp/~sakama

Abstract. *Nonmonotonic logic programming* (NMLP) and *inductive logic programming* (ILP) are two important extensions of logic programming. The former aims at representing incomplete knowledge and reasoning with commonsense, while the latter targets the problem of inductive construction of a general theory from examples and background knowledge. NMLP and ILP thus have seemingly different motivations and goals, but they have much in common in the background of problems, and techniques developed in each field are related to one another. This paper presents techniques for combining these two fields of logic programming in the context of *nonmonotonic inductive logic programming* (NMILP). We review recent results and problems to realize NMILP.

1 Introduction

Representing knowledge in computational logic gives formal foundations of artificial intelligence (AI) and provides computational methods for solving problems. Logic programming supplies a powerful tool for representing declarative knowledge and computing logical inference. However, logic programming based on classical Horn logic is not sufficiently expressive for representing incomplete human knowledge, and is inadequate for characterizing nonmonotonic commonsense reasoning. *Nonmonotonic logic programming* (NMLP) [3,5] is introduced to overcome such limitations of Horn logic programming by extending the representation language and enhancing the inference mechanism. The purpose of NMLP is to represent incomplete knowledge and reason with commonsense in a program.

On the other hand, *machine learning* concerns with the problem of building computer programs that automatically construct new knowledge and improve with experience [27]. The primary inference used in learning is *induction* which constructs general sentences from input examples. *Inductive Logic Programming* (ILP) [28,30,33] realizes inductive machine learning in logic programming, which provides a formal background to inductive learning and has advantages of using computational tools developed in logic programming. The goal of ILP is the inductive construction of first-order clausal theories from examples and background knowledge.

NMLP and ILP thus have seemingly different motivations and goals, however, they have much in common in the background of problems, and techniques

T. Eiter, W. Faber, and M. Truszczyński (Eds.): LPNMR 2001, LNAI 2173, pp. 62–80, 2001.
© Springer-Verlag Berlin Heidelberg 2001

developed in each field are related to one another. First, the process of discovering new knowledge by humans is the iteration of hypotheses generation and revision, which is inherently nonmonotonic. Indeed, induction is nonmonotonic reasoning in the sense that once induced hypotheses might be changed by the introduction of new evidences. Second, induction problems assume background knowledge which is incomplete, otherwise there is no need to learn. Therefore, representing and reasoning with incomplete knowledge are vital issues in ILP. Third, NMLP uses hypotheses in the process of commonsense reasoning, and hypotheses generation is particularly important in *abductive logic programming.* Abduction generates hypotheses in a different manner from induction, but they are both inverse deduction and extend theories to account for evidences. Indeed, abduction and induction interact, and work complementarily in many phases [14]. Fourth, in NMLP updates of general rules are considered in the context of *intentional knowledge base update* [6], while a similar problem is captured in ILP as *concept-learning* [26]. It is argued in [9] that these two researches handle the same problem when formulated in a logical framework. With these reasons, it is clear that both NMLP and ILP cope with similar problems and have close links to each other.

Comparing NMLP and ILP, NMLP performs default reasoning and derives plausible conclusions from incomplete knowledge bases. Various types of inferences and semantics are introduced to extract intuitive conclusions from a program. NMLP may change conclusions by the introduction of new information, but it has no mechanism of learning new knowledge from the input. By contrast, ILP extends a theory by constructing new rules from input examples and background knowledge. Discovered rules reveal hidden laws between examples and background knowledge, and are also used for predicting unseen phenomena. However, the present ILP mostly considers Horn logic programs or classical clausal programs as background knowledge, and has limited applications to nonmonotonic situations.

Thus, both NMLP and ILP have limitations in their present frameworks and complement each other. Since both commonsense reasoning and machine learning are indispensable for realizing intelligent information systems, combining techniques of the two fields in the context of *nonmonotonic inductive logic programming* (NMILP) is meaningful and important. Such combination will extend the representation language on the ILP side, while it will introduce a learning mechanism to programs on the NMLP side. Moreover, linking different extensions of logic programming will strengthen the capability of logic programming as a knowledge representation tool in AI. From the practical viewpoint, the combination will be beneficial for ILP to use well-established techniques in NMLP, and will open new applications of NMLP.

NMLP realizes nonmonotonic reasoning using *negation as failure* (NAF). Some researches in ILP, however, argue that negation as failure is inappropriate in machine learning. In [8], the authors say:

> For concept learning, negation as failure (and the underlying closed world assumption) is unacceptable because it acts as if everything is known.

Clearly, in learning this is not the case, since otherwise nothing ought to be learned.

Although the account is plausible, it does not justify excluding NAF in ILP. Suppose that background knowledge is given as a Horn logic program, and the CWA or NAF infers negative facts which are not derived from the program. When a new evidence E which is initially assumed false under the CWA or NAF is observed, this just means that the old assumption $\neg E$ is rebutted. The task of inductive learning is then to revise the old theory to explain the new evidence. On the other hand, if one excludes NAF in a background program, she loses the way of representing default negation in the program. This is a significant drawback in representing knowledge and restricts the application of ILP. In fact, NAF enables to write shorter and simpler programs and appears in many basic but practical Prolog programs such as computing set differences, finding union/intersection of two lists, etc [42]. Horn ILP precludes every program including these rules with NAF. Thus, NAF is also important in ILP, and the use of NAF never invalidates the need of learning.

In the field of ILP, it is often considered the so-called *nonmonotonic problem setting* [18]. Given a background Horn logic program P and a set E of *positive* examples, it computes a hypothesis H which is satisfied in the least Herbrand model of $P \cup E$. This is also called the *weak* setting of ILP [11]. In this setting, any fact which is not derived from $P \cup E$ is assumed to be false under the *closed world assumption* (CWA). By contrast, the *strong* setting of ILP computes a hypothesis H which, together with P, implies E, and does not imply *negative* examples. The strong setting is usually employed in ILP and is also considered in this paper (see Section 2.2).[1] The nonmonotonic setting is called "nonmonotonic" in the sense that it performs a kind of default reasoning based on the closed world assumption. Some systems take similar approaches using Clark's completion ([10], for instance). The above mentioned nonmonotonic setting is clearly different from our problem setting. The former still considers an induction problem within clausal logic, while we extend the problem to nonmonotonic logic programs.

This paper presents techniques for realizing inductive machine learning in nonmonotonic logic programs. The paper is not intended to provide a comprehensive survey of the state of the art, but mainly consists of recent research results of the author. The rest of this paper is organized as follows. Section 2 reviews frameworks of NMLP and ILP. Section 3 presents various techniques for induction in nonmonotonic logic programs. Section 4 summarizes the paper and addresses open issues.

---

[1] The weak setting is also called *descriptive/confirmatory induction*, while the strong setting is called *explanatory/predictive induction* [15].

2   Preliminaries

2.1   Nonmonotonic Logic Programming

Nonmonotonic logic programs considered in this paper are *normal logic programs*, logic programs with negation as failure.

A *normal logic program* (NLP) is a set of *rules* of the form:

$$A \leftarrow B_1, \ldots, B_m, not\, B_{m+1}, \ldots, not\, B_n \tag{1}$$

where each A, B_i $(1 \le i \le n)$ is an atom and *not* presents *negation as failure* (NAF). The left-hand side of $\leftarrow$ is the *head*, and the right-hand side is the *body* of the rule. The conjunction in the body of (1) is identified with the set $\{ B_1, \ldots, B_m, not\, B_{m+1}, \ldots, not\, B_n \}$. For a rule R, $head(R)$ and $body(R)$ denote the head of R and the body of R, respectively. The conjunction in the body is often written by the Greek letter Γ. A rule with the empty body $A \leftarrow$ is called a *fact*, which is identified with the atom A. A rule with the empty head $\leftarrow \Gamma$ with $\Gamma \ne \emptyset$ is also called an *integrity constraint*. Throughout the paper a program means a normal logic program unless stated otherwise. A program P is *Horn* if no rule in P contains NAF. A Horn program is *definite* if it contains no integrity constraint. The *Herbrand base* $\mathcal{HB}$ of a program P is the set of all ground atoms in the language of P. Given the Herbrand base $\mathcal{HB}$, we define $\mathcal{HB}^+ = \mathcal{HB} \cup \{ not\, A \mid A \in \mathcal{HB} \}$. Any element in $\mathcal{HB}^+$ is called an *LP-literal*, and an LP-literal of the form $not\, A$ is called an *NAF-literal*. We say that two LP-literals L_1 and L_2 have the same *sign* if either $(L_1 \in \mathcal{HB}$ and $L_2 \in \mathcal{HB})$ or $(L_1 \notin \mathcal{HB}$ and $L_2 \notin \mathcal{HB})$. For an LP-literal L, $pred(L)$ denotes the predicate in L and $const(L)$ denotes the set of constants appearing in L. A program, a rule, or an LP-literal is *ground* if it contains no variable. A program/rule containing variables is semantically identified with its ground instantiation, i.e., the set of ground rules obtained from the program/rule by substituting variables with elements of the Herbrand universe in every possible way.

An *interpretation* is a subset of $\mathcal{HB}$. An interpretation I *satisfies* the ground rule R of the form (1) if $\{B_1, \ldots, B_m\} \subseteq I$ and $\{B_{m+1}, \ldots, B_n\} \cap I = \emptyset$ imply $A \in I$ (written as $I \models R$). In particular, I satisfies the ground integrity constraint $\leftarrow B_1, \ldots, B_m, not\, B_{m+1}, \ldots, not\, B_n$ if either $\{B_1, \ldots, B_m\} \setminus I \ne \emptyset$ or $\{B_{m+1}, \ldots, B_n\} \cap I \ne \emptyset$. When a rule R contains variables, $I \models R$ means that I satisfies every ground instance of R. An interpretation which satisfies every rule in a program is a *model* of the program. A model M of a program P is *minimal* if there is no model N of P such that $N \subset M$. A Horn logic program has at most one minimal model called the *least model*.

For the semantics of NLPs, we consider the *stable model semantics* [17] in this paper. Given a program P and an interpretation M, the ground Horn logic program P^M is defined as follows: the rule $A \leftarrow B_1, \ldots, B_m$ is in P^M iff there is a ground rule of the form (1) in the ground instantiation of P such that $\{B_{m+1}, \ldots, B_n\} \cap M = \emptyset$. If the least model of P^M is identical to M, M is called a *stable model* of P. A program may have none, one, or multiple stable models in general. A program having exactly one stable model is called *categorical* [3].

A stable model coincides with the least model in a Horn logic program. A *locally stratified program* [36] has the unique stable model which is called the *perfect model*. Given a stable model M, we define $M^+ = M \cup \{\, not\, A \mid A \in \mathcal{HB} \setminus M \,\}$.

A program is *consistent* (under the stable model semantics) if it has a stable model; otherwise a program is *inconsistent*. Throughout the paper, a program is assumed to be consistent unless stated otherwise. If every stable model of a program P satisfies a rule R, it is written as $P \models_s R$. Else if no stable model of a program P satisfies a rule R, it is written as $P \models_s not\, R$. In particular, $P \models_s A$ if a ground atom A is true in every stable model of P; and $P \models_s not\, A$ if A is false in every stable model of P. By contrast, if every model of P satisfies R, it is written as $P \models R$. Note that when P is Horn, the meaning of $\models$ coincides with the classical entailment.

2.2   Inductive Logic Programming

A typical ILP problem is stated as follows. Given a logic program B representing background knowledge and a set E^+ of positive examples and a set E^- of negative examples, find hypotheses H satisfying[2]

1. $B \cup H \models e$ for every $e \in E^+$.
2. $B \cup H \not\models f$ for every $f \in E^-$.
3. $B \cup H$ is consistent.

The first condition is called *completeness* with respect to positive examples, and the second condition is called *consistency* with respect to negative examples. It is also implicitly assumed that $B \not\models e$ for some $e \in E^+$ or $B \models f$ for some $f \in E^-$, because otherwise there is no need to introduce H. A hypothesis H *covers* (resp. *uncovers*) an example e if $B \cup H \models e$ (resp. $B \cup H \not\models e$).

The goal of ILP is then to develop an algorithm which efficiently computes hypotheses satisfying the above three conditions. Induction algorithms are roughly classified into two categories by the direction of searching hypotheses. A *top-down* algorithm firstly generates a most general hypothesis and refines it by means of specialization, while a *bottom-up* algorithm searches hypotheses by generalizing (positive) examples. Each algorithm locally alternates search directions from general to specific and vice versa to correct hypotheses. Algorithms presented in Sections 3.1–3.3 of this paper are bottom-up on this ground.

An induction algorithm is *correct* if every hypothesis produced by the algorithm satisfies the above three conditions. By contrast, an induction algorithm is *complete* if it produces every rule satisfying the conditions. Note that the correctness is generally requested for algorithms, while the completeness is problematic in practice. For instance, consider the background program B and the positive example E such that

$$B:\ r(f(x)) \leftarrow r(x),$$
$$q(a) \leftarrow,\quad r(b) \leftarrow .$$
$$E:\ p(a).$$

---

[2] When there is no negative example, E^+ is just written as E.

Then, any of the following rules

$$p(x) \leftarrow q(x),$$
$$p(x) \leftarrow q(x),\ r(b),$$
$$p(x) \leftarrow q(x),\ r(f(b)),$$
$$\cdots$$

explains $p(a)$. Generally, there exist possibly infinite solutions for explaining an example, and designing a complete induction algorithm without any restriction is of little value in practice. In order to extract meaningful hypotheses, additional conditions are usually imposed on possible hypotheses to reduce the search space. Such a condition is called an *induction bias* and is defined as any information that syntactically or semantically influences learning processes.

In the field of ILP, most studies consider a Horn logic program as background knowledge and induce Horn clauses as hypotheses. In this paper, we consider an NLP as background knowledge and induce hypothetical rules possibly containing NAF. In the next section, we give several algorithms which realize this.

3   Induction in Nonmonotonic Logic Programs

3.1   Least Generalization

Generalization is a basic operation to perform induction. In his seminal work [34], Plotkin introduces generalization in clausal theories based on *subsumption*. Given two clauses C_1 and C_2, C_1 *θ-subsumes* C_2 if $C_1\theta \subseteq C_2$ for some substitution θ. Then, C_1 is *more general than* C_2 *under θ-subsumption* if C_1 θ-subsumes C_2. In normal logic programs, a subsumption relation between rules is defined as follows.

Definition 3.1. (subsumption relations between rules) Let R_1 and R_2 be two rules. Then, R_1 *θ-subsumes* R_2 (written as $R_1 \succeq_\theta R_2$) if $head(R_1)\theta = head(R_2)$ and $body(R_1)\theta \subseteq body(R_2)$ hold for some substitution θ. In this case, R_1 is said *more general than* R_2 *under θ-subsumption*.

Thus subsumption is defined for comparison of rules with the same predicate in the heads. The same definition is employed by Taylor [43]. Fogel and Zaverucha [16] discuss the effect of subsumption to reduce the search space in normal logic programs.

For generalization in clausal theories, *least generalizations* of clauses are particularly important. The notion is defined for nonmonotonic rules as follows.

Definition 3.2. (least generalization under subsumption) Let $\mathcal{R}$ be a finite set of rules such that every rule in $\mathcal{R}$ has the same predicate in the head. Then, a rule R is a *least generalization of $\mathcal{R}$ under θ-subsumption* if $R \succeq_\theta R_i$ for every rule R_i in $\mathcal{R}$, and for any other rule R' satisfying $R' \succeq_\theta R_i$ for every R_i in $\mathcal{R}$, it holds that $R' \succeq_\theta R$.

In the clausal language every finite set of clauses has a least generalization. In particular, every finite set of Horn clauses has a least generalization as a Horn clause [33,34].[3] When we consider normal logic programs, rules are syntactically regarded as Horn clauses by viewing NAF-literal $not\,p(x)$ as an atom $not\_p(x)$ with the new predicate not_p. Then the result of Horn logic programs is directly carried over to normal logic programs.

Theorem 3.1. *(existence of a least generalization) Let $\mathcal{R}$ be a finite set of rules such that every rule in $\mathcal{R}$ has the same predicate in the head. Then, every non-empty set $R \subseteq \mathcal{R}$ has a least generalization under θ-subsumption.*

A least generalization of two rules is computed as follows. First, a least generalization of two terms $f(t_1, \ldots, t_n)$ and $g(s_1, \ldots, s_n)$ is a new variable v if $f \neq g$; and is defined as $f(lg(t_1, s_1), \ldots, lg(t_n, s_n))$ if $f = g$, where $lg(t_i, s_i)$ means a least generalization of t_i and s_i. Next, a least generalization of two LP-literals $L_1 = (not)p(t_1, \ldots, t_n)$ and $L_2 = (not)q(s_1, \ldots, s_n)$ is undefined if L_1 and L_2 do not have the same predicate and sign; otherwise, it is defined as $lg(L_1, L_2) = (not)p(lg(t_1, s_1), \ldots, lg(t_n, s_n))$.

Then, a least generalization of two rules $R_1 = A_1 \leftarrow \Gamma_1$ and $R_2 = A_2 \leftarrow \Gamma_2$, where A_1 and A_2 have the same predicate, is obtained as

$$lg(A_1, A_2) \leftarrow \Gamma$$

where $\Gamma = \{\, lg(\gamma_1, \gamma_2) \mid \gamma_1 \in \Gamma_1,\ \gamma_2 \in \Gamma_2 \text{ and } lg(\gamma_1, \gamma_2) \text{ is defined}\,\}$. In particular, if A_1 and A_2 are empty, a least generalization of two integrity constraints $\leftarrow \Gamma_1$ and $\leftarrow \Gamma_1$ is given by $\leftarrow \Gamma$. A least generalization of a finite set of rules is computed by repeatedly applying the above procedure.

In ILP generalization is usually considered in relation to the background knowledge. Plotkin [35] extends subsumption to *relative subsumption* for this use. Given the background knowledge B as a clausal theory, a clause C *subsumes* D *relative to* B if there is a substitution θ such that $B \models \forall(C\theta \rightarrow D)$.

We apply relative subsumption to normal logic programs. Let $R = H \leftarrow A, \Gamma$ be a rule where A is an atom and Γ is a conjunction. Suppose that there is a rule $A' \leftarrow \Gamma'$ in a program P such that $A\theta = A'\theta$ for some substitution θ. Then, we say that the rule $(H \leftarrow \Gamma', \Gamma)\theta$ is obtained by *unfolding* R in P. We also say that R_k is obtained by unfolding R_0 in P if there is a sequence $R_0, \ldots, R_k$ of rules such that R_i $(1 \leq i \leq k)$ is obtained by unfolding R_{i-1} in P.

Definition 3.3. (relative subsumption) Let P be an NLP, and R_1 and R_2 be two rules. Then, R_1 θ-*subsumes* R_2 *relative to* P (written as $R_1 \succeq_\theta^P R_2$) if there is a rule R that is obtained by unfolding R_1 in P and R θ-subsumes R_2. In this case, R_1 is said *more general than* R_2 *relative to* P *under* θ-subsumption.

The above definition reduces to Definition 3.1 when P is empty. By the definition relative subsumption is also defined for two rules having the same

---

[3] If two clauses have no predicate with the same sign in common, the empty clause becomes the least generalization.

predicate in the heads. In clausal theories, Buntine [7] introduces *generalized subsumption* which is defined between definite clauses having the same predicate in the heads. Comparing two definitions, Buntine's definition is model theoretic, while our definition is operational. Taylor [43] introduces *normal subsumption* which extends Buntine's subsumption to normal logic programs and is defined in a model theoretic manner.

Example 3.1. Suppose the background program P, and two rules R_1 and R_2 as follows.

$$
\begin{aligned}
P : \ & has\_wing(x) \leftarrow bird(x),\ not\ ab(x), \\
& bird(x) \leftarrow sparrow(x), \\
& ab(x) \leftarrow broken\text{-}wing(x). \\
R_1 : \ & flies(x) \leftarrow has\_wing(x). \\
R_2 : \ & flies(x) \leftarrow sparrow(x),\ full\_grown(x),\ not\ ab(x).
\end{aligned}
$$

From P and R_1, the rule

$$
R_3 : \ flies(x) \leftarrow sparrow(x),\ not\ ab(x)
$$

is obtained by unfolding. As R_3 θ-subsumes R_2, $R_1 \succeq_\theta^P R_2$.

In clausal theories, a least generalization does not always exist under relative subsumption. However, when background knowledge is a finite set of ground atoms, a least generalization of two clauses is constructed [33,35]. The result is extended to nonmonotonic rules and is rephrased in our context as follows. Let P be a finite set of ground atoms, and R_1 and R_2 be two rules. Then, a least generalization of these rules under relative subsumption is constructed as a least generalization of R_1' and R_2' where $head(R_i') = head(R_i)$ and $body(R_i') = body(R_i) \cup B$.

Example 3.2. Suppose the background program P, and two (positive) examples R_1 and R_2 as follows.

$$
\begin{aligned}
P : \ & bird(tweety) \leftarrow, \quad bird(polly) \leftarrow . \\
R_1 : \ & flies(tweety) \leftarrow has\_wing(tweety),\ not\ ab(tweety). \\
R_2 : \ & flies(polly) \leftarrow sparrow(polly),\ not\ ab(polly).
\end{aligned}
$$

Then, R_1' and R_2' becomes

$R_1' : \ flies(tweety) \leftarrow bird(tweety),\ bird(polly),\ has\_wing(tweety),$
$$not\ ab(tweety),$$
$R_2' : \ flies(polly) \leftarrow bird(tweety),\ bird(polly),\ sparrow(polly),\ not\ ab(polly).$

The least generalization of R_1' and R_2' is

$$
flies(x) \leftarrow bird(tweety),\ bird(polly),\ bird(x),\ not\ ab(x).
$$

Removing redundant literals, it becomes

$$R : flies(x) \leftarrow bird(x), \, not \, ab(x).$$

In this case, it holds that $P \cup \{R\} \models_s R_i$ $(i = 1, 2)$.

3.2 Inverse Resolution

Inverse resolution [29] is based on the idea of inverting the resolution step between clauses. There are two operators that carry out inverse resolution, *absorption* and *identification*, which are called the *V-operators* together. Each operator builds one of the two parent clauses given the other parent clause and the resolvent. Suppose two rules $R_1 : B_1 \leftarrow \Gamma_1$ and $R_2 : A_2 \leftarrow B_2, \Gamma_2$. When $B_1\theta_1 = B_2\theta_2$, the rule $R_3 : A_2\theta_2 \leftarrow \Gamma_1\theta_1, \Gamma_2\theta_2$ is produced by unfolding R_2 with R_1. Absorption constructs R_2 from R_1 and R_3, while identification constructs R_1 from R_2 and R_3 (see figure).

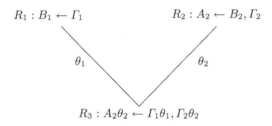

$$R_1 : B_1 \leftarrow \Gamma_1 \qquad\qquad R_2 : A_2 \leftarrow B_2, \Gamma_2$$

$$\theta_1 \qquad\qquad \theta_2$$

$$R_3 : A_2\theta_2 \leftarrow \Gamma_1\theta_1, \Gamma_2\theta_2$$

Given a normal logic program P containing the rules R_1 and R_3, absorption produces the program $A(P)$ such that

$$A(P) = (P \setminus \{R_3\}) \cup \{R_2\}.$$

On the other hand, given an NLP P containing the rules R_2 and R_3, identification produces the program $I(P)$ such that

$$I(P) = (P \setminus \{R_3\}) \cup \{R_1\}.$$

Note that there are multiple $A(P)$ or $I(P)$ exist in general according to the choice of the input rules in P. We write $V(P)$ to mean either $A(P)$ or $I(P)$.

When P is a Horn logic program, any information implied by P is also implied by $V(P)$, namely

$$V(P) \models P.$$

In this regard, the V-operators generalize a Horn logic program. In the presence of negation as failure in a program, however, the V-operators do not work as generalization operations in general.

Example 3.3. Let P be the program:

$$p(x) \leftarrow not\, q(x), \quad q(x) \leftarrow r(x), \quad s(x) \leftarrow r(x), \quad s(a) \leftarrow,$$

which has the stable model $\{\, p(a), s(a)\,\}$. Absorbing the third rule into the second rule produces $A(P)$:

$$p(x) \leftarrow not\, q(x), \quad q(x) \leftarrow s(x), \quad s(x) \leftarrow r(x), \quad s(a) \leftarrow,$$

which has the stable model $\{\, q(a), s(a)\,\}$. Then, $P \models_s p(a)$ but $A(P) \not\models_s p(a)$.

A counter-example for identification is constructed in a similar manner. The reason is clear, since in nonmonotonic logic programs newly proven facts may block the derivation of other facts which are proven beforehand. As a result, the V-operators may not generalize the original program. Moreover, the next example shows that the V-operators often make a consistent program inconsistent.

Example 3.4. Let P be the program:

$$p(x) \leftarrow q(x), not\, p(x), \quad q(x) \leftarrow r(x), \quad s(x) \leftarrow r(x), \quad s(a) \leftarrow,$$

which has the stable model $\{\, s(a)\,\}$. Absorbing the third rule into the second rule produces $A(P)$:

$$p(x) \leftarrow q(x), not\, p(x), \quad q(x) \leftarrow s(x), \quad s(x) \leftarrow r(x), \quad s(a) \leftarrow,$$

which has no stable model.

The above example shows that the V-operators have destructive effect on the meaning of programs in general. It is also known that they may destroy the syntactic structure of programs such as acyclicity and local stratification [37].

These observations give us a caution to apply the V-operators to NMLP. A condition for the V-operators to generalize an NLP is as follows.

Theorem 3.2. *(conditions for the V-operators to generalize programs) [37] Let P be an NLP, and R_1, R_2, R_3 be rules at the beginning of this section. For any NAF-literal not L in P,* [4]

(i) *if L does not depend on the head of R_3 in P, then $P \models_s N$ implies $A(P) \models_s N$ for any $N \in \mathcal{HB}$.*
(ii) *if L does not depend on the atom B_2 of R_2 in P, then $P \models_s N$ implies $I(P) \models_s N$ for any $N \in \mathcal{HB}$.*

---

[4] Here, *depends on* is a transitive relation defined as: A depends on B if there is a ground rule from P s.t. A appears in the head and B appears in the body of the rule.

Example 3.5. Suppose the background program P and a (positive) example E as follows.

$$P: \ flies(x) \leftarrow sparrow(x), \ not \ ab(x),$$
$$bird(x) \leftarrow sparrow(x),$$
$$sparrow(tweety) \leftarrow, \quad bird(polly) \leftarrow .$$
$$E: \ flies(polly).$$

Initially, $P \models_s flies(tweety)$ but $P \not\models_s flies(polly)$. Absorbing the second rule into the first rule in P produces the program $A(P)$ in which the first rule of P is replaced by the next rule in $A(P)$:

$$flies(x) \leftarrow bird(x), \ not \ ab(x).$$

Then, $A(P) \models_s flies(polly)$. Notice that $A(P) \models_s flies(tweety)$ also holds.

Taylor [43] introduces a different operator called *normal absorption*, which generalizes normal logic programs.

3.3   Inverse Entailment

Suppose an induction problem

$$B \cup \{H\} \models E$$

where B is a Horn logic program and H and E are each single Horn clauses. *Inverse entailment* (IE) [31] is based on the idea that a possible hypothesis H is deductively constructed from B and E by inverting the entailment relation as

$$B \cup \{\neg E\} \models \neg H.$$

When a background theory is a nonmonotonic logic program, however, the IE technique cannot be used. This is because IE is based on the *deduction theorem* in first-order logic, but it is known that the deduction theorem does not hold in nonmonotonic logics in general [41].

To solve the problem, Sakama [38] introduced the *entailment theorem* in normal logic programs. A *nested rule* is defined as

$$A \leftarrow R$$

where A is an atom and R is a rule of the form (1). An interpretation I satisfies a ground nested rule $A \leftarrow R$ if $I \models R$ implies $A \in I$. For an NLP P, $P \models_s (A \leftarrow R)$ if $A \leftarrow R$ is satisfied in every stable model of P.

Theorem 3.3. *(entailment theorem [38]) Let P be an NLP and R a rule such that $P \cup \{R\}$ is consistent. For any ground atom A, $P \cup \{R\} \models_s A$ implies $P \models_s A \leftarrow R$. In converse, $P \models_s A \leftarrow R$ and $P \models_s R$ imply $P \cup \{R\} \models_s A$.*

The entailment theorem corresponds to the deduction theorem and is used for inverting entailment in normal logic programs.

Theorem 3.4. *(IE in normal logic programs [38]) Let P be an NLP and R a rule such that $P \cup \{R\}$ is consistent. For any ground LP-literal L, if $P \cup \{R\} \models_s L$ and $P \models_s \leftarrow L$, then $P \models_s not\ R$.*

Thus, the relation

$$P \models_s not\ R \qquad (2)$$

provides a necessary condition for computing a rule R satisfying $P \cup \{R\} \models_s L$ and $P \models_s \leftarrow L$. When L is an atom (resp. NAF-literal), it represents a positive (resp. negative) example. The condition $P \models_s \leftarrow L$ states that the example L is initially false in every stable model of P. To simplify the problem, a program P is assumed to be *function-free* and *categorical* in the rest of this section.

Given two ground LP-literals L_1 and L_2, the relation $L_1 \sim L_2$ is defined if $pred(L_1) = pred(L_2)$ with a predicate of arity ≥ 1 and $const(L_1) = const(L_2)$. Let L be a ground LP-literal and S a set of ground LP-literals. Then, L_1 in S is *relevant* to L if either (i) $L_1 \sim L$ or (ii) L_1 shares a constant with an LP-literal L_2 in S such that L_2 is relevant to L.

Let P be a program with the unique stable model M and A a ground atom representing a positive example. Suppose that the relation $P \cup \{R\} \models_s A$ and $P \models_s \leftarrow A$ hold. By Theorem 3.4, the relation (2) holds, thereby

$$M \not\models R. \qquad (3)$$

Then, we start to find a rule R satisfying the condition (3). Consider the integrity constraint $\leftarrow \Gamma$ where Γ consists of ground LP-literals in M^+ which are relevant to the positive example A.[5] Since M does not satisfy this integrity constraint,

$$M \not\models\ \leftarrow \Gamma \qquad (4)$$

holds. That is, $\leftarrow \Gamma$ is a rule which satisfies the condition (3).

Next, by $P \models_s \leftarrow A$, it holds that $A \notin M$, thereby $not\ A \in M^+$. Since $not\ A$ is relevant to A, the integrity constraint $\leftarrow \Gamma$ contains $not\ A$ in its body. Then, shifting the atom A to the head produces

$$A \leftarrow \Gamma' \qquad (5)$$

where $\Gamma' = \Gamma \setminus \{not\ A\}$.

Finally, the rule (5) is generalized by constructing a rule R^* such that $R^*\theta = A \leftarrow \Gamma'$ for some substitution θ. It is verified that the rule R^* satisfies the condition (2), i.e., $P \models_s not\ R^*$.

The next theorem presents a sufficient condition for the correctness of R^* to induce A.

---

[5] Since P is function-free, Γ consists of finite LP-literals.

Theorem 3.5. *(correctness of the IE rule [39]) Let P be a function-free and categorical NLP, A a ground atom, and R^* a rule obtained as above. If $P \cup \{R^*\}$ is consistent and $pred(A)$ does not appear in P, then $P \cup \{R^*\} \models_s A$.*

Example 3.6. Let P be the program

$$bird(x) \leftarrow penguin(x),$$
$$bird(tweety) \leftarrow, \quad penguin(polly) \leftarrow .$$

Given the example $L = flies(tweety)$, it holds that $P \models_s \leftarrow flies(tweety)$. Our goal is then to construct a rule R satisfying $P \cup \{R\} \models_s L$.

First, the set M^+ of LP-literals becomes

$$M^+ = \{ bird(tweety), bird(polly), penguin(polly),$$
$$not\, penguin(tweety), not\, flies(tweety), not\, flies(polly) \}.$$

From M^+ picking up LP-literals which are relevant to L, the integrity constraint:

$$\leftarrow bird(tweety), not\, penguin(tweety), not\, flies(tweety)$$

is constructed. Next, shifting $flies(tweety)$ to the head produces

$$flies(tweety) \leftarrow bird(tweety), not\, penguin(tweety).$$

Finally, replacing $tweety$ by a variable x, the rule

$$R^* : \quad flies(x) \leftarrow bird(x), not\, penguin(x)$$

is obtained, where $P \cup \{R^*\} \models_s L$ holds.

The inverse entailment algorithm is also used for learning programs by negative examples [38].

3.4   Other Techniques

This section reviews other techniques for learning nonmonotonic logic programs.

Bain and Muggleton [2] introduce the algorithm called *Closed World Specialization* (CWS). In the algorithm, an initial program and an intended interpretation that a learned program should satisfy are given. In this setting, any atom which is not included in the interpretation is considered false. For instance, suppose the program:

$$P : \quad flies(x) \leftarrow bird(x),$$
$$bird(eagle) \leftarrow, \quad bird(emu) \leftarrow,$$

and the intended interpretation:

$$M : \quad \{ flies(eagle), bird(eagle), bird(emu) \},$$

where $flies(emu)$ is not in M and is interpreted false. As P implies $flies(emu)$, the CWS algorithm specializes P and produces

$$flies(x) \leftarrow bird(x),\ not\ ab(x),$$
$$bird(eagle) \leftarrow,\ \ bird(emu) \leftarrow,\ \ ab(emu) \leftarrow .$$

Here, $ab(x)$ is a newly introduced atom.[6] In this algorithm NAF is used for specializing Horn clauses and the CWS produces normal logic programs.

Inoue and Kudoh [19] propose an algorithm called *LELP* which learns *extended logic programs* (ELP) under the answer set semantics. The algorithm is close to Bain and Muggleton's method but is different from it on the point that [19] uses *Open World Specialization* (OWS) rather than the CWS under the 3-valued setting. The OWS does not use the closed world assumption to identify negative instances of the target concept.

Given positive and negative examples, LELP firstly constructs (monotonic) rules that cover positive examples by using an ordinary ILP algorithm,[7] then generates *default rules* to uncover negative examples by incorporating NAF literals to the bodies of rules. In addition, exceptions to rules are identified from negative examples and are then generalized to *default cancellation rules*. In LELP, hierarchical defaults can be learned by recursively calling the exception identification algorithm. Moreover, when some instances are possibly classified as both positive and negative, *nondeterministic rules* can also be learned so that there are multiple answer sets for the resulting program. Lamma *et al.* [22] formalize the same problem under the well-founded semantics. In their algorithms, different levels of generalization are strategically combined in order to learn solutions for positive and negative concepts.

Dimopoulos and Kakas [12] construct default rules with exceptions. For instance, suppose the background program:

$$\begin{aligned} P: \ & bird(x) \leftarrow penguin(x), \\ & penguin(x) \leftarrow super\_penguin(x), \\ & bird(a) \leftarrow,\ \ bird(b) \leftarrow, \\ & penguin(c) \leftarrow,\ \ super\_penguin(d) \leftarrow, \end{aligned}$$

and the positive and negative examples:

$$\begin{aligned} E^+: \ & flies(a),\ flies(b),\ flies(d). \\ E^-: \ & flies(c). \end{aligned}$$

Their algorithm first computes a rule which covers all the positive examples:

$$r_1: \ flies(x) \leftarrow bird(x).$$

---

[6] Such an atom is called *invented*.

[7] An "Ordinary ILP" means any top-down/bottom-up ILP algorithm which is used in clausal logic.

This rule also covers the negative example, then the algorithm next computes a rule which explains the negative example:

$$r_2 :\ \neg flies(x) \leftarrow penguin(x)\,.$$

In order to avoid drawing contradictory conclusions on c, the rule r_2 is given priority over r_1. Likewise, the algorithm next computes the rule

$$r_3 :\ flies(x) \leftarrow super\_penguin(x)$$

and r_3 is given priority over r_2. A unique feature of their algorithm is that they learn rules using an ordinary ILP algorithm, and represent exceptions by a prioritized hierarchy without using NAF.

Sakama [39] presents a method of computing inductive hypotheses using answer sets of extended logic programs. Given an ELP P and a ground literal L, suppose a rule R satisfying $P \cup \{R\} \models_{AS} L$, where $\models_{AS}$ is an entailment under the answer set semantics. It is shown that this relation together with $P \not\models_{AS} L$ implies $P \not\models_{AS} R$. This provides a necessary condition for any possible hypothesis R which explains L. A candidate hypothesis is then obtained by computing answer sets of P, and constructing a rule which is unsatisfied in an answer set. The method provides the same result as [38] in a much simpler manner. In function-free stratified programs the algorithm constructs inductive hypotheses in polynomial-time.

Bergadano et al. [4] propose the system called $TRACY^{not}$ which learns NLPs using the derivation information of examples. In this system candidate hypotheses are given in input to the system, and from those candidates the system selects hypotheses which cover/uncover positive/negative examples. Martin and Vrain [25] introduce an algorithm to learn NLPs under the 3-valued semantics. Given a 3-valued model of a background program, it constructs (possibly recursive) rules to explain examples. Seitzer [40] proposes a system called INDED. It consists of a deductive engine which computes stable models or the well-founded model of a background NLP, and an inductive engine which induces hypotheses using the computed models and positive/negative examples. It can learn unstratified programs. Fogel and Zaverucha [16] propose an algorithm for learning strict and call-consistent NLPs, which effectively searches the hypotheses space using subsumption and iteratively constructed training examples.

Finally, the algorithms presented in this paper are summarized in Table 1.

For related research, *learning abductive logic programs* [13,20,21,23] and *learning action theories* [24] are important applications of NMILP.

4   Summary and Open Issues

We presented an overview of techniques for realizing induction in nonmonotonic logic programs. Techniques in ILP have been centered on clausal logic so far, especially on Horn logic. However, as nonmonotonic logic programs are different

Table 1. Comparison of Algorithms

Learned Programs	Algorithms	References
NLP	Ordinary ILP + specialization	[2]
	Selection from candidates	[4]
	Top-down	[16,25,40]
	Inverse resolution	[37,43]
	Inverse entailment	[38]
	Least generalization	Section 3.1
ELP	Ordinary ILP	[12]
	Ordinary ILP + specialization	[19,22]
	Computing Answer Sets	[39]

from classical logic, existing techniques are not directly applicable to nonmonotonic situations. In contrast to clausal ILP, the field of nonmonotonic ILP is less explored and several issues remain open. Such issues include:

– *Generalization under implication*: In Section 3.1, we introduced the subsumption order between rules and provided an algorithm of computing a least generalization, which is an easy extension of the one in clausal logic. On the other hand, in clausal theories there is another generalization based on the *implication order* which uses the entailment relation $C_1 \models C_2$ between two clauses C_1 and C_2. Concerning generalizations under implication in NMLP, however, the result of clausal logic is not directly applicable to NMLP. This is because the entailment relation in NMLP is considered under the commonsense semantics, which is different from the classical entailment relation. For instance, under the stable model semantics, the relation $\models_s$ is used instead of $\models$. Generality relations under implication would have properties different from the subsumption order, and the existence of least generalizations and their computability are to be examined.

– *Generalization operations in nonmonotonic logic programs*: In clausal theories, operations by inverting resolution generalize programs, but as presented in Section 3.2, they do not generalize programs in nonmonotonic situations in general. Then, it is important to develop program transformations which generalize nonmonotonic logic programs (under particular semantics) in general. Such transformations would serve as fundamental operations in nonmonotonic ILP. An example of this kind of transformations is seen in [43].

– *Relations between induction and other commonsense reasoning*: Induction is a kind of nonmonotonic inference, hence theoretical relations between induction and other nonmonotonic formalisms, including nonmonotonic logic programming, are of interest. Such relations will enable us to implement ILP in terms of NMLP, and also open possibilities to integrate induction and commonsense reasoning. Researches in this direction are found in [1,14].

Ten years have passed since the first LPNMR conference was held in 1991. In [32] the preface says:

> ... there has been growing interest in the relationship between logic programming semantics and non-monotonic reasoning. It is now reasonably clear that there is ample scope for each of these areas to contribute to the other.

As a concluding remark, we rephrase the same sentence between NMLP and ILP. Combining NMLP and ILP in the framework of nonmonotonic inductive logic programming is an important step towards a better knowledge representation tool, and will bring fruitful advance in each field.

Acknowledgements

The author thanks Katsumi Inoue for comments on an earlier draft of this paper.

References

1. H. Ade and M. Denecker. AILP: abductive inductive logic programming. In: *Proc. 14th International Joint Conference on Artificial Intelligence*, Morgan Kaufmann, pp. 1201–1207, 1995. 77
2. M. Bain and S. Muggleton. Non-monotonic learning. In: S. Muggleton (ed.), *Inductive Logic Programming*, Academic Press, pp. 145–161, 1992. 74, 77
3. C. Baral and M. Gelfond. Logic programming and knowledge representation. *Journal of Logic Programming* 19/20:73–148, 1994. 62, 65
4. F. Bergadano, D. Gunetti, M. Nicosia, and G. Ruffo. Learning logic programs with negation as failure. In: L. De Raedt (ed.), *Advances in Inductive Logic Programming*, IOS Press, pp. 107–123, 1996. 76, 77
5. G. Brewka and J. Dix. Knowledge representation with logic programs. In: *Proc. 3rd Workshop on Logic Programming and Knowledge Representation, Lecture Notes in Artificial Intelligence* 1471, Springer-Verlag, pp. 1–51, 1997. 62
6. F. Bry. Intensional updates: abduction via deduction. In: *Proc. 7th International Conference on Logic Programming*, MIT Press, pp. 561–575, 1990. 63
7. W. Buntine. Generalized subsumption and its application to induction and redundancy. *Artificial Intelligence* 36:149–176, 1988. 69
8. L. De Raedt and M. Bruynooghe. On negation and three-valued logic in interactive concept learning. In: *Proc. 9th European Conference on Artificial Intelligence*, Pitmann, pp. 207–212, 1990. 63
9. L. De Raedt and M. Bruynooghe. Belief updating from integrity constraints and queries. *Artificial Intelligence* 53:291–307, 1992. 63
10. L. De Raedt and M. Bruynooghe. A theory of clausal discovery. In: *Proc. 13th International Joint Conference on Artificial Intelligence*, Morgan Kaufmann, pp. 1058–1063, 1993. 64
11. L. De Raedt and N. Lavrač. The many faces of inductive logic programming. In: *Proc. 7th International Symposium on Methodologies for Intelligent Systems, Lecture Notes in Artificial Intelligence* 689, Springer-Verlag, pp. 435–449, 1993. 64

12. Y. Dimopoulos and A. Kakas. Learning nonmonotonic logic programs: learning exceptions. In: *Proc. 8th European Conference on Machine Learning, Lecture Notes in Artificial Intelligence* 912, Springer-Verlag, pp. 122–137, 1995. 75, 77

13. Y. Dimopoulos and A. Kakas. Abduction and inductive learning. In: L. De Raedt (ed.), *Advances in Inductive Logic Programming*, IOS Press/Ohmsha, pp. 144–171, 1996. 76

14. P. A. Flach and A. C. Kakas (eds). *Abduction and Induction: Essays on their Relation and Integration*, Applied logic series 18, Kluwer Academic, 2000. 63, 77, 79

15. P. A. Flach. Logical characterisations of inductive learning. In: D. M. Gabbay and R. Kruse (eds.), *Handbook of Defeasible Reasoning and Uncertainty Management Systems*, vol. 4, Kluwer Academic Publishers, pp. 155–196, 2000. 64

16. L. Fogel and G. Zaverucha. Normal programs and multiple predicate learning. In: *Proc. 8th International Workshop on Inductive Logic Programming, Lecture Notes in Artificial Intelligence* 1446, Springer-Verlag, pp. 175–184, 1998. 67, 76, 77

17. M. Gelfond and V. Lifschitz. The stable model semantics for logic programming. In: *Proc. 5th International Conference and Symposium on Logic Programming*, MIT Press, pp. 1070–1080, 1988. 65

18. N. Helft. Induction as nonmonotonic inference. In: *Proc. 1st International Conference on Principles of Knowledge Representation and Reasoning*, Morgan Kaufmann, pp. 149–156, 1989. 64

19. K. Inoue and Y. Kudoh. Learning extended logic programs. In: *Proc. 15th International Joint Conference on Artificial Intelligence*, Morgan Kaufmann, pp. 176–181, 1997. 75, 77

20. K. Inoue and H. Haneda. Learning abductive and nonmonotonic logic programs. In: [14], pp. 213–231, 2000. 76

21. A. C. Kakas and F. Riguzzi. Learning with abduction. In: *Proc. 7th International Workshop on Inductive Logic Programming, Lecture Notes in Artificial Intelligence* 1297, Springer-Verlag, pp. 181–188, 1997. 76

22. E. Lamma, F. Riguzzi, and L. M. Pereira. Strategies in combined learning via logic programs. *Machine Learning* 38(1/2), pp. 63–87, 2000. 75, 77

23. E. Lamma, P. Mello, F. Riguzzi, F. Esposito, S. Ferilli, and G. Semeraro. Cooperation of abduction and induction in logic programming. In: [14], pp. 233–252, 2000. 76

24. D. Lorenzo and R. P. Otero. Learning to reason about actions. In: *Proc. 14th European Conference on Artificial Intelligence*, IOS Press, pp. 316–320, 2000. 76

25. L. Martin and C. Vrain. A three-valued framework for the induction of general logic programs. In: L. De Raedt (ed.), *Advances in Inductive Logic Programming*, IOS Press, pp. 219–235, 1996. 76, 77

26. R. S. Michalski. A theory and methodology of inductive learning. *Artificial Intelligence* 20:111-161, 1983. 63

27. T. M. Mitchell. *Machine Learning*, McGraw-Hill, 1997. 62

28. S. Muggleton (ed.). *Inductive Logic Programming*, Academic Press, 1992. 62, 79

29. S. Muggleton and W. Buntine. Machine invention of first-order predicate by inverting resolution. In: [28], pp. 261–280, 1992. 70

30. S. Muggleton and L. De Raedt. Inductive logic programming: theory and methods. *Journal of Logic Programming* 19/20:629–679, 1994. 62

31. S. Muggleton. Inverse entailment and Progol. *New Generation Computing* 13:245–286, 1995. 72

32. A. Nerode, W. Marek, and V. S. Subrahmanian (eds.). *Proc. First International Workshop of Logic Programming and Nonmonotonic Reasoning*, MIT Press, 1991. 78

33. S.-H. Nienhuys-Cheng and R. de Wolf. *Foundations of inductive logic programming. Lecture Notes in Artificial Intelligence* 1228, Springer-Verlag, 1997. 62, 68, 69

34. G. D. Plotkin. A note on inductive generalization. In: B. Meltzer and D. Michie (eds.), *Machine Intelligence* 5, Edinburgh University Press, pp. 153–63, 1970. 67, 68

35. G. D. Plotkin. A further note on inductive generalization. In: B. Meltzer and D. Michie (eds.), *Machine Intelligence* 6, Edinburgh University Press, pp. 101–124, 1971. 68, 69

36. T. C. Przymusinski. On the declarative semantics of deductive databases and logic programs. In: J. Minker (ed.), *Foundations of Deductive Databases and Logic Programming*, Morgan Kaufmann, pp. 193–216, 1988. 66

37. C. Sakama. Some properties of inverse resolution in normal logic programs. In: *Proc. 9th International Workshop on Inductive Logic Programming, Lecture Notes in Artificial Intelligence* 1634, Springer-Verlag, pp. 279–290, 1999. 71, 77

38. C. Sakama. Inverse entailment in nonmonotonic logic programs. In: *Proc. 10th International Conference on Inductive Logic Programming, Lecture Notes in Artificial Intelligence* 1866, Springer-Verlag, pp. 209–224, 2000. 72, 73, 74, 76, 77

39. C. Sakama. Learning by answer sets. In: *Proc. AAAI Spring Symposium on Answer Set Programming*, AAAI Press, pp. 181–187, 2001. 74, 76, 77

40. J. Seitzer. Stable ILP: exploring the added expressivity of negation in the background knowledge. In: *Proceedings of IJCAI-95 Workshop on Frontiers of ILP*, 1997. 76, 77

41. Y. Shoham. Nonmonotonic logics: meaning and utility. In: *Proc. 10th International Joint Conference on Artificial Intelligence*, Morgan Kaufmann, pp. 388–393, 1987. 72

42. L. Sterling and E. Shapiro. *The Art of Prolog*, 2nd Edition, MIT Press, 1994. 64

43. K. Taylor. Inverse resolution of normal clauses. In: *Proc. 3rd International Workshop on Inductive Logic Programming*, J. Stefan Institute, pp. 165–177, 1993. 67, 69, 72, 77

Strong Equivalence for Logic Programs and Default Theories (Made Easy)

Hudson Turner

Computer Science Department, University of Minnesota, Duluth
Duluth, MN 55812, USA
hudson@d.umn.edu

Abstract. Logic programs P and Q are strongly equivalent if, given any logic program R, programs $P \cup R$ and $Q \cup R$ are equivalent (that is, have the same answer sets). Strong equivalence is convenient for the study of equivalent transformations of logic programs: one can prove that a local change is correct without considering the whole program. Recently, Lifschitz, Pearce and Valverde showed that Heyting's logic of here-and-there can be used to characterize strong equivalence of logic programs. This paper offers a more direct characterization, and extends it to default logic. In their paper, Lifschitz, Pearce and Valverde study a very general form of logic programs, called "nested" programs. For the study of strong equivalence of default theories, it is convenient to introduce a corresponding "nested" version of default logic, which generalizes Reiter's default logic.

1 Introduction

Logic programs P and Q are "strongly equivalent" if, given any logic program R, $P \cup R$ and $Q \cup R$ are equivalent. Recent work by Lifschitz, Pearce and Valverde [4] uses Heyting's logic of here-and-there to characterize strong equivalence of logic programs under the answer set semantics [1,3]. Their proof utilizes Pearce's equilibrium logic [5,6]. In the current paper, strong equivalence of logic programs is characterized more directly, in terms of concepts used in the definition of answer sets—no knowledge of the logic of here-and-there is required. This simplifies the proof of the main strong equivalence theorem, and may also make the result easier to apply to specific cases. Moreover, this alternative characterization of strong equivalence is easily extended to Rieter's default logic [7].

Strong equivalence can help us reason about correctness of logic programs and default theories. For example, as discussed in [4], it can be used to establish the fact that in any logic program with a constraint of the form

$$\bot \leftarrow F, G,$$

the disjunctive rule

$$F; G \leftarrow \top$$

T. Eiter, W. Faber, and M. Truszczyński (Eds.): LPNMR 2001, LNAI 2173, pp. 81–92, 2001.

can be replaced by the pair of rules

$$F \leftarrow not\,G$$
$$G \leftarrow not\,F$$

without affecting the program's answer sets.

Lifschitz, Pearce and Valverde consider strong equivalence for a very general form of logic programs, called "nested" programs, introduced by Lifschitz, Tang and Turner [3]. For the study of strong equivalence of default theories, it is convenient to introduce similarly general "nested" default theories.

Section 2 reviews definitions for nested logic programming. Section 3 states and proves a simple characterization of strong equivalence for logic programs. Section 4 makes precise the relationship between our strong equivalence theorem and that obtained using the logic of here-and-there. Section 5 briefly investigates strongly equivalent transformations of logic programs. Taking advantage of the strong similarities between definitions for logic programming and default logic, Section 6 introduces "nested" default logic, and shows that it extends both nested logic programming and disjunctive default logic [2], which in turn extends Reiter's default logic. Section 7 states a characterization of strong equivalence for nested default theories similar to that for nested logic programs. Section 8 briefly investigates strongly equivalent transformations of default theories. Proofs related to nested default logic appear in Section 9.

2   Nested Logic Programming

This paper employs the definition of logic programs from [3], although the presentation differs in some details.

2.1   Syntax

The words *atom* and *literal* are understood here as in propositional logic. *Elementary formulas* are literals and the 0-place connectives ⊥ ("false") and ⊤ ("true"). *NLP formulas* are built from elementary formulas using the unary connective *not* and the binary connectives , (conjunction) and ; (disjunction). An *NLP rule* is an expression of the form

$$F \leftarrow G$$

where F and G are NLP formulas, called the *head* and the *body* of the rule.

A *nested logic program* is a set of NLP rules.

When convenient, a rule $F \leftarrow \top$ is identified with the formula F.

2.2   Semantics

Let us first define recursively when a consistent set X of literals *satisfies* an NLP formula F (symbolically, $X \models F$), as follows.

- For elementary F, $X \models F$ iff $F \in X$ or $F = \top$.
- $X \models (F, G)$ iff $X \models F$ and $X \models G$.
- $X \models (F; G)$ iff $X \models F$ or $X \models G$.
- $X \models not\ F$ iff $X \not\models F$.

A consistent set X of literals is *closed under* a program P if, for every rule $F \leftarrow G$ in P, $X \models F$ whenever $X \models G$.

The *reduct* of a formula F relative to a consistent set X of literals (written F^X) is obtained by replacing every maximal occurrence in F of a formula of the form $not\ G$ with $\bot$ if $X \models G$ and with $\top$ otherwise. The *reduct* of a program P relative to X (written P^X) is obtained by replacing the head and body of each rule in P by their reducts relative to X.

A consistent set X of literals is an *answer set* for P if it is minimal among the consistent sets of literals closed under P^X.

As discussed in [3], this definition agrees with previous versions of the answer set semantics on consistent answer sets (but does not allow for an inconsistent one).

3   Strong Equivalence of Logic Programs

Logic programs P and Q are *equivalent* if they have the same answer sets. They are *strongly equivalent* if, for any logic program R, $P \cup R$ and $Q \cup R$ are equivalent.

The following terminology is convenient. For program P, and consistent sets X, Y of literals with $X \subseteq Y$, call the pair (X, Y) an *SE-model* of P if both X and Y are closed under P^Y.

In Section 4, we will see that SE-models correspond to models in the logic of here-and-there.

Theorem 1. *Logic programs are strongly equivalent iff they have the same SE-models.*

Proof. Right to left: Assume that programs P and Q have the same SE-models. Take any program R. We need to show that $P \cup R$ and $Q \cup R$ are equivalent. Assume that X is an answer set for $P \cup R$. That is, X is a consistent set of literals closed under $(P \cup R)^X$, and no proper subset of X is closed under $(P \cup R)^X$. Since $(P \cup R)^X = P^X \cup R^X$, X is closed under both P^X and R^X. Since X is closed under P^X, it follows by assumption that X is closed under Q^X. So X is closed under $Q^X \cup R^X = (Q \cup R)^X$. Suppose a proper subset of X is closed under $(Q \cup R)^X$. Then it is closed under both Q^X and R^X. By assumption it is also closed under P^X, and thus under $(P \cup R)^X$, contradicting the choice of X. We conclude that every answer set for $P \cup R$ is an answer set for $Q \cup R$. By symmetry, every answer set for $Q \cup R$ is an answer set for $P \cup R$.

Left to right: Assume (wlog) that (X, Y) is an SE-model of program P but not of program Q. We need to show that P and Q are not strongly equivalent. Consider two cases.

Case 1: Y is not closed under Q^Y. Then Y is not closed under $(Q \cup Y)^Y = Q^Y \cup Y$, and so is not an answer set for $Q \cup Y$. On the other hand, one easily verifies that Y is an answer set for $P \cup Y$. Hence P and Q are not strongly equivalent.

Case 2: Y is closed under Q^Y. Take $R = X \cup \{F \leftarrow G : F, G \in Y \setminus X\}$. Clearly Y is closed under $(Q \cup R)^Y$. Let Z be a subset of Y closed under $(Q \cup R)^Y = Q^Y \cup R$. By choice of R, $X \subseteq Z$, and by assumption X is not closed under Q^Y, so $X \neq Z$. Hence some $L \in Y \setminus X$ belongs to Z. It follows by choice of R that $Y \setminus X \subseteq Z$. Consequently $Z = Y$, and so Y is an answer set for $Q \cup R$. On the other hand, X is a proper subset of Y that is closed under $(P \cup R)^Y = P^Y \cup R$. So Y is not an answer set for $P \cup R$, and we conclude again that P and Q are not strongly equivalent.   □

Although simpler (due to simpler definitions), this proof resembles in many details the proof of the main theorem in [4], including the fact that it demonstrates that if logic programs P and Q are not strongly equivalent then they can be distinguished by adding a logic program in which the head of each rule is a literal and the body of each rule is either a literal or $\top$.

4   HT-Models and the Logic of Here-and-There

Lifschitz, Pearce and Valverde identify logic program rules with formulas in the logic of here-and-there, and show that programs are strongly equivalent iff they are equivalent in the logic of here-and-there.

They consider nested programs, as described in Section 2, except that they do not allow classical negation. (That is, their programs do not contain the symbol ¬.) Accordingly, they define answer sets using sets of atoms in place of consistent sets of literals. For convenience, the term "stable model" will be used to refer to an answer set in their sense.

After establishing their strong equivalence theorem (with respect to stable models) for nested programs without classical negation, they explain that the result can be extended to all nested programs as follows. Take any nested program P. For each atom A in the language of P, add a new atom A', and let P' be the program in this extended language obtained by (i) replacing each occurrence of each negative literal ¬A with atom A', and (ii) adding the rule $\bot \leftarrow A, A'$ for every new atom A'. The answer sets for P are in one-to-one correspondence with the stable models of P'. More precisely, given any set X of literals, let X' be obtained by replacing each negative literal ¬$A \in X$ by A'. Then X is an answer set for P iff X' is a stable model of P'.

It follows that nested programs P and Q are strongly equivalent (in the sense of this paper) iff P' and Q' are strongly equivalent wrt stable models. Moreover, for any nested programs P and Q without classical negation, P and Q are strongly equivalent wrt stable models iff P' and Q' are.

In [4], an *HT-interpretation* is a pair (I^H, I^T) of sets of atoms, with $I^H \subseteq I^T$. Without going into details, we can observe that they define when an HT-interpretation is a model of a logic program in the sense of the logic of here-and-there.

Although it is not done here, one can easily verify that their Lemmas 1 and 2 together imply the following.

Proposition 1. *For any nested logic program P, (X, Y) is an SE-model of P iff (X', Y') is a model of P' in the logic of here-and-there.*

So these approaches are essentially equivalent with regard to logic programs. Each has advantages.

The primary advantage of the approach introduced here is its relative simplicity. The definition of SE-model is quite straightforward, based on concepts already introduced in the definition of answer sets. This in turn simplifies the proof of the strong equivalence theorem. Moreover, the (relatively) simple definition can make the theorem easier to apply to specific cases.

The definition introduced in this paper takes advantage of the special status of the symbol $\leftarrow$ in definitions of logic programming. By comparison, the logic of here-and-there treats $\leftarrow$ as just another connective, and even defines *not* in terms of it—*not F* is understood as an abbreviation for $\bot \leftarrow F$. The possibility of nested occurrences of $\leftarrow$ complicates the truth definition considerably.

It is important to note, though, that this complication takes a familiar form— the truth definition in the logic of here-and-there uses standard Kripke models. In fact, they are a special case of Kripke models for intuitionistic logic (which is, accordingly, slightly weaker). Thus, such an approach brings with it a range of associations that may help clarify intuitions about the meaning of connectives $\leftarrow$ and *not* in logic programming.

Even if we consider only convenience in the study of strong equivalence (or similar properties), the logic of here-and-there offers a potential advantage: it is a logic with known identities, deduction rules, and such, which can be used to establish strong equivalence in particular cases.

Nonetheless, when we wish to apply strong equivalence results, it seems likely that a model-theoretic argument using the definition from this paper will often be easier than a proof-theoretic argument using known properties of the logic of here-and-there.

5   Equivalent Transformations of Logic Programs

To demonstrate the use of Theorem 1, let us consider again the example from the introduction: for any NLP formulas F and G, programs P_1 and P_2 below have the same SE-models.

$$\begin{array}{ll} F; G & F \leftarrow not\ G \\ \bot \leftarrow F, G & G \leftarrow not\ F \\ & \bot \leftarrow F, G \end{array}$$

To see this, take any pair (X, Y) of consistent sets of literals such that $X \subseteq Y$, and consider four cases.

Case 1: $Y \models (F, G)^Y$. Then Y is not closed under either of P_1^Y or P_2^Y, so (X, Y) is not an SE-model of P_1 or P_2.

Case 2: $Y \models (F, not\,G)^Y$. So Y is closed under both P_1^Y and P_2^Y. Notice that not does not occur in G^Y. It follows that since $Y \not\models G^Y$ and $X \subseteq Y$, $X \not\models G^Y$. We can conclude that X is closed under P_1^Y iff $X \models F^Y$ iff X is closed under P_2^Y. So (X, Y) is an SE-model of P_1 iff it is an SE-model of P_2.
Case 3: $Y \models (not\,F, G)^Y$. Symmetric to previous case.
Case 4: $Y \models (not\,F, not\,G)^Y$. Similar to first case.

When strong equivalence is characterized using the logic of here-and-there, we immediately obtain a replacement theorem: strong equivalence is preserved under substitution of formulas that are equivalent in the logic of here-and-there. And of course it follows that if formulas F and G are satisfied by the same (here-and-there) models of a program P, then, for any program Q, occurrences of F in Q can be replaced by G without affecting the answer sets of $P \cup Q$. One can provide a similar facility using SE-models. Let us begin with two definitions.

We say that NLP formulas F and G are *equivalent* relative to logic program P if, for every SE-model (X, Y) of P, $X \models F^Y$ iff $X \models G^Y$.

An occurrence of a formula is *regular* if it is not an atom preceded by $\neg$.

Theorem 2. *Let P be a program, and let F and G be formulas equivalent relative to P. For any program Q, and any program Q' obtained from Q by replacing regular occurrences of F by G, programs $P \cup Q$ and $P \cup Q'$ are strongly equivalent.*

The restriction to regular occurrences is essential. For example, formulas p and q are equivalent relative to program $P_3 = \{p \leftarrow q, q \leftarrow p\}$, yet programs $P_3 \cup \{\neg p\}$ and $P_3 \cup \{\neg q\}$ are not strongly equivalent.

Theorem 2 is a more widely-applicable version of Proposition 3 from [3]. There we defined equivalence of formulas more strictly, and did not make it relative to a program. We also used a notion of "equivalence" of programs stronger than strong equivalence. Although it is not done here, a proof of Theorem 2 can be easily constructed based on the corresponding proof from the earlier paper. (Section 9 does include a similar proof—of the corresponding theorem for "nested" default logic.) Alternatively, just as Proposition 1 related the SE-models (X, Y) of a program P with the models (X', Y') of program P' under the logic of here-and-there, one can show that NLP formulas F and G are equivalent relative to program P iff the corresponding formulas F' and G' are satisfied by the same models of P' in the logic of here-and-there.

Many formula equivalences are proved in [3] (Proposition 4), and of course they also hold under our (weaker) definition (relative to the empty program). Thus, Theorem 2 implies, for instance, that replacing subformulas of the form $not\,(F, G)$ with $not\,F; not\,G$ yields a strongly equivalent program.

For another example using Theorem 2, observe that for any program Q, and any program Q' obtained from Q by replacing occurrences of $not\,F$ by G and/or $not\,G$ by F, programs $P_2 \cup Q$ and $P_2 \cup Q'$ are strongly equivalent.

6   Nested Default Logic

For the study of strong equivalence of default theories, it is convenient to introduce a "nested" version of default logic that generalizes disjunctive default logic [2], which in turn generalizes Reiter's default logic.

The relatively uniform syntax of nested default logic will make it more convenient for stating and using strong equivalence results. (We don't have to deal separately with a prerequisite and a set of justifications—they are expressed in a single formula.)

As one might expect, the definitions for nested default logic are almost exactly as for nested logic programs—essentially, allow arbitrary formulas of classical logic in place of literals, and use consistent, logically closed sets of formulas in place of consistent sets of literals. Accordingly, the strong equivalence theorem (and its proof!) is nearly identical too.

6.1   Syntax

Let us say *classical formula* to mean a formula of classical propositional logic.

NDL formulas are built from classical formulas using the unary connective *not* (negation as failure) and the binary connectives | (strong disjunction) and $\wedge$ (conjunction). (There is no need for a distinct "strong conjunction" connective.) An *NDL rule* is an expression of the form

$$\frac{F}{G}$$

where F and G are NDL formulas, called the *condition* and the *conclusion* of the rule.

A *nested default theory* is a set of NDL rules.

When convenient, a rule of the form $\frac{\top}{F}$ will be identified with formula F.

6.2   Semantics

Let us use the term *candidate set* for a consistent set of classical formulas that is closed under classical propositional logic.

We can recursively define when a candidate set X *satisfies* an NDL formula F (symbolically, $X \models F$), as follows.

- For classical F, $X \models F$ iff $F \in X$.
- $X \models (F \wedge G)$ iff $X \models F$ and $X \models G$.
- $X \models (F \,|\, G)$ iff $X \models F$ or $X \models G$.
- $X \models not\ F$ iff $X \not\models F$.

A candidate set X is *closed under* a default theory P if, for every rule $\frac{F}{G}$ in P, $X \models F$ implies $X \models G$.

The *reduct* of an NDL formula F relative to a candidate set X (written F^X) is obtained by replacing every maximal occurrence in F of a formula of the form *not G* with $\bot$ if $X \models G$ and with $\top$ otherwise. The reduct of a default theory P relative to X (written P^X) is obtained by replacing the condition and conclusion of each rule in P by their reducts relative to X.

A candidate set X is an *extension* of P if it is minimal among the candidate sets closed under P^X.

6.3   Relation to (Nested) Logic Programming

Essentially, nested logic programming is a special case of nested default logic. Every NLP formula F corresponds to the NDL formula $d(F)$ obtained by replacing occurrences of the connectives ; and , with $|$ and $\wedge$ respectively. A nested logic program corresponds to the default theory obtained by replacing each NLP rule $F \leftarrow G$ with $\dfrac{d(G)}{d(F)}$. A consistent set of literals corresponds to the candidate set whose formulas are its consequences (in classical logic).

Proposition 2. *The answer sets for any nested logic program correspond to the extensions of the corresponding nested default theory.*

6.4   Relation to (Disjunctive) Default Logic

Nested default logic generalizes disjunctive default logic [2], which in turn generalizes Reiter's default logic. Here we review the definition of disjunctive default logic and relate it to nested default logic.

A *disjunctive default rule* is an expression of the form

$$\frac{\alpha : \beta_1, \ldots, \beta_m}{\gamma_1 | \cdots | \gamma_n} \tag{1}$$

where $\alpha, \beta_1, \ldots, \beta_m, \gamma_1, \ldots, \gamma_n$ are classical formulas ($m \geq 0, n \geq 1$). Reiter's default logic corresponds to the special case when $n = 1$.[1]

A disjunctive default rule (1) corresponds to the NDL rule

$$\frac{\alpha \wedge not\, \neg\beta_1 \wedge \cdots \wedge not\, \neg\beta_m}{\gamma_1 | \cdots | \gamma_n}.$$

A *disjunctive default theory* is a set of disjunctive default rules.

Let P be a disjunctive default theory and X a set of classical formulas. Define

$$P^X = \left\{ \frac{\alpha :}{\gamma_1 | \cdots | \gamma_n} : \frac{\alpha : \beta_1, \ldots, \beta_m}{\gamma_1 | \cdots | \gamma_n} \in P \text{ and } \neg\beta_1, \ldots, \neg\beta_m \notin X \right\}.$$

A set Y of classical formulas is *closed under* P^X if, for every member of P^X, if $\alpha \in Y$ then at least one of $\gamma_1, \ldots, \gamma_n$ belongs to Y.

We say X is an *extension* of P if X is minimal among sets of formulas closed under propositional logic and closed under P^X.

---

[1] In Reiter's formulation, a default theory is a pair (P, W), where the second component W is a set of classical formulas. Here we suppress the second component, since every $\phi \in W$ can be equivalently represented in P by the rule $\dfrac{\top :}{\phi}$.

Proposition 3. *A candidate set X is an extension of a disjunctive default theory P iff it is an extension of the corresponding nested default theory.*

Proposition 3 restricts attention to candidate sets (which are by definition consistent) because, unlike nested default logic, disjunctive default logic allows for the possibility of an inconsistent extension.

7 Strong Equivalence of Default Theories

Nested default theories P and Q are *equivalent* if they have the same extensions. They are *strongly equivalent* if, for any nested default theory R, $P \cup R$ and $Q \cup R$ are equivalent.

For nested default theory P, and candidate sets X, Y with $X \subseteq Y$, the pair (X, Y) is an *SE-model* of P if both X and Y are closed under P^Y.

Theorem 3. *Nested default theories are strongly equivalent iff they have the same SE-models.*

A proof of Theorem 3 is easily obtained from the proof of Theorem 1, and so is not presented in this paper. (Essentially, replace references to "consistent sets of literals" with references to "candidate sets.")

The proof shows that any two nested default theories that are not strongly equivalent can be distinguished by adding a nested default theory in which the conditions and conclusions of all rules are classical formulas.

8 Equivalent Transformations of Default Theories

As with logic programs (using Theorem 1), Theorem 3 can be used, for example, to show that in any default theory containing the rule

$$\frac{F \wedge G}{\perp},$$

the rule

$$\frac{\top}{F \mid G}$$

can be replaced by the rules

$$\frac{not\ F}{G}, \frac{not\ G}{F}.$$

Moreover, it is clear that replacing any occurrence of one classical formula with another that is logically equivalent (in classical logic) yields a strongly equivalent default theory.

We can formulate an additional replacement theorem, similar to Theorem 2 for logic programming, thus extending our account of when an occurrence of one formula may be safely replaced by another. Again we need some definitions first.

We say that NDL formulas F and G are *equivalent* relative to nested default theory P if, for every SE-model (X, Y) of P, $X \models F^Y$ iff $X \models G^Y$.

An occurrence of a subformula in an NDL formula is called *regular* if it is not a proper subpart of an occurrence of a subformula formed by an application of $\neg$ or $\vee$.

Theorem 4. *Let P be a nested default theory, and let F and G be formulas equivalent relative to P. For any nested default theory Q, and any nested default theory Q' obtained from Q by replacing some regular occurrences of F by G, nested default theories $P \cup Q$ and $P \cup Q'$ are strongly equivalent.*

As with Theorem 2, the restriction to regular occurrences is essential. (And essentially the same example shows this.)

Theorem 4 can be used to show, for example, that in any nested default theory with rules

$$\frac{not\ F}{\neg F},\ \frac{not\ \neg F}{F}$$

any occurrence of NDL formula $F|G$ (for any classical formula G) can be safely replaced with $F \vee G$.

9 Proofs Related to Nested Default Logic

Proposition 2. *The answer sets for any nested logic program correspond to the extensions of the corresponding nested default theory.*

For any candidate set X, let $l(X)$ denote the set of all literals in X.

Lemma 1. *For any NLP formula F and candidate set X, $l(X) \models F$ iff $X \models d(F)$.*

Proof. Straightforward, by structural induction.   □

Lemma 2. *For any NLP formula F and candidate set X, $d(F^{l(X)}) = d(F)^X$.*

Proof. Follows easily from Lemma 1 and the definitions.   □

Lemma 3. *For any nested logic program P and candidate sets X and Y, $l(X)$ is closed under $P^{l(Y)}$ iff X is closed under $d(P)^Y$.*

Proof. Follows easily from Lemmas 1 and 2, and the definitions.   □

Proof of Proposition 2: Take any nested logic program P. Assume X is an answer set for P. So X is a consistent set of literals closed under P^X, and no proper subset of X is closed under P^X. Let Y be the candidate set corresponding to X. By Lemma 3, Y is closed under $d(P)^Y$. Suppose a candidate set Z with $Z \subseteq Y$ is closed under $d(P)^Y$. By Lemma 3, $l(Z)$ is closed under P^X. Since $Z \subseteq Y$, $l(Z) \subseteq X$. We conclude by choice of X that $l(Z) = X$. It follows that $Z = Y$. So Y is an extension of $d(P)$. Proof in the other direction is similar.   □

Proposition 3. *A candidate set X is an extension of a disjunctive default theory P iff it is an extension of the corresponding nested default theory.*

Proof. It is clear that for any disjunctive default theory P and corresponding nested default theory Q, and any candidate sets X and Y, X is closed under P^Y iff X is closed under Q^Y, from which the result follows. □

Theorem 4. *Let P be a nested default theory, and let F and G be formulas equivalent relative to P. For any nested default theory Q, and any nested default theory Q' obtained from Q by replacing some regular occurrences of F by G, nested default theories $P \cup Q$ and $P \cup Q'$ are strongly equivalent.*

The proof of Theorem 4 is very similar to the proof of Proposition 3 from [3], and illustrates how a proof of Theorem 2 might go.

We begin with an easily verified lemma.

Lemma 4. *For any NDL formula F and candidate set X, $X \models F$ iff $X \models F^X$.*

Lemma 5. *Let F and G be NDL formulas equivalent relative to nested default theory P. If an NDL formula H' can be obtained from an NDL formula H by replacing some regular occurrences of F by G, then H and H' are equivalent relative to P.*

Proof. Consider any SE-model (X, Y) of P. We need to show that $X \models H^Y$ iff $X \models (H')^Y$. Proof is by structural induction on H.

Case 1: H is an atom or $H = \neg H_1$ or $H = H_1 \vee H_2$. Then the only regular occurrence of a formula in H is H itself. Consequently $H = F$ and $H' = G$, and we're done.

Case 2: $H = H_1 \wedge H_2$. If $H = F$ and $H' = G$ we're done. Otherwise, $H' = H'_1 \wedge H'_2$ and, by the induction hypothesis, H_1 and H'_1 are equivalent relative to P, as are H_2 and H'_2. Then

$$
\begin{aligned}
X \models H^Y \ &\text{iff} \ X \models (H_1 \wedge H_2)^Y \\
&\text{iff} \ X \models H_1^Y \wedge H_2^Y \\
&\text{iff} \ X \models H_1^Y \ \text{and} \ X \models H_2^Y \\
&\text{iff} \ X \models (H'_1)^Y \ \text{and} \ X \models (H'_2)^Y \\
&\text{iff} \ X \models (H'_1)^Y \wedge (H'_2)^Y \\
&\text{iff} \ X \models (H'_1 \wedge H'_2)^Y \\
&\text{iff} \ X \models (H')^Y.
\end{aligned}
$$

Case 3: $H = H_1 | H_2$. Similar to Case 2.

Case 4: $H = not\, H_1$. If $H = F$ and $H' = G$ we're done. Otherwise, $H' = not\, H'_1$ and, by the induction hypothesis, H_1 and H'_1 are equivalent relative to P. Assume that $X \models (not\, H_1)^Y$. Then $(not\, H_1)^Y = \top$, so $Y \not\models H_1$. It follows by Lemma 4 that $Y \not\models H_1^Y$. Since (X, Y) is an SE-model of P, so is (Y, Y). Since H_1 and H'_1 are equivalent relative to P, we can conclude that $Y \not\models (H'_1)^Y$. By Lemma 4, $Y \not\models H'_1$. So $(not\, H'_1)^Y = \top$, and thus $X \models (not\, F)^Y$. The other direction is symmetric. □

Proof of Theorem 4: Assume that Q' can be obtained from Q by replacing some regular occurrences of F by a formula G that is equivalent relative to P. We must show that $P \cup Q$ and $P \cup Q'$ have the same SE-models.

Consider any SE-model (X, Y) of P. It is enough to show that both X and Y are closed under Q^Y iff both are closed under $(Q')^Y$. So consider any rule $\frac{H_1}{H_2} \in Q$, along with the corresponding rule $\frac{H_1'}{H_2'} \in Q'$. By Lemma 5, $X \models (H_1)^Y$ iff $X \models (H_1')^Y$, and similarly $X \models (H_2)^Y$ iff $X \models (H_2')^Y$. We conclude that X is closed under Q^Y iff it is closed under $(Q')^Y$. Since (Y, Y) is also an SE-model of P, the same argument can be used to show that Y is closed under Q^Y iff it is closed under $(Q')^Y$.   □

Acknowledgements

I am grateful to Vladimir Lifschitz and Michael Gelfond for helpful comments. This work partially supported by NSF Career Grant #0091773.

References

1. Michael Gelfond and Vladimir Lifschitz. Classical negation in logic programs and disjunctive databases. *New Generation Computing*, 9:365–385, 1991. 81
2. Michael Gelfond, Vladimir Lifschitz, Halina Przymusińska, and Miroslaw Truszczyński. Disjunctive defaults. In James Allen, Richard Fikes, and Erik Sandewall, editors, *Principles of Knowledge Representation and Reasoning: Proc. of the 2nd Int'l Conference*, pages 230–237, 1991. 82, 87, 88
3. Vladimir Lifschitz, L. R. Tang, and Hudson Turner. Nested expressions in logic programs. *Annals of Mathematics and Artificial Intelligence*, 25(2–3):369–390, 1999. 81, 82, 83, 86, 91
4. Vladimir Lifschitz, David Pearce, and Agustín Valverde. Strongly equivalent logic programs. *ACM Transactions on Computational Logic*, To appear, 2001. (Pre-print version available at www.cs.utexas.edu/users/vl/papers.html.) 81, 84
5. David Pearce. A new logical characterization of stable models and answer sets. In Jürgen Dix, Luis Pereira, and Teodor Przymusinski, editors, *Non-Monotonic Extensions of Logic Programming (Lecture Notes in Artificial Intelligence 1216)*, pages 57–70. Springer-Verlag, 1997. 81
6. David Pearce. From here to there: stable negation in logic programming. In D. Gabbay and H. Wansing, editors, *What is Negation?* Kluwer, 1999. 81
7. Raymond Reiter. A logic for default reasoning. *Artificial Intelligence*, 13(1,2):81–132, 1980. 81

On the Effect of Default Negation
on the Expressiveness of Disjunctive Rules[*]

Tomi Janhunen[**]

Helsinki University of Technology, Laboratory for Theoretical Computer Science
P.O.Box 5400, FIN-02015 HUT, Finland
Tomi.Janhunen@hut.fi

Abstract. In this paper, the expressive power of disjunctive rules involving default negation is analyzed within a framework based on polynomial, faithful and modular (PFM) translations. The analysis is restricted to the stable semantics of disjunctive logic programs. A particular interest is understanding what is the effect if default negation is allowed in the heads of disjunctive rules. It is established in the paper that occurrences of default negation can be removed from the heads of rules using a PFM translation when default negation is allowed in the bodies of rules. In this case, we may conclude that default negation appearing in the heads of rules does not affect expressive power of rules. However, in the case that default negation may not be used in the bodies of rules, such a PFM translation is no longer possible. Moreover, there is no PFM translation for removing default negation from the bodies of rules. Consequently, disjunctive logic programs with default negation in the bodies of rules are strictly more expressive than those without.

1 Introduction

Logic programming with *answer sets* [6,7] as proposed by Gelfond and Lifschitz has been recently recognized as a logic programming paradigm of its own [22,23]. This is mainly because problems from many domains such as *planning* [18], *configuration* [30] and *verification* [9] have attractive formulations as logic programs under the *answer set semantics* [6]. Much of the promise of the paradigm is also due to efficient implementations [17,24] that currently allow computing answer sets for logic programs with thousands of rules. Being able to handle programs of this scale has already turned out to be sufficient to enable industrial applications of the answer set programming approach.

Our interest in answer set programming is comparing the expressive powers of various types of rules that have been introduced by the logic programming community. This paper can be viewed as a continuation of previous work on

---

[*] A preliminary version of this paper was presented at the 5th Dutch-German Workshop on Nonmonotonic Reasoning Techniques and their Applications (DGNMR'01).

[**] Support from Academy of Finland (project 43963) is acknowledged with gratitude.

T. Eiter, W. Faber, and M. Truszczyński (Eds.): LPNMR 2001, LNAI 2173, pp. 93–106, 2001.

the expressive power of non-monotonic logics [8,10,12,13,14]. The author [15] extends similar techniques for some syntactically restricted classes of logic programs. The analysis is based on the existence of *polynomial, faithful* and *modular* (PFM) translation functions between classes. This gives rise to a hierarchy of classes of logic program ordered by expressive power. However, the results presented in [15] are limited to very special subclasses of *normal logic programs*, since the goal is studying how the number of positive body literals affects the expressiveness of rules. In this paper, more general classes of logic programs involving disjunction are taken into consideration. The semantics of programs in these classes is determined by respective generalizations [7,19] of the answer set semantics [6].

Historically speaking, the answer set semantics has its roots in the *stable model semantics* [5] of normal logic programs (also known as *general logic programs* [20]). This class is obtained from ordinary logic programs (that consist of rules that are effectively Horn clauses) by allowing the use of a form of negation – *negation as failure to prove* [20] – in the bodies of rules. Due to close interconnections to Reiter's *default logic* [28], this form of negation is also known as *default negation*. Default negation differs from classical negation and it is therefore quite natural that Gelfond and Lifschitz proposed a logic programming approach with both negations [6]. This is how the answer set semantics originated as a generalization of the stable model semantics. Later on, Gelfond and Lifschitz extended the answer set semantics to cover disjunctive logic programs with classical negation [7] (Przymusinski [26] presented similar ideas, but in a more general setting). The latest generalization [19,18] to answer set programming allows occurrences default negation in the heads of disjunctive rules as well.

In this paper, we restrict ourselves to the class of disjunctive logic programs without classical negation and use PFM translation functions to evaluate the effects of extending the rule language with default negation (i) in the bodies of rules, (ii) in the heads of rules, and (iii) in both. The rest of the paper is organized as follows. Section 2 gives a brief introduction to disjunctive logic programs and the stable model semantics. In Section 3, we present the analysis method based on PFM translation functions. The method is then applied in Section 4 to evaluate the effects of default negation on the expressiveness of disjunctive rules. After that some comparisons with related work are performed in Section 5. Finally, the paper ends with a discussion in Section 6.

2   Disjunctive Logic Programs

In this paper, we consider disjunctive logic programs in the propositional case[1]. We let $\sim$ stand for default negation in order to distinguish it from classical negation $\neg$. Given a (propositional) atom a, we define *positive and negative*

---

[1] Disjunctive programs with variables are also covered through Herbrand instantiation. In the presence of function symbols, Herbrand instantiation produces an infinite (but countable) propositional program out of a finite disjunctive program with variables.

literals as expressions of the forms a and ~a, respectively. To handle sets of negative literals nicely, we define $\sim A = \{\sim a \mid a \in A\}$ for a set of atoms A. In general, a *disjunctive logic program* P is a set of rules of the form

$$A \vee \sim B \leftarrow C \wedge \sim D \tag{1}$$

where A, B, C and D are sets of atoms. The literals in $A \cup \sim B$ form the *head* of the rule while the literals in $C \cup \sim D$ form the *body* of the rule. The intuition behind a rule of the form (1) is that if all the atoms in C can be inferred and none of the atoms in D can be inferred, then one of the atoms in A can be inferred *or* one of the atoms in B cannot be inferred. This is how the head of the rule is interpreted *disjunctively* while the body is subject to a *conjunctive* interpretation[2]. The Herbrand base $\mathrm{Hb}(P)$ of a disjunctive logic program P is the set of atoms that appear in P. The class of all disjunctive logic programs is denoted by $\mathcal{D}$. A disjunctive logic program P is *positive* if all rules (1) of P satisfy $B = \emptyset$ and $D = \emptyset$. Quite similarly, a program P is *head-positive* (alternatively *body-positive*), if all rules (1) of P satisfy $B = \emptyset$ (alternatively $D = \emptyset$). The respective classes of disjunctive logic programs are denoted by $\mathcal{D}^+$, $\mathcal{D}^{h+}$, and $\mathcal{D}^{b+}$. These definitions imply that $\mathcal{D}^+ \subset \mathcal{D}^{h+} \subset \mathcal{D}$ and $\mathcal{D}^+ \subset \mathcal{D}^{b+} \subset \mathcal{D}$.

2.1   Stable Models and Answer Sets

Because this paper is restricted to classes of disjunctive logic programs without classical negation, the forthcoming definition of stable models coincides with that of answer sets [19]. The standard way to define the semantics of a *positive* disjunctive logic program P is to distinguish models of P that are *minimal* as follows. An *interpretation* of P is simply a subset of $\mathrm{Hb}(P)$ and a rule $A \leftarrow C$ of P is satisfied in an interpretation $I \subseteq \mathrm{Hb}(P)$ of P if $C \subseteq I$ implies $A \cap I \neq \emptyset$. A set of atoms $M \subseteq \mathrm{Hb}(P)$ is a *model* of P if all rules of P are satisfied in M. A model M of P is a (subset) minimal model of P if there is no model M' of P such that $M' \subset M$. By this definition, it is possible that a positive disjunctive program has no minimal models ($P_1 = \{a \leftarrow , \leftarrow a\}$), a unique minimal model ($P_2 = \{a \leftarrow\}$) or even several minimal models ($P_3 = \{a \vee b \leftarrow\}$). By a slight abuse of notation, we write $M = \mathrm{Mm}(P)$ to declare that M is one of the minimal models of a positive disjunctive logic program P. Thus we may write $M_1 = \{a\} = \mathrm{Mm}(P_3)$ as well as $M_2 = \{b\} = \mathrm{Mm}(P_3)$ although these models are not unique.

The stable model semantics of disjunctive logic programs is obtained via the Gelfond-Lifschitz reduction of a disjunctive logic program P [7,18,19] which presumes a model candidate M. The reduced program

$$P^M = \{A \leftarrow C \mid A \vee \sim B \leftarrow C \wedge \sim D \in P,\ B \subseteq M,\ \text{and}\ D \cap M = \emptyset\} \tag{2}$$

is a positive one. A model M of a disjunctive logic program P is *stable* if M is a minimal model of P^M (not necessarily a unique one), i.e., $M = \mathrm{Mm}(P^M)$.

---

[2] Rather than using a set-based notation (1), heads and bodies of rules are often written as disjunctions and conjunctions, respectively. For instance, when $A = \{a\}$, $B = \{b\}$, $C = \{c\}$, and $D = \{d\}$, we write $a \vee \sim b \leftarrow c \wedge \sim d$ for the rule (1).

Example 1. Consider logic programs $P_1 = \{a \vee \sim a \leftarrow\}$ [19] and $P_2 = \{a \leftarrow a\}$. The former has two stable models $M_1 = \{a\}$ and $M_2 = \emptyset$ while M_2 is the unique stable model of P_2. Note that M_1 is also a model of P_2, but not a minimal one.

The program P_1 illustrates how the negative literal $\sim a$ in the head lets us express succinctly a *choice* regarding a: either a is in the model (a $\in M_1$) or a is not in the model (a $\notin M_2$). Simons [29] achieves the same effect by enriching normal logic programs with *choice rules*. Note that due to the negative literal $\sim a$ in the head of the only rule of P_1, the stable models M_1 and M_2 of P_1 break the well-known anti-chain property: $M_1 \subseteq M_2$ does not imply $M_1 = M_2$.

3   Polynomial, Faithful and Modular Translations

In this paper, we employ a framework of polynomial, faithful and modular translation functions for comparing the expressive powers of classes $\mathcal{C}$ of logic programs [15]. Some basic assumptions are imposed on any class $\mathcal{C}$ of logic programs. First of all, the class $\mathcal{C}$ is supposed to be *closed under unions*, i.e., given any two programs P and P' from $\mathcal{C}$, then also $P \cup P'$ belongs to $\mathcal{C}$. On the other hand, it is assumed that $\mathcal{C}$ has a semantic operator $\mathrm{Sem}_\mathcal{C}$ associated with it. The operator $\mathrm{Sem}_\mathcal{C}$ assigns a set of interpretations $I \subseteq \mathrm{Hb}(P)$ to each program P of $\mathcal{C}$. Typically, these interpretations are distinguished models of P. It is clear that the classes $\mathcal{D}$, $\mathcal{D}^+$, $\mathcal{D}^{h+}$, and $\mathcal{D}^{b+}$ satisfy these criteria. The semantic operator $\mathrm{Sem}_\mathcal{C}$ is the same for each class $\mathcal{C}$ of these: $\mathrm{Sem}_\mathcal{C}$ assigns $\{M \subseteq \mathrm{Hb}(P) \mid M = \mathrm{Mm}(P^M)\}$ to a program P whenever P is a member of the respective class $\mathcal{C}$.

In the following definition, we list the general requirements for a translation function Tr that transforms logic programs P of one class $\mathcal{C}$ into logic programs $\mathrm{Tr}(P)$ of another class $\mathcal{C}'$. The latter class is assumed to be a subclass or a superclass of $\mathcal{C}$. We let $||P||$ stand for the *length* of P in symbols.

Definition 1. *Given two classes of logic programs $\mathcal{C}$ and $\mathcal{C}'$ that are closed under unions and the respective semantic operators $\mathrm{Sem}_\mathcal{C}$ and $\mathrm{Sem}_{\mathcal{C}'}$, a translation function $\mathrm{Tr} : \mathcal{C} \to \mathcal{C}'$ is*

- **polynomial** *if for all logic programs $P \in \mathcal{C}$, the time required to compute the translation $\mathrm{Tr}(P) \in \mathcal{C}'$ is polynomial in $||P||$,*
- **faithful** *if (i) for all logic programs $P \in \mathcal{C}$, the base $\mathrm{Hb}(P) \subseteq \mathrm{Hb}(\mathrm{Tr}(P))$ and (ii) the models/interpretations in $\mathrm{Sem}_\mathcal{C}(P)$ and $\mathrm{Sem}_{\mathcal{C}'}(\mathrm{Tr}(P))$ are in a one-to-one correspondence and coincide up to $\mathrm{Hb}(P)$, and*
- **modular** *if (i) for all logic programs $P_1 \in \mathcal{C}$ and $P_2 \in \mathcal{C}$, the translation $\mathrm{Tr}(P_1 \cup P_2) = \mathrm{Tr}(P_1) \cup \mathrm{Tr}(P_2)$ and (ii) $\mathcal{C}' \subset \mathcal{C}$ implies that the translation $\mathrm{Tr}(P') = P'$ for all logic programs $P' \in \mathcal{C}'$.*

The faithfulness requirement implies that a translation function Tr may introduce new atoms, but the number of such atoms is clearly bounded by the polymiality requirement. Let us also note that if Tr is faithful, then $\mathrm{Sem}_\mathcal{C}(P) = \{M \cap \mathrm{Hb}(P) \mid M \in \mathrm{Sem}_{\mathcal{C}'}(\mathrm{Tr}(P))\}$ holds. The first part of the modularity condition enforces locality of Tr, since the translation of a program $P_1 \cup P_2$

is obtained as the union of the translations of the subprograms P_1 and P_2. This implies that programs can be translated rule by rule. The second part handles cases where programs of a class $\mathcal{C}$ are translated into programs in a proper subclass $\mathcal{C}'$ of $\mathcal{C}$. Such a class $\mathcal{C}'$ is typically obtained by restricting the syntax of the rules of the programs in $\mathcal{C}$. In this setting, we require that syntactically restricted rules remain intact by a translation function. Note that whenever $\mathcal{C}' \subset \mathcal{C}$ holds, the joint effect of the modularity conditions (i) and (ii) is that $\mathrm{Tr}(P' \cup P) = P' \cup \mathrm{Tr}(P)$ holds for all logic programs $P' \in \mathcal{C}'$ and $P \in \mathcal{C}$.

We say that a translation function $\mathrm{Tr} : \mathcal{C} \to \mathcal{C}'$ is PFM if it satisfies all the three criteria. If such a translation function exists, we write $\mathcal{C} \xrightarrow{\text{PFM}} \mathcal{C}'$ and consider $\mathcal{C}'$ *as expressive as* $\mathcal{C}$. In certain cases, we can find a counter-example which proves that a translation function satisfying our criteria does not exist. We use the notation $\mathcal{C} \xrightarrow{\text{PFM}} \mathcal{C}'$ in such cases. Any of the letters P, F, and M may be omitted from the notation if the corresponding criterion is not needed in the counter-example (note that $\mathcal{C} \xrightarrow{\text{FM}} \mathcal{C}'$ implies $\mathcal{C} \xrightarrow{\text{PFM}} \mathcal{C}'$, for instance).

More complex relations among classes of logic programs can be deduced from the base relations $\xrightarrow{\text{PFM}}$ and $\xrightarrow{\text{PFM}}$. A class $\mathcal{C}$ is *less expressive* than $\mathcal{C}'$ (denoted by $\mathcal{C} \xRightarrow{\text{PFM}} \mathcal{C}'$) if $\mathcal{C} \xrightarrow{\text{PFM}} \mathcal{C}'$ and $\mathcal{C}' \xrightarrow{\text{PFM}} \mathcal{C}$. Classes $\mathcal{C}$ and $\mathcal{C}'$ are *equally expressive* (denoted by $\mathcal{C} \xLeftrightarrow{\text{PFM}} \mathcal{C}'$) if $\mathcal{C} \xrightarrow{\text{PFM}} \mathcal{C}'$ and $\mathcal{C}' \xrightarrow{\text{PFM}} \mathcal{C}$. Classes $\mathcal{C}$ and $\mathcal{C}'$ are *mutually incomparable* (denoted by $\mathcal{C} \xleftrightarrow{\text{PFM}} \mathcal{C}'$) if $\mathcal{C} \xrightarrow{\text{PFM}} \mathcal{C}'$ and $\mathcal{C}' \xrightarrow{\text{PFM}} \mathcal{C}$. By these relations, we have accommodated the method proposed for non-monotonic logics [13] to the case of logic programs (c.f. [15] for a discussion on the main differences).

4   Expressive Power Analysis

Recall the inclusions $\mathcal{D}^+ \subset \mathcal{D}^{h+} \subset \mathcal{D}$ stated in Section 2. Since the semantic operators of these classes coincide, it follows by the existence of an *identity translation function* $\mathrm{Tr}_{\mathrm{id}}$ (i.e., $\mathrm{Tr}_{\mathrm{id}}(P) = P$ holds for any P from $\mathcal{D}^+$ or $\mathcal{D}^{h+}$) that $\mathcal{D}^+ \xrightarrow{\text{PFM}} \mathcal{D}^{h+}$ and $\mathcal{D}^{h+} \xrightarrow{\text{PFM}} \mathcal{D}$, but the strictness of these relationships remains open. So let us begin our analysis by establishing $\mathcal{D}^+ \xRightarrow{\text{PFM}} \mathcal{D}^{h+}$.

Theorem 1. $\mathcal{D}^{h+} \xrightarrow{\text{FM}} \mathcal{D}^+$.

Proof. Consider $P = \{a \leftarrow \sim a\}$ that clearly belongs to $\mathcal{D}^{h+}$. Then suppose there is a faithful and modular translation function that maps P to a *positive* logic program $\mathrm{Tr}(P)$ in $\mathcal{D}^+$. It follows by the faithfulness of Tr that $\mathrm{Hb}(P) \subseteq \mathrm{Hb}(\mathrm{Tr}(P))$. In addition, the translation $\mathrm{Tr}(P)$ does not have minimal models, since P does not have stable models. This implies that $\mathrm{Tr}(P)$ has no models, i.e., $\mathrm{Tr}(P)$ is an inconsistent positive logic program. Then consider $P' = P \cup \{a \leftarrow\}$ for which $\mathrm{Tr}(P') = \mathrm{Tr}(P) \cup \{a \leftarrow\}$ holds, as Tr is modular. But then $\mathrm{Tr}(P')$ does not have models nor minimal models so that P' does not have stable models, as Tr is faithful. A contradiction, since $M = \{a\}$ is a stable model of P'.   □

Let us then concentrate on establishing that $\mathcal{D} \xrightarrow{\text{PFM}} \mathcal{D}^{h+}$ which implies that $\mathcal{D} \xLeftrightarrow{\text{PFM}} \mathcal{D}^{h+}$. For this result, we have to find a way to translate disjunctive logic programs having occurrences of default negation in the heads of rules into head-positive disjunctive logic programs. For each atom a $\in$ Hb(P), we introduce a new atom a° which is to mean that a cannot be inferred by the rules. In analogy to [6], the atom a° can be understood as a "positive occurrence" of the negative literal $\sim$a. The difference is that we apply the idea to remove default negation while Gelfond and Lifschitz aim to remove negative literals formed with classical negation. For a set of atoms $A \subseteq$ Hb(P), we let $A°$ denote the set {a° | a $\in$ A}. For any $P \in \mathcal{D}$, we distinguish a particular subset of Hb(P): $\text{Hd}^{\sim}(P) = \bigcup\{B \mid A \vee \sim B \leftarrow C \wedge \sim D \in P\}$ is the set of atoms that appear negatively in the heads of the rules of P. Default negation can be removed from the heads of rules using a translation function $\text{Tr}_{\text{h+}}$ to be defined as follows.

Definition 2. *For a disjunctive logic program P, let $\text{Tr}_{\text{h+}}(P)$ denote the translation of P into a head-positive disjunctive logic program*

$$\{\leftarrow \text{a} \wedge \text{a°} \ , \ \text{a°} \leftarrow \sim\text{a} \mid \text{a} \in \text{Hd}^{\sim}(P)\} \ \cup$$
$$\{A \cup B° \leftarrow C \wedge \sim D \mid A \vee \sim B \leftarrow C \wedge \sim D \in P\} \tag{3}$$

Thus Hb($\text{Tr}_{\text{h+}}(P)$) = Hb(P) $\cup$ $\text{Hd}^{\sim}(P)°$. Let us establish that $\text{Tr}_{\text{h+}}$ is PFM.

Theorem 2. *Let P be a disjunctive logic program. If $M \subseteq$ Hb(P) is a stable model of P, then $M \cup (\text{Hd}^{\sim}(P) - M)°$ is a stable model of $\text{Tr}_{\text{h+}}(P)$.*

Proof. Let M be a stable model of P and $M' = M \cup (\text{Hd}^{\sim}(P) - M)°$. By the definitions of $\text{Tr}_{\text{h+}}(P)$ and M', the reduct of $\text{Tr}_{\text{h+}}(P)$ with respect to M' is

$$\{\leftarrow \text{a} \wedge \text{a°} \mid \text{a} \in \text{Hd}^{\sim}(P)\} \cup \{\text{a°} \leftarrow \mid \text{a} \in \text{Hd}^{\sim}(P) - M\} \ \cup$$
$$\{A \cup B° \leftarrow C \mid A \cup B° \leftarrow C \wedge \sim D \in \text{Tr}_{\text{h+}}(P) \text{ and } D \cap M' = \emptyset\}. \tag{4}$$

The rules of the forms $\leftarrow \text{a} \wedge \text{a°}$ and $\text{a°} \leftarrow$ in (4) are satisfied in M' directly by the definition of M'. Let us then assume that some of the rules $A \cup B° \leftarrow C$ in (4) is not satisfied in M', i.e., $C \subseteq M'$ and $(A \cup B°) \cap M' = \emptyset$. It follows by the definition of M' that $C \subseteq M$, $A \cap M = \emptyset$ and $B \subseteq M$. Also $D \cap M = \emptyset$ holds by (4) and the definition of M'. Thus the rule $A \leftarrow C$ belongs to P^M and it is not satisfied by M. Thus M is not a model of P^M, a contradiction. Hence the rule $A \cup B° \leftarrow C$ is satisfied by M'. To conclude, we have established that M' is a model of the reduct (4). It remains to establish the minimality of M'.

So let us assume that M' is not a minimal model of (4), i.e., there is a model N' of (4) such that $N' \subset M'$. Now N' and M' must coincide on the atoms of $\text{Hd}^{\sim}(P)°$, because $N' \subset M'$, N' is a model of (4), and the rule $\text{a°} \leftarrow$ is included in (4) for each a $\in \text{Hd}^{\sim}(P) - M$. Thus $N \subset M$ holds for $N = N' \cap \text{Hb}(P)$. Then assume that N is not a model of P^M, i.e., there is a rule $A \leftarrow C \in P^M$ such that $C \subseteq N$ and $A \cap N = \emptyset$. So there is a rule $A \vee \sim B \leftarrow C \wedge \sim D$ in P such that $B \subseteq M$ and $D \cap M = \emptyset$. Consequently, $A \cup B° \leftarrow C \wedge \sim D$ belongs to $\text{Tr}_{\text{h+}}(P)$ and $D \cap M' = \emptyset$ implying that $A \cup B° \leftarrow C$ belongs to (4). Moreover, it follows by the definitions of N and M' and the relationship $N' \subset M'$ that $A \cap N' = \emptyset$, $B° \cap N' = \emptyset$ and $C \subseteq N'$. Thus $A \cup B° \leftarrow C$ is not satisfied in N', a contradiction. Hence N is a model of P^M. Then $N \subset M$ implies that M is not a minimal model of P^M, contradicting the stability of M. Thus M' is a minimal model of (4), i.e., a stable model of $\mathrm{Tr}_{h+}(P)$. $\qquad\square$

Theorem 3. *Let P be a disjunctive logic program. If $M' \subseteq \mathrm{Hb}(P) \cup \mathrm{Hd}^\sim(P)^\circ$ is a stable model of $\mathrm{Tr}_{h+}(P)$, then $M = M' \cap \mathrm{Hb}(P)$ is a stable model of P.*

Proof. Let $M' \subseteq \mathrm{Hb}(P) \cup \mathrm{Hd}^\sim(P)^\circ$ be a stable model of $\mathrm{Tr}_{h+}(P)$ and define $M = M' \cap \mathrm{Hb}(P)$. Consider any a $\in \mathrm{Hd}^\sim(P)$. (i) Suppose that a $\in M$ and a$^\circ \in M'$. Then a $\in M'$ and $\leftarrow$ a $\wedge$ a$^\circ \in \mathrm{Tr}_{h+}(P)^{M'}$ is not satisfied in M', a contradiction. (ii) Then assume that a $\notin M$ and a$^\circ \notin M'$. Since a $\in \mathrm{Hd}^\sim(P) \subseteq \mathrm{Hb}(P)$ and $M = M' \cap \mathrm{Hb}(P)$, it follows that a $\notin M'$. This implies that a$^\circ \leftarrow$ belongs to $\mathrm{Tr}_{h+}(P)^{M'}$. Since M' is a model of $\mathrm{Tr}_{h+}(P)^{M'}$, it holds necessarily that a$^\circ \in M'$, a contradiction. Now (i) and (ii) imply for any a $\in \mathrm{Hd}^\sim(P)$ that a $\notin M \Leftrightarrow$ a$^\circ \in M'$. Thus $M' = M \cup (\mathrm{Hd}^\sim(P) - M)^\circ$.

Then consider any rule $A \vee \sim B \leftarrow C \wedge \sim D$ of the original program P. Now (iii) $A \leftarrow C \in P^M \Leftrightarrow B \subseteq M$ and $D \cap M = \emptyset \Leftrightarrow B^\circ \cap M' = \emptyset$ and $D \cap M' = \emptyset$ $\Leftrightarrow B^\circ \cap M' = \emptyset$ and $A \cup B^\circ \leftarrow C \in \mathrm{Tr}_{h+}(P)^{M'}$.

Let us then assume that M is not a model of P^M. So there is a rule $A \leftarrow C$ in P^M such that $C \subseteq M$ and $A \cap M = \emptyset$. This implies by (iii) that $B^\circ \cap M' = \emptyset$ and the rule $A \cup B^\circ \leftarrow C$ belongs to $\mathrm{Tr}_{h+}(P)^{M'}$. It follows that $C \subseteq M'$ and $(A \cup B^\circ) \cap M' = \emptyset$. Thus $A \cup B^\circ \leftarrow C$ is not satisfied in M', i.e., M' is not a model of $\mathrm{Tr}_{h+}(P)^{M'}$, a contradiction. Hence M is a model of P^M.

Finally, let us assume that M is not a minimal model of P^M. Then there is a model N of P^M such that $N \subset M$. Define a model $N' = N \cup (\mathrm{Hd}^\sim(P) - M)^\circ$ so that $N' \subset M'$ is the case. Let us assume that N' is not a model of $\mathrm{Tr}_{h+}(P)^{M'}$, i.e., the reduct contains a rule which is not satisfied in N'. Three cases arise. (a) A rule $\leftarrow$ a $\wedge$ a$^\circ$ of $\mathrm{Tr}_{h+}(P)^{M'}$ is false in N'. This implies that a $\in \mathrm{Hd}^\sim(P)$, a $\in N'$ and a$^\circ \in N'$. By the relationship $N' \subset M'$, we obtain that a $\in M'$ and a$^\circ \in M'$, a contradiction. (b) A rule a$^\circ \leftarrow$ of $\mathrm{Tr}_{h+}(P)^{M'}$ is false in N'. It follows that a $\in \mathrm{Hd}^\sim(P)$ and a$^\circ \notin N'$ so that a$^\circ \notin M'$ holds, as N' and M' coincide on the atoms of $\mathrm{Hd}^\sim(P)^\circ$. Then M' is not a model of $\mathrm{Tr}_{h+}(P)^{M'}$, a contradiction. (c) A rule $A \cup B^\circ \leftarrow C$ of $\mathrm{Tr}_{h+}(P)^{M'}$ is false in N'. It follows that $C \subseteq N'$ and $(A \cup B^\circ) \cap N' = \emptyset$ so that $C \subseteq N$ and $A \cap N = \emptyset$. Moreover, $B^\circ \cap M' = \emptyset$ holds, as N' and M' coincide on the atoms of $\mathrm{Hd}^\sim(P)^\circ$. Thus $A \leftarrow C$ belongs to P^M by (iii). In addition, this particular rule is not satisfied in N which contradicts the fact that N is a model of P^M.

By the preceding case analysis, N' is a model of $\mathrm{Tr}_{h+}(P)^{M'}$, a contradiction. Hence M is a minimal model of P^M and a stable model of P. $\qquad\square$

Theorem 4. $\mathcal{D} \xrightarrow{\mathrm{PFM}} \mathcal{D}^{h+}$.

Proof. It is obvious that Tr_{h+} is polynomial and modular. To establish faithfulness we note that Theorem 2 gives rise to a mapping f_1 that maps a stable model M of P to a stable model $f_1(M) = M \cup (\mathrm{Hd}^\sim(P) - M)^\circ$ of $\mathrm{Tr}_{h+}(P)$. Then consider any two stable models M and N of P such that $f_1(M) = f_2(N)$. It follows that $M = N$ so that f_1 is injective. On the other hand, a mapping f_2 that maps a stable model M' of $\mathrm{Tr}_{h+}(P)$ to a stable model $f_2(M') = M' \cap \mathrm{Hb}(P)$ of P is obtained from Theorem 3. If we have two stable models M' and N' of $\mathrm{Tr}_{h+}(P)$ such that $M = f_2(M') = f_2(N') = N$, it follows by the proof of Theorem 3 that $M' = M \cup (\mathrm{Hd}^\sim(P) - M) = N \cup (\mathrm{Hd}^\sim(P) - N) = N'$. This indicates that f_2 is injective. Thus it is clear that f_1 and f_2 are bijective and inverses of each other. Consequently, the stable models of P and $\mathrm{Tr}_{h+}(P)$ are in a one-to-one correspondence and they coincide up to $\mathrm{Hb}(P)$. $\qquad\square$

Having established the equivalence of $\mathcal{D}$ and $\mathcal{D}^{h+}$, we are ready to proceed to the analysis of *body-positive* programs. Recall that any $P \in \mathcal{D}^{b+}$ is a set of rules of the form $A \vee {\sim} B \leftarrow C$. By the denial of negative subgoals in the bodies of rules, the semantic definitions are simplified accordingly. Given $P \in \mathcal{D}^{b+}$ and a model candidate $M \subseteq \mathrm{Hb}(P)$, the reduct P^M contains a rule $A \leftarrow C$ whenever $B \subseteq M$ for some rule $A \vee {\sim} B \leftarrow C \in P$. The definition of stable models remains intact, i.e., $M = \mathrm{Mm}(P^M)$. However, the properties of P^M let us establish interesting results for the programs of $\mathcal{D}^{b+}$ as follows.

Lemma 1. *If $Q \in \mathcal{D}^{b+}$, $P \subseteq Q$, and $M_1 \subseteq M_2 \subseteq \mathrm{Hb}(Q)$, then $P^{M_1} \subseteq Q^{M_2}$.*

Indeed, the reduct P^M grows monotonically with respect to P and M. This is in contrast with head-positive programs $P \in \mathcal{D}^{h+}$ that satisfy $P^{M_2} \subseteq P^{M_1}$ for $M_1 \subseteq M_2 \subseteq \mathrm{Hb}(P)$. The monotonicity properties of P^M let us to extend well-known properties of minimal models of positive disjunctive programs to cover stable models of body-positive disjunctive programs.

Lemma 2. *If $P \in \mathcal{D}^{b+}$ and $M \subseteq \mathrm{Hb}(P)$ is a model of P^M, then P has a stable model $N \subseteq \mathrm{Hb}(P)$ such that $N \subseteq M$.*

Proof sketch. Let $M \subseteq \mathrm{Hb}(P)$ be a model of P^M for $P \in \mathcal{D}^{b+}$. Then we may use transfinite induction to construct a descending sequence of interpretations $M_0 \supseteq M_1 \supseteq M_2 \supseteq \ldots$ such that (i) $M_0 = M$, (ii) $M_\alpha \subseteq M_{\alpha-1}$ can be chosen as $\mathrm{Mm}(P^{M_{\alpha-1}})$ for a successor ordinal α, and (iii) M_α is defined as the limit $\bigcap_{\beta<\alpha} M_\beta$ for a limit ordinal α. The construction can be done so that M_α remains a model of P^{M_α} for any ordinal α. Moreover, it follows for a sufficiently large successor ordinal α ($|\alpha| > |\mathrm{Hb}(P)|$) that $M_\alpha = M_{\alpha-1}$. This implies by (ii) that $M_\alpha = \mathrm{Mm}(P^{M_\alpha})$ so that $N = M_\alpha$ is a stable model of P. In an extreme case, N may become empty. This is demonstrated in Example 2. $\qquad\square$

Example 2. Consider an infinite body-positive disjunctive logic program $P = \{\mathsf{b}_i \vee {\sim}\mathsf{b}_{i-1} \leftarrow \,|\, i > 0\}$. It is clear that $M_0 = \mathrm{Hb}(P) = \{\mathsf{b}_i \,|\, i \geq 0\}$ is a model of $P^{M_0} = \{\mathsf{b}_i \leftarrow \,|\, i \geq 1\}$, but not a minimal one, as $M_1 = \{\mathsf{b}_i \,|\, i \geq 1\}$ is the unique minimal model of P^{M_0}. Similarly, for any $j > 0$, $M_{j-1} = \{\mathsf{b}_i \,|\, i \geq j-1\}$ is not a minimal model of $P^{M_{j-1}} = \{\mathsf{b}_i \leftarrow \,|\, i \geq j\}$, but $M_j = \{\mathsf{b}_i \,|\, i \geq j\}$ is. It follows that $\bigcap_{i \geq 0} M_i = \emptyset$ and $N = \emptyset$ is a stable model of P. This is obvious, since the reduct $P^N = \emptyset$. Note that N is in fact the unique stable model of P. $\qquad\square$

Proposition 1. *Consider $P \in \mathcal{D}^{b+}$ and $Q \in \mathcal{D}^{b+}$ such that $P \subseteq Q$. (i) If Q has a stable model $M \subseteq \mathrm{Hb}(Q)$ then P has a stable model $N \subseteq \mathrm{Hb}(P)$ such that $N \subseteq M$. (ii) If P has no stable models, neither has Q.*

Proof. Suppose that M is a stable model of Q, i.e., $M = \mathrm{Mm}(Q^M)$. Since $P^{M'} \subseteq Q^M$ holds for $M' = M \cap \mathrm{Hb}(P)$ by Lemma 1, we know that M and M' are models of $P^{M'}$. Thus P has a stable model $N \subseteq M' \subseteq M$ by Lemma 2. The claim (ii) of this proposition follows easily from (i) by contrapositive argumentation.   □

To characterize the expressive power of the class $\mathcal{D}^{b+}$, we note that $\mathcal{D}^{+} \xrightarrow[\text{PFM}]{} \mathcal{D}^{b+}$ and $\mathcal{D}^{b+} \xrightarrow[\text{PFM}]{} \mathcal{D}$ hold directly by the relationships $\mathcal{D}^{+} \subset \mathcal{D}^{b+} \subset \mathcal{D}$ and the identity translation function $\mathrm{Tr}_{\mathrm{id}}$. The latter relationship is shown to be a strict one in the following theorem. Thus body-positive disjunctive programs are strictly less expressive than general as well as head-positive disjunctive programs, as implied by the fact that $\mathcal{D}^{b+} \xrightarrow[\text{PFM}]{\Longrightarrow} \mathcal{D}$ and Theorem 4.

Theorem 5. $\mathcal{D} \xrightarrow[\text{FM}]{\nrightarrow} \mathcal{D}^{b+}$.

Proof. Consider $P = \{a \leftarrow \sim a\}$ from $\mathcal{D}$. Suppose there is a faithful and modular translation function Tr that maps P to a program $\mathrm{Tr}(P)$ of $\mathcal{D}^{b+}$. Since P has no stable models, neither has $\mathrm{Tr}(P)$ by the faithfulness of Tr. As Tr is modular, we know that $\mathrm{Tr}(P') = \mathrm{Tr}(P) \cup \{a \leftarrow\}$ holds for $P' = P \cup \{a \leftarrow\}$. Thus $\mathrm{Tr}(P')$ has no stable models by Proposition 1. This contradicts the faithfulness of Tr, since P' has a unique stable model $M = \{a\}$.   □

Let us then address the relationship $\mathcal{D}^{+} \xrightarrow[\text{PFM}]{} \mathcal{D}^{b+}$. Our last theorem provides a concrete counter-example to establish that body-positive disjunctive programs are strictly more expressive than positive ones, i.e., $\mathcal{D}^{+} \xrightarrow[\text{PFM}]{\Longrightarrow} \mathcal{D}^{b+}$ holds.

Theorem 6. $\mathcal{D}^{b+} \xrightarrow[\text{PFM}]{\nrightarrow} \mathcal{D}^{+}$.

Proof. Consider a body-positive logic program $P = \{a \vee \sim b \leftarrow\}$. Suppose there is a PFM translation function Tr from $\mathcal{D}^{b+}$ to $\mathcal{D}^{+}$ that maps P to a positive program $\mathrm{Tr}(P)$ such that $\mathrm{Hb}(P) \subseteq \mathrm{Hb}(\mathrm{Tr}(P))$. It follows by the modularity of Tr that $P \cup \{b \leftarrow a\}$ is translated into $\mathrm{Tr}(P \cup \{b \leftarrow a\}) = \mathrm{Tr}(P) \cup \{b \leftarrow a\}$. Note that $\mathrm{Hb}(P \cup \{b \leftarrow a\}) = \mathrm{Hb}(P)$ and $\mathrm{Hb}(\mathrm{Tr}(P \cup \{b \leftarrow a\})) = \mathrm{Hb}(\mathrm{Tr}(P))$.

Now $P \cup \{b \leftarrow a\}$ has two stable models $M_1 = \emptyset$ and $M_2 = \{a, b\}$. This implies by the faithfulness of Tr that $\mathrm{Tr}(P) \cup \{b \leftarrow a\}$ has exactly two minimal models $N_1 \subseteq \mathrm{Hb}(\mathrm{Tr}(P))$ and $N_2 \subseteq \mathrm{Hb}(\mathrm{Tr}(P))$ such that $M_1 = N_1 \cap \mathrm{Hb}(P)$ and $M_2 = N_2 \cap \mathrm{Hb}(P)$. It follows that both N_1 and N_2 are models of $\mathrm{Tr}(P)$, but not necessarily minimal ones. Consequently, there exist minimal models N_1' and N_2' of $\mathrm{Tr}(P)$ such that $N_1' \subseteq N_1$ and $N_2' \subseteq N_2$. Since P has a unique stable model $M = \emptyset$, it follows by the faithfulness of Tr that N_1' and N_2' must be the same minimal model of $\mathrm{Tr}(P)$, say N'. Moreover, $N' \subseteq N_1 \cap N_2$ and $N' \cap \mathrm{Hb}(P) = M = \emptyset$. But then the rule $b \leftarrow a$ is satisfied by N' which is therefore a model of $\mathrm{Tr}(P) \cup \{b \leftarrow a\}$ such that $N' \subseteq N_1 \cap N_2$. Recall that N_1 and N_2 form an antichain as minimal models of $\mathrm{Tr}(P) \cup \{b \leftarrow a\}$. It follows that $N' \subset N_1$ and $N' \subset N_2$ – contradicting minimality of N_1 and N_2.   □

5   Related Work

Antoniou et al. [1] apply a modularity condition when developing normal forms for Nute's *defeasible logic* [25]. Since the syntax of defeasible logic is based on rules, too, it is worth comparing their notion of modularity with the one applied in this paper. According to Antoniou et al., a translation function Tr is *modular*, if $D_1 \cup D_2 \equiv_{L(D_1) \cup L(D_2)} D_1 \cup \mathrm{Tr}(D_2)$ for any defeasible theories D_1 and D_2. Here $\equiv$ denotes semantical equivalence, i.e., the theories yield exactly the same conclusions in the union of the respective languages $L(D_1)$ and $L(D_2)$ of D_1 and D_2. Similarly, Tr is *correct*, if $D \equiv_{L(D)} \mathrm{Tr}(D)$ for every D, and *incremental*, if $D_1 \cup D_2 \equiv_{L(D_1) \cup L(D_2)} \mathrm{Tr}(D_1) \cup \mathrm{Tr}(D_2)$ for every D_1 and D_2. Thus any modular transformation is also incremental and correct [1]. Note that the part (i) of our definition of modularity in Definition 1 corresponds to incrementality. The main difference is that our definition of modularity is purely syntactical: a modular translation need not be faithful (i.e., correct in the terminology of Antoniou et al.). The notions of faithfulness differ, too, since the skeptical semantics of defeasible theories is based on proofs rather than models.

Inoue and Sakama [11] present an alternative way for removing default negation from the heads of rules. Their idea is to translate (1) into $A^* \cup B^* \leftarrow C \cup \sim D$ where $A^* = \{a^* \mid a \in A\}$ and $B^* = \{a^* \mid a \in B\}$ are sets of new atoms. In addition, the rules $a \leftarrow a^*$, $a^* \leftarrow \{a\} \cup B$, $\leftarrow b \wedge b^*$, and $\leftarrow a^* \wedge \sim b$ have to be introduced for each $a \in A$ and $b \in B$. The resulting translation function $\mathrm{Tr_{IS}}$ is clearly modular, but *quadratic* in the worst case. In contrast to this, the translation function $\mathrm{Tr_{h+}}$ in Definition 2 is *linear*. The translational idea behind $\mathrm{Tr_{h+}}$ is also simpler than that of $\mathrm{Tr_{IS}}$. Inoue and Sakama [11, Remark 6.3] note anyway that the stable models of a disjunctive program P and $\mathrm{Tr_{IS}}(P)$ are in a one-to-one correspondence. Thus $\mathrm{Tr_{IS}}$ is also PFM and Theorem 4 is also implied by the results in [11]. Inoue and Sakama [11, Section 6.3] propose yet another polynomial and modular translation function for removing default negation from head-positive programs. However, Theorem 1 implies that $\mathrm{Tr_{IS}}$ cannot be faithful. This explains why Inoue and Sakama need an additional stability condition on minimal models to establish faithfulness. The resulting semantics of positive programs is expressive enough to capture head-positive programs.

Eiter and Gottlob [4] study the computational complexity of disjunctive logic programs by ranking the main decision problems (brave and cautious reasoning with stable/minimal models) in *polynomial time hierarchy* (PH). To summarize their results, these decision problems of positive and head-positive programs are complete problems on the second level of PH. By the tight semantical correspondences embodied in the relationships $\mathcal{D} \xleftrightarrow{\mathrm{PFM}} \mathcal{D}^{\mathrm{h+}}$, $\mathcal{D}^+ \xleftrightarrow{\mathrm{PFM}} \mathcal{D}^{\mathrm{b+}} \xrightarrow{\mathrm{PFM}} \mathcal{D}$, these results extend for the classes allowing default negation in the heads of rules, too.

Corollary 1. *For disjunctive programs in $\mathcal{D}$ and $\mathcal{D}^{\mathrm{b+}}$, (i) brave reasoning with stable models forms a Σ_2^{p}-complete decision problem, and (ii) cautious reasoning with stable models forms a Π_2^{p}-complete decision problem.*

The results concerning the class $\mathcal{D}$ appeared first in [11, Theorem 6.4]. Further differences in expressive power can be detected if the computational complexity of checking the existence of stable models is taken into consideration. For disjunctive programs in $\mathcal{D}^{h+}$, this forms a Σ_2^p-complete decision problem. The same holds for $\mathcal{D}$ by the relationship $\mathcal{D} \xrightarrow{\text{PFM}} \mathcal{D}^+$ as well as [11, Theorem 6.4]. However, for any disjunctive program P from $\mathcal{D}^+$ it is sufficient to find one (even non-minimal) model to solve this decision problem. This is an indication of the fact that the problem is Σ_1^p-complete (i.e., **NP**-complete) [4]. By Lemma 2 and the relationship $\mathcal{D}^+ \xleftarrow{\text{PFM}} \mathcal{D}^{b+}$, we may conclude that the corresponding decision problem is also Σ_1^p-complete for the class of body-positive programs $\mathcal{D}^{b+}$.

6   Conclusions and Further Research

In this paper, we apply a framework based on polynomial, faithful and modular (PFM) translation functions to study the effect of default negation on the expressiveness of disjunctive rules. Three subclasses of the class of disjunctive logic programs $\mathcal{D}$ are identified: the classes of positive programs $\mathcal{D}^+$, head-positive programs $\mathcal{D}^{h+}$, and body-positive programs $\mathcal{D}^{b+}$. To summarize the relationships established by Theorems 1, 4, 5, and 6, we have obtained an expressive power hierarchy (EPH) for disjunctive programs with the following structure: $\mathcal{D}^+ \xrightarrow{\text{PFM}} \mathcal{D}^{b+} \xrightarrow{\text{PFM}} \mathcal{D} \xleftarrow{\text{PFM}} \mathcal{D}^{h+}$. Therefore, we conclude that permitting default negation in the heads of rules does not increase the expressive power of rules given that default negation is allowed in the bodies of rules. The translation function Tr_{h+} given in Definition 2 removes such occurrences of default negation in a straightforward way. However, this is no longer possible when default negation is banned in the bodies of rules so that the expressive power of body-positive disjunctive programs exceeds that of positive disjunctive programs. Moreover, it is clear by the structure of the hierarchy that the expressive power of rules is properly increased by introducing default negation in the bodies of rules.

However, the expressive powers of the four classes are the *same* if measured by the computational complexity of brave and cautious reasoning with stable models. This follows by the results of Eiter and Gottlob [4], Inoue and Sakama [11], and this paper (Corollary 1). On the other hand, the classes $\mathcal{D}^+$ and $\mathcal{D}^{b+}$ can be differentiated from the classes $\mathcal{D}^{h+}$ and $\mathcal{D}$ if the complexity of deciding the existence of a stable model is taken into account, but $\mathcal{D}^+$ and $\mathcal{D}^{b+}$ remain equivalent even under this additional measure. Since $\mathcal{D}^+ \xrightarrow{\text{PFM}} \mathcal{D}^{b+}$ holds, we conclude that the measure based on PFM translations provides a refined view on the expressiveness of disjunctive rules involving default negation. This is because polynomial transformations involved in PH preserve just the plain yes/no answers of decisions problems. Compared to this, the notions of faithfulness and modularity (c.f. Definition 1) constitute a much stronger constraint. Let us also point out that the hierarchy EPH deduced in this paper remains valid even in the unlikely event that the complexity classes **P** and **NP** coincide and PH collapses.

It is to be expected that the results of this paper can be extended and generalized in several ways. (i) Currently, our results do not cover the classes of *extended* disjunctive programs where *classical literals*, i.e., atoms a and their classical negations ¬a, may appear wherever atoms appear in ordinary disjunctive rules (1). In order to generalize our framework for the case of extended disjunctive programs, we have to extend languages associated with disjunctive programs and revise the notion of faithfulness accordingly. The basic technique for obtaining translations will be the one by Gelfond and Lifschitz [6]: classical negative literals are simply rewritten as new atoms. (ii) Furthermore, it will be interesting to study the effect of *integrity constraints*, i.e., rules (1) with $A = \emptyset$, using the framework proposed in this paper. (iii) The current notion of modularity could be split in two, i.e., notions of *weak* and *strong modularity*. The latter would correspond to the current notion while the former could be introduced to strengthen intranslatability results. For instance, the proof of Theorem 1 remains valid even if we introduce a notion of modularity requiring that head-positive rules can be translated in separation of rules that are not head-positive. (iv) So far our analysis covers only the stable semantics, but a wide variety of alternative semantics for disjunctive logic programs have been proposed (see, e.g., [2,3,21,27,31]). Due to our recent experiences with non-monotonic logics [14], we expect (in)translatability results regarding other semantics as well. Our first results in this respect on Przymusinski's *partial stable models* [26] can be found in [16].

References

1. G. Antoniou, D. Billington, G. Governatori, and M. Maher. Representation results for defeasible logic. *ACM Transactions on Computational Logic*, 2(2):255–287, April 2001. 102

2. S. Brass and J. Dix. Disjunctive semantics based on partial and bottom-up evaluation. In *Proceedings of the 12th International Conference on Logic Programming*, pages 199–213, Tokyo, June 1995. The MIT Press. 104

3. P. Dung. An argumentation theoretic foundation for logic programming. *Journal of Logic Programming*, 22:151–177, 1995. 104

4. T. Eiter and G. Gottlob. On the computational cost of disjunctive logic programming: Propositional case. *Annals of Mathematics and Artificial Intelligence*, 15:289–323, 1995. 102, 103

5. M. Gelfond and V. Lifschitz. The stable model semantics for logic programming. In *Proceedings of the 5th International Conference on Logic Programming*, pages 1070–1080, Seattle, USA, August 1988. The MIT Press. 94

6. M. Gelfond and V. Lifschitz. Logic programs with classical negation. In *Proceedings of the 7th International Conference on Logic Programming*, pages 579–597, Jerusalem, Israel, June 1990. The MIT Press. 93, 94, 98, 104

7. M. Gelfond and V. Lifschitz. Classical negation in logic programs and disjunctive databases. *New Generation Computing*, 9:365–385, 1991. 93, 94, 95

8. G. Gottlob. Translating default logic into standard autoepistemic logic. *Journal of the Association for Computing Machinery*, 42(2):711–740, 1995. 94

9. K. Heljanko. Using logic programs with stable model semantics to solve deadlock and reachability problems for 1-safe Petri nets. *Fundamenta Informaticae*, 37(3):247–268, 1999. 93

10. T. Imielinski. Results on translating defaults to circumscription. *Artificial Intelligence*, 32:131–146, 1987. 94

11. Katsumi Inoue and Chiaki Sakama. Negation as failure in the head. *Journal of Logic Programming*, 35(1):39–78, 1998. 102, 103
12. T. Janhunen. Classifying semi-normal default logic on the basis of its expressive power. In M. Gelfond, N. Leone, and G. Pfeifer, editors, *Proceedings of the 5th International Conference on Logic Programming and Non-Monotonic Reasoning, LPNMR'99*, pages 19–33, El Paso, Texas, December 1999. Springer-Verlag. LNAI. 94
13. T. Janhunen. On the intertranslatability of non-monotonic logics. *Annals of Mathematics in Artificial Intelligence*, 27(1-4):79–128, 1999. 94, 97
14. T. Janhunen. Capturing stationary and regular extensions with Reiter's extensions. In Ojeda-Aciego M. et al., editors, *Logics in Artificial Intelligence, European Workshop, JELIA 2000*, pages 102–117, Málaga, Spain, September/October 2000. Springer-Verlag. LNAI 1919. 94, 104
15. T. Janhunen. Comparing the expressive powers of some syntactically restricted classes of logic programs. In J. Lloyd et al., editors, *Computational Logic, First International Conference*, pages 852–866, London, UK, July 2000. Springer-Verlag. LNAI 1861. 94, 96, 97
16. T. Janhunen, I. Niemelä, P. Simons, and J. You. Unfolding partiality and disjunctions in stable model semantics. In A. G. Cohn, F. Guinchiglia, and B. Selman, editors, *Proceedings of the Seventh International Conference on Principles of Knowledge Representation and Reasoning*, pages 411–419, Breckenridge, Colorado, USA, April 2000. Morgan Kaufmann Publishers. 104
17. N. Leone et al. Dlv. http://www.dbai.tuwien.ac.a t/proj/dlv/, 2000. A Disjunctive Datalog System. 93
18. V. Lifschitz. Answer set planning. In D. De Schreye, editor, *Logic Programming, Proceedings of the 1999 International Conference on Logic Programming*, pages 23–37. MIT Press, November-December 1999. 93, 94, 95
19. V. Lifschitz and T. Woo. Answer sets in general nonmonotonic reasoning (preliminary report). In *Proceedings of the Third International Conference on Principles of Knowledge Representation and Reasoning*, pages 603–614, 1992. 94, 95, 96
20. J. W. Lloyd. *Foundations of Logic Programming*. Springer-Verlag, Berlin, 1987. 94
21. J. Lobo, J. Minker, and A. Rajasekar. *Foundations of Disjunctive Logic Programming*. The MIT Press, 1992. 104
22. W. Marek and M. Truszczyński. Stable models and an alternative logic programming paradigm. In *The Logic Programming Paradigm: a 25-Year Perspective*, pages 375–398. Springer-Verlag, 1999. 93
23. I. Niemelä. Logic programming with stable model semantics as a constraint programming paradigm. *Annals of Mathematics and Artificial Intelligence*, 25(3,4):241–273, 1999. 93
24. I. Niemelä, P. Simons, and T. Syrjänen. Smodels: a system for answer set programming. In *Proceedings of the 8th International Workshop on Non-Monotonic Reasoning*, Breckenridge, Colorado, USA, April 2000. cs.AI/0003033. 93
25. D. Nute. Defeasible logic. In D. M. Gabbay, C. J. Hogger, and J. A. Robinson, editors, *Handbook of Logic in Artificial Intelligence and Logic Programming*, chapter 7, pages 353–395. Oxford Science Publications, 1994. 102
26. T. C. Przymusinski. Stable semantics for disjunctive programs. *New Generation Computing*, 9:401–424, 1991. 94, 104
27. T. C. Przymusinski. Static semantics for normal and disjunctive logic programs. *Annals of Mathematics and Artificial Intelligence, Special Issue on Disjunctive Programs*, 14:323–357, 1995. 104

28. R. Reiter. A logic for default reasoning. *Artificial Intelligence*, 13:81–132, 1980.
    94

29. P. Simons. Extending the stable model semantics with more expressive rules.
    In *Proceedings of the 5th International Conference on Logic Programming and
    Nonmonotonic Reasoning*, pages 305–316, El Paso, Texas, USA, December 1999.
    Springer-Verlag. 96

30. T. Soininen, I. Niemelä, J. Tiihonen, and R. Sulonen. Unified configuration knowl-
    edge representation using weight constraint rules. In *Workshop Notes of the
    ECAI'2000 Configuration Workshop*, pages 79–84, Berlin, Germany, August 2000.
    93

31. J. You and L. Yuan. A three-valued semantics for deductive databases and logic
    programs. *Journal of Computer and System Sciences*, 49:334–361, 1994. 104

On the Expressibility
of Stable Logic Programming

V. W. Marek[1] and J. B. Remmel[2]

[1] Department of Computer Science, University of Kentucky
[2] Department of Mathematics, University of California, San Diego

Abstract. Schlipf [Sch95] proved that Stable Logic Programming (SLP) solves all *NP* decision problems. We extend Schlipf's result to prove that SLP solves all search problems in the class *NP*. Moreover, we do this in a uniform way as defined in [MT99]. Specifically, we show that there is a single DATALOG⌐ program P_{Trg} such that given any Turing machine M, any polynomial p with non-negative integer coefficients and any input σ of size n over a fixed alphabet Σ, there is an extensional database $edb_{M,p,\sigma}$ such that there is a one-to-one correspondence between the stable models of $edb_{M,p,\sigma} \cup P_{Trg}$ and the accepting computations of the machine M that reach the final state in at most $p(n)$ steps. Moreover, $edb_{M,p,\sigma}$ can be computed in polynomial time from p, σ and the description of M and the decoding of such accepting computations from its corresponding stable model of $edb_{M,p,\sigma} \cup P_{Trg}$ can be computed in linear time. A similar statement holds for Default Logic with respect to Σ_2^P-search problems.

We also show that there is single program *Meta* which is a metainterpreter for SLP programs. That is, for any program Q, there there is an encoding of Q as an extensional data base edb_Q such that the stable models of $Meta \cup edb_Q$ are in one-to-one correspondence with the stable models of Q.

1 Introduction

The main motivation for this paper comes from recent developments in Knowledge Representation, especially the appearance of a new generation of systems [CMT96,NS96,ELM+97] based on the so-called Answer Set Programming (ASP) paradigm [Nie98,CP98,MT99,Lif98]. In particular, these systems suggest that we need to revisit one of the basic issues in the foundations of ASP, namely, how can we characterize what such ASP systems can theoretically compute. Throughout this paper, we shall focus mostly on one particular ASP formalism, namely, the Stable Semantics for Logic Programs (SLP) [GL88]. We note that the underlying methods of ASP are similar to those used in Logic Programming [Ap90] and Constraint Programming [JM94,MS99]. That is, like Logic Programming, ASP is a declarative formalism and the semantics of all ASP systems are based on logic. Like Constraint Programming, certain clauses of an ASP program act as *constraints*. There is a fundamental difference between ASP

T. Eiter, W. Faber, and M. Truszczyński (Eds.): LPNMR 2001, LNAI 2173, pp. 107–120, 2001.
© Springer-Verlag Berlin Heidelberg 2001

programs and Constraint Logic programs, however. That is, in Constraint Programming, the constraints act on individual elements of Herbrand base of the program while the constraint clauses in ASP programs act more globally in that they place restrictions on what subsets of the Herbrand base can be acceptable answers for program. For example, suppose that we have a problem Π whose solutions are *subsets* of some Herbrand base H. In order to solve the problem, an ASP programmer essentially writes a logic program P that describes the constraints on the subsets of H which can be answers to Π. The basic idea is that the program P should have the property that there is an easy decoding of solutions of Π from stable models of P and that all solutions of Π can be obtained from stable models of P through this decoding. The program P is then submitted to the ASP engine such as *smodels* [NS96], dlv [ELM+97] or DeReS [CMT96] which computes the stable models of the program P. Thus the ASP engine finds the stable models of the program (if any exists) and we read-off the solutions to Π from these stable models. Notice that the idea here is that all solutions are equally good in the sense that any solution found in the process described above is acceptable. Currently, the systems based on ASP paradigm are being tested on the problems related to planning, product configuration, combinatorial optimization problems and other domains.

It is a well known fact that the semantics of existing Logic Programming systems such as Prolog, Mercury and LDL have serious problems. For instance, the unification algorithm used by most dialects of Prolog do not enforce the occur check and hence these systems can produce incorrect results [AP94]. Moreover, the processing strategies of Prolog and similar languages have the effect that correct logic programs can be non-terminating [AP93]. While good programming techniques can overcome these problems, it is clear that such deficiencies have restricted the appeal of the Logic Programming systems for ordinary programmers and system analysts. The promise of ASP and, in particular, of SLP and its extensions, such as Disjunctive Logic Programming [GL91,ELM+97], is that a new generation of logic programming systems can be built which have a clear semantics and are easier to program than the previous generation of Logic Programming systems. In particular, both of the problems referred to above, namely, the occurs check problem and the termination problem, do not exist in SLP. Of course, there is a price to pay, namely, SLP systems only accept programs without function symbols. Consequently, one of the basic data structures used in Prolog, specifically, the *term*, is not available in SLP. Thus SLP systems require the programmer to explicitly construct many data structures. In SLP programming, predicates are used to construct the required data structures and clauses that serve as constraints are used to ensure that the predicates behave properly with respect to semantics of the program. SLP programs are always terminating because the Herbrand base is finite and hence there are only a finite number of stable models. In addition, unlike the case of usual Logic Programming, the order of the clauses of the program does not affect the set of stable models of the program[1]. Finally the stable semantics of logic programs is well understood so that SLP programs have clear semantics.

We note that the restriction that ASP programs do not allow function symbols is crucial. First, it is well known that once one allows function symbols in a logic program P, the Herbrand base becomes infinite. Moreover, the stable models of logic programs *with* function symbols can be immensely complex. For example, for stratified logic programs [ABW88,Prz88], the perfect model is the unique stable model of that program [GL88]. Apt and Blair [AB90] showed that perfect models of stratified logic programs capture precisely the arithmetic sets. That is, they show that for a given arithmetic set X of natural numbers, there is a finite stratified logic program P_X such that in the perfect model of P_X, some predicate p_X is satisfied by precisely the numbers in X. This was the first result that showed that it is not possible to have meaningful practical programming with general stratified programs *if we allow* unlimited use of function symbols. The result of [AB90] was extended in [BMS95] where Blair, Marek, and Schlipf showed that the set of stable models of a locally stratified program can capture any set in the hyperarithmetic hierarchy. Marek, Nerode, and Remmel [MNR94] showed that the problem of finding a stable model of a finite (predicate) logic program P is essentially equivalent to finding a path through an infinite branching recursive tree. That is, given an infinite branching recursive tree $T \subseteq \omega^{<\omega}$, there is a finite program P_T such that there is a one-to-one degree preserving correspondence between the infinite paths through T and the stable models of P_T and, vice versa, given an finite program P, there is a recursive tree T_P such that there is one-to-one degree preserving correspondence between the stable models of P and the infinite paths through T_P. One consequence of this result is that the problem of determining whether a finite predicate logic program has a stable model is a Σ_1^1-complete. More results on the structure of the family of stable models of the programs can be found in [CR99].

All the results mentioned in the previous paragraph show that stable semantics for logic programs admitting function symbols can be used only in a very limited setting. This is precisely what the XSB system attempts to do. When well-founded semantics is total, the resulting model is the unique stable model of the program. XSB attempts to query that model. Unfortunately, the class of programs for which it succeeds is not intuitive [RRS+97]. ASP systems propose a more radical solution to the problem of complexity of stable models of logic programs with function symbols, namely, abandoning function symbols entirely. Once this is accepted, the semantics of logic program P can be defined in two stages. First, we assume, as in standard Logic Programming, that we interpret P over the Herbrand universe of P determined by the predicates and constants that occur in P. Since, the set of constants occurring in the he program is finite, we can grounded the program in these constants to obtain a finite propositional logic program P_g. The stable models of P are by definition the stable models P_g. The process of grounding is performed by a separate grounding engine such as

---

[1] However it is the case that the order of the clauses can affects the processing time of the ASP engine.

lparse [NS96]. The grounded program is then passed to the engine computing the stable models. It is then easy to check that the features of SLP mentioned above, i.e., the absence of occurs check and termination problems and the independence of the semantics from the ordering of the clauses of the program, automatically hold.

The language of logic programming without function symbols was studied by the database community with the hope that it could lead to new, more powerful, database language [Ull88]. This language is called DATALOG and some database systems such as DB2 implement the positive part of DATALOG. The fact that admitting negation in the bodies of clauses leads to multiple stable models was unacceptable from the database perspective. Hence the database community preferred other semantics for DATALOG program with negation such as the well-founded semantics [VRS91] or the inflationary semantics [AHV95].

The main purpose of this paper is to revisit the question of what can be computed by logic programs without functions symbols under the stable model semantics. First, consider the case of finite propositional programs. Here the situation is simple. Given a set At of propositional atoms, let $\mathcal{F}$ be a finite antichain of subsets of At (i.e. whenever $X, Y \in \mathcal{F}$, $X \subseteq Y$, then $X = Y$). Then one can show that there is a logic program $P_{\mathcal{F}}$ such that $\mathcal{F}$ is precisely the class of all stable models of $P_{\mathcal{F}}$ [MT93]. Moreover, the family of stable models of any program P forms such an antichain. Thus in the case of finite propositional logic programs, we have a complete characterization of the possible sets of stable models. Note, however, this result does not tell us anything about the uniformity and the effectiveness of the construction. The basic complexity result for SLP propositional programs is due to Marek and Truszczyński [MT91] who showed that the problem of deciding whether a finite propositional logic program has a stable model is *NP*-complete.

To formulate our question about what can be computed by logic programs without functions symbols under the stable model semantics, we first recall the notion of *search problem* [GJ79] and of a *uniform* logic program [MT99]. A search problem is a set $\mathcal{S}$ of finite instances [GJ79] such that, given any instance $I \in \mathcal{S}$, we have a set S_I of solutions to $\mathcal{S}$ for instance I. For example, the search problem may be to find Hamiltonian paths in a graph. Thus, the set of instances of the problem is the set of all finite graphs and, for any given instance I, S_I is the set of all Hamiltonian paths of I. An algorithm solves the search problem $\mathcal{S}$ if it returns a solution $s \in S_I$ whenever S_I is non-empty and it returns the string "empty" otherwise. We say that a search problem $\mathcal{S}$ *is in NP* if there is such an algorithm which can be computed by a non-deterministic polynomial time Turing machine. We say that search problem $\mathcal{S}$ *is solved by a uniform logic program* if there exists:

1. a polynomial time encoding $edb_{\mathcal{S}}$ under which every instance I of $\mathcal{S}$ is mapped to a finite set of facts, i.e. clauses with empty bodies and no variables, and

2. a *single* logic program $P_{\mathcal{S}}$ such that there is a polynomial time computable function $sol_{\mathcal{S}}(\cdot, \cdot)$ such that for every instance I of $\mathcal{S}$, $sol_{\mathcal{S}}(I, \cdot)$ maps the set of stable models of the $edb_{\mathcal{S}}(I) \cup P$ onto the set of solutions S_I of I.

We note that decision problems can be viewed as special cases of search problems. Schlipf [Sch95] has shown that the class of *decision* problems in *NP* is captured precisely by uniform logic programs. Specifically he proved that a decision problem is solved by a uniform logic program if and only if it is in *NP*. An excellent review of the complexity and expressivity results for Logic programming can be found in [DEGV99].

The goal of this paper is to prove a strengthening of Schlipf's result as well as prove a number of related facts. First, we will prove that the Schlipf's result can be extended to all *NP search* problems. That is, we shall show that there is a single logic program P_{Trg} that is capable of simulating polynomial time nondeterministic Turing machines in the sense that given any polynomial time nondeterministic Turing machine M, any input σ, and any run-time polynomial $p(x)$, there is a set of facts $edb_{M,p,\sigma}$ (depending on M, $p(x)$ and σ) such that a stable model of $P_{Trg} \cup edb_{M,p,\sigma}$ codes an accepting computation of M started with input σ that terminates in $p(|\sigma|)$ steps and any such accepting computation of M is coded by some stable model of $P_{Trg} \cup edb_{M,p,\sigma}$. This result will show that logic programs without function symbols under the stable logic semantics capture all *NP*-search problems[2]. The converse implication, that is, a search problem computed by a uniform logic program P is an *NP*-search problem is obvious since one can compute a stable model SM of a program by first guessing SM and then doing a polynomial time check that SM is a stable model of the program.

2   Technical Preliminaries

In this section we formally introduce several notions that will be needed for the proof of our main result. Our proof of this result uses essentially the same idea used by Cook [Co71] in his proof of the *NP*-completeness of the satisfiability problem.

First, we introduce the set of logic programs that we will study. We will consider here only so called DATALOG$^{\neg}$ programs. Specifically, a clause is an expression of the form

$$p(\overline{X}) \leftarrow q_1(\overline{X}), \ldots, q_m(\overline{X}), \neg \, r_1(\overline{X}), \ldots, \neg \, r_n(\overline{X}) \tag{1}$$

where $p, q_1, \ldots, q_m, r_1, \ldots, r_n$ are atoms, possibly with variables and/or constants. A program is a finite set P of clauses of the form (1). Each program determines its language (based on the predicates occurring in the program). Since there are no function symbols in our programs, both the Herbrand universe and the Herbrand base of the program are finite.

---

[2] As pointed by M. Truszczynski, for our goal of describing the complexity of the Stable Logic Programming, a weaker result is sufficient. That is, we need only show that for each instance I of an *NP* search problem Π, there is a program P_I and a polynomial time projection from the collection of stable models of P_I to the set of solutions of I. Our result shows that this property holds in a stronger form, namely, there is a single program with a varying extensional database.

A ground instance of the clause C of the form (1) is the result of a simultaneous substitution of constants for variables occurring in C. Given a program P, P_g is the propositional program consisting of all ground substitutions of clauses of P.

Given a propositional program P and a set M included in its Herbrand base, H_P, the Gelfond-Lifschitz transformation of P by means of M, $GL(P, M)$ is the program $GL(P, M)$ arising from P as follows. First, eliminate all clauses C in P such that for some j, $1 \leq j \leq n$, $r_j \in M$. Finally, in any remaining clauses, we eliminate all negated atoms. The resulting set of clauses forms a program, $GL(P, M)$, which is a Horn program and hence it possesses a least model N_M. We say that M is a *stable model of the propositional program* P if $M = N_M$. Finally, we say that M is a stable model of a program P (now possibly with variables), if M is a stable model of the propositional program P_g.

A (nondeterministic) Turing Machine is a structure of the form

$$M = (Q, \Sigma, \Gamma, D, \delta, s, f),$$

where Q is a finite set of states and Σ is a finite alphabet of input symbols. We assume Q always contains two special states, s_0, the start state, and f, the final state. We assume that there is special symbol B for "blank" such that $B \notin \Sigma$. The set $\Gamma = \Sigma \cup \{B\}$ is the set of tape symbols. The set D of move directions will consist of elements l, r, and λ where l is the "move left" symbol, r is the "move right" symbol and λ is the "stay put" symbol. The function $\delta : Q \times \Gamma \to \mathcal{P}(Q \times \Gamma \times D)$ is the transition function of the machine M. We can think of δ as a 5-ary relation. We assume M operates on a one-way infinite tape where the cells of the tape are labeled from left to right by $0, 1, 2, \ldots$. To visualize the behavior of the machine M, we shall talk about the read-write head of the machine. At any given time, in a computation, the read-write head of M is always in some state $s \in Q$ and is reading some symbol $p \in \Gamma$. It then picks an instruction $(s1, p1, d) \in \delta(s, p)$ and then replaces the symbol p by $p1$, changes its state to state $s1$, and moves according to d.

Suppose we are given a Turing machine M whose runtimes are bounded by a polynomial $p(x) = a_0 + a_1 x + \cdots + a_k x^k$ where each $a_i \in N = \{0, 1, 2, \ldots\}$ and $a_k \neq 0$. That is, on any input of size n, an accepting computation terminates in at most $p(n)$ steps. Then any accepting computation on input σ can affect at most the first $p(n)$ cells of the tape. Thus in such a situation, there is no loss in only considering tapes of length $p(n)$. Hence in what follows, one shall implicitly assume that that the tape is finite. Moreover, it will be convenient to modify the standard operation of M in the following ways.

1. We shall assume $\delta(f, a) = \{(f, a, \lambda)\}$ for all $a \in \Gamma$.

2. Given an input x of length n, instead of immediately halting when we first get to the final state f reading a symbol a, we just keep executing the instruction (f, a, λ) until we have completed $p(n)$ steps. That is, we remain in state f, we never move, and we never change any symbols on the tape after we get to state f.

The main effect of these modifications is that all accepting computations will run for exactly $p(n)$ steps on an input of size n.

3 Uniform Coding of Turing Machines by a Logic Program

In this section, we shall describe the logic program P_{Trg} and our extensional data base coding $edb_{M,p,\sigma}$ described above. The key to our construction is the fact that at any given moment of time, the behavior of a Turing machine M depends only on the current state of tape, the position of the read-write head and the set of available instructions. Our coding of Turing machine computation will reflect this observation.

First, we define the language (i.e. a signature) of the program P_{Trg}. The set of predicates that will occur in our extensional database are the following: $time(X)$ for "X is a time step", $cell(X)$ for "X is a cell number", $symb(X)$ for "X is a symbol", $state(S)$ for "S is a state", $i\_position(P)$ for "P is the initial position of the read-write head", $data(P,Q)$ for "Initially, the tape stores the symbol Q at the cell P", $delta(X,Y,X1,Y1,Z)$ for "the triple $(X1,Y1,Z)$ is an executable instruction when the read-write head is in state X and reads symbols Y" (thus $delta$ represents the five-place relation δ), $neq(X,Y)$ for "$X \neq Y$" [3], $succ(X,Y)$ for $Y = X + 1$.

Next we describe the constants that will be used in our description of time, cell numbers, cell contents and specific machines. The last two families of constants will be "machine-dependent", since we did not specify any restrictions on the finite sets Q and Σ. Thus we have the following set of constant symbols: (1) $0, 1, \ldots, p(n)$ where n is the length of the input σ and p is the runtime polynomial, (2) s, for each $s \in S$. Note two constants s_0 (for initial state), and f (for final state) will be present in every extensional database. (3) x for each $x \in \Sigma$, and B (blank symbol), and finally (4) r, l, λ.

This given, we can easily define the extensional database $ext_{M,p,\sigma}$. That is, given input $\sigma = \sigma_1 \ldots \sigma_n$, runtime polynomial $p(x)$, we let $edb_{M,\sigma,p}$ consist of the following set of facts that describe the machine M, the segment of integers $0, \ldots, p(n)$ and the initial configuration of the tape.

1. $state(s) \leftarrow$ for $s \in Q$
2. $symb(x) \leftarrow$ for $x \in \Gamma$
3. $delta(s,x,s1,x1,d) \leftarrow$ for every pair $(s,x) \in Q \times \Gamma$ and every triple $(s1,x1,d) \in \delta(s,x)$
4. $succ(i,i+1) \leftarrow$ for $0 \leq i < p(n)$.
5. $time(i) \leftarrow$ for $0 \leq i \leq p(n)$
6. $cell(i) \leftarrow$ for $0 \leq i \leq p(n) - 1$.
7. $data(m, \sigma(m))$ for $0 \leq m \leq |\sigma| - 1$
8. $data(m, B)$ for $|\sigma| \leq m \leq p(n) - 1$
9. $dir(l), dir(r), dir(\lambda)$
10. $i\_position(0)$
11. $neq(a,b) \leftarrow$ for all $a, b \in S \cup \Gamma \cup \{0, \ldots, p(n)\}$ with $a \neq b$.

---

[3] Technically, we should use a separate inequality relation for each type, but we will not use different symbols for these inequality relations.

The remaining predicates of P_{Trg} are the following: $tape(P, Q, T)$ for "the tape stores symbol Q at cell P at time T", $position(P, T)$ for "the read-write head reads the content cell P at time T", $state(S, T)$ for "the read-write head is in state S at time T" (notice that we have both a unary predicate $state/1$ with the content consisting of states, and $state/2$ to describe the evolution of the machine), $instr(S, Q, S1, Q1, D, T)$ for "Instruction $(S1, Q1, D)$ belonging to $\delta(S, Q)$ has been selected for execution at time T", $otherInstr(S, Q, S1, Q1, D, T)$ for "Instruction other than $(S1, Q1, D)$ belonging to $\delta(S, Q)$ has been selected for execution at time T", $instr\_def(T)$ for "there is an instruction to be executed at time T", $completion$ for "computation successfully completed", and A, a propositional letter[4].

In the program P_{Trg}, there should be no constants. We will not be absolutely strict in this respect. For ease of presentation, we will use the constants 0, f, and s_0. These can easily be eliminated by introducing appropriate unary predicates. Also we shall write $y = x + 1$ for $succ(x, y)$. Finally to simplify the clauses, we will follow here the notation used in the $smodels$ syntax. That is, we will use $p(X_1; \ldots, X_k)$ as an abbreviation for $p(X_1), \ldots, p(X_k)$.

This given, we are now ready to write the program P_{Tng}.

Group 1. Our first four clauses are used to describe the position of the read-write head at any given time t.
  (1.1) $position(P, T) \leftarrow T = 0, i\_position(P)$
  (1.2) $position(P, T1) \leftarrow T1 = T + 1, position(P1, T), state(S, T),$
        $tape(P1, Q, T), instr(S, Q, S1, Q1, D, T), D = l, neq(P1, 0), P1 = P + 1$
  (1.3) $position(P, T1) \leftarrow T1 = T + 1, position(P1, T), state(S, T),$
        $tape(P1, Q, T), instr(S, Q, S1, Q1, D, T), D = r, P = P1 + 1$
  (1.4) $position(P, T1) \leftarrow T1 = T + 1, position(P, T), state(S, T),$
        $tape(P1, Q, T), instr(S, Q, S1, Q1, D, T), D = \lambda$
Group 2. Our next three clauses describe how the contents of the tape change as instructions get executed.
  (2.1) $tape(P, Q, T) \leftarrow T = 0, data(P, Q)$
  (2.2) $tape(P, Q1, T1) \leftarrow T1 = T + 1, position(P, T), state(S, T),$
        $tape(P, Q, T), instr(S, Q, S1, Q1, D, T)$
  (2.3) $tape(P, Q, T1) \leftarrow T1 = T + 1, tape(P, Q, T), position(P1, T),$
        $neq(P, P1)$
Group 3. Our next two clauses describe how the state of the read-write head evolves in time.
  (3.1) $state(S, T) \leftarrow T = 0, S = s_0$
  (3.2) $state(S, T1) \leftarrow T1 = T + 1, position(P, T), state(S1, T),$
        $tape(P, Q, T), instr(S1, Q, S, Q1, D, T)$

---

[4] The propositional letter A will be used whenever we write clauses acting as constraints. That is, the symbol A will occur in the following syntactical configuration. A will be the head of some clause, and the negation of A will also occur in the body of that same clause. In such situation a stable model *cannot* satisfy the remaining atoms in the body of that clause.

Group 4. Our next two clauses describe how we select a unique instruction to be executed at time T.

(4.1) Selecting instruction at step 0.

$instr(S, Q, S1, Q1, D, T) \leftarrow state(S; S1), symb(Q; Q1), dir(D),$
$time(T), T = 0, S = s_0, i\_position(P), tape(P, Q, T),$
$delta(S, Q, S1, Q1, D), \neg otherInstr(S, Q, S1, Q1, D, T)$

(4.2) Selecting instruction at other steps.

$instr(S, Q, S1, Q1, D, T) \leftarrow state(S; S1), symb(Q; Q1),$
$dir(D), time(T), position(P, T), state(S, T), tape(P, Q, T),$
$delta(S, Q, S1, Q1, D), \neg otherInstr(S, Q, S1, Q1, D, T)$

Group 5. Our next set of clauses define the *otherInstr* predicate and (5.6) and (5.7) ensure that exactly one instruction is selected for execution at any given time T.

(5.1) $otherInstr(S, Q, S1, Q1, D1, T) \leftarrow state(S; S'; S1; S2),$
$symb(Q; Q'; Q1; Q2), time(T), dir(D; D2),$
$instr(S', Q', S2, Q2, D2, T), neq(S2, S1)$

(5.2) $otherInstr(S, Q, S1, Q1, D1, T) \leftarrow state(S; S'; S1; S2),$
$symb(Q; Q'; Q1; Q2), time(T), dir(D; D2),$
$instr(S', Q', S2, Q2, D2, T), neq(Q2, Q1)$

(5.3) $otherInstr(S, Q, S1, Q1, D1, T) \leftarrow state(S; S'; S1; S2),$
$symb(Q; Q'; Q1; Q2), time(T), dir(D; D2),$
$instr(S', Q', S2, Q2, D2, T), neq(D2, D1)$

(5.4) $otherInstr(S, Q, S1, Q1, D1, T) \leftarrow state(S; S'; S1; S2),$
$symb(Q; Q'; Q1; Q2), time(T), dir(D; D2),$
$instr(S', Q', S2, Q2, D2, T), neq(S', S)$

(5.5) $otherInstr(S, Q, S1, Q1, D1, T) \leftarrow state(S; S'; S1; S2),$
$symb(Q; Q'; Q1; Q2), time(T), dir(D; D2),$
$instr(S', Q', S2, Q2, D2, T), neq(Q', Q)$

(5.6) The definition of the *instr_def* predicate.

$instr\_def(T) \leftarrow state(S; S1), symb(Q; Q1), dir(D), time(T),$
$instr(S, Q, S1, Q1, D, T)$

(5.7) The clause to ensure that there is an instruction to be executed at any given time.

$A \leftarrow time(T), \neg instr\_def(T), \neg A$

Group 6. Constraints for the coherence of the computation process.

(6.1) When the task is completed.

$completion \leftarrow instr(f, Q, f, Q, \lambda, p(n))$

(6.2) The atom *completion* belongs to every stable model.

$A \leftarrow \neg completion, \neg A$

4   Main Results

Our first proposition immediately follows from our construction.

Proposition 1. *There is a polynomial q so that for every machine M, polynomial p, and an input σ, the size of the extensional database $edb_{M,p,\sigma}$ is equal to $q(|M|, |\sigma|, p(|\sigma|))$.*

In the full version of the paper, we shall prove that for any nondeterministic Turing Machine M, runtime polynomial $p(x)$, and input σ of length n, the stable models of $edb_{M,p,\sigma} \cup P_{Trg}$ encode the sequences of tapes of length $p(n)$ which occur in the steps of an accepting computation of M starting on σ and that any such sequence of steps can be used to produce a stable model of $edb_{M,p,\sigma} \cup P_{Trg}$.

Theorem 1. *The mapping of Turing machines to DATALOG$^\neg$ programs defined by $M \mapsto edb_{M,p,\sigma} \cup P_{Tng}$ has the property that there is a 1-1 polynomial time correspondence between the set of stable models of $edb_{M,p,\sigma} \cup P_{Tng}$ and the set of computations of M of the length $p(n)$ ending in the state f.*

Corollary 1. *A search S problem can be solved by means of a uniform logic program in SLP if and only if S is an NP-search problem.*

One can also show that all supported models of $edb_{M,p,\sigma} \cup P_{Tng}$ are stable. This fact implies that the similar corollary holds for Supported Logic Programming, SuLP.

Corollary 2. *A search S problem can be solved by means of a uniform logic program in SuLP if and only if S is an NP-search problem.*

Finally we can prove similar results for default logic programs without function symbols with respect to nondeterministic Turing machines with an oracle for 3-SAT. It thus follows that a search problem S can be solved by means of a uniform default logic program if and only if S is in Σ_2^P. A decision version of this result has been proved in [CEG97].

Theorem 2. *For each $n \in N$ there is a default theory $\langle W_n, D_n \rangle$ such that for every 3-SAT oracle Turing machine M, every polynomial $p \in N[x]$, and every finite input σ where $|\sigma| = n$, there is a polynomial-time one-to-one correspondence between the accepting computations of length $p(n)$ of M on input σ and the Reiter extensions of the default theory $\langle edb_{M,p,\sigma} \cup W_n, D_n \rangle$.*

5   Metainterpreters

The results of section 4 suggest that there should be a universal logic program P_{Meta} for the stable model semantics in the sense that for any logic program Q, there exists an extensional database edb_Q describing Q such that there is a one-to-one correspondence between the stable models of $P_{Meta} \cup edb_Q$ and the stable models of Q. We call such a program program a metainterpreter for SLP programs.

First, we will describe a metainterpreter for the class of so-called 0-2 programs. A propositional program P is a *0-2 program* if for every clause C of P has either no positive literal in the body, or exactly 2 positive literals in the body. Blair proved that 0-2 programs semi-represent all propositional programs (see [MT93], Ch. 5, for the discussion of semirepresentability). The following result is due to Blair.

Proposition 2 (Blair). *There is a linear-lime computable function f that assigns to each propositional program P, a 0-2 program $f(P)$ such that there is a one-to-one projection from the family of stable models of $f(P)$ to the family of stable models of P.*

We will describe a metainterpreter (which we will call *Meta1*) that computes stable models of 0-2 propositional programs. To this end we need a data structure that expresses the given 0-2 program. The extensional predicates describing the input program are as follows: $atom(\cdot)$, to describe atoms, $clause(\cdot)$, to describe clauses, $head(\cdot, \cdot)$ to describe the head of a clause, $neg(\cdot, \cdot)$ to state that an atom occurs negatively in the body of a clause, $first(\cdot, \cdot)$ to state that an atom is the first of two positive atoms occurring in the body of a clause, and $second(\cdot, \cdot)$ to state that an atom is the second of two positive atoms occurring in the body of a clause.

The description of a propositional program Q (the data for the program *Meta1* consists of the following facts: $atom(a) \leftarrow$ for all atoms a occurring in Q, $clause(c) \leftarrow$ for all clauses c of Q, $head(a, c) \leftarrow$ whenever a is the head of clause c in Q, $first(a, c) \leftarrow$ and $second(b, c) \leftarrow$ whenever a and b are the first and the second atoms in the body of clause c in Q, respectively. We call this collection edb_Q.

The remaining predicates of *Meta1* are the following: $nempty(\cdot)$, to describe that there are atoms occurring positively in the body of a clause, $empty(\cdot)$, to describe that there are no atoms occurring positively in the body of a clause, $in(\cdot)$, to describe the stable model of the input program itself, $out(\cdot)$, to describe the complement of the stable model of the input program, $unusable(\cdot)$, to describe the clauses not involved in the computation of the stable model, $usable(\cdot)$, to describe the clauses involved in the computation of the stable model, $computed(\cdot)$, to describe the computed atoms, and A, a propositional atom.

This given, *Meta1* consists of the following clauses.

1. Generating the model.
   (a) $in(B) \leftarrow atom(B), \neg out(B)$
   (b) $out(B) \leftarrow atom(B), \neg in(B)$
2. Computing Gelfond-Lifschitz reduct.
   (a) $unusable(C) \leftarrow clause(C), atom(B), neg(B, C), in(B)$
   (b) $usable(C) \leftarrow clause(C), \neg unusable(C)$
3. Classifying clauses.
   (a) $nempty(C) \leftarrow clause(C), atom(B), first(B, C)$
   (b) $empty(C) \leftarrow clause(C), \neg nempty(C)$
4. Computation process.
   (a) $computed(B) \leftarrow clause(C), empty(C), usable(C), head(B, C)$
   (b) $computed(B) \leftarrow clause(C), first(B1, C), second(B2, C),$
       $computed(B1), computed(B2), head(B, C)$
5. Constraints.
   (a) $A \leftarrow atom(B), in(B), \neg computed(B), \neg A$
   (b) $A \leftarrow atom(B), out(B), computed(B), \neg A$

We then can prove the following.

Proposition 3. *There is a one-to-one projection that for every propositional program Q maps stable models of Meta1 ∪ edb$_Q$ to stable models of Q.*

In the full version of this paper, we construct yet another metainterpreter *Meta2* for SLP, that accepts all propositional programs (not only 0 − 2-programs) and have the property that its supported models are automatically stable. The size of the representation of the extensional database is, however, larger. A number of metainterpreters for various classes of programs have been constructed in [EFLP01].

Acknowledgments

Work partially supported by the NSF grant IRI-9619233 .

References

Ap90.   K. R. Apt. Logic Programming. in *Handbook of Theoretical Computer Science*, pp. 475–574. Elsevier, 1990. 107
AB90.   K. R. Apt and H. A. Blair. Arithmetical classification of perfect models of stratified programs. *Fundamenta Informaticae*, 12:1–17, 1990. 109
ABW88.   K. Apt, H. A. Blair, and A. Walker. Towards a theory of declarative knowledge. In J. Minker, editor, *Foundations of deductive databases and logic programming*, pages 89–142, Los Altos, CA, 1988. Morgan Kaufmann. 109
AP93.   K. R. Apt and D. Pedreschi. Reasoning about termination of pure Prolog programs. *Information and Computation* 106:109–157, 1994. 108
AP94.   K. R. Apt and A. Pellegrini. On the occur-check free pure Prolog programs. *ACM Toplas* 16:687–726, 1994. 108
AHV95.   S. Abiteboul, R. Hull, and V. Vianu. *Foundations of Databases*. Addison-Wesley Publishing Company, 1995. 110
BMS95.   H. A. Blair, W. Marek, and J. Schlipf. The expressiveness of locally stratified programs. *Annals of Mathematics and Artificial Intelligence*, 15:209–229, 1995. 109
BK82.   K. A. Bowen and R. A. Kowalski. Amalgamating language and metalanguage in Logic Programming. In: *Logic Programming,* pp. 153–172, Academic Press, 1982.
CP98.   M. Cadoli and L. Palipoli. Circumscribing datalog: expressive power and complexity. *Theoretical Computer Science*, 193:215–244, 1998. 107
CEG97.   M. Cadoli, T. Eiter and G. Gottlob. Default logic as a query language. *IEEE Transactions on Knowledge and Data Engineering*, 9:448–463, 1997. 116
CR99.   D. Cenzer and J. B. Remmel. Π_1^0 Classes in Mathematics. *Handbook of Recursive Mathematics* pp. 623–821, Elsevier 1999. 109
CMT96.   P. Cholewiński, W. Marek, and M. Truszczyński. Default reasoning system DeReS. In *Proceedings of KR-96*, pages 518–528. Morgan Kaufmann, 1996. 107, 108
Co71.   S. Cook. The complexity of theorem-proving procedures. *Proceedings of Third Annual ACM Symposium on Theory of Computing* pp. 151–158. 1971. 111

DEGV99.   E. Dantsin, T. Eiter, G. Gottlob and A. Voronkov. Complexity and Expres-
          sive Power of Logic Programming, Technical Report of Institut für Infor-
          mationssysteme, Technische Universität Wien", INFSYS RR-1843-99-05,
          1999, To appear in: *ACM Computing Surveys.* 111
DK89.   P. M. Dung and K. Kanchanasut. On the generalized predicate completion
          of non-Horn programs, In: Logic programming, Proceedings of the North
          American Conference, pp. 587–603, MIT Press, 1989.
EFLP01.   T. Eiter, W. Faber, N. Leone and G. Pfeifer, Computing Preferred and
          Weakly Preferred Answer Sets by Meta-Interpretation in Answer Set Pro-
          gramming, In: Proceedings AAAI 2001 Spring Symposium on Answer
          Set Programming: Towards Efficient and Scalable Knowledge Representa-
          tion and Reasoning, Stanford, CA (Workshop Technical Report SS-01-01),
          AAAI Press, 2001. 118
ELM+97.   T. Eiter, N. Leone, C. Mateis, G. Pfeifer, and F. Scarcello. A deductive
          system for non-monotonic reasoning. In *Proceedings of the 4th International
          Conference on Logic Programming and Nonmonotonic Reasoning*, pages
          363–374, 1997. Springer LN in Computer Science 1265. 107, 108
GJ79.   M. R. Garey and D. S. Johnson. *Computers and intractability; a guide to
          the theory of NP-completeness.* W. H. Freeman, 1979. 110
GL88.   M. Gelfond and V. Lifschitz. The stable semantics for logic programs. In
          Proceedings of the 5th International Symposium on Logic Programming,
          pages 1070–1080, Cambridge, MA, 1988. MIT Press. 107, 109
GL91.   M. Gelfond and V. Lifschitz. Classical negation in logic programs and
          disjunctive databases. *New Generation Computing* 9:365–385, 1991. 108
JM94.   J. Jaffar and M. J. Maher. Constraint logic programming: A survey. *Journal
          of Logic Programming*, 19(20):503–581, 1994. 107
Lif98.   V. Lifschitz. Action languages, answer sets and planning. *The Logic Pro-
          gramming Paradigm*, pp. 357–373. Series Artificial Intelligence, Springer-
          Verlag, 1999. 107
MNR94.   W. Marek, A. Nerode, and J. B. Remmel. The stable models of predicate
          logic programs. *Journal of Logic Programming*, 21(3):129–154, 1994. 109
MT91.   W. Marek and M. Truszczyński. Autoepistemic logic. *Journal of the ACM*,
          38:588–619, 1991. 110
MT93.   V. W. Marek and M. Truszczyński. *Nonmonotonic Logic – Context-
          Dependent Reasoning.* Series Artificial Intelligence, Springer-Verlag, 1993.
          110, 116
MT99.   V. W. Marek and M. Truszczyński. Stable Models and an Alternative Logic
          Programming Paradigm. *The Logic Programming Paradigm*, pp. 375–398.
          Series Artificial Intelligence, Springer-Verlag, 1999. 107, 110
MS99.   K. Marriott and P. J. Stuckey. *Programming with Constraints: An Intro-
          duction.* MIT Press, Cambridge, MA, 1998. 107
Nie98.   I. Niemelä. Logic programs with stable model semantics as a constraint
          programming paradigm. In *Proceedings of the Workshop on Computational
          Aspects of Nonmonotonic Reasoning*, pages 72–79, 1998. 107
NS96.   I. Niemelä and P. Simons. Efficient implementation of the well-founded and
          stable model semantics. In *Proceedings of JICSLP-96*. MIT Press, 1996.
          107, 108, 110
Prz88.   T. Przymusiński. On the declarative semantics of deductive databases and
          logic programs. In *Foundations of deductive databases and logic program-
          ming*, pages 193–216, Los Altos, CA, 1988. Morgan Kaufmann. 109

RRS⁺97.   P. Rao, I. V. Ramskrishnan, K. Sagonas, T. Swift, D. S. Warren, and J. Freire. XSB: A system for efficiently computing well-founded semantics. In *Proceedings of LPNMR'97*, pages 430–440, Lecture Notes in Computer Science, 1265, Springer-Verlag, 1997. 109

Sch95.   J. Schlipf. The expressive powers of the logic programming semantics. *Journal of the Computer Systems and Science*, 51:64–86, 1995. 107, 111

Ull88.   J. D. Ullman. *Principles of Database and Knowledge-Base Systems*. Computer Science Press, Rockville, MD, 1988. 110

VRS91.   A. Van Gelder, K. A. Ross, and J. S. Schlipf. Unfounded sets and well-founded semantics for general logic programs. *Journal of the ACM*, 38:620–650, 1991. 110

On the Relationship between Defeasible Logic and Well-Founded Semantics

Gerhard Brewka

University of Leipzig, Dep. of Computer Science
Augustusplatz 10-11, 04109 Leipzig, Germany
brewka@informatik.uni-leipzig.de

Abstract. We investigate in this paper the relationship between an ambiguity propagating defeasible logic recently proposed by Antoniou et al. [3] and well-founded semantics with priorities [6] under a straightforward translation from defeasible theories to extended logic programs. It turns out that a slightly restricted version of defeasible logic is correct wrt well-founded semantics yet incomplete. We also investigate the sources of the incompleteness and argue that the additional conclusions obtained by prioritized well-founded semantics are indeed desired.

1 Introduction

Defeasible Logic was originally proposed by Donald Nute in 1987 [13] (for an overview see the handbook article [14]). The logic was never as prominent as, say, default logic [17] or circumscription [11]. Yet it has received considerable attention in recent years. This is at least partly due to a very active group of researchers at Griffith University which has worked on theoretical foundations, further development and implementations of defeasible logic(s) [1,2,3,12].

The main advantage of defeasible logic is certainly computational: the computation of conclusions is polynomial and highly efficient implementations exist [12]. A second advantage are its built in preference handling facilities.

In the meantime several variants of Defeasible Logic have been proposed. All of them are defined proof theoretically. Defeasible logic(s) belong to a class of nonmonotonic approaches which can be called directly sceptical. By this we mean sceptical approaches where the conclusions, rather than being defined as the intersection of extensions or answer sets, are constructed directly.

In the area of logic programming well-founded semantics can be viewed as a directly sceptical semantics. It is interesting to see, therefore, what the exact relationship between these two approaches is. Since the preference handling techniques of defeasible logic have no counterpart in standard well-founded semantics the comparison will be based on an extension of well-founded semantics which was recently proposed by the author of this paper.[1]

---

[1] Although numerous prioritized version of logic programs under stable model or answer set semantics exist (see [7] for a discussion of some of these approaches) not much work has been done on prioritizing well-founded semantics.

T. Eiter, W. Faber, and M. Truszczyński (Eds.): LPNMR 2001, LNAI 2173, pp. 121–132, 2001.

To be precise, we will compare one of the arguably most interesting defeasible logics, an ambiguity propagating variant presented in [3], with the prioritized version of well-founded semantics for extended logic programs. This semantics was originally proposed in [6]. In this paper we use a considerably simplified version. The simplification is possible since for the purposes of this paper we do not need the ability to represent preferences in the logical language.

The major result of this paper is the correctness of the considered defeasible logic under the condition that no defeasible rule is preferred to a strict rule. We also investigate reasons for the incompleteness of the logic and argue that the additional conclusions obtained by well-founded semantics are desirable. The paper may thus be read as a critique of defeasible logic.

The rest of the paper is organized as follows. Sect. 2 describes the ambiguity propagating defeasible logic used for comparison in this paper. Sect. 3 presents a simplified version of the preferred well-founded semantics in [6]. Sect. 4 introduces the translation from defeasible logic to extended logic programs. Sect. 5 establishes the correctness result and Sect. 6 incompleteness. Sect. 7 concludes.

The analysis in the paper is performed in a propositional setting, that is, we consider propositional defeasible theories and propositional extended logic programs.

2 Defeasible Logic

Defeasible logic was first introduced by Nute [13]. It is based on strict rules of the form $A \to p$ and defeasible rules of the form $A \Rightarrow p$. In both cases A is a set of literals and p a literal. We omit set brackets whenever A is a singleton set. Facts are represented as strict rules with empty set of antecedents (in which case the arrow is left out). Nute also introduced a third type of rules called defeaters which can block the derivation of a literal without giving rise to the derivation of the complementary literal. In [2] it is shown that defeaters are not essential in the sense that they can be simulated by the other rules. We will therefore not discuss defeaters in this paper.

To solve conflicts among rules Nute used a preference relation $>$ among rules: $r > r'$ intuitively stands for: r has higher priority than r'. The preference relation is required to be acyclic, i.e. its transitive closure must be irreflexive.

Nute's original defeasible logic was not ambiguity propagating. Consider the following example:

Example 1:
1) $\Rightarrow p$
2) $\Rightarrow \neg p$
3) $\Rightarrow q$
4) $p \Rightarrow \neg q$

Since p is not defeasibly provable (because of the conflicting second rule) rule 4) is disregarded and q is defeasibly provable in Nute's logic. This seems highly questionable since, although p is not accepted, there is an argument supporting $\neg q$ which should not be disregarded in a sceptical approach.

For this reason Antoniou and colleagues [3] defined an "ambiguity propagating defeasible logic without team defeat" which behaves as desired in the example. We consider this logic as one of the most interesting variants of defeasible logic and use it for our comparison in this paper.

A defeasible theory is a pair $T = (R, >)$ where R is a finite set of strict and defeasible rules and $>$ is the preference relation among R. A conclusion of T is a tagged literal: $+\Delta q$ means q is strictly provable, $+\delta q$ means q is defeasibly provable, and $+\sigma q$ means q is supported.[2] The tags preceded by minus-signs stand for corresponding negated expressions. A proof is a finite sequence P of tagged literals. $P(i)$ denotes the i-th element in the sequence, $P(1..i)$ its initial segment of length i. The complement of a literal q is denoted $-q$. $R[q]$ is the set of rules with head q, $R_s[q]$ the subset of $R[q]$ consisting of all strict rules. The antecedents of a rule r are denoted $A(r)$.

Inference rules are phrased as conditions on proofs as follows:[3]

$+\Delta$: If $P(i+1) = +\Delta q$ then
$\quad$ $\exists r \in R_s[q]$ $\forall a \in A(r) : +\Delta a \in P(1..i)$.

$-\Delta$: If $P(i+1) = -\Delta q$ then
$\quad$ $\forall r \in R_s[q]$ $\exists a \in A(r) : -\Delta a \in P(1..i)$.

$+\delta$: If $P(i+1) = +\delta q$ then
$\quad$ (1) $+\Delta q \in P(1..i)$ or
$\quad$ (2.1) $-\Delta - q \in P(1..i)$ and
$\quad$ (2.2) $\exists r \in R[q]$ such that
$\quad\quad\quad$ $\forall a \in A[r] : +\delta a \in P(1..i)$ and
$\quad\quad\quad$ $\forall s \in R[-q]$:
$\quad\quad\quad\quad\quad$ $\exists a \in A[s] : -\sigma a \in P(1..i)$ or
$\quad\quad\quad\quad\quad$ $r > s$.

$-\delta$: If $P(i+1) = -\delta q$ then
$\quad$ (1) $-\Delta q \in P(1..i)$ and
$\quad$ (2.1) $+\Delta - q \in P(1..i)$ or
$\quad$ (2.2) $\forall r \in R[q]$:
$\quad\quad\quad$ $\exists a \in A[r] : -\delta a \in P(1..i)$ or
$\quad\quad\quad$ $\exists s \in R[-q]$ such that
$\quad\quad\quad\quad\quad$ $\forall a \in A[s] : +\sigma a \in P(1..i)$ and
$\quad\quad\quad\quad\quad$ $r \not> s$.

$+\sigma$: If $P(i+1) = +\sigma q$ then
$\quad$ $+\Delta q \in P(1..i)$ or

---

[2] We use σ here rather than the less readable and less mnemonic symbol used in [3].
[3] The rule for $+\sigma$ in [3] had a mistake in the last line (G. Antoniou, personal communication) which is corrected here.

$\exists r \in R[q]$ such that
$\quad \forall a \in A[r] : +\sigma a \in P(1..i)$ and
$\quad \forall s \in R[-q]$:
$\quad\quad \exists a \in A[s] : -\delta a \in P(1..i)$ or
$\quad\quad s \not> r.$

$-\sigma :$ If $P(i+1) = -\sigma q$ then
$\quad -\Delta q \in P(1..i)$ and
$\quad \forall r \in R[q]$:
$\quad\quad \exists a \in A[r] : -\sigma a \in P(1..i)$ or
$\quad\quad \exists s \in R[-q]$ such that
$\quad\quad\quad \forall a \in A[s] : +\delta a \in P(1..i)$ and
$\quad\quad\quad s > r.$

Consider the following example:

Example 2:
1) p
2) $p \rightarrow q$
3) $q \Rightarrow r$
4) $\Rightarrow \neg r$

Assume there are no priorities. Here is a proof for $+\sigma r$:

$$+\Delta p, +\Delta q, +\sigma q, +\sigma r.$$

If we add the preference $4 > 3$ the last step in the proof does not go through. Indeed, we now have the following proof for $+\delta \neg r$:

$$-\Delta r, +\delta \neg r.$$

3   Prioritized Well-Founded Semantics

In this section we present a simplified version of the well-founded semantics for extended logic programs with priorities which was defined in [6]. The simplification is possible because we are not interested here in expressing preference information in the logical language (for a discussion why this may be useful see [6]).

A (propositional) extended logic program is a finite set of rules of the form

$$c \leftarrow a_1, \ldots, a_n, not\ b_1, \ldots, not\ b_m$$

where the a_i, b_j and c are propositional literals, i.e., either propositional atoms or such atoms preceded by the classical negation sign. The symbol *not* denotes negation by failure (default negation), $\neg$ denotes strong negation. An extended logic program is a finite set P of rules. A prioritzed logic program is a pair $(P, >)$ where P is an extended logic program and $>$ an acyclic preference relation on P: as in defeasible logic $r > r'$ stands for r is preferred over r'. In [6] $>$ was required to be transitive. This restriction is not necessary and dropped here for the purpose of comparison. Note also that in the earlier paper the "smaller" rules were preferred rather than the "bigger" rules as in this paper.

Well-founded semantics is an inherently sceptical semantics that refrains from drawing conclusions whenever there is a potential conflict. Its original formulation for general logic programs by Gelder, Ross and Schlipf [9] is based on a certain partial model. Przymusinski reconstructed this definition in 3-valued logic [15,16]. A reformulation based on the least fixed point of a monotone operator, namely the twofold application of the Gelfond/Lifschitz γ-operator [8], was first given by Baral and Subrahmanian [5]. The straightforward extension of this formulation to extended logic programs that underlies our approach was used by several authors, e.g. [4,10].

Let us first introduce the γ-operator. We say a rule r of the form above is defeated by a literal l if $l = b_i$ for some $i \in \{1, \ldots, m\}$. We say r is defeated by a set of literals X if X contains a literal that defeats r.

Let P be a logic program, X a set of literals. The X-reduct of P, denoted P^X, is the program obtained from P by deleting each rule defeated by X. For a set of rules R, the closure $Cl(R)$ is the smallest set of literals closed under R and the consequences $Cn(R)$ the smallest set of literals that is (1) closed under R, and (2) logically closed, i.e., either consistent or equal to the set of all literals. For the computation of the closure we simply neglect default negated literals.

The Gelfond/Lifschitz operator γ_P now is defined as follows:

$$\gamma_P(X) = Cn(P^X)$$

For normal logic programs (that is programs without strong negation) the atoms true according to well-founded semantics are just the least fixed point of the twofold application of γ. It was argued in [6] that for the extension of well-founded semantics to extended logic programs with two kinds of negation it is favourable to slightly modify the fixed point operator: rather than computing the least fixed point of γ^2 Brewka proposed to compute the least fixed point of $\gamma\gamma^*$ where γ^* rather than yielding the consequences $Cn(P^X)$ yields the closure $Cl(P^X)$. This leads to a larger set of well-founded conclusions without violating correctness wrt answer set semantics.

The intuition behind well-founded semantics can be described as follows: given a set of literals S already known to be derivable, $\gamma^*(S)$ produces a set of potential conclusions which still might defeat rules in P. The conclusions of rules not defeated by any of the potential defeaters are clearly derivable. Starting with the empty set, we thus generate larger and larger sets S until a fixed point is reached. The following terminology reflects this intuition:

Definition 1. *Let P be an extended logic program.*

- *A literal l is an S-potential defeater iff l is in the closure of the rules in P not defeated by S.*
- *A rule r is S-undefeatable iff r is not defeated by any S-potential defeater.*

– *A literal l is S-derivable iff l is a consequence of S-undefeatable rules in P.*

It is obvious that l is S-derivable iff $l \in \gamma(\gamma^*(S))$. The least fixed point of $\gamma\gamma*$ is called $WFS(P)$, or simply WFS if P is clear from context.

To take preferences into account we first introduce a notion of dominance. Intuitively, a rule r dominates a rule r' in the context of a set of literals S if r has higher priority and if the application of r in context S actually defeats r'. As pointed out in [6] the second condition is necessary to guarantee that prioritized well-founded semantics is an extension of well-founded semantics. Here is the formal definition

Definition 2. *Let r and r' be rules, S a set of literals. We say r S-dominates r' iff*

1. $r > r'$, *and*
2. $Cl(\{r\} \cup \{s : s$ *is S-undefeatable*$\})$ *defeats r'.*

For the case of prioritized programs Def. 1 becomes

Definition 3. *Let $(P, >)$ be a prioritized logic program.*

– *A literal l is an S-potential r-defeater iff l is in the closure of rules in P which are (1) not defeated by S and (2) not S-dominated by r.*
– *A rule r is S-safe iff r is not defeated by any S-potential r-defeater.*
– *A literal l is S-derivable iff l is a consequence of the set of S-safe rules in P.*

The definition for prioritized logic programs is different from the one for non-prioritized programs in two respects. Firstly, there is not a single set of potential defeaters for all rules but each rule r has its own set of potential defeaters. Secondly, the rules which are used to derive potential defeaters must satisfy an additional condition: to potentially defeat r a rule must not be dominated by r in context S. Since fewer rules can be used to derive potential defeaters for a rule the safe rules are a superset of the undefeatable rules. We thus obtain more derivable literals. For the special case where $>$ is empty the two definitions of S-derivable clearly coincide.

The set of S-derivable literals grows monotonically with S. We thus can start as usual with the empty set of literals and iterate the computation of S-derivable formulas until a fixed point is reached.

Here is a small example illustrating the definition.

Example 3:
1) $c \leftarrow not\ \neg c, a$
2) $\neg c \leftarrow not\ c$
3) a

Let $1 > 2$. Clearly, rule 3 is $\emptyset$-safe since there is no way of defeating a rule without default negation. But also 1) is $\emptyset$-safe since the closure of 1 together with the $\emptyset$-undefeatable rule 3 defeats 2 and thus 1 $\emptyset$-dominates 2. Therefore the set of $\emptyset$-derivable literals is $\{c, a\}$. This set is already the least fixed point.

4   The Translation

We use a straightforward modular translation $Trans$ from defeasible theories $T = (R, >)$ to extended logic programs $Trans(T) = (Trans(R), >')$ where $Trans(R) = \{Trans(r) : r \in R\}$ and the translation of each rule is defined as follows:

$$\{a_1, \ldots, a_n\} \rightarrow b \qquad \text{becomes} \qquad b \leftarrow a_1, \ldots, a_n$$
$$\{a_1, \ldots, a_n\} \Rightarrow b \qquad \text{becomes} \qquad b \leftarrow not - b, a_1, \ldots, a_n$$

Furthermore, we require that $Trans(r) >' Trans(r')$ iff $r > r'$. (in the rest of the paper we use the same symbol for the two preference relations because we don't expect this to cause any confusion).

The prioritized logic programs obtained this way are a proper subset of prioritized extended logic programs which we call defeasible logic programs. Defeasible logic programs use default negation in a highly restricted way (corresponding to normal defaults in default logic).

5   (In)correctness

We first investigate correctness of defeasible logic wrt prioritized well-founded semantics, that is, the question whether for each defeasible conclusion $+\delta p$ of a defeasible theory T we have $p \in WFS(Trans(T))$. The answer for the general case will be no, but for a somewhat restricted case correctness can be established.

The negative answer for the general case can be demonstrated by the following counterexample (we put the defeasible logic rules and their translation into the same line):

Example 4:

1) $\Rightarrow p$ $\qquad\qquad\qquad$ $p \leftarrow not \neg p$
2) $p \rightarrow q$ $\qquad\qquad\qquad$ $q \leftarrow p$
3) $\Rightarrow \neg q$ $\qquad\qquad\qquad$ $\neg q \leftarrow not \, q$

Assume $3 > 2$. Now $+\delta \neg q$ is a conclusion which can be established through the following derivation:

$$-\Delta p, -\Delta q, +\delta \neg q$$

Well-founded semantics, on the other hand, concludes q but not $\neg q$: although 3 has higher priority than 2 it does not dominate 2 since a strict rule can never be defeated. From this we have the following proposition:

Proposition 1. *Defeasible logic is incorrect wrt prioritized well-founded semantics: there is a defeasible theory $T = (R, >)$ and a formula q such that $+\delta q$ is a consequence of T but $q \notin WFS(Trans(T))$.*

The example already hints at the source of the incorrectness. In defeasible logic a strict rule can be overridden by a defeasible rule with higher priority. This can never happen in well-founded semantics where the conclusion of a strict rule is accepted whenever its antecedents are accepted no matter what the preferences are. Indeed, a restriction on the admissable preferences turns out to be sufficient for obtaining correctness.

Proposition 2. *Let $T = (R, >)$ be a defeasible theory such that $>$ is defined on defeasible rules only, $Trans(T) = (P, >)$ its translation. If $+\delta q$ is a conclusion of T then $q \in WFS(Trans(T))$.*

Proof. For the proof we show the following lemmata: Let $S = S_0 \cup S_1 \cup \ldots$ be the least fixed point reached for $Trans(T)$, that is, $S_0 = \emptyset$ and for all $i > 0$, S_i is the set of S_{i-1}-derivable literals. Then the following results hold:

Lemma 1. *If $+\Delta q$ is a conclusion of T, then $q \in S_1$ (and henceforth in all S_j for $j \geq 1$).*

Lemma 2. *If $+\delta q$ is a conclusion of T, then $q \in S_i$ for some i (and henceforth in all S_j for $j \geq i$).*

Lemma 3. *If $-\sigma q$ is a conclusion of T, then q is not an S-potential defeater, that is there is an i such that q is not an S_i- potential defeater (and henceforth not an S_j-potential defeater for all $j \geq i$).*

Note that our proposition is equivalent to Lemma 2. Lemma 1 is immediate since strict rules can never be defeated.

The proof for Lemmas 2 and 3 is by joint induction on the length n of the shortest proof of the corresponding tagged literals. The base case can be checked easily. For the inductive step we assume that Lemmas 2 and 3 hold for tagged literals whose shortest proofs are of length at most $n - 1$. We have to distinguish 2 cases representing the possible tagged literals appearing in the lemmata:

case $+\delta q$:
there are two alternatives
a) $+\Delta q$ appears in the proof before $+\delta q$, then according to Lemma 1, q is already in S_1 and thus in S, or
b) there is a rule r with head q whose antecedents are, by induction hypothesis, in S_j for some j, and for all conflicting rules r': an antecedent is, by induction hypothesis, not an S_k-potential defeater, for some k, or r' is S_j dominated by r. Hence r is S_m-safe for sufficiently large m and thus $q \in S$. Note that for domination to hold we need the fact that r' is a defeasible rule, otherwise r could not dominate r'.

case $-\sigma q$:
we know that for each rule r with head q one of the following 2 alternatives holds:
a) there is an antecedent which is, by induction hypothesis, not an S_j-potential defeater for some j, or

b) there is a conflicting rule s whose antecedents are, by induction hypothesis, already in S_i, for some i, and which S_i-dominates r (since $s > r$ rule r must be defeasible and thus domination follows from the fact that the rules have complementary heads).

Let k be the smallest integer such that for each rule r with head q an antecedent of r is not an S_k-potential defeater (case a) or r is S_k-dominated by a rule with complementary head (case b). Let D be the set of rules with head q for which case b) holds but not case a). There are two possibilities: if D is empty then q is not a potential S_k-defeater. If D is not empty then, since $>$ is acyclic, there must be a rule r' among the rules S_k-dominating elements of D which is itself not S_k-dominated and thus S_k-safe. S_{k+1} therefore contains $-q$, all rules for which case b) holds are thus S_{k+1}-defeated and q is not an S_{k+1}-potential conclusion.

6 Incompleteness

We next discuss completeness. It turns out that defeasible logic is incomplete wrt prioritized well-founded semantics:

Proposition 3. *Let $T = (R, >)$ be a defeasible theory, and $Trans(T) = (P, >)$ its translation. $q \in WFS(Trans(T))$ does not imply that $+\delta q$ is a conclusion of T.*

To prove the proposition we will discuss some counterexamples which also illustrate the sources of the incompleteness.

Here is a first counterexample:

Example 5:

| 1) | $\Rightarrow \neg p$ | $\neg p \leftarrow not\ p$ |
| 2) | $p \Rightarrow p$ | $p \leftarrow p$ |

Assume there are no preferences. There is no proof for $+\delta \neg p$. Although the conflicting rule 2 can never be used to derive p, the mere existence of the rule is regarded as sufficient reason not to conclude $\neg p$. Well-founded semantics, on the other hand, concludes $\neg p$: p is not a potential $\emptyset$-defeater, 1 is thus $\emptyset$-undefeatable and used to derive $\neg p$. Well-founded semantics thus implicitly performs the kind of loop checking which is lacking in defeasible logic.

For the next counterexample consider again the rules of Example 4:

Example 6:

1)	$\Rightarrow p$	$p \leftarrow not\ \neg p$
2)	$p \rightarrow q$	$q \leftarrow p$
3)	$\Rightarrow \neg q$	$\neg q \leftarrow not\ q$

This time we assume no priorities. Clearly $q \in WFS(Trans(T))$ but $+\delta q$ is not a conclusion of T. This illustrates a major difference in the way strict rules are treated. In well-founded semantics a strict rule is applied whenever its antecedents are accepted, independently of whether the antecedents are derived using strict or defeasible rules. In defeasible logic strict rules have a different role, depending on whether all antecedents have strict proofs or not. If this is the case, then the rule is applied. If one of the antecedents is only defeasibly derivable then the strict rule is treated like a defeasible rule and may be blocked by a conflicting defeasible rule, as in our example.

Is this ambivalent role of rules adequate? In other words, is well-founded semantics sometimes not cautious enough? We do not think so. As the authors of [3] point out "strict rules are intended to define relationships that are definitional in nature". The example they give is $emu(X) \rightarrow bird(X)$. If there is a definitional relationship between emus and birds it seems fully adequate to accept, say $bird(Tweety)$ if $emu(Tweety)$ is accepted. The additional conclusions obtained by well-founded semantics in examples like the one above seem perfectly reasonable.

The next example shows that well-founded semantics takes more preferences into account than defeasible logic.

Example 7:

1)	$\Rightarrow p$	$p \leftarrow not\neg p$
2)	$p \rightarrow \neg q$	$\neg q \leftarrow p$
3)	$\Rightarrow q$	$q \leftarrow not\neg q$
4)	$q \rightarrow \neg p$	$\neg p \leftarrow q$

Assume $1 > 3$. Defeasible logic does not conclude $+\delta p$. The reason is that only preferences of rules with complementary heads play a role in the proof theory of defeasible logic. Preferences among other rules are simply disregarded. Well-founded semantics, on the other hand, concludes p in the example. Rule 1 is $\emptyset$-safe since the closure of 1 together with the $\emptyset$-undefeatable rule 2 defeats 3, that is 1 $\emptyset$-dominates 3.

Again we believe that the additional conclusions obtained by well-founded semantics are perfectly reasonable.

7   Conclusions

In this paper we have analyzed the relationship between defeasible logic and well-founded semantics for prioritized extended logic programs with two types of negation. For the comparison we used a straightforward modular translation of defeasible theories to extended logic programs. The analysis was based on the arguably most attractive variant of defeasible logic, the ambiguity propagating defeasible logic presented in [3]. The prioritized well-founded semantics we used is a considerably simplified version of a semantics proposed in [6]. The simplification was possible since for the purpose of this paper the ability to represent preference information in the logical language was not essential.

It turned out that, although correctness does not hold in general, a minor restriction is sufficient to guarantee correctness: if we admit preferences between defeasible rules only, then all defeasibly provable literals are true in prioritized well-founded semantics. It should be mentioned that the use of the ambiguity propagating variant of defeasible logic without team defeat clearly is essential for this result. Nute's original version is obviously incorrect (see Example 1) as any other variant without ambiguity propagation.

We also analyzed the sources of the incompleteness of defeasible logic. It turned out that three factors contribute to the incompleteness: 1) the lack of loop checking, 2) the somewhat ambivalent role of strict rules which - so to speak - turn into defeasible rules if not all antecedents are strictly provable, and 3) the preference handling which completely neglects preferences between rules which do not have complementary literals.

From a semantical point of view well-founded semantics seems to have clear advantages: the additional conclusions obtained seem perfectly reasonable. Moreover, in comparison with the complex rules of defeasible logic the definition of well-founded semantics is quite simple and elegant. Finally, the semantics is defined for a much larger class of programs than those obtained by translating defeasible theories.

What remains is the computational aspect. In both approaches the computation of conclusions is polynomial in the size of the rule base. In [6] the variant of well-founded semantics where preference information is expressed in the language is reported to be of cubic complexity. In [12] Nute's defeasible logic is reported to be of linear complexity. It remains an issue for further study how these results transfer to the variants discussed in this paper, and whether there are applications where a possible computational advantage of defeasible logic can outweigh its semantical disadvantages.

Acknowledgements

I would like to thank G. Antoniou for several helpful discussions on defeasible logic.

References

1. Antoniou, G., Billington, D., Governatori, G., Maher, M. J., A Flexible Framework for Defeasible Logics, Proc. 17th American National Conference on Artificial Intelligence, AAAI-2000, 405-410   121
2. Antoniou, G., Billington, D., Governatori, G., Maher, M. J., Representation Results for Defeasible Logics, *ACM Transactions on Computational Logic*, in print   121, 122
3. Antoniou, G., Billington, D., Governatori, G., Maher, M. J., Rock, A., A Family of Defeasible Reasoning Logics and its Implementation, Proc. European Conference on Artificial Intelligence ECAI-2000, 459-463   121, 122, 123, 130
4. Baral, C., Gelfond, M., Logic Programming and Knowledge Representation, *Journal of Logic Programming*, 19,20:73-148, 1994   125

5. Baral, C., Subrahmanian, V. S., Duality between Alternative Semantics of Logic Programs and Nonmonotonic Formalisms, Intl. Workshop on Logic Programming and Nonmonotonic Reasoning, 1991   125

6. Brewka, G., Well-Founded Semantics for Extended Logic Programs with Dynamic Preferences. *Journal of Artificial Intelligence Research*, 4:19–36, 1996   121, 122, 124, 125, 126, 130, 131

7. Brewka, G., Eiter, T., Preferred Answer Sets for Extended Logic Programs. *Artificial Intelligence* 109, 297–356, 1999   121

8. Gelfond, M., Lifschitz, V., Logic Programs with Classical Negation, Proc. 7th Intl. Conference on Logic Programming, 1990   125

9. van Gelder, A., Ross, K., Schlipf, J., The Well-Founded Semantics for General Logic Programs, *Journal of ACM*, 221-230, 1990   125

10. Lifschitz, V., Foundations of Declarative Logic Programming, in: G. Brewka (ed.), Principles of Knowledge Representation, Studies in Logic, Language and Information, CSLI publications, 1996   125

11. McCarthy, J., Circumscription – A Form of Nonmonotonic Reasoning, *Artificial Intelligence* 13, 1980   121

12. Maher, M. J., Rock, A., Antoniou, G., Billington, D., Miller, T., Efficient Defeasible Reasoning Systems, Proc. 12th IEEE International Conference on Tools with Artificial Intelligence, ICTAI-2000, 384-392   121, 131

13. Nute, D., Defeasible Reasoning, in Proc. 20th Hawaii International Conference on on Systems Science, IEEE Press, 1987, 470-477   121, 122

14. Nute, D., Defeasible Logic, in D. M. Gabbay, C. J. Hogger, J. A. Robinson (eds.) Handbook of Logic in Artificial Intelligence and Logic Programming, Vol. 3, Oxford University Press, 1994, 353-395   121

15. Przymusinski, T., The Well-Founded Semantics Coincides with the Three-Valued Stable Semantics, *Fundamenta Informaticae*, 1989   125

16. Przymusinski, T., Stable Semantics for Disjunctive Programs, *New Generation Computing*, 9:401-424, 1991   125

17. Reiter, R., A Logic for Default Reasoning, *Artificial Intelligence* 13 (1980) 81-132   121

A Comparative Study of Well-Founded Semantics for Disjunctive Logic Programs

Kewen Wang*

Institut für Informatik, Universität Potsdam
Postfach 60 15 53, D–14415 Potsdam, Germany
`kewen@cs.uni-potsdam.de`

Abstract. Much work has been done on extending the well-founded semantics to general disjunctive logic programs and various approaches have been proposed. However, no consensus has been reached about which semantics is the most intended. In this paper we look at disjunctive well-founded reasoning from different angles. We show that there is an intuitive form of the well-founded reasoning in disjunctive logic programming which can be equivalently characterized by several different approaches including program transformations, argumentation, unfounded sets (and resolution-like procedure). We also provide a bottom-up procedure for this semantics. The significance of this work is not only in clarifying the relationship among different approaches, but also in providing novel arguments in favor of our semantics.

1 Introduction

The importance of representing and reasoning about disjunctive information has been addressed by many researchers. Disjunctive logic programming (DLP) is widely believed to be a suitable tool for formalizing disjunctive reasoning and it has received extensive study in recent years. Since DLP admits both default negation and disjunction, the issue of finding a suitable semantics for disjunctive programs is more difficult than it is in the case of normal (i. e. non-disjunctive) logic programs. Usually, skepticism and credulism represent two major semantic intuitions for knowledge representation in artificial intelligence. The well-founded semantics [12] is a formalism of skeptical reasoning in normal logic programming while the stable semantics [6] formalizes credulous reasoning. Recently, considerable effort has been paid to generalize these two semantics to disjunctive logic programs. However, the task of generalizing the well-founded model to disjunctive programs has proven to be complex. There have been various proposals for defining the well-founded semantics for general disjunctive logic programs [8]. As argued by some authors (for instance [2,10,13]), each of the previous versions of the disjunctive well-founded semantics bears its own drawbacks. Moreover, no consensus has been reached about what constitutes an intended well-founded semantics for disjunctive logic programs. The semantics D-WFS [1,2], STATIC [10]

---

* On leave from Tsinghua University, Beijing.

T. Eiter, W. Faber, and M. Truszczyński (Eds.): LPNMR 2001, LNAI 2173, pp. 133–146, 2001.

and WFDS [13] are among the most recent approaches to defining disjunctive well-founded semantics. D-WFS is based on a series of abstract properties and it is the weakest (least) semantics that is invariant under a set of program transformations. STATIC has its root in autoepistemic logic and is based on the notion of *static expansions* for belief theories. The semantics STATIC(P) for a disjunctive program P is defined as the least static expansion of P_{AEB} where P_{AEB} is the belief theory corresponding to P. The basic idea of WFDS is to transform P into an argumentation framework and WFDS(P) is specified by the least acceptable hypothesis of P. Although these semantics stem from very different intuitions, all of them share a number of attractive properties. In particular, each of these semantics extends both the well-founded semantics [12] for normal logic programs and the generalized closed world assumption (GCWA) [9] for positive disjunctive programs (i. e. without default negation).

It has been proven that D-WFS is equivalent to a restricted version of STATIC [3]. But the relation of these semantics to the argumentation-based semantics and unfounded sets are as yet unclear. In this paper, we modify some existing semantics to make them more intuitive and report further equivalence results. First, we define a transformation-based semantics denoted D-WFS* by introducing a new transformation into Brass and Dix's set $\mathbf{T}_{WFS}$ of program transformations. This semantics naturally extends D-WFS and enjoys all the important properties that have been proven for D-WFS. We prove that WFDS is equivalent to D-WFS*. We also provide a bottom-up evaluation procedure for WFDS (and D-WFS*). Second, we define a new notion of unfounded sets which is a generalization of the unfounded sets defined in [7,5]. Based on this new notion of unfounded sets, we define a well-founded semantics U-WFS for disjunctive programs. We show that U-WFS is equivalent to WFDS (and thus D-WFS*). Moreover, in [14] we have developed a top-down procedure D-SLS Resolution which is sound and complete with respect to our semantics. D-SLS extends both SLS-resolution [11] and SLI-resolution [8]. Altogether we obtain the following equivalence results:

$$\text{WFDS} \equiv \text{D-WFS}^* \equiv \text{U-WFS} \equiv \text{D-SLS}.$$

We consider these results to be quite significant: (1) Our results clarify the relationship among quite several different approaches to defining disjunctive well-founded semantics, including argumentation-based, transformation-based, unfounded sets-based and resolution-based approaches. (2) Since the four semantics are based on very different intuitions, these equivalent characterizations in turn provide yet more powerful arguments in favor of our semantics. (3) Both the top-down procedure D-SLS Resolution [14] and the bottom-up query evaluation proposed in this paper pave two different ways for implementing our semantics.

The rest of this paper is arranged as follows. In Section 2 we recall some basic definitions and notation; we present in Section 3 a slightly restricted form of the well-founded semantics WFDS. In Section 4 we introduce a new program transformation *Head reduction* and then define the transformation-based semantics D-WFS*, which naturally extends D-WFS. In Section 5, we first provide a bottom-up query evaluation for D-WFS* (and WFDS) and then prove the equivalence of D-WFS* and WFDS. Section 6 introduces the new notion of unfounded sets and defines the well-founded semantics U-WFS. We also show that U-WFS is equivalent to WFDS. Section 7 is our conclusion. Proofs of the theorems are given in the full version of this paper.

2   Preliminaries

We briefly review most of the basic notions used throughout this paper.

A *disjunctive logic program* is a finite set of rules of the form

$$a_1 \vee \cdots \vee a_n \leftarrow b_1, \ldots, b_m, not\ c_1, \ldots, not\ c_t, \tag{1}$$

where a_i, b_i, c_i are atoms and $n > 0$. The default negation '*not a*' of an atom a is called a *negative literal*. In this paper we consider only propositional programs although many definitions and results hold for predicate logic programs.

P is a *normal* logic program if it contains no disjunctions.

If a rule of form (1) contains no negative body literals, it is called *positive*; P is a positive program if every rule of P is positive.

If a rule of form (1) contains no body atoms, it is called *negative*; P is a negative program if every rule of P is negative.

Following [2], we also say a negative rule r is a *conditional fact*. That is, a conditional fact is of form $a_1 \vee \cdots \vee a_n \leftarrow not\ c_1, \cdots, not\ c_m$, where a_i and c_j are (ground) atoms for $1 \leq k \leq n$ and $0 \leq j \leq m$.

For a rule r of form (1), $body(r) = body^+(r) \cup body^-(r)$ where $body^+(r) = \{b_1, \ldots, b_m\}$ and $body^-(r) = \{not\ c_1, \ldots, not\ c_t\}$; $head(r) = a_1 \vee \cdots \vee a_n$. When no confusion is caused, we also use $head(r)$ to denote the set of atoms in $head(r)$. For instance, $a \in head(r)$ means that a appears in the head of r. If X is a set of atoms, $head(r) - X$ is the disjunction obtained from $head(r)$ by deleting the atoms in X. The set $head(P)$ consists of all atoms appearing in rule heads of P.

As usual, B_P is the *Herbrand base* of disjunctive logic program P, that is, the set of all (ground) atoms in P. A *positive (negative) disjunction* is a disjunction of atoms (negative literals) in P. A *pure disjunction* is either a positive one or a negative one. The disjunctive base of P is $DB_P = DB_P^+ \cup DB_P^-$ where DB_P^+ is the set of all positive disjunctions in P and DB_P^- is the set of all negative disjunctions in P. If A and $B = A \vee A'$ are two disjunctions, then we say A is a *sub-disjunction* of B, denoted $A \subseteq B$.

A *model state* of a disjunctive program P is a subset of DB_P. Usually, a well-founded semantics for a disjunctive logic program is defined by a model state.

If S is an expression (a set of literals, a disjunction or a set of disjunctions), $atoms(S)$ denotes the set of all atoms appearing in S.

For simplicity, we assume that all model states are closed under implication of pure disjunctions. That is, for any model state S, if A is a sub-disjunction of a pure disjunction B and $A \in S$, then $B \in S$. For instance, if $S = \{a, b \lor c\}$, then $a \lor b \lor c \in S$.

Given a model state S and a pure disjunction A, we also say A is satisfied by S, denoted $S \models A$, if $A \in S$.

We assume that all disjunctions have been simplified by deleting the repeated literals. For example, the disjunction $a \lor b \lor b$ is actually the disjunction $a \lor b$.

3   Argumentation and Well-Founded Semantics

As illustrated in [13][1], argumentation provides an unifying semantic framework for DLP. The basic idea of the argumentation-based approach for DLP is to translate each disjunctive logic program into an argument framework $\mathbf{F}_P = \langle P, \mathrm{DB}_P^-, \leadsto_P \rangle$. In the framework defined in [13], an *assumption* of P is a negative disjunction of P, and a *hypothesis* is a set of assumptions; $\leadsto_P$ is an attack relation among the hypotheses. An *admissible hypothesis* Δ is one that can attack every hypothesis which attacks it. The intuitive meaning of an assumption $not\ a_1 \lor \cdots \lor not\ a_m$ is that $a_1 \land \cdots \land a_m$ can not be proven from the disjunctive program.

Given a hypothesis Δ of disjunctive program P, similar to the GL-transformation [6], we can easily reduce P into another disjunctive program without default negation.

Definition 1. *Let Δ be a hypothesis of disjunctive program P, then the reduct of P with respect to Δ is the disjunctive program*

$$P_\Delta^+ = \{head(r) \leftarrow body^+(r) \mid r \in P \text{ and } body^-(r) \subseteq \Delta\}.$$

The following definition introduces a special resolution $\vdash_P$ which resolves default-negation literals with a disjunction.

Definition 2. *Let Δ be a hypothesis of disjunctive program P and $A \in DB_P^+$. If there exists $B \in DB_P^+$ and $not\ b_1, \ldots, not\ b_m \in \Delta$ such that $B = A \lor b_1 \lor \cdots \lor b_m$ and $P_\Delta^+ \models B$. Then Δ is said to be a* supporting hypothesis *for A, denoted $\Delta \vdash_P A$. Here $\models$ is the inference relation of the classical propositional logic.*

The set of all positive disjunctions supported by Δ is denoted:

$$cons_P(\Delta) = \{A \in DB_P^+ \mid \Delta \vdash_P A\}.$$

To derive suitable hypotheses for a given disjunctive program, some constraints will be required to filter out unintuitive hypotheses.

Definition 3. *Let Δ and Δ' be two hypotheses of disjunctive program P. If at least one of the following two conditions holds:*

---

[1] You et al in [15] also defined an argumentative extension to the disjunctive stable semantics. However, their framework does not lead to an intuitive well-founded semantics for DLP as the authors have observed.

1. *there exists* $\beta = \text{not } b_1 \vee \cdots \vee \text{not } b_m \in \Delta'$, $m > 0$, *such that* $\Delta \vdash_P b_i$, *for all* $i = 1, \ldots, m$; *or*
2. *there exist* $\text{not } b_1, \ldots, \text{not } b_m \in \Delta', m > 0$, *such that* $\Delta \vdash_P b_1 \vee \cdots \vee b_m$, *then we say* Δ *attacks* Δ', *and denoted* $\Delta \leadsto_P \Delta'$.

Intuitively, $\Delta \leadsto_P \Delta'$ means that Δ causes a direct contradiction with Δ' and the contradiction may come from one of the above two cases.

Example 1.

$$a \vee b \leftarrow$$
$$c \leftarrow d, \text{not } a, \text{not } b$$
$$d \leftarrow$$
$$e \leftarrow \text{not } e$$

Let $\Delta' = \{\text{not } c\}$ and $\Delta = \{\text{not } a, \text{not } b\}$, then $\Delta \leadsto_P \Delta'$.

The next definition specifies what is an acceptable hypothesis.

Definition 4. *Let Δ be a hypothesis of disjunctive program P. An assumption B of P is* admissible *with respect to Δ if $\Delta \leadsto_P \Delta'$ holds for any hypothesis Δ' of P such that $\Delta' \leadsto_P \{B\}$.*
   Denote $\mathcal{A}_P(\Delta) = \{\text{not } a_1 \vee \cdots \vee \text{not } a_m \in DB_P^- \mid \text{not } a_i \text{ is admissible wrt } \Delta \text{ for some } i, 1 \leq i \leq m\}$.

Originally, $\mathcal{A}_P$ also includes some other negative disjunctions. To compare with different semantics, we omit them here. Another reason for doing this is that information in form of negative disjunctions does not participate in inferring positive information in DLP.

   For any disjunctive program P, $\mathcal{A}_P$ is a monotonic operator. Thus, if P is finite then $\mathcal{A}_P$ has the least fixpoint $\text{lfp}(\mathcal{A}_P)$ and $\text{lfp}(\mathcal{A}_P) = \mathcal{A}_P^k(\emptyset)$ for some $k \geq 0$.

Definition 5. *The* well-founded disjunctive hypothesis *$WFDH(P)$ of disjunctive program P is defined as the least fixpoint of the operator $\mathcal{A}_P$. That is, $WFDH(P) = \mathcal{A}_P \uparrow \omega$.*
   The well-founded disjunctive semantics *$WFDS$ for P is defined as the model state $WFDS(P) = WFDH(P) \cup cons_P(WFDH(P))$.*

By the above definition, $WFDS(P)$ is uniquely determined by $WFDH(P)$.
   For the disjunctive program P in Example 1, $WFDH(P) = \{\text{not } c\}$ and $WFDS(P) = \{a \vee b, d, \text{not } c\}$. Notice that e is unknown.

4   Transformation-Based Semantics

In this section we study the relation of the argumentation-based semantics to the transformation-based semantics. We first introduce a new program transformation so as to simplify the rule heads of disjunctive programs and then define a new transformation-based semantics (called D-WFS*) as the most skeptical semantics that satisfies both our new program transformation and Brass and Dix's set $\mathbf{T}_{\text{WFS}}$ of program transformations. Our new semantics D-WFS* naturally extends the D-WFS in [2] and is no less skeptical than D-WFS. In fact, this extension is meaningful because D-WFS seems too skeptical to derive useful information from some disjunctive programs as the next example shows.

Example 2. John is traveling in Europe but we are not sure which city he is visiting. We know that, if there is no evidence to show that John is in Paris, he should be either in London or in Berlin. Also, we are informed that John is now visiting either London or Paris. This knowledge base can be conveniently expressed as the following disjunctive logic program P:

$$b \vee l \leftarrow not\ p$$
$$l \vee p \leftarrow$$

Here, b, l and p denote that John is visiting *Berlin, London* and *Paris*, respectively.

Intuitively, *not b* (i. e. John is not visiting Berlin) should be inferred from P. It can be verified that neither b nor its negation *not b* can be derived from P under D-WFS and STATIC while *not b* can be derived under WFDS.

The intuition behind Minker's Generalized Closed World Assumption (GCWA) [9] can be read off its proof-theoretic characterization:

If, for every positive disjunction A, $P \vdash a \vee A$ implies $P \vdash A$, then *not a* is derivable from P, where $\vdash$ is the inference relation in the classical logic and P is considered as a classical logic theory.

The above principle for positive DLP can be reformulated in general DLP as follows:

If, for every conditional fact $a \vee A \leftarrow not\ C$, $P \vdash (a \vee A \leftarrow not\ C)$ implies $P \vdash (A \leftarrow not\ C)$, then not a is derivable from P, where $\vdash$ is the inference relation in the classical logic and P is considered as a classical logic theory.

However, D-WFS does not obey the above principle as Example 2 shows. In fact, $P \vdash (b \vee l \leftarrow not\ p)$ implies $P \vdash (l \leftarrow not\ p)$ since $l \vee p \leftarrow$ is in P. But $b \notin$ D-WFS(P).

According to [2], an abstract semantics can be defined as follows.

Definition 6. *A semantics $\mathcal{S}$ is a mapping which assigns to every disjunctive program P a set $\mathcal{S}(P)$ of pure disjunctions such that the following conditions are satisfied:*

1. *if Q' is a sub-disjunction of pure disjunction Q and $Q' \in \mathcal{S}(P)$, then $Q \in \mathcal{S}(P)$;*
2. *if the rule $A \leftarrow$ is in P for a (positive) disjunction A, then $A \in \mathcal{S}(P)$;*
3. *if a is an atom and $a \notin head(P)$ (i. e. a does not appear in the rule heads of P), then not $a \in \mathcal{S}(P)$.*

It should be noted that a semantics satisfying the above conditions is not necessarily a *suitable* one because Definition 6 is still very general.

Besides the program transformations $\mathbf{T}_{\text{WFS}}$ in [2], we also need a new program transformation called *Head reduction* to define our semantics. This definition is designed just to reflect the semantic intuition behind the GCWA as mentioned at the beginning of this section.

Definition 7. *An atom a in disjunctive program P is called* GCWA*-negated if, for any rule r in P of form $a \vee A \leftarrow B, not\ c_1, \ldots, not\ c_t$, there is a rule $A' \leftarrow$ in P such that A' is a sub-disjunction of $A \vee c_1 \vee \cdots \vee c_t$.*

For instance, b can be *GCWA-negated* for the disjunctive program in Example 2.

Definition 8. *A rule r is an* implication *of another rule r' if $head(r') \subseteq head(r)$, $body(r') \subseteq body(r)$ and at least one inclusion is proper.*

The definition of our new semantics D-WFS* will be based on the set $\mathbf{T}^*_{\text{WFS}}$ of the following six program transformations. In the sequel, P_1 and P_2 are disjunctive programs:

- **Unfolding**: P_2 is obtained from P_1 by unfolding if there is a rule $A \leftarrow b, B, not\ C$ in P_1 such that

$$P_2 = P_1 - \{A \leftarrow b, B, not\ C\}$$
$$\cup \{A \vee (A' - \{b\}) \leftarrow B, B', not\ C, not\ C') \mid$$
$$\text{there is a rule of } P_1 : A' \leftarrow B', not\ C' \text{ such that } b \in A'\}.$$

- **Elimination of tautologies**: P_2 is obtained from P_1 by elimination of tautologies if there is a rule $A \leftarrow B, not\ C$ in P_1 such that $A \cap B \neq \emptyset$ and $P_2 = P_1 - \{A \leftarrow B, not\ C\}$.
- **Elimination of nonminimal rules**: P_2 is obtained from P_1 by elimination of nonminimal rules if there are two distinct rules r and r' of P_1 such that r is an implication of r' and $P_2 = P_1 - \{r\}$.
- **Positive reduction**: P_2 is obtained from P_1 by positive reduction if there is a rule $A \leftarrow B, not\ C$ in P_1 and $c \in C$ such that $c \notin head(P_1)$ and $P_2 = P_1 - \{A \leftarrow B, not\ C\} \cup \{A \leftarrow B, not\ (C - \{c\})\}$.
- **Negative reduction**: P_2 is obtained from P_1 by negative reduction if there are two rules $A \leftarrow B, not\ C$ and $A' \leftarrow$ in P_1 such that $A' \subseteq C$ and $P_2 = P_1 - \{A \leftarrow B, not\ C\}$.
- **Head reduction** P_2 is obtained from P_1 by head reduction if there is a rule $a \vee A \leftarrow B, not\ C$ in P_1 such that a is GCWA-negated and $P_2 = P_1 \cup \{A \leftarrow B, not\ C\} - \{a \vee A \leftarrow B, not\ C\}$.

Example 3. Consider the disjunctive program P in Example 2. Since the atom b is GCWA-negated, P can be transformed into the following disjunctive program P' by *Head reduction*:

$$l \leftarrow not\ p$$
$$l \vee p \leftarrow$$

Suppose that $\mathcal{S}$ is a semantics. Then by Definition 6, $l \vee p \in \mathcal{S}$ and $not\ b \in \mathcal{S}$.

We say a semantics S satisfies a program transformation T (or, S is invariant under T) if $S(P_1) = S(P_2)$ for any two disjunctive programs P_1 and P_2 with $P_2 = T(P_1)$.

Let S and S' be two semantics. S is *weaker* than S' if $S(P) \subseteq S'(P)$ for any disjunctive program P.

We present the main definition of this section as follows.

Definition 9. *(D-WFS***) The semantics D-WFS** *for disjunctive programs is defined as the weakest semantics allowing all program transformations in* $\mathbf{T}^*_{WFS}$.

This definition is not constructive and thus it can not be directly used to compute the semantics D-WFS* (a bottom-up procedure will be given in the next section). In the rest of this section, we first look at some properties of D-WFS*.

As the following theorem shows, D-WFS$^*(P)$ is well-defined for every disjunctive program P. This is guaranteed by the following two lemmas.

Lemma 1. *There is a semantics that satisfies all the program transformations in* $\mathbf{T}^*_{WFS}$.

Lemma 2. *Let* S_1 *and* S_2 *be two semantics satisfying* $\mathbf{T}^*_{WFS}$. *Then their intersection* $S = S_1 \cap S_2$ *is also a semantics and satisfies* $\mathbf{T}^*_{WFS}$.

Therefore, we have the following result which shows that semantics D-WFS* assigns the unique model state D-WFS$^*(P)$ for each disjunctive program P.

Theorem 1. *For any disjunctive program* P, *D-WFS*$^*(P)$ *is well-defined.*

Since the set $\mathbf{T}_{WFS}$ of program transformations in [2] is a subset of $\mathbf{T}^*_{WFS}$, our D-WFS* extends the original D-WFS in the following sense.

Theorem 2. *Let* P *be a disjunctive program. Then*

$$D\text{-}WFS(P) \subseteq D\text{-}WFS^*(P).$$

The converse of Theorem 2 is not true in general. As we will see in Section 5, for the disjunctive program P in Example 2, *not* $b \in$ D-WFS$^*(P)$ but *not* $b \notin$ D-WFS(P). This theorem also implies that D-WFS* extends the restricted STATIC since the D-WFS* is equivalent to the restricted STATIC [3].

5   Bottom-Up Computation

Parallel to the computation for D-WFS [2], we will first provide a bottom-up procedure for D-WFS* and then show the equivalence of D-WFS* and WFDS. As a result, we actually provide a bottom-up computation for WFDS.

Let P be a disjunctive program. Our bottom-up computation for D-WFS$^*(P)$ consists of two stages. At the first stage, P is equivalently transformed into a negative program Lft(P) called the *least fixpoint transformation*. The details of this transformation can be found in [2,13]. The basic idea is to first evaluate body atoms of the rules in P but delay the negative body literals. The second stage is to further simplify Lft(P) into res$^*(P)$ from which the semantics D-WFS$^*(P)$ can be directly read off.

5.1   Strong Residual Program

In general, the negative program $Lft(P)$ can be further simplified by deleting unnecessary rules, unnecessary body literals and unnecessary head atoms. This leads to the idea of so-called *reductions*, which was firstly studied in [4] and then generalized to the case of disjunctive logic programs in [2]. The reduction of a disjunctive program P is called the residual program of P. The following is a generalization of Brass and Dix's residual programs.

Let N_{GCWA} be the set of atoms that are GCWA-negated in disjunctive program N. The reduction operator R^* is defined as, for any negative program N (i. e. a set of conditional facts),

$$R^*(N) = \{ (A - a) \leftarrow not\ (C \cap head(N)) \mid$$
$$\text{there is rule } r \in N : A \leftarrow not\ C \text{ such that}$$
$$(1) \text{ no rule of form } (A' \leftarrow) \text{ with } A' \subseteq C,$$
$$(2) \text{ no rule } r' \text{ s.t. } r \text{ is an implication of } r',$$
$$(3)\ a \in N_{\text{GCWA}} \text{ and } A - N_{\text{GCWA}} \neq \emptyset\}.$$

The notion of the *implication* of rules can be found in Definition 8. For any disjunctive program P, we can first transform it into the negative disjunctive program $Lft(P)$. Then, *fully* perform the reduction R^* on $Lft(P)$ to obtain a simplified negative program $res^*(P)$ (the *strong residual program* of P). The iteration procedure of R^* will finally stop in finite steps because B_P contains finite number of atoms and the total number of atoms occurring in each N is reduced by R^*. This procedure is precisely formulated in the next definition, which has the same form as Definition 3.4 in [2] (the difference is only in that we have a new reduction operator R^* here).

Definition 10. *(strong residual program) Let P be a disjunctive program. Then we have a sequence of negative programs $\{N_i\}_{i\geq 0}$ with $N_0 = Lft(P)$ and $N_{i+1} = R^*(N_i)$. Let $N_{t+1} = R^*(N_t)$. Then we call N_t is the strong residual program of P and denote it as $res^*(P)$.*

Since the Head reduction has been directly embedded into the operator R^*, the following result can be obtained from Theorem 4.3 in [2], which guarantees the completeness of our bottom-up computation.

Theorem 3. *Let P and P' be two disjunctive programs. If P is transformed into P' by a program transformation in $\mathbf{T}^*_{WFS}$, then $res^*(P) = res^*(P')$.*

This theorem has the following interesting corollary.

Corollary 1. *Let $\mathcal{S}$ be a semantics satisfying $\mathcal{S}(P) = \mathcal{S}(res^*(P))$ for all disjunctive program P. Then $\mathcal{S}$ allows all program transformations in $\mathbf{T}^*_{WFS}$.*

This corollary implies that, if $\mathcal{S}_0$ is a mapping from the set of all strong residual programs to the set of model states and it satisfies all properties in Definition 6, then the mapping defined by $\mathcal{S}(P) = \mathcal{S}(res^*(P))$ is a semantics. Therefore, the following lemma is obtained from the fact that D-WFS* is the weakest semantics.

Lemma 3. *Given disjunctive program P, we have*

$$D\text{-}WFS^*(res^*(P)) = D\text{-}WFS^*_+(P) \cup D\text{-}WFS^*_-(P)$$

where

$$D\text{-}WFS^*_+(res^*(P)) = \{A \in DB^+_P \mid rule \; A' \leftarrow \; is \; in \; res^*(P)$$
$$for \; some \; sub\text{-}disjunction \; A' \; of \; A\}$$

$$D\text{-}WFS^*_-(res^*(P)) = \{A \in DB^-_P \mid if \; a \notin head(res^*(P))$$
$$for \; some \; atom \; a \; appearing \; in \; A.\}$$

Thus, for any disjunctive program P, it is an easy task to get the semantics D-WFS$^*(res^*(P))$ of its strong residual program.

The main theorem in this section can be stated as follows.

Theorem 4. *For any disjunctive program P, we have*

$$D\text{-}WFS^*(P) = D\text{-}WFS^*_+(P) \cup D\text{-}WFS^*_-(P)$$

where

$$D\text{-}WFS^*_+(P) = \{A \in DB^+_P \mid rule \; A' \leftarrow \; is \; in \; res^*(P)$$
$$for \; some \; sub\text{-}disjunction \; A' \; of \; A\}$$

$$D\text{-}WFS^*_-(P) = \{A \in DB^-_P \mid if \; a \notin head(res^*(P))$$
$$for \; some \; atom \; a \; appearing \; in \; A.\}$$

Example 4. Consider again the disjunctive program P in Example 2. The strong residual program $res^*(P)$ is as follows:

$$l \leftarrow not \; p$$
$$l \vee p \leftarrow$$

Thus, D-WFS$^*(P) = \{l \vee p, not \; b\}$ [2].

5.2   Equivalence of WFDS and D-WFS*

Before we present the main theorem of this section, we need some properties of WFDS. First, we can justify that WFDS is a semantics in the sense of Definition 6. Moreover, it possesses the following two properties which can be verified directly.

Proposition 1. *WFDS satisfies all program transformations in* $\mathbf{T}^*_{WFS}$.

---

[2] D-WFS$^*(P)$ should include all pure disjunctions implied by either $l \vee p$ or $not \; b$. However, the little abusing of notion here simplifies our notation.

This proposition implies that the argumentation-based semantics WFDS is always at least as strong as the transformation-based semantics D-WFS*.

The next result convinces that the strong residual program $res^*(P)$ of disjunctive program P is equivalent to P w.r.t. the semantics WFDS. Therefore, we can first transform P into $res^*(P)$ and then compute $WFDS(res^*(P))$.

Proposition 2. *For any disjunctive program P,*

$$WFDS(P) = WFDS(res^*(P)).$$

It has been shown in [2] that Lft and their reduction operator R can be simulated by $\mathbf{T}_{WFS} = \mathbf{T}^*_{WFS} - \{\text{Head reduction}\}$, we have that Lft and R^* can be simulated by $\mathbf{T}^*_{WFS}$. Thus, the above proposition holds.

Now we can state the main result of this section, which asserts the equivalence of D-WFS* and WFDS.

Theorem 5. *For any disjunctive logic program P,*

$$WFDS(P) = D\text{-}WFS^*(P).$$

An important implication of this result is that the well-founded semantics WFDS also enjoys a bottom-up procedure similar to the D-WFS.

6   Unfounded Sets

The first definition of the well-founded model [12] is given in term of *unfounded sets* and it has been proved that the notion of unfounded sets constitutes a powerful and intuitive tool for defining semantics for logic programs. This notion has also been generalized to characterizing stable semantics for disjunctive logic programs in [7,5]. However, the two kinds of unfounded sets defined in [7,5] can not be used to define an intended well-founded semantics for disjunctive programs.

Example 5. [3]
$$a \vee b \leftarrow$$
$$c \leftarrow not\ a, not\ b$$

Intuitively, *not c* should be derived from the above disjunctive program and actually, many semantics including DWFS, STATIC and WFDS assign a truth value *'false'* for c. However, according to the definitions of unfounded sets in [7,5], c is not in any n-fold application of the well-founded operators on the empty set. For this reason, a more reasonable definition of the unfounded sets for disjunctive programs is in order.

In this section, we will define a new notion of unfounded sets for disjunctive programs and show that the well-founded semantics U-WFS defined by our notion is equivalent to D-WFS* and WFDS.

---

[3] This example is due to Jürgen Dix (personal communication)

We say $body(r)$ of $r \in P$ is *true* wrt model state S, denoted $S \models body(r)$, if $body(r) \subseteq S$; $body(r)$ is *false* wrt model state S, denoted $S \models \neg body(r)$ if either (1) the complement of a literal in $body(r)$ is in S or (2) there is a disjunction $a_1 \vee \cdots \vee a_n \in S$ such that $\{not\ a_1, \ldots, not\ a_n\} \subseteq body(r)$.

In Example 5, the second rule is false wrt $S = \{a \vee b\}$.

Definition 11. *Let S be a model state of disjunctive program P, a set X of ground atoms is an* unfounded set *for P wrt S if, for each $a \in X$ and each rule $r \in P$ such that $a \in head(r)$, at least one of the following conditions holds:*

1. *the body of r is false wrt S;*
2. *there is $x \in X$ such that $x \in body^+(r)$;*
3. *if $S \models body(r)$, then $S \models (head(r) - X)$.*

Notice that the above definition generalized the notions of unfounded sets in [7,5] in two ways. Firstly, the original ones are defined only for interpretations (sets of ground literals) rather than for model states. An interpretation is a model state but not vice versa. Secondly, though one can redefine the original notions of unfounded sets for model states, such unfounded sets are still too weak to capture the intended well-founded semantics of some disjunctive programs. Consider Example 5, let $S = \{a \vee b\}$. According to definition 11, the set $\{c\}$ is an unfounded set of P wrt S, but $\{c\}$ is not an unfounded set in the sense of Leone or Eiter.

Having the new notion of unfounded sets, we are ready to define the well-known operator $\mathcal{W}_P$ for any disjunctive program P.

If P has the greatest unfounded set wrt a model state, we denote it $\mathcal{U}_P(S)$. However, $\mathcal{U}_P(S)$ may be undefined for some S. For example, let $P = \{a \vee b\}$ and $S = \{a, b\}$. Then $X_1 = \{a\}$ and $X_2 = \{b\}$ are two unfounded sets wrt S but $X = \{a, b\}$ is not. Here we will not discuss the operator $\mathcal{U}_P(S)$ in detail.

Definition 12. *Let P be a disjunctive program, the operator $\mathcal{T}_P$ is defined as, for any model state S,*

$$\mathcal{T}_P(S) = \{A \in DB_P \mid \text{there is a rule } r \in P : A \vee a_1 \vee \cdots \vee a_n \leftarrow body(r)$$
$$\text{such that } S \models body(r) \text{ and not } a_1, \ldots, not\ a_n \in S\}.$$

Notice that $\mathcal{T}_P(S)$ is a set of positive disjunctions rather than just a set of atoms.

Definition 13. *Let P be a disjunctive program, the operator $\mathcal{W}_P$ is defined as, for any model state S,*

$$\mathcal{W}_P(S) = \mathcal{T}_P(S) \cup not.\mathcal{U}_P(S).$$

where $not.\mathcal{U}_P(S) = \{not\ p \mid p \in \mathcal{U}_P(S)\}$.

In general, $\mathcal{W}_P$ is a partial function because there may be no greatest unfounded set wrt model state S as mentioned previously.

However, we can prove that $\mathcal{W}_P$ has the least fixpoint. Given a disjunctive program P, we define a sequence of model states $\{W_k\}_{k \in \mathcal{N}}$ where $W_0 = \emptyset$ and $W_k = \mathcal{W}_P(W_{k-1})$ for $k > 0$.

Similar to Proposition 5.6 in [7], we can prove the following proposition.

Proposition 3. *Let P be a disjunctive program. Then*

1. Every model state W_k is well-defined and the sequence $\{W_k\}_{k \in \mathcal{N}}$ is increasing.

2. the limit $\cup_{k \geq 0} W_k$ of the sequence $\{W_k\}_{k \in \mathcal{N}}$ is the least fixpoint of $\mathcal{W}_P$.

Since we consider only finite propositional programs in this paper, there is some $t \geq 0$ such that $W_t = W_{t+1}$.

The well-founded semantics U-WFS is defined by

$$\text{U-WFS}(P) = \text{lfp}(\mathcal{W}_P).$$

For the program P in Example 5, U-WFS$(P) = \{a \vee b, not\ c\}$.

An important result is that WFDS (and thus D-WFS*) can also be equivalently characterized in term of the unfounded sets defined in this section.

Theorem 6. *For any disjunctive program P,*

$$WFDS(P) = U\text{-}WFS(P).$$

Theorem 6 provides further evidence for suitability of WFDS (equivalently, D-WFS*) as the intended well-founded semantics for disjunctive logic programs.

By the following lemma, we can directly prove Theorem 6.

Lemma 4. *Let P be a disjunctive program. Then $W_k = S_k$ for any $k \geq 0$.*

This lemma also reveals a kind of correspondence between the well-founded disjunctive hypotheses and the unfounded sets.

7   Conclusion

In this paper we have investigated recent approaches to defining well-founded semantics for disjunctive logic programs. We first provided a minor modification of the argumentative semantics WFDS defined in [13]. Based on some intuitive program transformations, we proposed an extension to the D-WFS in [2]. In our approach, we introduce a new program transformation called Head reduction. This transformation plays a similar role in DLP as the GCWA [9] in positive DLP. We have also given a new definition of the unfounded sets for disjunctive programs, which is a generalization of the unfounded sets investigated by [7,5]. This new notion of unfounded sets fully takes disjunctive information into consideration and provides another characterization for disjunctive well-founded semantics. The main contribution of this paper is the equivalence of U-WFS, D-WFS and WFDS. We have also provided a bottom-up computation for our semantics. A top-down procedure is presented in [14], which is sound and complete with respect to our semantics. These results show that there exists a disjunctive well-founded semantics which can be characterized in terms of argumentation, program transformations, unfounded sets and resolution. The fact that different starting points lead to the same semantics provides strong support for WFDS. Future work will concentrate on more efficient algorithms and applications.

Acknowledgments

The author would like to thank Philippe Besnard, James Delgrande, Thomas Linke and Torsten Schaub for helpful comments on this work. This work was supported by DFG under grant FOR 375/1-1, TP C and NSFC under grant 69883008.

References

1. S. Brass, J. Dix. Characterizations of the Disjunctive Well-founded Semantics: Confluent Calculi and Iterated GCWA. *Journal of Automated Reasoning*, 20(1):143–165, 1998. 133
2. S. Brass, J. Dix. Semantics of disjunctive logic programs based on partial evaluation. *Journal of Logic programming*, 38(3):167-312, 1999. 133, 135, 138, 139, 140, 141, 143, 145
3. S. Brass, J. Dix, I. Niemelä, T. Przymusinski. On the equivalence of the Static and Disjunctive Well-founded Semantics and its computation. *Theoretical Computer Science*, 258(1-2): 523-553, 2001. 134, 140
4. F. Bry. Negation in logic programming: A formalization in constructive logic. In: D. Karagiannis ed. *Information Systems and Artificial Intelligence: Integration Aspects (LNCS 474)*, Springer, pages 30-46, 1990. 141
5. T. Eiter, N. Leone and D. Sacca. On the partial semantics for disjunctive deductive databases. *Annals of Math. and AI.*, 19(1-2): 59-96, 1997. 134, 143, 144, 145
6. M. Gelfond, V. Lifschitz. The stable model semantics for logic programming. In: *Proceedings of the 5th Symposium on Logic Programming*, MIT Press, pages 1070-1080, 1988. 133, 136
7. N. Leone, P. Rullo and F. Scarcello. Disjunctive stable models: unfounded sets, fixpoint semantics, and computation. *Information and Computation*, 135(2): 69-112, 1997. 134, 143, 144, 145
8. J. Lobo, J. Minker and A. Rajasekar. *Foundations of Disjunctive Logic Programming*. MIT Press, 1992. 133, 134
9. J. Minker. On indefinite databases and the closed world assumption. LNCS 138, pages 292-308, 1982. 134, 138, 145
10. T. Przymusinski. Static semantics of logic programs. *Annals of Math. and AI.*, 14: 323-357, 1995. 133
11. K. Ross. A procedural semantics for well-founded negation in logic programs. *Journal of Logic programming*, 13(1): 1-22, 1992. 134
12. A. Van Gelder, K. A. Ross and J. Schlipf. The well-founded semantics for general logic programs. *J. ACM*, 38(3): 620-650, 1991. 133, 134, 143
13. K. Wang. Argumentation-based abduction in disjunctive logic programming. *Journal of Logic programming*, 45(1-3): 105-141, 2000. 133, 134, 136, 140, 145
14. K. Wang. A top-down procedure for disjunctive well-founded semantics. In: *Proceedings of the International Joint Conference on Automated Reasoning (IJCAR'01)*, Springer, 2001. 134, 145
15. J. You, L. Yuan and R. Goebel. An abductive approach to disjunctive logic programming. *Journal of Logic programming*, 44(1-3): 101-127, 2000. 136

Reasoning with Open Logic Programs

Piero A. Bonatti

Dipartimento di Tecnologie dell'Informazione
Università di Milano
bonatti@dti.unimi.it

Abstract. This paper motivates and introduces entailment problems over nonmonotonic theories some of whose predicates—called *open predicates*—are not (completely) specified. More precisely, we are interested in those inferences that hold for some or all possible axiomatizations of the open predicates. Since a complete specification of an open predicate may model incomplete knowledge about the world, this kind of inference should distinguish missing object-level knowledge from missing parts of the specification, and restrict nonmonotonic inference accordingly. We formalize some interesting forms of such *open entailment* problems, and provide formal proof techniques for some of them in a logic programming framework.

1 Introduction

In this paper we tackle the problem of deciding whether a given formula is entailed by a nonmonotonic theory which has not been completely specified. The motivation for this work stems from several applications areas, including the following:

- *Agent programs verification.* Given a logic-based agent—such as an IMPACT agent [13]—it may be necessary to verify its correct behavior by proving that certain actions will never be executed, or that some action will surely be taken under given circumstances. The agent's actions are determined by entailment from a logic program whose details cannot be fully specified at verification time (e.g., the precise definition of the agent's beliefs and goals would most likely be unavailable).
- *Reasoning about actions and change* when the effects of some actions, or the causal links between certain fluents, have not been specified (e.g., because they have not yet been identified).
- *Security policy verification.* Security policies are often modelled and specified by means of nonmonotonic theories, either directly [14,12] or indirectly, by translating the specifications into logic programs with negation [2,4]. Part of the security policy may be unknown [4], e.g., because it is to be decided by a different organization, or because it is subject to changes. Thus, some of the predicates in the corresponding logic program are undefined at policy design time. Policies should be verified by proving that certain authorizations will/will not be granted (i.e., certain atoms will/will not be derivable), no matter how the missing details are filled in (see [4] for further details).

T. Eiter, W. Faber, and M. Truszczyński (Eds.): LPNMR 2001, LNAI 2173, pp. 147–159, 2001.
© Springer-Verlag Berlin Heidelberg 2001

In all these examples, standard nonmonotonic semantics would treat missing predicates as if they were false for all arguments. Clearly, this is not appropriate for the above reasoning tasks. One should rather consider all the possible complete definitions of those predicates. More generally, if a predicate is partially specified, all the complete definitions compatible with the available details should be considered. In classical logic, this would be equivalent to proving that a certain formula is a logical consequence of the incomplete specification. In a nonmonotonic setting, we must identify hybrid inference mechanisms, that lie somewhere in between classical and nonmonotonic deduction. In particular, negation as failure should *not* be applied to any predicate whose definition is not complete.

We start a formal investigation of these aspects by focussing on normal logic programs under the stable model semantics (that underlies—more or less explicitly—all the aforementioned verification problems). Using existing terminology [6], by *open program* we mean a normal logic program whose domain and predicates are not completely specified. Section 3 formalizes open programs and some related, interesting inference problems. Section 4 introduces provably sound and complete techniques for solving some of those problems, under suitable assumptions. These techniques are based on the skeptical resolution calculus—that can handle open domains—which is recalled in Section 2. Section 6 concludes the paper with a list of interesting open problems and some related work.

2   Preliminaries

We assume the reader to be familiar with the standard notation and results on logic programming [10] and the stable model semantics [8].

Let metavariable P range over normal logic programs, and let $\mathsf{Ground}(P)$ denote the ground instantiation of P. We recall that a *support* of a ground atom A from P is a set of negative literals obtained by recursively unfolding A and its positive subgoals in $\mathsf{Ground}(P)$, until only negative literals are left.

In the main part of the paper, the skeptical resolution calculus introduced in [3] will be adapted to open entailment. In the rest of this section we recall the basic definitions.

A *ground countersupport* for a ground atom A from P is a set of positive literals K such that:

1. each $B \in K$ is the complement of some literal belonging to a support of A from P;
2. conversely, each support of A from P contains a literal whose complement is in K.

A (nonground) *countersupport* of an arbitrary atom A from P is a pair $\langle K, \theta \rangle$ such that for all ground instances $A\theta\sigma$, $K\sigma$ is a ground countersupport of $A\theta\sigma$.

The skeptical resolution calculus is formulated independently of any specific mechanism for computing negation as failure. Such mechanism is abstracted by a function CounterSupp that maps each atom A onto a (possibly empty) set of nonground countersupports for A.

Let P be an arbitrary given program. A *(simple) goal* is a finite sequence of literals. A *goal with hypotheses* (*h-goal* for short) is a pair $(G \mid H)$, where G is a simple goal and H is a multiset of (positive or negative) literals called *hypotheses*. Roughly speaking, the answer to a query $(G \mid H)$ should be *yes* if G holds in all the stable models that satisfy H. Finally, a *skeptical goal* (*s-goal* for short) is a finite sequence of h-goals; the empty sequence is denoted by $\square$.

A *skeptical derivation from P and* CounterSupp *with restart goal G_0* is a (possibly infinite) sequence of s-goals $\mathcal{G}_0, \mathcal{G}_1, \ldots$, where each $\mathcal{G}_{i+1}$ is obtained from $\mathcal{G}_i$ through one of the following rewrite rules (Γ and Δ are sequences of h-goals).[1]

Resolution. This rule may take two forms; a literal can be unified with either a program rule or a hypothesis. First suppose that L_i is an atom, $A \leftarrow B_1, \ldots, B_k$ is a standardized apart variant of a rule of P, and θ is the *mgu* of L_i and A. Then the following is an instance of the rule.

$$\frac{\Gamma \ (L_1 \ldots L_{i-1}, L_i, L_{i+1} \ldots L_n \mid H) \ \Delta}{[\Gamma \ (L_1 \ldots L_{i-1}, B_1, \ldots, B_k, L_{i+1} \ldots L_n \mid H) \ \Delta] \theta} .$$

Secondly, let L_i be a (possibly negative) literal, let L' be a hypothesis, and let θ be the *mgu* of L_i and L'. Then the following is an instance of the rule.

$$\frac{\Gamma \ (L_1 \ldots L_{i-1}, L_i, L_{i+1} \ldots L_n \mid H, L') \ \Delta}{[\Gamma \ (L_1 \ldots L_{i-1}, L_{i+1} \ldots L_n \mid H, L') \ \Delta] \theta} .$$

Failure. Suppose that $L_i = \neg A$, and $\langle \{B_1, \ldots, B_k\}, \theta \rangle \in$ CounterSupp(A). Then the following is an instance of the Failure rule.

$$\frac{\Gamma \ (L_1 \ldots L_{i-1}, L_i, L_{i+1} \ldots L_n \mid H) \ \Delta}{[\Gamma \ (L_1 \ldots L_{i-1}, B_1, \ldots, B_k, L_{i+1} \ldots L_n \mid H) \ \Delta] \theta} .$$

Contradiction. This rule tries to prove $(G \mid H)$ by showing that H cannot be satisfied by any stable model of P.

$$\frac{\Gamma \ (G \mid H, L) \ \Delta}{\Gamma \ (\bar{L} \mid H, L) \ \Delta} .$$

Split. Essentially, this rule is needed to compute floating conclusions and discover contradictions. It splits the search space by introducing a new hypothesis. Let G_0 be the restart goal, L be an arbitrary literal and σ be the composition of the *mgus* previously computed during the derivation; the Split rule is:

$$\frac{\Gamma \ (G \mid H) \ \Delta}{\Gamma \ (G \mid H, L) \ (G_0\sigma \mid H, \bar{L}) \ \Delta} .$$

The h-goals $(G \mid H, L)$ and $(G_0\sigma \mid H, \bar{L})$ are called *restart h-goals*.

---

[1] The restart goal G_0 will be needed in the Splitting rule below.

Success.

$$\frac{\Gamma \ (\square \mid H) \ \Delta}{\Gamma \ \Delta} \ .$$

A skeptical derivation is *successful* if the last s-goal is $\square$; in this case we say that the first s-goal $\mathcal{G}_0$ has a successful skeptical derivation from P. As usual, the composition of the *mgus* computed during the derivation, restricted to the variables of $\mathcal{G}_0$, is called *answer substitution*. Skeptical resolution is sound and complete w.r.t. the skeptical stable model semantics, under a completeness assumption over CounterSupp (see [3] for further details).

There exist derivation strategies that restrict the application of the split rule. Such strategies are strictly goal-directed for call-consistent programs. A prototype implementation based on a semi-naive metainterpreter has been implemented in XSB Prolog (http://xsb.sourceforge.net). (Further details can be found in the journal version of [3].)

3   Open Programs and Open Entailment

In order to avoid ill-formed, possibly paradoxical definitions, assume two fixed, infinite sets of function and predicate symbols are given, and denote them with Func and Pred, respectively (as usual, constant symbols are identified with 0-ary functions). Moreover, let Var be an infinite set of variable symbols (following Prolog's conventions, they will be denoted with uppercase letters). ¿From now on, we shall consider only normal logic programs built from these sets (when we write "for all programs" or "there exists a program" we implicitly restrict the quantification accordingly).

Intuitively, an open program is a partially specified program P. Some predicates, called "open predicates", are not completely specified in P, in the sense that their definition might be completely missing, or it might contain only some of the rules that define the predicate. The set of open predicates will be identified with a set of symbols $O \subseteq$ Pred. Moreover, the missing clauses might contain function symbols that do not appear in P. Such symbols are listed in a set $F \subseteq$ Func.

Definition 1 (Open program). *An* open program *is a triple* $\langle\, P, F, O\,\rangle$ *where* P *is a normal logic program,* $F \subset$ Func, *and* $O \subset$ Pred. *The symbols in* F *should not occur in* P *(while the symbols in* O *may occur in* P).

For any given open program $\langle\, P, F, O\,\rangle$, an *open atom* (resp. literal) is any atom (resp. literal) whose predicate belongs to O.

The next definition models all the possible ways of filling in the missing details of an open program.

Definition 2 (Open program completions). *Let* $\Omega = \langle\, P, F, O\,\rangle$ *be an open program. A normal program* P' *is a* completion[2] *of* Ω *if the following conditions hold:*

---

[2] The word "completion", referred to normal programs, traditionally denotes Clark's completion [10]. Unfortunately, the author could not find any suggestive alternative.

1. $P' \supseteq P$;
2. the function symbols occurring in P' but not in P belong to F;
3. for all $r \in P' \setminus P$, the predicate symbol in the head of r belongs to O.

The set of all possible completions of Ω will be denoted by $\mathsf{Comp}(\Omega)$ or, equivalently, by $\mathsf{Comp}(P, F, O)$.

Example 3. Consider an open program Ω with

$$P = \{p(a, X) \leftarrow \neg q(X)\},$$
$$F = \{b\},$$
$$O = \{q\}.$$

Some of the completions in $\mathsf{Comp}(\Omega)$ are:

$$P_1 = P \cup \{q(a)\},$$
$$P_2 = P \cup \{q(b)\},$$
$$P_3 = P \cup \{q(X) \leftarrow \neg p(X, Y)\},$$
$$P_4 = P \cup \{q(b) \leftarrow \neg q(b)\}.$$

These programs differ in many respects. The Herbrand domain of P_1 and P_3 coincides with the domain of P, while the domain of P_2 and P_4 is extended with b. Programs P_1 and P_2 are stratified while P_3 and P_4 are not. Program P_3 has two stable models, while P_4 has no stable models.   □

In the context of a given open program $\langle P, F, O \rangle$, a ground literal is a variable-free literal belonging to the language of some $P' \in \mathsf{Comp}(P, F, O)$—or, equivalently, any ground literal built with the symbols occurring in P, F and O.

We are ready to formalize entailment from open programs. In the following, by *consistent program* we mean a normal logic program with at least one stable model.

Definition 4 (Open inference). *For all open programs $\Omega = \langle P, F, O \rangle$ and all first-order sentences Ψ,*

1. *(Credulous open inference) $\Omega \models^c \Psi$ iff for some $P' \in \mathsf{Comp}(\Omega)$, P' credulously entails Ψ.*
2. *(Skeptical open inference) $\Omega \models^s \Psi$ iff for all $P' \in \mathsf{Comp}(\Omega)$, P' skeptically entails Ψ.*
3. *(Mixed open inference I) $\Omega \models^{cs} \Psi$ iff for some consistent $P' \in \mathsf{Comp}(\Omega)$, P' skeptically entails Ψ.*
4. *(Mixed open inference II) $\Omega \models^{sc} \Psi$ iff for all consistent $P' \in \mathsf{Comp}(\Omega)$, P' credulously entails Ψ.*

Note that without the consistency requirement on P', mixed open inference would be trivial in most cases. It is often possible to build a pathological rule

$p(a) \leftarrow \neg p(a)$ from the symbols in F and O, and obtain an inconsistent $P' \in$ Comp(Ω). Then (without the consistency requirement) for *all* sentences Ψ we would have $\Omega \models^{cs} \Psi$ and $\Omega \not\models^{sc} \Psi$.

The four forms of open entailment combine two aspects:

– The quantification on P' captures the kind of property to be verified. We may be interested either in proving that in some case something happens (e.g., if open predicates are completed in certain ways, then the program may do errors) or that in all cases some property is guaranteed (e.g., the program will always operate correctly, no matter how missing details are fixed).
– Credulous and skeptical stable model semantics are the two basic semantics available at the underlying application level.

Example 5. Consider the open program and the completions illustrated in Example 3. Since $p(a, a)$ is true in the unique stable model of P_2, then we have both $\Omega \models^c p(a, a)$ and $\Omega \models^{cs} p(a, a)$. However, $p(a, a)$ is not in the stable model of P_1, so $\Omega \not\models^s p(a, a)$. The sentence $q(a)$ is skeptically entailed by P_1 and P_3, but not by P_2 (P_4 is ignored because it is inconsistent), so $\Omega \not\models^{sc} q(a)$.   □

When Ω is not intrinsically inconsistent, then the four kinds of entailment can be compared as stated by the next proposition.

Proposition 6. *Suppose there exists a consistent $P' \in$ Comp(Ω). Then, for all sentences Ψ,*

1. *$\Omega \models^s \Psi$ implies $\Omega \models^{cs} \Psi$ and $\Omega \models^{sc} \Psi$;*
2. *$\Omega \models^{cs} \Psi$ implies $\Omega \models^c \Psi$;*
3. *$\Omega \models^{sc} \Psi$ implies $\Omega \models^c \Psi$.*

Thus, we get a lattice of entailment relations, where skeptical open entailment is the strongest and credulous open entailment the weakest.

There is also a duality between pairs of entailments, which is helpful, as the four inference problems can be reduced to only two problems.

Proposition 7. *For all open programs Ω and all sentences Ψ,*

1. *$\Omega \models^c \Psi$ iff $\Omega \not\models^s \neg\Psi$;*
2. *$\Omega \models^{sc} \Psi$ iff $\Omega \not\models^{cs} \neg\Psi$.*

Therefore, in the following we shall focus on $\models^s$ and $\models^{cs}$. They are based on skeptical inference, that—unlike credulous approaches—does not need the program to be instantiated before reasoning. Since, in general, the set of terms is not exactly specified, such instantiation may be expensive or even impossible (e.g., theoretically speaking, in the security policy verification problem the set of constants has no fixed a priori bound, as constants correspond to user names and data objects; in practice, their number is only bounded by operating system limitations, and is considerably high). Currently, it is not clear to what extent credulous approaches to open entailment are feasible.

4   Approaches to Skeptical Open Entailment

The skeptical resolution calculus can be adapted to open entailment by a few modifications. Some of them essentially state that open literals (both positive and negative ones) should be treated like negative literals.

Accordingly, an open program $\langle P, F, O \rangle$ is *range restricted* if each variable occurring within an open or negative literal in the body of a rule $r \in P$, occurs either in the head of r or in a positive, non-open literal of r.

Moreover, an *open support* for a ground atom A w.r.t. an open program $\Omega = \langle P, F, O \rangle$ and $P' \in \mathsf{Comp}(\Omega)$, is a goal G obtained by unfolding A in $\mathsf{Ground}(P')$, until all the literals in G are either open or negative.

A *ground open countersupport* for A w.r.t. Ω and P' is a set of ground literals K such that

1. each $L \in K$ is the complement of some literal belonging to an open support of A w.r.t. Ω and P';
2. conversely, each open support of A w.r.t. Ω and P' contains a literal whose complement is in K.

In the open setting, the Failure rule should work no matter how the Herbrand domain can be extended. This requirement leads to the following definitions.

Let a P'-*substitution* be a substitution whose range is contained in the language of P'.

A (non-ground) *open countersupport* of an arbitrary atom A w.r.t. $\Omega = \langle P, F, O \rangle$ is a pair $\langle K, \theta \rangle$, where θ is a P-substitution, such that for all $P' \in \mathsf{Comp}(\Omega)$ and all grounding P'-substitutions σ, $K\sigma$ is a ground open countersupport for $A\theta\sigma$ w.r.t. Ω and P'.

Example 8. Consider again the open program of Example 3. Atom $p(a, b)$ has one open support, $\neg q(b)$, and a ground open countersupport $q(b)$ (w.r.t. P_2 and P_4). Moreover, $p(Y, X)$ has a nonground countersupport $\langle \{q(X)\}, \{Y = a\} \rangle$ (according to the intuition that $p(a, X)$ is false whenever $q(X)$ is true).   □

Example 9. In [4], an identically empty (or inconsistent) policy template is presented as an example of verification of partially specified policies. The corresponding open program (where irrelevant details have been simplified away) has the following structure:

$$P = \{p_1(X) \leftarrow p_2(X), \neg r(X),$$
$$p_1(X) \leftarrow p_3(X), r(X),$$
$$p_2(X) \leftarrow q(X), r(X),$$
$$p_3(X) \leftarrow q(X), \neg r(X)\},$$
$$F = \text{an infinite set of identifiers},$$
$$O = \{q, r\}.$$

The atom $p_1(X)$ has the following open countersupports, where ϵ denotes the empty substitution:

$$\langle \{\neg q(X)\}, \epsilon \rangle, \quad \langle \{r(X)\}, \epsilon \rangle, \quad \langle \{\neg r(X)\}, \epsilon \rangle.$$

Note that countersupports may contain negative literals, because open atoms are treated like negative literals during open support computation.   □

In the rest of the paper, we assume a function $\mathsf{CounterSupp}_\Omega$ that maps each atom A onto a (possibly empty) set of (non-ground) open countersupports for A w.r.t. Ω. By analogy with the original skeptical resolution calculus, $\mathsf{CounterSupp}_\Omega$ is an abstract model of the actual implementation of negation as failure (possibly including issues related to loop-checking, or tabulation and delay), largely independent of particular implementation choices (cf. [3]).

Definition 10 (OSK-Derivations). *An open skeptical derivation from $\Omega = \langle P, F, O \rangle$ (OSK-derivation, for short) is a skeptical derivation from P where the Failure rule is based upon $\mathsf{CounterSupp}_\Omega$, and is never applied to any open atom.*

Example 11. Consider again the open program and the open countersupports illustrated in Example 9. The following is a formalized version of the proof that the partially specified policy is inconsistent.

$$
\begin{array}{ll}
(\neg p_1(X) \mid \ ) & \text{Failure, using } \langle \{r(X)\}, \epsilon \rangle \\
(r(X) \mid \ ) & \text{Split} \\
(r(X) \mid r(X)) \ (\neg p_1(X) \mid \neg r(X)) & \text{Resol. with hyp.} \\
(\Box \mid r(X)) \ (\neg p_1(X) \mid \neg r(X)) & \text{Success} \\
(\neg p_1(X) \mid \neg r(X)) & \text{Failure, using } \langle \{\neg r(X)\}, \epsilon \rangle \\
(\neg r(X) \mid \neg r(X)) & \text{Resol. with hyp.} \\
(\Box \mid \neg r(X)) & \text{Success} \\
\Box
\end{array}
$$

The answer substitution is empty, which means that $\Omega \models^s \forall X. \neg p(X)$ (cf. Theorem 13 below).

Note the mix of negation as failure (Failure rules and countersupports) and "classical" reasoning by cases (Split rule), that considers the possible values that $r(X)$ may take in different completions.

Space limitations do not allow more complex examples. Interested readers can find a complex policy for a hospital in [4], together with the translation into logic programs and a clear indication of what predicates are to be left open. Several policy verification proofs are included. They are all open skeptical entailment problems.   □

The completeness of open skeptical derivations w.r.t. open entailment depends on the completeness of $\mathsf{CounterSupp}_\Omega$.

Definition 12. *$\mathsf{CounterSupp}_\Omega$ is complete (w.r.t. Ω) if for all ground atoms $A\gamma$ and all ground open countersupports K for $A\gamma$ (w.r.t. Ω and some $P' \in \mathsf{Comp}(\Omega)$) there exist an open countersupport $\langle K', \theta \rangle \in \mathsf{CounterSupp}_\Omega(A)$ and a substitution σ such that $A\theta\sigma = A\gamma$ and $K'\sigma = K$.*

The following theorem states that open skeptical resolution is sound and complete for open skeptical entailment. Note that the initial goal G is restricted to the language of P. The other goals cannot be inferred with open skeptical inference, but resolution would not treat them properly. For example, from $P = \{p(X)\}$ one could erroneously derive all goals $p(a)$ such that $a \in F$.

Theorem 13. *Let G be a simple goal whose symbols occur in P. If G has a successful OSK-derivation from Ω with answer substitution θ, then $\Omega \models^s \forall G\theta$. Conversely, if $\mathsf{CounterSupp}_\Omega$ is complete and $\Omega \models^s G\sigma$ for some grounding σ, then G has a successful OSK-derivation from Ω with answer substitution θ more general than σ.*

In general, implementing a complete function $\mathsf{CounterSupp}_\Omega$ is a nontrivial (and sometimes impossible) task, and an extensive investigation of this issue must be deferred to an extended version of the paper. However, we have identified two interesting special cases where completeness can be easily achieved:

- If $F = \emptyset$ (i.e., the Herbrand domain is completely specified), then computing open countersupports is not harder than computing standard countersupports from a normal program. Open supports can be obtained by unfolding the given atom A in $\mathsf{Ground}(P)$ until all the literals are either open or negative. Ground countersupports can then be obtained by collecting one literal from each support and negating it. This basic approach can be optimized in various ways, reducing redundancy, deriving nonground countersupports, etc.
- Suppose $\langle P, F, O \rangle$ is range restricted and *generic*,[3] that is, the terms occurring in P are all variables. (This is precisely the kind of programs we are using to verify the policy templates introduced in [4], cf. Example 9.) Then the countersupport construction illustrated in the previous point can be carried out from P rather than $\mathsf{Ground}(P)$, and yields a provably complete function $\mathsf{CounterSupp}_\Omega$.

Example 14. As an example of nonempty open predicate specifications, consider an open program Ω modelling reachability in a directed graph:

$$P = \{e(X, v) \leftarrow \neg e(v, X), \tag{1}$$
$$l(X, Y) \leftarrow e(X, Y), \tag{2}$$
$$l(X, Y) \leftarrow e(Y, X), \tag{3}$$
$$r(X, X), \tag{4}$$
$$r(X, Y) \leftarrow l(X, Z), r(Z, Y)\}, \tag{5}$$
$$F = \text{an infinite set of identifiers, not including } v,$$
$$O = \{e\}.$$

The graph's edges are specified by the open predicate e. All we know about the graph is that it has a star-shaped subgraph with central node v, which is directly connected to each other node X either by an edge (v, X) or by (X, v). The other predicates model graph connectivity regardless of the edges' direction. Predicate

---

[3] We borrow this term from the theory of database queries.

$l(X, Y)$ holds if there is an edge between X and Y, in some direction. Predicate r is the reflective and transitive closure of l. We can prove that the graph is strongly connected (in all completions) by carrying out a successful OSK-derivation for $r(X, Y)$ with empty answer substitution (which means $\Omega \models^s \forall X.\forall Y.r(X, Y)$). The derivation is the following:

$(r(X, Y) \mid \ )$	Resolution with (5)
$(l(X, Z), r(Z, Y) \mid \ )$	Resolution with (2)
$(e(X, Z), r(Z, Y) \mid \ )$	Split
$(e(X, Z), r(Z, Y) \mid e(X, Z))\ (r(X, Y) \mid \neg e(X, Z))$	Resolution with hyp.
$(r(Z, Y) \mid e(X, Z))\ (r(X, Y) \mid \neg e(X, Z))$	Resolution with (4) $(Z = Y)$
$(\Box \mid e(X, Y))\ (r(X, Y) \mid \neg e(X, Y))$	Success
$(r(X, Y) \mid \neg e(X, Y))$	Resolution with (5)
$(l(X, Z'), r(Z', Y) \mid \neg e(X, Y))$	Resolution with (3)
$(e(Z', X), r(Z', Y) \mid \neg e(X, Y))$	Resolution with (1)
$(\neg e(X, Z'), r(Z', Y) \mid \neg e(X, Y))$	Resolution with hyp. $(Z' = Y)$
$(r(Y, Y) \mid \neg e(X, Y))$	Resolution with (4)
$(\Box \mid \neg e(X, Y))$	Success
$\Box$	

$\Box$

5   Restricted Mixed Open Inference of Type I

A general approach to mixed inference is still an open problem. In this paper we sketch a preliminary approach that applies to completely undefined open predicates and unbounded domains. More precisely, in the context of an open program $\langle P, F, O \rangle$, we assume that the predicates in O do not occur in the head of any rule of P, and F is infinite.

The ground open resolution calculus should be extended with a new rule, called *abduction rule*:

$$\frac{(G_1 \mid H_1) \ldots (G_{j-1} \mid H_{j-1})(G', L, G'' \mid H_j)(G_{j+1} \mid H_{j+1}) \ldots (G_n \mid H_n)}{(G_1 \mid L, H_1) \ldots (G_{j-1} \mid L, H_{j-1})(G', G'' \mid L, H_j)(G_{j+1} \mid L, H_{j+1}) \ldots (G_n \mid L, H_n)}$$

where the predicate in L belongs to O, and under the restriction that each $\{L, H_i\}$ must be consistent $(1 \leq i \leq n)$. Intuitively, open predicates can be abduced as needed to complete the derivation.

Simple mixed derivations extend OSK-derivations with zero or more instances of the abduction rule.

Definition 15. Simple mixed derivations *(SM-derivations, for short) are recursively defined as follows:*

- *An OSK-derivation is an SM-derivation.*
- *If $\mathcal{G}_0, \ldots, \mathcal{G}_n$ is an SM-derivation and $\frac{\mathcal{G}_n}{\mathcal{G}_{n+1}}$ is an instance of the abduction rule, then $\mathcal{G}_0, \ldots, \mathcal{G}_{n+1}$ is an SM-derivation.*

The following theorem states that SM-derivations are sound and complete under the restrictions stated at the beginning of this section, and the further assumption that P is call-consistent.

Theorem 16. *Let $\Omega = \langle P, F, O \rangle$, where P is call-consistent, F is infinite and the predicates in O do not occur in the head of any rule of P. Let G be any ground simple goal. If G has a successful, ground SM-derivation then $\Omega \models^{cs} G$. Conversely, if CounterSupp$_\Omega$ is complete and $\Omega \models^{cs} G$, then G has a successful, ground SM-derivation.*

Example 17. Let Ω be defined as follows:

$$
\begin{aligned}
P &= \{p(X) \leftarrow \neg q(X), r(X), \\
&\qquad q(X) \leftarrow \neg p(X)\}, \\
F &= \{a, b\}, \\
O &= \{r\}.
\end{aligned}
$$

All the completions entailing $\neg r(a)$ entail also $q(a)$. Accordingly, there exists the following ground SM-derivation:

$$
\begin{array}{lll}
(q(a) \mid \ ) & \text{Resolution with } q(X) \leftarrow \neg p(X) \\
(\neg p(a) \mid \ ) & \text{Failure with } \langle \{\neg r(a)\}, \epsilon \rangle \\
(\neg r(a) \mid \ ) & \text{Abduction rule} \\
(\Box \mid \neg r(a)) & \text{Success} \\
\qquad \Box
\end{array}
$$

$\Box$

It should be possible to remove the restriction to ground derivations by keeping all the goals with hypotheses of the form $(\Box \mid H)$ in the derivation (e.g., by "turning off" the Success rule), and performing a final check that all such H can be instantiated to consistent sets of hypotheses using the symbols in F.

Example 18. A nonground version of the derivation illustrated in the previous example, starting with $(q(X) \mid \ )$, would terminate with the goal $(\Box \mid \neg r(X))$. Clearly, the hypothesis $\neg r(X)$ can be consistently instantiated using the constants in F. $\Box$

Example 19. Let $P = \{p(a) \leftarrow q(X), \neg q(a)\}$ and $O = \{q\}$. Consider the SM-derivation

$$
\begin{array}{ll}
(p(a) \mid \ ) & \text{Resolution with } p(a) \leftarrow q(X), \neg q(a) \\
(q(X), \neg q(a) \mid \ ) & \text{Abduction rule} \\
(\neg q(a) \mid q(X)) & \text{Abduction rule} \\
(\Box \mid q(X), \neg q(a)) & \text{Success} \\
\qquad \Box
\end{array}
$$

We have $\Omega \models^{cs} p(a)$ iff F is not empty. Accordingly, the final hypotheses $q(X), \neg q(a)$ can be instantiated to a consistent set iff $F \neq \emptyset$. $\Box$

Similarly, it should be possible to remove the restriction to completely undefined open predicates by closing the hypotheses H under the partial definitions of open programs during the final check.

The final check is in fact a particular *constraint satisfaction problem*. Detailed solutions to this problem are interesting subjects for further research.

6   Final Discussion and Related Work

The definitions of open programs and open entailment can be immediately extended from logic programs to all nonmonotonic logics. On the contrary, the proof techniques based on skeptical resolution are tailored to logic programs. For a more general approach, other calculi (and extensions thereof) should be considered (e.g., [1,5,11]).

At the current stage of investigation, we see no appealing way of approaching open entailment with credulous engines or calculi, because these techniques need to instantiate the theory. This is in contrast with the need of handling (possibly unbounded) open domains. On closed domains, we are planning an experimental comparison of credulous and skeptical approaches. The latter might be more efficient on open programs due to their goal-directed nature, that might focus proof efforts on relevant completions.

The theoretical investigation of open programs and entailment is still in a very early stage, and many interesting questions are to be answered. More work is needed to obtain more general solutions to the entailment problems. Important (and partially related) issues such as the computational complexity of open entailment, expressiveness (i.e., which classes of properties can be checked via open entailment and skeptical resolution), syntactic restrictions on completions (e.g., restricting completions to stratified programs) have not yet been explored.

Moreover, there is some interesting related literature whose relationships with our work have not yet been investigated.

In [9], a semantic approach to reasoning with open domains was introduced. In the most optimistic perspective, open skeptical resolution might eventually be adapted to reason with the programs introduced in [9]. Another approach compatible with open domains can be found in [11]. Both works support first-order quantification.

The original notion of open programs (e.g., [6]) adopted a fixed underlying universe and was introduced for characterizing a compositional semantics for logic programs. Some of those results could be of use for understanding inherent limitations of open entailment.

Later on [7] the term "open logic program" has been used in a framework for integrating logic programming and classical first-order logic. There, open predicates are those defined by a classical first-order theory. The alphabet is fixed.

Acknowledgements

The work reported in this paper was partially supported by the European Community within the Fifth (EC) Framework Programme under contract IST-1999-11791 – FASTER project.

References

1. G. Amati, L. Carlucci Aiello, D. Gabbay, and F. Pirri. A proof theoretical approach to default reasoning I: tableaux for default logic. *J. Logic and Comput. 6*, 2, 205–231. 158
2. E. Bertino, C. Bettini, E. Ferrari and P. Samarati. A temporal access control mechanism for database systems. *IEEE Trans. on Knowledge and Data Engineering*, 8(1):67–80, 1996. 147
3. P. A. Bonatti. Resolution for skeptical stable semantics. *Journal of Automated Reasoning*. To appear. Preliminary version in Proc. of LPNMR'97, LNAI 1265, Springer Verlag, 1997. 148, 150, 154
4. P. A. Bonatti, S. De Capitani Di Vimercate, P. Samarati. An algebra for composing access control policies. *ACM Transactions on Information and System Security, 5(1), 2002*, to appear. Preliminary version in Proc. of the 7th ACM Conference on Computer and Communication Security, CCS'2000, Atene, 2000. 147, 153, 154, 155
5. P. A. Bonatti, N. Olivetti. Sequent calculi for propositional nonmonotonic logics. *ACM Transactions on Computational Logic*, to appear. Electronic version available at http://www.acm.org/tocl/accepted.html 158
6. A. Bossi, M. Gabbrielli, G. Levi, and M. C. Meo. Contributions to the Semantics of Open Logic Programs. In *Proc. of the International Conference on Fifth Generation Computer Systems 1992*, 570–580, 1992. 148, 158
7. M. Denecker. A Terminological Interpretation of (Abductive) Logic Programming, *Proc. of LPNMR95*, Springer, 1995. 158
8. M. Gelfond, V. Lifschitz. The stable model semantics for logic programming. In *Proc. of the 5th ICLP*, pp.1070-1080, MIT Press, 1988. 148
9. M. Gelfond, H. Przymusinska, "Reasoning in Open Domains", In *Logic Programming and Nonmonotonic Reasoning*, 397–413, MIT press, 1993. 158
10. J. Lloyd. *Foundations of logic programming*. Springer-Verlag, 1984. 148, 150
11. R. Rosati. Towards first-order nonmonotonic reasoning. In *Proc. of LPNMR'99*, LNAI 1730, 332–346, Springer Verlag, Berlin, 1999. 158
12. P. Samarati S. Jajodia and V. S. Subrahmanian. A logical language for expressing authorizations. In *Proc. IEEE Symp. on Security and Privacy*, pages 94–107, Oakland, CA, 1997. 147
13. V. S. Subrahmanian, P. A. Bonatti, J. Dix, T. Eiter, S. Kraus, F. Ozcan, R. Ross. *Heterogeneous Active Agents*. MIT Press, 2000. 147
14. T. Y. C. Woo and S. S. Lam. Authorizations in distributed systems: A new approach. *Journal of Computer Security*, 2(2,3), 1993. 147

Representation of Incomplete Knowledge by Induction of Default Theories

Pascal Nicolas and Béatrice Duval

LERIA – University of Angers – France
2, boulevard Lavoisier, F-49045 Angers Cedex 01
{pascal.nicolas|beatrice.duval}@univ-angers.fr

Abstract. We present a method to learn simultaneously definitions for a concept and its negation. This problem is relevant when we have to deal with a complex domain where it is difficult to acquire a complete theory and where we have to reason from incomplete knowledge. We use default logic to represent such incomplete theories. This paper specifies the problem of learning a default theory from a set of examples and a background knowledge. We propose an operational method to inductively construct such a theory. Our learning process relies on a generalization mechanism defined in the field of Inductive Logic Programming. We first consider the case where the initial knowledge is sure because it contains only ground facts. Then, we extend the framework to the case where the initial knowledge is a default theory.

1 Introduction

We present here a method that enables to construct a default theory from a set of positive and negative examples and an initial background knowledge. The learning process that we propose is strongly related to research realized in the field of Inductive Logic Programming (ILP). ILP investigates theory and methods to induce first-order clausal theories from examples and background knowledge [18]. More precisely, in the normal framework of ILP, if B is the background knowledge and E^+ and E^- are the sets of positive and negative examples respectively, the aim is to induce hypotheses H such that $B \wedge H \models E^+$ and $B \wedge H \wedge E^- \not\models \perp$. In most cases, E^+ and E^- are examples of a single target predicate and B and H are definite Horn clauses (but some systems [6] induce full first-order theories). The ILP community has also considered the problem of using more expressive formalisms, specially in systems that construct clauses containing the negation as failure operator [1,2,15].

The problem that we consider in this paper extends [9] and concerns the simultaneous learning of definitions for a predicate p and its negation $\neg p$. So in our framework, negative examples for a predicate p will play the full role of leading to explicit definitions of $\neg p$. The relevance of this approach has been first pointed out by De Raedt [5] who argued that the closed world assumption is not suited to the learning paradigm because we cannot assume that everything is known. Our proposition follows the same idea and is concerned with the construction

T. Eiter, W. Faber, and M. Truszczyński (Eds.): LPNMR 2001, LNAI 2173, pp. 160–172, 2001.

of theories where it seems difficult to apply the closed world assumption. Let us imagine a secretary-agent that must learn from observations when it must pass on a phone call to the manager. This concept seems difficult to define completely. So it is a good representation for the agent to define explicitly situations where the call can be passed on, and situations where the manager must not be disturbed. This formalism enables the agent to recognize cases where the concept remains undefined according to the current learned theory. A situation may also be undetermined because it satisfies at the same time a positive and a negative definition.

In order to give explicitly definitions of p and $\neg p$ and to deal with possible inconsistencies between them, we propose to represent the learned knowledge by a default theory. *Default logic* [22] is a powerful language to represent incomplete knowledge, which enables our method to obtain compact theories where the relationships between the definitions for p and $\neg p$ appear clearly. In default logic, knowledge is represented by a default theory (W, D), where W is a set of classical formulas (the sure knowledge) and D is a set of *default rules* (or *defaults*) that represent non completely specified inference rules, often considered as *rules with exceptions*. Formally, a default $\frac{\alpha\,:\,\beta}{\gamma}$ has a *consequent* γ and two types of antecedents: a *prerequisite* α and a *justification* β[1]. Then, the intuitive meaning of a default rule is : "if α is proved, and if $\neg\beta$ is not deducible (in other words if β is coherent) then conclude γ". In whole generality, α, β and γ can be any first order logic formula. But in our work, they will be formulas with free variables, like $p(X, Y)$, so our defaults are said to be *open*. As usual in default logic, each formula $p(X, Y)$ represents the set of all ground formulas $p(a, b)$ that can be obtained by instantiation with the constants of the domain. In this work, we only consider finite domains (without symbol function) and then our set of open defaults is in fact a compact representation of a finite set of *closed defaults* (without free variables) obtained by instanciation over the constant set.

We recall below the definition of an *extension* that is a set of plausible conclusions infered from a given *closed default theory* (see [22] for more details on default logic). A default theory is said to be closed if all its defaults are closed.

Definition 1. *[22] Let (W, D) be a closed default theory. For any set of closed formulas S, let $\Gamma(S)$ be the smallest set satisfying :*
- *$W \subseteq \Gamma(S)$*
- *$Th(\Gamma(S)) = \Gamma(S)$*
- *For any $\frac{\alpha\,:\,\beta}{\gamma} \in D$, if $\alpha \in \Gamma(S)$ and $\neg\beta \notin S$, then $\gamma \in \Gamma(S)$.*

A set of closed formulas E is an extension of (W, D) iff $E = \Gamma(E)$.

A fundamental feature of default logic is its ability to represent incomplete knowledge, so it is not surprising that a default theory may have multiple extensions : one for each point of view that we can adopt in front of the missing information. For instance $(W, D) = \left(\{a\}, \left\{\frac{a\,:\,b}{c}, \frac{a\,:\,\neg c}{\neg b}\right\}\right)$ has two extensions $E_1 = Th(W \cup \{c\})$ and $E_2 = Th(W \cup \{\neg b\})$. That is why it is necessary

---

[1] If δ is a default rule, $pre(\delta)$, $jus(\delta)$ and $cons(\delta)$ respectively denote the prerequisite, the justification and the consequent of δ.

to distinguish between *skeptical* (or *cautious*) *theorems* and *credulous theorems*. The former are formulas that occur in every extension ($c \vee \neg b$ in our previous example) and can be considered as sure deductions. The later are formulas that occur in at least one extension (c in our previous example) and are only hypothetical conclusions. As it will be described later, this distinction is central in the paradigm that we present in our work.

The rest of the paper is organised as follows : section 2 considers default learning in the case where the initial theory does not contain defaults. Our methodology is illustrated on examples in section 3. In section 4, we develop the more general framework of learning with an initial theory that contains defaults. Then, we compare our work with other approaches in section 5.

2   Learning Default Theories

2.1   Definition and Algorithm

The following definition formally precises the framework of learning a default theory; it is inspired by a well known semantic specification of ILP. In this section, we consider the special case where the initial background knowledge is expressed by ground facts.

Definition 2. *Let* $E^+ = \{p(a_1), \ldots, p(a_n)\}$ *be a set of positive examples and* $E^- = \{\neg p(a'_1), \ldots, \neg p(a'_m)\}$ *a set of negative examples of a target predicate* p. *Let* W *be an initial set of ground facts containing no occurrence of* p *or* $\neg p$,

Learning a default theory for the concept described by p *and* $\neg p$ *consists in finding a default theory* (W', D') *such that:*

- *D' is a set of defaults, the consequents of which are p or $\neg p$*
- *$W' = W \cup E_p$, where E_p is a set of examples that cannot be generalized*
- *$(\bigwedge_{e \in E^+} e) \wedge (\bigwedge_{e \in E^-} e))$ is a skeptical theorem of (W', D').*

Definition 3. *An example* e *($p(a)$ or $\neg p(a)$) is **covered by a default theory*** (W, D) *if* e *is a credulous theorem of* (W, D).

An example e *($p(a)$ or $\neg p(a)$) is an **exception** to a default theory* (W, D) *if* $\neg e$ *is a credulous theorem of* (W, D).

Our approach considers that the training examples constitute a sure knowledge from which we induce default rules. As a default theory may have multiple extensions mutually inconsistent, our definition requires that the training examples become skeptical theorems of the induced default theory. For instance, let $E^+ = \{flies(1)\}$, $E^- = \{\neg flies(2)\}$ and $W = \{bird(1), bird(2), penguin(2)\}$, and let D' be the default set $D' = \left\{ \frac{bird(X) : flies(X)}{flies(X)}, \frac{penguin(X) : \neg flies(X)}{\neg flies(X)} \right\}$. The theory (W, D') does not satisfy definition 2. In fact, (W, D') has two extensions $E_1 = Th(W \cup \{flies(1), flies(2)\})$ and $E_2 = Th(W \cup \{flies(1), \neg flies(2)\})$ and consequently, $\neg flies(2)$ is not a skeptical theorem. The reader can easily check that if we take $D' = \left\{ \frac{bird(X) : flies(X) \wedge \neg penguin(X)}{flies(X)}, \frac{penguin(X) : \neg flies(X)}{\neg flies(X)} \right\}$, then (W, D') is a solution to this simple learning problem.

The main idea is to give symetric roles to positive and negative examples; the positive examples are used to build defaults defining p and the negative examples are used to build defaults defining $\neg p$. Generalization of positive examples leads to a general rule defining p but this definition may admit exceptions, that are found by examining the negative examples. Generalization from such a set of exceptions enables to specialize the rule defining p and moreover gives a general definition of $\neg p$. A symetric treatment is also applied to generalization of negative examples. To resume, our method to construct a set of defaults alternates generalization and specialization steps.

The generalization process is based on a generic ILP algorithm named here $\mathbf{Gen}(q, \mathcal{E}^+, T, \varphi)$ that, from a set of positive examples $\mathcal{E}^+$ of the predicate q and a background theory T, induces one definition $\varphi(X)$ that characterizes a part of $\mathcal{E}^+$. More precisely, that means that the theory T and the clause $(q(X) : -\varphi(X))$ enables to prove all the examples $q(a)$ generalized by φ (see section 3 for details).

Formally, the algorithms that we propose are the followings.

Algorithm **DefaultLearning**
$\quad$ In : $p(X), W, E^+, E^-$; Out : W', D'
Begin
$\quad W' \leftarrow W \qquad D' \leftarrow \emptyset$
$\quad \overline{E^+} \leftarrow E^+$
$\quad$ While $\overline{E^+} \neq \emptyset$
$\qquad \mathbf{Gen}(p, \overline{E^+}, W, \varphi)$ searches φ that generalizes a part of $\overline{E^+}$
$\qquad$ If a formula φ is found, then
$\qquad\qquad$ Add to D' the default $\delta = \frac{\varphi(X) : p(X)}{p(X)}$
$\qquad\qquad$ Remove from $\overline{E^+}$ the examples generalized by φ
$\qquad\qquad Exc \leftarrow \{e \in E^- \mid e \text{ is an exception to}(W', D')\}$
$\qquad\qquad$ If $Exc \neq \emptyset$ then $\mathbf{Specialise}(Exc, W, \delta, W', D', \{pre(\delta)\})$
$\qquad$ else
$\qquad\qquad W' \leftarrow W' \cup \overline{E^+} \qquad \overline{E^+} \leftarrow \emptyset$
$\quad$ Endwhile
$\quad JUS(X) \leftarrow \wedge \neg pre(\delta)$, for all $\delta \in D'$ s. t. $cons(\delta) = p(X)$
$\quad \overline{E^-} \leftarrow \{e \in E^- \mid e \text{ is not covered by }(W', D')\}$
$\quad$ While $\overline{E^-} \neq \emptyset$
$\qquad \mathbf{Gen}(\neg p, \overline{E^-}, W, \varphi)$ searches φ that generalizes a part of $\overline{E^-}$
$\qquad$ If a formula φ is found, then
$\qquad\qquad$ Add to D' the default $\frac{\varphi(X) : \neg p(X) \wedge JUS(X)}{\neg p(X)}$
$\qquad\qquad$ Simplify $JUS(X) = \wedge_{i=1}^k \neg J_i(X)$ by removing each $J_i(X)$ s.t. there is no constant tuple $\overline{X}$ satisfying $p(\overline{X}) \in E^+$ and $W \vdash \varphi(\overline{X}) \wedge J_i(\overline{X})$
$\qquad\qquad$ Remove from $\overline{E^-}$ the examples generalized by φ
$\qquad$ else
$\qquad\qquad W' \leftarrow W' \cup \overline{E^-} \qquad \overline{E^-} \leftarrow \emptyset$
$\quad$ Endwhile
End

Algorithm **Specialise**
$\quad$ In : Exc, W; InOut : δ, W', D'; In: $ForbForm$
Begin
$\quad \overline{Exc} \leftarrow Exc$
$\quad$ While $\overline{Exc} \neq \emptyset$
$\qquad \mathbf{Gen}(\neg cons(\delta), \overline{Exc}, W, \psi_{Exc})$ searches ψ_{Exc} that generalizes a part of $\overline{Exc}$
$\qquad$ If ψ_{Exc} is found and $\psi_{Exc} \notin ForbForm$, then
$\qquad\qquad jus(\delta) \leftarrow jus(\delta) \wedge \neg \psi_{Exc}$
$\qquad\qquad$ Add to D' the default $\delta_{Exc} = \frac{\psi_{Exc}(X) : \neg cons(\delta)}{\neg cons(\delta)}$
$\qquad\qquad$ Remove from $\overline{Exc}$ the examples generalized by ψ_{Exc}
$\qquad\qquad$ /* E stands for E^+ (resp. E^-) if $cons(\delta) = p(X)$ (resp. $cons(\delta) = \neg p(X)$)*/
$\qquad\qquad Exc_{Exc} \leftarrow \{e \in E \mid e \text{ is an exception to}(W', D')\}$

$\quad$ If $Exc_{Exc} \neq \emptyset$ then **Specialise**$(Exc_{Exc}, W, \delta_{Exc}, W', D', ForbForm \cup \{pre(\delta_{Exc})\})$
$\quad$ else
$\qquad W' \leftarrow W' \cup \overline{Exc} \qquad \overline{Exc} \leftarrow \emptyset$
$\quad$ Endwhile
End

In our main algorithm **DefaultLearning**, p stands for the predicate to learn, E^+ and E^- are the set of positive and negative examples of the concept; W is the initial theory; W' is the theory W which may be augmented by some examples that cannot be generalized; D' is a set of defaults the consequents of which are p and $\neg p$. For clarity, the algorithm is written by assuming that we begin by learning p. But as our method deals with positive and negative examples in a symetric manner, it could as well begin by learning $\neg p$ by exchanging the roles of E^+ and E^-.

The process starts by a generalization step, that means that the learning algorithm **Gen** is applied to E^+ in order to compute one formula φ that represents a subset of E^+. If it is possible to find such a formula, the default $\delta = \frac{\varphi(X) : p(X)}{p(X)}$ is build into D'.

This default δ may admit exceptions (see definition 3). The set of exceptions is obtained by checking for each $\neg p(e)$ in E^- whether $p(e)$ is a theorem of (W', D'). If the set of exceptions is not empty, we must specialize δ. **Gen** is used to induce a formula ψ that generalizes these exceptions and we modify the default δ into $\frac{\varphi(X) : p(X) \wedge \neg \psi(X)}{p(X)}$. By this way, this default is no longer applicable to the negative examples that verify $\psi(X)$. At the same time, these negative examples, generalized by $\psi(X)$, lead to a general definition of $\neg p$, represented by the default $\frac{\psi(X) : \neg p(X)}{\neg p(X)}$. This default is specialized on its turn if it is necessary. This recursive process always ends because we use the set of forbidden formula, $ForbForm$, that avoids possible loops in the situations where exceptions and examples are generalized by the same formula. For instance, with $E^+ = \{flies(1), flies(2)\}$, $E^- = \{\neg flies(3), \neg flies(4)\}$ and $W = \{bird(1), bird(2), bird(3), bird(4)\}$, we obtain the first default $\delta_1 = \frac{bird(X) : flies(X)}{flies(X)}$ which has the exceptions E^-. If we specialize δ_1 without taking into account $ForbForm$, we obtain the new default $\delta_2 = \frac{bird(X) : \neg flies(X)}{\neg flies(X)}$ and δ_1 is specialized in $\delta_1' = \frac{bird(X) : flies(X) \wedge \neg bird(X)}{flies(X)}$. This is not acceptable because the positive examples $flies(1), flies(2)$ are no longer covered by this theory, and become exceptions to δ_2, which leads to a loop in this recursive specialization. The use of $ForbForm$ enables to find the final theory $(W \cup \{\neg flies(3), \neg flies(4)\}, \{\frac{bird(X) : flies(X)}{flies(X)}\})$, because an example e that cannot be generalized is simply added to W' as a ground fact. This ensures that e is a skeptical theorem of (W', D').

When all the positive examples are generalized (first Endwhile), we check whether there are still any negative examples not covered by the current theory. If it is the case, we begin to complete the definition of $\neg p$ by a similar process. At this time, all the positive examples, that are the potential exceptions for defaults defining $\neg p$, have already been treated. So the formulas to characterize these possible exceptions have already been computed: they are the prerequisites of some defaults defining p. That is why all the new defaults that are introduced for $\neg p$ are constrained by a justification JUS that is the conjunction of all the prerequisites of all defaults concluding p. By this way, we avoid the computation of exceptions, which is an expensive process. The counterpart of this strategy is that the justifications of these last defaults are certainly too complex and they are simplified by a mechanism that checks for each new default whether these formulas really correspond to some exceptions.

A last point to notice is that in our algorithm the sets of examples that are not yet covered ($\overline{E^+}$ and $\overline{E^-}$) decrease each time that **Gen** generalizes a subset of examples: this is the principle of iterative covering common to many learning algorithms. But when we have to determine the exceptions to a current theory, we must take into account the initial sets of examples E^+ and E^-. This is necessary to be sure that we have found all the possible exceptions.

2.2   Correctness

The work presented here extends a previous method [9] that concerned only Lukaszewicz' default theories where the existence of an extension is guaranted. In Reiter's default logic, this point must be more carefully studied.

Theorem 1. *The algorithm **DefaultLearning** induces a default theory that has always an extension.*

Proof: In [14] it is shown that a Reiter's default theory has at least one extension if its *block-graph* contains only even cycles. For a default theory (W, D), the block-graph is a pair $(\overline{D}, A)$. The vertex set $\overline{D}$ contains all closed defaults obtained from D except those that are incompatible with W, ie: defaults δ s.t. $W \vdash \neg jus(\delta)$. In our particular case, the arc set A contains the pair (δ, δ') if δ "blocks" δ', i.e.: $W \vdash pre(\delta)$ and $W \cup cons(\delta) \vdash \neg jus(\delta')$. By construction, each induced default is normal or semi-normal[2] and its consequent is $p(\overline{X})$ or $\neg p(\overline{X})$. So, it is obvious that only even cycle may exist and then our learned default theories have always an extension. $\square$

When it ends, our algorithm guarantees that all examples are covered (each given example e is a credulous theorem) and that there are no remaining exceptions (for each given example e, $\neg e$ is not a credulous theorem). So we have to prove that it is sufficient to make all the examples skeptical theorems, as it is required by definition 2.

Theorem 2. *Let (W, D) be a default theory induced by the algorithm **Default-Learning** and e a given example.*

If e is a credulous theorem of (W, D) and $\neg e$ is not a credulous theorem of (W, D), then e is a skeptical theorem of (W, D).

Proof: Without loss of generality we fix that e is a positive example $p(a)$ (the proof for a negative example is similar) such that $p(a)$ is a credulous theorem and $\neg p(a)$ is not a credulous theorem. Since $p(a)$ is a credulous theorem it means

---

[2] A default is semi-normal if it is like $\frac{\alpha \,:\, \beta \wedge \gamma}{\gamma}$.

that there exists a closed default $\delta = \frac{\alpha(a) \, : \, p(a) \wedge \beta(a)}{p(a)}$ (particularly we may have $\beta(a) = true$) with $W \vdash \alpha(a)$.

Let us suppose that $p(a)$ is not a skeptical theorem. In other words, there exists an extension E not containing $p(a)$, then δ is blocked in E that is $E \vdash \neg p(a) \vee \neg \beta(a)$. Since $\neg p(a)$ is not a credulous theorem, it is never possible to obtain $\neg p(a)$, so the only way to block δ is to derive $\neg \beta(a)$. $\neg \beta(a)$ cannot be obtained by a default δ' because its consequent can only be $p(X)$. So, we must have $\neg \beta(a) \in W$. But in this case, δ is always blocked and $p(a)$ is not a credulous theorem. This contradiction gives our result. $\square$

The next section gives examples illustrating our methodology.

3   Commented Examples

In order to test the relevance of our method, we have simulated its main steps on some artificial examples. It is fundamental in our work to compute generalization formulas that may have exceptions. This can be realized in ILP systems (like FOIL [21] for instance) by allowing a certain level of noise. But it is difficult to adjust this parameter: if we accept a high level of noise, we find too general formulas, if the level of noise is too weak, the generalization is too specific or impossible because of the exceptions. To avoid this difficulty that must be studied carefully for each application domain, we use a generalization mechanism that rely only on positive examples. The ILP system Progol [16] has the ability to learn from positive data only [17] and we use it as the generalization tool described by the function **Gen** in our algorithm. Progol is an ILP system based on inverse entailment. The input file for Progol specifies the set of positive examples and the initial background theory that may contain definite Horn clauses but also integrity constraints expressed by headless Horn clauses. Moreover, the user specifies type and mode declarations for the predicates. These biases are very important to determine the space of possible generalizations that Progol searches with an A*-like algorithm in order to return a clause that realizes the best data compression.

In the following examples, the different stages of our method have been simulated by switching learning steps of p and $\neg p$. When learning p, the theory with only E^+ was considered and in order to learn $\neg p$, the negative examples are considered with $\neg p$ renamed in an ad-hoc predicate *not_p*. The covering tests, that are necessary to determine which examples are not yet generalized and also to determine exceptions to a default, require either extension calculus or query answering in Reiter's default logic. For both tasks, operational systems exist (for instance DeRes [4], GADEL [19], XRay [20]), and they could be integrated in a whole system for default theory learning.

Example 1. The initial theory W concerns a set of people and a set of dishes[3].

$$W = \begin{Bmatrix} hb(1), ..., hb(45), hb(46), ..., hb(50), hb(51), ..., hb(55) \\ v(46), ..., v(50), diab(51), ..., diab(55) \\ a(mutton), a(beef), a(fish), \\ di(mutton), di(beef), di(fish), \\ oa(egg), oa(milk), di(egg), di(milk), \\ sug(ice\_cream), sug(cake), di(ice\_cream), di(cake) \end{Bmatrix}$$

The aim is to induce what people eat and what they do not eat from the following sets of examples.

$$E^+ = \begin{Bmatrix} eats(2, egg), ..., eats(50, egg), \\ eats(1, milk), ..., eats(50, milk), eats(1, mutton), ..., eats(45, mutton), \\ eats(1, beef), ..., eats(45, beef), eats(1, fish), ..., eats(45, fish) \end{Bmatrix}$$

$$E^- = \begin{Bmatrix} \neg eats(1, egg), \\ \neg eats(46, mutton), ..., \neg eats(50, mutton), \\ \neg eats(46, beef), ..., \neg eats(50, beef), \\ \neg eats(46, fish), ..., \neg eats(50, fish), \\ \neg eats(51, ice\_cream), ..., \neg eats(55, ice\_cream), \\ \neg eats(51, cake), ..., \neg eats(55, cake) \end{Bmatrix}$$

Let us suppose that we begin to learn the definition of $eats(X, Y)$. So we run Progol in order to generalize from the examples E^+ and W. The best clause according to Progol evaluation is $(eats(X, Y) :\!\!- hb(X), oa(Y))$, which means that all the persons eat dishes that have an animal origin (eggs and milk). From this formula we build into D' a first default $\delta_1 = \frac{hb(X) \wedge oa(Y) : eats(X,Y)}{eats(X,Y)}$. By examining the set of negative examples, we find that this default admits only one exception $\neg eats(1, egg)$, that cannot lead to a relevant generalization. So this exception $\neg eats(1, egg)$ is added to W'. There are still some positive examples that are not covered by (W', D') and a second call to the generalization of Progol returns the clause $(eats(X, Y) :\!\!- hb(X), a(Y))$. So we build the default $\delta_2 = \frac{hb(X) \wedge a(Y) : eats(X,Y)}{eats(X,Y)}$. But this default admits a set of exceptions $Exc_{\delta_2} = \{\neg eats(46, mutton), ..., \neg eats(50, fish)\}$. In order to characterize these exceptions by a general formula, we submit this subset of examples to Progol (after a replacement of $\neg eats$ by not_eats. Progol returns the clause $(not\_eats(X, Y) :\!\!- v(X) \wedge a(Y))$. So δ_2 is specialized into $\delta'_2 = \frac{hb(X) \wedge a(Y) : eats(X,Y) \wedge \neg(v(X) \wedge a(Y))}{eats(X,Y)}$ and at the same time, we build $\delta_3 = \frac{v(X) \wedge a(Y) : \neg eats(X,Y)}{\neg eats(X,Y)}$. This default δ_3 admits no exception.

At this moment, we have finished the covering of all the positive examples and we consider the negative examples that are not yet covered by $(W', \{\delta_1, \delta'_2, \delta_3\})$, namely $\{\neg eats(51, ice\_cream), ..., \neg eats(55, cake)\}$. To generalize these instances, Progol finds the formula $(diab(X) \wedge sug(Y))$ and we build a default δ_4 with this formula as prerequisite. To take into account the whole job that has been realised during the learning of the positive part $eats(X, Y)$, this default has a justi-

---

[3] The following notations are used: hb stands for human_being, v for vegetarian, di for dish and *diab* for diabetic; a for animal qualifies dishes that are animal flesh, and oa for animal_origin qualifies dishes that have an animal origin, *sug* qualifies sugary food.

fication which is the conjunct of the prerequisites of defaults defining $eats(X, Y)$:
$\delta_4 = \frac{diab(X) \wedge sug(Y) : \neg eats(X,Y) \wedge \neg(hb(X) \wedge oa(Y)) \wedge \neg(hb(X) \wedge a(Y))}{\neg eats(X,Y)}$. The justification in
δ_4 is simplified by checking that there does not exist a couple (X, Y) such that
$eats(X, Y) \in E^+$ and $(diab(X) \wedge sug(Y))$ and $(hb(X) \wedge oa(Y))$ are true simultaneously. So $(hb(X) \wedge oa(Y))$ is removed from the justification of δ_4. The same
is true for $(hb(X) \wedge a(Y))$ and finally, we obtain $\delta_4' = \frac{diab(X) \wedge sug(Y) : \neg eats(X,Y)}{\neg eats(X,Y)}$.
The simplification process relies on theorem proving in Horn logic and is much
less expensive than the computation of exceptions that requires theorem proving
in default logic. One can easily check that all the positive and all the negative
examples are skeptical theorems of $(W', \{\delta_1, \delta_2', \delta_3, \delta_4'\})$.

The following example illustrates that a learned default theory may have
multiple extensions.

Example 2. Let us consider that we want to learn the predicate p^4 with $W = \{q(b1), q(b2), q(b3), q(nixon), r(t1), r(t2), r(nixon)\}$, $E^+ = \{p(b1), p(b2), p(b3)\}$
and $E^- = \{\neg p(t1), \neg p(t2)\}$.
Let us note that *nixon* is not given as a positive example nor as a negative
one. So the simplification step applies to the second default, inducing $D' = \{\frac{q(X) : p(X)}{p(X)}, \frac{r(X) : \neg p(X)}{\neg p(X)}\}$. As it is required by our definition, the conjunct of
all the examples is a skeptical theorem of (W, D') even if this theory has two
distinct extensions $E_1 = Th(W \cup \{p(b1), p(b2), p(b3), \neg p(t1), \neg p(t2), p(nixon)\})$
and $E_2 = Th(W \cup \{p(b1), p(b2), p(b3), \neg p(t1), \neg p(t2), \neg p(nixon)\})$. Knowledge
about *nixon* remains undefined since it is not a training example.

4   Learning with Initial Defaults

In both previous sections we consider special default theories where W only contains ground facts. This requirement was necessary to make a bridge between
default logic where the sure knowledge can be expressed by any first order formula and ILP where the initial background knowledge is expressed by Prolog
clauses, that are not equivalent to implications. In the case of the example 1, the
whole initial theory is expressed by ground facts, whereas some general Prolog
clause like $(hb(X) :- v(X))$ could have been used. Let us notice that such an
oriented rule could be written in default logic by $\frac{v(X) : true}{hb(X)}$.

We consider now that we want to learn a new concept from an initial default theory and a set of examples. The initial default theory may have multiple
extensions, but this difficulty can be resolved if the learning process relies only
on the sure initial knowledge. That is why we propose a method where generalization uses a background knowledge including only all the ground facts that
are skeptical theorems of our initial theory. This new learning problem can be
stated as followed.

Definition 4. *Let E^+ and E^- be positive and negative examples of a target
predicate p. Let (W_0, D_0) be an initial default theory containing no occurences
of p or $\neg p$.*

---

[4] r stands for republican, q for quaker and p for pacifist.

Learning a default theory for the concept described by p and $\neg p$ consists to build a default theory (W', D') such that:

- $D' = D_0 \cup D_p$, where D_p is a set of defaults, the consequents of which are p or $\neg p$
- $W' = W_0 \cup E_p$, where E_p is a set of examples that cannot be generalized
- $(\wedge_{e \in E+} e) \wedge (\wedge_{e \in E-} e))$ is a skeptical theorem of (W', D').

We propose the following method to induce W' and D' in such a case. First, we compute W the set of ground facts that are skeptical theorems from the initial default theory (W_0, D_0). Then the algorithm to learn the default theory (W', D') is the same as the one given in subsection 2.1, except the two following modifications:

- **DefaultLearning** works on the inputs: $p(X), W, W_0, D_0, E^+, E^-$
- the two first initializations $W' \leftarrow W$ and $D' \leftarrow \emptyset$ are replaced by
$$W' \leftarrow W_0 \qquad D' \leftarrow D_0$$

So the background knowledge used for generalization by **Gen** is always W, the set of skeptical theorems of (W_0, D_0). But each time we have to compute a set of exceptions, we consider the exceptions of the current theory (W', D'). This current theory contains the initial default theory (W_0, D_0) augmented by some new defaults defining p or $\neg p$ and eventually by some examples that cannot be generalized. So, generalization relies on sure knowledge but the search of exceptions takes into account the credulous theorems of (W_0, D_0). This is necessary to insure that each example will be a skeptical theorem of the resulting default theory (W', D').

Example 3. Let us consider the initial theory (W_0, D_0) with $W_0 = \{q(b1), q(b2),$ $q(nixon), r(t1), r(t2), r(nixon), usp(nixon), p(john)\}$ and $D_0 = \{\frac{q(X) : p(X)}{p(X)},$ $\frac{r(X) : \neg p(X)}{\neg p(X)}\}$. Let $E^+ = \{no(b1), no(b2), no(john)\}$[5] and $E^- = \{\neg no(t1),$ $\neg no(t2), \neg no(nixon)\}$

The initial theory (W_0, D_0) has two extensions and we consider only the set W of ground facts that are skeptical theorems in order to learn a definition of no. As $W = W_0 \cup \{p(b1), p(b2), \neg p(t1), \neg p(t2)\}$, our method constructs the first default $\delta_1 = \frac{p(X) : no(X)}{no(X)}$. The negative example $\neg no(nixon)$ is an exception for δ_1 since there exists an extension where δ_1 can be applied to $nixon$. A generalization of this exception leads to the formula $usp(X)$. Then δ_1 is specialized into $\delta_1' = \frac{p(X) : no(X) \wedge \neg usp(X)}{no(X)}$ and at the same time we build the default $\delta_2 = \frac{usp(X) : \neg no(X)}{\neg no(X)}$ that has no exceptions. The learning process completes the definition of $\neg no$ by the default $\delta_3 = \frac{\neg p(X) : \neg no(X)}{\neg no(X)}$. We can check that each example is a skeptical theorem of (W', D') with $W' = W_0$ and $D' = D_0 \cup \{\delta_1', \delta_2, \delta_3\}$. This final resulting default theory (W', D') has two extensions because of the remained incomplete specification about $p(nixon)$ and $\neg p(nixon)$. But, each of these extensions contains the conclusion $\neg no(nixon)$ as it is required by our objective.

---

[5] *no* stands for nuclear_opponent and *usp* stands for US President.

5 Related Works

The problem of learning non-monotonic theories by learning both a concept and its negation has been pointed as very interesting for many years. In [5] a concept and its negation are effectively learned, but in the framework of definite clauses : the negative concept is represented by a new predicate not_p and the learning algorithm checks that no contradiction occurs between the definitions of p and not_p. The framework proposed in [8] learns a concept and its exceptions by means of general rules, and conflicts between rules are solved by additional priority relations. This framework captures the notion of *specificity* of a rule as it is done in [3] in *prioritized default logic*. But, it is known [23] that specificity can be handled by means of *semi-normal* defaults and that is exactly what our method does. In [7] the problem of contradiction between definition of p and $\neg p$ is solved by using integrity constraints in order to restrict the conclusions derivable from too general rules.

More recently, some works deal with this problem in the context of extended logic programs [11,13,12]. Extended Logic Programs (ELP) have been introduced by Gelfond and Lifschitz [10] to extend the class of normal logic programs by allowing explicit negation. A rule in an ELP has the form $L_0 \leftarrow L_1, \ldots, L_m, not\ L_{m+1}, \ldots, not\ L_n$, where each L_i is a literal (positive or negative). [11,13] propose methods to learn an ELP that contains a definition of p and a definition of $\neg p$. Each definition may have exceptions that are described by abnormality predicates, and these abnormality predicates are defined by normal clauses. So, the aim of these works is the same as ours. The main difference is that we do not rely on abnormality predicates to specialize overgeneral rules. For instance, the algorithm presented in [13] learns rules for p and specializes them if they have exceptions, then it computes on the same manner a set of rules for $\neg p$. For our example 3, the following rules

$p(X) : -q(X), not\ \neg p(X).$ ab1(X) :- usp(X). $\neg p(X) : -r(X), not\ p(X).$
$no(X) : -p(X), not\ ab1(X).$ $\neg no(X) : -usp(X).$

are learned. We can observe that the algorithm has dealt twice with the set of US presidents, once when US presidents are considered as a characterization of $ab1$ and another time when US presidents are considered as examples of the concept $\neg no$. This illustrates that using abnormality predicates to specialize rules hides the deep relationships that exist between definitions of no and $\neg no$ and this leads to redundancy in the learning process and in the resulting rules. Furthermore, the complete theory induced by [13] would in fact transform the rule defining no into the two rules : $(no(X) : -p(X), not\ ab1(X), not\ \neg no(X).)$ and $(no(X) : -p(X), undefined(\neg no(X)).)$ and similarly for the other rules concluding $\neg no(X)$. The well founded semantics requires these modifications in order to deal correctly with the examples where the definitions of no and $\neg no$ overlap.

The method we have presented, like those described in [11,13,12], is a method to build a consistent theory in a non-monotonic framework. The common feature of our work and those presented in [11,13,12] is to rely on a standard ILP procedure to compute definitions for the positive and the negative parts of the concept; then we use a theorem prover for default logic (a theorem prover for the answer set semantics in [11] and for WFSX semantics in [13,12]) to compute the potential exceptions to the definitions that have been induced. So, the central point is to study for each used semantics how to agreggate these definitions into non monotonic rules able to deal with potential contradictions.

A more recent work [25,24] presents another approach where the induction of hypotheses is realized directly from the answer sets of the initial program. So this work redefines the learning process accordingly to the framework used. In the case of a background program having multiple answer sets, the author proposes to learn different rules for each answer set, which is very different from our proposition of part 4. Of course, further study and also experimentation of those formalisms on real problems are necessay to decide whether induction must rely on credulous or skeptical knowledge.

6   Conclusion

We have presented a framework to induce default theories from training examples. Default logic is probably the most general framework that we can imagine to represent at the same time a concept and its negation and the recent tools realized for extension calculus or query answering enable to consider its application to some real domains. This paper has shown how to control the inductive construction of a default theory to insure that it correctly represents the knowledge contained in the training examples. The availability of ILP systems allowed us to check the relevance of this approach on some artificial examples. We have now to further study the generalization process, specially on real examples. We think that our method can be the basis of a system that helps a user to formalize its knowledge in default logic.

References

1. M. Bain and S. Muggleton. Non-monotonic learning. In S. Muggleton, editor, *Inductive Logic Programming*, pages 145–161. Academic Press, 1992. 160
2. F. Bergadano, D. Gunetti, M. Nicosia, and G. Ruffo. Learning logic programs with negation as failure. In L. De Raedt, editor, *Proceedings of Inductive Logic Programming conference*, pages 33–51, K. U. Leuven, 1995. 160
3. G. Brewka. Adding priorities and specificity to default logic. In L. Pereira and D. Pearce, editors, *European Workshop on Logics in Artificial Intelligence (JELIA'94)*, Lecture Notes in Artificial Intelligence, pages 247–260. Springer Verlag, 1994. 170
4. P. Cholewiński, V. Marek, A. Mikitiuk, and M. Truszczyński. Computing with default logic. *Artificial Intelligence*, 112:105–146, 1999. 166
5. L. De Raedt and M. Bruynooghe. On negation and three-valued logic in interactive concept learning. In *Proceedings of the 9th European Conference on Artificial Intelligence*, pages 207–212. Pitman, 1990. 160, 170
6. L. De Raedt and M. Bruynooghe. A theory of clausal discovery. In R. Bajcsy, editor, *Proceedings of the 13th International Joint Conference on Artificial Intelligence*, pages 1058–1063. Morgan Kaufmann Publishers, 1993. 160

7. Y. Dimopoulos, S. Džeroski, and A. Kakas. Integrating explanatory and descriptive learning in ILP. In *Proceedings of the International Joint Conference on Artificial Intelligence*, volume 2, pages 900–906. Morgan Kaufmann Publishers, 1997. 170

8. Y. Dimopoulos and A. Kakas. Learning non-monotonic logic programs: Learning exceptions. In N. Lavrač and S. Wrobel, editors, *European Coonference on Machine Learning'95*, volume 912 of *Lecture Notes in Artificial Intelligence*, pages 122–137. Springer Verlag, 1995. 170

9. B. Duval and P. Nicolas. Learning default theories. In S. Parsons A. Hunter, editor, *Qualitative and Quantitative Approaches to Reasoning with Uncertainty*, volume 1638 of *Lecture Notes in Artificial Intelligence*. Springer Verlag, 1999. 160, 165

10. M. Gelfond and V. Lifschitz. Classical negation in logic programs and disjunctive databases. *New Generation Computing*, 9(3-4):363–385, 1991. 170

11. K. Inoue and Y. Kudoh. Learning Extended Logic Programs. In *Proceedings of the International Joint Conference on Artificial Intelligence*, volume 1, pages 176–181. Morgan Kaufmann Publishers, 1997. 170, 171

12. E. Lamma, F. Riguzzi, and L. M. Pereira. Strategies in combined learning via logic programs. *Machine Learning*, 38(1/2):63–87, January 2000. 170, 171

13. E. Lamma, F. Riguzzi, and L. M. Pereira. Learning with extended logic programs. In *Worshop Learning Programming and non monotonic reasoning. Principles of Knowledge Representation and Reasoning*, Trento, 1998. 170, 171

14. T. Linke and T. Schaub. Alternative foundations for Reiter's default logic. *Artificial Intelligence*, 124:31–86, 2000. 165

15. L. Martin and C. Vrain. A three-valued framework for the induction of general logic programs. In L. De Raedt, editor, *Advances in Inductive Logic Programming*, pages 219–235. IOS Press, 1996. 160

16. S. Muggleton. Inverse entailment and Progol. *New generation Computing*, 13:245–286, 1995. 166

17. S. Muggleton. Learning from positive data. In S. Muggleton, editor, *Proceedings of the 6th International Workshop on Inductive Logic Programming*, volume 1314 of *Lecture Notes in Artificial Intelligence*, pages 358–376. Springer-Verlag, 1996. 166

18. S. Muggleton and L. De Raedt. Inductive Logic programming: Theory and Methods. *Journal of Logic Programming*, 19/20:629–679, 1994. 160

19. P. Nicolas, F. Saubion, and I. Stéphan. Gadel : a genetic algorithm to compute default logic extensions. In *Proceedings of the European Conference on Artificial Intelligence*, pages 484–488, 2000. 166

20. P. Nicolas and T. Schaub. The XRay system : An implementation platform for local query-answering in default logics. In Simon Parsons Antony Hunter, editor, *Applications of Uncertainty Formalisms*, volume 1455 of *Lecture Notes in Computer Science*, pages 254–378. Springer Verlag, 1998. 166

21. J. R. Quinlan. Learning logical definitions from relations. *Machine Learning*, 5:239–266, 1990. 166

22. R. Reiter. A logic for default reasoning. *Artificial Intelligence*, 13(1-2):81–132, 1980. 161

23. R. Reiter and G. Criscuolo. On interacting defaults. In *Proceedings of the International Joint Conference on Artificial Intelligence*, pages 270–276, 1981. 170

24. C Sakama. Learning by answer sets. In *AAAI Spring Symposium: Answer set programming*. 171

25. C Sakama. Inverse entailment in nonmonotonic logic programs. volume 1866 of *Lecture Notes in Artificial Intelligence*, pages 209–224. Springer-Verlag, 2000. 171

Explicitly Using Default Knowledge in Concept Learning: An Extended Description Logics Plus Strict and Default Rules

Véronique Ventos[1], Pierre Brézellec[2], and Henry Soldano[3]

[1] Université Paris-Sud
LRI Bat. 490, 91405 Orsay, France
ventos@lri.fr
[2] Université de Versailles-St-Quentin
LGI Av. des Etats-Unis, 78035, Versailles Cedex
brezel@genetique.uvsq.fr
[3] Université Paris-Nord
LIPN, av. J.B. Clément, 93430 Villetaneuse, France
soldano@lipn.univ-paris13.fr

Abstract. This work concerns the use of default knowledge in concept learning from positive and negative examples. Two connectives are added to a description logics, C-CLASSIC, previously defined for concept learning. The new connectives (δ and ϵ) allow to express the idea that some properties of a given concept definition are default properties, and that some properties that should belong to the concept definition actually do not (these are excepted properties). When performing concept learning both hypotheses and examples are expressed in this new description logics but prior to learning, a saturation process using default and non default rules has to be applied to the examples in order to add default and excepted properties to their definition. As in the original C-CLASSIC, disjunctive learning is performed using a standard greedy set covering algorithm whose generalization operator is the Least Common Subsumer operator of C-CLASSIC$_{\delta\epsilon}$. We exemplify concept learning using default knowledge in this framework and show that explicitly expressing default knowledge may result in simpler concept definitions.

1   Introduction

The general aim of concept learning consists of inducing hypotheses from a set of examples of an unknown target concept. The choice of the concept (and therefore hypothesis) and example languages is very important in this framework. Inductive Logic Programming (ILP, [15,17]) studies learning within the framework provided by clausal logic. However, the language is often restricted to Horn clauses for complexity reasons. Description Logics (DLs) are other restrictions of first-order logic[1] in which the subsumption computation and its complexity have

---

[1] Note that comparing the expressive power of DLs and restrictions of First Order Logic used in ILP is still an open issue [7].

T. Eiter, W. Faber, and M. Truszczyński (Eds.): LPNMR 2001, LNAI 2173, pp. 173–185, 2001.

been deeply studied [11]. Several ILP approaches presented a learning framework where the learned theories or the entailment relation are non-monotonic (e.g. [1,9]) in order to put emphasis on the problems that cannot be captured by classical definite logic programs. We propose here to learn in a framework combining rules, default rules and a description logics allowing to handle default knowledge. In our approach, concept learning is performed in two steps. First, we use both default rules and strict rules in order to extend the definitions of the examples by adding default properties and excepted properties. Then, concept learning is performed using subsumption and Least Common Subsumer algorithms that handle examples and hypothesis including such default and excepted properties.

The description logics used here, C-CLASSIC$_{\delta\epsilon}$ [23,22], extends C-CLASSIC with two non classical connectives (δ,ϵ) used to represent default knowledge. C-CLASSIC is one of the most expressive previously known tractable DL, which preserves its good computational properties both for subsumption and PAC-learnability. The connective δ intuitively represents the common notion of default. For instance, having $\delta Viviparous$ as a conjunct in the definition of the concept $Mammal$ states that mammals are generally viviparous. The connective ϵ is used to represent a property that is not present in the description of the concept or of the instance but that should be. Thus, for instance, being a mammal, an ornithorynchus[2] should be viviparous since mammals are generally viviparous. However, an ornithorynchus is "exceptional" w.r.t. this property (i.e. it has the property $Viviparous^\epsilon$) as it is an oviparous mammal.

Default and excepted properties can be deduced by applying default rules closely related to Reiter's normal defaults. For instance, the Reiter's normal default $\frac{Bird(x):Fly(x)}{Fly(x)}$ is interpreted as "if x is a bird and if it is consistent that x can fly then infer that x can fly". Note that this default rule handles in the same way particular birds that cannot fly, as penguins, and non flying animals as cats for instance: nothing is deduced. In our framework, the rule corresponding to the previous normal default is $Bird(x) \rightarrow_d Fly(x)$ which is interpreted as "if x is a bird and if it is consistent (i.e. not incoherent) that x can fly then infer that x generally flies (δFly(x) is inferred) else infer that x is exceptional w.r.t. Fly (Fly^ϵ(x) is inferred). In this framework, we infer that a bird generally flies, that penguins are exceptional w.r.t. Fly and nothing is deduced concerning cats.

Such default rules together with strict rules (i.e. non default rules) allowing to express incoherences (e.g. $Fly \sqcap Inapt\text{-}to\text{-}fly \rightarrow \bot^3$) are used to extend the description of the examples prior to learning.

As in the original C-CLASSIC, disjunctive learning is performed using a standard greedy set covering algorithm whose generalization operator is the Least Common Subsumer operator of C-CLASSIC$_{\delta\epsilon}$. The computation of the subsumption relation of C-CLASSIC$_{\delta\epsilon}$, that is used to check whether a hypothesis covers an example, has been proved to be correct, complete and polynomial. Furthermore, C-CLASSIC$_{\delta\epsilon}$ is PAC-learnable [23,21,25].

---

[2] Ornithoryncus = duck-billed platypus.

[3] $\bot$ is used to denote incoherences

This paper is organized as follows. Section 2 gives some needed background information on the C-CLASSIC$_{\delta\epsilon}$ description logics. Learning and saturation process in C-CLASSIC$_{\delta\epsilon}$ are described in sections 3 and 4 together with a comparison with learning in C-CLASSIC. Finally, in section 5 we briefly discuss related work in DLs and ILP fields and we present future work.

2   C-CLASSIC$_{\delta\epsilon}$

Description Logics are a family of knowledge representation formalisms which stem from KL-ONE [3]. Several systems have been built based on DLs (e.g. CLASSIC [2], FLEX [18]) and they have been used in real-world applications (e.g. CLASSIC in [20]). Besides, DLs facilitate the use of background knowledge and are more expressive than attribute-value representations. The field of DLs has received increased attention over the recent years in the Machine Learning community (e.g. [14,7,6]). These previous approaches used terminological languages unable to define concepts with default properties whereas allowing for default properties in concept definitions is frequently required in applications where few concepts can be strictly defined with necessary and sufficient properties [12].

In DLs, a concept is defined as a set of properties satisfied by individuals that are instances of the concept. These properties are expressed by terms that are built from atomic concepts and roles and from a set of connectives. Concepts are partially ordered by a subsumption relation which expresses the inclusion relation between concepts and is usually based on a standard model-based logical semantics. The subsumption relation in C-CLASSIC$_{\delta\epsilon}$ which is central for the learning task is presented in section 2.2. Knowledge is mainly separated into two components: a terminological component (T-box) which contains the definition of concepts and an assertional component (A-box) containing statements about individuals. We assume here that the A-box is empty since we represent the examples using the terminological language presented in section 2.1 (see section 3 for more details about examples). Section 2.3 presents the Least Common Subsumer operation in C-CLASSIC$_{\delta\epsilon}$ which is the generalization operator used during the learning process.

2.1   Terminological Language

The connectives of C-CLASSIC$_{\delta\epsilon}$ are the connectives of C-CLASSIC [7] plus the connectives δ and ϵ introduced in $\mathcal{AL}_{\delta\epsilon}$ [8]. The terminological language of C-CLASSIC$_{\delta\epsilon}$ is defined using a set **R** of atomic roles, a set **P** of atomic concepts, the constants $\top$ and $\bot$, a set **I** of individuals (called *classic-individuals*), and the following syntactic rule (C and D are concepts, P is a atomic concept, R is a atomic role, u is a real, n is an integer and I_i are classic-individuals):

$C, D \rightarrow$	$\top$	the most general concept
	$\mid \bot$	the most specific concept
	$\mid P$	atomic concept

$ONE\text{-}OF\ \{I_1 \ldots I_n\}$	concept in extension
$MINu$	u is a real number
$MAXu$	u is a real number
$C \sqcap D$	concept conjunction
$\forall R : C$	value restriction
$R\ FILLS\ \{I_1 \ldots I_n\}$	subset of values for R
$R\ AT\text{-}LEAST\ n$	cardinality for R (minimum)
$R\ AT\text{-}MOST\ n$	cardinality for R (maximum)
δC	default concept
C^ϵ	exception to the concept C

This syntactic rule is used to define *terms* of C-CLASSIC$_{\delta\epsilon}$.

Example: *Student* $\sqcap$ $\delta(publications\ AT\text{-}LEAST\ 4)$ $\sqcap$ $\forall age{:}MAX\ 27 \sqcap publications$ *FILLS* $\{JAIR,AI\}$ $\sqcap$ $\forall publications{:}\ (\forall year{:}\ ONE\text{-}OF\{97,98,99\})$ describes all the students who generally have at least four publications, are less than 27 years old, have at least one publication in JAIR and AI, and whose publications have been published in the years 97, 98 or 99.

Defining a concept[4] means giving a name A to a *term* T of the C-CLASSIC$_{\delta\epsilon}$ language using the expression $A \equiv C$.

Example: *Mammal* $\equiv$ *Animal* $\sqcap$ $\delta Viviparous$ $\sqcap$ *Vertebrate*

A T-box of C-CLASSIC$_{\delta\epsilon}$ is composed of concept definitions.

2.2 Subsumption in C-CLASSIC$_{\delta\epsilon}$

In DLs, concepts are organized in a taxonomy via a subsumption relation. Concerning the strict part of C-CLASSIC$_{\delta\epsilon}$, subsumption in C-CLASSIC$_{\delta\epsilon}$ is equivalent to subsumption in C-CLASSIC. More precisely, a concept C is subsumed by a concept D if C has (explicitly or implicitly) all properties of D. In our framework, we must distinguish strict and default properties. Roughly speaking, a concept C is subsumed by a default property if its definition contains either the default property, the strict property or the excepted property. For instance, δFly subsumes concepts having explicitly or implicitly either δFly, Fly or Fly^ϵ in their definition, while concepts whose definition does not mention anything (strict, default, exception, exception of exception ...) about Viviparous are not subsumed by $\delta Viviparous$.

Example :

Bird $\equiv$ *Animal* $\sqcap$ *Has-Wings* $\sqcap$ $\delta Flies$ (a bird generally flies)

Penguin $\equiv$ *Animal* $\sqcap$ *Has-Wings* $\sqcap$ $\delta(Flies^\epsilon)$ (a penguin is generally exceptional w.r.t. Flies) $\sqcap$ $\delta Inapt\text{-}to\text{-}fly$ (a penguin is generally inapt to fly)

SuperPenguin $\equiv$ *Animal* $\sqcap$ *Has-Wings* $\sqcap$ $(Flies^\epsilon)^\epsilon$ (a Superpenguin is an exception to an exception since it is an exceptional Penguin) $\sqcap$ *Inapt-to-fly*$^\epsilon$ (a SuperPenguin is exceptional w.r.t. Inapt-to-Fly since it can fly)

With these definitions, *Bird* subsumes *Penguin* and *SuperPenguin* ($\delta Flies$ both subsumes $\delta(Flies^\epsilon)$ and $(Flies^\epsilon)^\epsilon$). *SuperPenguin* is subsumed by *Penguin* ($\delta(Flies^\epsilon)$ subsumes $(Flies^\epsilon)^\epsilon$ and δ *Inapt-to-fly* subsumes *Inapt-to-fly*$^\epsilon$). Note that if *Bird* and *SuperPenguin* were defined with the strict property *Fly* and *Penguin* with the strict property *Inapt-to-fly*, *Penguin* would no

---

[4] Note that cyclic concept definitions are not allowed.

more be subsumed by *Bird* and *SuperPenguin* would no more be subsumed by *Penguin*.

More formally, let C and D be two elements of C-CLASSIC$_{\delta\epsilon}$, $C \sqsubseteq D$, i.e. D subsumes C, iff C satisfies the strict properties of D, and satisfies or is explicitly "exceptional" w.r.t. the default properties of D.

The definition of the subsumption of C-CLASSIC$_{\delta\epsilon}$ is based on an "equational system" fully defined in [22] called EQ. EQ is a set of axioms defining the main properties of the C-CLASSIC$_{\delta\epsilon}$ connectives (e.g. the axiom $A \sqcap B = B \sqcap A$ expresses the commutativity of concept conjunction, the axioms $A \sqcap \delta A = A$ and $A^\epsilon \sqcap \delta A = A^\epsilon$ express a subsumption relationship between A and δA (A is subsumed by δA) and between A^ϵ and δA (A^ϵ is subsumed by δA), the axiom $\delta\delta A = \delta A$ expresses the idempotence of δ).

Let $=_{EQ}$ denote the equality (modulo EQ axioms) between two *terms* of C-CLASSIC$_{\delta\epsilon}$. Subsumption in C-CLASSIC$_{\delta\epsilon}$ is defined as follows.

Definition 1 (Subsumption) *Let C and D be two elements of C-CLASSIC$_{\delta\epsilon}$, $C \sqsubseteq D$, i.e. D subsumes C, iff $C \sqcap D =_{EQ} C$.*

In DLs, the subsumption computation (for instance $C \sqsubseteq D$) is performed in two steps. First C and D are expanded (i.e. their definition is then exclusively made up of atomic concepts and roles). This expansion step allows us to take into account the background knowledge linked to the T-box. Then, a subsumption algorithm is applied on them.

In [23,22], a polynomial-time, complete and correct subsumption algorithm based on the equational system has been designed for C-CLASSIC and C-CLASSIC$_{\delta\epsilon}$. This algorithm computes normal form of concepts according to the equational system, this normalisation step will be used during the saturation process. This subsumption is not a pure syntactic relation like θsubsumption. It is a semantic relation like logical implication or generalized subsumption [4]. Indeed, the subsumption takes into account the whole T-box which expresses a kind of background knowledge. In other words, the subsumption relation corresponds to logical implication within C-CLASSIC$_{\delta\epsilon}$.

2.3   Least Common Subsumer in C-CLASSIC$_{\delta\epsilon}$

As mentioned above, learning in C-CLASSIC$_{\delta\epsilon}$ relies both on the subsumption relation and on the computation of the Least Common Subsumer (LCS)[5] of two concept definitions. The definition of the LCS in C-CLASSIC$_{\delta\epsilon}$ is as follows:

Definition 2 (LCS in C-CLASSIC$_{\delta\epsilon}$) *$LCS(A,B) \rightarrow C \in$ C-CLASSIC$_{\delta\epsilon}$ if and only if $A \sqsubseteq C$ and $B \sqsubseteq C$ (C subsumes both A and B), $\not\exists D$, $D \in$ C-CLASSIC$_{\delta\epsilon}$ such that $A \sqsubseteq D$, $B \sqsubseteq D$ and D is strictly subsumed by C.*

An LCS algorithm has been designed for C-CLASSIC$_{\delta\epsilon}$ in [23,24]. It has been proved that this algorithm is correct and polynomial, and that the LCS is unique.

---

[5] In the framework of DLs, the notion of Least Common Subsumer has been introduced by Borgida, Cohen and Hirsh in [5].

Example:

C ≡ *Animal* ⊓ *Vertebrate* ⊓ *With-beak* ⊓ *Oviparous* ⊓ *Has-teats* ⊓ Viviparous$^\epsilon$ ⊓ ∀*weight:MIN 20* ⊓ ∀*age:MAX 15*

D ≡ *Animal* ⊓ *Vertebrate* ⊓ *Has-teats* ⊓ *Viviparous* ⊓ ∀*weight:MIN 10* ⊓ ∀*age:MAX 10*

LCS(C,D) = *Animal* ⊓ *Vertebrate* ⊓ *Has-teats* ⊓ δ*Viviparous* ⊓ ∀*weight:MIN 10* ⊓ ∀*age:MAX 15*

3   Learning in C-CLASSIC

Cohen and Hirsh [7,6] give theoretical and experimental results on the learnability of description logics. In particular, they prove that C-CLASSIC is PAC-learnable.

From a practical point of view, the authors propose several algorithms allowing to learn concepts of C-CLASSIC from positive and negative examples of these concepts. The language of both concepts and examples is the terminological language of the DL.

The *covers relation* that specifies how hypotheses relate to examples is the subsumption relation: an hypothesis H covers an exemple e if and only if $e \sqsubseteq H$ (i.e. H subsumes e). The aim is then to find a hypothesis H that covers all positive examples (completeness) and none of the negative examples (consistency). As C-CLASSIC only contains a limited kind of disjunction (the ONE-OF connective), many target concepts of practical interest cannot be expressed using a single term of C-CLASSIC. One way to overcome this limitation is to consider algorithms which learn a disjunction of terms rather than a single term, i.e. a hypothesis H such that $H \equiv H_1 \lor H_2 \ldots \lor H_n$ (however, note that the connectives δ et ε allow to limit the number of disjuncts used to represent concepts (see section 4.3)). The cover of an example is then as follow :

If $H \equiv H_1 \lor H_2 \ldots \lor H_n$ and e is a concept, then H covers e if and only if ∃ H_i, $e \sqsubseteq H_i$ (i.e. H_i subsumes e)

The basic idea behind the LCSLEARNDISJ algorithm described in [7] is to use the LCS to implement a specific-to-general greedy search for hypotheses that cover many positive examples and no negative examples (this approach is similar to GOLEM [16] where multi-clause Prolog predicates are learned).

Example 1

Let $E^+ = \{e_1, e_2, e_3, e_4\}$ be a set of positive examples of the concept to learn and $E^- = \{ce_1\}$ a set of negative examples of this concept.

e_1 ≡ *Animal* ⊓ *Viviparous* ⊓ *Vertebrate* ⊓ *Barks.*

e_2 ≡ *Animal* ⊓ *Vertebrate* ⊓ *Oviparous* ⊓ *Has-teats.*

e_3 ≡ *Animal* ⊓ *Vertebrate* ⊓ *Flies* ⊓ *Quacks.*

e_4 ≡ *Animal* ⊓ *Vertebrate* ⊓ *Lives-in-Antartica* ⊓ *Has-Wings* ⊓ *Inapt-to-fly.*

ce'_1 ≡ *Animal* ⊓ *Vertebrate* ⊓ *Lives-in-the-sea* ⊓ *Scales.*

Results :

LCSLEARNDISJ computes the Least Common Subsumer of various subsets of positive examples. Since all the computed LCS (e.g. *Animal* ⊓ *Vertebrate*) cover the negative example, no consistent generalization can be performed. As a consequence, LCSLEARNDISJ returns the disjunction of the description of the four positive examples: (*Animal* ⊓ *Viviparous* ⊓ *Vertebrate* ⊓ *Barks*) ∨ (*Animal* ⊓ *Vertebrate* ⊓ *Oviparous* ⊓ *Has-teats*) ∨ (*Animal* ⊓ *Vertebrate* ⊓ *Flies* ⊓ *Quacks*) ∨ (*Animal* ⊓ *Vertebrate* ⊓ *Lives-in-Antartica* ⊓ *Has-Wings* ⊓ *Inapt-to-fly*).

In this example, we can see that for instance e_1 and e_2 have more in common than *Animal* ⊓ *Vertebrate* since e_1 is viviparous and e_2 has teats. However, the relationship between *Viviparous* and *Has-teats* can not be expressed in C-CLASSIC since it is not a strict knowledge (i.e. it is neither true that all animals that have teats are viviparous nor that all animals being viviparous have teats) and we can not add *Viviparous* to e_2 since it is oviparous (the same problem appears with e_3 that flies and e_4 which has wings but which is inapt to fly). In other words, e_2 and e_4 have exceptional properties but C-CLASSIC does not allow to express these exceptional properties. We show in section 4 how the saturation process allow to learn a more suited concept in C-CLASSIC$_{\delta\epsilon}$ without explictly expressing the exceptional properties of e_2 and e_4.

4   Learning in C-CLASSIC$_{\delta\epsilon}$

Learning in C-CLASSIC$_{\delta\epsilon}$ is similar to learning in C-CLASSIC. C-CLASSIC$_{\delta\epsilon}$ has been proved PAC-learnable [23,21]. The same LCSLEARNDISJ algorithm can be used as polynomial subsumption and Least Common Subsumer algorithms have been defined on C-CLASSIC$_{\delta\epsilon}$.

However, the example definitions have to be saturated prior to learning using background knowledge. A part of this background knowledge is related to default and excepted properties and it is used to add such properties in the positive and negative examples. The learning problem for our framework is therefore defined as follows:

Given: a set of T-box statements, a finite set of rules[6] β (background knowledge), and sets of C-CLASSIC$_{\delta\epsilon}$ concepts E^+, E^- (positive and negative examples).

Build: sets of saturated examples $E^{+'}$ and $E^{-'}$ ($E^{+'}$ and $E^{-'}$ are the result of the saturation process linked to β and applied on E^+ and E^-).

Find: a hypothesis H (disjuncts of C-CLASSIC$_{\delta\epsilon}$ terms), such that H is complete w.r.t. $E^{+'}$ and consistent w.r.t. $E^{-'}$.

4.1   Background Knowledge

The background knowledge β is composed of two sets of rules (C and D are terms of C-CLASSIC$_{\delta\epsilon}$): a set *Def* of default rules in the form C $\rightarrow_d$ D meaning that if a concept is subsumed by C, it is generally subsumed by D, together with a set *Inc* of strict incoherence rules in the form C $\rightarrow$ ⊥ meaning that if a concept is subsumed by C, it is incoherent. More precisely, the definition of *Def* and *Inc* are the following:

---

[6] The syntax of these rules is defined in section 4.1.

Definition 3 (Def) *Def is composed of m rules called $R_1,\ldots,R_m$ such that $R_i = precondition_i \rightarrow_d Conclusion_i$ where $precondition_i$ is a term of $C\text{-}CLASSIC^7$ and $Conclusion_i$ a term of C-CLASSIC where the only allowed concept conjunctions are in the value restriction of roles.*

Definition 4 (Inc) *Inc is composed of n rules called $R_1,\ldots,R_n$ such that $R_i = precondition_i \rightarrow \perp$ where $precondition_i$ is a term of C-CLASSIC.*

A rule of Def or Inc is applicable if its precondition subsumes the example.

4.2   Saturation Process

One of the main operations of the saturation process is to detect a potential incoherence between the definition of an example and the conclusion of an applicable default rule in order to add a default property (no incoherence has been detected) or an excepted property (an incoherence has been detected) to the example.

We distinguish two kinds of incoherences: incoherences of type 1 and incoherences of type 2.

An incoherence of type 1 corresponds to an incoherence linked to one or more general axioms concerning the connectives of the language. For instance, *child AT-LEAST* 2 ⊓ *child AT-MOST* 1 is incoherent and more generally for all role R, R *AT-LEAST* m ⊓ R *AT-MOST* n is incoherent if m > n. These axioms are expressed in the equational system of C-CLASSIC [23].

An incoherence of type 2 corresponds to an incoherence linked to a rule belonging to *Inc* (e.g. *Inapt-to-fly* ⊓ *Flies* is incoherent).

It must be highlighted that in our framework incoherences are only linked to strict knowledge. Indeed, a default property cannot be incoherent. This is the reason why when there is no conflict between the conclusion of the default rule and the current description of e' we add δConclusion rather than Conclusion which could later be in conflict with knowledge issued from other rules. Besides, an excepted property never leads to an incoherence since an exception to a concept does not correspond to a negation of this concept. For instance, Fly^ϵ ⊓ Fly is not incoherent.

The fact that incoherences are linked only to strict knowledge has two implications. First, it allows us to be sure that the addition of default and excepted properties will not further lead to incoherences. This guarantees the monotonicity of the extension process. Besides, we can state that a term T of $C\text{-}CLASSIC_{\delta\epsilon}$ is incoherent if and only if the term T' equivalent to T without default and excepted properties is incoherent. Thus, incoherence of type 1 can be detected by translating a term of $C\text{-}CLASSIC_{\delta\epsilon}$ into a term of C-CLASSIC (i.e. by removing

---

[7] We could extend the process by using terms of $C\text{-}CLASSIC_{\delta\epsilon}$ in the theory but our goal is to show that we can obtain default and excepted properties from rules whose precondition and conclusion are described using strict properties.

default and excepted properties) and by applying the normalization procedure defined for C-CLASSIC in [23][8].

The sketch of the extension algorithm is the following. Let e be an example described by a term C of C-CLASSIC$_{\delta\epsilon}$, for each rule of *Def* we check whether C is subsumed by the premisse of the rule. In order to achieve this task default and excepted properties of C are removed and C' the term of C-CLASSIC obtained is compared with the premisse of the rule by applying the subsumption algorithm designed for C-CLASSIC. If the premisse subsumes C', we check if the conclusion of the default rule is incoherent with C' (i.e. if it leads to incoherences of type 1 or 2). Incoherences of type 1 are detected by computing the normal form of C' $\sqcap$ Conclusion using the normalization algorithm of C-CLASSIC terms. If this normal form is equivalent to the denotation of $\perp$, there is an incoherence. Incoherences of type 2 are detected by verifying whether a premisse of a rule belonging to *Inc* subsumes C' $\sqcap$ Conclusion. If any incoherence is detected the conclusion is excepted and added to C (i.e. Conclusion$^\epsilon$ is added to C) otherwise the conclusion of the rule by default (i.e. δConclusion) is added to C.

The extension algorithm is as follows :

Inputs: a term C of C-CLASSIC$_{\delta\epsilon}$, a set Def $=\{R_1,\ldots,R_n\}$ of "default rules", a set Inc $= \{R'_1,\ldots,R'_m\}$ of strict incoherence rules.

Output: ENF-C the extended normal form of C.

External procedures used:
Remove$\delta\epsilon$(d): transforms a term d of C-CLASSIC$_{\delta\epsilon}$ into a term of C-CLASSIC by removing default and excepted properties of d (since incoherences concern only strict properties).
Subsume(C,D): returns **true** if C subsumes D, C and D being two terms of C-CLASSIC.
NF'(d): computes the normal form of a term d of C-CLASSIC.
BEGIN
C' $\leftarrow$ Remove$\delta\epsilon$(C)
    For all R$_i$ of Def such that Premisse$_i$ $\rightarrow$ Conclusion$_i$ and Subsume(Premisse$_i$,C')
    begin
      Add $\leftarrow$ **false** {* Add is true if an excepted property has been added *}
      * Search for incoherences of type 1
      if NF'(C' $\sqcap$ Conclusion$_i$) $= \perp$ {* Conclusion$_i$ is incoherent with the description of C' and C *}
          then begin
          C $\leftarrow$ C $\sqcap$ (Conclusion $_i$)$^\epsilon$
          Add $\leftarrow$ **true**
          end
      * Search for incoherences of type 2
      if not Add **then if** there exists in Inc a premisse D such that Subsume(D,C' $\sqcap$ Conclusion$_i$)

---

[8] Applying this procedure on an incoherent term leads to normalize the term by $\perp$ which denotes incoherences.

then $C \leftarrow C \sqcap (\text{Conclusion}_i)^\epsilon$ **else** $C \leftarrow C \sqcap \delta\text{Conclusion}_i$
end For all
END

Example

We consider example 1 described in section 3.

Let β a background knowledge made of two sets *Inc* and *Def*.

Def = {R1: *Animal* $\sqcap$ *Has-teats* $\rightarrow_d$ *Viviparous*, R2: *Animal* $\sqcap$ *Has-Wings* $\rightarrow_d$ *Flies*, R3: *Animal* $\sqcap$ *Lives-in-the-sea* $\sqcap$ *Scales* $\rightarrow_d$ *Gills* } is a set of default rules meaning that generally animals having teats are viviparous, that generally animals having wings fly and that generally animals with scales and living in the sea have gills.

Inc = {R4: *Viviparous* $\sqcap$ *Oviparous* $\rightarrow \perp$, R5: *Inapt-to-fly* $\sqcap$ *Flies* $\rightarrow \perp$} is a set of strict rules respectively meaning that an example can not be both oviparous and viviparous and that it is impossible to fly and to be inapt to fly. We illustrate now the saturation process on the example 1.

$e'_1 \equiv e_1$

$e'_2 \equiv e_2 \sqcap Viviparous^\epsilon$

$e'_3 \equiv e_3$

$e'_4 \equiv e_4 \sqcap Flies^\epsilon$.

$ce'_1 \equiv ce_1 \sqcap \delta Gills$.

Some explanations about the saturation of e_2:

e_2 verifies (i.e. is subsumed by) the precondition of R1. The addition of *Viviparous* to e_2 leads to an incoherence (*Viviparous* $\sqcap$ *Oviparous* is subsumed by $\perp$ from R4). The property *Viviparous$^\epsilon$* is added to e_2. Adding this property makes it possible to highlight that a part of e_2 (*Oviparous*) is incoherent with *Animal* $\sqcap$ *Has-teats* $\rightarrow_d$ *Viviparous*. This information can be useful during the learning process described in the next section.

4.3   Learning in C-CLASSIC$_{\delta\epsilon}$ vs. C-CLASSIC

Using the example 1 and the background knowledge described in the previous section, we show now that, given the same positive and negative examples, C-CLASSIC$_{\delta\epsilon}$ allows to learn disjunctive concepts represented with less disjuncts than concepts learned in C-CLASSIC.

LCSLEARNDISJ is applied on the saturated examples. The first disjunct learned by the algorithm is LCS(e'_1,e'_2) (i.e. *Animal* $\sqcap$ $\delta Viviparous^9$ $\sqcap$ *Vertebrate*). The examples e'_1 and e'_2 are then removed from the learning set. The next learned disjunct is LCS(e'_3,e'_4) that covers these two positives examples and no negative examples. The algorithm returns the following hypothesis: (*Animal* $\sqcap$ $\delta Viviparous$ $\sqcap$ *Vertebrate*) $\vee$ (*Animal* $\sqcap$ $\delta Flies$ $\sqcap$ *Vertebrate*).

The following instance: $e \equiv$ *Animal* $\sqcap$ *Vertebrate* $\sqcap$ *Lives-in-Australia* $\sqcap$ *Wings*

---

[9] Note that this property does not belong to the LCS computed from the C-CLASSIC definitions of e_1 and e_2. Now, this property is crucial since it prevents the negative example to be subsumed (let us remind that ce'_1 has the properties *Animal* $\sqcap$ *Vertebrate*).

$\sqcap$ *Big-feet* $\sqcap$ *Inapt-to-fly* is recognized by the definition learned in C-CLASSIC$_{\delta\epsilon}$: the saturation process adds *Flies*$^\epsilon$ to e and *Animal* $\sqcap$ δ*Flies* $\sqcap$ *Vertebrate* subsumes the saturated instance. Note that e is not recognized by the definition learned in C-CLASSIC (see section 3).

5 Related and Further Work

Cohen and Hirsh suggest that learning systems based on description logics may prove to be a useful complement to ILP systems. One issue is the investigation of combining our framework and non-monotonic frameworks in ILP. In [9], the authors present a framework for learning non-monotonic logic programs. Hence given a background theory and a set of examples they generate a hypothesis within the language bias of a subclass of non-monotonic logic programs[10] that covers all the positive examples and none of the negative examples. In such theories in order to decide if an atom, A, holds they need to show that A can be derived classically using some rule, r, for A and that ¬A can not be derived classically using some rule r' which is designated higher than the rule r by the priority relation on the program.

For instance, consider the background theory B:

bird(x) ← *penguin(x)*

penguin(x) ← *superpenguin(x)*

bird(a), bird(b), penguin(c), penguin(d), superpenguin(e), superpenguin(f)

Consider also the set of examples $E = E^+ \cup E^-$ where $E^+ = \{flies(a), flies(b),$ *flies(e), flies(f)*$\}$ and $E^- = \{flies(c), flies(d)\}$.

The result of the algorithm is the hypothesis H :

R1 : *flies(x)* ← *bird(x)*

R2 : ¬ *flies(x)* ← *penguin(x)*

R3 : *flies(x)* ← *superpenguin(x)*

where R1 has lower priority than R2 and R2 has lower priority than R3.

In such a non-monotonic framework, the goal is to learn strict predicates (e.g. *Fly* whose penguin is a negative example) by generating default rules. This approach is not suited to learn strict concepts having default properties in their definition (e.g. *Bird* whose penguin is a positive example despite the fact it is exceptional w.r.t. the *Fly* property). A further work could consist in using default rules learned in this non-monotonic framework (e.g. R1, R2, R3[11]) in order to improve learning in C-CLASSIC$_{\delta\epsilon}$ (for instance, positive and negative examples of the concept *Bird* could be saturated with $\delta(Flies^\epsilon)$ or $(Flies^\epsilon)^\epsilon$ using R1, R2 and R3). Note that the problem of learning with a non-monotonic background knowledge is one of the possible directions for further research listed in [9].

Abduction [10,13] also is the basis for non-monotonic learning frameworks by

---

[10] Theories where their set of contradictory rules can be separated into classes where the rules in each class are totally ordered by the priority relation of the theory.

[11] The presence of ¬ is not a problem since it is straighforward to add the negation on atomic concepts in C-CLASSIC$_{\delta\epsilon}$ (and the axiom A $\sqcap$ ¬A $\equiv$ ⊥ in the equational system in order to take into account such incoherences.

providing a uniform technique to handle negation as failure, incomplete predicates and integrity constraints. We need also to compare our work with these approaches.

As a conclusion, in this paper we have defined a problem setting concerning learning concept in a framework combining a description logics allowing to define concepts with default and excepted properties, and a background knowledge represented by rules and default rules. We proposed a prior saturation of the examples using the background knowledge and we showed that learning from extended examples can lead to the construction of a more satisfactory learned concept. More precisely, the learned concepts are smaller in size (they have less disjuncts) and they are more general covering more examples which can be identified as belonging to the target concept. The presence of defaults is a way to improve the expressive power of the DL (few concepts can be defined with necessary and sufficient properties using only strict knowledge) and therefore to improve the learning process. Finally, note that the application of default rules is difficult since it can lead to ambiguities. For instance, in [19] the authors integrated defaults in DLs using incident rules of the form c1 $\rightarrow_d$ c2 meaning "whenever an object is an instance of c1 it is also an instance of c2 unless this is in conflict with some other piece of knowledge". This approach requires to handle multi extensions by defining preference criteria (e.g. the preferred models contain the most specific knowledge or the most applied defaults). In our framework, the connectives δ and ϵ allow us to avoid this problem.

References

1. M. Bain and S. Muggleton, 'Non-monotonic learning', in *Knowledge Representation and Organization in Machine Learning*, ed., Stephen Muggleton, 289–319, ACADEMIC PRESS LIMITED, (1992). 174
2. A. Borgida and P. F. Patel-Schneider, 'Complete algorithm for subsumption in the CLASSIC description logic', *Artificial Intelligence Research*, **1**, 278–308, (1994). 175
3. R. J. Brachman, 'A structural paradigm for representing knowledge', Technical Report 3605, BBN Report, (1978). 175
4. W. Buntine, 'Generalized subsumption and its application to induction and redundancy', *Artificial Intelligence*, **36**, (1988). 177
5. W. W. Cohen, A. Borgida, and H. Hirsh, 'Computing least common subsumers in description logics', in *10th National Conference of the American Association for Artificial Intelligence*, pp. 754–760, San Jose, California, (1992). 177
6. W. W. Cohen and H. Hirsh, 'The learnability of description logics with equality constraints', *Machine Learning*, **2**(4), 169–199, (1994). 175, 178
7. W. W. Cohen and H. Hirsh, 'Learning the CLASSIC description logic: theoretical and experimental results', in *International Conference on Knowledge Representation and Reasoning*, 121–133, (1994). 173, 175, 178
8. P. Coupey and C. Fouqueré, 'Extending conceptual definitions with default knowledge', *Computational Intelligence*, **13**(2), (1997). 175
9. Y. Dimopoulos and A. Kakas, 'Learning non-monotonic logic programs: learning exceptions', in *Proceedings of the 11th European Conference on Artificial Intelligence, 1995*, ed., Springer-Verlag, pp. 107–121, (1995). 174, 183

10. Y. Dimopoulos and A. Kakas, 'Abduction and inductive learning', in *Advances in Inductive Logic Programming*, ed., L. De Raedt, pp. 144–171, (1996). 183
11. F. M. Donini, M. Lenzerini, D. Nardi, and W. Nutt, 'The complexity of concept languages', in *Principles of Knowledge Representation and Reasoning: 2nd International Conference*, eds., J. A. Allen R. Fikes and E Sandewall, pp. 151–162, Cambridge, Mass., (1991). 174
12. J. Doyle and R. S. Patil, 'Two theses of knowledge representation: language restrictions, taxonomic classification, and the utility of representation services', *Artificial Intelligence*, **48**(3), 261–297, (1991). 175
13. K. Inoue and C. Sakama, 'Abducing priorities to derive intended conclusions', in *16th International Joint Conference on Artificial Intelligence*, pp. 44–49, Japan, (1999). 183
14. J. U. Kietz and K. Morik, 'A polynomial approach to the constructive induction of structural knowledge', *Machine Learning*, **14**(2), 193–217, (1994). 175
15. S. Muggleton, 'Inductive logic programming', *New Generation Computing*, **8**, 295–318, (1991). 173
16. S. Muggleton and C. Feng, 'Efficient induction of logic programs', in *Inductive Logic programming*, ACADEMIC PRESS, (1992). 178
17. S. Muggleton and L. De Raedt, 'Inductive logic programming: Theory and methods', *Journal of Logic Programming*, **19**, (1994). 173
18. J. Quantz, G. Dunker, F. Bergmann, and I. Kellner, 'The flex system', Technical report, KIT-Report, Technische Universität, Berlin, Germany, (1996). 175
19. J. Quantz and V. Royer, 'A preference semantics for defaults in terminological logics', in *Principles of Knowledge Representation and Reasoning: 3rd International Conference*, 294–305, Bernhard Nebel, Charles Rich and William Swartout, Cambridge, MA., USA, (1992). 184
20. J. R. Wright, E. S. Weixelbaum, K. Brown, G. T. Vesonder, S. R. Palmer, J. I. Berman, and H. H. Moore, 'A knowledge-based configurator that supports sales, engineering and manufacturing at att bell network systems', in *Proceedings of the Innovative Applications of Artificial Intelligence Conferences*, pp. 183–193, Menlo Park, California, USA, (1993). 175
21. V. Ventos, P. Brézellec, P. Coupey, and H. Soldano, 'C-classic$_{\delta\epsilon}$: un langage de descriptions pac-learnable', in *Actes Journées Acquisition Validation Apprentissage, JAVA95*, pp. 192–196, Grenoble, France, (1995). 174, 179
22. V. Ventos, 'A deductive study of c-classic$_{\delta\epsilon}$', in *Proceedings of the International Workshop in Description Logics 96*, pp. 192–196, Boston, USA, (1996). 174, 177
23. V. Ventos, *C-CLASSIC$_{\delta\epsilon}$: une logique de descriptions pour la définition et l'apprentissage de concepts avec défauts et exceptions*, PhD thesis, France, 1997. 174, 177, 179, 180, 181
24. V. Ventos, P. Brézellec, P. Coupey, and H. Soldano, 'Lcs operation in c-classic$_{\delta\epsilon}$: formal properties and applications', in *International KRUSE Symposium Knowledge Retrieval, Use, and Storage for Efficiency*, pp. 124–135, Vancouver, Canada, (1997). 177
25. V. Ventos, P. Brézellec, H. Soldano, and D. Bouthinon 'Learning concepts in c-classic$_{\delta\epsilon}$', in *Proceedings of the International Workshop on Description Logics 98*, pp. 50–54, Trento, Italy, (1998). 174

Declarative Specification and Solution of Combinatorial Auctions Using Logic Programming

Chitta Baral and Cenk Uyan

Department of Computer Sc. and Engg., Arizona State University
Tempe, Arizona 85287
{chitta,cuyan}@asu.edu

Abstract. In a combinatorial auction problem bidders are allowed to bid on a bundle of items. The auctioneer has to select a subset of the bids so as to maximize the price it gets, and of course making sure that it does not accept multiple bids that have the same item as each item can be sold only once. In this paper we show how the combinatorial auction problem and many of its extensions can be expressed in logic programming based systems such as Smodels and dlv. We propose this as an alternative to the standard syntax specific specialized implementations that are much harder to modify and extend when faced with generalizations and additional constraints.

1   Introduction and Motivation

In a simple auction several bidders bid for an item and the auctioneer selects the highest bid. Often bidders need a bundle of items, where the worth of the whole bundle – to the bidder – may be more than the sum of the individual worth of each item in the bundle. For example, let A and B be two adjacent real estate plots. A single developer can often make more money developing both plots together than two different developers developing A and B separately without co-operating with each other. This happens if say both A and B are needed to create a lucrative golf course while A and B separately can only be used for less profitable purposes. The opposite may be true in some cases too. The cases that are often mentioned with regards to both are airport landing slots [9], bandwidth auctions, real estate auctions, and transportation exchanges [11].

In such cases participating in parallel or sequential auctions for each items in a bundle desired by a bidder is risky as the bidder may not win all items in the bundle. Moreover it would be difficult for him to individually price each item in the bundle. One way to avoid such problems is to have *combinatorial auctions* where bidders are allowed to bid on bundles. Although this is good for the bidder, the seller's problem of deciding which bids to accept becomes harder, as different bidders can make up their own bundle on which they bid on .

Recently, there has been a lot of interest in this problem because of its applicability in Internet based auctions, B2B exchanges, and multi-agent systems [16,7]. There have been several papers [12,13,2,4,6,15,10] that analyze this

T. Eiter, W. Faber, and M. Truszczyński (Eds.): LPNMR 2001, LNAI 2173, pp. 186–199, 2001.
© Springer-Verlag Berlin Heidelberg 2001

problem and present algorithms and techniques to solve it and a few of its generalizations. One starting point that guides research on this is the result from [10] which shows the problem of finding the optimal set of bids (that maximize the seller's take) to be NP-Complete.

So far there are three different approaches for solving this problem: complete algorithms [12,2,10] that find an optimal solution in the general case, incomplete methods [4] that find high quality solutions quickly, and identification of tractable special cases and algorithms for those cases [15,13]. The other possible approach of finding approximation algorithms is blocked by the result from [12] that shows that no polynomial algorithm can guarantee a solution that is close to optimal.

In this paper we follow the first approach of obtaining optimal solutions in the general case. Our methodology is different from the earlier approaches [12,2,10] in that we would like to represent the problem in a declarative knowledge representation language such that optimal 'models' of the representation correspond to optimal solutions. This is similar to the methodology of satisfiability based planning [5] where the planning problem is represented as a propositional theory, and each model of this theory encodes a plan. *The main motivation behind our approach of using a declarative knowledge representation language is that we would like the process of adding additional constraints, or making a generalization to be easier.* This differs from the other approaches [12,13,2,6] where major changes were needed to move from single unit combinatorial auctions to multi-unit combinatorial auctions. Also, as mentioned in [13] additional generalizations necessitates change in the code, which requires the knowledge of the structure of the code and hence can only be done by people adequately familiar with the original code. In contrast we will show that when using a declarative knowledge representation language additional generalization, or addition of new constraints often leads to adding a few extra rules, without needing the detailed knowledge of the original code or its structure.

The declarative language that we will use throughout this paper is Smodels [8,14][1], an extension of logic programming with answer set semantics [3]. It has new constructs such as cardinality and weight constraints, and optimization statements. It is preferable over propositional logic as it is more expressive in terms of being able to express transitive closure, causality, and aggregation. Moreover, it is a non-monotonic language and hence more suitable for knowledge representation and finally it includes optimization statements. (A more detailed argument about the advantages of logic programming with answer set semantics over other logics is given in the draft of a book by the first author available at

---

[1] Strictly speaking, Smodels is a system that started of as implementing the answer set semantics of logic programs and now has several new constructs. By the Smodels language we refer to the extension of logic programs that is used by the Smodels system.

We would like to mention that some of the encodings in this paper can also be expressed in the language of the dlv system [1]. Due to lack of space we only focus on the Smodels system.

http://www.public.asu.edu/~cbaral/.) Smodels is preferable over ILP (integer linear programming) because it can represent logical specifications more easily. Although ILP can accommodate propositional logic, it has not been shown how it can accommodate non-monotonic features of a logic program.

Our goal in this paper is to show how single unit and multi unit combinatorial auction problems can be specified and declaratively solved using Smodels, and how it is easy to add additional constraints and further generalizations to the original problem using Smodels. We hope this representation will serve as a benchmark to the logic programming, knowledge representation and declarative problem solving communities to develop more efficient implementations of the Smodels language such that the timing of obtaining solutions of combinatorial auction problems specified in Smodels is comparable to that of the specialized algorithms/programs in [12,13,2,6].

2   Background: The Smodels Language

A logic program is a collection of rules of the form

$$a_0 \leftarrow a_1, \ldots, a_m, not\ a_{m+1}, \ldots, not\ a_n \tag{1}$$

where a_i's are atoms. For an atom a, "*not a*" is referred to as a naf-literal. Intuitively, the above rule means that if $a_1 \ldots a_m$ are true and $a_{m+1} \ldots a_n$ can be assumed to be false then a_0 must be true. Logic programs whose rules do not have *not* in the body – referred to as definite programs – have unique answer sets, which are the least models of the theory obtained by treating rules of the form $a_0 \leftarrow a_1, \ldots, a_m$ as the classical formula $a_1 \wedge \ldots \wedge a_m \supset a_0$. Given a logic program P and a set of atoms S, the Gelfond-Lifschitz transformation P^S is defined as the set of rules obtained from P by removing all rules from P whose body contains *not b* such that $b \in S$, and then removing the naf-literals from the rest of the rules. *A set S of atoms is said to be an answer set of a logic program P if S is the answer set of the definite program P^S.*

In the Smodels language, each of the $a_0, \ldots, a_m$ can be replaced by cardinality expressions and weight expressions. An example of a cardinality expression is:

$$3\ \{sold(X) : item(X)\}\ 6$$

which is true in an answer set if the number of items that are sold is between (inclusively) 3 and 6. We can encode the value each item is sold by a weight declaration of the form:

$$\mathrm{weight}sold(a) = 8.$$

which would mean that item a was sold for \$8. Now the weight expression

$$23\ [sold(X) : item(X)]\ 36$$

will be true in an answer set if the total value of those items that are sold is between (inclusively) 23 and 36.

Optimization statements are syntactically similar to weight and cardinality expressions except that the left and right range are replaced by the label *maximize* or *minimize* in the left hand side. For example, if we want to obtain the answer sets where the number of items that is sold is maximum then we need to write the following:

$$maximize \ \{sold(X) : item(X)\}.$$

Smodels allows multiple optimization statements and treats them as a compound optimization through a lexicographic ordering
among the optimizations statements. A more formal characterization of the Smodels language is given in [14].

3   Single Unit Combinatorial Auction

We explain the single unit combinatorial auction problem through an example. The auctioneer has the set of items $\{1, 2, 3, 4\}$, and the buyers submit bids $\{a, b, c, d, e\}$ where a constitutes of $\langle\{1, 2, 3\}, 24\rangle$, meaning that the bid a is for the bundle $\{1, 2, 3\}$ and its price is \$24. Similarly b constitutes of $\langle\{2, 3\}, 9\rangle$, c constitutes of $\langle\{3, 4\}, 8\rangle$, d constitutes of $\langle\{2, 3, 4\}, 25\rangle$, and e constitutes of $\langle\{1, 4\}, 15\rangle$. The *winner determination* problem is to accept a subset of the bids with the stipulation that no two bids containing the same item can be accepted, so as to maximize the total price fetched. We now present an Smodels encoding (which is both a specification and a program.) of this example.

3.1   Specifying the Domain

1. We specify the bid names and their values as follows:

   bid(a). weight sel(a) = 24. bid(b). weight sel(b) = 9. bid(c). weight sel(c) = 8. bid(d). weight sel(d) = 25. bid(e). weight sel(e) = 15.
2. We specify the items as follows: item(1..4).
3. We specify the composition of each bids – in terms of what items it consists of, as follows.

   in(1,a). in(2,a). in(3,a).   in(2,b). in(3,b).   in(3,c). in(4,c). in(2,d). in(3,d). in(4,d).   in(1,e). in(4,e).

3.2   The General Rules

We have the following general rules which together with the domain specific rules from the previous subsection, when run using Smodels will give us the winning bids.

1. The following two rules label each bid as either selected or not selected.
   $sel(X) \leftarrow bid(X), not \ not\_sel(X).$
   $not\_sel(X) \leftarrow bid(X), not \ sel(X).$
   They can be replaced by the following single Smodels rule:

   $\{sel(X)\} \leftarrow bid(X).$

2. The following enforces the constraint that two different bids with the same items can not be both selected.

$\leftarrow sel(X), sel(Y), X \neq Y, in(I, X), in(I, Y).$

The above Smodels rule does not follow the syntax of rules in Section 2. Such rules of the form

$\leftarrow a_1, \ldots, a_m, not\ a_{m+1}, \ldots, not\ a_n.$

with empty head mean that there can not be answer sets that evaluate the body true. Such rules can be thought of as the following rule, where f is a new atom, that satisfies the syntax of (1) in Section 2.

$f \leftarrow not\ f, a_1, \ldots, a_m, not\ a_{m+1}, \ldots, not\ a_n.$

3. The following optimization statement specifies that we must select bids such that their total price is maximized.

$maximize\ [sel(X) : bid(X)].$

When we run the above program in the Smodels system using the command
lparse auc1.sm | smodels 0
the system first outputs the answer set $\{a\}$, and then outputs the optimal answer set $\{d\}$, indicating that the latter has a higher total price.

3.3   Formal Characterization

In a combinatorial auction (single unit case), the auctioneer has m items $M = \{1, \ldots, m\}$ and the buyers submit n bids $B = \{B_1, \ldots, B_n\}$, where each bid is a tuple $B_i = \langle S_i, p_i \rangle$, with $S_i \subseteq M$, and p_i is a price. The *winner determination problem* [13] is an assignment of bids as *accepted* ($x_i = 1$) or not ($x_i = 0$), for $1 \leq i \leq n$ that satisfies the constraint

$$(\sum_{1 \leq i \leq n, j \in S_i} x_i) \leq 1 \qquad \text{for } 1 \leq j \leq m; \text{ and maximizes} \qquad \sum_{i=1}^{n} p_i \times x_i.$$

The above characterization can be related to the Smodels encoding as follows:

Theorem 1. *For a single unit combinatorial auction problem with integer prices, each solution to the winner determination problem corresponds to an optimal answer set of the encoding described in 3.1-3.2 and vice-versa.*

3.4   Encoding in dlv

The dlv system [1] is also an implementation of an extension of logic programming with additional constructs. It allows disjunctions in the head of rules and captures the second level of polynomial hierarchy. Among its additional constructs are weak constraints which are of the form:

$$:\sim p_1, \ldots, p_m, not\ q_1, \ldots, not\ q_n.[weight : level]$$

Given a program with weak constraints its *best* answer sets are obtained by first obtaining the answer sets without considering the weak constraints and ordering each of them based on the weight and priority level of the set of weak constraints they violate, and then selecting the ones that violate the minimum. In presence of both weight and priority level information, the minimization is done with respect to the weight of the constraints of the highest priority, then the next highest priority and so on.

The encoding in Section 3.1 and 3.2 can be alternatively encoded in dlv[2] as follows:

1. We have the *bid* atoms from part 1 of Section 3.1, and *in* atoms from part 3 of Section 3.1.
2. We can either have the rules in part 1 of Section 3.2 or use disjunction and have the rule: $sel(X) \lor not\_sel(X) \leftarrow bid(X)$.
3. We have the constraint in part 2 of Section 3.2.
4. Finally instead of the optimization statement in part 3 of Section 3.3, we have the following weak constraints.
   $:\sim not\ sel(a).[24:1]$
   $:\sim not\ sel(b).[9:1]$
   $:\sim not\ sel(c).[8:1]$
   $:\sim not\ sel(d).[25:1]$
   $:\sim not\ sel(e).[15:1]$

4   Combinatorial Auction with CNF Bids

In this section we show how the single unit combinatorial auction specification can be generalized such that a bidder can specify some options between his bids. For example a bidder may want to specify that only one of his bids g and h be accepted, but not both. This can be generalized further to such that a bidder can specify a CNF[3] bid [4] which is a conjunction of (ex-or) disjunction of items such that one item from each of the conjuncts is awarded to the bidder. (An alternative way to achieve this is by opening up the CNF to several bids and adding a dummy [2] item to each of the bids so that exactly one of them is selected.) As before we show our encoding with respect to an example.

1. We will have the domain specification as in part 1 and 2 of Section 3.1 and the general rules in part 1 and 3 of Section 3.2.
2. Recall that a CNF bid is not a bundle of items, rather it could be of the following form: $a = (g1 \oplus h1) \land (g2 \oplus h2) \land (g3 \oplus h3)$
   which means that the bid a can be satisfied by granting one of the items $g1$ and $h1$, one of the items $g2$ and $h2$ and one of the items $g3$ and $h3$. We can represent this in Smodels as follows:

---

[2] In the future we plan to compare the timings using the dlv system with the timings using the Smodels system.

[3] Although the use of CNF is somewhat misleading, we use it to be consistent with the original terminology in [4].

conj(c1, a). disj(g1, c1). disj(h1, c1).
conj(c2, a). disj(g2, c2). disj(h2, c2).
conj(c3, a). disj(g3, c3). disj(h3, c3).
This will replace the representation in part 3 of Section 3.1.

3. Now it is not enough to just label bids as selected or un-selected. After labeling a bid as selected we must identify which items are granted as part of that selected bid. We have the following rules to encode that.

$other\_granted(X, C, G) \leftarrow granted(X, C, G'), G' \neq G.$
$granted(X, C, G) \leftarrow sel(X), conj(C, X),$
$$disj(G, C), not \ other\_granted(X, C, G).$$

Intuitively, $granted(X, C, G)$ means that as part of the selection of bid X, to satisfy the conjunct C, item G is granted; and $other\_granted(X, C, G)$ means that some item other than G has been granted. The above two rules ensure that for any selected bid X, and its conjunct C exactly one item in that conjunct is granted in each answer set.

4. Because of the difference between a CNF bid and a simple bid consisting of a bundle, part 2 of Section 3.2 needs to be replaced by the following rule, so as to enforce that we should not select two bids and grant the same item with respect to both.

$\leftarrow bid(X), bid(Y), granted(X, C, G), granted(Y, C', G), X \neq Y.$

5   Multi-unit Combinatorial Auction

Multi-unit combinatorial auction is a generalization of the single unit case, where the auctioneer may have multiple identical copies of each item and the bids may specify multiple units of each item. The goal here is same as before: to maximize the total price that is fetched; but the condition is that the bids should be selected such that for any item the total number that is asked by the selected bids should not be more than the number that is originally available for that item. As before, we describe our Smodels encoding with respect to an example: first the specification for a particular domain, and then a set of general rules.

5.1   Specifying the Domain

1. The bid names and their values are specified as in part 1 of 3.1.
   bid(a). weight sel(a) = 23.
   bid(b). weight sel(b) = 9.
   bid(c). weight sel(c) = 8.
   bid(d). weight sel(d) = 25.
   bid(e). weight sel(e) = 15.
2. We specify the items and their initial quantities as follows:
   item(i). item(j). item(k). item(l).
   limit(i,8). limit(j,10). limit(k,6). limit(l,12).
3. We specify the composition of each bid as follows:
   in(i,a,6). in(j,a,4). in(k,a,4).

Intuitively, the above means that, bid 'a' is for 6 units of item 'i', 4 units of item 'j', and 4 units of item 'k'.
in(j,b,6). in(k,b,4).
in(k,c,2). in(l,c,10).
in(j,d,4). in(k,d,2). in(l,d,4).
in(i,e,6). in(l,e,6).

5.2   The General Rules

We have the following general rules which together with the domain specific rules of the previous subsection, when run using Smodels will give us the winning bids.

1. The following two rules label each bid as either selected or not selected.
   $sel(X) \leftarrow bid(X), not\ not\_sel(X).$
   $not\_sel(X) \leftarrow bid(X), not\ sel(X).$
2. The following rule defines $sel\_in(I, X, Z)$, which intuitively means that bid X is selected, and Z units of item I is in bid X.
   $sel\_in(I, X, Z) \leftarrow item(I), bid(X), sel(X), in(I, X, Z).$
3. The following weight declaration assigns the weight Z to the atom
   $sel\_in(X, Y, Z).$ $weight\ sel\_in(X, Y, Z) = Z.$
   The above weight assignment is used in the next step to compute the total quantity of each item in the selected bids.
4. The following rule enforces the constraint that for each item, the total quantity that is to be encumbered towards the selected bids must be less than or equal to the initial available quantity of that item.
   $\leftarrow Y'[sel\_in(I, X, Z) : bid(X) : num(Z)], item(I), limit(I, Y), Y' = Y + 1.$
5. As before we have the following optimization statement.
   $maximize\ [sel(X) : bid(X)].$

When the above program is run through Smodels using the command
   lparse file.sm | smodels 0
the system first outputs the answer set $\{sel(d), sel(a)\}$, and then outputs another answer set $\{sel(e),\ sel(d),\ sel(b)\}$ and mentions that the latter one is optimal.

Thus the Smodels system starts off with a sub-optimal solution, and keeps giving better and better solutions until an optimal solution is found. We refer to this as exhibiting a weak anytime behavior as after the first solution is found, a user may interrupt the system at any time and get a sub-optimal solution which improves with time. Since there is no guarantee that the first solution will be found within a certain time bound we use the qualifier 'weak' with the adjective 'anytime'.

5.3   Formal Characterization

In the multi-unit case, the auctioneer has u_j units of each item j, $1 \leq j \leq m$, and each bid B_i is of the form $\langle (\lambda_i^1, \ldots, \lambda_i^m), p_i \rangle$, where λ_i^j denotes the number of units of item j that is part of the bid B_i. In this case, the *winner determination problem* [13] is an assignment of bids as *accepted* ($x_i = 1$) or not ($x_i = 0$), for $1 \leq i \leq n$ that satisfies the constraint

$$(\sum_{i=1}^{n} \lambda_i^j \times x_i) \leq u_j \qquad \text{for } 1 \leq j \leq m; \text{ and maximizes} \qquad \sum_{i=1}^{n} p_i \times x_i.$$

Theorem 2. *For a multi-unit combinatorial auction problem integer prices, each solution to the winner determination problem corresponds to an answer set of the encoding described in 5.1-5.2 and vice-versa.*

6   Combinatorial Exchanges

A combinatorial exchange is a further generalization, where we have buyers and sellers. The buyers bid as before, while the sellers offer their items for a price. The job of the exchange is to accept a subset of the bids of the buyers and sellers such that it maximizes the surplus (the amount it obtains from the buyers minus the amount it has to pay to the sellers), subject to the condition that for each item, the total number it obtains from the selected seller bids is more than what it has to give in lieu of the selected buyer bids. Note that the maximization condition guarantees that the exchange does not lose money outright. This is because by not accepting any bids the surplus will be zero. So when the exchange accepts some bids its surplus would have to be positive. We now describe our Smodels encoding for multi-unit combinatorial exchanges through a slight modification of the example in Section 5. The modification is that instead of specifying the initial quantity of each item, we create a seller f, who offers those quantities for a price.

1. We have part 1 and part 3 of Section 5.1 and only the items listing of part 2 of 5.2. We do not have the description of the initial quantity for the items. Instead the bid for the seller f is specified as follows:

   bid(f). weight sel(f) = -50.
   in(i,f,-8). in(j,f,-10). in(k,f,-6). in(l,f,-12).

   A sellers bid is distinguished from a buyers bid by having a negative price for the whole bid (meaning the seller wants money for those items, instead of being ready to give a certain amount of money), and similarly the atom $in(i, f, -8)$ means that the seller f has 8 units of item i to *sell*, while $in(i, a, 6)$ would mean that the buyer a wants to *buy* 6 units of item i.

2. We have part 1, 2, 3, and 5 of Section 5.2 and we replace part 4 by the following rule.

   $$\leftarrow Y \, [sel\_in(I, X, Z) : bid(X) : num(Z)] \, Y, item(I), Y > 0.$$

The above rule enforces the constraint that for each item I, the *total number* encumbered with respect to the selected buyer bids should be less than or equal to the sum that is available from the selected seller bids. Note that the use of the same variable Y as the upper and lower bound of the weight constraint serves the purpose of computing the aggregate. [4]

3. Although the following rule is normally not necessary, as it is taken care of by the maximize statement, by having it we can exploit the weak anytime behavior. It also eliminates selections, where the exchange may lose money, earlier in the process.

$$\leftarrow Y[sel(X):bid(X)]Y, Y < 0.$$

When we run the above program through Smodels it tells us to not select any bids. This is expected because the maximum amount that can be obtained from the buyers is $49 by selecting b, d and e; but to satisfy that we have to select f, which costs $50, resulting in a net loss to the exchange. On the other hand if we change our example, and assign -45 as the weight of sel(f), then the Smodels output is indeed to select b, d, e, and f.

6.1   Formal Characterization

In case of a combinatorial exchange, instead of a single auctioneer, we have many sellers, who also present bids, but in their bids the λ_i^js and p_is are negative numbers denoting the fact that they want to sell (instead of buy) those items and they want to be paid (rather than they are willing to pay). Here the *winner determination problem* [13] is an assignment of bids as *accepted* ($x_i = 1$) or not ($x_i = 0$), for $1 \leq i \leq n$ that satisfies the constraint

$$(\sum_{i=1}^{n} \lambda_i^j \times x_i) \leq 0 \qquad \text{for } 1 \leq j \leq m; \text{ and maximizes} \qquad \sum_{i=1}^{n} p_i \times x_i.$$

Theorem 3. *For a multi-unit combinatorial exchange problem with integer prices, each solution to the winner determination problem corresponds to an optimal answer set of the above encoding and vice-versa.*

7   Expressing Additional Constraints

In this section we show how further generalizations and additional constraints can be easily expressed in Smodels.

---

[4] But the Smodels requirement of having a domain variable for Y (not shown in the above rule) makes it an inefficient way to compute aggregation. Having an efficient computation of aggregates together with the answer set semantics remains a challenge.

1. Suppose we would like to express the constraint that item 1 must be sold. We can achieve this by adding the following rules:

   $sold(X) \leftarrow item(X), bid(Y), sel(Y), in(X, Y).$
   $\leftarrow not\ sold(1).$

2. Suppose we would like to have reserve prices[5] in the single unit combinatorial auction. This can be encoded by the following modification of the program in Section 3. The main change is that we replace $bid(X)$ by $bid(X, Y)$ where Y was originally the weight of $bid(X)$. This change allows us to compare the sum of the reserve prices of the items in a bid with the bid price, which now is the parameter Y instead of the weight of $bid(X)$.

   As regards to the specification of the domain, the bids are specified as follows: bid(a,24). bid(b,9). bid(c,8). bid(d,25). bid(e,15).

   The composition of items and bids are as in part 2, and 3 of 3.1. The general rules, as described below are different from the ones in 3.2.

   (a) The following two rules label each bid as either selected or not selected. The third rule assigns a weight to $sel(X, Y)$.
       $sel(X, Y) \leftarrow bid(X, Y), not\ not\_sel(X, Y).$
       $not\_sel(X, Y) \leftarrow bid(X, Y), not\ sel(X, Y).$
       $weight\ sel(X, Y) = Y.$
   (b) The following enforces the constraint that two different bids with the same items can not be both selected.
       $\leftarrow sel(X, N), sel(Y, N'), X \neq Y, item(I), in(I, X), in(I, Y).$
   (c) We have the following optimization statement.
       $maximize\ [sel(X, Y) : bid(X, Y)].$
   (d) We express the reserve price of each item by the following:
       rp(1,2). rp(2,8). rp(3,8). rp(4,12).
   (e) The following rules compute the sum of the reserve prices of bids and compare them with the bid price and eliminate possible answer sets where the bid price of a selected bid is less than the sum of the reserve prices of items in that bid.
       $in\_rp(Item, Bid, Res\_pr) \leftarrow in(Item, Bid), rp(Item, Res\_pr).$
       $weight\ in\_rp(Item, Bid, Res\_pr) = Res\_pr.$
       $item\_num(X, Y) \leftarrow item(X), num(Y).$
       $\leftarrow C\ [in\_rp(Item, Bid, Res\_pr) : item\_num(Item, Res\_pr)]\ C,$
       $\quad bid(Bid, Bid\_pr), sel(Bid, Bid\_pr), Bid\_pr < C.$

3. Suppose we would like to have a constraint that item 1 and 3 must not go to the same bidder. In the simple case if we assume that each bid is by a different bidder we can encode this by the following rule.
   $\leftarrow bid(X, Y), sel(X, Y), in(1, X), in(3, X).$

---

[5] In simple auctions reserve price of an item is the minimum price a seller would accept for that item. Its extension [13] to combinatorial auctions will become clear below.

4. In the more general case where each bid has an associated bidder we first need to express this association as follows:
   bidder(a, john). bidder(b, mary). bidder(c, john).
   bidder(d,mary). bidder(e, peter).
   Next we need the following rules:
   $goes\_to(Item, Bidder) \leftarrow in(Item, X), bidder(X, Bidder), sel(X, Y).$
   $\leftarrow goes\_to(1, B), goes\_to(3, B).$
   Similarly, if we want to specify that the items 1 and 3 must go to the same bidder, then the last rule can be replaced by the following rules.
   $\leftarrow goes\_to(1, B), not\ goes\_to(3, B).$
   $\leftarrow goes\_to(3, B), not\ goes\_to(1, B).$

5. Suppose we would like to represent the constraint that every bidder must return happy, i.e., at least one of her bid must be satisfied. This can be expressed by the following:
   $happy(Bidder) \leftarrow bidder(X, Bidder), bid(X, Y), sel(X, Y).$
   $\leftarrow bidder(Bid, Bidder), not\ happy(Bidder).$

6. Suppose the seller wants to only deal with whole sellers. I.e., it wants to have the constraint that it only selects bids of a bidder if the total money to be obtained from that bidder is more than \$100. This can be achieved by adding the following rules.
   $sel(Bid, Value, Bidder) \leftarrow bid(Bid, Value), sel(Bid, Value),$
   $bidder(Bid, Bidder).\ weight\ sel(Bid, Value, Bidder) = Value.$
   $total(Bidder, C) \leftarrow C\ [sel(Bid, Value, Bidder) : bid(Bid, Value)]\ C.$
   $\leftarrow total(Bidder, C), C < 100.$

7. Suppose the seller wants to avoid bid 'a' as it came late, unless it includes an item that is not included in any other bids. This can be expressed by the following rules.
   $ow\_covered(Bid, Item) \leftarrow in(Item, Bid'), Bid \neq Bid'.$
   $not\_ow\_covered(Bid) \leftarrow in(Item, Bid), not\ ow\_covered(Bid, Item).$
   $\leftarrow sel(a, Value), not\ not\_ow\_covered(a).$

8. To check inventory costs the seller may require that no more than 5 unsold items should be left after the selection. This can be expressed by the following rules.
   $sold(I) \leftarrow item(I), bid(X, Y), sel(X, Y), in(I, X).$
   $unsold(I) \leftarrow item(I), not\ sold(I).$
   $\leftarrow C\ \{unsold(I) : item(I)\}\ C, C > 5.$

9. To contain shipping and handling costs the seller may require that bids should be accepted such that at least 5 items go to each bidder. This can be expressed by the following rules.
   $count(Bidder, C) \leftarrow C\ \{goes\_to(Item, Bidder) : item(Item)\}\ C,$
   $bidder(B, Bidder).$
   $\leftarrow bidder(B, Bidder), count(Bidder, C), C < 5.$

10. If item 'a' is a family treasure the seller may require that it can only be sold to bidder john or mary, his relatives. This can be expressed by the following rule.
    $\leftarrow goes\_to(a, X), X \neq john, X \neq mary.$

The above shows how additional constraints and generalizations can be easily expressed as new Smodels rules and often we do not have to change the original program, but just have to add new rules.

8 Conclusion

In this paper we showed[6] how the combinatorial auction problem and its generalizations can be expressed and solved using the declarative knowledge representation language of Smodels. We argued that the declarativeness of Smodels allows us to easily make generalizations and add additional constraints. Although our focus was more on knowledge representation, we ran some experiments with respect to synthetic examples following the approach of [6,12]. In case of single-unit bids, our results have been comparable to those reported in [12]. In case of multiunit bids with synthetic data drawn from a decay distribution [6] we obtained reasonable timings for bundle sizes up to 1500, with 150 items. Our timings were worse than [6] though. We did not compare with the timings in [4,13], as the first one is about an incomplete algorithm and the second one does not report timings. We hope the programs in this paper would serve as a benchmark and a challenge to researchers in logic programming, declarative problem solving and knowledge representation in terms of having faster implementations of Smodels.

Acknowledgments

This work was supported by the NASA grant NCC2-1232 and the NSF grants IRI-9501577 and NSF 0070463. We thank the anonymous reviewers for their comments.

References

1. T. Eiter, N. Leone, C. Mateis, G. Pfeifer, and F. Scarcello. A deductive system for nonmonotonic reasoning. In *Proc. of KR 98*, pages 406–417, 1998. 187, 190
2. Y. Fujisima, K. Leyton-Brown, and Y. Shoham. Taming the computational complexity of combinatorial auctions. In *Proc. of IJCAI 99*, pages 548–553, 1999. 186, 187, 188, 191
3. M. Gelfond and V. Lifschitz. The stable model semantics for logic programming. In R. Kowalski and K. Bowen, editors, *Logic Programming: Proc. of the Fifth Int'l Conf. and Symp.*, pages 1070–1080. MIT Press, 1988. 187
4. H. Hoos and C. Boutilier. Solving combinatorial auctions using stochastic local search. In *Proc. of AAAI'00*, 2000. 186, 187, 191, 198

---

[6] The Smodels system [8,14] requires each rule to be strongly range restricted. That means every variable that appears in a rule must appear in a positive domain literal in the body of a rule. For simplifying the presentation we have omitted domain literals in some of the rules. For clarification, some of the Smodels and dlv code that we developed while testing the programs in this paper are available at http://www.public.asu.edu/~cbaral/comb-auc/.

5. H. Kautz and B. Selman. Planning as satisfiability. In *Proc. of ECAI-92*, pages 359–363, 1992. 187

6. K. Leyton-Brown, Y. Shoham, and M. Tennenholtz. An algorithm for multi-unit combinatorial auctions. In *Proc. of AAAI'00*, 2000. 186, 187, 188, 198

7. D. Monderer and M. Tennenholtz. Optimal auctions revisited. *Artificial Intelligence*, 2000. 186

8. I. Niemela and P. Simons. Smodels – an implementation of the stable model and well-founded semantics for normal logic programs. In *Proc. 4th international conference on Logic programming and non-monotonic reasoning*, pages 420–429, 1997. 187, 198

9. S. Rassenti, V. Smith, and R. Bulfin. A combinatorial auction mechanism for airport time slot allocation. *Bell J. of Economics*, 13:402–417, 1982. 186

10. M. Rothkopf, A. Pekec, and R. Harstad. Computationally manageable combinatorial auctions. *Management Science*, 44(8):1131–1147, 1998. 186, 187

11. T. Sandholm. An implementation of the contract net protocol based on marginal cost calculations. In *Proc. of AAAI 93*, pages 256–262, 1993. 186

12. T. Sandholm. An algorithm for optimal winner determination in combinatorial auctions. In *Proc. of IJCAI 99*, pages 542–547, 1999. 186, 187, 188, 198

13. T. Sandholm and S. Suri. Improved algorithms for optimal winner determination in combinatorial auctions and generalizations. In *Proc. of AAAI'00*, 2000. 186, 187, 188, 190, 194, 195, 196, 198

14. P. Simons. Extending the stable model semantics with more expressive rules. In *Proc. of International Conference on Logic Programming and Nonmonotonic Reasoning, LPNMR'99*, 1999. 187, 189, 198

15. M. Tennenholtz. Some tractable combinatorial auctions. In *Proc. of AAAI'00*, 2000. 186, 187

16. M. Wellman, W. Walsh, P. Wurman, and J. Mackie-Mason. Auction protocols for decentralized scheduling. *Games and Economic bahavior*, 1999. 186

Bounded LTL Model Checking with Stable Models*

Keijo Heljanko and Ilkka Niemelä

Helsinki University of Technology, Dept. of Computer Science and Engineering
Laboratory for Theoretical Computer Science
P.O. Box 5400, FIN-02015 HUT, Finland
{Keijo.Heljanko, Ilkka.Niemela}@hut.fi

Abstract. In this paper bounded model checking of asynchronous concurrent systems is introduced as a promising application area for answer set programming. As the model of asynchronous systems a generalization of communicating automata, 1-safe Petri nets, are used. It is shown how a 1-safe Petri net and a requirement on the behavior of the net can be translated into a logic program such that the bounded model checking problem for the net can be solved by computing stable models of the corresponding program. The use of the stable model semantics leads to compact encodings of bounded reachability and deadlock detection tasks as well as the more general problem of bounded model checking of linear temporal logic. Some experimental results on solving deadlock detection problems using the translation and the Smodels system are presented.

1   Introduction

In this paper we put forward symbolic model checking [2,3] as a promising application area for answer set programming systems. In particular, we demonstrate how bounded model checking problems of asynchronous concurrent systems can be reduced to computing stable models of logic programs.

Verification of asynchronous systems is typically done by enumerating the set of reachable states of the system. Tools based on this approach (with various enhancements) include, e.g., the SPIN system [12], which supports extended state machines communicating through FIFO queues, and the PROD tool [17] based on Petri nets. The main problem with enumerative model checkers is the amount of memory needed to store the set of reachable states.

Symbolic model checking is widely applied especially in hardware verification. The main analysis technique is based on (ordered) binary decision diagrams (BDDs). In many cases the set of reachable states can be represented very compactly using a BDD encoding. Although the approach has been successful, there

---

* This is an extended version of a paper titled "Answer Set Programming and Bounded Model Checking"[11] presented at the AAAI Spring 2001 Symposium on Answer Set Programming, Stanford, March 2001. The financial support of Academy of Finland (Projects 43963, 47754) and Tekniikan Edistämissäätiö are gratefully acknowledged.

T. Eiter, W. Faber, and M. Truszczyński (Eds.): LPNMR 2001, LNAI 2173, pp. 200–212, 2001.
© Springer-Verlag Berlin Heidelberg 2001

are difficulties in applying BDD-based techniques, in particular, in areas outside hardware verification. The key problem is that some Boolean functions do not have a compact representation as BDDs and the size of the BDD representation of a Boolean function is very sensitive to the variable ordering used. Bounded model checking [1] has been proposed as a technique for overcoming the space problem by replacing BDDs with satisfiability (SAT) checking techniques because typical SAT checkers use only polynomial amount of memory. The idea is roughly the following. Given a sequential digital circuit, a (temporal) property to be verified, and a bound n, the behavior of a sequential circuit is unfolded up to n steps as a Boolean formula S and the negation of the property to be verified is represented as a Boolean formula $\overline{R}$. The translation to Boolean formulae is done so that $S \wedge \overline{R}$ is satisfiable iff the system has a behavior violating the property of length at most n. Hence, bounded model checking provides directly interesting and practically relevant benchmarks for any answer set programming system capable of handling propositional satisfiability problems.

Until now bounded model checking has been applied to synchronous hardware verification and little attention has been given to knowledge representation issues such as developing concise and efficient logical representation of system behavior. In this work we study the knowledge representation problem and employ ideas used in reducing planning to stable model computation [15]. The aim is to develop techniques such that the behavior of an asynchronous concurrent system can be encoded compactly and the inherent concurrency in the system could be exploited in model checking the system. To illustrate the approach we use a simple basic Petri net model of asynchronous systems, 1-safe Place/Transition nets, which is an interesting generalization of communicating automata [5].

The structure of the rest of the paper is the following. In the next section we introduce Petri nets and the bounded model checking problem. Then we develop a compact encoding of bounded model checking as the problem of finding stable models of logic programs. We first show how to treat reachability properties such as deadlocks and then demonstrate how to extend the approach to cope with properties expressed in linear temporal logic (LTL). We discuss initial experimental results and end with some concluding remarks.

2   Petri Nets and Bounded Model Checking

We will now introduce P/T-nets. They are one of the simplest forms of Petri nets. We will use as a running example the P/T-net presented in Fig. 1.

A triple $\langle P, T, F \rangle$ is a *net* if $P \cap T = \emptyset$ and $F \subseteq (P \times T) \cup (T \times P)$. The elements of P are called *places*, and the elements of T *transitions*. Places and transitions are also called *nodes*. The places are represented in graphical notation by circles, transitions by squares, and the *flow relation* F with arcs. We identify F with its characteristic function on the set $(P \times T) \cup (T \times P)$. The *preset* of a node x, denoted by $\bullet x$, is the set $\{y \in P \cup T \,|\, F(y, x) = 1\}$. In our running example, e.g., $\bullet t2 = \{p1, p2\}$. The *postset* of a node x, denoted by $x^\bullet$, is the set $\{y \in P \cup T \,|\, F(x, y) = 1\}$. Again in our running example $p2^\bullet = \{t2, t3, t5\}$.

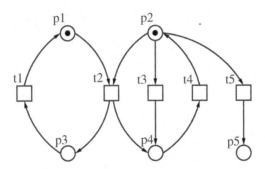

Fig. 1. Running Example

A *marking* of a net $\langle P, T, F \rangle$ is a mapping $P \mapsto \mathbb{N}$. A marking M is identified with the multi-set which contains $M(p)$ copies of p for every $p \in P$. A 4-tuple $\Sigma = \langle P, T, F, M_0 \rangle$ is a *net system* (also called a *P/T-net*) if $\langle P, T, F \rangle$ is a net and M_0 is a marking of $\langle P, T, F \rangle$. A marking is graphically denoted by a distribution of tokens on the places of the net. In our running example in Fig. 1 the net has the initial marking $M_0 = \{p1, p2\}$.

A marking M enables a transition $t \in T$ if $\forall p \in P : F(p, t) \leq M(p)$. If t is enabled, it can *occur* leading to a new marking (denoted $M \xrightarrow{t} M'$), where M' is defined by $\forall p \in P : M'(p) = M(p) - F(p, t) + F(t, p)$. In the running example $t2$ is enabled in the initial marking M_0, and thus $M_0 \xrightarrow{t2} M'$, where $M' = \{p3, p4\}$.

A marking M_n is *reachable* in Σ if there is an *execution*, i.e., a (possibly empty) sequence of transitions $t_1, t_2, \ldots, t_n$ and markings $M_1, M_2, \ldots, M_{n-1}$ such that: $M_0 \xrightarrow{t_1} M_1 \xrightarrow{t_2} \ldots M_{n-1} \xrightarrow{t_n} M_n$. A marking M is reachable within a bound n, if there is an execution with $\leq n$ transitions, with which M is reachable.

A marking M is 1-safe if $\forall p \in P : M(p) \leq 1$. A P/T-net is 1-safe if all its reachable markings are 1-safe. We will restrict ourselves to finite P/T-nets which are 1-safe, and in which each transition has both nonempty pre- and postsets.

Given a 1-safe P/T-net Σ, we say that a set of transitions $S \subseteq T$ is *concurrently enabled* in the marking M, if (i) all transitions $t \in S$ are enabled in M, and (ii) for all pairs of transitions $t, t' \in S$, such that $t \neq t'$, it holds that $^\bullet t \cap {}^\bullet t' = \emptyset$. If a set S is concurrently enabled in the marking M, we can fire it in a *step* (denoted $M \xrightarrow{S} M'$), where M' is the marking reached after firing all of the transitions in the step S in arbitrary order. It is easy to prove by using the 1-safeness of the P/T-net Σ that all possible interleavings of transitions in a step S are enabled in M, and that they all lead to the same final marking M'. In our running example in the marking $M' = \{p3, p4\}$ the step $\{t1, t4\}$ is enabled, and will lead back to the initial marking M_0. This is denoted by $M' \xrightarrow{\{t1, t4\}} M_0$. Notice also that for any enabled transition, the singleton set containing only that transition is always (trivially) a step.

We say that a marking M_n is *reachable in step semantics* in a 1-safe P/T-net if there is a *step execution*, i.e., a (possibly empty) sequences $S_1, S_2, \ldots, S_n$ of steps and $M_1, M_2, \ldots, M_{n-1}$ of markings such that: $M_0 \xrightarrow{S_1} M_1 \xrightarrow{S_2} \ldots M_{n-1} \xrightarrow{S_n} M_n$. A marking M is reachable within a bound n in the step semantics, if there is a step execution with at most n steps, with which M is reachable.

We will refer to the "normal semantics" as *interleaving semantics*. Note that if a marking is reachable in n transitions in the interleaving semantics, it is also reachable in n steps in the step semantics. However, the converse does not necessarily hold. We have, however, the following theorem.

Theorem 1. *For finite 1-safe P/T-nets the set of reachable markings in the interleaving and step semantics coincide.*

Linear temporal logic (LTL). The linear temporal logic LTL is one of the most widely used logic for specifying properties of reactive systems [3]. The basic idea is to specify properties that the system should have using LTL. A model checker is then used to check whether all (infinite) behaviors of the system are models of the specification formula. If not, then the model checker outputs a behavior of the system which violates the given specification.

Given a finite set AP of atomic propositions, the syntax of LTL[1] is given by:

$$\varphi ::= p \in AP \mid \neg \varphi_1 \mid \varphi_1 \vee \varphi_2 \mid \varphi_1 \wedge \varphi_2 \mid \varphi_1 \, U \, \varphi_2 \mid \varphi_1 \, R \, \varphi_2 \, .$$

An ω-word over 2^{AP} is an infinite sequence $w = x_0 \, x_1 \, \ldots$ such that $x_i \in 2^{AP}$ for all $i \geq 0$. For an ω-word w we define $w_{(i)} = x_i$, and denote by $w^{(i)}$ the suffix of w starting at x_i. We define the relation $w \models \varphi$ inductively as follows:

- $w \models p$ iff $p \in w_{(0)}$ for $p \in AP$
- $w \models \neg \varphi_1$ iff not $w \models \varphi_1$
- $w \models \varphi_1 \vee \varphi_2$ iff $w \models \varphi_1$ or $w \models \varphi_2$
- $w \models \varphi_1 \wedge \varphi_2$ iff $w \models \varphi_1$ and $w \models \varphi_2$
- $w \models \varphi_1 \, U \, \varphi_2$ iff there exists a $j \geq 0$ such that $w^{(j)} \models \varphi_2$ and for all $0 \leq i < j$, $w^{(i)} \models \varphi_1$
- $w \models \varphi_1 \, R \, \varphi_2$ iff for all $j \geq 0$, if for every $i < j \; w^{(i)} \not\models \varphi_1$ then $w^{(j)} \models \varphi_2$.

We define some shorthand LTL formulas: $\top \equiv p \vee \neg p$ for some arbitrary fixed $p \in AP$, $\bot \equiv \neg \top$, $\Diamond \varphi \equiv (\top \, U \, \varphi)$, $\Box \varphi \equiv (\bot \, R \, \varphi)$, and $\varphi_1 \rightarrow \varphi_2 \equiv \neg \varphi_1 \vee \varphi_2$.

The temporal operators are called: U for "until", R for "release", $\Diamond$ for "eventually", and $\Box$ for "globally". Some examples of practical use of LTL formulas in specification are: $\Box \neg (cs_1 \wedge cs_2)$ (it always holds that two processes are not at the same time in a critical section), $\Box(req \rightarrow \Diamond ack)$ (it is always the case that a request is eventually followed by an acknowledgement), and $((\Box \Diamond sch_1) \wedge (\Box \Diamond sch_2)) \rightarrow (\Box(tr_1 \rightarrow \Diamond cs_1))$ (if both process 1 and 2 are scheduled infinitely often, then always the entering of process 1 in the trying section is followed by the process 1 eventually entering the critical section).

---

[1] Note that we do not define the often used next-time operator $X \, \varphi$. This is a tradeoff which allows the use of step semantics.

Given a 1-safe P/T net Σ, we use a chosen subset of the places as the atomic propositions AP. An infinite (interleaving) execution $M_0 \xrightarrow{t_1} M_1 \xrightarrow{t_2} \ldots$ satisfies φ iff the corresponding ω-word $w = (M_0 \cap AP), (M_1 \cap AP), \ldots$ satisfies φ. We say that Σ satisfies φ iff every infinite execution starting from the initial marking M_0 satisfies φ. Alternatively, Σ does not satisfy φ if there exists an infinite execution starting from M_0 which satisfies $\neg\varphi$. We call such an execution a *counterexample*.

The temporal logic LTL specifies properties of infinite executions. In many cases it suffices to reason about simple temporal properties. A typical example is the reachability of a marking satisfying some condition C which roughly corresponds to finding a counterexample for a formula $\Box\neg C$. An important reachability based property is deadlock detection.

Definition 1. (Deadlock) *Given a 1-safe P/T-net Σ, is there a reachable marking M which does not enable any transition of Σ?*

Most analysis questions including deadlock detection and LTL model checking are PSPACE-complete in the size of a 1-safe Petri net, see e.g., [6]. In *bounded model checking* we fix a bound n and look for counterexamples which are shorter than the given bound n. For example, in the case of *bounded deadlock detection* in step semantics we look for step executions reaching a deadlock in n steps. It is easy to show that, e.g., the bounded deadlock detection problem in step semantics is NP-complete (when the bound n is given in unary coding).

This idea can also be applied to LTL model checking. Biere et.al. [1] introduce *bounded LTL model checking*. They also discuss how to ensure that a given bound n is sufficient to guarantee completeness. Unfortunately, getting an exact bound is often computationally infeasible, and easily obtainable upper bounds are too large. In the case of 1-safe P/T-nets they are exponential in the number of places in the net. Therefore the bounded model checking results are usually not conclusive if a counterexample is not found. Thus bounded model checking is at its best in "bug hunting", and not as easily applicable in verifying systems to be correct.

3 From Bounded Model Checking to Answer Set Programming

In this section we show how to solve bounded LTL model checking problems using answer set programming. We start with the simpler reachability properties and then extend the approach to handle full LTL model checking.

For encoding bounded model checking problems we use normal logic programs with the stable model semantics [8]. A normal rule is of the form

$$a \leftarrow b_1, \ldots, b_m, \text{not } c_1, \ldots, \text{not } c_n \tag{1}$$

where each a, b_i, c_j is a ground atom. We employ three extensions which can be seen as compact shorthands for normal rules. We use *integrity constraints*, i.e., rules with empty head. Such a constraint like the one on the left can be taken as a shorthand for a rule given on the right

$$\leftarrow b, \text{not } c \qquad \rightsquigarrow \qquad f \leftarrow \text{not } f, b, \text{not } c$$

where f is a new atom. For expressing the choice whether to include an atom in a stable model we use *choice rules*. They are normal rules where the head is in brackets with the idea that the head can be included in a stable model only if the body holds but it can be left out, too. Such a construct can be represented using normal rules by introducing a new atom. For example, the choice rule on the left corresponds to the two normal rules on the right where a' is a new atom.

$$\{a\} \leftarrow b, \text{not } c \qquad \rightsquigarrow \qquad \begin{array}{l} a \leftarrow \text{not } a', b, \text{not } c \\ a' \leftarrow \text{not } a \end{array}$$

Finally, a compact encoding of *conflicts* is needed, i.e., rules of the form

$$\leftarrow 2\{a_1, \ldots, a_n\} \qquad\qquad (2)$$

saying that a stable model cannot contain any two atoms out of a set of atoms $\{a_1, \ldots, a_n\}$. Such a rule can be expressed, e.g., by adding a rule $f \leftarrow \text{not } f, a_i, a_j$ for each pair a_i, a_j from $\{a_1, \ldots, a_n\}$, i.e., using $\mathcal{O}(n^2)$ rules. Choice and conflict rules are simple cases of cardinality constraint rules [16]. The Smodels system (http://www.tcs.hut.fi/Software/smodels/) provides an implementation for cardinality constraint rules and includes primitives supporting directly such constraints without translating them first to corresponding normal rules.

3.1   Reachability Checking

Now we devise a method for translating bounded reachability problems of 1-safe P/T-nets to tasks of finding stable models. Consider a net $N = \langle P, T, F \rangle$ and a step bound $n \geq 1$. We construct a logic program $\Pi_A(N, n)$, which captures the possible executions of N up to n steps, as follows.

- For each place $p \in P$, include a choice rule $\{p(0)\} \leftarrow$.
- For each transition $t \in T$, and for all $i = 0, 1, \ldots, n - 1$, include a rule

$$\{t(i)\} \leftarrow p_1(i), \ldots, p_l(i) \qquad\qquad (3)$$

  where $\{p_1, \ldots, p_l\}$ is the preset of t. Hence, a stable model can contain a transition instance in step i only if its preset holds at step i.
- For each place $p \in P$, for each transition t_k in the preset of p, and for all $i = 0, 1, \ldots, n - 1$, include a rule

$$p(i + 1) \leftarrow t_k(i) . \qquad\qquad (4)$$

  These say that p holds in the next step if at least one of its preset transitions is in the current step.

$$
\begin{array}{llll}
\{t1(i)\} \leftarrow p3(i) & p1(i+1) \leftarrow t1(i) & p1(i+1) \leftarrow p1(i), \text{not } t2(i) & \{p1(0)\} \leftarrow \\
\{t2(i)\} \leftarrow p1(i), p2(i) & p2(i+1) \leftarrow t4(i) & p2(i+1) \leftarrow p2(i), \text{not } t2(i), & \{p2(0)\} \leftarrow \\
\{t3(i)\} \leftarrow p2(i) & p3(i+1) \leftarrow t2(i) & \qquad \text{not } t3(i), \text{not } t5(i) & \{p3(0)\} \leftarrow \\
\{t4(i)\} \leftarrow p4(i) & p4(i+1) \leftarrow t2(i) & p3(i+1) \leftarrow p3(i), \text{not } t1(i) & \{p4(0)\} \leftarrow \\
\{t5(i)\} \leftarrow p2(i) & p4(i+1) \leftarrow t3(i) & p4(i+1) \leftarrow p4(i), \text{not } t4(i) & \{p5(0)\} \leftarrow \\
& p5(i+1) \leftarrow t5(i) & p5(i+1) \leftarrow p5(i) & \\
& \leftarrow 2\{t2(i), t3(i), t5(i)\} & \text{where } i = 0, 1, \ldots n-1 &
\end{array}
$$

Fig. 2. Program $\Pi_A(N, n)$

- For each place $p \in P$, and for all $i = 0, 1, \ldots, n-1$, include a rule

$$
\leftarrow 2\{t_1(i), \ldots, t_l(i)\} \tag{5}
$$

where $\{t_1, \ldots, t_l\}$ is the set of transitions having each p in their preset and $l \geq 2$. This rule states that at most one of the transitions that are in conflict w.r.t. p can occur.
- For each place p, and for all $i = 0, 1, \ldots, n-1$,

$$
p(i+1) \leftarrow p(i), \text{not } t_1(i), \ldots, \text{not } t_l(i) \tag{6}
$$

where $\{t_1, \ldots, t_l\}$ is the set of transitions having p in their preset. This is the *frame axiom* for p stating that p holds if no transition using it occurs.

Consider net N in Fig. 1 for which program $\Pi_A(N, n)$ is given in Fig. 2. In $\Pi_A(N, n)$ the initial marking is not constrained but any Boolean combination C of marking conditions can be captured with a set of rules $\Pi_M(C, i)$ [16]. For example, to eliminate stable models not satisfying a condition C at step i saying that $M(p_1) = 1$ and ($M(p_2) = 0$ or $M(p_3) = 1$), it is sufficient to use rules $\Pi_M(C, i)$:

$$
\begin{array}{ll}
\leftarrow \text{not } c(i) & c_{\bar{p}_2 \vee p_3}(i) \leftarrow \text{not } p_2(i) \\
c(i) \leftarrow p_1(i), c_{\bar{p}_2 \vee p_3}(i) & c_{\bar{p}_2 \vee p_3}(i) \leftarrow p_3(i)
\end{array}
$$

Our approach can solve a reachability problem for a set of initial markings given by a condition C_0 where the markings to be reached are specified by another condition C.

Theorem 2. *Let $N = \langle P, T, F \rangle$ be a 1-safe P/T-net for all initial markings satisfying a condition C_0. Net N has an initial marking satisfying C_0 such that a marking satisfying a condition C is reachable in at most n steps iff $\Pi_M(C_0, 0) \cup \Pi_A(N, n) \cup \Pi_M(C, n)$ has a stable model.*

The deadlock detection problem is now just a special case of a reachability property, just add rules $\Pi_M(C, n) = \Pi_D(N, n)$ eliminating stable models where some transition is enabled. Program $\Pi_D(N, n)$ includes for each transition $t \in T$ and its preset $\{p_1, \ldots, p_l\}$, a rule

$$
\leftarrow p_1(n), \ldots, p_l(n) . \tag{7}
$$

For our running example, the rules $\Pi_D(N, n)$ are

$$
\leftarrow p3(n) \qquad \leftarrow p1(n), p2(n) \qquad \leftarrow p2(n) \qquad \leftarrow p4(n) .
$$

3.2   Bounded LTL Model Checking

Our strategy for finding counterexamples for LTL formula φ (i.e., executions satisfying $\neg\varphi$) is exactly the same as in [1]. There it is shown to be an approximation of the unbounded version which becomes equivalent to the unbounded case if the bound used is sufficiently increased. We (as they do) require that all reachable states of the system have a successor (i.e., there are no deadlocks). In this case the reachability of a marking satisfying a condition C is equivalent to finding a counterexample for an LTL formula of the form $\square\neg C$.

We look for two different kinds of counterexamples. On the left in Fig. 3 is a *loop counterexample*, and on the right is a *counterexample without loop*. Loop counterexamples specify an infinite execution themselves, while counterexamples without a loop specify a prefix of an execution, which can be always extended to an infinite execution (by the deadlock freeness assumption). The arcs of the figure denote the "next state" of each state. Notice in the loop counterexample that if $M_{(i-1)}$ is equivalent to the last state M_n, the state M_i is the "next state" of M_n. Our semantics is cautious in the case without loop, and extending the execution into an infinite one in any way will yield a counterexample.[2]

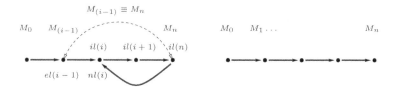

Fig. 3. Two counterexample possibilities

An LTL formula is said to be in *positive normal form* when all negations in the formula appear directly before an atomic proposition. A formula can be put into positive normal form with the following equivalences (and their duals): $\neg\neg\varphi \equiv \varphi$, $\neg(\varphi_1 \vee \varphi_2) \equiv \neg\varphi_1 \wedge \neg\varphi_2$, and $\neg(\varphi_1 \, U \, \varphi_2) \equiv \neg\varphi_1 \, R \, \neg\varphi_2$.

Given an LTL formula f in positive normal form (when the formula to be model checked is φ, the formula f is equivalent to $\neg\varphi$ with negations pushed in), and a bound $n \geq 1$ we construct a program $\Pi_{\mathrm{LTL}}(f, n)$ as follows.

- Guess which state is equivalent to the last. For all $0 \leq i \leq n - 1$ add rule

$$\{el(i)\} \leftarrow . \tag{8}$$

- Disallow guessing two or more. (Guessing none is allowed though.) Add rule

$$\leftarrow 2\{el(0), el(1), \ldots, el(n - 1)\} . \tag{9}$$

---

[2] Actually the counterexamples without loop are exactly the informative safety counterexamples of [13].

Formula type	Translation	Formula type	Translation
p, for $p \in AP$	$f(i) \leftarrow p(i)$	$\neg p$, for $p \in AP$	$f(i) \leftarrow$ not $p(i)$
$f_1 \vee f_2$	$f(i) \leftarrow f_1(i)$ $f(i) \leftarrow f_2(i)$	$f_1 \wedge f_2$	$f(i) \leftarrow f_1(i), f_2(i)$
$f_1 \, U \, f_2$	$f(i) \leftarrow f_2(i)$ $f(i) \leftarrow f_1(i), f(i+1)$ $f(n+1) \leftarrow nl(i), f(i)$	$f_1 \, R \, f_2$	$f(i) \leftarrow f_2(i), f_1(i)$ $f(i) \leftarrow f_2(i), f(i+1)$ $f(n+1) \leftarrow nl(i), f(i)$ $f(n+1) \leftarrow l,$ not $cstate(f)$ $cstate(f) \leftarrow il(i),$ not $f_2(i)$

Fig. 4. Translation of an LTL formula f

- Check that the guess is correct. For all $0 \leq i \leq n-1$, $p \in P$ include rules

$$\leftarrow el(i), p(i), \text{not } p(n) \qquad \leftarrow el(i), p(n), \text{not } p(i) \ .$$

- Specify auxiliary loop related atoms. For all $0 \leq i \leq n-1$, include rules

$$l \leftarrow el(i) \qquad nl(i+1) \leftarrow el(i) \qquad il(i+1) \leftarrow el(i) \qquad il(i+1) \leftarrow il(i) \ .$$

See Fig. 3 for an example. The $nl(i)$ atom is in a model for the "next state" of the last state, while $il(i)$ is in the model for all states in the loop.
- Require that if a loop exists, the last step contains a transition to disallow looping by idling. Add the rule

$$\leftarrow l, \text{not } t_1(n-1), \ldots, \text{not } t_k(n-1) \tag{10}$$

where $\{t_1, \ldots, t_k\} = T$, i.e., the set of all transitions.
- Allow at most one visible transition in a step to eliminate steps which cannot be interleaved to yield a counterexample. For all $0 \leq i \leq n-1$, add rule

$$\leftarrow 2\{t_1(i), \ldots, t_k(i)\} \tag{11}$$

where $\{t_1, \ldots, t_k\}$ is the set of *visible transitions*, i.e., the transitions whose firing changes the marking of a place p appearing in the formula f.

We recursively translate the formula f by first translating its subformulae, and then f as follows. For all $0 \leq i \leq n$, add the rules given by Fig. 4.[3] Finally we require that the top level formula f should hold in the initial marking

$$\leftarrow \text{not } f(0) \ . \tag{12}$$

With this program $\Pi_{\mathrm{LTL}}(f, n)$ we get our main main result.

Theorem 3. *Let f be an LTL formula in positive normal form and $N = \langle P, T, F \rangle$ be a 1-safe and deadlock free P/T-net for all initial markings satisfying a condition C_0. If $\Pi_{\mathrm{M}}(C_0, 0) \cup \Pi_{\mathrm{A}}(N, n) \cup \Pi_{\mathrm{LTL}}(f, n)$ has a stable model, then there is an execution of N from an initial marking satisfying C_0 which satisfies f.*

---

[3] An equivalence explaining the release translation: $f_1 \, R \, f_2 \equiv (\Box f_2) \vee (f_2 \, U \, (f_2 \wedge f_1))$.

The size of the program in Theorem 3 is linear in the size of the net and formula, i.e., $\mathcal{O}((|P| + |T| + |F| + |f|) \cdot n)$. The semantics of LTL is defined over interleaving executions. A novelty of the translation is that it allows concurrency between invisible transitions.

Forcing interleaving semantics. We can create the interleaving semantics versions of bounded model checking problems by adding a set of rules $\Pi_I(N, n)$. It includes for each time step $0 \leq i \leq n - 1$ a rule

$$\leftarrow 2\{t_1(i), \ldots, t_m(i)\} \tag{13}$$

where $\{t_1, \ldots, t_m\}$ is the set of all transitions. These rules eliminate all stable models having more than one transition firing in a step.

Corollary 1. *Let* $\Pi_S(N, n)$ *be a program solving a bounded model checking problem in the step semantics using any of the translations above. Then the program* $\Pi_S(N, n) \cup \Pi_I(N, n)$ *solves the same problem in the interleaving semantics.*

3.3   Relation to Previous Work

In previous work on bounded model checking little attention has been given to the knowledge representation problem of encoding succinctly the unfolded behavior and the temporal property. We address this problem and develop an encoding of the behavior of an asynchronous system which is linear in the size of the system description (Petri net) and in the number of steps. Moreover, it allows the exploitation of the inherent concurrency of the system in model checking.

Our approach could be used as a basis for a similar treatment using propositional logic and satisfiability (SAT) checkers. For simple temporal properties such as reachability and deadlock this is fairly straightforward to develop using the ideas of Clark's completion and Fages' theorem [7]. This is because our encoding produces acyclic programs except for the choice rules which need a special treatment. To achieve a compact SAT encoding is more challenging because propositional logic lacks cardinality constraint rules (2). Their mapping to propositional formulae can result to a quadratic blow-up which is sometimes significant as conflicts may involve even hundreds of transitions.

For general LTL model checking a succinct SAT encoding is challenging. The compactness of our encoding is due to the fact that stable model semantics supports the smallest fixed point evaluation of recursive rules which is exploited in translating the U and R operators. Because of these recursive rules a similar compact SAT encoding is not immediate. In [1] a SAT encoding is given. However, it is more complicated than our linear size encoding but remains polynomial.

4   Experiments

We have implemented the deadlock detection and LTL model checking translations presented in the previous section. The translation is given a fixed initial marking M_0, which allows the following optimizations to be implemented:

Problem	$|P|$	$|T|$	St. n	St. s	Int. n	Int. s	States
DARTES(1)	331	257	32	0.5	32	0.5	>1500000
DP(6)	36	24	1	0.0	6	0.1	728
DP(8)	48	32	1	0.0	8	0.3	6560
DP(10)	60	40	1	0.0	10	3.3	59048
DP(12)	72	48	1	0.0	12	617.4	531440
ELEV(1)	63	99	4	0.0	9	0.4	163
ELEV(2)	146	299	6	0.5	12	3.9	1092
ELEV(3)	327	783	8	5.6	15	139.0	7276
ELEV(4)	736	1939	10	157.2	>13	1215.2	48217
HART(25)	127	77	1	0.0	>5	1.0	>1000000
HART(50)	252	152	1	0.0	>5	5.7	>1000000
HART(75)	377	227	1	0.0	>5	15.5	>1000000
HART(100)	502	302	1	0.0	>5	35.9	>1000000
KEY(2)	94	92	>25	1937.9	>26	56.1	536
MMGT(3)	122	172	7	11.1	10	87.2	7702
MMGT(4)	158	232	8	687.3	>11	1874.1	66308
Q(1)	163	194	9	0.1	>17	2733.7	123596

Fig. 5. Experiments

- Place and transition atoms are added only from the time step they can first appear on. Only atoms for places $p(0)$ in the initial marking are created for time $i = 0$. Then for each $0 \le i \le n - 1$: (i) Add transition atoms for all transitions $t(i)$ such that all the place atoms in the preset of $t(i)$ exist. (ii) Add place atoms for all places $p(i + 1)$ such that either the place atom $p(i)$ exists or some transition atom in the preset of $p(i + 1)$ exists.
- Duplicate rules are removed. Duplicates can appear in (5),(7).

As benchmarks we use a set of deadlock detection benchmarks collected by Corbett [4], converted to 1-safe P/T-nets by Melzer and Römer [14]. The models were picked from those which have a deadlock. For each model and both semantics we incremented the used bound until a deadlock was found. We report the time for Smodels to find the first stable model using this bound. In some cases a model could not be found within a reasonable time in which case we report the time used to prove that there is no deadlock within the reported bound. Unfortunately, we did not have a large collection of LTL model checking examples, and benchmarking the LTL translation is left for further work. The experimental results can be found in Fig. 5. The columns are:

- Problem: The problem name with the size of the instance in parenthesis.
- $|P|$: Number of places in the original net.
- $|T|$: Number of transitions in the original net.
- St. n: The smallest integer n such that a deadlock could be found using the step semantics / in case of $> n$ the largest integer n for which we could prove that there is no deadlock within that bound using the step semantics.
- St. s: The time in seconds to find the first stable model / to prove that there is no stable model. (See St. n above.)
- Int. n and Int. s: defined as St. n and St. s but for the interleaving semantics.
- States: Number of reachable states of the P/T-net (if known).[4]

---

[4] These differ from the ones reported in [11] where unfortunately there are some errors.

The times reported are the average of 5 runs of the time for `smodels 2.26`
as reported by the `/usr/bin/time` command on a 450Mhz Pentium III PC
running Linux. The used tools, nets, and logic programs are available from:
`<http://www.tcs.hut.fi/~kepa/experiments/LPNMR2001/>`.

In many of the experiments the step semantics version found a deadlock with
a smaller bound than the interleaving one. Also, when the bound needed to find
the deadlock was fairly small, the bounded model checker was performing well.
In the examples ELEV(4), HART(x) and Q(1) we were able to find the counterexample only when using step semantics. In the KEY(2) example we were
not able to find a counterexample with either semantics, even though the problem is known to have only a small number of reachable states. In contrast, the
DARTES(1) problem has a large state-space, and despite of it a counterexample
of length 32 was obtained. Overall, the results are promising, in particular, for
small bounds and the step semantics.

5   Conclusions

We introduce bounded model checking of asynchronous concurrent systems modeled by 1-safe P/T-nets as an interesting application area for answer set programming. We present mappings from bounded reachability, deadlock detection and
LTL model checking problems of 1-safe P/T-nets to stable model computation.
Our approach is capable of doing model checking for a set of initial markings at
once. This is usually difficult to achieve in current enumerative model checkers
and often leads to state space explosion. We handle asynchronous systems using
a step semantics whereas previous work on bounded model checking only uses
the interleaving semantics [1]. Furthermore, our encoding is more compact than
the previous approach employing propositional satisfiability [1]. This is because
our rule based approach allows to represent executions of the system, e.g. frame
axioms, succinctly and supports directly the recursive fixed point computation
needed to evaluate LTL formulae.

The first experimental results indicate that stable model computation is quite
a competitive approach to searching for short executions of the system leading
to deadlock and worth further study. More experimental work and comparisons
are needed to determine the strength of the approach. In particular, for comparing with SAT checking techniques, it would be interesting to develop a similar
treatment of asynchronous systems using a SAT encoding and compare it to the
logic program based approach.

Relating the net unfolding method (see [9,14] and further references there)
to bounded model checking would be interesting. There are also alternative semantics to the two presented in this work [10], applying them to bounded LTL
model checking is left for further work.

References

1. A. Biere, A. Cimatti, E. Clarke, and Y. Zhu. Symbolic model checking without BDDs. In *Tools and Algorithms for the Construction and Analysis of Systems (TACAS'99)*, pages 193–207. Springer, March 1999. 201, 204, 207, 209, 211
2. J. Burch, E. Clarke, K. McMillan, D. Dill, and L.Hwang. Symbolic model checking: 10^{20} states and beyond. *Information and Computation*, 98(2):142–170, 1992. 200
3. E. Clarke, O. Grumberg, and D. Peled. *Model Checking*. The MIT Press, 1999. 200, 203
4. J. C. Corbett. Evaluating deadlock detection methods for concurrent software. Technical report, Department of Information and Computer Science, University of Hawaii at Manoa, 1995. 210
5. J. Desel and W. Reisig. Place/Transition Petri nets. In *Lectures on Petri Nets I: Basic Models*, pages 122–173. Springer-Verlag, 1998. 201
6. J. Esparza. Decidability and complexity of Petri net problems – An introduction. In *Lectures on Petri Nets I: Basic Models*, pages 374–428. Springer-Verlag, 1998. 204
7. F. Fages. Consistency of Clark's completion and existence of stable models. *Journal of Methods of Logic in Computer Science*, 1:51–60, 1994. 209
8. M. Gelfond and V. Lifschitz. The stable model semantics for logic programming. In *Proceedings of the 5th International Conference on Logic Programming*, pages 1070–1080, Seattle, USA, August 1988. The MIT Press. 204
9. K. Heljanko. Using logic programs with stable model semantics to solve deadlock and reachability problems for 1-safe Petri nets. *Fundamenta Informaticae*, 37(3):247–268, 1999. 211
10. K. Heljanko. Bounded reachability checking with process semantics. In *Proceedings of the 12th International Conference on Concurrency Theory (Concur'2001)*, Aalborg, Denmark, August 2001. Accepted for publication. 211
11. K. Heljanko and I. Niemelä. Answer set programming and bounded model checking. In *Proceedings of the AAAI Spring 2001 Symposium on Answer Set Programming: Towards Efficient and Scalable Knowledge Representation and Reasoning*, pages 90–96, Stanford, USA, March 2001. AAAI Press, Technical Report SS-01-01. 200, 210
12. G. Holzmann. The model checker SPIN. *IEEE Transactions on Software Engineering*, 23(5):279–295, 1997. 200
13. O. Kupferman and M. Y. Vardi. Model checking of safety properties. In *Proceeding of 11th International Conference on Computer Aided Verification (CAV'99)*, pages 172–183. Springer-Verlag, 1999. 207
14. S. Melzer and S. Römer. Deadlock checking using net unfoldings. In *Proceeding of 9th International Conference on Computer Aided Verification (CAV'97)*, pages 352–363, Haifa, Israel, Jun 1997. Springer-Verlag. 210, 211
15. I. Niemelä. Logic programming with stable model semantics as a constraint programming paradigm. *Annals of Mathematics and Artificial Intelligence*, 25(3,4):241–273, 1999. 201
16. I. Niemelä and P. Simons. Extending the Smodels system with cardinality and weight constraints. In Jack Minker, editor, *Logic-Based Artificial Intelligence*, pages 491–521. Kluwer Academic Publishers, 2000. 205, 206
17. K. Varpaaniemi, K. Heljanko, and J. Lilius. PROD 3.2 - An advanced tool for efficient reachability analysis. In *Proceedings of the 9th International Conference on Computer Aided Verification (CAV'97)*, pages 472–475, Haifa, Israel, June 1997. Springer-Verlag. 200

Diagnosing Physical Systems in A-Prolog

Michael Gelfond[1], Marcello Balduccini[1], and Joel Galloway[2]

[1] Department of Computer Science, Texas Tech University
Lubbock, TX 79409, USA
{mgelfond,balduccini}@cs.ttu.edu
http://www.cs.ttu.edu/~mgelfond
[2] Dupont Pharmaceuticals
San Diego, CA, USA
Joel.R.Galloway@dupontpharma.com

Abstract. In this paper we suggest an architecture for a software agent which operates a physical device and is capable of making observations and of testing and repairing the device components. We present novel definitions of the notions of symptom, candidate diagnosis, and diagnosis which are based on the theory of action language $\mathcal{AL}$. The new definitions allow one to give a simple account of the agent's behavior in which many of the agent's tasks are reduced to computing stable models of logic programs.

1 Introduction

In this paper we continue the investigation of applicability of A-Prolog (a loosely defined collection of logic programming languages under the answer set semantics [6]) to knowledge representation and reasoning. The focus is on the development of an architecture for a software agent acting in a changing environment. We assume that the agent and the environment (sometimes referred to as a dynamic system) satisfies the following simplifying conditions.

1. The agent's environment is viewed as a transition diagram whose states are sets of fluents (relevant properties of the domain whose truth values may depend on time) and whose arcs are labeled by actions.
2. The agent is capable of making correct observations, performing actions, and remembering the domain history.

These assumptions hold in many realistic domains and are suitable for a broad class of applications. In many domains, however, the effects of actions and the truth values of observations can only be known with a substantial degree of uncertainty which cannot be ignored in the modeling process. It remains to be seen if some of our methods can be made to work in such situations. The above assumptions determine the structure of the agent's knowledge base. It consists of three parts. The *first part*, called an *action* (or *system*) *description*, specifies the transition diagram representing possible trajectories of the system. It contains descriptions of domain's actions and fluents, together with the definition

T. Eiter, W. Faber, and M. Truszczyński (Eds.): LPNMR 2001, LNAI 2173, pp. 213–225, 2001.
© Springer-Verlag Berlin Heidelberg 2001

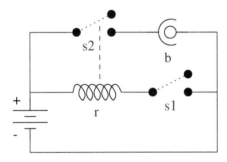

Fig. 1. $\mathcal{AC}$

of possible successor states to which the system can move after an action a is executed in a state σ. The *second part* of the agent's knowledge, called *history description*, contains observations made by the agent together with a record of its own actions. It defines a collection of paths in the diagram which can be interpreted as the system's possible pasts. If the agent's knowledge is complete (i.e., it has complete information about the initial state and the occurrences of actions) and the system's actions are deterministic then there is only one such path. The *third part* of agent's knowledge base contains a collection of the agent's goals. All this knowledge is used and updated by the agent who repeatedly executes the following steps:

1. observe the world and interpret the observations;
2. select a goal;
3. plan;
4. execute part of the plan.

In this paper we concentrate on agents operating physical devices and capable of testing and repairing the device components. We are especially interested in the first step of the loop, i.e. in agent's interpretations of discrepancies between agent's predictions and the system's actual behavior. The following example will be used throughout the paper:

Example 1. Consider a system S consisting of an analog circuit $\mathcal{AC}$ from figure 1. We assume that switches s_1 and s_2 are mechanical components which cannot become damaged. Relay r is a magnetic coil. If not damaged, it is activated when s_1 is closed, causing s_2 to close. Undamaged bulb b emits light if s_2 is closed. For simplicity we consider an agent capable of performing only one action, $close(s_1)$. The environment can be represented by two damaging exogenous actions: brk, which causes b to become faulty, and srg, which damages r and also b assuming that b is not protected. Suppose that the agent operating this device is given a goal of lighting the bulb. He realizes that this can be achieved by closing the first switch, performs the operation, and discovers that the bulb is not lit. The goal of the paper is to specify the agent's behavior after this discovery.

We start with presenting our definitions of the notions of symptom, candidate diagnosis, and diagnosis which are based on the theory of action language $\mathcal{AL}$ [1]. These definitions are used to give a simple account of the agent's behavior in which many of the agent's tasks are reduced to computing stable models of logic programs.

Background

By a physical system S we mean a triple $\langle C, F, A \rangle$ of finite sets. Elements of C are called *components* of S. Elements of F are referred to as *fluents*. By *fluent literals* we mean fluents and their negations (denoted by $\neg f$). The set A of *elementary actions* is partitioned into two disjoint sets, A_s and A_e; A_s consists of actions performed by an agent and A_e consists of exogenous actions whose occurrence can cause system components to malfunction.

A system S will be associated with the transition diagram $T(S)$ (or simply T). States of T are labeled by complete and consistent sets of fluent literals corresponding to possible physical states of S. The arcs are labeled by subsets of A called *compound actions*. Execution of a compound action $\{a_1, \ldots, a_k\}$ corresponds to the simultaneous execution of its components. Paths of T correspond to possible behaviors (or trajectories) of S. To reason about S we need to have a concise and convenient way to define its transition diagram. This will be done by a system description $SD(S)$ (or simply SD) consisting of rules of A-Prolog defining components of S, its fluent and actions, *causal laws* determining the effects of these actions, and the actions' *executability conditions*. We assume that SD has a unique answer set which defines an action description of $\mathcal{AL}$. (In our further discussion we will identify this action description with SD.) Causal laws of SD can be divided into two parts. The first part, SD_n, contains laws describing normal behavior of the system. Their bodies usually contain special fluent literals of the form $\neg ab(c)$. As usual $ab(c)$ is read as "component c of S is abnormal". Its use in diagnosis goes back to [15]. The second part, SD_b, describes effects of exogenous actions damaging the components. Such laws normally contain relation ab in the head or positive parts of the bodies.

In addition to describing all possible trajectories of S, we need to describe the history of S up to a current moment n. This is done by a collection Γ_n of statements in the 'history description' part of $\mathcal{AL}$. We assume that the system's time is discrete and t_i and t_{i+1} stand for two consecutive moments of time in the interval $0 \ldots n$. Statements of Γ_n have the form:

1. $obs(l, t)$ - 'fluent literal l was observed to be true at moment t';
2. $hpd(a, t)$ - elementary action $a \in A$ was observed to happen at moment t

where $0 \le t < n$. For simplicity we only consider histories with *observations closed under the static causal rules of $\mathcal{AL}$*, (i.e. if every state of S must satisfy a constraint 'fluent literal l_0 is true if fluent literals from P are true' and literals from P are observed in Γ then so must be l_0). Let S be a system with the transition diagram T and let Γ_n be a history of S up to moment n. A path $\sigma_0, a_0, \sigma_1, \ldots, a_{n-1}, \sigma_n$ in T is a *model* of Γ_n iff

1. $a_k = \{a : hpd(a, k) \in \Gamma_n\}$;
2. if $obs(l, k) \in \Gamma_n$ then $l \in \sigma_k$.

Γ_n is *consistent* (with respect to T) if it has a model. A fluent literal l holds in a model M at time $k \leq n$ ($M \models h(l, k)$) if $l \in \sigma_k$. Finally, $\Gamma_n \models h(l, k)$ if, for every model M of Γ_n, $M \models h(l, k)$. Notice that, in contrast to action description language $\mathcal{L}$ from [2], [3] a domain description of $\mathcal{AL}$ is consistent only if changes in the observations of system's states can be explained without assuming occurrences of any action not recorded in Γ_n.

The following is a description, SD, of system S from Example 1:

$$\text{Fluents:}$$

$comp(r)$.	$comp(b)$.	$switch(s_1)$.	$switch(s_2)$
$f(active(r))$.	$f(on(b))$.	$f(prot(b))$.	
$f(closed(SW)) \leftarrow$		$switch(SW)$.	
$f(ab(X)) \quad\quad \leftarrow$		$comp(X)$.	

Agent Actions: Exogenous Actions
$a\_act(close(s_1))$. $x\_act(brk)$.
$x\_act(srg)$.

Causal Laws and Executability Conditions describing normal functioning of S:

$$SD_n \begin{cases} causes(close(s_1), closed(s_1), [\,]). \\ caused(active(r), [closed(s_1), \neg ab(r)]). \\ caused(closed(s_2), [active(r)]). \\ caused(on(b), [closed(s_2), \neg ab(b)]). \\ caused(\neg on(b), [\neg closed(s_2)]). \\ impossible\_if(close(s_1), [closed(s_1)]). \end{cases}$$

($causes(A, L, P)$ says that execution of action A in a state satisfying fluent literals from P causes fluent literal L to become true in a resulting state; $caused(L, P)$ means that every state satisfying P must also satisfy L, $impossible\_if(A, P)$ indicates that action A is not executable in states satisfying P.) The system's malfunctioning information is given by:

$$SD_b \begin{cases} causes(brk, ab(b), [\,]). \\ causes(srg, ab(r), [\,]). \\ causes(srg, ab(b), [\neg prot(b)]). \\ caused(\neg on(b), [ab(b)]). \\ caused(\neg active(r), [ab(r)]). \end{cases}$$

Now consider a history, Γ_0 of S:

$$\Gamma_0 \begin{cases} hpd(close(s_1), 0). \\ obs(\neg closed(s_1), 0). \\ obs(\neg closed(s_2), 0). \\ obs(\neg ab(b), 0). \\ obs(\neg ab(r), 0). \\ obs(prot(b), 0). \end{cases}$$

It is easy to see that the path $\langle \sigma_0, close(s_1), \sigma_1 \rangle$ is the only model of Γ_0 and that $\Gamma_0 \models h(on(b), 1)$

2   Basic Definitions

Let S be a system with the transition diagram T, n be a moment of time, O_n be a collection of observations made by the agent starting at n, and Γ_{n-1} be the previous history of S. We say that a pair

$$S = \langle \Gamma_{n-1}, O_n \rangle \tag{1}$$

is a *symptom* of the system's malfunctioning if Γ_{n-1} is consistent (w.r.t. T) and $\Gamma_{n-1} \cup O_n$ is not. Our definition of a candidate diagnosis of symptom (1) is based on the notion of *explanation* from [1]. In our terminology, an explanation, E, of symptom (1) is a collection of statements

$$E = \{hpd(a_i, t) : 0 \le t < n \text{ and } a_i \in A_e\} \tag{2}$$

such that $\Gamma_{n-1} \cup O_n \cup E$ is consistent.

Definition 1. A *candidate diagnosis* D of symptom (1) consists of an explanation $E(D)$ of (1) together with the set $\Delta(D)$ of components of S which could possibly be damaged by actions from $E(D)$. More precisely, $\Delta(D) = \{c : M \models h(ab(c), n-1)\}$ for some model M of $\Gamma_{n-1} \cup O_n \cup E(D)$.

Definition 2. We say that a *diagnosis* of a symptom $S = (\Gamma_{n-1}, O_n)$ is a candidate diagnosis in which all components in Δ are faulty.

3   Computing Candidate Diagnoses

In this section we show how the need for diagnosis can be determined and candidate diagnoses found by the techniques of answer set programming [10].

Consider a system description SD of S whose behavior up to the moment $n-1$ from some interval $[0, N]$ is described by history Γ_{n-1}. (We assume that N is sufficiently large for our application.) We start by describing an encoding of SD into programs of A-Prolog suitable for execution by SMODELS [14]. Since SMODELS takes as an input programs with finite Herbrand bases, references to lists should be eliminated from SD. To do that we expand the signature of SD by new terms - names of the corresponding causal laws - and consider a mapping α defined as follows:

1. $\alpha(causes(a, l_0, [l_1 \ldots l_m]))$ is the collection of atoms $d\_law(d)$, $head(d, l_0)$, $action(d, a)$, $prec(d, i, l_i)$ for $1 \leq i \leq m$, and $prec(d, m + 1, nil)$ (Here and below d will refer to the name of the corresponding law).
2. $\alpha(caused(l_0, [l_1 \ldots l_m]))$ is the collection of atoms $s\_law(d)$, $head(d, l_0)$, $prec(d, i, l_i)$ for $1 \leq i \leq m$, and $prec(d, m + 1, nil)$.
3. $\alpha(impossible\_if(a, [l_1 \ldots l_m]))$ is a constraint

$$\leftarrow h(l_1, T), \ldots, h(l_n, T),$$
$$o(a, T).$$

where $o(a, t)$ stands for *action a occurred at time t*.

By $\alpha(SD)$ we denote the result of applying α to the laws of SD. Finally, for any history, Γ, of S

$$\alpha(SD, \Gamma) = \Pi \cup \alpha(SD) \cup \Gamma$$

where Π is defined as follows:

$$\Pi \begin{cases}
\text{1. } h(L, T') & \leftarrow d\_law(D), \\
& \quad head(D, L), \\
& \quad action(D, A), \\
& \quad o(A, T), \\
& \quad prec\_h(D, T). \\
\text{2. } h(L, T) & \leftarrow s\_law(D), \\
& \quad head(D, L), \\
& \quad prec\_h(D, T). \\
\text{3. } all\_h(D, N, T) & \leftarrow prec(D, N, nil). \\
\text{4. } all\_h(D, N, T) & \leftarrow prec(D, N, P), \\
& \quad h(P, T), \\
& \quad all\_h(D, N', T). \\
\text{5. } prec\_h(D, T) & \leftarrow all\_h(D, 1, T). \\
\text{6. } h(L, T') & \leftarrow h(L, T), \\
& \quad not\ h(\overline{L}, T'). \\
\text{7. } o(A, T) & \leftarrow hpd(A, T). \\
\text{8. } h(L, 0) & \leftarrow obs(L, 0). \\
\text{9. } & \leftarrow obs(L, T), \\
& \quad not\ h(L, T).
\end{cases}$$

Here D, A, L are variables for the names of laws, actions, and fluent literals respectively, T, T' denote consecutive time points from the interval $[0, N]$, and N, N' are variables for consecutive integers. (The corresponding typing predicates in the bodies of some rules of Π are omitted to save space; o is used instead of hpd to distinguish between actions observed and actions hypothesized). The following terminology will be useful for describing the relationship between answer sets of $\alpha(SD, \Gamma_{n-1})$ and models of Γ_{n-1}.

We say that an answer set $\mathcal{AS}$ of $\alpha(SD, \Gamma_{n-1})$ *defines the trajectory* $p = \sigma_0, a_0, \sigma_1, \ldots, a_{n-2}, \sigma_{n-1}$ where $\sigma_k = \{l : h(l, k) \in \mathcal{AS}\}$ and $a_k = \{a : o(a, k) \in \mathcal{AS}\}$.

The following theorem establishes the relationship between the theory of actions in $\mathcal{AL}$ and logic programming.

Theorem 1. *If the initial situation of Γ_{n-1} is complete, i.e. for any fluent f of SD, Γ_{n-1} contains $obs(f,0)$ or $obs(\neg f,0)$ then M is a model of Γ_{n-1} iff M is a trajectory defined by some answer set of $\alpha(SD,\Gamma_{n-1})$.*

(The theorem is similar to the result from [18] which deals with a different language and uses the definitions from [11]).

Now let S be a symptom of the form (1), and let

$$TEST(S) = \alpha(SD,\Gamma_{n-1}) \cup O_n \cup R \qquad (3)$$

where

$$R \begin{cases} obs(f,0) & \leftarrow not\ obs(\neg f,0). \\ obs(\neg f,0) & \leftarrow not\ obs(f,0). \end{cases}$$

for any fluent $f \in F$. The rules of R are sometimes called the *awareness axioms*. They guarantee that initially the agent considers all possible values of the domain fluents. (If the agent's information about the initial state of the system is complete these axioms can be omitted.) The following corollary forms the basis for our diagnostic algorithms.

Corollary 1. *Let $S = \langle \Gamma_{n-1}, O_n \rangle$ where Γ_{n-1} is consistent. Then S is a symptom of system's malfunctioning iff the program $TEST(S)$ has no answer set.*

To diagnose the system, S, we construct a program, DM, defining an *explanation space* of our diagnostic agent - a collection of sequences of exogenous events which could happen (unobserved) in the system's past and serve as possible explanations of unexpected observations. We call such programs *diagnostic modules* for S. The simplest diagnostic module, DM_0, is defined by rules:

$$DM_0 \begin{cases} o(A,T) & \leftarrow 0 \leq T < n,\ x\_act(A), \\ & \quad not\ \neg o(A,T). \\ \\ \neg o(A,T) & \leftarrow 0 \leq T < n,\ x\_act(A), \\ & \quad not\ o(A,T). \end{cases}$$

or, in the more compact, *choice rule*, notation of SMODELS ([16])

$$\{o(A,T) : x\_act(A)\} \leftarrow 0 \leq T < n.$$

(Recall that a choice rule has the form

$$m\{p(\overline{X}) \ : \ q(\overline{X})\}n \leftarrow body$$

and says that, if the body is satisfied by an answer set AS of a program then AS must contain between m and n atoms of the form $p(\overline{t})$ such that $q(\overline{t}) \in AS$.)

Finding candidate diagnoses of symptom (1) can be reduced to finding answer sets of a *diagnostic program*

$$\mathcal{D}_0(\mathcal{S}) = TEST(\mathcal{S}) \cup DM_0 \qquad (4)$$

It is not difficult to see that DM_0 generates every possible sequence of the past occurrences of exogenous actions and hence, by Theorem 1, $\mathcal{D}_0(\mathcal{S})$ finds all the candidate diagnoses of $\mathcal{S}$.

Example 2. Let us again consider system S from Example 1. According to Γ_0 initially the switches s_1 and s_2 are open, all circuit components are ok, s_1 is closed by the agent, and b is protected. It is predicted that b will be *on* at 1. Suppose that, instead, the agent observes that at time 1 bulb b is *off*, i.e. $O_1 = \{obs(\neg on(b), 1)\}$. Intuitively, this is viewed as a symptom $\mathcal{S}_0 = \langle \Gamma_0, O_1 \rangle$ of malfunctioning of S. By running SMODELS on $TEST(\mathcal{S}_0)$ we discover that this program has no answer sets and therefore, by corollary 1, $\mathcal{S}_0$ is indeed a symptom. Diagnoses of $\mathcal{S}_0$ can be found by running SMODELS on $\mathcal{D}_0(\mathcal{S}_0)$ and extracting the necessary information from the computed answer sets. It is easy to check that, as expected, there are three candidate diagnoses:

$$D_1 = \langle \{o(brk, 0)\}, \{b\} \rangle$$
$$D_2 = \langle \{o(srg, 0)\}, \{r\} \rangle$$
$$D_3 = \langle \{o(brk, 0), o(srg, 0)\}, \{b, r\} \rangle$$

which corresponds to our intuition. Theorem 1 guarantees correctness of this computation.

The basic diagnostic module $\mathcal{D}_0$ can be modified in many different ways. For instance, a simple modification, $\mathcal{D}_1(\mathcal{S})$ which eliminates some candidate diagnoses containing actions unrelated to the corresponding symptom can be constructed as follows: Let

$$DM_1 = DM_0 \cup REL$$

where

$$REL \begin{cases} 1. & rel(A, L) \leftarrow d\_law(D), \\ & \qquad head(D, L), \\ & \qquad action(D, A), \\ & \qquad x\_act(A). \\ 2. & rel(A, L) \leftarrow s\_law(D), \\ & \qquad head(D, L), \\ & \qquad prec(D, P), \\ & \qquad rel(A, P), \\ & \qquad x\_act(A). \\ 3. & rel(A) \quad\leftarrow obs(L, T), \\ & \qquad T \geq n, \\ & \qquad rel(A, L). \\ 4. & \qquad\quad\leftarrow T < n, \\ & \qquad o(A, T), \\ & \qquad not\ hpd(A, T), \\ & \qquad not\ rel(A). \end{cases}$$

and let
$$\mathcal{D}_1(\mathcal{S}) = TEST(\mathcal{S}) \cup DM_1$$

It is easy to see that this modification is *safe*, i.e. $\mathcal{D}_1$ will not miss any useful predictions about the malfunctioning components.[1]

Example 3. Let us expand the system S from Example 1 by a new component, c, unrelated to the circuit, and an exogenous action a which damages this component. It is easy to see that diagnosis $\mathcal{S}_0$ from Example 1 will still be a symptom of malfunctioning of a new system, S_a, and that the basic diagnostic module applied to S_a will return diagnoses $D_1 - D_3$ from Example 2 together with new diagnoses containing a and $ab(c)$, e.g.

$$D_4 = \langle \{o(brks, 0), o(a, 0)\}, \{b, c\} \rangle$$

Diagnostic module $\mathcal{D}_1$ will ignore actions unrelated to $\mathcal{S}$ and return only $D_1 - D_3$.

It may be worth noticing that the distinction between hpd and o allows actions unrelated to observations at n to actually happen at moment $n - 1$. Constraint (4) of REL only prohibits generating such actions in our search for diagnosis. Even more unrelated actions can be eliminated from the search space of our diagnostic modules by considering relevance relation rel depending on time. The diagnostic module $\mathcal{D}_1$ can also be further modified by limiting its search to recent occurrences of exogenous actions. This can be done by

$$\mathcal{D}_2(\mathcal{S}) = TEST(\mathcal{S}) \cup DM_2$$

where DM_2 is obtained by replacing an atom $0 \leq T < n$ in the bodies of rules of DM_0 by $n - m \leq T < n$. The constant m determines the time interval in the past that an agent is willing to consider in it's search for possible explanations. To simplify our discussion in the rest of the paper we *assume that* $m = 1$. Finally, the rule

$$\leftarrow k\{o(A, n - 1)\}.$$

added to DM_2 will eliminate all diagnoses containing more than k actions. Of course the resulting module $\mathcal{D}_3$ as well as $\mathcal{D}_2$ can miss some diagnoses and deepening of the search and/or increase of k may be necessary if no diagnosis of a symptom is found. There are many other interesting ways of constructing efficient diagnostics modules. We are especially intrigued by the possibilities of using new features of answer sets solvers such as weight rules of SMODELS and soft constraints of DLV [19] to specify a preference relation on diagnosis. This however is a subject of further investigation. Suppose now the diagnostician has a candidate diagnosis D of a symptom $\mathcal{S}$. Is it indeed a diagnosis?

---

[1] In the full paper we will make this and other similar statements mathematically precise.

4   Finding a Diagnosis

To answer this question the agent should be able to test components of $\Delta(D)$. Assuming that *no exogenous actions occur during testing* a diagnosis can be found by the following simple algorithm, $Find\_Diag(\mathcal{S})$:

function $Find\_Diag(\mathcal{S})$
   repeat
      $(E, \Delta) := Candidate\_Diag(\mathcal{S})$;
      $diag := true$; $\Delta_0 := \Delta$;
      while $\Delta_0 \neq \emptyset$ **and** $diag$ **do**
         select $c \in \Delta_0$; $\Delta_0 := \Delta_0 \setminus \{c\}$;
         if $faulty(c)$ **then**
            $O_n := O_n \cup obs(ab(c), n)$;
         else
            $O_n := O_n \cup obs(\neg ab(c), n)$;
            $diag := false$;
         end
      end {while}
   until $diag$ or $\Delta = \emptyset$;
   return (E, Δ).

The algorithm uses functions $Candidate\_Diag(\mathcal{S})$ which returns a candidate diagnosis (E, Δ) of $\mathcal{S}$ and $faulty(c)$ which checks if a component c of S is faulty. Notice that $\Delta = \emptyset$ indicates that no diagnosis is found - the diagnostician failed. To illustrate the algorithm, consider

Example 4. Consider the system S from Example 1 and a history Γ_0 in which b is not protected, all components of S are ok, both switches are open, and the agent closes s_1 at time 0. At time 1, he observes that the bulb b is not lit, considers $\mathcal{S} = \langle \Gamma_0, O_1 \rangle$ where $O_1 = \{obs(\neg on(b), 1)\}$ and calls function $Need\_Diag(\mathcal{S})$ which searches for an answer set of $TEST(\mathcal{S})$. There are no such sets, the diagnostician realizes he has a symptom to diagnose and calls function $Find\_Diag(\mathcal{S})$. Let us assume that the first call to $Candidate\_Diag$ returns

$$PD_1 = \langle \{o(srg, 0)\}, \{r, b\} \rangle$$

Suppose that the agent selects component r from Δ and determines that it is not faulty. Observation $obs(\neg ab(r), 1)$ will be added to O_1, $diag$ will be set to $false$ and the program will call $Candidate\_Diag$ again with the updated symptom $\mathcal{S}$ as a parameter. $Candidate\_Diag$ will return another possible diagnosis

$$PD_2 = \langle \{o(brk, 0)\}, \{b\} \rangle$$

The agent will test bulb b, find it to be faulty, add observation $obs(ab(b), 1)$ to O_1 and return PD_2.

Now let us consider a different scenario:

Example 5. Let Γ_0 and observation O_1 be as in Example 4 and suppose that the program's first call to *Candidate_Diag* returns PD_1, b is found to be faulty, $obs(ab(b), 1)$ is added to O_1, and *Find_Diag* returns PD_1. The agent proceeds to have b repaired but, to his disappointment, discovers that b is still not on! Intuitively this means that PD_1 is a wrong diagnosis - there must have been a power surge at 0.

The example shows that, *in order to find a correct explanation of a symptom, it is essential for an agent to repair damaged components and observe the behavior of the system after repair.* For simplicity we assume that, similar to testing, repair occurs in well controlled environment, i.e. *no exogenous actions happen during the repair process.* To formally model this process we introduce a special action, $repair(c)$ for every component c of S. The effect of this action will be defined by the causal law:

$$causes(repair(c), \neg ab(c), [])$$

The diagnostic process will be now modeled by the following algorithm: (Here $S = \langle \Gamma_{n-1}, O \rangle$) and $\{obs(f_i, k)\}$ is a collection of observations the diagnostician makes to test his repair at moment k.)

procedure $Diagnose(S;$
   $k := n;$
  while $Need\_Diag(S)$ **do**
      $\langle E, \Delta \rangle = Find\_Diag(S);$
      if $\Delta = \emptyset$ **then**
         no diagnosis
      else
         $Repair(\Delta);$
         $O := O \cup \{hpd(repair(c), k) : c \in \Delta\};$
         $k := k + 1;$
         $O := O \cup \{obs(f_i, k)\};$
     end
  end

Example 6. To illustrate the above algorithm let us go back to the agent from Example 5 who just discovered diagnosis D_1. He will repair the bulb and check if the bulb is lit. It is not, and therefore a new observation is recorded as follows:

$$O_1 := O_1 \cup \{hpd(repair(b), 1), obs(\neg on(b), 2)\}$$

$Need\_Diag(S)$ will detect a continued need for diagnosis, $Find\_Diag(S)$ will return D_3, which, after new repair and testing will hopefully prove to be the right diagnosis.

The diagnosis produced by the above algorithm can be viewed as a reasonable interpretation of discrepancies between the agent's predictions and actual observations. To complete our analysis of step 1 of the agent's acting and reasoning loop we need to explain how this interpretation can be incorporated in the agent's history. If the diagnosis discovered is unique then the answer is obvious - O is simply added to Γ_{n-1}. If however faults of the system components can be caused by different sets of exogenous actions the situation becomes more subtle. Complete investigation of the issues involved is the subject of further research.

5   Related Work

There is a numerous number of papers on diagnosis many of which substantially influenced the authors views on the subject. The roots of our approach go back to [15] where diagnosis for a static environment were formally defined in logical terms. Recent expansions of this work [17,12,3] which take into account the dynamics of system's behavior served as the starting point of the work presented in this paper. We

1. substantially simplified the basic definitions of [3];
2. presented reasonable efficient and provenly correct algorithms for computing 'dynamic' diagnosis;
3. showed how to combine diagnostics with planning and other activities of a reasoning agent.

The simplification of basic definitions from [3]is achieved by a careful choice of the 'history description' language - $\mathcal{AL}$ seems to be more suitable for our purposes that $\mathcal{L}$ used in [3]. The reasoning algorithms are based on recent discoveries of close relationship between A-Prolog and reasoning about effects of actions [11] and the ideas from answer set programming [10,13,9]. This approach of course would be impossible without existence of efficient answer set reasoning systems. Finally, the integration of a diagnostic and other activities is based on the agent architecture from [1].

6   Conclusion

The paper describes an ongoing work on the development of a diagnostic problem solving agent in A-Prolog. In particular we are looking for for good modeling techniques with clear and provenly correct algorithms. The following can be of interest to people who share these interests:

• definitions of a symptom, candidate diagnosis, and diagnosis which we believe to be substantially simpler than other similar approaches;

• a new algorithm for computing candidate diagnoses. (The algorithm is based on answer set programming and views the search for candidate diagnoses as 'planning in the past');

• a simple account of diagnostics, testing and repair based on the use of answer set solvers.

In the full paper we plan to give mathematical analysis of correctness of the corresponding algorithms and test them on medium size examples.

References

1. Baral, C., and Gelfond, M. Reasoning agents in dynamic domains. In Minker, J,. ed., *Logic-Based Artificial Intelligence*, Kluwer Academic Publishers, (2000), 257–279, 215, 217, 224

2. Baral, C., Gelfond, M., and Provetti, A. Reasoning about actions: laws, observations, and hypotheses. In *Journal of Logic Programming*, volume 31, 201–244, 1994. 216

3. Baral, C., McIlraith, S., and Son, T. Formulating diagnostic problem solving using an action language with narratives and sensing. In *Proceedings of the 2000 KR Conference*, 311-322, 2000. 216, 224

4. de Kleer, J., Mackworth, A., and Reiter, R. Characterizing diagnoses and systems. In *Artificial Intelligence*, volume 56(2-3), 197–222, 1992.

5. Gelfond, M., and Lifschitz, V. The stable model semantics for logic programming. In *Logic Programming: Proc. of the Fifth Int'l Conf. and Symp.*, 1070–1080, 1988.

6. Gelfond, M., and Lifschitz, V. Classical negation in logic programs and disjunctive databases. In *New Generation Computing*, 365–387, 1991. 213

7. Gelfond, M., and Lifschitz, V. Representing actions in extended logic programs. In *Proc. of Joint International Conference and Symposium on Logic Programming*, 559–573, 1992.

8. Gelfond, M., and Lifschitz, V. Action languages. In *Electronic Transactions on AI*, volume 3(16), 1998.

9. Lifschitz, V. Action languages, Answer Sets, and Planning. In *The Logic Programming Paradigm: a 25-Year Perspective*. 357–373, Springer Verlag, 1999. 224

10. Marek, W., and Truszczynski, M. Stable models and an alternative logic paradigm. In *The Logic Programming Paradigm: a 25-Year Perspective*, 375–398, Springer Verlag, 1999. 217, 224

11. McCain, T., and Turner, H. A causal theory of ramifications and qualifications. In *Artificial Intelligence*, volume 32, 57–95, 1995. 219, 224

12. McIlraith, T. Explanatory diagnosis conjecturing actions to explain observations. In *Proceedings of the 1998 KR Conference*, 167–177, 1998. 224

13. Niemela, I. Logic programs with stable model semantics as a constraint programming paradigm. In *Annals of Mathematics and Artificial Intelligence*, 25(3-4), 241–273, 1999. 224

14. Niemela, I., and Simons, P. SMODELS - an implementation of the well-founded and stable model semantics for normal logic programs. In *Proc. of LPNMR'97*, volume 1265 of Lecture Notes in Computer Science, 420–429, 1997. 217

15. Reiter, R. A theory of diagnosis from first principles. In *Artificial Intelligence*, volume 32, 57–95, 1987. 215, 224

16. Simons, P. Extending the stable model semantics with more expressive rules. In *5th International Conference, LPNMR'99*, 305–316, 1999. 219

17. Thielscher, M. A theory of dynamic diagnosis. In *Linkoping Electronic Articles in Computer and Information Science*, volume 2(11), 1997. 224

18. H. Turner. Representing actions in logic programs and default theories. In *Journal of Logic Programming*, 31(1-3):245–298, May 1997. 219

19. Eiter, T., Faber, Leone, N., Pfeifer, G. Declarative Problem Solving in DLV In Minker, J,. ed., *Logic-Based Artificial Intelligence*, Kluwer Academic Publishers, 257–279, 2000. 221

Planning with Different Forms of Domain-Dependent Control Knowledge – An Answer Set Programming Approach

Tran Cao Son[1], Chitta Baral[2], and Sheila McIlraith[3]

[1] Department of Computer Science, New Mexico State University
PO Box 30001, MSC CS, Las Cruces, NM 88003, USA
tson@cs.nmsu.edu
[2] Department of Computer Science and Engineering, Arizona State University
Tempe, AZ 85287, USA
chitta@asu.edu
[3] Knowledge Systems Laboratory, Computer Science, Stanford University
Stanford, CA 94305, USA
sam@ksl.stanford.edu

Abstract. In this paper we present a declarative approach to adding domain-dependent control knowledge for Answer Set Planning (ASP). Our approach allows different types of domain-dependent control knowledge such as hierarchical, temporal, or procedural knowledge to be represented and exploited in parallel, thus combining the ideas of control knowledge in HTN-planning, GOLOG-programming, and planning with temporal knowledge into ASP. To do so, we view domain-dependent control knowledge as sets of independent constraints. An advantage of this approach is that domain-dependent control knowledge can be modularly formalized and added to the planning problem as desired. We define a set of constructs for constraint representation and provide a set of domain-independent logic programming rules for checking constraint satisfaction.

1 Introduction

Planning is hard. The complexity of classical planning is known to be PSPACE-complete for finite domains and undecidable in the general case [8,12]. By fixing the length of plans, the planning problem reduces to NP-complete or worse. Planning systems such as FF [16], HSP [6], Graphplan [5], and Blackbox [18] have greatly improved the performance of their systems on benchmark planning problems by exploiting domain-independent search heuristics, clever encodings of knowledge, and efficient data structures [30]. Nevertheless, despite impressive improvements in performance, there is a growing belief that planners that exploit *domain-dependent* control knowledge may provide the key to future performance gains [30]. This conjecture is supported by the impressive performance of planners such as TLPlan [1], TALplan [11] and SHOP [26], all of which exploit domain-dependent control knowledge.

T. Eiter, W. Faber, and M. Truszczyński (Eds.): LPNMR 2001, LNAI 2173, pp. 226–239, 2001.
© Springer-Verlag Berlin Heidelberg 2001

A central issue in incorporating domain-dependent control knowledge into a planner is to identify the classes of knowledge to incorporate and to devise a means of representing and reasoning with this knowledge. In the past, planners such as TLPlan and TALplan have exploited domain-dependent *temporal knowledge*; SHOP and various hierarchical task network (HTN) planners have exploited domain-dependent *hierarchical and partial-order knowledge*; and satisfiability-based planners such as Blackbox have experimented with a variety of domain-dependent control knowledge encoded as propositional formulae. In this paper, we propose to exploit temporal knowledge and hierarchical knowledge as well as, what we refer to as, *procedural knowledge* within the paradigm of answer set planning. We show how these classes of domain-dependent control knowledge can be represented using a normal logic program and how they can be exploited by a basic answer set planner. We demonstrate the improvement in the efficiency of our answer set planner.

The set of programming language constructs provided by the logic programming language GOLOG (e.g., sequence (;), if-then-else, while, etc.) [20] provides an example of the class of procedural knowledge we incorporate into our planner. For example, a procedural constraint written as $a_1; a_2; (a_3|a_4|a_5); f$? tells the planner that it should make a plan where a_1 is the first action, a_2 is the second action and then it should choose one of a_3, a_4 or a_5 such that after their execution f will be true. This type of domain-dependent control knowledge is different from temporal knowledge where plans are restricted to action sequences that agree with a given set of temporal formulas. Procedural knowledge is also different from hierarchical and partial-order constraints where tasks are divided into smaller tasks, with some partial ordering and other constraints between them. These three classes of domain-dependent control knowledge differ in their structure and while there may be transformations available between one form and another, it is often natural for a user to express knowledge in a particular form.

To exploit the above classes of domain-dependent planning constraints we use the declarative problem-solving paradigm exemplified by satisfiability-based planners. We refer to such an approach to planning as *model-based planning*, to indicate that plans are *models* of the logical theory describing the planning problem. One advantage of this approach is that planner development is divided into two parts: development of model generators for logical languages, and planner encoding as a logical theory. This enables those developing logical encodings of model-based planning problems to exploit the diversity of domain-independent model generators being developed for different tasks.

In this paper, we use an answer set programming appraoch to model-based planning. We use logic programming as the logical language to encode our model-based planning problem. From a knowledge representation perspective, there are many advantages to a logic programming encoding, as compared to a simple propositional logic encoding. These include: parsimonious encoding of solutions to the frame problem in the presence of qualification and ramification constraints; the presence of the non-classical '←' operator that not only helps in encoding causality but also can be exploited when searching for models; and many fundamental theoretical results [3] that help construct proofs of the correctness of encodings. In contrast, few of the encodings of satisfiability-based planners have proofs of correctness, while most logic programming encodings are accompanied by a proof of correctness. From the perspective of computation, planners based on propositional encodings still fare better. There are currently more implementations of propositional solvers than of logic programming answer set generators, and the best propositional solvers tend to be faster than the best answer set generators.

The rest of this paper is organized as follows: we will review the basics of action language and answer set planning in the next section. We then introduce different constructs for domain-dependent control knowledge representation. For each construct, we provide a set of logic programming rules as its implementation (Subsections 3.1-3.3). We use Smodels, an implemented system for computing stable models of logic programs [27], in our experiments. As such, the rules developed in this paper are written in Smodels syntax and can be used as input to Smodels program[1]. In Subsection 3.4, we describe some experimental results and conclude in Section 4.

2   Preliminaries

2.1   Action Theories

We use the high-level action description language $\mathcal{B}$ of [15] to represent action theories. In such a language, an action theory consists of two finite, disjoint sets of names called *actions* and *fluents*. Actions transition the system from one state to another. Fluents are propositions whose truth value can change as the result of actions. Unless otherwise stated, a is used to denote an action. f and p are used to denote fluents. The action theory also comprises a set of propositions of the following form:

$$\mathbf{caused}(\{p_1, \ldots, p_n\}, f) \tag{1}$$

$$\mathbf{causes}(a, f, \{p_1, \ldots, p_n\}) \tag{2}$$

$$\mathbf{executable}(a, \{p_1, \ldots, p_n\}) \tag{3}$$

$$\mathbf{initially}(f) \tag{4}$$

where f and p_i's are fluent literals (a *fluent literal* is either a fluent g or its negation $\neg g$, written as $neg(g)$) and a is an action. (1) represents a static causal law, i.e., a ramification constraint. It conveys that whenever the fluent literals $p_1, \ldots, p_n$ hold, so does f. (2), referred to as a *dynamic causal law*, represents the (conditional) effect of a. Intuitively, a proposition of the form (2) states that f is guaranteed to be true after the execution of a in any state of the world where $p_1, \ldots, p_n$ are true. (3) captures an *executability condition* of a. It says that a is executable in a state in which $p_1, \ldots, p_n$ hold. Finally, propositions of

---

[1]   Although we use Smodels, we believe that the code presented here could easily be used with DLV [9], following simple modifications to reflect differences in syntax.

the form (4) are used to describe the initial state. (4) states that f holds in the initial state.

An *action theory* is a pair (D, Γ) where D consists of propositions of the form (1)-(3) and Γ consists of propositions of the form (4). For the purpose of this paper, it suffices to note that the semantics of such an action theory is given by a transition graph, represented by a relation t, whose nodes are the alternative (complete) states of the action theory and whose links (labeled with actions) represent the transition between its states (see details in [15]). That is, if $\langle s, a, s' \rangle \in t$, then there exists a link with label a from state s to state s'.

A *trajectory* of the system is denoted by a sequence $s_0 a_1 s_1 \ldots a_n s_n$ where s_i's are states and a_i's are actions and $\langle s_i, a_{i+1}, s_{i+1} \rangle \in t$ for $i \in \{0, \ldots, n - 1\}$. $s_0 a_1 s_1 \ldots a_n s_n$ is a trajectory of a fluent formula Δ if Δ holds in s_n.

In this paper, we will assume that Γ is *complete*, i.e., for every fluent f, either **initially**(f) or **initially**$(neg(f))$ belongs to Γ. We will also assume that (D, Γ) is *consistent* in the sense that there exists a non-empty relation t representing the transition graph of (D, Γ).

2.2   Answer Set Planning

A *planning problem* is specified by a triple $\langle D, \Gamma, \Delta \rangle$ where (D, Γ) is an action theory and Δ is a fluent formula (or *goal*), representing the goal state. A sequence of actions $a_1, \ldots, a_m$ is a *possible plan for* Δ if there exists a trajectory $s_0 a_1 s_1 \ldots a_m s_m$ such that s_0 and s_m satisfy Γ and Δ, respectively[2].

Given a planning problem $\langle D, \Gamma, \Delta \rangle$, answer set planning solves it by translating it into a logic program $\Pi(D, \Gamma, \Delta)$ (or Π, for short) consisting of *domain-dependent* rules that describe D, Γ, and Δ respectively, and *domain-independent* rules that generate action occurrences and represent the transitions between states.

● **Goal representation.** To encode Δ, we define formulas and provide a set of rules for formula evaluation. We consider formulas that are bounded classical formulas with each bound variable associated with a sort. They are formally defined as follows.

- A literal is a formula.
- The negation of a formula is a formula.
- A finite conjunction of formulas is a formula.
- A finite disjunction of formulas is a formula.
- If $X_1, \ldots, X_n$ are variables that can have values from the sorts $s_1, \ldots, s_n$, and $f_1(X_1, \ldots, X_n)$ is a formula then $\forall X_1, \ldots, X_n . f_1(X_1, \ldots, X_n)$ is a formula.

---

[2]   Note that the notion of plan employed here is weaker than the conventional one where the goal must be achieved on every possible trajectory. This is because an action theory with causal laws can be non-deterministic. Note however, that if D is deterministic, i.e., for every pair (s, a) there exists at most one state s' such that $\langle s, a, s' \rangle \in t$, then every possible plan for Δ is also a plan for Δ.

– If $X_1, \ldots, X_n$ are variables that can have values from the sorts $s_1, \ldots, s_n$, and $f_1(X_1, \ldots, X_n)$ is a formula then $\exists X_1, \ldots, X_n.f_1(X_1, \ldots, X_n)$ is a formula.

A sort called *formula* is introduced and each non-atomic formula is associated with a unique name and defined by (possibly) a set of rules. For example, the conjunction $f \wedge g \wedge h$ is represented by the set of atoms $\{conj(f'), in(f, f'), in(g, f'), in(h, f')\}$ where f' is the name assigned to $f \wedge g \wedge h$; $\forall X_1, \ldots, X_n.f_1(X_1, \ldots, X_n)$ can be represented by the rule

$$formula(forall(f, f_1(X_1, \ldots, X_n))) \leftarrow in(X_1, s_1), \ldots, in(X_n, s_n)$$

where f is the name assigned to the formula. In keeping with previous notation, negation is denoted by the function symbol *neg*. For example, if f is the name of a formula then $neg(f)$ is a formula denoting its negation. Rules to check when a formula holds or does not hold can be written in a straightforward manner and are omitted here to save space. (Details can be downloaded from the Web[3].)

• **Action theory representation.** Since each set of literals $\{p_1, \ldots, p_n\}$ in (1)-(3) can be represented by a conjunction of literals, D can be encoded as a set of facts of Π as follows. First, we assign to each set of fluent literals that occurs in a proposition of D a distinguished name. The constant *nil* denotes the set $\{\}$. A set of literals $\{p_1, \ldots, p_n\}$ will be replaced by the set of atoms $Y = \{conj(s), in(p_1, s), \ldots, in(p_n, s)\}$ where s is the name assigned to $\{p_1, \ldots, p_n\}$. With this representation, propositions in D can be easily translated into a set of facts of Π. For example, a proposition $causes(a, f, \{p_1, \ldots, p_n\})$ with $n > 0$ is encoded as a set of atoms consisting of $causes(a, f, s)$ and the set Y (s is the name assigned to $\{p_1, \ldots, p_n\}$).

• **Domain independent rules.** The domain independent rules of Π are adapted mainly from [14,10,21,22]. The main predicates in these rules are:

– $holds(L, T)$: L holds at time T,
– $possible(A, T)$: action A is executable at time T,
– $occ(A, T)$: action A occurs at time T, and
– $hf(\varphi, T)$: formula φ holds at time T.

The main rules are given next. In these rules, T is a variable of the sort *time*, L, G are variables denoting *fluent literals* (written as F or $neg(F)$ for some fluent F), S is a variable set of the sort *conj* (conjunction), and A, B are variables of the sort *action*.

$$holds(L, T+1) \leftarrow occ(A, T), causes(A, L, S), hf(S, T). \tag{5}$$

$$holds(L, T) \leftarrow caused(S, L), hf(S, T). \tag{6}$$

$$holds(L, T+1) \leftarrow contrary(L, G), holds(L, T), not\ holds(G, T+1). \tag{7}$$

$$possible(A, T) \leftarrow executable(A, S), hf(S, T). \tag{8}$$

$$holds(L, 0) \leftarrow literal(L), initially(L). \tag{9}$$

$$nocc(A, T) \leftarrow A \neq B, occ(B, T), T < length. \tag{10}$$

$$occ(A, T) \leftarrow T < length, possible(A, T), not\ nocc(A, T). \tag{11}$$

---

3   http://www.cs.nmsu.edu/~tson/asp_planner

Here, (5) encodes the effects of actions, (6) encodes the effects of static causal laws, and (7) is the inertial rule. (8) defines a predicate that determines when an action can occur and (9) encodes the initial situation. (10)-(11) generate action occurrences, one at a time. We omit most of the auxiliary rules such as rules for defining contradictory literals etc. The source code and examples can be retrieved from our Web site.

Let $\Pi_n(D, \Gamma, \Delta)$ (or Π_n when it is clear from the context what D, Γ, and Δ are) be the logic program consisting of

- the set of domain-independent rules in which the domain of T is $\{0, \ldots, n\}$,
- the set of atoms encoding D and Γ, and
- the rule $\leftarrow not\ hf(\Delta, n)$ that encodes the requirement that Δ holds at n.

The following result (adapted from [22]) shows the equivalence between trajectories of Δ and stable models of Π_n. Let S be a stable model of Π_n, define $s(i) = \{f \mid holds(f, i) \in S\}$ and $A[i, j] = a_i, \ldots, a_j$ where i or j are integers, f is a fluent, a_t's are actions, and for every t, $i \leq t \leq j$, $occ(a_t, t) \in S$.

Theorem 1. *For a planning problem $\langle D, \Gamma, \Delta \rangle$,*

- *if $s_0 a_0 \ldots a_{n-1} s_n$ is a trajectory of Δ, then there exists a stable model S of Π_n such that $A[0, n-1] = [a_0, \ldots, a_{n-1}]$ and $s_i = s(i)$ for $i \in \{0, \ldots, n\}$, and*
- *if S is a stable model of Π_n with $A[0, n-1] = [a_0, \ldots, a_{n-1}]$ then $s(0)a_0 \ldots a_{n-1}s(n)$ is a trajectory of Δ.*

3   Control Knowledge as Constraints

In this section, we add domain-dependent control knowledge to ASP by viewing it as constraints on the stable models of the program Π. For each type of control knowledge[4], we introduce new constructs for its encoding and present a set of rules that check when a constraint is satisfied.

3.1   Temporal Knowledge

In [1], temporal knowledge is used to prune the search space. Temporal constraints are specified using a linear temporal logic with a precisely defined semantics. It is easy to add them to (or remove them from) a planning problem since their representation is separate from the action and goal representation. Planners exploiting temporal knowledge to control search have proven to be highly efficient and to scale up well [2]. In this paper, we represent temporal knowledge using temporal formulas. In our notation, a temporal formula is either

---

[4] We henceforth abbreviate domain-dependent control knowledge as *control knowledge*.

- a formula (as defined in previous section), or
- a formula of the form $until(\phi, \psi)$, $always(\phi)$, $eventually(\phi)$, or $next(\phi)$ where ϕ and ψ are temporal formulas.

For example, in a logistics domain, let P and L denote a package and its location, respectively. The following formula:

$$always((goal(P, L) \wedge at(P, L)) \Rightarrow next(\neg holding(P))) \tag{12}$$

can be used to express that if the goal is to have a package at a particular location and if the package is indeed at that location then it's always the case that the agent will not be holding the package in the next state. This has the effect of preventing the agent from picking up the package once it's at its goal location.

Like non-atomic formulas, temporal formulas can be encoded in ASP using constants, atoms, and rules. For example, the formula $until(f, next(g))$ is represented by the set of atoms $\{tf(n_1, next(g)), tf(n_2, until(f, n_1))\}$ where tf stands for "temporal formula" and n_1 and n_2 are the new constants assigned to $next(g)$ and $until(f, neg(g))$, respectively. The semantics of these temporal operators is the standard one.

To complete the encoding of temporal constraints, we provide the rules for temporal formula evaluation. The key rules, which define the satisfiability of a temporal formula N at time T ($htf(N, T)$) and between T and T' ($hd(N, T, T')$), are given below.

$$htf(N, T) \leftarrow formula(N), hf(N, T) \tag{13}$$
$$hf(N, T) \leftarrow tf(N, N_1), htf(N_1, T) \tag{14}$$
$$htf(N, T) \leftarrow tf(N, until(N_1, N_2)), hd(N_1, T, T'), htf(N_2, T'). \tag{15}$$
$$htf(N, T) \leftarrow tf(N, always(N_1)), hd(N_1, T, length+1). \tag{16}$$
$$htf(N, T) \leftarrow tf(N, eventually(N_1)), htf(N_1, T'), T \leq T'. \tag{17}$$
$$htf(N, T) \leftarrow tf(N, next(N_1)), htf(N_1, T + 1). \tag{18}$$
$$not\_hd(N, T, T') \leftarrow not\ htf(N, T''), T \leq T'' < T'. \tag{19}$$
$$hd(N, T, T') \leftarrow htf(N, T), not\ not\_hd(N, T, T') \tag{20}$$

Having defined temporal constraints and specified when they are satisfied, adding temporal knowledge to a planning problem in ASP is easy. We must: (i) encode the knowledge as a temporal formula, say ϕ; (ii) add the rules (13)-(20) to Π; and (iii) add the constraint $\leftarrow not\ htf(\phi, 0)$ to Π. Step (iii) eliminates models of Π in which ϕ does not hold. For example, if Π is the program for planning in the logistics domain, adding the constraint (12) to Π will eliminate all models whose corresponding trajectory admits an action occurrence that causes the $holding(P)$ to be true after P is delivered at its destination. As a concrete example, given the goal formula $at(p, l_2)$, there exists no model of Π that corresponds to the sequence of actions $pick\_up(p, l_1), move(l_1, l_2), drop(p, l_2), pick\_up(p, l_2)$. (We appeal to the users for the intuitive meaning of the effects of actions, the initial setting, and the goal of the problem.)

3.2   Procedural Knowledge

Procedural knowledge can be thought of as an (under-specified) sketch of the plans to be generated. This type of control knowledge has been used in GOLOG, an Algol-like logic programming language for agent programming, control and execution, based on a situation calculus theory of actions [20]. GOLOG has been primarily used as a programming language for high-level agent control in dynamical environments (see e.g. [7]). More recently, Golog has been used for general planning [13]. In the planning context, a GOLOG program specifies an arbitrarily incomplete plan that includes non-deterministic choice points that are filled in by the planner (the deductive machinery of a GOLOG-interpreter). For example, a simple GOLOG program $\mathbf{a_1}; \mathbf{a_2}; (\mathbf{a_3}|\mathbf{a_4}|\mathbf{a_5}); \mathbf{f}$? represents plans which have a_1 followed by a_2, followed by one of a_3, a_4, or a_5 such that f is true upon termination of the plan. The interpreter, when asked for a solution to this program, needs only to decide which one of a_3, a_4, or a_5 it should choose. To encode procedural knowledge, we introduce a set of Algol-like constructs such as sequence, loop, conditional, and nondeterministic choice of arguments/actions. These constructs are used to encode partial procedural control knowledge in the form of programs which are defined inductively as follows. For an action theory (D, Γ) we define a program syntactically as follows.

- an action a is a program,
- a formula ϕ is a program[5],
- if p_i's are programs then $p_1; \ldots; p_n$ is a program,
- if p_i's are programs then $p_1| \ldots |p_n$ is a program,
- if p_1 and p_2 are programs and ϕ is a formula then "**if** ϕ **then** p_1 **else** p_2" is a program,
- if p is a program and ϕ is a formula then "**while** ϕ **do** p" is a program, and
- if X is a variable of sort s, $p(X)$ is a program, and $f(X)$ is a formula, then **pick**$(X, f(X), p(X))$ is a program.

As is common practice with Smodels, we will assign to each program a name (with the exception of actions and formulas), provide rules for the construction of programs, and use prefix notation. A sequence $\alpha = p_1; \ldots; p_n$ will be represented by the atoms $proc(p)$, $head(p, n_1)$, $tail(p, n_2)$ and the set of atoms representing $p_2; \ldots; p_n$, where p, n_1, and n_2 are the names assigned to α, p_1 (if it is not a primitive action or a formula), and $p_2; \ldots; p_n$, respectively.

The operational semantics of programs specifies when a trajectory $s_0 a_0 s_1 \ldots a_{n-1} s_n$, denoted by α, is *a trace of a program* p and is defined as follows.

- for $p = a$ and a is an action, $n = 1$ and $a_0 = a$,
- for $p = \phi$, $n = 0$ and ϕ holds in s_0,
- for $p = p_1; p_2$, there exists an i such that $s_0 a_0 \ldots s_i$ is a trace of p_1 and $s_i a_i \ldots s_n$ is a trace of p_2,

---

[5] This is analogous to the GOLOG test action f? which tests the truth value of a fluent.

- for $p = p_1 | \ldots | p_n$, α is a trace of p_i for some $i \in \{1, \ldots, n\}$,
- for $p = \textbf{if } \phi \textbf{ then } p_1 \textbf{ else } p_2$, α is a trace of p_1 if ϕ holds in s_0 or α is a trace of p_2 if $neg(\phi)$ holds in s_0,
- for $p = \textbf{while } \phi \textbf{ do } p_1$, $n = 0$ and $neg(\phi)$ holds in s_0 or ϕ holds in s_0 and there exists some i such that $s_0 a_0 \ldots s_i$ is a trace of p_1 and $s_i a_i \ldots s_n$ is a trace of p, and
- for $p = \textbf{pick}(X, f(X), q(X))$, then there exists a constant x of the sort of X such that $f(x)$ holds in s_0 and α is a trace of $q(x)$.

The logic programming rules that realize this semantics follow. We define a predicate $trans(p, t_1, t_2)$ which holds in a stable model S iff $s(t_1) a_{t_1} \ldots s(t_2)$ is a trace of p[6].

$$trans(P, T_1, T_2) \leftarrow proc(P), head(P, P_1), tail(P, P_2), \tag{21}$$
$$trans(P_1, T_1, T_3), trans(P_2, T_3, T_2).$$

$$trans(A, T, T+1) \leftarrow action(A), A \neq null, occ(A, T). \tag{22}$$

$$trans(null, T, T) \leftarrow \tag{23}$$

$$trans(N, T_1, T_2) \leftarrow choiceAction(N), \tag{24}$$
$$in(P_1, N), trans(P_1, T_1, T_2).$$

$$trans(F, T_1, T_1) \leftarrow formula(F), hf(F, T_1). \tag{25}$$

$$trans(I, T_1, T_2) \leftarrow if(I, F, P_1, P_2), \tag{26}$$
$$hf(F, T_1), trans(P_1, T_1, T_2).$$

$$trans(I, T_1, T_2) \leftarrow if(I, F, P_1, P_2), \tag{27}$$
$$not\ hf(F, T_1), trans(P_2, T_1, T_2).$$

$$trans(W, T_1, T_2) \leftarrow while(W, F, P), hf(F, T_1), T_1 \le T_3 \le T_2, \tag{28}$$
$$trans(P, T_1, T_3), trans(W, T_3, T_2).$$

$$trans(W, T, T) \leftarrow while(W, F, P), not\ hf(F, T). \tag{29}$$

$$trans(S, T_1, T_2) \leftarrow choiceArgs(S, F, P), \tag{30}$$
$$hf(F, T_1), trans(P, T_1, T_2).$$

Finding a valid instantiation of a program P can be viewed as a planning problem $\langle D, \Gamma, \Delta \rangle$ where Δ is the constraint $\leftarrow not\ trans(P, 0, n)$. Let Π_n^T be the program obtained from Π_n by (i) adding the rules (21)-(30), and (ii) replacing the goal constraint with $\leftarrow not\ trans(P, 0, n)$. The following theorem is similar to Theorem 1.

Theorem 2. *Let (D, Γ) be an action theory and P be a program. Then, (i) for every stable model S of Π_n^T, $s(0) a_0 \ldots a_{n-1} s(n)$ is a trace of P; and (ii) if $s_0 a_0 \ldots a_{n-1} s_n$ is a trace of P then there exists a stable model S of Π_n^T such that $s_j = s(j)$ and $occ(a_i, i) \in S$ for $j \in \{0, \ldots, n\}$ and $i \in \{0, \ldots, n-1\}$.*

---

[6] Recall that we define $s(i) = \{holds(f, i) \in S \mid f \text{ is a fluent}\}$ and assume $occ(a_i, i) \in S$.

3.3 HTN Knowledge

GOLOG programs are good for representing procedural knowledge but prove cumbersome for encoding partial orderings between programs and do not allow temporal constraints. For example, to represent that any sequence containing the n programs $p_1, \ldots, p_n$, in which p_1 occurs before p_2, is a valid plan for a goal Δ, one would need to list all the possible sequences and then use the non-deterministic construct[7]. This can be easily represented by an HTN consisting of the set $\{p_1, \ldots, p_n\}$ and a constraint expressing that p_1 must occur before p_2. HTNs also allows maintenance constraints of the form $always(\phi)$ to be represented. However, HTNs do not have complex constructs such as procedures, conditionals, or loops. Attempts to combine hierarchical constraints and GOLOG-like programs (e.g., [4]) have fallen short since they do not allow complex programs to occur within these HTN programs. We will show next that, under the ASP framework, this restriction can be eliminated by adding the following item to the definition of programs in the previous section.

– If $p_1, \ldots, p_n$ are programs then a pair (S, C) is a program where $S = \{p_1, \ldots, p_n\}$ and C is a set of ordering or truth constraints (defined below).

Let $S = \{p_1, \ldots, p_k\}$ be a set of programs. Assume that n_i, $1 \leq i \leq k$, is the name assigned to the program p_i. An ordering constraint over S has the form $n_i \prec n_j$ where $n_i \neq n_j$ and a truth constraint is of the form (n_i, ϕ), (ϕ, n_i), or (n_i, ϕ, n_t) where ϕ is a formula. In our encoding, we will represent a program (S, C) by an atom $htn(p, Sn, Cn)$ where p, Sn, and Cn are the names assigned to (S, C), S, and C respectively. To complete our extension, we need to define when a trajectory is a trace of a program with the new construct and provide logic program rules for checking its satisfaction. A trajectory $s_0 a_0 \ldots a_{n-1} s_n$ is a trace of a program (S, C) if there exists a sequence $j_0 = 0 \leq j_1 \leq \ldots \leq j_k = n$ and a permutation $(i_1, \ldots, i_k)$ of $(1, \ldots, k)$ such that the sequence of trajectories $\alpha_1 = s_0 a_0 \ldots s_{j_1}$, $\alpha_2 = s_{j_1} a_{j_1} \ldots s_{j_2}$, $\ldots$, $\alpha_k = s_{j_{k-1}} a_{j_{k-1}} \ldots s_n$ satisfies the following conditions:

– for each l, $1 \leq l \leq k$, α_l is a trace of p_{i_l},
– if $n_t \prec n_l \in C$ then $i_t < i_l$,
– if $(\phi, n_l) \in C$ (or $(n_l, \phi) \in C$) then ϕ holds in the state $s_{j_{l-1}}$ (or s_{j_l}), and
– if $(n_t, \phi, n_l) \in C$ then ϕ holds in $s_{j_t}, \ldots, s_{j_{l-1}}$.

We will extend the predicate $trans$ to allow the new type of programs to be considered. Rules for checking the satisfaction of a program $htn(N, S, C)$ are given next.

$$trans(N, T_1, T_2) \leftarrow htn(N, S, C), \tag{31}$$
$$not\ nok(N, T_1, T_2).$$
$$1\{begin(N, I, T_3, T_1, T_2) : between(T_3, T_1, T_2)\}1 \leftarrow htn(N, S, C), in(I, S), \tag{32}$$

---

[7] For $n = 3$, the three possibilities are $p_1; p_2; p_3$, $p_1; p_3; p_2$, and $p_3; p_1; p_2$. Using a concurrent construct $\|$, these three programs can be packed into two programs $p_1; p_2 \| p_3$ and $p_1; p_3; p_2$.

$$trans(N, T_1, T_2).$$
$$1\{end(N, I, T_3, T_1, T_2) : between(T_3, T_1, T_2)\}1 \leftarrow htn(N, S, C), \qquad (33)$$
$$in(I, S),$$
$$trans(N, T_1, T_2).$$
$$nok(N, T_1, T_2) \leftarrow htn(N, S, C), \qquad (34)$$
$$in(I, S), T_3 > T_4,$$
$$begin(N, I, T_3, T_1, T_2),$$
$$end(N, I, T_4, T_1, T_2).$$
$$nok(N, T_1, T_2) \leftarrow htn(N, S, C), \qquad (35)$$
$$in(I, S), T_3 \leq T_4,$$
$$begin(N, I, T_3, T_1, T_2),$$
$$end(N, I, T_4, T_1, T_2),$$
$$not \ trans(I, T_3, T_4).$$
$$nok(N, T_1, T_2) \leftarrow htn(N, S, C), \qquad (36)$$
$$not \ trans(N, T_1, T_2).$$

In the above rules, the predicates $begin(N, I, T_3, T_1, T_2)$ and $end(N, I, T_4, T_1, T_2)$ are used to record the beginning and the end of the program I, a member of N. Rules (32)-(33) make sure that each program will have start and times. These two rules are not logic programming rules but are unique to Smodels encodings. They were introduced to simplify the encoding of choice rules [28], and can be translated into a set of normal logic program rules. The predicate $nok(N, T_1, T_2)$ states that the assignments for programs are not acceptable. (We omit the rules that check for the satisfiability of constraints in C of a program $htn(N, S, C)$. They can be downloaded from our Web site.) Theorem 2 will still hold.

3.4   Demonstration Experiments

We tested our implementation with some domains from the general planning literature and from the AIPS planning competition [2]. We chose problems for which procedural control knowledge appeared to be easier to exploit than other types of control knowledge. Our motivation was: (i) it has already been established that well-chosen temporal and hierarchical constraints will improve a planner's efficiency; (ii) we have previously experimented with the use of temporal knowledge in the ASP framework [29]; and (iii) we are not aware of any empirical results indicating the utility of procedural knowledge in planning, especially in ASP. ([13] concentrates on using GOLOG to do planning in domains with incomplete information, not on exploiting procedural knowledge in planning.)

We selected the elevator example from [20] (elp1-elp3) and the Miconic-10 elevator domain (s1-0,...,s5-0s2), proposed by Schindler Lifts Ltd. for the AIPS 2000 competition [2]. Note that some of the planners, that competed in AIPS 2000, were unable to solve this problem. Due to the space limitation we cannot present the action theories and the Smodels encoding of the programs here. They can be found at the URL mentioned previously. The time taken to compute one model with and without control knowledge are given in column 5 and 6 of the table below, respectively.

Problem	Plan Length	# Person	# Floors	With Control Knowledge	Without Control Knowledge
elp1	10	2	6	0.600	**0.560**
elp2	14	3	6	1.411	6.729
elp3	18	4	6	3.224	120.693
s1-0	4	1	2	0.100	**0.020**
s2-0	8	2	4	1.802	**0.921**
s3-0	12	3	6	22.682	34.519
s4-0	15	4	8	164.055	314.101
s5-0s1	19	5	4	57.952	> 2 hours
s5-0s2	19	5	5	105.040	> 2 hours

As can be seen, the encoding with control knowledge yields substantially better performance in situations where the minimal plan length is great. For large instances (the last two rows), Smodels can find a plan using control knowledge in a short time and cannot find a plan in 2 hours without control knowledge. In some small instances (the time in column 6 is in boldface), the speed up cannot make up for the overhead needed in grounding the control knowledge. The output of Smodels for each run is given in the file *result* at the above URL. For larger instances of the elevator domain [2] (5 persons or more and 10 floors or more), our implementation terminated prematurely with either a stack overflow error or a segmentation fault error[8].

4   Discussions and Future Work

In this paper we presented a declarative approach to adding domain-dependent control knowledge to ASP. Our approach enables different types of control knowledge such as hierarchical, temporal, or procedural knowledge to be represented and exploited in parallel; thus combining the ideas of HTN-planning, GOLOG-programming, and planning with temporal knowledge into ASP. For example, one can find a valid instantiation of a GOLOG program that satisfies some temporal constraints. This distinguishes our work from other related work [17,19,4,25] where only one or two types of constraints were considered or combined. Moreover, in a propositional environment, ASP with procedural knowledge can be viewed as an off-line interpreter for a GOLOG program. Because of the declarative nature of logic programming the correctness of this interpreter is easier to prove than an interpreter written in Prolog. We view domain-dependent

---

[8] Experiments were run on a an HP OmniBook 6000 laptop with 130,544 Kb Ram and an Intel Pentium III 600 MHz processor).

control knowledge as independent sets of constraints. An advantage of this approach is that domain-dependent control knowledge can be modularly formalized and added to planning problems as desired.

Our experimental result demonstrates that ASP can scale up better with domain-dependent control knowledge. In keeping with the experience of researchers who have incorporated control knowledge into SATplan (e.g., [19]), we do not expect ASP with only one type of domain-dependent knowledge to do better than TLPLAN [1], as Smodels is a general purpose system. But in the presence of near deterministic procedural constraints, our approach may do better. More rigorous experimentation with a variety of domains including those used in the AIPS planning competition will be a significant focus of our future work.

Acknowledgements

The first two authors would like to acknowledge the support of the NASA grant NCC2-1232. The third author would like to acknowledge the support of NASA grant NAG2-1337. The work of Chitta Baral was also supported in part by the NSF grants IRI-9501577 and NSF 0070463. The work of Tran Cao Son was also supported in part by NSF grant EIA-981072.

References

1. F. Bacchus and F. Kabanza. Using temporal logics to express search control knowledge for planning. *Artificial Intelligence*, 116(1,2):123–191, 2000. 226, 231, 238
2. F. Bacchus, H. Kautz, D. E. Smith, D. Long, H. Geffner, and J. Koehler. AIPS-00 Planning Competition, http://www.cs.toronto.edu/aips2000/. 231, 236, 237
3. C. Baral. *Knowledge Representation, reasoning, and declarative problem solving with Answer sets (Book draft)*. 2001. 228
4. C. Baral and T. C. Son. Extending ConGolog to allow partial ordering. In *ATAL, LNCS, Vol. 1757*, pages 188–204, 1999. 235, 237
5. A. Blum and M. Furst. Fast planning through planning graph analysis. *Artificial Intelligence*, 90:281–300, 1997. 226
6. B. Bonet and H. Geffner. Planning as heuristic search. *Artificial Intelligence - Special issue on Heuristic Search*, 129(1-2):5-33, 2001. 226
7. W. Burgard, A. B. Cremers, D. Fox, D. Hähnel, G. Lakemeyer, Schulz D., W. Steiner, and S. Thrun. The interactive museum tour-guide robot. In *AAAI-98*, pages 11–18, 1998. 233
8. T. Bylander. The computational complexity of propositional STRIPS planning. *Artificial Intelligence*, 69:161–204, 1994. 226
9. S. Citrigno, T. Eiter, W. Faber, G. Gottlob, C. Koch, N. Leone, C. Mateis, G. Pfeifer, and F. Scarcello. The dlv system: Model generator and application frontends. In *Proceedings of the 12th Workshop on Logic Programming*, pages 128–137, 1997. 228
10. Y. Dimopoulos, B. Nebel, and J. Koehler. Encoding planning problems in non-monotonic logic programs. In *Proceedings of European Conference on Planning*, pages 169–181, 1997. 230

11. P. Doherty and J. Kvarnstom. TALplanner: An Empirical Investigation of a Temporal Logic-based Forward Chaining Planner, TIME'99, 1999. 226
12. K. Erol, D. Nau, and V. S. Subrahmanian. Complexity, decidability and undecidability results for domain-independent planning. *Artificial Intelligence*, 76(1-2):75–88, 1995. 226
13. A. Finzi, F. Pirri, and R. Reiter. Open world planning in the situation calculus. In *AAAI-00*, page 754–760, 2000. 233, 236
14. M. Gelfond. Posting on TAG-mailing list, 1999. 230
15. M. Gelfond and V. Lifschitz. Action languages. *ETAI*, 3(6), 1998. 228, 229
16. J. Hoffmann and B. Nebel. The FF planning system: Fast plan generation through heuristic search. *JAIR*, 14:253-302, 2001. 226
17. Y. C. Huang, B. Selman, and H. Kautz. Control knowledge in planning: Benefits and tradeoffs. In *AAAI-99*, pages 511–517, 1999. 237
18. H. Kautz and B. Selman. BLACKBOX: A new approach to the application of theorem proving to problem solving. In *Workshop Planning as Combinatorial Search*, AIPS-98. 226
19. H. Kautz and B. Selman. The role of domain-specific knowledge in the planning as satisfiability framework. In *Proceedings of AIPS*, 1998. 237, 238
20. H. Levesque, R. Reiter, Y. Lesperance, F. Lin, and R. Scherl. GOLOG: A logic programming language for dynamic domains. *Journal of Logic Programming*, 31(1-3):59–84, 1997. 227, 233, 236
21. V. Lifschitz. Answer Set Planning. In *ICLP'99*, pages 23–37, 1999. 230
22. V. Lifschitz and H. Turner. Representing transition systems by logic programs. In *LPNMR'99*, pages 92–106, 1999. 230, 231
23. A. Lotem and S. Dana Nau. New advances in GraphHTN: Identifying independent subproblems in large HTN domains. In *AIPS*, pages 206–215, 2000.
24. J. McCarthy and P. Hayes. Some philosophical problems from the standpoint of artificial intelligence. In B. Meltzer and D. Michie, editors, *Machine Intelligence*, volume 4, pages 463–502. Edinburgh University Press, Edinburgh, 1969.
25. S. McIlraith. Modeling and programming devices and web agents. In *Proceedings of the NASA Goddard Workshop on Formal Approaches to Agent-Based Systems, LNCS*, 2000. 237
26. D. Nau, Y. Cao, A. Lotem, and H. Muñoz-Avila. SHOP: Simple Hierarchical Ordered Planner. In *AAAI-99*, pages 968–973, 1999. 226
27. I. Niemelä and P. Simons. Smodels - an implementation of the stable model and well-founded semantics for normal logic programs. In *ICLP & LPNMR*, pages 420–429, 1997. 228
28. I. Niemelä, P. Simons, and T. Soininen. Stable model semantics for weight constraint rules. In *LPNMR'99*, pages 315–332, 1999. 236
29. L. Tuan and C. Baral. Effect of knowledge representation on model based planning: experiments using logic programming encodings. In *AAAI Spring Symposium on "Answer Set Programming"*, pages 110–115, 2001. 236
30. D. Wilkins and M. desJardines. A call for knowledge-based planning. *AI Magazine*, 22(1):99–115, Spring 2001. 226

Encoding Solutions of the Frame Problem in Dynamic Logic

Norman Foo, Dongmo Zhang, Yan Zhang, Samir Chopra, and Bao Quoc Vo

Knowledge Systems Group, School of Computer Science and Engineering
University of New South Wales, Australia

Abstract. We investigate the relationship amongst some solutions to the frame problem. We encode Pednault's syntax-based solution [20], Baker's state-minimization policy [1], and Gelfond & Lifchitz's Action Language $\mathcal{A}$ [7] in the propositional dynamic logic (PDL). The formal relationships among these solutions are given. The results of the paper show that dynamic logic, as one of the formalisms for reasoning about dynamic domains, can be used as a formal tool for comparing and unifying logics of action.

Keywords: relationships between formalisms, frame problem, dynamic logic.

1 Introduction

Among the established formalisms for specifying and reasoning about actions are the situation calculus [19,23], STRIPS [3], the event calculus [17], action languages [7] and some other monotonic or nonmonotonic logics such as in [9]. Fundamental problems in this area, such as the frame problem, ramification problem, and qualification problem, have been widely investigated with varying degrees of success. Clearly, the time has come to analyze, compare and systematize these formalisms and solutions in order to obtain a more complete and unified (if possible) theory of action.

This paper focuses on solutions to the frame problem. We compare and analyze the main solutions to the frame problem in the literature by encoding them in the propositional dynamic logic (PDL). The reasons for choosing PDL as the medium are twofold. First, the language of dynamic logic is expressive. It provides built-in expression of compound actions (i.e., generated from primitive actions by the program connectives ; , $\cup$, ?, $\ast$), non-deterministic effects and qualifications of actions. It has also been extended to represent concurrent actions [10], non-execution of actions [8], indirect effects of actions [11,26]. Second, dynamic logic features a sound and complete axiomatic deductive system and a well-developed Kripkean semantics. Its proof and model theory have reached a high degree of sophistication through the development of theoretical computer science. Some features, such as decidability and the finite model property of PDL, and techniques such as bisimulation and filtration, are well understood.

T. Eiter, W. Faber, and M. Truszczyński (Eds.): LPNMR 2001, LNAI 2173, pp. 240–253, 2001.
© Springer-Verlag Berlin Heidelberg 2001

In contrast to other formalisms, such as the situation calculus [23] and action languages [7], *PDL* does not have a built-in solution to the frame problem (*PDL*-based solutions to the frame problem have been proposed via extensions [2,8,22]). In this paper, however, we show that three solutions to the frame problem (Pednault's syntax-based approach [20], Baker's circumscription [1] and the action language $\mathcal{A}$ [7]) can be encoded in *PDL*. The relationship amongst these solutions is clarified and we prove that in the case that action descriptions are in normal form and queries are simple, these solutions to the frame problem are essentially equivalent. In contrast to the work in [14], our results show that the equivalence of the solutions heavily depends on the syntactical restrictions of action descriptions and queries.

Due to the limitation of space, we omit all the proofs of theorems. [1]

2 Reasoning about Action in *PDL*

In dynamic logic, a causal relation between an action α and its effect A is expressed by a modal formula: $[\alpha]A$, read as α *always causes* A. For instance, $[Shoot]\neg alive$ represents "shooting at a turkey kills the turkey". The formula $\langle\alpha\rangle A$ reads as α *is executable and possibly causes* A *to be true*, where $\langle\alpha\rangle$ is the dual operator of $[\alpha]$. In particular, $\langle\alpha\rangle\top$ represents α is executable, where $\top$ represents the logical constant **true**. $\prec \alpha \succ A$ denotes "$\langle\alpha\rangle\top \to \langle\alpha\rangle A$", meaning "*if α is executable, then α may cause A.*" A language of *PDL* consists of a set Flu of fluent symbols (propositional variables) and a set Act_P of primitive action symbols. We will use f, f_1, f_2, *etc.*, to denote fluents, and use a, a_1, a_2, *etc.*, for primitive actions. The formulas ($A \in Fma$) and actions ($\alpha \in Act$) can be defined as usual [18]. A formula which does not include modal operators is referred to as a *propositional formula* ($\varphi \in Fma_P$). The semantics and deductive system of *PDL* can be found in any standard introductory text e.g [18].

2.1 Action Description

PDL provides a formal language to describe behaviors and internal relations of a dynamic system. Those sentences which describe the generic effects of actions, domain constraints and causal ramifications are generally called *action description*. In this paper, an action description of a dynamic system is any finite set of *PDL* formulas.

Example 1 Consider the Yale Shooting Problem [12] described by the following action description:

$$\Sigma = \left\{ \begin{array}{l} \neg loaded \to [Load]loaded \\ loaded \to [Shoot]\neg alive \\ loaded \to [Shoot]\neg loaded \\ \langle Load\rangle\top, \langle Wait\rangle\top, \langle Shoot\rangle\top \end{array} \right\}$$

---

[1] They are available at http://www.cse.unsw.edu.au/~ksg/Pubs/ksgworking.html.

The first three sentences state the effects of action *Load* and *Shoot* on fluent *loaded* and *alive* (effect axioms). The last three represent the executability of actions (qualification axioms).

An action description Σ is *normal* if each formula in Σ is of the form:

- $\varphi \rightarrow [a]l$ (*deterministic action law*)
- $\varphi \rightarrow\prec a \succ l$ (*non-deterministic action law*)
- $\varphi \rightarrow \langle a \rangle \top$ (*qualification law*)
  where $\varphi \in Fma_P$, $a \in Act_P$ and l is a fluent literal.[2]

It is easy to see that the action description in Example 1 is normal.

2.2   Reasoning with Action Description

A formula in an action description is different from an ordinary formula. The sentence "*loaded* → [*Shoot*]¬*alive*" states that whenever *loaded* is true, *Shoot* must cause ¬*alive*. In the situation calculus this is written as $\forall s(loaded(s) \rightarrow \neg alive(do(Shoot, s)))$ instead of $loaded(s) \rightarrow \neg alive(do(Shoot, s))$ for some particular situation s. A simple approach to the problem in dynamic logic, which was introduced in [26], is to treat an action description as a set of extra axioms of PDL.

Definition 1 [26] Let Σ be an action description. A formula A is Σ-*provable*, written $\vdash^\Sigma A$, if it belongs to the smallest set of formulas which contains all theorems of PDL all elements of Σ, and is closed under *modus ponens* and *modal generalization* [18].

Consider the action description Σ in Example 1. We can prove that $\vdash^\Sigma$ ¬*loaded* → [*Load*; *Shoot*]¬*alive*.[3]

2.3   Consistency of Action Description

An action description Σ is *consistent*[4] if $\not\vdash^\Sigma \perp$, where $\perp$ represents logical constant "**false**". Let Σ be a normal action description. For any fluent f and any primitive action a, if we merge the action laws about a and $f(\neg f)$ in each form together, there are at most five laws about a and f in Σ:

$$\varphi_0 \rightarrow \langle a \rangle \top$$
$$\varphi_{1,1} \rightarrow [a]f, \; \varphi_{1,2} \rightarrow [a]\neg f$$
$$\varphi_{2,1} \rightarrow\prec a \succ \neg f, \; \varphi_{2,2} \rightarrow\prec a \succ f$$

---

[2] In [25], the normal form of action descriptions is defined in a more general version to express indirect effects of actions based on the extended PDL [26].

[3] By using PDL axioms and Definition 1.

[4] In [26], it is called *uniformly consistent*, distinguishing from the consistency of normal set of formulas.

It is easy to see that if φ_0, $\varphi_{1,1}$ and $\varphi_{1,2}$ are true simultaneously, then the action description will contain a contradiction. Similarly for φ_0, $\varphi_{1,j}$ and $\varphi_{2,j}$ ($j = 1$ or $j = 2$). We call a normal action description Σ is *safe* if it is satisfies the following assumption:

$$\vdash \neg\varphi_0 \vee \neg\varphi_{1,1} \vee \neg\varphi_{1,2} \text{ and } \vdash \neg\varphi_0 \vee \neg\varphi_{1,j} \vee \neg\varphi_{2,j} \ (j = 1, 2)$$

The following theorem shows that the safety is a sufficient condition of the consistency of normal action descriptions.

Theorem 1 [25]*Let Σ be a normal action description. If Σ is safe, then it is consistent.*

Since the action description in Example 1 is safe, it is consistent.

We remark that the normal form is quite expressive though not every action description can be expressed in normal form. Any action description written in the form of pre-condition axioms and successor state axioms in the *propositional* situation calculus language (that is, there are no sort *object* and function symbols in the language [23]) can be translated into normal form and moreover the resultant action descriptions are safe. Action descriptions written in $\mathcal{A}$ or in STRIPS can also be expressed in normal form. Additionally, the determinism of action (i.e., for any initial state there exists one and only one next state) can be expressed by normal form.

3 Properties of PDL Models

We now present some special properties of PDL models which are not included in the standard discourse of dynamic logic but are useful for the purpose of the paper.

3.1 PDL Models

A model for a PDL language is a structure of the form $M = (W, \{R_a : a \in Act_P\}, V)$, with R_a a binary relation on W for each primitive action. Note that we only consider the accessibility relations of primitive actions. Those for compound actions can be defined by using the standard model conditions [18]. The satisfiability relation is defined as usual. A model M *satisfying* a formula A in world w is denoted $M \models_w A$. A is *valid* in M, denoted by $M \models A$, if $M \models_w A$ for all $w \in W$. Let Σ be an action description. A model M is a Σ-*model* if $M \models A$ for any $A \in \Sigma$. Intuitively, a model is a Σ-model if Σ is true in every world of the model; $Mod(\Sigma)$ denotes the set of all Σ-models. In [26], it is shown that *for any action description Σ, $\vdash^\Sigma A$ iff A is valid in all Σ-models.* We now investigate models which are relevant to the models of action language and situation calculus.

Definition 2 A model $M = (W, \mathcal{R}, V)$ is *saturated* if for each interpretation I of Flu, there exists $w \in W$ such that $M \models_w I$. We use $Mod_S(\Sigma)$ to denote the set of all saturated Σ-models.

Proposition 1 *If Σ is normal and safe, then $\vdash^{\Sigma} A$ iff $M \models A$ for any $M \in Mod_S(\Sigma)$.*

We will show in section 6 that the saturation of PDL models corresponds to the Existence of Situation Axioms (ESA) [1]. Note that Proposition 1 depends on the definition of the normal form of action description. If we allow a normal action description to describe domain constraints or indirect effects, this proposition will cease to hold.

Definition 3 A model $M = (W, \mathcal{R}, V)$ is *natural* if
1. W is the set of all interpretations of Flu,
2. for any $f \in Flu$, $w \in V(f)$ iff $f \in w$.
We denote the set of all natural Σ-models by $Mod_N(\Sigma)$.

It is easy to see that any natural model is saturated.

Proposition 2 *If Σ be normal and safe, then $\vdash^{\Sigma} \varphi \to [a_1; \cdots; a_n]l$ iff $M \models \varphi \to [a_1; \cdots; a_n]l$ for any $M \in Mod_N(\Sigma)$.*

A formula in the form $\varphi \to [a_1; \cdots; a_n]l$ is referred to as *a simple query*, where φ is a propositional formula, l a literal. Notice that Proposition 2 is only true for simple queries. For instance, let $\Sigma = \emptyset$, $Flu = \{f\}$ and $Act_P = \{a\}$. Let $A = f\vee \prec a \succ \neg f\vee \prec a \succ \prec a \succ f\vee \prec a \succ \prec a \succ \prec a \succ f$. Then A is valid in all the natural models but $\not\vdash^{\Sigma} A$. This proposition is a key lemma of Theorem 2.

Definition 4 A model $M = (W, \mathcal{R}, V)$ is *functional* if for any $a \in Act_P$, R_a is a function on W. We denote the set of all natural functional Σ-models by $Mod_{NF}(\Sigma)$.

The syntactical condition with respect to functional models is so-called *determinism*, which means that each state can have and only have one next state after an action.

Definition 5 *Let $\Xi = \{\langle a\rangle f \to [a]f : a \in Act_P \text{ and } f \in Flu\} \cup \{\langle a\rangle\top : a \in Act_P\}$. An action description is deterministic[5] if $\Sigma \vdash \Xi$.*

Note that $\langle a\rangle f \to [a]f$ can be expressed in normal form in the following way: $f' \to [a]f$, $\neg f' \to [a]\neg f$, where f' is a new fluent symbol (in most cases, we can put the descriptions of determinism and effects of actions together without introducing new fluent symbols).

Proposition 3 *Let Σ be normal and safe. If Σ is deterministic, then $\vdash^{\Sigma} A$ iff $M \models A$ for any $M \in Mod_{NF}(\Sigma)$.*

Note the difference between Proposition 2 and 3. We can relax the restriction of simple query at the price of allowing only deterministic action descriptions.

---

[5] Here we assume that a deterministic action is always executable for simplicity. It can be relaxed at the price of a more complex formalization.

3.2   Minimizing PDL Models

Let $M = (W, \mathcal{R}, V)$ be a PDL model. For any $w \in W$, let $||w|| = \{f \in Flu : M \models_w f\} \cup \{\neg f : f \in Flu \ \& \ M \models_w f\}$. We denote $Chg(M) = \{(a, f, w) : \exists w'(wR_a w' \ \& \ f \in (||w||\backslash||w'||) \cup (||w'||\backslash||w||)\}$. In words, $(a, f, w) \in Chg(M)$ iff there exists an accessible world w' to w on action a such that the truth value of f is different at w and w'.

Definition 6 For any M_1, $M_2 \in Mod(\Sigma)$, $M_1 \sqsubset M_2$ iff
   1. $W_1 = W_2$,
   2. $V_1(f) = V_2(f)$,
   3. $Chg(M_1) \subset Chg(M_2)$.
   We denote the set of $\sqsubset$-minimal models in $Mod(\Sigma)$ as $\min(Mod(\Sigma))$. Intuitively, $M_1 \sqsubset M_2$ means M_1 has lesser state change than M_2.

4   Pednault's Solution to the Frame Problem

We first encode Pednault's syntax-based solution [20] to the frame problem in PDL. Before doing this, let's recall the meaning of the frame problem.

   To formalize the effects of actions in a dynamic system, it is necessary to provide all the effect axioms of actions (which specify what is affected by actions). Often this is easy because most actions affect only a few of the relevant fluents. In contrast, listing all the frame axioms (which specify what is not affected by actions) is tedious. Moreover, they are much more numerous than effect axioms. For instance, in Example 1, only effect axioms were listed. There are nine frame axioms, such as $alive \rightarrow [Load]alive$, $loaded \rightarrow [Wait]loaded$ etc., that were not listed. Without these axioms, the action description is incomplete. We cannot even establish the intuitive assertion $\vdash^\Sigma alive \rightarrow [Load]alive$. The frame problem is how to invent an inference mechanism for reasoning about effect of action with incomplete action descriptions.

   Pednault [20] introduced an approach to the frame problem with which frame axioms can be automatically generated from effect axioms and qualification axioms. Consider an normal action description Σ without non-deterministic action laws. Suppose that the positive and negative effect axioms and qualification axioms about action a and fluent f in an action description Σ are:

$$\varphi_0 \rightarrow \langle a \rangle \top, \ \varphi_1 \rightarrow [a]f, \ \varphi_2 \rightarrow [a]\neg f.$$

According to the *Completeness Assumption* [23], we have the following frame axioms:
   $FA_{a,f}^+ : (\neg\varphi_0 \vee \neg\varphi_2) \wedge f \rightarrow [a]f$
   $FA_{a,f}^- : (\neg\varphi_0 \vee \neg\varphi_1) \wedge \neg f \rightarrow [a]\neg f$
   All frame axioms generated by this procedure are referred to as *the frame axioms with respect to Σ*. For instance, $\neg loaded \wedge alive \rightarrow [Shoot]alive$ is a frame axiom about *Shoot* and *alive* with respect to the action description in Example

1. Suppose that Δ is the set of all the generated frame axioms with respect to Σ. Then we are able to prove that $\{\neg loaded\} \vdash^{\Sigma \cup \Delta} [Load; Wait; Shoot] \neg alive$.

In general, given a set Σ of effect axioms, we generate all the frame axioms with the above procedure. Let Δ be all the generated frame axioms. Then $\Sigma \cup \Delta$ will be the complete action description with respect to Σ. Therefore, to answer a query A, we only have to make the inference $\vdash^{\Sigma \cup \Delta} A$.

The following theorem establishes the semantic condition for Pednault's solution. It also gives the relationship between syntax-based and minimization-based approaches.

Observation 1 *Let Σ be a normal action description without non-deterministic action laws. If Σ is safe, then $\vdash^{\Sigma \cup \Delta} A$ iff $M \models A$ for any $M \in min(Mod_S(\Sigma))$ where Δ is the set of frame axioms with respect to Σ.*

It is not hard to extend Pednault's solution to non-deterministic case.

5   Encoding the Action Language $\mathcal{A}$ in PDL

The action languages [6] offer a simple and elegant solution to the frame problem. In this section, we show that the action language $\mathcal{A}$ can be embedded into PDL. Our approach can also be extended to the action language $\mathcal{B}$ and $\mathcal{C}$ if we base on the extended propositional logic (EPDL) [26].

An action description Σ in the language $\mathcal{A}$ [6] is a set of expressions of the form: a **causes** l **if** φ, where a is a primitive action, l is a fluent literal, and φ is a conjunction of literals. The state of a dynamic domain is expressed by a set of *axioms* of the form: **now** l. A query in action language $\mathcal{A}$ is an expression of the form: **necessarily** φ **after** $a_1, \cdots, a_n$, where φ is a propositional formula and $a_1, \cdots, a_n$ are primitive actions.

A structure $T = (W, \{R_a \subseteq W \times W : a \in Act_P\}, V)$ is a *transition system* of an action description Σ if

1. W is the set of all interpretations of Flu,
2. V is a function from Flu to 2^W such that $f \in V(w)$ iff $f \in w$.
3. $(w, w') \in R_a$ iff $E(a, w) \subseteq w' \subseteq E(a, w) \cup w$, where $E(a, w)$ is the set of the head l of all expression "a **causes** l **if** φ" in Σ such that w satisfies φ.

Let Γ be a set of expressions in the form: **now** l. A query "**necessarily** φ **after** $a_1, \cdots, a_n$" is a consequence of Γ in T if, for any chain $(w_0, w_1) \in R_{a_1}$, $\cdots, (w_{n-1}, w_n) \in R_{a_n}$, whenever w_0 satisfies l for each **now** $l \in \Gamma$, w_n satisfies φ. A query "**necessarily** φ **after** $a_1, \cdots, a_n$ is a consequence of Γ with respect to an action description Σ if it is a consequence of Γ in any transition system of Σ.

According to the translation between $\mathcal{A}$ and PDL shown in the Appendix, we can easily transform an action description and a state description between two languages. Since such a translation is one-to-one, we will only use PDL language to describe action descriptions, initial states and queries. They are easily recognized with context. It is easy to see that an action description in language $\mathcal{A}$ is always normal and safe. There is an important difference between the semantics of action language and PDL. In $\mathcal{A}$, there is no explicit expression for qualification of actions. An underlying assumption, called *Qualification Completeness,* in the semantics is that *an action is always executable unless the action description implies that it is not.* In PDL, there is no such assumption. Thus qualification of actions must be explicitly specified.

Let Σ be a finite action description in $\mathcal{A}$. Suppose the action laws about an action a and fluent f are $\varphi_1 \rightarrow [a]f$ and $\varphi_2 \rightarrow [a]\neg f$. This implies that a is not executable when $\varphi_1 \wedge \varphi_2$. Collecting all the conditions of non-executability: $\varphi_1^1 \wedge \varphi_2^1, \cdots, \varphi_1^n \wedge \varphi_2^n$, we know that a is not executable if $(\varphi_1^1 \wedge \varphi_2^1) \vee \cdots \vee (\varphi_1^n \wedge \varphi_2^n)$. By *Qualification Completeness,* we assume that $(\neg(\varphi_1^1 \wedge \varphi_2^1) \wedge \cdots \wedge \neg(\varphi_1^n \wedge \varphi_2^n)) \rightarrow \langle a \rangle \top$; such a condition is an *induced qualification law* . Let Λ be the set of all such laws from Σ. Then we have

Observation 2 *Let Σ be a finite action description and Γ a finite set of axioms, both in $\mathcal{A}$. A query "**necessarily** φ after $a_1, \cdots, a_n$" is a consequence of Γ with respect to Σ iff $\vdash^{\Sigma \cup \Lambda \cup \Delta} (\bigwedge \Gamma) \rightarrow [a_1; \cdots; a_n]l$, where Δ is the frame axioms with respect to $\Sigma \cup \Lambda$.*

Clearly, the expressive power of $\mathcal{A}$ is quite restricted. Action descriptions can only be normal. And queries can only be simple in our terminology.

6   Encoding Baker's Solution in PDL Models

Finally we consider Baker's solution. First, we have to recall the basic assumption of the approach.

6.1   Models of Situation Calculus

A model of the situation calculus [1,19], (an SC-model), consists of the various domains: the domain of situations $|\mathcal{M}|_s$, the domain of actions $|\mathcal{M}|_a$ and the domain of fluents $|\mathcal{M}|_f$; as well as interpretations for the constants:
  1. Interpretations for the relations $Holds$ and Ab:
     $$Holds^{\mathcal{M}} \subseteq |\mathcal{M}|_f \times |\mathcal{M}|_s, \quad Ab^{\mathcal{M}} \subseteq |\mathcal{M}|_a \times |\mathcal{M}|_f \times |\mathcal{M}|_s,$$
  2. Interpretation for the *Result* function:
     $$Result^{\mathcal{M}} \in (|\mathcal{M}|_a \times |\mathcal{M}|_s \rightarrow |\mathcal{M}|_s).$$

The following axioms were used in Baker's circumscriptive solution to the frame problem:

1. Unique names axioms:
   - Unique Name Axioms for fluents (UNAF): for any $f_1, f_2 \in Flu$, $f_1 \neq f_2$.
   - Unique Name Axioms for Actions(UNAA): for any $a_1, a_2 \in Flu$, $a_1 \neq a_2$.
2. Commonsense Law of Inertia (CLI):
   $\neg Ab(a, f, s) \leftrightarrow (Holds(f, Result(a, s)) \leftrightarrow Holds(f, s))$
3. Domain Closure Axioms:

- Domain Closure Axiom for Fluents (DCAF):
    $f = f_1 \vee f = f_2 \vee \cdots \vee f = f_n \vee \cdots$
- Domain Closure Axiom for Actions (DCAA):
    $a = a_1 \vee a = a_2 \vee \cdots \vee a = a_n \vee \cdots$

4. Existence of Situation Axioms (ESA):
    $\exists s (Holds(f_1, s) \wedge Holds(f_2, s) \wedge \cdots \wedge Holds(f_n, s) \wedge \cdots)$
    $\exists s (Holds(f_1, s) \wedge \neg Holds(f_2, s) \wedge \cdots \wedge Holds(f_n, s) \wedge \cdots)$
    $\cdots$
    $\exists s (\neg Holds(f_1, s) \wedge \neg Holds(f_2, s) \wedge \cdots \wedge \neg Holds(f_n, s) \wedge \cdots)$

For the sake of simplicity, we omit the formal presentation of domain closure and existence of situation axioms and ignore language differences in the representation of an action description based on the translation in the Appendix. Therefore, Σ is an action description in the situation calculus if it is a translation from an action description in PDL. Furthermore, an SC model $\mathcal{M}$ is a Σ-model if $\mathcal{M}$ satisfies all the formulas in Σ.

6.2   Relations between SC Models and PDL Models

First, we translate an SC model to a PDL model.

Definition 7 Let $\mathcal{M}$ be an SC model. A PDL model $M = (W, \mathcal{R}, V)$ is the *corresponding model* of $\mathcal{M}$ if
1. $W = |\mathcal{M}|_s$,
2. $(s_1^{\mathcal{M}}, s_2^{\mathcal{M}}) \in R_a$ iff $s_2^{\mathcal{M}} = Result^{\mathcal{M}}(a^{\mathcal{M}}, s_1^{\mathcal{M}})$,
3. $s^{\mathcal{M}} \in V(f)$ iff $Holds^{\mathcal{M}}(f^{\mathcal{M}}, s^{\mathcal{M}})$.

Lemma 1 Let $M = (W, \mathcal{R}, V)$ be a PDL model and $\mathcal{M}$ the corresponding model of M. Then
1. $M \models_{s^{\mathcal{M}}} \varphi$ iff $\mathcal{M} \models Holds(\varphi, s)$.
2. M is functional.
3. If $\mathcal{M}$ satisfies the common sense law of inertia, then $(a, f, s^{\mathcal{M}}) \in Chg(M)$ iff $(a^{\mathcal{M}}, f^{\mathcal{M}}, s^{\mathcal{M}}) \in Ab^{\mathcal{M}}$.
4. If Σ is a normal action description, then M is a Σ-model iff $\mathcal{M}$ is a Σ-model.
5. If $\mathcal{M}$ satisfies Existence of Situation Axioms, then M is saturated.

Next, we consider the transformation of PDL models to SC models.

Definition 8 Let $M = (W, \mathcal{R}, V)$ be a functional PDL model. An SC model $\mathcal{M}$ is the *corresponding model* of M if
1. $|\mathcal{M}|_f = Flu$, $|\mathcal{M}|_a = Act_P$, $|\mathcal{M}|_s = W$.
2. $s' = Result^{\mathcal{M}}(a, s)$ iff $(s, s') \in R_a$.
3. $(f, s) \in Holds^{\mathcal{M}}$ iff $f \in V(s)$.
4. $(a, f, s) \in Ab^{\mathcal{M}}$ iff $(a, f, s) \in Chg(M)$.

Lemma 2 *Let $\mathcal{M}$ be the corresponding model of a functional PDL model $M = (W, \mathcal{R}, V)$. Then*

    1. $\mathcal{M} \models Holds(\varphi, s)$ iff $M \models_{s^{\mathcal{M}}} \varphi$

    2. $\mathcal{M}$ satisfies the Commonsense Law of Inertia.

    3. $\mathcal{M}$ satisfies Domain Closure Axioms for Fluents and Actions.

    4. $\mathcal{M}$ satisfies Unique Names Axioms for Fluents and Actions.

    5. If Σ is a normal action description, then $\mathcal{M}$ is a Σ-model iff M is a Σ-model.

    6. If M is saturated, then $\mathcal{M}$ satisfies Existence-of-Situation Axiom.

The following shows the relationship between SC models and PDL models.

Lemma 3 *Let M be a functional PDL model. If $\mathcal{M}$ is the corresponding model of M, then M is the corresponding model of $\mathcal{M}$. Conversely, suppose that $\mathcal{M}$ is an SC model and M the corresponding model of $\mathcal{M}$. If $\mathcal{M}$ satisfies:*

    1. Domain Closure Axioms for Fluents and Actions,

    2. Unique Names Axioms for Fluents and Actions,

    then $\mathcal{M}$ is the corresponding model of M.

6.3 Relationship between Baker's Circumscription Policy and *PDL*-Model-Based Minimization

Since the $Holds$ function cannot be nested, not every formula in PDL can be translated into the situation calculus language. We call an action description is SC-expressible if it can be translated into situation calculus language.

Observation 3 *Let Σ be a deterministic and SC-expressible action description.*

    1. $M \in min(Mod_F(\Sigma))$ if and only if its corresponding SC model is a model of $CIRCUM(\Sigma \cup \Psi; Ab; Result)$.

    2. $\mathcal{M}$ is a model of $CIRCUM(\Sigma \cup \Psi; Ab; Result)$ if and only if its corresponding model in $min(Mod_F(\Sigma))$.

    where Ψ is the set of UNAF, UNAA, DCAF and DCAA.

Note that the action description in the observation is not necessarily normal. However, if we impose syntactical restrictions on action description and queries, we can prove that all the solutions to the frame problem we considered thus far are equivalent. This result corresponds to the one in [14].

Corollary 1 *Let Σ be a normal action description, Γ a finite set of literals. If Σ is deterministic and safe, then the following statements are equivalent:*

    1. $\vdash^{\Sigma \cup \Delta} (\bigwedge \Gamma) \rightarrow [a_1; \cdots; a_n]l$, where Δ is the set of frame axioms with respect to Σ.

    2. For any model $M \in min(Mod_{NF}(\Sigma))$, $M \models (\bigwedge \Gamma) \rightarrow [a_1; \cdots; a_n]l$.

    3. "necessarily l after $a_1, \cdots, a_n$" is a consequence of Γ with respect to Σ.

    4. $CIRCUM(\Sigma \cup \Psi; Ab; Result) \models \forall s(Holds((\bigwedge \Gamma), s) \rightarrow Holds(l, Result(a_1, \cdots, a_n, s)))$.

where Ψ is the set of UNAF, UNAA, DCAF, DCAA and ESA.

7   Conclusion and Discussion

We have encoded three typical solutions to the frame problem: Pednault's syntax-based solution, Baker's circumscription and Gelfond & Lifchitz's action language A, in PDL in either syntax or semantics. Three observations have been given which show the formal relationships among these solutions, which are helpful for a fuller and deeper understanding of the frame problem and the associated solutions. As a corollary of these observations, we know that for *normal and safe* action descriptions and *simple* queries, all the solutions to the frame problem are equivalent. This corresponds to the result in [14], where Pednault's, Reiter's and Baker's solutions to the frame problem were compared based on action language $\mathcal{A}$. A crucial difference between Kartha's result and ours is the following. Action language $\mathcal{A}$ is the least expressive language among the formalisms of action. Under its restrictions we cannot see the difference among the solutions (Corollary 1). In contrast, dynamic logic is the highest with regard to a certain level (propositional or first-order). This makes a systematic comparison of formalisms on action possible. Additionally, the soundness and completeness of dynamic logic bridge the syntax and semantics, which makes the unification of different approaches possible.

With help of the formal results in the paper, we would like to make the following remarks:

Syntactical restrictions: The equivalence among the solutions to the frame problem relies heavily on the syntactical restrictions on action description and queries. For instance, if Σ is not normal, the validity of a formula A in all the natural saturated Σ-models does not guarantee $\vdash^{\Sigma} A$. Thus the link between the Σ-provability in PDL and provability from transition systems of action language $\mathcal{A}$ will not exist. Additionally, the form of queries is also crucial to the equivalence. Fortunately, the link between minimizing PDL models and minimizing SC models does not depend on the normality of action description.

Extensibility of action formalisms: Each formalism of action has been or is intended to be extended to accommodate *non-deterministic and indirect effects* of actions and *compound and concurrent* actions. Compatible extensions of these formalisms will approximate dynamic logic in expressiveness. For instance, to extend $\mathcal{A}$ to express general queries requires transition systems to allow "non-natural" models according to Proposition 2. Currently, to express programs or compound actions, dynamic logic might be the best formalism among the existent ones.

Epistemic minimization and physical minimization: We know that Baker's circumscriptive policy (varying $Result$) corresponds exactly to the minimization of PDL models. We may remember that we took a detour, varying $Holds$, before we reached the "right solution": state-minimization [24]. Such a detour does not seem necessary in PDL models or transition systems. There is a subtle difference between circumscriptive first-order models and minimizing PDL models. With circumscription we minimize abnormality whereas in PDL we minimize change of worlds. We refer to the former kind of minimization as to be *epistemic* and the latter as to be *physical*.

Action-oriented frame problem: We have considered Pednault's syntax-based solution and Baker's model-based solution to the frame problem. However, these solutions only work for the so-called *fluent-oriented frame problem* (see [13]). A remaining challenge is to encode the solutions to the action-oriented frame problem, i.e, how to make it the default in PDL that only actions mentioned in the action description have effects. A typical approach to the action-oriented frame problem is using action variables to range over all actions which have effects. A compact representation of frame axioms can then be offered by using the *Explanation Closure Assumption* and quantifying over action variables [23,13]. Such an approach cannot be encoded in PDL because there are no action variables (even in first-order versions). In [5], it was shown that given a normal and safe action description Σ, if $\vdash^{\Sigma \cup \Delta} A$, where Δ is the set of all the frame axioms with respect to Σ, then there is a subset Δ' of Δ such that all the action symbols occur in Δ' occur in A. This means that if we postpone listing frame axioms till a query arises, frame axioms in which the actions are irrelevant to the query are not needed for answering the query. Therefore, the action-oriented frame problem is not a problem in this sense.

Appendix: Translations between Languages

We now provide an intertranslation between dynamic logic, situation calculus and action languages. This intertranslation is not formal. For instance, a fluent symbol stands for a proposition in PDL but is an individual in situation calculus. Again, $Holds(\varphi, S_0)$ make sense only in the extended predicate of $Holds$. Additionally, all these translations depend on the semantics of the associated action logics.

1. Expressions for describing initial state:

Dynamic Logic	Situation Calculus	Action Language $\mathcal{A}$
f	$Holds(f, S_0)$	**now** f
$\neg f$	$\neg Holds(f, S_0)$	**now** $\neg f$
φ	$Holds(\varphi, S_0)$	

2. Expressions for describing queries

Dynamic Logic	Situation Calculus	Action Language $\mathcal{A}$
$[a_1, \cdots, a_n]\varphi$	$Holds(\varphi, Result([a_1, \cdots, a_n], s))$	φ **after** $a_1, \cdots, a_n$

3. Expressions for describing causation between propositions

Dynamic Logic	Situation Calculus	Action Language $\mathcal{B}$
$[\varphi]\psi$	$Holds(\varphi, s) \rightarrow Caused(\psi, true, s)$	ψ **if** φ

4. Expressions for describing domain axioms:

Dynamic Logic	Situation Calculus	Action Language $\mathcal{A}$ or $\mathcal{C}$
$\varphi \rightarrow [a]l$	$\forall s(Holds(\varphi, s) \rightarrow Holds(L, Result(a, s)))$	a **causes** l **if** φ
$\varphi \rightarrow \prec a \succ l$		a **may cause** l **if** φ
$\varphi \rightarrow \langle a \rangle \top$	$\forall s(Holds(\varphi, s) \rightarrow Poss(a, s))$	**executable** a **if** φ

References

1. A. Baker, Nonmonotonic reasoning in the framework of situation calculus, *Artificial Intelligence*, 49:5-23, 1991.   240, 241, 244, 247
2. M. A. Castilho, O. Gasquet, and A. Herzig, Formalizing action and change in modal logic I: the frame problem, *J. of Logic and Computations*, 5(9):701-735, 1999.   241
3. R. Fikes and N. Nilsson, STRIPS: a new approach to the application of theorem proving to problem solving, In: *Proceedings of the 2nd International Joint Conference on Artificial Intelligence*, William Kaufmann, 608-620, 1971.   240
4. N. Foo and D. Zhang, Dealing with the ramification problem in extended propositional dynamic logic, To appear in F. Wolter, H. Wansing, M. de Rijke, and M. Zakharyaschev eds, *Advances in Modal Logic, Volume 3*, CSLI Publications, 2001.
5. N. Foo and D. Zhang, Lazy-formalization to the frame problem, manuscript. (available at http://www.cse.unsw.edu.au/~ksg/Pubs/ksgworking.html).   251
6. M. Gelfond and V. Lifschitz, Representing actions and change by logic programs, *Journal of Logic Programming*, vol. 17, no. 2,3,4, 301–323, 1993.   246
7. M. Gelfond and V. Lifschitz, Action languages, *Electronic Transactions on AI*, 16(3), 1998.   240, 241
8. G. Giacomo and M. Lenzerini, PDL-based framework for reasoning about actions, In M. Gori and G. Soda (Eds.), *Topics in Artificial Intelligence*, LNAI 992,103-114, 1995.   240, 241
9. M. L. Ginsberg, *Nonmonotonic Reasoning* , Morgan Kaufmann, 1988.   240
10. L. Giordano, A. Martelli, and C. Schwind, Dealing with concurrent actions in modal action logics, *ECAI'98*, 537-541, 1998.   240
11. L. Giordano, A. Martelli and C. Schwind, Ramification and causality in a modal action logic, *J. Logic Computat.* 5(10), 615-662, 2000.   240
12. S. Hanks and D. McDermott, Nonmonotonic logic and temporal projection, *Artificial Intelligence*, 33(3):379-412, 1987.   241
13. F. Lin and Y. Shoham, Provably correct theories of action, *AAAI-91*, 349-354, 1991.   251
14. G. Kartha, Soundness and completeness theorems for three formalization of action, *IJCAI-93*, 724-729, 1993.   241, 249, 250
15. G. Kartha, V. Lifschitz: Actions with indirect effects (Preliminary Report), *KR'94*, 341-350, 1994
16. G. Kartha: On the range of applicability of Baker's approach to the frame problem. *AAAI-96* ,664-669, 1996.
17. R. A. Kowalski and M. J. Sergot, A logic-based calculus of events, *New Generation Computing*, Vol. 4, 67-95, 1986.   240
18. D. Kozen and J. Tiuryn, Logics of programs, In J. van Leeuwen ed. *Handbook of Theoretical Computer Science*, Elsevier, 789-840, 1990.   241, 242, 243
19. J. McCarthy and P. Hayes, Some philosophical problems from the standpoint of artificial intelligence, In B. Meltzer and D. Michie edits, *Machine Intelligence* 4, Edinburgh University Press, 463-502, 1969.   240, 247
20. E. Pednault, ADL: exploring the middle ground between STRIPS and the situation calculus, *KR-89*, 324-332.   240, 241, 245
21. Peleg, D. Concurrent dynamic logic, *J. ACM*, 34(2):450-479,1987.
22. H. Prendinger and G. Schurz, Reasoning about action and change: A dynamic logic approach, *J. of Logic, Language, and Information*, 5:209-245, 1996.   241

23. R. Reiter, The frame problem in the situation calculus: a simple solution (sometimes) and a completeness result for goal regression, In V. Lifschitz editor, *Artificial Intelligence and Mathematical Theory of Computation*, Academic Press, 1991, 359-380.   240, 241, 243, 245, 251

24. M. Shanahan, *Solving the frame problem: a mathematical investigation of the common sense law of inertia*, The MIT Press, 1997.   250

25. D. Zhang and S. Chopra, Consistency analysis of action descriptions, in *Proceedings of Australian Workshop on Computational Logic 2001, 107-116.*   242, 243

26. D. Zhang and N. Foo, EPDL: a logic for causal reasoning, to appear in *Proceedings of IJCAI-01.*   240, 242, 243, 246

$\mathcal{E}$-RES: Reasoning about Actions, Events and Observations

Antonis Kakas[1], Rob Miller[2], and Francesca Toni[3]

[1] Department of Computer Science, University of Cyprus
antonis@ucy.ac.cy
[2] School of Library, Archive and Information Studies, University College London, UK
rsm@ucl.ac.uk
[3] Department of Computing,Imperial College of Science, Technology and Medicine,
London, UK
ft@doc.ic.ac.uk

Abstract. The language $\mathcal{E}$ for reasoning about actions and change can be translated into an argumentation framework. In this paper, we extend this translation of the basic language and show how it can, together with methods from abduction, form the basis for a principled implementation of $\mathcal{E}$. The extension we have considered concerns the addition of new type of sentences in the language as well as allowing theories where the narrative of events given is incomplete.

A system, called $\mathcal{E}$-RES, is developed within the argumentation framework of Logic Programming without Negation as Failure (*LPwNF*). This can support directly a variety of modes of common sense reasoning such as: default persistence in credulous or sceptical form, assimilation of observations and their diagnosis possibly under incomplete information, as well as combinations of these. To improve the efficiency of the system we have considered the integration of a SAT solver within the *LPwNF* computation, to carry out the of validating the time universal constraints imposed by ramification statements.

1 Introduction

General formalisms of action and change can provide a natural framework for a variety of AI problems such as diagnosis, planning and cognitive robotics. They can offer a high level of expressivity and a basis for the development of a computational framework to solve these problems. In this paper we study how one such formalism, the Language $\mathcal{E}$ [10], can be developed into a framework capable of supporting a variety of basic reasoning modes needed to address this type of AI applications.

The computational foundation of this framework and its associated system, called $\mathcal{E}$-RES, is a re-formulation of the Language $\mathcal{E}$ in terms of argumentation [2], within the framework of Logic Programming without Negation as Failure (*LPwNF*) [3], together with a synthesis of methods from abductive reasoning [9]. This allows a principled implementation of the $\mathcal{E}$-RES system in a way that separates issues of expressiveness and efficiency. It is then possible to examine how

T. Eiter, W. Faber, and M. Truszczyński (Eds.): LPNMR 2001, LNAI 2173, pp. 254–267, 2001.
© Springer-Verlag Berlin Heidelberg 2001

we can use in a modular way "external" solvers, e.g. a SAT solver [6] or a notion of relevancy of part of the theory to the goal at hand, for improving the computational behaviour of the framework.

2 The Language E and Its Model Semantics

The vocabulary of the Language $\mathcal{E}$ consists of a set Φ of *fluent constants*, a set of *action constants*, and a partially ordered set $\langle \Pi, \preceq \rangle$ of *time-points*. This vocabulary depends each time on the domain being modeled. A *fluent literal* is either a fluent constant F or its negation $\neg F$. In the current implementation of the $\mathcal{E}$-RES system the only time structure that is supported is that of the natural numbers, so we restrict our attention here to domains of this type.

Domain descriptions in the Language $\mathcal{E}$ are collections of the following kinds of statements (where A is an action constant, T is a time-point, F is a fluent constant, L is a fluent literal and C is a set of fluent literals):

- *t-propositions*: L holds-at T
- *h-propositions*: A happens-at T
- *c-propositions*: A initiates F when C, or A terminates F when C
- *r-propositions*: L whenever C
- *p-propositions*: A needs C.

T-propositions are used to record observations that particular fluents hold or do not hold at particular time-points. H-propositions are used to state that particular actions occur at particular time-points. C-propositions state general "action laws" – the intended meaning of "A initiates F when C" is "C is a minimally sufficient set of conditions for an occurrence of A to initiate F". R-propositions serve a dual role in that they describe both static constraints between fluents and ways in which fluents may be indirectly affected by action occurrences. P-propositions state necessary conditions for an action to occur.

The semantics of $\mathcal{E}$ is based on a notion of a *model* of a domain D. A map, $H : \Phi \times \Pi \mapsto \{true, false\}$, is an interpretation of D. Given a time point T and a fluent constant F we first define the notion of an *initiation-point* (*termination-point* resp.) *for F in H relative to D* as follows. Consider first the case where D contains no r-propositions. Then T is an **initiation-point** (**termination-point** resp.) **for F in H relative to D** iff there is an action constant A such that (i) D contains both an h-proposition A happens-at T and a c-proposition A initiates (terminates, resp.) F when C, and (ii) H satisfies C at T (i.e for each $F \in C$, $H(F, T) = true$, and for each F' such that $\neg F' \in C$, $H(F', T) = false$).

When the domain D contains r-propositions this definition has to be extended to allow for initiation or termination points that are generated recursively through such these r-propositions.

Definition 1. *(Initiation/termination point) Let H be an interpretation of $\mathcal{E}$, and D be a domain description. Let $\mathcal{W}$ be the set $2^{\Phi \times \Pi} \times 2^{\Phi \times \Pi}$ and let the operator $\mathcal{F} : \mathcal{W} \mapsto \mathcal{W}$ be defined as follows. For each, $\langle In, Te \rangle \in \mathcal{W}$ denote*

$\mathcal{F}(\langle \mathcal{In}, \mathcal{Te} \rangle)$ *by* $\langle \mathcal{In}', \mathcal{Te}' \rangle$. *Then for any* $F \in \Phi$ *and* $T \in \Pi$, (F, T) *is in* $\mathcal{In}'$ *(resp. in* $\mathcal{Te}'$*) iff one of the following two conditions holds.*

1. *There is an* $A \in \Delta$ *s.t. (i) there is both an h-proposition in* D *of the form* "A happens-at T" *and a c-proposition in* D *of the form* "A initiates F when C" *(resp.* "A terminates F when C"*) and (ii)* H *satisfies* C *at* T.
2. *There is an r-proposition in* D *of the form* "F whenever C" *(resp.* "$\neg F$ whenever C"*) and a partition* $\{C_1, C_2\}$ *of* C *such that (i)* C_1 *is non-empty, for each fluent constant* $F' \in C_1$, $(F', T) \in \mathcal{In}$, *and for each fluent literal* $\neg F' \in C_1$, $(F', T) \in \mathcal{Te}$, *and (ii) there is some* $T_2 \in \Pi$, $T \prec T_2$, *such that for all* T_1, $T \preceq T_1 \preceq T_2$, H *satisfies* C_2 *at* T_1.

Let $\langle \mathcal{In}^f, \mathcal{Te}^f \rangle$ *be the least fixed point of the (monotonic) operator* $\mathcal{F}$ *starting from the empty tuple* $\langle \emptyset, \emptyset \rangle$. T *is an initiation-point (resp. termination-point) for* F *in* H *relative to* D *iff* $(F, T) \in \mathcal{In}^f$ *(resp.* $(F, T) \in \mathcal{Te}^f$*).*

It is useful to note that any initiation or termination point at some time T relative to D, defined in this way, must refer to at least one known h-proposition at T in the domain D.

Given this notion of an initiation and termination point then an interpretation H is a **model** of D iff, for every fluent constant F and time-points $T_1 \prec T_3$:

1. If there is no initiation- or termination-point T_2 for F in H such that $T_1 \preceq T_2 \prec T_3$, then $H(F, T_1) = H(F, T_3)$.
2. If T_1 is an initiation-point for F in H, and there is no termination-point T_2 for F in H such that $T_1 \prec T_2 \prec T_3$, then $H(F, T_3) = true$.
3. If T_1 is a termination-point for F in H, and there is no initiation-point T_2 for F in H such that $T_1 \prec T_2 \prec T_3$, then $H(F, T_3) = false$.
4. H satisfies the following constraints:
   - For all F holds-at T in D, $H(F, T) = true$, and for all "$\neg F$ holds-at T'" in D, $H(F, T') = false$.
   - For all A needs C in D and A happens-at T in D, H satisfies C at T.
   - For all L whenever C in D, and time-points T, if H satisfies C at T then H satisfies $\{L\}$ at T.

A domain D **entails** (written $\models$) the t-proposition F holds-at T ($\neg G$ holds-at T, resp.), iff for every model H of D, $H(F, T) = true$ ($H(G, T) = false$, resp.).

The first three conditions for a model encapsulate a notion of *default persistence* for fluents whereas the fourth condition imposes other constraints on the model from explicit information about the fluents given in D. This separation allows a modular extension of the language and, as we will see, facilitates the development of a proof theory for it.

Example 1. (Bulb Domain: D_b)

SwitchOn initiates *Light* when {*Normal*}	(D_b1)
SwitchOff terminates *Light*	(D_b2)
Break terminates *Normal*	(D_b3)
$\neg Light$ whenever {$\neg Normal$}	(D_b4)
SwitchOn needs {$\neg Light$}	(D_b5)
SwitchOn happens-at 2	(D_b6)
Normal holds-at 0	(D_b7)

In this example, D_b entails *Light* holds-at 4 but not when D_b is extended with *Break* happens-at 3.

The above semantics assumes that no events occur other than those explicitly given in the domain description D. This is not always a valid assumption and it is possible to have domains where some action types are **open**, e.g. in the example above *Break* could be considered as open. Following work on abduction [9], we define a notion of **generalized model** of D as any model of $D \cup Ab$, where Ab is any set of h-propositions over the open action types in D. A corresponding entailment is then defined in terms of these generalized models.

3   An Argumentation Proof Theory for $\mathcal{E}$

The basic subset of the language $\mathcal{E}$, comprising only of h- and c-propositions, has been re-formulated into the argumentation framework of *LPwNF* in [11]. In this section, we give a brief review of the argumentation formulation of $\mathcal{E}$ and show how it can be extended when we extend the syntax of the basic language or when we allow open action types in a domain description. This results in a proof theory for $\mathcal{E}$ which in turn will form the basis of the $\mathcal{E}$-RES system implementing the language.

The argumentation re-formulation of $\mathcal{E}$ translates a domain D, over the basic subset of the language, into an **argumentation program** $P_{\mathcal{E}}(D) = (B(D), \mathcal{A}_{\mathcal{E}}, <_{\mathcal{E}})$ in *LPwNF*. The background monotonic logic $(\mathcal{L}, \vdash)$ of the *LP-wNF* framework is:

- $\mathcal{L}$ consists of all sentences $\lambda_0 \leftarrow \lambda_1, \ldots, \lambda_n$ $(n \geq 0)$, with λ_i, $0 \leq i \leq n$, positive or negative (via a negation or complement operator, $\neg$,) literals, and all variables implicitly universally quantified from the outside, and
- $\vdash$ is obtained by repeatedly applying the classical modus ponens inference rule $\dfrac{X \leftarrow Y, \quad Y}{X}$ with $X \leftarrow Y$ any ground instance of a sentence in $\mathcal{L}$.

Given D, $B(D)$, called the **background theory for D**, is given by:

- If A happens-at $T \in D$, then $Happens(A, T) \in B(D)$.
- If A initiates F when {$L_1, \ldots, L_n$} $\in D$, then $B(D)$ contains a rule for *Initiation*:

$Initiation(F,t) \leftarrow Happens(A,t), HoldsAt(L_1,t), \ldots, HoldsAt(L_n,t).$
Similarly, for "terminates" c-propositions a rule for *Termination* is given in
$B(D)$. (Here and below $HoldsAt(\neg F_i, t)$ stands for $\neg HoldsAt(F_i, t)$).

The rest of $P_{\mathcal{E}}(D)$ is independent of any given domain D. $\mathcal{A}_{\mathcal{E}}$, called the **argumentation theory** consists of:

Generation rules:

$HoldsAt(f, t_2) \leftarrow Initiation(f, t_1), t_1 \prec t_2$ $(PG[f, t_2; t_1])$

$\neg HoldsAt(f, t_2) \leftarrow Termination(f, t_1), t_1 \prec t_2$ $(NG[f, t_2; t_1])$

Persistence rules:

$HoldsAt(f, t_2) \leftarrow HoldsAt(f, t_1), t_1 \prec t_2$ $(PP[f, t_2; t_1])$

$\neg HoldsAt(f, t_2) \leftarrow \neg HoldsAt(f, t_1), t_1 \prec t_2$ $(NP[f, t_2; t_1])$

Assumption rules:

$HoldsAt(f, t)$ $(PA[f, t])$

$\neg HoldsAt(f, t)$ $(NA[f, t])$

Also, $<_{\mathcal{E}}$ is a **priority relation** defined over $\mathcal{A}_{\mathcal{E}}$ by:
$NP[f, t; t_1] <_{\mathcal{E}} PG[f, t; t_2]$ iff $t_1 \preceq t_2$,
$NG[f, t, t_1] <_{\mathcal{E}} PG[f, t; t_2]$ iff $t_1 \prec t_2$,
$PA[f, t] <_{\mathcal{E}} NG[f, t; t'], PA[f, t] <_{\mathcal{E}} NP[f, t; t'],$
together with the corresponding cases where positive rules are replaced by negative rules and vice versa.

The essential element of this translation is that it formalizes that the effects of later events take priority over the effects of earlier events. The argumentation semantics of $P_{\mathcal{E}}(D)$ is given via the *admissible* extensions of $B(D)$. These are subsets, S, of argument rules from $\mathcal{A}_{\mathcal{E}}' \subset \mathcal{A}_{\mathcal{E}}$ consisting only of generation or assumption rules, which are added to $B(D)$. An extension S is **admissible** iff:

- it is consistent i.e. *non-self-attacking*, and
- *(counter-)attacks* any set of arguments *attacking* it.

A set of argument rules, A, **attacks** another such set, B, if the two sets are in conflict, by monotonicaly deriving (in $\vdash$), together with $B(D)$, complimentary literals λ and $\neg\lambda$, respectively, and A is *not of lower priority* than B. A set A is of lower priority than B if it has a rule of lower priority than some rule in B and does not contain any rule of higher priority than some rule in B.

Given this translation it can be shown, under some quite general restrictions on D, that the models of D correspond exactly to the maximally (w.r.t. set inclusion) admissible extensions of $P_{\mathcal{E}}(D)$. We can then use this translation to develop an argumentation-based proof theory for $\mathcal{E}$. This proof theory is defined in terms of *derivations of trees*, whose nodes are sets of arguments in $\mathcal{A}_{\mathcal{E}}$ attacking the arguments in their parent nodes.

Let S_0 be a (non-self-attacking) set of arguments in $\mathcal{A_E}'$ such that $B(D) \cup S_0 \vdash (\neg)HoldsAt(F,T)$. Then, two kinds of derivations are defined:

- *Successful derivations* $S_0, ..., S$, building, from a tree consisting only of the root S_0, a tree whose root S is an admissible subset of $\mathcal{A_E}'$ such that $S \supseteq S_0$.
- *Finitely failed derivations*, guaranteeing the absence of any admissible set of arguments containing S_0.

Then, the given literal, $L = (\neg)HoldsAt(F,T)$, we say that L is a **sceptical** consequence of D iff (i) there exists a successful derivation starting with S_0 and, (ii) for every set S_0' of argument rules in $\mathcal{A_E}'$ such that $B(D) \cup S_0'$ derives (in $\vdash$) the complement of L, every derivation for S_0' is finitely failed. If only the first condition, (i), holds we say that L is a **credulous** consequence of D.

The formal details of the derivations are not needed for this paper. Informally, both kinds of derivation incrementally consider all attacks against the root and, whenever this does not counter-attack one of its attacks, a new set of arguments that can do this is added to the root. Then, the process is repeated, until every attack has been counter-attacked successfully (successful derivation) by the extended root or until some attack cannot be counter-attacked by any extension of the root (finitely failed derivations). Examples of this proof theory will be presented in the next section.

An important feature of the argumentation re-formulation of $\mathcal{E}$ is the fact that this is modular with respect to the addition of new type of sentences in the language. This follows primarily from the fact that the translation is faithful at the level of the models of the language and so it can reflect the modular separation of the model definition into two parts: conditions (1-3) encapsulating default persistence and condition 4 for extra constraints. When we add r-propositions we only need to extend the background definitions of *Initiation* and *Termination* in $B(D)$ without changing the type of arguments in $P_{\mathcal{E}}(D)$. For each, L `whenever` C a fact $Whenever(L, C)$, is added to $B(D)$, and the definitions of *Initiation* and *Termination* are augmented with:

$$Start(l, t) \leftarrow Whenever(l, c), Select(c, l1, \{l_2, \ldots, l_n\}),$$
$$Start(l1, t), HoldsAt(l_2, t_+), \ldots, HoldsAt(l_n, t_+)$$

where for a positive literal $l = F$, $Start(l, t)$, is to be read as $Initiation(F, t)$ and for a negative literal, $l = \neg F$, as $Termination(F, t)$, and t_+ is the next immediate time after t. Hence every event that brings about any literal, l_1, of C while the rest of this, $\{l_2, \ldots, l_n\}$, continues to hold also brings about, through the r-proposition, L.

In turn, the only extension required to the proof theory is to add, for any r-proposition L `whenever` $\{L_1, \ldots, L_k\}$, to the root S of any derivation a set of arguments, S_r, so that that $B(D) \cup S \cup S_r \vdash \phi$ where ϕ is the (classical) formula $HoldsAt(L, t) \leftarrow HoldsAt(L_1, t), \ldots, HoldsAt(L_k, t)$. Similarly, when we extend the language with t and p-propositions we need to extend the proof theory by adding to the root of a derivation a set of arguments, S_t and S_p, so that they can derive (with $B(D)$) the $HoldsAt$ literals corresponding to these sentences. The proof theory continues then as before but now with the extra attacks against S_r, S_t and S_p to be considered.

Finally, when we have *open* action types in the domain D the proof theory is extended to allow the *abduction* of a new set of events, H, and hence new generation arguments can be added to the root. Derivations are now defined in terms of tuples, $< H, S >$. In this extended proof theory it is possible for new attacks to be generated during the derivation due to the new events abduced. The proof theory therefore now includes **suspended** attacks which can become actual attacks when H grows. If this happens then these attacks need to be counter-attacked as usual, otherwise, suspended attacks that remain so until the end of the derivation are ignored.

Theorem 1. *(Soundness and Completeness of the Extended Proof Theory)*
Let D^1 be a description domain possibly with open action types and S_0 a consistent set of arguments. If there exists a successful extended derivation from $< \emptyset, S_0 >$ to $< H, S >$ then there exists a generalized model, M, of D such that (i) M is also a model of $D \cup H$ and (ii) M satisfies L for any literal L s.t. $B(D \cup H) \cup S \vdash L$. Also, if every extended derivation from $< \emptyset, S_0 >$ is finitely failed, then there exists no generalized model, M, of D such that M satisfies L for every literal L s.t. $B(D \cup H) \cup S_0 \vdash L$ where H is the set of h-propositions corresponding to M.
Conversely, let M be a generalized model of D such that its corresponding set of h-propositions H is finite and M satisfies L. Then there exists a set of arguments S_0 and a successful extended derivation from $< \emptyset, S_0 >$ to $< H', S >$ such that $B(D \cup H') \cup S_0 \vdash L$ and $H' \subseteq H$.

4   Reasoning with the Language $\mathcal{E}$

The language $\mathcal{E}$ can support in a natural way a variety of modes of reasoning with actions and observations. The argumentation-based computational model for E, described in the previous section, allows a principled implementation of these forms of reasoning. In this section we present some of these forms of reasoning and explain briefly how they are mapped into argumentation.

4.1   Default Persistence

The argumentation translation of the language $\mathcal{E}$ maps the basic reasoning of default persistence captured by the model theoretic semantics of $\mathcal{E}$ into an argumentation reasoning. Consider the following example where vaccine A provides protection only for people with blood type O, and vaccine B for people with blood type other than O.

---

[1] All results in this paper refer to domains with discrete linear time, a finite number of h-propositions and a restriction that limits the possibility for events to simultaneously initiate and terminate the same fluent.

Example 2. (Vaccinations - No open actions)
InjectA initiates *Protected* when {*TypeO*} (D_v1)
InjectB initiates *Protected* when {¬*TypeO*} (D_v2)
InjectA happens-at 2 (D_v3)
InjectB happens-at 3 (D_v4)

Given this domain, we can show that at any time T_f after 3 $G = \{Protected$ holds-at $T_f\}$ is a sceptical consequence of D_v whereas for times less or equal to 3 *Protected* is only a credulous consequence. An argument S_0 for G is given by $S_0 = \{PG[Protected, T_f; 2], PA[Type0, 2]\}$ i.e. a generation argument based on the event of *InjectA* at time 2 together with an assumption argument for *Type0* at time 2. All attacking arguments against this can be counter-attacked (defended) by S_0 itself. This gives a successful derivation for S_0 and thus G is a credulous consequence. To show that it is a sceptical consequence we consider the opposite goal ¬G.

The only way to derive this is through the argument $R_1 = \{NA[Protected, T_f]\}$ (there are no generation arguments for ¬G). This is attacked by S_0 given above, which can be counterattacked (only) if R_1 is extended to R_2 with the assumption argument $NA[Type0, 2]$. But R_1 and thus also R_2 are also attacked by $\{PG[Protected, T_f; 3], NA[Type0, 3]\}$ via the event *InjectB* at time 3. To defend against this it is now necessary to add $PA[Type0, 3]$ to R_2 to give $R_3 = \{NA[Protected, T_f], NA[Type0, 2], PA[Type0, 3]\}$. But then we have a new attack against R_3 given by $\{NP[Type0, 3; 2], NA[Type0, 2]\}$ through a persistence argument from time 2 to time 3. This attack can only be counterattacked via a generation argument for $HoldsAt(Type0, 3)$. But no such arguments exist in D_v and hence the derivation for ¬G finitely fails, as required.

This example shows how the argumentation reasoning deals correctly with default persistence under incomplete information. For a more complex example consider the same goal G in the domain below where the fluents *TypeO* and *Strong* are incompletly specified.

Example 3. (Vaccinations Cnt.)
InjectB initiates *Protected* when {¬*TypeO*} (D_r1)
InjectC initiates *Protected* when {*Strong*} (D_r2)
Strong whenever {*TypeO*} (D_r3)
InjectB happens-at 2 (D_r4)
InjectC happens-at 3 (D_r5)

As above, derivations for ¬G finitely fail. The two attacks against ¬G, via the two injection events, can only be counterattacked by $\{PA[Type0, 2]\}$ and $\{NA[Strong, 3]\}$. But then the satisfaction of the ramification statement requires $\{PA[Strong, 2]\}$ to be added. In turn this gives a new persistence attack of *Strong* from time 2 to 3 which can not be counterattacked as there is no generation rule for ¬*Strong*.

4.2   Assimilating Observations and Diagnosis

A domain description in the language $\mathcal{E}$ may contain observations (t-propositions) about some of its fluents. The observations can refer either to some initial time or any other time point. An argument for a default conclusion to be valid must also be extensible to an admissible superset that is able to confirm these observations. This extra requirement gives a form of reasoning from effects to causes both forward and backward in time.

Example 4. Infections - No open actions

Expose initiates *Infected* when $\{TypeA\}$	(D_i1)
Expose initiates *Infected* when $\{TypeB\}$	(D_i2)
Allergic whenever $\{TypeA, Infected\}$	(D_i3)
Allergic whenever $\{TypeB\}$	(D_i4)
Expose happens-at 3	(D_i5)
$\neg Infected$ holds-at 1	(D_i6)
Infected holds-at 6	(D_i7)

The observation at time 6 requires that a generation rule argument for *Infected* at 6 is added to the root of any derivation. The weaker assumption argument $PA[Infected; 6]$ cannot defend against its persistence attack starting from time 1 where the observation of $\neg Infected$ is given. The only possibility for such a generation rule is the one based on the event of *Expose* at time 3 with either *TypeA* or *TypeB* assumed at time 3, and consequently at any other time before or after 3. Under any one of these assumptions the two r-propositions imply that *Allergic* would hold from 6. The argumentation reasoning is thus able to derive that $\neg Allergic$ cannot be derived credulously and hence that *Allergic* holds sceptically from 6 onwards.

Effectively, these observations are explained in terms of missing information on incomplete fluents. When a domain contains open action types this gives us a form of *diagnosis* of the observations in terms of assumptions both on incomplete fluents and on unknown (in D) events.

Definition 2. *(Diagnosis in $\mathcal{E}$)*
Let D be a given domain description[2] and O a set of observations. A (strong) **diagnosis** *for O in D is a set H of h-propositions s.t. $D \cup H$ is consistent and $D \cup H \models O$.*

A weaker form of diagnosis useful when we have incomplete information on fluents whose truth cannot be affected by any action (e.g at some initial time point), is as follows.

Definition 3. *(Conditional Diagnosis in $\mathcal{E}$)*
Let D be a domain description and O a set of observations. Then a **weak diagnosis** *for O in D is a set H of h-propositions s.t. there exists a model M of*

---

[2] For simplicity of presentation we will assume that the domain does not contain any p-propositions, P. If this is the case then we have an extra requirement on the diagnosis that $D \cup H \models P$.

$D \cup H$ *where* $M \models O$. H is conditional on a set of assumptions Δ *iff Δ is a set of t-propositions ($\Delta \cap O = \emptyset$) such that H is a (strong) diagnosis for O in $D \cup \Delta$. The tuple, $< H, \Delta >$, is called a **conditional diagnosis** for O in D.*

Note that the assumptions Δ in a conditional plan can refer to any time point not necessarily to an initial time point only. In the previous example the empty set $H = \emptyset$ is a weak diagnosis for the observation *Infected* holds-at 6 in the domain D_i given by the sentences D_i1-D_i5. Two conditional diagnoses are $< \emptyset$, *TypeA* holds-at 3 > and $< \emptyset$, *TypeB* holds-at 3 >. Note that $< \emptyset$, *TypeA* holds-at 1 > is also a conditional diagnosis. The assumption that *TypeA* holds at some time point (e.g. an initial time point 1) implies that it also holds at any other time point as no action in D_i can affect the value of this fluent. Typically, if we have incomplete information on fluents that cannot be affected by any action or the information is incomplete at some initial time point before which actions can not occur then a conditional diagnosis is appropriate.

Theorem 2. *Let D be a given domain description and O a set of observations. Let also $S_0 \subseteq \mathcal{A}_\mathcal{E}$ be a set of arguments and H_0 a set of action facts such that $B(D \cup H_0) \cup S_0 \vdash O$. If there exists a successful extended derivation in D from $< H_0, S_0 >$ to $< H, S >$ then$< H, \Delta >$ is a conditional diagnosis for O in D, where $\Delta = \{F$ holds-at $T | PA[F, T] \in S\} \cup \{\neg F$ holds-at $T | NA[F, T] \in S\}$.*

To illustrate this computation of conditional diagnoses let us consider again example 1 where D_b7 is absent and *Break* is an open action type. Suppose we are given the observations: *Light* holds-at 4 and $\neg Light$ holds-at 6.

To assimilate the first observation we can use a generation argument, $S_0 = \{PG[Light, 4; 2], PA[Normal, 2]\}$, based on the given event of *SwitchOn*. This can defend itself against all its attacks except possibly an attack via a generation argument based on an event of *Break* at a time after 2 and before 4. As we have no such event in our computed diagnosis this remains suspended. Also, because the p-proposition in D requires that $\neg Light$ holds at 2, S_0 will be extended to S_1 with $NA[Light, 2]$. To assimilate the second observation the only way we can extend, S_1, is via a generation argument based on an event of *Break* at a time before 6. Hence S_1 is extended to $S_2 = S_1 \cup \{NG[Light, 4; T]\}$ and H_0 to $H_1 = \{Break$ happens-at $T\}$ for $T < 6$. Note that this generation of $\neg Light$ is *indirect* through the ramification statement in the theory.

Adding this new event results in the re-examination of the suspended attack from before. In general, there are two ways to deal with this situation. One way is to constrain the time of the new event so that it does not lead to an actual attack. The other is to counter-attack this attack in the usual way. In this case, the second option is not available as we cannot assume *SwitchOn* events. Hence we are forced to set $T \geq 4$. The computation then concludes successfully with $< H_1, S_2 >$ giving the (a set of) conditional diagnosis (one for each T in [4,6)) $< \{Break$ happens-at $T\}, \{Normal$ holds-at 2, $\neg Light$ holds-at 2$\} >$.

A computed conditional diagnosis $< H, \Delta >$ in D can be tested to see if this is a strong diagnosis by checking whether the assumptions Δ follow sceptically from $D \cup H$. In the previous example, $\{Normal$ holds-at 2$\}$ is not a sceptical consequence (the domain is incomplete on this fluent) and hence the diagnosis needs this condition.

5   The $\mathcal{E}$-RES System: Implementing $\mathcal{E}$

The argumentation based proof theory described in section 3 forms the basis of a principled implementation of the language $\mathcal{E}$ into a system, called $\mathcal{E}$-RES. The computational effectiveness of this system depends on two main factors: (a) reducing the number of attacks considered for the goal at hand by restricting only to attacks that are necessary, and (b) improving the effeciency of the satisfaction of the global constraints imposed by the t,p and r-propositions. A major optimization that we can apply with respect to the first factor concerns the consideration of persistence attacks.

Definition 4. *A* **restricted attack** *against a set S is a minimal attack on S which does not contain any persistence rule $PP[F,T';T]$ (resp. $NP[F,T';T]$) unless S contains the assumption rule $NA[F,T]$ (resp. $PA[F,T]$) and $B(D) \cup S \vdash HoldsAt(F,T')$ (resp. $B(D) \cup S \vdash \neg HoldsAt(F,T')$).*

Lemma 1. *Let D be a domain and S a set of argument rules that is consistent and attacks all the restricted attacks against it. Then there exists a superset of S which is admissible.*

This means that we only need to consider those persistence attacks against a set S that start from assumptions that are in S. In the implementation of $\mathcal{E}$-RES we exploit this lemma by considering a notion of *suspended* persistence attacks on an assumption which are activated whenever the contrary assumption (at another time point) is added to S.

5.1   Satisfiability of Constraints in $\mathcal{E}$-RES

The global constraints imposed by the t,p and r-propositions can be computationally demanding. Although most of these constraints refer to a single time point, those imposed by the ramification statements need to be satisfied at every time point and hence could be a major source of inefficiency. The lemma below allows us to address this by confining this task to a specific set of time points.

Lemma 2. *Let D be a domain and T_1, T_2 ($T_1 < T_2$) be time points such that there is no h-proposition in D at any time T in (T_1, T_2). Suppose also that there exists a partial model M_p of D defined over the whole time line minus the interval $(T_1, T_2]$, except at times points in $(T_1, T_2]$ where t-propositions are given in D where M_p satisfies the conditions imposed by these. M_p also satisfies any p-propositions at T_2. Then if there exists a time point T in $(T_1, T_2]$ such that M_p can be extended to a partial model covering also T then M_p can be extended to a full model of D.*

Hence when D contains only a finite number of h-propositions we can split the (linear) time line to a finite number of time intervals and satisfy the ramification constraints only at one time point in each of these intervals. $\mathcal{E}$-RES implements an interleaved process of (a) satisfiability of the ramification statements as classical implications at these time points and (b) cross-check of the assumptions required in (a) under the language $\mathcal{E}$ default persistence.

As the number of (ground) ramification constraints at each time point can be large we can employ a SAT solver [6] within the $\mathcal{E}$-RES system to carry out this process (a) of generating a classical model for these. Furthermore, we have considered a notion of *relevancy* of ramifications to the query at hand which, assuming that D is consistent, selects at each time point only a subset of ramification constraints. Therefore we now have an iterative (over the finite number of time points) process of interleaving between: (i) projecting the assumptions, that we have added to S so far, to the current time point and selecting the relevant ramification constraints based on these, (ii) generating a classical model of these constraints using a SAT solver given the partial instatiation generated in (i), and (iii) ensuring the compatibility of this model with the arguments S computed so far at the previous time points. Note that the output of steps (ii) and (iii) could affect the set of relevant ramifications computed in (i) and hence we need to repeat the whole process before going to the next time point.

Initial experiments with this iterative method indicate a significant reduction in the computation. Note however that we are still left with the problem of deciding which t-propositions are relevant to the query/goal at hand. Currently, we assume that these are selected externally to the system.

The $\mathcal{E}$-RES system is currently implemented in Prolog (Eclipse 4.2). An interface allows the user to define directly in the syntax of the language $\mathcal{E}$ the domain description. The system also supports some extra forms of auxiliary information, e.g. that a fluent is *constant* and so does not change over time. Open action types are specified together with their associated p-propositions and priority information amongst them that might exist. In addition, although $\mathcal{E}$ is defined as a propositional language the $\mathcal{E}$-RES system allows domain descriptions to be given in a non-propositional form under some restrictions. An early version of the system with examples is available from http://www.ucl.ac.uk/~uczcrsm/LanguageE/. New versions of the system will be added to this web site in the near future.

6   Related Work and Conclusions

Recently there has been a wide interest in developing specialized action languages [5]. These efforts have concentrated on the formal semantics of such languages and how they can be applied to specific problems. Examples of these are the language *Golog* [12] or the Fluent Calculus as developed in [15] for cognitive robotics, a circumscriptive Event Calculus [14] and the language $\mathcal{C}$ [8] for planning, and the language $\mathcal{L}$ together with others related to it [1,4] for the problem of diagnosis. Our work focuses on the general computational aspects of such languages using argumentation and abduction as a basis for a principled implementation of the language $\mathcal{E}$. A system, called Causal Calculator [13], which is based on the language $\mathcal{C}$ translates the whole representation into a propositional theory and then uses a SAT solver to find a solution to its query. A systematic comparison of the $\mathcal{E}$-RES system with these systems would be useful.

An interesting feature of our approach is the possibility it opens of synthesizing, in the implementation of these languages, the resolution based computation of argumentation and abduction in Logic Programming with the propositional satisfiability methods of SAT solvers. A SAT-based procedure has also been used recently in $\mathcal{C}$ [7] for planning. This hybrid computational model, that could also include other methods e.g. constraint solving, is an important topic of future work. Currently, the system is designed with emphasis on the complexity of reasoning that it can perform rather than on the efficiency of large scale computation. We are studying ways to improve this by investigating further notions of relevancy in order to dynamically focus the computation only on the parts of the theory, especially of t-propositions, that are needed for the query at hand.

References

1. C. Baral, S. McIlraith, and T. Son. Formulating diagnostic problem solving using an action language with narratives and sensing. In *KR-00*, 2000. 265
2. A. Bondarenko, P. M. Dung, R. A. Kowalski, and F. Toni. An abstract, argumentation-theoretic framework for default reasoning. *Journal of Artificial Inelligence*, 93(1-2):63–101, 1997. 254
3. D. Dimopoulos and A. C. Kakas. Logic programming without negation as failure. In *Proc. of ILPS'95*, volume pp. 369-383, 1995. 254
4. M. Gelfond and J. Galloway. Diagnosing dynamic systems in a-prolog. In *Answer Set Programming, AAAI Symposium (to appear)*, 2001. 265
5. M. Gelfond and V. Lifschitz. Action languages. In *ETAI*, volume 3(16), 1998. 265
6. I. Gent, H. van Maaren, and T. Walsh. *Highlights of Satisfiability Research in the Year 2000*. IOS Press, 2000. 255, 265
7. E. Giuchiglia. Planning as satisfiability with expressive action languages. In *KR-00*, 2000. 266
8. E. Giuchiglia and V. Lifschitz. An action language based on casual explanation. In *AAAI-98*, pages 623–630, 1998. 265
9. A. C. Kakas, R. A. Kowalski, and F. Toni. The role of abduction in logic programming. In *Handbook of Logic in AI and Logic Programming*, volume 5, pages 235–324. OU Press, 1998. 254, 257
10. A. C. Kakas and R. S. Miller. A simple declarative language for describing narratives with actions. In *JLP 31(1-3), pp. 157-200*, 1997. 254
11. A. C. Kakas, R. S. Miller, and F. Toni. An argumentation framework for reasoning about actions and change. In *LPNMR'99, 78–91, Springer Verlag*, 1999. 257
12. H. Levesque, R. Reiter, Y. Lesperance, F. Lin, and R. Scherl. Golog: A logic programming language for dynamic domains. *Logic Programming*, 31:59–84, 1997. 265
13. N. McCain. *Causality in Commonsense Reasoning about Actions*. PhD thesis, University of Texas at Austin, 1997. 266
14. M. Shanahan. An abductive event calculus planner. *Logic Programming*, 44(1-3):207–239, 2000. 265

15. M. Thielscher. Representing the knowledge of a robot. In *Proc.KR00*, pages 109–120, 2000. 265

Omega-Restricted Logic Programs

Tommi Syrjänen

Helsinki University of Technology, Dept. of Computer Science and Eng., Laboratory
for Theoretical Computer Science,
P.O.Box 5400, FIN-02015 HUT, Finland
Tommi.Syrjanen@hut.fi

Abstract. We define a new syntactic class of logic programs, omega-restricted programs. We divide the predicate symbols of a logic program into two parts: domain and non-domain predicates, where the domain predicates are defined by the maximal stratifiable subset of the rules of the program. We extend the usual definition of stratification by adding a special omega-stratum that holds all unstratifiable predicates of the program. We demand that all variables that occur in a rule also occur in the rule body in a positive literal that is on a lower stratum than rule head. This restriction is syntactic and can be checked efficiently. The existence of a stable model of an omega-restricted program is decidable even when function symbols are allowed. We prove that the problem is 2-**NEXP**-complete and identify subclasses of omega-restricted programs such that the problem stays in **NEXP** or **NP**. The class of omega-restricted programs is implemented in the SMODELS system.

1 Introduction

The answer set programming (ASP) paradigm has gained popularity in the recent years as a number of ASP systems have become available (for example, DeReS [3], dlv [6], and SMODELS [12]). The basic idea of ASP is to encode a problem as a logic program such that the answer sets (stable models) of the program correspond to the solutions of the problem. We then use a logic program engine to find the answer sets of the program. The underlying formal semantics is usually based on some extension of the stable model semantics of normal logic programs [7].

The inference engines of the existing systems work with ground programs, that is, programs without variables. A rule with variables represents the set of ground rules that can be created by replacing the variables in it by constant terms that occur in the program. This instantiation is done in a preprocessing step before the actual inference engine is used. This bottom-up approach to variable use has prevented the use of function symbols since even one function symbol in a program forces its Herbrand instantiation to be infinite. However, in most cases it is enough to examine only a small subset of the Herbrand instantiation since vast majority of the rules will have unsatisfiable bodies so they can be left out without affecting the set of stable models. This holds true

T. Eiter, W. Faber, and M. Truszczyński (Eds.): LPNMR 2001, LNAI 2173, pp. 267–280, 2001.
© Springer-Verlag Berlin Heidelberg 2001

even when function symbols are allowed; it is possible that all answer sets of a program are finite and computable even if the Herbrand instantiation is infinite.

The aim of this work is to define a new class of logic programs, ω-restricted programs, that are syntactically guaranteed to be decidable even when function symbols are used. The basic idea is to construct a hierarchy of predicates such that the predicates on the lowest level are defined using only ground facts and all variables that occur in a rule of level $n + 1$ have to also occur in a positive literal of level n or lower in the rule body. The definition of the hierarchy extends the usual concept of stratification [1] by adding a special ω-stratum to hold the unstratifiable part of a program.

It turns out that this syntactic restriction is strong enough to guarantee finite answer sets. In fact, we will see that deciding whether an ω-restricted program has an answer set is 2-**NEXP**-complete. Since the stable model semantics of logic programs without functions is **NEXP**-complete [4], we can conclude that by using ω-restricted functions we move up one step in the exponential hierarchy. This result also implies that we cannot solve all computable problems using ω-restricted programs. Recently P. Bonatti [2] has proposed a computationally complete class of logic programs called finitary programs. However, together with Turing equivalence comes semi-decidability of general reasoning problems.

The ω-restricted programs have been implemented in the SMODELS system [12] that has been designed in Helsinki University of Technology. The SMODELS system is available at http://www.tcs.hut.fi/Software/smodels.

In the following sections we will use the following program to illustrate the basic concepts of ω-restriction:

$$
\begin{aligned}
number(0) &\leftarrow\ ;\cdots;number(n) \leftarrow \\
odd(x+1) &\leftarrow number(x), even(x) \\
even(x+1) &\leftarrow number(x), odd(x) \\
even(0) &\leftarrow \\
two\_divides(x) &\leftarrow even(x) \\
interesting(x) &\leftarrow number(x), \text{not } dull(x) \\
dull(x) &\leftarrow number(x), \text{not } interesting(x) \\
interesting\_odd(x) &\leftarrow odd(x), interesting(x)\ .
\end{aligned}
\tag{1}
$$

2   The Stable Model Semantics

The basic component of a logic program is an *atom* of the form:

$$
p(t_1, \ldots, t_n)
\tag{2}
$$

where p is a n-ary predicate symbol ($n \geq 0$) and t_1, ..., t_n are terms. A *term* is either a variable v, a constant c, or an m-ary function symbol $f(t_1, \ldots, t_m)$ where t_1, ..., t_m are terms. We denote the predicate symbol of an atom A by $pred(A)$. A *literal* is either an atom A or its negation not A.

The set $\mathcal{V}(t)$ of variables that *occur in* a term is defined as follows:

$$\mathcal{V}(t) = \begin{cases} \emptyset & \text{, if } t \text{ is a constant;} \\ \{t\} & \text{, if } t \text{ is a variable; and} \\ \bigcup_{i=1}^{m} \mathcal{V}(t_i) & \text{, if } t \text{ is a function } f(t_1, \ldots, t_m) \ . \end{cases} \tag{3}$$

A variable occurs in a literal if it occurs in at least one of its arguments:

$$\mathcal{V}(a(t_1, \ldots, t_n)) = \bigcup_{i=1}^{n} \mathcal{V}(t_i) \ . \tag{4}$$

An inference *rule* R is of the form:

$$h \leftarrow l_1, \ldots, l_n \ , \tag{5}$$

where the *head* h is an atom and l_1, ..., l_n in the *body* are literals. The sets of positive and negative literals in the body of R are denoted by $body^+(R)$ and $body^-(R)$ respectively. Intuitively, a rule asserts that if all literals in the rule body are true, then the head must be true also. A *logic program* P is a finite set of rules. We denote the set of predicate symbols that occur in P with $preds(P)$.

The set of variables that occur in a rule R is defined in terms of variables that occur in its literals:

$$\mathcal{V}(R) = \mathcal{V}(head(R)) \cup \bigcup_{l \in body(R)} \mathcal{V}(l) \ . \tag{6}$$

A rule is *ground* if $\mathcal{V}(R) = \emptyset$.

Let P be a variable-free logic program and M be a set of atoms that occur in P. Then, the Gelfond-Lifschitz reduct P^M is obtained by:

1. removing each rule with a negative literal not A in its body where $A \in M$.
2. removing all negative literals form the bodies of the remaining rules.

Since P^M is negation-free, it has a unique least model M'. If the model M' coincides with M, then M is a *stable model* of P.

The *Herbrand universe* $\mathbf{HU}(P)$ of a logic program P is the set of constant terms that can be formed using the constants and function symbols of P. A *ground instance* of a literal or a rule can be obtained by replacing variables in it by terms in $\mathbf{HU}(P)$. The *Herbrand instantiation* P_G is the set of all possible instantiations of rules in P. The set of stable models of a logic program P with variables is defined to be the set of stable models of its instantiation P_G. In practice, we usually do not have to construct the full Herbrand instantiation to be able to construct all stable models. Hereafter we will use the term *instantiation* of P to mean any subset of P_G that has the same set of stable models.

Example 1. Let P be the program:

$$\begin{aligned} a(1) &\leftarrow ; \qquad a(2) \leftarrow \\ b(x) &\leftarrow a(x), \text{not } c(x) \\ c(x) &\leftarrow a(x), \text{not } b(x) \ . \end{aligned} \tag{7}$$

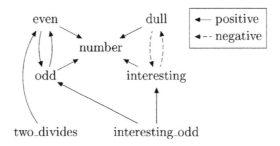

Fig. 1. The dependency graph of Program (1)

Then, the instantiation P_G is:

$$
\begin{array}{ll}
a(1) \leftarrow & a(2) \leftarrow \\
b(1) \leftarrow a(1), \text{not } c(1) & b(2) \leftarrow a(2), \text{not } c(2) \\
c(1) \leftarrow a(1), \text{not } b(1) & c(2) \leftarrow a(2), \text{not } b(2) \ .
\end{array}
\tag{8}
$$

Now, P_G has four stable models: $M_1 = \{a(1), a(2), b(1), b(2)\}$, $M_2 = \{a(1), a(2), b(1), c(2)\}$, $M_3 = \{a(1), a(2), c(1), b(2)\}$, and $M_4 = \{a(1), a(2), c(1), c(2)\}$. Consider M_1. The reduct $P_G^{M_1}$ is the program:

$$
b(1) \leftarrow; \quad b(2) \leftarrow; \quad a(1) \leftarrow; \quad a(2) \leftarrow \ .
\tag{9}
$$

The least model of $P_G^{M_1} = \{a(1), a(2), b(1), b(2)\} = M_1$, so we see that M_1 is really a stable model of P_G and hence of P.

A *spitting set* of a normal logic program P is a set of ground atoms U such that for all rules R in P_G if $head(R)$ is in U, then all atoms occurring in the rule body are also in U. We denote the set of ground rules whose heads are in U with $b_U(P_G)$. Given an an evaluation I of atoms in U, we denote by $e_U(P_G, I)$ the set of ground rules that is obtained by removing from P_G all rules that have a literal l containing an atom of U that is not satisfied by I and removing all literals l containing a member of U from the bodies of the remaining rules. By Splitting Set Theorem [8], M is a stable model of P_G only if $M = I \cup J$ where I is a stable model of $b_U(P_G)$ and J is a stable model of $e_U(P_G \setminus b_U(P), I)$.

3   Omega-Restricted Logic Programs

In this section we give a formal definition for ω-restricted programs. The main idea is to construct a stratification of the predicate symbols such that a predicate p is on a higher level than a predicate q if p is defined in terms of q. We start by formalizing the concept of dependency between predicate symbols.

Definition 1. *Let P be a logic program. Then, the one-step dependency relation $D_1(P) \subseteq preds(P) \times preds(P)$ is defined as follows:*

1. $D_1^+(P) = \{\langle pred(a), pred(l) \rangle \mid \exists R \in P : a = head(R) \wedge l \in body^+(R)\}$
2. $D_1^-(P) = \{\langle pred(a), pred(l) \rangle \mid \exists R \in P : a = head(R) \wedge l \in body^-(R)\}$
3. $D_1(P) = D_1^+(P) \cup D_1^-(P)$.

The one-step dependency relation may be drawn as a graph. For example, the dependency graph of Program (1) is shown in Figure 1.

We now generalize the one-step dependency relation to a full dependency relation. The intuition is that a predicate p depends on a predicate q if there is a path from p to q in the dependency graph. If at least one of the edges between p and q is negative, then p depends negatively on q.

Definition 2. *A* dependency path π_P *of a logic program P is a sequence*

$$\pi_P = \langle p_1, p_2, \ldots, p_n \rangle \tag{10}$$

where $p_i \in preds(P)$ for $1 \leq i \leq n$ and $\langle p_j, p_{j+1} \rangle \in D_1(P)$ for $1 \leq j < n$. A path π_P is negative (denoted by $\overline{\pi}_P$) if and only if $\langle p_j, p_{j+1} \rangle \in D_1^-(P)$ for some $1 \leq j < n$.

Definition 3. *The* dependency relation $D(P) \subseteq preds(P) \times preds(P)$ *of a logic program P is defined as follows:*

1. $D^+(P) = \{\langle p, q \rangle \mid \exists \pi_P : \pi_P = \langle p, \ldots, q \rangle\}$;
2. $D^-(P) = \{\langle p, q \rangle \mid \exists \overline{\pi}_P : \overline{\pi}_P = \langle p, \ldots, q \rangle\}$; *and*
3. $D(P) = D^+(P) \cup D^-(P)$.

Next, we define the concept of ω-stratification. The definition extends the traditional definition of stratification [1] by adding a new stratum, the ω-stratum, for the predicates that depend negatively on each other.

Definition 4. *An ω-stratification of a program P is a function $\mathcal{S} : preds(P) \rightarrow \mathbb{N} \cup \{\omega\}$ such that:*

1. $\forall p_1 \forall p_2 (\langle p_1, p_2 \rangle \in D^+(P) \Rightarrow \mathcal{S}(p_1) \geq \mathcal{S}(p_2))$; *and*
2. $\forall p_1 \forall p_2 (\langle p_1, p_2 \rangle \in D^-(P) \Rightarrow \mathcal{S}(p_1) > \mathcal{S}(p_2) \vee \mathcal{S}(p_1) = \omega)$.

We use the convention that $\omega > n$ for all $n \in \mathbb{N}$. The first condition asserts that a predicate p_1 that depends positively on a predicate p_2 has to be on at least as high stratum as p_2. The second condition states that if p_1 depends negatively on p_2, then p_1 has to be on a higher stratum or they both must be in the ω-stratum. In practice, we are interested in stratifications that are strict in the sense that $\mathcal{S}(p_1) > \mathcal{S}(p_2)$ whenever p_1 depends on p_2 but not vice versa.

Example 2. Consider Program (1). We can construct an ω-stratification $\mathcal{S}$ for it by looking at its dependency graph. As there are no edges leading from *number*, we can set $\mathcal{S}(number) = 0$. Predicates *even* and *odd* depend on *number* and each other, so we set $\mathcal{S}(even) = \mathcal{S}(odd) = 1$. Continuing this, *two_divides* depends on *even* so $\mathcal{S}(two\_divides) = 2$. The negative cycle of *interesting* and *odd* forces that $\mathcal{S}(interesting) = \mathcal{S}(odd) = \mathcal{S}(interesting\_odd) = \omega$. This stratification is shown in Figure 2.

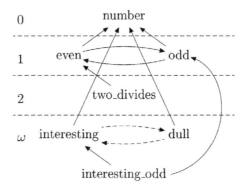

Fig. 2. A stratification of Program (1)

Next, we will extend the ω-stratification to cover also rules and variables by defining the concept of an ω-valuation.

Definition 5. *The ω-valuation of a rule R under an ω-stratification $\mathcal{S}$ is the function:*

$$\Omega(R, \mathcal{S}) = \mathcal{S}(pred(head(R)))$$

The ω-valuation of a variable v in a rule R under an ω-stratification $\mathcal{S}$ is the function:

$$\Omega(v, R, \mathcal{S}) = \min(\{\mathcal{S}(pred(a)) \mid a \in body^+(R) \wedge v \in \mathcal{V}(a)\} \cup \{\omega\})$$

Example 3. Let $\mathcal{S}$ be as defined in Example 2. Consider the rule

$$R: \quad interesting(x) \leftarrow number(x), not\ dull(x)\ .$$

Now

$$\Omega(R, \mathcal{S}) = \mathcal{S}(interesting) = \omega$$
$$\Omega(x, R, \mathcal{S}) = \min\{\mathcal{S}(number), \mathcal{S}(dull), \omega\} = \min\{0, \omega\} = 0\ .$$

A rule is ω-restricted if all variables that occur in it also occur in a positive body literal that belongs to a strictly lower stratum than the head.

Definition 6. *Let R be a rule in a logic program P. Then R is ω-restricted if and only if there exists an ω-stratification $\mathcal{S}$ such that:*

$$\forall v \in \mathcal{V}(R): \Omega(v, R, \mathcal{S}) < \Omega(R, \mathcal{S})\ .$$

Definition 7. *Let P be an logic program. Then P is ω-restricted if and only if all rules $R \in P$ are ω-restricted.*

Example 4. Consider the rule:

$$s(x+1) \leftarrow s(x)$$

This rule is not ω-restricted since for all ω-stratifications, $\Omega(R, \mathcal{S}) = \Omega(x, R, \mathcal{S})$.

Finally, we divide the predicate symbols into two classes, domain predicates that are on finite strata and non-domain predicates that are on the ω-stratum. The domain predicates are defined by the maximal stratifiable subset of the rules of the program.

Definition 8. *Let P be an ω-restricted program. Then a predicate $p \in preds(P)$ is a* domain predicate *if and only if there exists an ω-stratification $\mathcal{S}$ such that $\mathcal{S}(p) < \omega$. The set of rules defining domain predicates of P is denoted by $\mathcal{D}(P)$.*

4   Domain Predicates and Instantiation

The subprogram $\mathcal{D}(P)$ defining the domain predicates of P is stratified, so it has a unique least model $M_{\mathcal{D}(P)}$. It is easy to verify that $M_{\mathcal{D}(P)}$ is a splitting set of P. Thus, we can compute the stable models of P by first computing $M_{\mathcal{D}(P)}$ and then extending it to cover the atoms on ω-stratum. Moreover, each variable that occurs in a rule R occurs also in a positive domain literal so we can create all relevant ground instances of R by computing the natural join of extensions of the domain literals in $body(R)$.

We can compute $M_{\mathcal{D}(P)}$ and the instantiation P_{NG} of $P_N = P \setminus \mathcal{D}(P)$ using the following algorithm:

1. Find all strongly connected components of the dependency graph of P. Each component becomes a new stratum with the exception that all components that have a path to a negative dependency cycle are put on the ω-stratum. Order the different strata by doing a depth-first search over the strongly connected components.
2. Instantiate the predicates on finite strata starting from the lowest one. After instantiation, compute the deductive closure of the new ground rules and store the resulting atoms as facts in a database. These facts are then used to give domains for variables when we instantiate the rules on higher strata.
3. Finally, instantiate all rules on the ω-stratum and output them along with the domain facts.

5   Computational Complexity

In this section we examine the computational complexity of ω-restricted programs. We are interested in two problems:

− In INSTANTIATION we have an ω-restricted program P and a ground atom $p(t_1, \ldots, t_n)$ and we want to find whether one of the following conditions holds:

Table 1. Computational complexity

		INSTANTIATION	MODEL
No variables		—	**NP**-complete
Fixed variables	No functions	**P**-complete	**NP**-complete
	With functions	**EXP**-complete	**NEXP**-complete
Unlimited variables	No functions	**EXP**-complete	**NEXP**-complete
	With functions	2-**EXP**-complete	2-**NEXP**-complete

    1. $p(t_1, \ldots, t_n) \in M_{\mathcal{D}(P)}$; or
    2. There is a rule $p(t_1, \ldots, t_n) \leftarrow l_1, \ldots, l_n$ in P_{NG}.
 – In MODEL we want to find out whether an ω-restricted program P has an
  answer set.

The instantiation complexity is included in the model complexity in all cases
since we may have to construct the full instantiation of a program before we
know whether it has any stable models at all.

    In addition to proving complexity results for the whole class of ω-restricted
programs, we examine how the computational complexities of INSTANTIATION
and MODEL change when we restrict our attention to some subclasses of programs. We use two parameters to divide the ω-restricted programs into four
classes:

 – The maximum number of variables in a rule is either fixed to some constant d
  or it is unlimited; and
 – Function symbols are either allowed or not.

    The main complexity results are presented in Table 1. The MODEL complexi-
ties of function-free normal logic programs with the stable model semantics have
been presented in earlier literature [10,4]. The corresponding complexity classes
of function-free ω-restricted programs are the same so we see that at least in
these categories ω-restricted programs are as expressive as normal logic programs. Since the MODEL problem of the unrestricted case is 2-**NEXP**-complete,
we know that ω-restricted programs are decidable:

Theorem 1. *Both* INSTANTIATION *and* MODEL *are decidable for ω-restricted
programs.*

5.1   Turing Machine Translation

Most of the complexity results of this work are derived by proving that the
computations of a deterministic Turing machine M can be simulated by a logic
program P such that the size of P is polynomial with respect to the size of M.

Definition 9. *A deterministic Turing machine $M = (K, \Sigma, \delta, s)$ where K is a
finite set of states, Σ is a finite alphabet containing the blank symbol $\sqcup$, $s \in K$
is the initial state and δ is a transition function $\delta : K \times \Sigma \to (K \cup \{y, n\}) \times \Sigma \times
\{-1, 0, 1\}$.*

A computation of a Turing machine M given an input x starts from the configuration $(s, \sqcup x)$ and each computation step yields a new configuration according to δ until one of the halting states y (*accept*) or n (*reject*) is reached.

We encode the states of a Turing machine M using the predicate $state(q)$, the alphabet using $symbol(\sigma)$, and the transitions using $transition(q_1, \sigma_1, q_2, \sigma_2, d)$, where $d \in \{-1, 0, +1\}$. The atom $at\text{-}place(\sigma, p, t)$ is used to denote that the input tape cell p contains the symbol σ at the time step t. The predicate $current\text{-}state(q, p, \sigma, t)$ indicates that the machine is in the state q and the head is over the tape cell p looking at the symbol σ at the time step t.

We encode one computation step using the two rules:

$$\begin{aligned}
at\text{-}place(s_2, p, t+1) \leftarrow{}& transition(q_1, s_1, q_2, s_2, d), \\
& current\text{-}state(q_1, p, s_1, t), \quad\quad (11) \\
& place(p), time(t)
\end{aligned}$$

$$\begin{aligned}
current\text{-}state(q_2, p+d, s_3, t+1) \leftarrow{}& transition(q_1, s_1, q_2, s_2, d), \\
& current\text{-}state(q_1, p, s_1, t), \quad\quad (12) \\
& at\text{-}place(s_3, p+d, t), time(t), \\
& place(p), symbol(s_3) \;.
\end{aligned}$$

Here we have used the notation $t + 1$ to denote the successor of t. How the successor relation is actually defined depends on the program class that we want to examine. The same thing holds also for predecessor relation that is used in the case of $p - 1$.

The rules above handle the cell where the read/write-head is currently positioned. In addition, we have to assert that the state of the other tape cells stays constant:

$$\begin{aligned}
at\text{-}place(s_1, p_1, t+1) \leftarrow{}& current\text{-}state(q, p_2, s_2, t), \\
& at\text{-}place(s_1, p_1, t), time(t), \\
& symbol(s_1), symbol(s_2), state(q), \quad\quad (13) \\
& place(p_1), place(p_2), not\ equal(p_1, p_2) \;.
\end{aligned}$$

In the initial configuration all tape cells that are not part of the input are empty:

$$at\text{-}place(\sqcup, p, 1) \leftarrow place(p), not\ part\text{-}of\text{-}input(p) \;. \quad\quad (14)$$

The first $|x|$ tape cells are initialized from the input and they also belong to the extension of $part\text{-}of\text{-}input/1$. Finally, we want to recognize whether the Turing machine halts in an accepting state or not:

$$\begin{aligned}
accept \leftarrow{}& current\text{-}state(y, p, s, t), place(p), symbol(s), time(t) \\
& \quad\quad\quad\quad\quad\quad\quad\quad\quad\quad\quad\quad\quad\quad\quad\quad (15) \\
reject \leftarrow{}& current\text{-}state(n, p, s, t), place(p), symbol(s), time(t) \;.
\end{aligned}$$

Note that we have not yet given definitions for the predicates $time/1$ and $place/1$ that encode the time steps and tape cells. In the following complexity proofs we show how we can define them in a polynomial number of rules using tools that are available for the four different ω-restricted program classes.

Since all rules except (13) and (14) in the translation are negation-free and both negations are over a predicate with a fixed extension that is linear to the size of the input program, the least model of the instantiation can be found in a linear time with respect to its size [5]. All predicates are domain predicates and we can easily find whether *accept* or *reject* is true in $M_{\mathcal{D}(P)}$.

We can generalize the translation to allow non-deterministic Turing machines by forcing the machine to choose between possible transitions at all computation steps. Due to space constraints, we do not include the details here but one possible translation has been presented by V. W. Marek and J. B. Remmel [9]. The existence of such a translation is enough to prove the following lemma:

Lemma 1. *If the* INSTANTIATION *problem of a subclass of the ω-restricted programs is* **C**-*complete for some complexity class* **C***, the corresponding* MODEL *problem is* **NC**-*complete.*

5.2   Complexity Results

Theorem 2. *The* INSTANTIATION *of an ω-restricted program is* **P**-*complete when the number d of variables occurring in it is fixed ($d \geq 3$) and no function symbols are allowed.*

Proof. We construct the proof in two parts:

(a) *Inclusion.* Let P be a program with d distinct variables. Then, each rule has at most n^d ground instances, where n is the number of constants in the program.

(b) *Hardness.* The **P**-complete problem BOOLEAN CIRCUIT VALUE [11] can be expressed as an ω-restricted logic program as follows:

$$true(G) \leftarrow nand\text{-}gate(G, L, R), false(L)$$
$$true(G) \leftarrow nand\text{-}gate(G, L, R), false(R) \tag{16}$$
$$false(G) \leftarrow nand\text{-}gate(G, L, R), true(L), true(R) \ .$$

Here we suppose that the Boolean circuit is implemented using only not-and gates and that the truth values of the input gates are given as facts.

Corollary 1. *The* MODEL *problem for a fixed number d of variables and no function symbols is* **NP**-*complete, if $d \geq 3$.*

Theorem 3. *The* INSTANTIATION *of an unlimited-variable ω-restricted program is* **EXP**-*complete if no function symbols are allowed.*

Proof. For inclusion, see Dantsin *et.al.* [4]. The hardness can be proved by noting that a deterministic **EXP**-time Turing machine M uses at most 2^{n^k} time steps for some k when the length of the input is n. We have to show that we can generate an exponential number of atoms representing time steps and tape cells using a program whose size is polynomial with respect to the size of M. To do this, we need to implement a n^k-bit binary counter that runs from 0 to $2^{n^k} - 1$. This can be done by encoding the numbers as vectors of binary variables:

$$
\begin{aligned}
number(0, \ldots, 0) &\leftarrow \\
number(y_1, \ldots, y_{n^k}) &\leftarrow bit(y_1), \ldots, bit(y_{n^k}), \\
&\quad number(x_1, \ldots, x_{n^k}), \\
&\quad next(x_1, \ldots, x_{n^k}, y_1, \ldots, y_{n^k}) \ .
\end{aligned}
\tag{17}
$$

The predicate $bit/1$ is an auxiliary with the extension $\{bit(0), bit(1)\}$ that is used to ensure that the rule is ω-restricted. The successor relation can be encoded with the rule:

$$
\begin{aligned}
next(x_1, \ldots, x_{n^k}, y_1, \ldots, y_{n^k}) &\leftarrow add(x_1, 1, y_1, c_1), \\
&\quad add(x_2, c_1, y_2, c_2), \\
&\quad \vdots \\
&\quad add(x_{n^k}, c_{n^k-1}, y_{n^k}, c_{n^k})
\end{aligned}
\tag{18}
$$

where $add/4$ is defined using the following four facts:

$$
\begin{aligned}
add(0,1,1,0) &\leftarrow & add(0,0,0,0) &\leftarrow \\
add(1,0,1,0) &\leftarrow & add(1,1,0,1) &\leftarrow \ .
\end{aligned}
\tag{19}
$$

We can implement the predecessor function by switching the arguments of the $next$ predicate. Now the time steps and tape positions can be defined in terms of numbers:

$$
\begin{aligned}
time(x_1, \ldots, x_{n^k}) &\leftarrow number(x_1, \ldots, x_{n^k}) \\
place(x_1, \ldots, x_{n^k}) &\leftarrow number(x_1, \ldots, x_{n^k}) \ .
\end{aligned}
\tag{20}
$$

Finally, we replace all references to $time/1$ and $place/1$ by $time/n^k$ and $place/n^k$ and add all necessary domain predicates to the rule bodies.

Theorem 4. *The* INSTANTIATION *of a fixed-variable ω-restricted program that uses function symbols is* **EXP***-complete, if $d \geq 8$.*

Proof.

(a) *Inclusion.* Without a loss of generality we may assume that there are k strata with c rules each in P. Let us use a_n to denote the number of ground instances of rules that belong to the first n strata.

Since the number d of variables is fixed, a rule on the $n + 1$-stratum may have at most a_n^d ground instances. Now we can establish an upper bound for the number of ground instances of rules on the stratum $n + 1$ or lower:

$$
\begin{aligned}
a_{n+1} = c \cdot a_n^d + a_n &\leq c \cdot a_n^d + c \cdot a_n^d \qquad \text{(when } d \geq 1\text{)} \\
&= 2c \cdot a_n^d \\
&= 2^{d^{n-1}+d^{n-2}+\cdots+d+1} \cdot c^{d^n+d^{n-1}+\cdots+d+1} \\
&= 2^{(\log_2 c)d^n + (\log_2 c+1)d^{n-1}\cdots+(\log_2 c+1)}
\end{aligned}
\tag{21}
$$

As both c and d are linear with respect to the size of the program, a_n grows $O(2^{n^{2k}})$ so the problem is in **EXP**.

(b) *Hardness.* As in the proof of Theorem 3, we need only to construct a binary counter from 0 up to $2^{n^k} - 1$. We do this by encoding an m-bit binary number x as a function $b_1(b_2(\cdots b_m(0)\cdots))$ where b_i is f if the ith bit of x is 0 and t if it is 1. The m-bit binary numbers can be generated recursively from $m-1$-bit numbers by the following two rules:

$$
\begin{aligned}
number_m(t(x)) &\leftarrow number_{m-1}(x) \\
number_m(f(x)) &\leftarrow number_{m-1}(x)
\end{aligned}
\tag{22}
$$

Here we need $m+1$ different *number* predicates since otherwise the rules would not be ω-restricted. As the basic basic case of the recursion, we define one 0-bit number as:

$$number_0(0) \leftarrow \quad . \tag{23}$$

The successor relation can also be defined recursively:

$$
\begin{aligned}
next_m(t(x), t(y)) &\leftarrow next_{m-1}(x, y) \\
next_m(f(x), f(y)) &\leftarrow next_{m-1}(x, y) \\
next_m(f(x), t(y)) &\leftarrow last_{m-1}(x), first_{m-1}(y)
\end{aligned}
\tag{24}
$$

where $last_m/1$ and $first_m/1$ are defined as:

$$
\begin{aligned}
last_m(t^m(0)) &\leftarrow \\
first_m(f^m(0)) &\leftarrow \quad .
\end{aligned}
\tag{25}
$$

The translation uses $7n^k + 3$ rules to create all n^k-bit numbers so we now have a polynomial reduction from **EXP**-time Turing machines to ω-restricted programs using only function symbols and the proof is completed.

Corollary 2. *The* MODEL *problem of a fixed-variable ω-restricted program that uses function symbols is* **NEXP***-complete, if $d \geq 8$.*

Theorem 5. *The* INSTANTIATION *of an ω-restricted program is* 2-**EXP***-complete.*

Proof. We can combine the proofs of Theorems 3 and 4 to see that the problem is in 2-**EXP** and that it is possible to implement all 2^{n^k}-bit integers putting together the two different exponential constructions.

Corollary 3. *The* MODEL *problem of an ω-restricted program is* 2-**NEXP***-complete.*

6   Conclusions

We defined a new class of logic programs, ω-restricted programs, that are decidable even when function symbols are used. We showed that the computational complexity of the program class is 2-**NEXP**-complete. If we make further restrictions either by fixing the maximum number of variables that may occur in a rule or by disallowing the function symbols, the complexity drops to **NEXP**-complete. If both restrictions are in effect, the complexity stays **NP**-complete. We have implemented the ω-restricted programs in the SMODELS system.

Acknowledgements

The author is grateful for the anonymous referees for their comments. The financial support of HeCSE graduate school, Academy of Finland (project no. 43963), and Tekniikan edistämissäätiö are gratefully acknowledged.

References

1. K. R. Apt and R. Bol. Logic programming and negation: A survey. *Journal of Logic Programming*, 19–20:9–71, 1994. 268, 271
2. Piero A. Bonatti. Resoning with infinite stable models. In *Proceedings of the 17th International Joint Conference on Artificial Intelligence*, August 2001. 268
3. Paweł Cholewiński, Victor W. Marek, and Miroslaw Truszczyński. Default reasoning system DeReS. In Luigia Carlucci Aiello, Jon Doyle, and Stuart Shapiro, editors, *KR'96: Principles of Knowledge Representation and Reasoning*, pages 518–528. Morgan Kaufmann, San Francisco, California, 1996. 267
4. Evgeny Dantsin, Thomas Eiter, Georg Gottlob, and Andrei Voronkov. Complexity and expressive power of logic programming. In *Proceedings of the Twelfth Annual IEEE Conference on Computational Complexity*, pages 82–101, Ulm, Germany, June 1997. IEEE Computer Society Press. 268, 274, 276
5. W. F. Dowling and J. H. Gallier. Linear-time algorithms for testing the satisfiability of propositional Horn formulae. *Journal of Logic Programming*, 3:267–284, 1984. 276
6. Eiter, T., Leone, N., Pfeifer G., Mateis C., and Scarcello, F. The kr system dlv: Progress report, comparisons and benchmarks. In *Proceedings of the Sixth International Conference on Principles of Knowledge Representation and Reasoning (KR'98)*, pages 406–417. Morgan Kaufmann Publishers, 1998. 267
7. M. Gelfond and V. Lifschitz. The stable model semantics for logic programming. In *Proc. of the 5th ICLP*, pages 1070–1080. The MIT Press, 1988. 267
8. Vladimir Lifschitz and Hudson Turner. Splitting a logic program. In *Proceedings of the Eleventh International Conference on Logic Programming*, pages 23–37, 1994. 270
9. V. W. Marek and J. B. Remmel. On the foundations of answer set programming. In *Answer Set Programming: Towards Efficient and Scalable Knowledge Representation and Reasoning*, pages 124–131. AAAI Press, March 2001. 276
10. W. Marek and M. Truszczyński. Autoepistemic logic. *Journal of the Association for Computing Machinery*, 38:588–619, 1991. 274

11. Christos H. Papadimitriou. *Computational Complexity*. Addison-Wesley Publishing Company, Inc, 1994. 276
12. Tommi Syrjänen and Ilkka Niemelä. The smodels system. In *Proceedings of the 6th International Conference on Logic Programming and Nonmonotonic Reasoning*, Vienna, Austria, September 2001. Springer-Verlag. 267, 268

Improving ASP Instantiators by Join-Ordering Methods

Nicola Leone[1], Simona Perri[1], and Francesco Scarcello[2]

[1] Department of Mathematics, University of Calabria
I-87030 Rende (CS), Italy
leone@unical.it
sperri@si.deis.unical.it
[2] D.E.I.S., University of Calabria
87030 Rende (CS), Italy
scarcello@deis.unical.it

Abstract. Most Answer Set Programming (ASP) systems, including **DLV** and Smodels, are endowed with an instantiation module. The instantiator generates a new program which is equivalent to the input program, but does not contain any variables (i.e., it is ground). Normal (i.e., disjunction-free) stratified programs are completely solved by the instantiator, which generates the output model directly.

The instantiation process may be computationally expensive in some cases, and the instantiator is crucial for the efficiency of the entire ASP system. In this paper, we propose to employ join-ordering techniques to improve the instantiation process. We design a new join-ordering method, and adapt a classical database method to this context. We implement these techniques in the ASP system **DLV**, and we carry out an experimentation activity on a collection of benchmark problems taken from different domains. The results of experiments are very positive, the new techniques improve sensibly the efficiency of the **DLV** system, whose instantiation module confirms to be a main strong point of **DLV** w.r.t. the other ASP systems.

1 Introduction

The recent implementation of knowledge base systems which efficiently support expressive logic-based languages, like **DLV** [5], Smodels [14], DCS [1], XSB [17] , QUIP [2], and CCALC [13], has renewed the interest in the area of non-monotonic reasoning and declarative logic programming. The advances made in this area allow us to use ASP systems, like **DLV** and Smodels, for solving real-world problems in a number of application areas, including planning, scheduling as well as for complex data manipulations [3] [19]. For instance, Smodels is being used for the automatic configuration of software distributions; while the latest application of **DLV**, issued by the italian national statistics institute (ISTAT), concerns the automatic correction of census data.

These systems support a fully declarative programming style, called *Answer Set Programming* (ASP). The knowledge representation language of ASP is very

T. Eiter, W. Faber, and M. Truszczyński (Eds.): LPNMR 2001, LNAI 2173, pp. 280–294, 2001.

expressive: function-free logic programs where nonmonotonic negation may occur in the bodies of the rules, and possibly (i.e., for some systems) with classical negation and disjunction in the heads of the rules. The semantics of an ASP program P is given by its *answer sets* [10], which are subset-minimal models of P, and are "grounded" in a precise sense. The idea of answer set programming is to represent a given computational problem by an ASP program whose answer sets correspond to solutions, and then use an answer set solver to find such a solution [12].

As an example, consider the well-known problem of 3-colorability, which is the assignment of three colors to the nodes of a graph in such a way that adjacent nodes have different colors. This problem is known to be NP-complete. Suppose that the nodes and the arcs are represented by a set F of facts with predicates *node* (unary) and *arc* (binary), respectively (*node* and *arc* can be stored in the tables representing the input database). Then, the following ASP program allows us to determine the admissible ways of coloring the given graph.

$$r_1: \quad color(X, r) \vee color(X, y) \vee color(X, g) \leftarrow node(X)$$
$$r_2: \quad \leftarrow arc(X, Y), color(X, C), color(Y, C)$$

Rule r_1 above states that every node of the graph is colored **red** or **yellow** or **green**, while r_2 forbids the assignment of the same color to any adjacent nodes. The minimality of answer sets guarantees that every node is assigned only one color. Thus, there is a one-to-one correspondence between the solutions of the 3-coloring problem and the answer sets of $F \cup \{r_1, r_2\}$. The graph is 3-colorable if and only if $F \cup \{r_1, r_2\}$ has some answer set.

ASP is very expressive: *every* problem in the complexity class Σ_2^P (i.e., in $\mathrm{NP^{NP}}$) can be directly encoded in an ASP program which can then be used to solve all problem instances in a uniform way [4]. The high expressiveness of answer set programming comes at the price of a high computational cost in the worst case. Indeed, computing an answer set of a disjunctive (resp. normal) propositional ASP program is Σ_2^P-hard (resp., NP-hard). The design and the implementation of suitable optimization techniques is therefore fundamental for ASP systems.

The kernel modules of the ASP systems operate on a ground instantiation of the input program, i.e., a program that does not contain any variables, but is (semantically) equivalent to the original input [5]. Therefore, an efficient instantiation procedure is of utmost importance.[1] The efficiency of an instantiation procedure can be measured in terms of the size of its output and the time needed to generate this instantiation. In a previous work, the **DLV** team has presented some rewriting techniques which reduce the size of the generated grounding instantiation [6]. In this paper we optimize the execution time needed to generate the grounding instantiation. The main contribution of the paper is the following:

– We propose the use of join-ordering techniques to improve the efficiency of the instantiation procedures of ASP systems. In particular, a join-optimization

---

[1] Note that the disjunction-free stratified programs are "solved" by the instantiation procedure, which provides the answer and does not generate any instantiation in this case. Thus, the instantiator alone has the full power of a deductive database system.

technique can be employed to re-order the body literals of a rule during the instantiation process.
– We design a new join-ordering method, and adapt a classical database method to our context.
– We implement the above join-ordering methods in the ASP system **DLV**.
– To check the impact of our methods on the instantiator of **DLV**, we experimentally compare the techniques that we implemented.
– To assess the validity of our results more in general, we compare also the instantiator of **DLV**, resulting from our enhancements, to the newest version of the instantiator of Smodels, released on March 2001.

The results of the experiments are very positive, it seems that the new techniques improve sensibly the efficiency of the **DLV** instantiator, which compares favourably against the instantiator of Smodels.

2   The Instantiation Procedure of DLV

In this section, we provide a short description of the overall instantiation module of the **DLV** system, and focus on the "heart" procedure of this module which produces all ground instances of a given rule, which will be optimized in the next sections through the introduction of the join-ordering methods. We assume that the reader is familiar with ASP syntax and semantics. An extensive description can be found in [10] and [3].

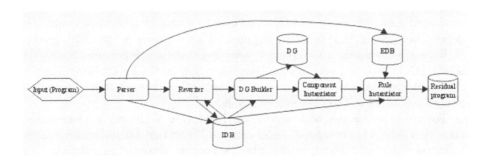

Fig. 1. Architecture of **DLV**'s Instantiator

The aim of the instantiator is mainly twofold: (i) to evaluate (∨-free) stratified programs components, and (ii) to generate the instantiation of disjunctive or unstratified components (if the input program is disjunctive or unstratified).
In order to evaluate efficiently stratified programs (components), **DLV** uses an improved version of the generalized semi-naive technique [20] implemented for the evaluation of linear and non-linear recursive rules.

If the input program is normal (i.e., ∨-free) and stratified, the instantiator evaluates completely the program and no further module is employed after the grounding; the program has a single answer set, namely the set of the facts and the atoms derived by the instantiation procedure. If the input program is disjunctive or unstratified, the instantiation procedure cannot evaluate completely the program. However, the optimization techniques mentioned above are useful to generate efficiently the instantiation of the non-monotonic part of the program. Two aspects are crucial for the instantiation:

(a) the number of generated ground rules,
(b) the time needed to generate such an instantiation.

The size of the generated instantiation is important because it strongly influences the computation time of the other modules of the system. A slower instantiation procedure generating a smaller grounding may be preferable to a faster one generating a large grounding. However, the time needed by the former can not be ignored otherwise we could not really have a computation time gain.

The main reason of large groundings even for small input programs is that each atom of a rule in $\mathcal{P}$ may be instantiated to many atoms in $B_{\mathcal{P}}$, which leads to combinatorial explosion. However, most of these atoms may not be derivable whatsoever, and hence such instantiations do not render applicable rules. The instantiator module generates ground instances of rules containing only atoms which can possibly be derived from $\mathcal{P}$.

In Figure 1 we have depicted the general structure of the instantiator module. An input program $\mathcal{P}$ is first analyzed from the parser, which also builds the extensional database from the facts in the program, and encodes the rules in the intensional database in a suitable way. Then, a rewriting procedure (see [6]), optimizes the rules in order to get an equivalent program $\mathcal{P}'$ that can be instantiated more efficiently and that can lead to a smaller ground program. The dependency graph (DG) builder computes the dependency graph of $\mathcal{P}'$, its connected components, and a topological ordering of these components. Finally, $\mathcal{P}'$ is instantiated one component at a time, starting from the lowest components in the topological ordering, i.e., those components that depend on no other component according to the dependency graph.

For space reasons we omit a detailed description of the whole instantiation algorithm here. The interested reader can find the instantiation algorithm in the technical report [7]. Below, we describe the process of rule's instantiation – the "heart" of the instantiation module – which we optimize in the next section by introducing join-ordering methods.

Let us first introduce some notations. We denote by $H(r)$ the set $\{a_1, ..., a_n\}$ of the head atoms, and by $B(r)$ the set $\{b_1, ..., b_k, \neg b_{k+1}, ..., \neg b_m\}$ of the body literals. $B^+(r)$ (resp., $B^-(r)$) denotes the set of atoms occurring positively (resp., negatively) in $B(r)$. For a literal L, $var(L)$ denotes the set of variables occurring in L. For a conjunction (or a set) of literals C, $var(C)$ denotes the set of variables occurring in the literals in C, and, for a rule r, $var(r) = var(H(r)) \cup var(B(r))$.

The procedure *InstantiateRule*, shown in Figure 2, generates the ground instances of a rule r of a program $\mathcal{P}$. When this procedure is called for the rule r,

Forward Procedure *FirstMatch*(θ: Substitution, A: Atom, var MatchFound: Boolean, var θ': Substitution);

(* Given a partial substitution θ for the rule's variables, and an atom A of the body, the procedure computes the first tuple t of the relation corresponding to A which matches with θ. It returns in θ' the extension of θ, where the free variables of A have been instantiated with the corresponding constants in t. The boolean variable MatchFound evaluates True iff such a matching tuple has been found; otherwise it evaluates False, and θ' is meaningless. *)

Forward Procedure *NextMatch*(θ: Substitution, A: Atom, var MatchFound: Boolean, var θ': Substitution);   (* Similar to FirstMatch, but finds the next matching tuple. *)

Function *InstantiateConjunction*(C: Conjunction; θ: Substitution) : SetOfSubsts;
var MatchFound:Boolean; A:Atom; B:Conjunction; θ':Substitution; S:SetOfSubsts;
begin
    if C is empty (* the end of the body has been reached,
        θ is a legal substitution *)
    then return($\{\theta\}$);
    $S := \emptyset$; $A :=$ first_conjunct(C); $B :=$ rest_conjunct(C);
    FirstMatch(θ,A,MatchFound,θ');
    while MatchFound **do**
        $S := S \cup$ InstantiateConjunction(B,θ');
        NextMatch(θ,A,MatchFound,θ');
    end_while;
    return(S);
end;

Function *InstantiateRule*(r: Rule): SetOfGroundRules;
var θ: Substitution; S: SetOfSubstitutions;
begin
    Let B_r^+ denote the Conjunction of the positive literals in the body of r;
    Order_Body(B_r^+);
    $\theta :=$ empty_substitution;
    S := InstantiateConjunction(B_r^+,θ);
    return ($\{\gamma r \mid \gamma \in S\}$);
end;

Fig. 2. The process of rule's instantiation

for each atom A occurring in the body of r, the set of ground instances I_A for A previously computed by the instantiator is collected in a relation $rel(A)$ that we call the extension of A. Each ground instance for $a \in I_A$ corresponds to a tuple in $rel(A)$ and vice versa. More precisely, each tuple of constants in the relation $rel(A)$ corresponds to a substitution $\theta : var(A) \to U_{\mathcal{P}}$ such that $\theta A \in I_a$, and vice versa. Such a substitution θ is called a valid substitution for r with respect to the given extensions of the atoms occurring in its body. Intuitively, *Instantiate Rule* performs the natural join of the relations associated with the positive body literals of the rule. Since the rule is safe, each rule's variable appears also in a positive body literal of the rule. Therefore, such a join is in a one-to-one correspondence with the set of all ground instances of the rule which are constructable from the set of available instances for the body atoms; each tuple of this join corresponds to a valid substitution for r with respect to the given extensions of atoms.

Roughly, InstantiateRule first orders the conjunction B_r^+ of the positive body literals of the rule r to be instantiated (by a call to procedure Order_Body, which will be described in the next section), and then calls the function InstantiateConjunction which actually computes the legal instantiations of B_r^+. This function starts from the first atom A in the conjunction B_r^+. It finds, by a call to function FirstMatch, the first tuple t matching with A in the relation $rel(A)$ associated with A, and binds its variables to the corresponding constants in t. Then, by a recursive call to InstantiateConjunction itself, this function takes the second atom, say A' in B_r^+, and binds its free variables (note that some variables of A' are already bound, if they appear also in A) by finding the first matching tuple in $rel(A')$. The process goes on until either (i) the end of the conjunction has been reached (C is empty in function InstantiateConjunction), or (ii) no matching tuple is found for some body atom (a call to a match function returned MatchFound=False). In the latter case, the (partial) substitution θ at hand is not good, since no instance of the current atom agrees with θ. Therefore, the current run of function InstantiateConjunction terminates, the calling function changes θ by finding another matching tuple, and restarts the forward instantiation phase. In the former case (i.e., in case (i)), the substitution at hand (the parameter θ previously computed by the matching functions) is returned, as it instantiates all rule's variables and hence induces a ground instance of the rule r. The calling function adds θ to the set S of the computed substitutions, and finds another match for the atom at its hand to generate further ground instances of r. The process terminates when no more match are found (i.e., no more ground instances can be generated).

3   Join-Ordering Methods

From the previous section, it should be clear enough that computing all the possible instantiations of a rule given the relations associated to the atoms occurring in its body is equivalent to computing all the answers of the conjunctive query joining the relations of the positive literals of the rule's body. A key issue for the efficient instantiation of (the non-trivial rule) r is thus the optimal ordering of literals in the body. This problem clearly corresponds to the choice of an optimal execution ordering for the join operations in a conjunctive query.

A good ordering dramatically affects the overall computation time. Many relevant real-world examples containing large relations (see next section) cannot be solved without a suitable ordering of the body atoms.

It is worthwhile noting that in ASP programs we have to instantiate many rules and, for recursive programs, we have to instantiate the same rule many times, possibly with different relations (until we reach a fixpoint). Therefore, the ordering procedure is called very often and should be done efficiently.

Let r be a rule and B_r^+ the conjunction of the atoms occurring in its body. Our procedure *Order_Body* gets as its input B_r^+ and modifies the ordering of atoms in this conjunction in order to minimize the instantiation time of r.

To choose an optimal ordering, we exploit some information about the relations associated to the atoms in B_r^+, also called the extensions of these atoms. For each atom A occurring in B_r^+, we know the number $T(A)$ of tuples in its associated relation $rel(A)$ and, for each variable $X \in var(A)$, the number $V(X, A)$ of distinct values for X over $rel(A)$ (i.e., the number of tuples in the projection of $rel(A)$ onto X).

Recall that the relations associated to the atoms of r change, in general, at each call to *InstantiateRule(r)*. Of course, there is more than one call only if r belongs to some recursive component of the program.

In order to meet both the requirements of efficiency of the optimization procedure and of efficiency of the instantiation procedure, we employed a greedy algorithm, very similar to the one used in traditional database systems for selecting an optimal left-deep join tree for a given conjunctive query [9]. Roughly, at each step $i > 1$, we have placed the first $i - 1$ atoms, and we make a greedy choice to select the ith atom in the final ordering of B_r^+. This atom, say A, is chosen if A is minimal with respect to some selectivity criterion.

For the sake of simplicity, we will use the name of an atom A to represent both the atom and its extension $rel(A)$, whenever no confusion arises. We will denote by B_{i-1} the set of the first $i - 1$ atoms and by $rel(B_{i-1})$ (or, simply, by B_{i-1}) the relation obtained computing the join of all the extensions of the first $i - 1$ atoms. Hence, the number of tuples $T(B_{i-1})$ in this relation is equal to the number of consistent substitutions for the atoms in $B(i-1)$. Moreover, we denote by $var(B_{i-1})$ the set of variables occurring in B_{i-1}. These variables are called the *bound variables* at step i. Therefore, for any bound variable $X \in var(B_{i-1})$, $V(X, B_{i-1})$ is the number of distinct values that X may take over the computed relation B_{i-1} (or, equivalently, over the set of consistent substitutions for the atoms in B_{i-1}). We estimate these numbers during the ordering procedure from the statistics we have for the single atoms, rather than explicitly computing them at each step. Indeed, in this phase, we do not compute any join (or substitution).

We next describe three selectivity criteria that we implemented in the **DLV** system. The first is the one used in the current version of **DLV** [8], the second is an adapted version of a criterion used in the context of traditional database systems [9], and the third is specifically designed for our purposes.

3.1   Old-DLV Criterion

This is the simple method implemented in the current versions of **DLV** [8]. Let D be the set of all atoms in $B_r^+ - B_{i-1}$ having some bound variable at this step, i.e., having a variable in common with some atom in B_{i-1}.

We select the atom A to be placed in the ith position of the ordered body as follows:

- if $D \neq \emptyset$, then A is the atom belonging to D whose extension has the smallest cardinality over the atoms in D;
- otherwise, i.e., no remaining atom has any bound variable (at step i), A is the atom whose extension has the smallest cardinality over all atoms in $B_r^+ - B_{i-1}$.

Therefore, this method gives the maximum priority to the binding of variables, and then chooses on the basis of the cardinality of the extensions.

Example 1. Assume that we are computing the ground instantiation of a rule r and that we already placed the first $i-1$ atoms. Let X and Y be the bound variables at step i, i.e., $var(B_{i-1}) = \{X, Y\}$. Moreover, Let $P(X, X')$, $Q(Y, Y')$, and $R(X, Y, X', Y')$ the remaining atoms in the body of r, i.e., the atoms in $B(r) - B_{i-1}$, and assume the number of tuples in their extensions are $T(P) = 30$, $T(Q) = 6$, and $T(R) = 300$, respectively.

The Old-**DLV** criterion first looks for atoms having some bound variable. In this example, either X or Y occurs in every remaining atom. Thus, the Old-**DLV** criterion chooses $Q(Y, Y')$ as the ith atom because its extension has the smallest cardinality.

3.2   Join Selectivity Criterion

This method is widely used in relational database systems [9]. We take as the ith atom in the ordered body the atom $A \in B_r^+ - B_{i-1}$ that minimizes the following selectivity index: $sel_j(A) = T(B_{i-1} \bowtie A)/T(B_{i-1})$.
Thus, we take the atom A which leads to the smallest intermediate relation size, over all atoms that are still to be ordered.

The size of a join operation between two relations R and S is $T(R) \cdot T(S)$ if they do not have any variable in common; otherwise, it is estimated as follows:

$$T(R \bowtie S) = \frac{T(R) \cdot T(S)}{\prod_{X \in var(R) \cap var(S)} \max\{V(X, R), V(X, S)\}},$$

where $\prod$ denotes the product operation.

Example 2. Consider again the rule r in Example 1. We next show how the ith atom is chosen according to the join-selectivity criterion. In this case, we need some additional statistics. Let $V(X, B_{i-1}) = 30$ and $V(Y, B_{i-1}) = 5$ be the current estimation for the number of different values for the bound variables at step i, i.e., for X and Y. Moreover, assume the statistics for the bound variables occurring in the remaining atoms are $V(X, P) = 30$, $V(Y, Q) = 5$, $V(X, R) = 30$, and $V(Y, R) = 5$. Consider the atom $P(X, X')$. The Join-selectivity criterion assigns to this atom the following selectivity index:

$$sel(P) = \frac{T(B_{i-1}) \cdot T(P)}{\max\{V(X, B_{i-1}), V(X, P)\}} \cdot \frac{1}{T(B_{i-1})} = \frac{30}{30} = 1.$$

Similarly, the other atoms get $sel(Q) = 1.2$ and $sel(R) = 2$. Thus, according to the Join-selectivity criterion, the ith atom is $P(X, X')$.

Note that the above estimation of the size of a join is based on the following simplifying assumptions:

Containment of value sets. If $V(X, R) \leq V(X, S)$, then every possible value for variable X in R is also a possible value for X in S.

Preservation of value sets. If $Y \in var(S)$ is not a join attribute, i.e., $Y \notin var(R) \cap var(S)$, then $V(Y, R \bowtie S) = V(Y, S)$. That is, performing a join operation, we do not lose values for non-join variables.

The interested reader can find a more detailed discussion of these assumptions and of this selectivity criterion in [9].

Here, we just observe that, because of the above assumptions, after the choice of atom A, we update the statistics of the value sets of its variables as follows: $V(X, B_i) = \min\{V(X, A), V(X, B_{i-1})\}$, if X is a bound variable at step i; otherwise, $V(X, B_i) = V(X, A)$.

3.3   Combined Criterion

This selectivity criterion explicitly deals with both the size of the intermediate result and the binding of variables, trying to minimize both these factors.

For this criterion we exploit, as additional statistics, the size of the (active) domains for the variables occurring in r (with respect to the current call of *InstantiateRule(r)*). We estimate this number, denoted by $dom(X)$, by $\max_{A \in B_r^+} V(X, A)$. In other words, we assume that there is a relation $rel(A)$, associated to some $A \in B_r^+$, which provides the active domain for X, i.e., which contains all values for X that also occur in the extensions of other atoms in r. In practice, this is the case most of the times and, if not, $dom(X)$ is usually very close to the cardinality of the actual domain for X.

The combined criterion takes as the ith atom in the ordered body the atom $A \in B_r^+ - B_{i-1}$ that minimizes the selectivity index $sel_c(A) = sel_s(A) \cdot sel_b(A)$, where

$$sel_s(A) = \frac{T(B_{i-1} \ltimes A)}{\prod_{X \in Z} dom(X)}, \quad \text{and} \quad sel_b(A) = \prod_{Y \in var(B_{i-1}) \cap var(A)} \frac{V(Y, A)}{dom(Y)^2},$$

where Z is the set of variables that A has in common with some other atom occurring in B_r^+, $\ltimes$ denotes the semijoin operation, and $sel_b(A) = 1$ in the trivial case $var(B_{i-1}) \cap var(A) = \emptyset$.

Example 3. We show how the combined criterion acts on the same rule considered in Example 1 and Example 2. We estimate the cardinality of the active domains for the variables. From the given statistics, we get $dom(X) = 100$, $dom(Y) = 100$, $dom(X') = 20$ and $dom(Y') = 20$. For the atom $P(X, X')$, according to the Combined criterion, we compute

$$T(B_{i-1} \ltimes P) = T(P) \cdot \frac{V(X, B_{i-1})}{dom(X)} = 30 \cdot \frac{30}{100} = 9, \quad \text{and hence}$$

$$sel_s(P) = \frac{T(B_{i-1} \ltimes P)}{dom(X) \cdot dom(X')} = \frac{9}{100 \cdot 20} \quad \text{and} \quad sel_b(P) = \frac{V(X, P)}{dom(X)^2} = \frac{30}{100^2}.$$

Then, the selectivity index for P is

$$sel_c(P) = sel_s(P) * sel_b(P) = \frac{9}{100 \cdot 20} \cdot \frac{30}{100^2} = 1.35e^{-5}.$$

Similarly, for Q and R, we get $sel_c(Q) = 7.5e^{-8}$ and $sel_c(R) = 1.69e^{-12}$. It follows that, according to the Combined criterion we choose $R(X, Y, X', Y')$ as the ith atom in the ordered body of r. Note that, after the choice of this atom, all the variables become bound.

Note that the selectivity index $sel_s(A)$ is a measure of how much the choice of A reduces the search space for possible substitutions. In fact, for the set of variables Z that A has in common with some other atom in B_r^+, the full search space counts $\prod_{X \in Z} dom(X)$ possible substitutions (or, equivalently, this is the size of the full relation over these variables). However, only $m = T(B_{i-1} \bowtie A)$ tuples of A are compatible with the previously chosen atoms. Thus, m represents the new maximum number of tuples of values for the variables in Z. Note that this criterion leans to prefer the atoms with large arities. Assume the extensions of two atoms A' and A'' have the same cardinality, that the domains of all variables are the same, and that the arity of A' is greater than the arity of A''. Then, $sel_c(A')$ and $sel_c(A'')$ have the same numerators, however $sel_c(A')$ has a bigger denominator, and in fact, most likely, it provides a better reduction of the search space.

The selectivity index $sel_b(A)$ takes into account the bound variables of A. Indeed, by preferring atoms with already bound variables, we may detect very fast possible inconsistencies. The index $sel_b(A)$ is 1, if A has no variable in common with the previously chosen atoms; otherwise, it is always ≤ 1. It leans to prefer the atoms with the large number of bound variables, and having the smaller fraction of values with respect to the full domain cardinalities. Indeed, these atoms are the most promising for detecting possible inconsistencies with the previously chosen atoms.

In the implementation of this criterion, we make a further use of variables' domains for removing the assumption about containment of value sets. However, we keep the assumption, implicit in the classical join-size estimation, that values are distributed uniformly over their domains. It follows that the size of the semijoin operation can be estimated as follows:

$$T(R \bowtie S) = T(S) \cdot \prod_{X \in var(R) \cap var(S)} \frac{V(X, R)}{dom(X)}.$$

Moreover, after we choice an atom A, we update the statistics of the value sets of its variables as follows: $V(X, B_i) = V(X, B_{i-1}) \cdot (V(X, A)/dom(X))$, if X is a bound variable at step i; otherwise, $V(X, B_i) = V(X, A)$.

4   Experimental Results and Conclusion

4.1   Benchmark Programs

In order to check the efficiency of the proposed methods, we have implemented the methods in the grounding engine of the **DLV** system, and we have run them on a collection of benchmark programs taken from different domains. We mainly selected programs where the instantiation process is hard, and it takes a relevant part of the entire computation (like, e.g., CRISTAL, HANOI, RAMSEY), but we considered also a couple of problems where the instantiation process is easy compared to the process of model generation (like BLOCKSWORLD and HAMILTONIAN-PATH). For space limitation, we cannot include the code of the benchmark programs in the paper. Rather, we provide below a very short description of the problems which are encoded in the benchmark programs. The programs encoding these problems, as well as the binaries used for our experiments, can be found at url: `www.dbai.tuwien.ac.at/staff/leone/join-ordering/`

RAMSEY(3,6) $\neq$ **17** Prove that 17 is not the Ramsey number Ramsey(3,6)[16].

HANOI[6discs,63steps] Hanoi Towers with 6 discs and 63 steps.

CRISTAL deductive databases application that involves complex knowledge manipulations on databases, developed at CERN in Switzerland.

K-DECOMP Decide whether a conjunctive query has hypertree width at most K [11].

TIMETABLING A timetable problem for the first year of the faculty of Science of the University of Calabria.

HAMILTONIAN PATH Hamiltonian Path on a random graph with 700 edges and 85 nodes.

BLOCKSWORLD A typical planning problem where some blocks, placed on a table, have to be moved from an initial position to a desidered final position.

CONSTRAINT-3COL 3col, constraint-satisfaction like encoding, on a graph with 30 nodes and 40 edges.

4.2   Old-DLV Instantiator vs. the New Methods

We implemented in **DLV** the three criteria described in Section 3 and we compared them by using the above benchmark problems. All experiments were performed on an Athlon/750 machine with 256MB of main memory running FreeBSD 4.2. The binaries were produced with GCC 2.95.2.

Table 1. A comparison of the join-ordering methods of Section 3

Program	Old-DLV	JoinSel	Combined
RAMSEY(3,6)$\neq$ 17	64.10	8.98	8.50
HANOI[6discs,63steps]	12.20	71.65	14.58
CRISTAL	19.53	14.73	13.37
K-DECOMP	30.78	37.84	29.82
TIMETABLING	283.15	269.03	238.35
HAMILTONIAN-PATH	2.55	2.43	2.41
BLOCKSWORLD	3.17	3.48	2.99
CONSTRAINT-3COL	84.01	34.98	31.64

The results of our tests are shown in Table 1. There, the first column describes the benchmark program; Colums 2–4 report the running times employed to generate the instantiation by **DLV**, when method *Old*-**DLV**, *JoinSel* and *Combined* is used, respectively. All running times are expressed in seconds.

Old-**DLV**, the original technique employed in the **DLV** system, is the worst in most cases and it is outperformed by both *JoinSel* and *Combined*. It is worth noting, however, that Old-**DLV**criterion is not a "naive" method, it takes into account both the binding of variables and the size of the extensions of atoms. In fact, it performs quite well on a number of problems, e.g., HAMILTONIAN-PATH, BLOCKSWORLD, and K-DECOMP. In particular, in the latter case, it is better than the Join-selectivity approach. However, it gets worse for problems where rules contain many atoms or/and atoms with large extensions, like, e.g., RAMSEY and TIMETABLING.

The Join-selectivity criterion guarantees good performance on a large number of programs, because it is based on the minimization of the intermediate partial relation computed at each step. In some way, its formulation also takes into account the binding of variables. Indeed, a larger number of bound variables in an atom leads to more selective joins (i.e., joins with a smaller index).

The combined criterion yields the best performance for the considered problems on average. The main advantage of this criterion comes from the exploitation that large arity atoms can reduce the number of allowed substitutions for many variables at once, provided that their extensions are not too big. For this reason, the procedure based on this method outperforms the Join-selectivity method on HANOI, K-DECOMP and TIMETABLING. Thus, the combined criterion, that we proposed in this paper, seems to be appropriate for the purpose of body reordering. It is worthwhile noting that we also tried a number of variants of this criterion for tuning the contribution of the different factors. However, for the considered examples, the formula described in Section 3.3 has given the better results, on average.

4.3   The Enhanced DLV Instantiator vs. lparse

Finally, we compared the instantiator of **DLV** against *lparse*, the instantiator of Smodels [14] – a prominent ASP system[2]. The newest version of *lparse* (release 1.0.4, 03-21-2001) accepts logic programs respecting *extended-domain restriction*. This condition enforces each rule's variable to occur in a positive body literal, called domain literal, which (i) is not mutually recursive with the head, and (ii) is not unstratified nor (transitively) depends on an unstratified literal (see Smodels manual in [18] for details). To instantiate a rule r, lparse employs a nested loop scanning the extensions of the domain predicates occurring in its body, and generates the ground instances of r accordingly (i.e., by applying the substitutions obtained from the domain atoms and disregarding the substitutions violating either some built-in predicate or some variable patterns). Table 2 shows

---

[2] Since the benchmark programs are *head-cycle free* we could eliminate disjunction, and traslate them in the language accepted by lparse.

a comparison between the instantiator of **DLV** (with the combined criterion) and *lparse* (release 1.0.4). For both systems, we report the time (CPU+I/O time) they take to instantiate the program and the size (number of rules) of the output instantiation. The symbol '−' means that the instantiator did not terminate within 20 minutes.

Note that, even if both **DLV** and lparse compute ground programs that are equivalent (with respect to the answer set semantics), the sizes of the respective instantiations may differ significantly. This is due to the different ways they instantiate a rule r: **DLV** computes the join of the extensions of the positive literals in the body of r; while lparse enumerates with a nested loop all the extensions of the domain predicates in a rule. Thus, the strategy of lparse is computationally less expensive (since no join is computed) if the cartesian product of these extensions is small, i.e., if there are few domains to scan or they have small extensions. However, lparse may produce an unusefully larger instantiation than **DLV**, since the rules generated by lparse may contain non-domain body literals which are certainly not derivable (i.e., they do not appear in the head of any rule of the instantiation having an applicable body). Indeed, the results in Table 2 show that lparse is sometimes very fast and in fact faster than **DLV** (e.g., for K-DECOMP, TIMETABLING and HAMILTONIAN-PATH, where there are a few domain predicates in each rule); but the size of the lparse's instantiation is always larger than the size of the instantiation computed by **DLV**. The size difference is relevant if several atoms (directly or transitively) depend on unstratified literals, like, e.g., in TIMETABLING.

Table 2. The new instantiator of **DLV** vs the instantiator of Smodels

Program	DLV		lparse	
	time	size	time	size
RAMSEY(3,6)≠ 17	8.50	13,344	-	-
HANOI[6discs,63steps]	14.58	62,413	-	-
CRISTAL	13.37	20,978	-	-
K-DECOMP	29.82	121,798	9.81	123,165
TIMETABLING	238.35	199,551	88.60	3,002,700
HAMILTONIAN-PATH	2.41	49,674	1.04	52,511
BLOCKSWORLD	2.99	46,872	9.73	459,706
CONSTRAINT-3COL	31.64	7	805.4	7

However, realistic applications often work on large domains or require several variables per rule. It follows that, for meaningful problems like, e.g., CRISTAL, HANOI and RAMSEY,[3] lparse is not able to compute the instantiation in a

---

[3] HANOI and RAMSEY are the benchmark problems proposed at the AAAI Spring Symposium on ASP Programming, March 2001.

reasonable time (we stopped the program after 20 minutes). In CONSTRAINT-
3COL and RAMSEY variables domains are not large; however some rule contains
a large number of domains, whose cartesian product is big and slows down the
technique adopted by lparse.[4]

Moreover, in order to evaluate the quality of the ground program produced by
the two instantiators, we are making a number of experiments running Smodels on both the ground programs produced by the **DLV** instantiator and by
lparse. Our preliminary results on the benchmark examples are very interesting. For instance, lparse is faster than **DLV** in producing a ground program for
HAMILTONIAN-PATH. However, Smodels performs very bad with this program as its input, while it is very fast on the ground program produced by the
DLV instantiator.

Concluding, the experiments confirm that the database techniques that we
implemented in **DLV** are very useful. Even further techniques and results from
the field of database optimization should be carried out to the area of knowledge
base systems to improve the efficiency of these systems.

References

1. D. East and M. Truszczyński. dcs: An implementation of DATALOG with Constraints. In C. Baral and M. Truszczyński, editors, *Proc. of NMR'2000*, Colorado,
   USA, 2000.   280
2. U. Egly, T. Eiter, H. Tompits, and S. Woltran. Solving Advanced Reasoning Tasks
   using Quantified Boolean Formulas. In *Proc. of AAAI'00*, pp. 417–422.   280
3. T. Eiter, W. Faber, N. Leone, and G. Pfeifer. Declarative Problem-Solving Using
   the DLV System. In J. Minker, editor, *Logic-Based Artificial Intelligence*, pp. 79–
   103. Kluwer Academic Pub., 2000.   280, 282
4. T. Eiter, G. Gottlob, and H. Mannila. Disjunctive Datalog. *ACM TODS*,
   22(3):364–418, 1997.   281
5. T. Eiter, N. Leone, C. Mateis, G. Pfeifer, and F. Scarcello. A Deductive System
   for Nonmonotonic Reasoning. In *Proc. of LPNMR'97*, LNAI 1265, pp. 363–374,
   Berlin, 1997, Springer.   280, 281
6. W. Faber, N. Leone, C. Mateis, and G. Pfeifer. Using Database Optimization
   Techniques for Nonmonotonic Reasoning. In *Proc. of DDLP'99*, pp. 135–139. 1999.
   281, 283
7. W. Faber, N. Leone, C. Mateis, and G. Pfeifer. Using Database Optimization Techniques for Nonmonotonic Reasoning. Technical Report DBAI-TR-99-33, Institut
   für Informationssysteme, Technische Universität Wien, Austria, May 1999.   283
8. W. Faber and G. Pfeifer. **DLV** homepage. www.dbai.tuwien.ac.at/proj/dlv/.
   286
9. H. Garcia-Molina, J. D. Ullman, and J. Widom. *Database System Implementation*.
   Prentice Hall, 2000.   286, 287, 288

---

[4] Note that each disjunctive rule with 2 head-atoms is rewritten in 2 or-free rules for
lparse. Moreover, weight constraints – the higher level constructs of Smodels – could
provide a more succint encoding in some cases including, e.g., TIMETABLING and
BLOCKSWORLD, even if they do not appear helpful in RAMSEY, CRISTAL and
HANOI.

10. M. Gelfond and V. Lifschitz. Classical Negation in Logic Programs and Disjunctive Databases. *New Generation Computing*, 9:365–385, 1991. 281, 282

11. G. Gottlob, N. Leone, and F. Scarcello. Hypertree decompositions and tractable queries. In *Proc. of PODS'99*, pp. 21–32, May 1999. To appear in *JCSS*. 290

12. V. Lifschitz. Answer set planning. In D. D. Schreye, editor, *Proc. of ICLP'99*, pp. 23–37, Las Cruces, New Mexico, USA, Nov. 1999. The MIT Press. 281

13. N. McCain and H. Turner. Satisfiability planning with causal theories. *Proc. of KR'98*, pp. 212–223. Morgan Kaufmann Pub., 1998. 280

14. I. Niemelä and P. Simons. Smodels – an implementation of the stable model and well-founded semantics for normal logic programs. In *Proc. of LPNMR'97*, LNAI 1265, pp. 420–429, Dagstuhl, Germany, July 1997. Springer Verlag. 280, 291

15. T. C. Przymusinski. Stable Semantics for Disjunctive Programs. *New Generation Computing*, 9:401–424, 1991.

16. S. Radziszowski. Small Ramsey Numbers. *The Electronic Journal of Combinatorics*, 1, 1999. 290

17. P. Rao, K. F. Sagonas, T. Swift, D. S. Warren, and J. Freire. XSB: A System for Efficiently Computing Well-Founded Semantics. In *Proc. of LPNMR'97*, LNAI 1265, pp. 2–17, Dagstuhl, Germany, July 1997. Springer Verlag. 280

18. P. Simons. Smodels homepage. <www.tcs.hut.fi/Software/smodels/>. 291

19. P. Simons. *Extending and Implementing the Stable Model Semantics*. PhD thesis, Helsinki University of Technology, Finland, 2000. 280

20. J. D. Ullman. *Principles of Database and Knowledge Base Systems*. Computer Science Press, 1989. 282

Optimizing the Computation of Heuristics for Answer Set Programming Systems[*]

Wolfgang Faber[1], Nicola Leone[2], and Gerald Pfeifer[1]

[1] Institut für Informationssysteme, TU Wien
A-1040 Wien, Austria
faber@kr.tuwien.ac.at
pfeifer@dbai.tuwien.ac.at
[2] Department of Mathematics, University of Calabria
87030 Rende (CS), Italy
leone@unical.it

Abstract. Most SAT solvers and Answer Set Programming (ASP) systems employ a backtracking search by repeatedly assuming the truth of literals. The choice of these branching literals is crucial for the performance of these systems.

Competitive ASP systems employ advanced heuristics to select branching literals, which are usually based on "look-ahead" techniques: To evaluate the heuristic value of a literal L, truth and falsity of L are assumed in the current interpretation, consequences are derived, and the quality of the resulting interpretations is evaluated. This process can be very expensive, and often consumes most of the time taken by an ASP system.

In this paper, we present two techniques to optimize the computation of the heuristics in the ASP system DLV. The first technique singles out pairs of literals $\langle A, not\ B \rangle$ having precisely the same consequences, which allows for making only one look-ahead for each of these pairs. The second technique (inspired by SAT solvers) is a 2-layered heuristic, in which a simple heuristic criterion reduces the set of literals to be looked-ahead. We implement both techniques in the ASP system DLV and evaluate their efficiency on a number of benchmark problems taken from various domains. The experiments confirm the usefulness of both techniques, sensibly improving the performance of DLV.

1 Introduction

DLV is a knowledge representation system based on disjunctive logic programming (DLP) [Min82,GL91] offering front-ends to several Knowledge Representation (KR) formalisms [ELM+98b,ELM+98a,EFLP99]. A strong point of DLV is its highly expressive language, which allows elegant and natural representations of very hard problems (up to Σ_2^P-hard problems). DLV supports a declarative

---

[*] This work was supported by FWF (Austrian Science Funds) under the projects Z29-INF and P14781 and MURST under project COFIN-2000 "From Data to Information (D2I)".

T. Eiter, W. Faber, and M. Truszczyński (Eds.): LPNMR 2001, LNAI 2173, pp. 295–308, 2001.

programming style which has recently been termed *Answer Set Programming (ASP)*, hence it is referred to as an *ASP system*. The idea of ASP is to represent a given computational problem by a logic program whose answer sets correspond to solutions, and then use an answer set solver (like DLV) to compute them [Lif99].

An efficient support for the highly expressive language of DLV requires the use of smart algorithms and data structures as well as sophisticated optimization techniques in order to deal with such hard computational tasks.

DLV employs backtracking search by repeatedly assuming the truth of literals [FLP99], and in order to improve the efficiency of the DLV system, in a previous paper [FLP01] we have experimented with a number of heuristics for deciding which branching literal to assume. These heuristics are based on "look-ahead" techniques: to evaluate the heuristic value of a literal L w.r.t. the interpretation I at hand, truth and falsity of L are assumed in the current interpretation, and its consequences are derived by computing its deterministic extensions $I' = DetCons(I \cup \{L\})$ (the interpretation I' is guaranteed to be contained precisely in the same answer sets containing $I \cup \{L\}$) and $I'' = DetCons(I \cup \{\text{not } L\})$. Note that I' and I'' can be inconsistent, in which case the search space can be pruned early.

The heuristic value of L is a measure of the "quality" of the resulting interpretations I' and I''. Some of these heuristics proved to be very useful, as they drastically reduce the number of choice-points arising in an ASP computation. However, the computation of these heuristics is very expensive, since the number of literals to be "looked-ahead" is very large in some cases, and the cost of a look-ahead is linear in the size of the Herbrand Base in the worst case. The computation of the heuristics thus often consumes most of the total time taken by an ASP system, and may slow down the ASP system significantly.

In this paper, we try to reduce the amount of time needed to evaluate the heuristics, by reducing the number of look-aheads that need to be performed. The main contributions of the paper are the following:

A. We define a new condition which is sufficient to guarantee that, at a given stage of the computation, two literals $\langle A, \text{not } B \rangle$ have precisely the same set of deterministic consequences w.r.t. the interpretation I at hand, that is, $DetCons(I \cup \{A\}) = DetCons(I \cup \{\text{not } B\})$. Consequently, A and *not* B are guaranteed to have precisely the same heuristic values, and we avoid the look-ahead for one of them.

   This technique allows us to save 50% of the look-aheads in several cases including, e.g., Hamiltonian Path and 3SAT programs.

B. We design a 2-layered heuristic. A computationally cheap heuristic criterion reduces the set of literals to be considered, and the look-ahead to select the branching literal is applied only to the literals in this set. This method significantly reduces the number of look-aheads, but, unlike the previous technique, it is not an "exact" method, that is, it might exclude literals which would otherwise have had high heuristic values. Also some literals for which the look-ahead detects inconsistency can be missed in this way, so there will be less pruning in general.

C. We implement the above techniques in the ASP system DLV and evaluate their efficiency on a number of benchmark problems taken from various domains. The results of the experiments are very positive and both techniques prove to be useful. Moreover, they are orthogonal and their integration performs at least as well as the best individual technique, resulting in a relevant improvement of the performance of the DLV system.

In addition to the above contributions, we explain in detail the heuristic criterion adopted in DLV for the selection of the branching literal, and the way how it is computed.

It is worthwhile noting that techniques for reducing the number of look-aheads have been employed in SAT solvers and in other ASP systems. In particular, the ASP system Smodels makes a drastic pruning of the look-aheads by eliminating each literal which has been derived during a previous look-ahead at the same branch-point: For each literal $B \in DetCons(I \cup \{A\})$, the look-ahead for B is not performed, because B is guaranteed to be worse than A w.r.t. the heuristic function of Smodels. This technique eliminates a higher number of look-aheads than our technique described in Item A; but our technique is more general and it is applicable to a wider class of heuristic functions. Indeed, the technique of Smodels relies on a monotonicity property of the heuristic: $DetCons(I \cup \{B\}) \subset DetCons(I \cup \{A\})$ implies that B is worse than A w.r.t. the heuristic function of Smodels. Our technique, instead, is applicable to every criterion determining the heuristic value from the result of the look-ahead (i.e., the heuristic value of A depends only on $DetCons(I \cup \{A\})$). In fact, our technique can also be applied in Smodels, while the optimization employed by Smodels cannot be used in DLV, since the heuristic employed in DLV is not monotonic in the sense described above. A 2-layered heuristic similar to the technique of Item B above has been successfully employed in the SAT solver SATZ [LA97].

2   Answer Set Programming Language

In this section, we provide a formal definition of the syntax and semantics of the ASP language supported by DLV: disjunctive datalog extended with strong negation. For further background, see [GL91,EFLP00].

ASP Programs A *(disjunctive) rule r* is a formula

$$a_1 \ \lor \ \cdots \ \lor \ a_n \ \text{:-} \ b_1, \cdots, b_k, \ \text{not} \ b_{k+1}, \cdots, \ \text{not} \ b_m.$$

where $a_1, \cdots, a_n, b_1, \cdots, b_m$ are classical literals (atoms possibly preceded by the classical negation symbol $\neg$) and $n \geq 0$, $m \geq k \geq 0$. The disjunction $a_1 \lor \cdots \lor a_n$ is the *head* of r, while the conjunction $b_1, \cdots, b_k,$ not $b_{k+1}, \cdots,$ not b_m is the *body*, $b_1, \cdots, b_k$ the *positive body*, and not $b_{k+1}, \cdots,$ not b_m the *negative body* of r. The sets of literals in head, body, positive body and negative body of r, are denoted by $H(r)$, $B(r)$, $B^+(r)$, and $B^-(r)$, respectively. Comparison operators (like $=, <, >, <>$) are built-in predicates in ASP systems, and may appear in the bodies of rules. A *disjunctive datalog program* (also called *ASP program* in this paper) $\mathcal{P}$ is a finite set of rules.

As usual, an object (atom, rule, etc.) is called *ground* or *propositional*, if it contains no variables.

Answer Sets We describe the semantics of consistent answer sets, which has originally been defined in [GL91].

Given a program $\mathcal{P}$, let the *Herbrand Universe* $U_\mathcal{P}$ be the set of all constants appearing in $\mathcal{P}$ and the *Herbrand Base* $B_\mathcal{P}$ be the set of all possible combinations of predicate symbols appearing in $\mathcal{P}$ with constants of $U_\mathcal{P}$, possibly preceded by $\neg$.

Given a rule r, $Ground(r)$ denotes the set of rules obtained by applying all possible substitutions σ from the variables in r to elements of $U_\mathcal{P}$. Similarly, given a program $\mathcal{P}$, the *ground instantiation* $Ground(\mathcal{P})$ of $\mathcal{P}$ is the set $\bigcup_{r \in \mathcal{P}} Ground(r)$.

For every program $\mathcal{P}$, we define its answer sets using its ground instantiation $Ground(\mathcal{P})$ in two steps, following [Lif96]:

A set L of literals is said to be *consistent* if, for every literal $\ell \in L$, its complementary literal is not contained in L. An interpretation I is a consistent set of ground literals. An interpretation $I \subseteq B_\mathcal{P}$ is *closed under* $\mathcal{P}$ (where $\mathcal{P}$ is a positive program), if, for every $r \in Ground(\mathcal{P})$, at least one literal in the head is true whenever all literals in the body are true. I is an *answer set* for $\mathcal{P}$ if it is minimal w.r.t. set inclusion and closed under $\mathcal{P}$.

The *reduct* or *Gelfond-Lifschitz transform* of a general ground program $\mathcal{P}$ w.r.t. an interpretation I is the positive ground program $\mathcal{P}^I$, obtained from $\mathcal{P}$ by (i) deleting all rules $r \in \mathcal{P}$ whose negative body is false w.r.t. I, (ii) deleting the negative body from the remaining rules. An answer set of a general program $\mathcal{P}$ is an interpretation I such that I is an answer set of $Ground(\mathcal{P})^I$.

3   Answer Set Computation

In this section, we describe the main steps of the computational process performed by ASP systems. We will refer particularly to the computational engine of the DLV system, but also other ASP systems, like Smodels employ a very similar procedure.

An answer set program $\mathcal{P}$ in general contains variables. The first step of a computation of an ASP system eliminates these variables, generating a ground instantiation of $\mathcal{P}$.[1] The hard part of the computation is then performed on this ground ASP program.

The heart of the computation is performed by the Model Generator, which is sketched in Figure 1. Roughly, the Model Generator produces some "candidate"

---

[1] This ground instantiation is required to have precisely the same answer sets as $\mathcal{P}$, and is usually much smaller than $Ground(\mathcal{P})$ [FLMP99].

Forward Function DetCons(I: Interpretation): Interpretation;
(* Extends I with the literals that can be deterministically inferred and returns the
   resulting interpretation or the set of all literals $\mathcal{L}$ upon inconsistency. [FLP99] *)
Forward Procedure Select(var I: Interpretation, var L: ClassicalLiteral);
(* Selects the classical literal L having the highest heuristic value (see Section 4 *)

Function ModelGenerator(var I: Interpretation): Boolean;
 (* The function returns True iff I can be extended to an answer set. *)
var   inconsistency: Boolean;
begin
    I := DetCons(I);
    if I = $\mathcal{L}$ **then return** False;   (* inconsistency detected *)
    if no literal is undefined in I **then return** IsAnswerSet(I);
    Select(I,L);
    if ModelGenerator($I \cup \{L\}$) **then return** True;
    else return ModelGenerator($I \cup \{\text{not } L\}$);
end;

Fig. 1. Computation of Answer Sets

answer sets. The stability of each of these is subsequently verified by the function
IsAnswerSet(I), which checks whether the given "candidate" I is a minimal
model of the program $Ground(\mathcal{P})^I$, the reduct of $Ground(\mathcal{P})$ w.r.t. I.

The ModelGenerator function is first invoked with parameter I set to the
empty interpretation.[2] If the program $\mathcal{P}$ has an answer set, the function returns
True, setting I to that answer set; otherwise it returns False. The Model Generator is similar to the Davis-Putnam procedure employed by SAT solvers. It
first calls the function DetCons, which extends I with those literals that can
be deterministically inferred from I. DetCons is similar to a unit propagation
procedure employed by SAT solvers, but exploits the peculiarities of ASP for
making further inferences (e.g., it exploits the knowledge that every answer set
is a minimal model). If DetCons does not detect any inconsistency, a classical
literal L is selected according to a heuristic criterion by a call to the Select procedure. ModelGenerator is then recursively called on $I \cup \{L\}$; if this call does
not generate an answer set (i.e., $I \cup \{L\}$ is not contained in any answer set), it is
called on $I \cup \{\text{not } L\}$. The classical literal L plays the role of a branching variable
of a SAT solver. And indeed the selection of a "good" literal L is crucial for the
performance of an ASP system. In the next section, we describe the heuristic
criterion adopted by DLV for the selection of such branching literals, and how
Select is implemented.

---

[2]   Observe that the interpretations built during the computation are 3-valued and an
   interpretation I is a set of ground literals. A ground classical literal A is True (resp.
   False) w.r.t. to I if $A \in I$ (resp. not $A \in I$); otherwise A is Undefined w.r.t. I.

4   Evaluation of the Heuristic Function

In this section, we define the heuristic criterion adopted in the DLV system and we describe how it is evaluated.

The heuristics of DLV is a "dynamic heuristics" (the ASP equivalent of UP heuristics for SAT), that is, the heuristic value of a literal Q depends on the result of taking Q true as well as false and computing its consequences, respectively. In order to reduce the number of look-aheads, the DLV system does not evaluate the heuristic value of *all* undefined classical literals; rather, it considers only a subset of the undefined classical literals, called *possibly-true* literals. The correctness of this strategy, adopted since the first release of DLV, is shown in [LRS97].

Definition 1. A *Possibly-True (PT) literal* of $\mathcal{P}$ w.r.t. an interpretation I is an undefined classical literal p such that there exists a rule $r \in Ground(\mathcal{P})$ for which all of the following conditions hold:

1. p is in the head of r: $p \in H(r)$;
2. the head of r is not true w.r.t. I: $H(r) \cap I = \emptyset$;
3. the positive body of r is true w.r.t. I: $B^+(r) \subseteq (I)$;
4. the negative body of r is not false w.r.t. I: $I \cap \{a : \mathtt{not}\ a \in B^-(r)\} = \emptyset$.

The set of all PT literals of $\mathcal{P}$ w.r.t. I is denoted by $PT_{\mathcal{P}}(I)$.   □

Example 1. Consider the program $\mathcal{P} = \{a \vee b \text{ :- } c.\ d \text{ :- not } a, \mathtt{not}\ f.\ e \vee f \text{:-} k.\}$ and let $I = \{c\}$ be an interpretation for $\mathcal{P}$, then $PT_{\mathcal{P}}(I) = \{a, b, d\}$.

As shown in Figure 2 (initial **foreach** statement), DLV's heuristic function is evaluated only on the PT literals. It is worthwhile noting, however, that the PT literals do not always restrict the set of classical literals to be looked-ahead, since *all* undefined literals are PT in some cases. For instance, in the program encoding 3SAT (see Section 7.1) every undefined literal is a PT literal, as it occurs in the head of a rule having a true (empty) body. In contrast, in the program HAMPATH, at a given stage of the computation, the PTs are only those literals of the form $inPath(a, b)$ or $outPath(a, b)$, where a is a node already reached from the start ($reached(a)$ is True) and (a, b) is an arc of the input graph.

Let us now turn our attention to the heuristic criterion adopted in DLV to choose the "best" among the PT literals.

A peculiar property of answer sets is *supportedness*: For each true classical literal A in an answer set I, there exists a rule r of the program such that the body of r is true w.r.t. I and A is the only true literal in the head of r (r is then called a *supporting rule* for A). Since an ASP system must eventually converge to a supported interpretation, ASP systems try to keep the interpretations "as much supported as possible" during the intermediate steps of the computation. To this end, the DLV system counts the number of *UnsupportedTrue (UT)* literals, i.e., classical literals which are true in the current interpretation but still miss a supporting rule (in [FLP99] UTs, called MBTs there, are discussed in detail). For instance, the rule :- *not x* implies that x must be true in each answer set of

Procedure Select(var I: Interpretation, var L: ClassicalLiteral);
var I_A^+, I_A^-: Interpretation;
begin
   $L := NULL$;
   foreach $A \in PT_\mathcal{P}(I)$ **do**
        $I_A^+ := \text{DetCons}(I \cup \{A\})$;   (* look-ahead for A *)
        if $I_A^+ = \mathcal{L}$ **then** $I := I \cup \{\text{not } A\}$;
        else $I_A^- := \text{DetCons}(I \cup \{\text{not } A\})$; (* look-ahead for **not** A *)
            if $I_A^- = \mathcal{L}$ **then** $I := I \cup \{A\}$; **endif**
        endif
        if $I_A^+ \neq \mathcal{L}$ **and** $I_A^- \neq \mathcal{L}$ **then** (* no inconsistency has arisen *)
            if $L = NULL$ **then** $L := A$; (* first literal, no comparison *)
            (* compare A against L w.r.t. the heuristic; *)
            elseif ($UT(I_A^+) + UT(I_A^-)$) $<$ ($UT(I_L^+) + UT(I_L^-)$) **then** $L := A$;
            elseif ($UT_2(I_A^+) + UT_2(I_A^-)$) $<$ ($UT_2(I_L^+) + UT_2(I_L^-)$) **then** $L := A$;
            elseif ($UT_3(I_A^+) + UT_3(I_A^-)$) $<$ ($UT_3(I_L^+) + UT_3(I_L^-)$) **then** $L := A$;
            elseif ($US(I_A^+) + US(I_A^-)$) $<$ ($US(I_L^+) + US(I_L^-)$) **then** $L := A$;
   endfor
end;

Fig. 2. Selection of the Branching Literal by DLV's Heuristic

the program, but it does not give a "support" for x. Thus, in the DLV system x is assumed true in the current interpretation to satisfy that rule, and it is added to the set of UnsupportedTrue literals; it will be removed from this set once a supporting rule for x will be found (e.g., $x \lor b$:-c is a supporting rule for x in the interpretation $I = \{x, \text{not } b, c\}$).

Intuitively, since the set of UnsupportedTrue literals must eventually be empty when an answer set is reached, the heuristic of DLV tries to minimize the number of UT literals, taking particular care of those UT literals which are more "in danger" (an UT literal appearing in the head of fewer rules is more in danger than a literal appearing in the head of many rules).

Given an interpretation I, let $UT(I)$ be the number of UT literals in I. Moreover, let $UT_2(I)$ and $UT_3(I)$ be the number of UT literals occurring, respectively, in the heads of 2 and 3 rules (which are not already satisfied w.r.t. I, and can therefore be potentially used to support the UT literal).[3] The heuristic of DLV considers $UT(I)$, $UT_2(I)$ and $UT_3(I)$ in a prioritized way to favor literals yielding interpretations with fewer $UT/UT_2/UT_3$ literals (which should more likely lead to a supported model). If all UT counters are equal, then the heuristic minimizes $US(I)$ the number of unsatisfied rules w.r.t. I.

Since the failure of the computation branch selecting A True starts a new branch assuming **not** A (see last instruction in Figure 1), the heuristic criterion considers the effect of choosing a literal A and its complement **not** A in a balanced way. To this end, the counters $UT(I_A^+)$, $UT_2(I_A^+)$, $UT_3(I_A^+)$, and $US(I_A^+)$,

---

[3] UT_1 literals do not exist in DLV computations. Whenever a rule r is the last potentially supporting rule for an UT literal A, then A is inferred via r (see [FLP99]).

resulting from the look-ahead on $I \cup \{A\}$, are ordinately added to the counters $UT(I_A^-)$, $UT_2(I_A^-)$, $UT_3(I_A^-)$, and $US(I_A^-)$, resulting from the look-ahead on $I \cup \{\text{not } A\}$, when evaluating the heuristics.

5   Look-Ahead Equivalences

Dynamic heuristics vary only in the interpretation resulting from the function $DetCons(I_A^+)$ (resp. $DetCons(I_A^-)$). It is therefore interesting to identify cases where two literals L and L' are *look-ahead equivalent*, i.e., $DetCons(I_L) = DetCons(I_{L'})$, since one of the two look-ahead computations could be saved. This notion of equivalence is formalized next.

Definition 2. *Let p and q be two undefined literals w.r.t. an interpretation I. p and q are* look-ahead equivalent *if $DetCons(I \cup \{p\}) = DetCons(I \cup \{q\})$.*

To single out a sufficient and efficiently checkable condition which guarantees such an equivalence, we first define the notion of a *potentially supporting rule*:

Definition 3. *Given a program $\mathcal{P}$, a classical literal a, and a (3-valued) interpretation I, a rule $r \in \mathcal{P}$ is a* potentially supporting rule *for a w.r.t. I, if the following conditions are satisfied: (i) a occurs in the head of r, (ii) no literal in $H(r) - \{a\}$ is true w.r.t. I, and (iii) no literal in the body of r is false w.r.t. I. Let $psupp_{\mathcal{P}}(a, I)$ denote the number of potentially supporting rules for a.*

We can now formulate the following:

Proposition 1. *If two undefined classical literals a and b occur in the head of a rule r in a program $\mathcal{P}$, and a and b are the only undefined literals w.r.t. an interpretation I in r (where we assume that there is no multiple occurrence of classical literals in rules), then it holds that:*

1. *If $psupp_{\mathcal{P}}(b, I) = 1$, then a and $\text{not } b$ are look-ahead equivalent.*
2. *If $psupp_{\mathcal{P}}(a, I) = 1$, then $\text{not } a$ and b are look-ahead equivalent.*

Proof. *(Sketch)* Suppose $psupp_{\mathcal{P}}(b, I) = 1$. Then r is the only rule in $\mathcal{P}$ which might derive b. Since the body of r is already true in I, such a derivation is performed iff a becomes false. Therefore, $DetCons(I)$ either contains both a and $\text{not } b$ or it contains none of them. A symmetric argument shows item 2. □

Example 2. Consider the program $\{a \vee b.\}$ and $I = \emptyset$. Both a and b are PT literals, so look-ahead for a, $\text{not } a$, b, and $\text{not } b$ is performed, i.e. we compute $DetCons(\{a\}) = \{a, \text{not } b\}$, $DetCons(\{\text{not } a\}) = \{\text{not } a, b\}$, $DetCons(\{b\}) = \{\text{not } a, b\}$, and $DetCons(\{\text{not } b\}) = \{a, \text{not } b\}$. In this example we can save the look-aheads for $\text{not } b$ and b because of proposition 1, and thus save half of the look-aheads.

In DLV computations, we can recognize the applicability of Proposition 1 very efficiently and avoid extraneous look-aheads. Experimental results reported in Section 8 will show that we avoid up to 50% of look-aheads in some cases (e.g. on 3SAT) by exploiting this simple condition.

6   2-Layered Heuristic

In [LA97] a different idea on reducing look-aheads is presented: An easy-to-compute heuristics is defined as a first layer, and look-ahead is only computed on those possible choices which look promising w.r.t. to this easier heuristics. This gives a kind of 2-layered heuristic.

The simple heuristic criteria defined in [LA97] involve the number of *binary clauses* a classical literal occurs in. The rationale is that this is the number of immediate propagations that can be performed during the look-ahead. This idea can be directly transferred to our ASP framework:

Definition 4. *A binary clause is a rule which contains exactly two undefined classical literals w.r.t. an interpretation I. The number of binary occurrences of an undefined literal a is the number of binary clauses a occurs in.*

Note that this notion directly corresponds to the number of immediate propagations which can be performed by assuming a and not a, so it matches the intuition of [LA97]. To reduce the number of literals to be looked-ahead, we adopt the following criterion:

First-Layer Heuristic S_{bin}. Let $PT_{\mathcal{P}}(I)$ be the set of PT literals of a program $\mathcal{P}$ w.r.t. an interpretation I, and let $S_{bin} \subseteq PT_{\mathcal{P}}(I)$ be the set of PT literals having more than the average number of binary occurrences w.r.t. all literals in $PT_{\mathcal{P}}(I)$. Then, consider only the literals in S_{bin} for the selection of the branching literals (i.e., make look-ahead only on these literals).

Note that our first-layer heuristics is inspired by the same intuition as the first-layer heuristics in [LA97], even though it is not precisely the same.

7   Benchmarks

7.1   Benchmark Programs

To evaluate the impact of the two optimization techniques presented in the previous sections, we chose a couple of benchmark problems: 3SAT, Blocksworld Planning, Hamiltonian Path, and Strategic Companies.

3SAT is one of the best researched problems in AI and generally used for solving many other problems by translating them to 3SAT, solving the 3SAT problem, and transforming the solution back to the original domain:

> Let Φ be a propositional formula in conjunctive normal form (CNF) $\Phi = \bigwedge_{i=1}^{n}(d_{i,1} \vee \ldots \vee d_{i,3})$ where the $d_{i,j}$ are literals over the propositional variables $x_1, \ldots, x_m$. Φ is satisfiable, iff there exists a consistent conjunction I of literals such that $I \models \Phi$.

3SAT is a classical NP-complete problem and can be easily represented in our formalism as follows: For each propositional variable x_i ($1 \leq i \leq$ m), we add the following rule which ensures that we either assume that variable x_i or its complement nx_i true: $x_i \vee nx_i$.   For each clause $d_1 \vee \ldots \vee d_3$ in Φ we add the constraint $:\text{- not } \bar{d}_1, \ldots, \text{not } \bar{d}_3$.   where $\bar{d}_i$ ($1 \leq i \leq 3$) is x_j if d_i is a positive literal x_j, and nx_j if d_i is a negative literal $\neg x_j$.

Hamiltonian Path (HAMPATH) is another classical NP-complete problem from
the area of graph theory:

> Given an undirected graph $G = (V, E)$, where V is the set of vertices of G
> and E is the set of edges, and a node $a \in V$ of this graph, does there exist a
> path of G starting at a and passing through each node in V exactly once?

Suppose that the graph G is specified by using two predicates $node(X)$ and
$arc(X, Y)$[4], and the starting node is specified by the unary predicate *start* which
contains only a single tuple. Then, the following program solves the problem
HAMPATH.

```
% Each node has to be reached.
:-node(X),not reached(X).  reached(X):-start(X).  reached(X):-inPath(Y,X).
% Guess whether to take a path or not.
inPath(X,Y) ∨ outPath(X,Y):-reached(X),arc(X,Y).
% At most one incoming/outgoing arc!
:-inPath(X,Y),inPath(X,Z),Y<>Z.  :-inPath(X,Y),inPath(Z,Y),X<>Z.
```

Blocksworld (BW) is a classic problem from the planning domain, and one of
the oldest problems in AI:

> Given a table and a number of blocks in a (known) initial state and a desired
> goal state, try to reach that goal state by moving one block at a time, such
> that only unoccupied blocks are moved on top of other unoccupied blocks
> or the table.

Figure 3 shows a simple example that can be solved in three time steps: First
we move block c to the table, then block b on top of a, and finally c on top of b.
Due to space restrictions we refer to [Erd99,FLMP99] for complete encodings.

Fig. 3. Simple BW Example

Strategic Companies (STRATCOMP) finally, is a Σ_2^P-complete problem, which
has been first described in [CEG97]:

> A holding owns companies $C(1),\dots,C(c)$, each of which produces some
> goods. Some of these companies may jointly control another one. This is
> modeled by means of predicates $prod(P, C1, C2)$ — product P is produced
> by companies $C1$ and $C2$ — and $contr(C, C1, C2, C3)$ — company C is
> jointly controlled by $C1$, $C2$ and $C3$.

---

[4] Predicate *arc* is symmetric, since undirected arcs are bidirectional.

Now, some companies should be sold, under the constraint that all goods can still be produced, and that no company is sold which would still be controlled by the holding afterwards. A company is strategic, if it belongs to a *strategic set*, which is a minimal set of companies satisfying these constraints.

The answer sets of the following natural program correspond one to one to the strategic sets. Checking whether any given company C is strategic is done by brave reasoning: "Is there *any* answer set containing C?"

$strategic(C1) \lor strategic(C2) \; :- \; prod(P, C1, C2).$
$strategic(C) \; :- \; contr(C, C1, C2, C3), strategic(C1), strategic(C2), strategic(C3).$

As in [CEG97] we assume that each product is produced by at most two companies and each company is jointly controlled by at most three companies.

7.2   Benchmark Data

For 3SAT, we have randomly generated 3CNF formulas over n variables (where n denotes the size as plotted on the x-axis of the graphs in Section 8) using a tool by Selman and Kautz [SK97]. For each size we generated 8 instances, where we kept the ratio between the number of clauses and the number of variables near the cross-over point of 4.3.

The instances for HAMPATH were generated by a tool by Patrik Simons which has been used to compare Smodels against SAT solvers (cf. [Sim00])[5]. Again, for each problem size n we generated 8 instances, always assuming node 1 as the starting node.

The blocksworld problems P3 and P4 have been employed in [Erd99] to compare ASP systems, and can be solved in 8 and 9 steps, respectively. We augmented these by problem P5 which requires 11 steps. For each of these problems, we generated 8 random permutations of the input.

For STRATCOMP, finally, we randomly generated 8 instances for each problem size n, with n companies and n products. Each company O is controlled by one to five companies (two groups of companies, where each of these groups controls the same company O, must have at least one member in common), where the actual number of companies is uniform randomly chosen. On average this results in 1.5 *contr* relations per company.

All experiments were performed on a Pentium III/733 machine with 256MB of main memory running GNU/Linux. The binaries were generated with GCC 2.95.2. The input files used for the benchmarks are available on the web at http://www.dbai.tuwien.ac.at/proj/dlv/lpnmr01.tar.gz.

8   Experimental Results and Conclusion

The results of our experiments are displayed in the graphs of Figures 4-7. For each problem domain we report two graphs: In both graphs the horizontal axis

---

[5] available at http://tcs.hut.fi/Software/smodels/misc/hamilton.tar.gz

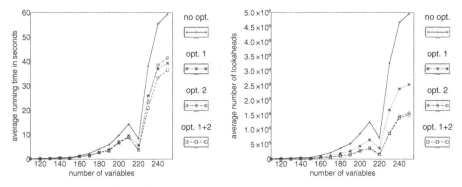

Fig. 4. 3SAT problems, average running times and look-aheads

reports a parameter representing the size of the instance, while on the vertical axis we report the running time (expressed in seconds) and the number of look-aheads, respectively, averaged over the 8 instances of the same size we have run (see previous section). The curves labeled by "no opt.", "opt. 1", "opt. 2", and "opt. 1+2", denote, respectively, the initial (unoptimized) version, the look-ahead equivalence optimization, the 2-layered optimization, and the combination of both look-ahead equivalence and 2-layered optimization.

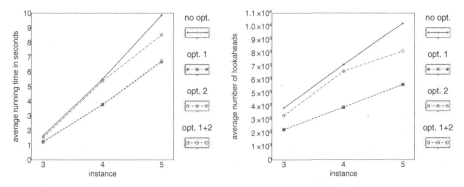

Fig. 5. Blocksworld problems, average running times and look-aheads

Observe first that both optimizations always bring some gain over the original version, as the "no optimization" curve is always on top of the other three curves in all graphs.

The two optimizations have different impact, depending on the problem domain: For Blocksworld, the equivalence optimization performs better than the 2-layered approach, while for Strategic Companies and 3SAT the opposite holds. For Hamiltonian Path both optimizations behave roughly equal.

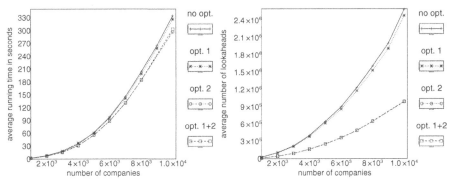

Fig. 6. Strategic Companies, average running times and look-aheads

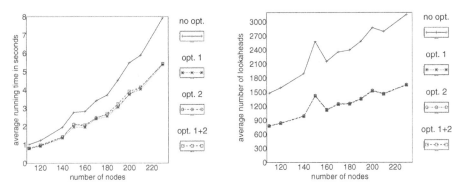

Fig. 7. Hamiltonian Path problems, average running times and look-aheads

The combination of the two optimizations combines the benefits in the sense that performance is always as good as for the best of the two strategies. Indeed, the curve combining the two strategies (opt.1+2) often nearly coincides with the curve of the best of opt.1 and opt.2, e.g. for Blocksworld opt.1+2 and opt.1 are almost equal, while for Strategic Companies opt.1+2 and opt.2 coincide. On Hamiltonian Path opt.1, opt.2, and opt.1+2 all give the same speed-up. Finally, in the case of 3SAT there are even better results for opt.1+2 than for any of the two methods alone.

Note that for opt.2 (and opt.1+2), the runtime and the number of look-aheads need not correlate, as fewer look-aheads are performed but the quality of the PTs may be worse, which may lead to larger trees. For opt.1 the choices remain the same, but only the number of look-aheads can be reduced, so avoided look-aheads directly reduce the runtime in this case.

Thus, both optimizations turned out to be useful, and we have incorporated their combination in the version of DLV released in June 2001. We believe that this is a promising way towards the improvement of ASP systems that should be subject of further investigation. Indeed, besides optimizing the implementation of the techniques proposed in this paper, we have already planned future work to explore other promising ways to reduce the number of look-aheads.

References

CEG97.   M. Cadoli, T. Eiter, and G. Gottlob. Default Logic as a Query Language. *IEEE TKDE*, 9(3):448–463, 1997. 304, 305

EFLP99.   T. Eiter, W. Faber, N. Leone, and G. Pfeifer. The Diagnosis Frontend of the dlv System. *AI Communications*, 12(1–2):99–111, 1999. 295

EFLP00.   T. Eiter, W. Faber, N. Leone, and G. Pfeifer. Declarative Problem-Solving Using the DLV System. *Logic-Based Artificial Intelligence*, pp. 79–103. Kluwer, 2000. 297

ELM⁺98a. T. Eiter, N. Leone, C. Mateis, G. Pfeifer, and F. Scarcello. Progress Report on the Disjunctive Deductive Database System dlv. *FQAS'98*, pp. 148–163. Springer. 295

ELM⁺98b. T. Eiter, N. Leone, C. Mateis, G. Pfeifer, and F. Scarcello. The KR System dlv: Progress Report, Comparisons and Benchmarks. *KR'98*, pp. 406–417. Morgan Kaufmann Publishers, 1998. 295

Erd99.   E. Erdem. Applications of Logic Programming to Planning: Computational Experiments. Unpublished draft. http://www.cs.utexas.edu/users/esra/papers.html, 1999. 304, 305

FLMP99.   W. Faber, N. Leone, C. Mateis, and G. Pfeifer. Using Database Optimization Techniques for Nonmonotonic Reasoning. *DDLP'99*, pp. 135–139. 298, 304

FLP99.   W. Faber, N. Leone, and G. Pfeifer. Pushing Goal Derivation in DLP Computations. *LPNMR'99*, pp. 177–191. 296, 299, 300, 301

FLP01.   W. Faber, N. Leone, and G. Pfeifer. Experimenting with heuristics for answer set programming. In *IJCAI 2001*, Seattle, WA, USA, August 2001. To appear. 296

GL91.   M. Gelfond and V. Lifschitz. Classical Negation in Logic Programs and Disjunctive Databases. *New Generation Computing*, 9:365–385, 1991. 295, 297, 298

LA97.   C. L. Li and Anbulagan. Heuristics based on unit propagation for satisfiability problems. In *IJCAI 1997*, pp. 366–371. 297, 303

Lif96.   V. Lifschitz. Foundations of logic programming. *Principles of Knowledge Representation*, pp. 69–127. CSLI Publications, Stanford, 1996. 298

Lif99.   V. Lifschitz. Answer set planning. *ICLP'99*, pp. 23–37. The MIT Press. 296

LRS97.   N. Leone, P. Rullo, and F. Scarcello. Disjunctive stable models: Unfounded sets, fixpoint semantics and computation. *Information and Computation*, 135(2):69–112, 1997. 300

Min82.   J. Minker. On Indefinite Data Bases and the Closed World Assumption. *CADE'82*, LNCS 138, pp. 292–308, New York, 1982. Springer. 295

Sim00.   P. Simons. *Extending and Implementing the Stable Model Semantics*. PhD thesis, Helsinki University of Technology, Finland, 2000. 305

SK97.   B. Selman and H. Kautz, 1997. ftp://ftp.research.att.com/dist/ai/. 305

New Generation Systems for Non-monotonic Reasoning

Pascal Nicolas, Frédéric Saubion, and Igor Stéphan

LERIA, Université d'Angers
2 Bd Lavoisier, F-49045 Angers Cedex 01
{Pascal.Nicolas,Frederic.Saubion,Igor.Stephan}@univ-angers.fr

Abstract. Default Logic is recognized as a powerful framework for knowledge representation and incomplete information management. Its expressive power is suitable for non monotonic reasoning, but the counterpart is its very high level of computational complexity. The purpose of this paper is to show how heuristics such as Genetic Algorithms, Ant Colony Optimization and Local Search can be used to elaborate an efficient non monotonic reasoning system.

1 Introduction

People are often used to manage and reason from incomplete information. Every day they make decisions without knowing every aspect of their environment. In many cases, this type of rough reasoning, based on natural and intuitive knowledge approximations, appears easier and more efficient than applying formal logical or mathematical deduction systems. From these remarks, one could expect that an Artificial Intelligence system would be easy to conceive and would be very efficient. Unfortunately, this is not the case. Twenty years ago [14] stated the foundations of *Default Logic* which is nowadays recognized as one of the best frameworks to capture and formalize common sense reasoning from incomplete information. Default Logic provides a representation of non completely specified rules by means of rules with exceptions and defines a deduction mechanism to get conclusions even if some data are not available. Unfortunately, this approach has a very high theoretical level of complexity. As a matter of fact, computing a set of plausible conclusions (called an extension) of a finite propositional default theory is $\Sigma_2^p - complete$ [5]. The difference in performances between human and artificial approaches relies on the fact that human reasoning can avoid many verifications while default logic builds a set of coherent conclusions and discards some kind of inconsistencies.

Previous works [11,2] have already investigated this computational aspect of default logic and even if some systems have good performances on certain classes of default theories, there is no efficient system for general extension calculus. Due to this computational complexity, a deterministic method based on the whole exploration of the search space would not be efficient for non trivial theories, even if it uses some sophisticated pruning methods.

T. Eiter, W. Faber, and M. Truszczyński (Eds.): LPNMR 2001, LNAI 2173, pp. 309–321, 2001.

We argue that non deterministic approaches [10,13] can be (on average) more efficient, in spite of their incompleteness.

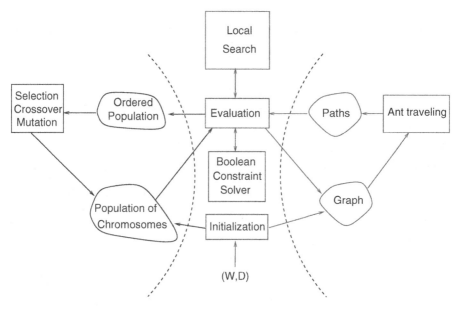

Fig. 1. GA, ACO + LS systems for Default Logic

In this paper, we present different approaches, sometimes complementary, that we have implemented in operational systems able to perform default reasoning on non trivial knowledge bases. The purpose of our different algorithms is to progressively improve a given initial configuration in order to reach a solution. Three general approaches are considered here. Genetic Algorithms are based on the principles of natural selection. Populations of possible solutions evolve through a process of mutation and crossover in order to generate better and better configurations. Ant Colony Optimization is inspired by the observation of the collective behavior of ants when they are seeking food. Its goal is to find an optimal path in a graph encoding the problem to solve. At last, Local Search relies on an incremental improvement of a potential solution to a given problem by local moves from a configuration to its neighbors. Local Search will be used here as an additional optimization mechanism and combined with previous methods. The general architecture of our system is summarized in figure 1 and detailled in sections 3, 4 and 5.

2   Extension Computation in Default Logic

In Default Logic [14] knowledge is represented by a *default theory* (W, D) where W contains the safe knowledge (in this work it is a finite set of propositional formulas) and D is a finite set of *default rules* (or defaults). A *default* $\delta = \frac{\alpha : \beta_1,...,\beta_n}{\gamma}$ is an inference rule (α, γ and all β_i are propositional formulas) whose meaning is "if the *prerequisite* α is proved, and if for all $i = 1,\ldots,n$ each *justification* β_i is individually consistent (in other words if nothing proves its negation) then one concludes the *consequent* γ[1]".

Given a default theory, Reiter has defined a set of its plausible conclusions, named an *extension*, by means of a fixpoint operator. In addition, he has given the following result:

Theorem 1. *[14] Let (W, D) be a default theory and E a formula set. We define $E_0 = W$ and for all $k \geq 0$,*

$$E_{k+1} = Th(E_k) \cup \left\{ \gamma \,\middle|\, \begin{array}{l} \frac{\alpha : \beta_1,...,\beta_n}{\gamma} \in D, E_k \vdash \alpha, \\ and\ E \not\vdash \neg\beta_i, \forall i = 1,\ldots,n \end{array} \right\}$$

Then, E is an extension of (W, D) iff $E = \bigcup_{k=0}^{\infty} E_k$.

Note that E, the whole extension to build, is used in its own definition. This non constructive characterization is also an argument to choose a "guess and check" method as we have done in this work.

It is important to note that a default theory may have one or multiple extensions and sometimes no extension at all. Now, we give some additional materials useful for the understanding of the rest of the paper.

Definition 1. *Let E be an extension of a default theory (W, D), its Generating Default Set is*

$$GD(W, D, E) = \left\{ \frac{\alpha : \beta_1,...,\beta_n}{\gamma} \in D \,\middle|\, \begin{array}{l} E \vdash \alpha\ and \\ E \not\vdash \neg\beta_i, \forall i = 1,\ldots,n \end{array} \right\}$$

Furthermore, given a default theory (W, D), computing its extension E is equivalent to finding its *Generating Default Set* Δ since $E = Th(W \cup cons(\Delta))$ [15].

Definition 2. *[16] Given a default theory (W, D), a set of defaults $\Delta \subseteq D$ is grounded if Δ can be ordered as a sequence $(\delta_1,\ldots,\delta_n)$ satisfying : $\forall i = 1,\ldots,n, W \cup cons(\{\delta_1,\ldots,\delta_{i-1}\}) \vdash pre(\delta_i)$.*

Lemma 1. *[16] Every generating default set is grounded.*

---

[1] If δ is a default rule, $pre(\delta)$, $jus(\delta)$ and $cons(\delta)$ respectively denotes the prerequisite, the set of justifications and the consequent of δ. These definitions will be also extended for sets of defaults.

The problem we address in this paper consists in an Extension Computation Problem (ECP) that can be defined w.r.t. our heuristic approach by the following components.

Definition 3. ECP

- A default theory (W, D)
- The set $\mathcal{CGD} = 2^D$ of possible configurations called candidate generating default sets.
- Given a candidate generating default set $C \in \mathcal{CGD}$, the candidate extension associated to C is

$$CE(W, D, C) = Th(W \cup \{cons(\delta) \mid \delta \in C\})^2$$

Given an ECP, a solution is a candidate generating default set $C \in \mathcal{CGD}$ such that $CE(W, D, C)$ is an extension w.r.t. theorem 1.

The last step of our heuristic approach consists in defining an evaluation function in order to compute the fitness of a candidate generating default set C w.r.t. the notion of solution. This evaluation relies on the four intermediate functions described below.

f_0 rates if the candidate extension is consistent or not.

$$f_0(C) = \begin{cases} 0 \ if \ CE(C) \ \text{is consistent} \\ 1 \ otherwise \end{cases}$$

f_1 rates the correctness of the candidate generating default set with respect to the definition 1.

$$f_1(C) = \Sigma_{i=1}^n \pi(\delta_i) \ where \ n = card(D)$$

with π defined as follows.

$\delta_i \in C$	$CE(C) \vdash \alpha_i$	$\exists j, CE(C) \vdash \neg\beta_i^j$	π
true	true	true	k
true	true	false	0
true	false	true	k
true	false	false	k
false	true	true	0
false	true	false	k
false	false	true	0
false	false	false	0

k is a positive number that represents a penalty given to each default that has been wrongly applied or wrongly not applied.

f_2 rates the level of groundedness of the candidate generating default set.

$$f_2(C) = card(\Gamma)$$

where Γ is the maximal grounded subset of C.

---

2 We use $CE(C)$ instead of $CE(W, D, C)$ when it is clear from context.

f_3 definitely checks this property

$$f_3(C) = \begin{cases} 0 \ if \ C \ is \ grounded \\ 1 \ otherwise \end{cases}$$

The complete evaluation function is defined w.r.t. previous components by taking into account experimental tuning and theoretical properties.

Definition 4. *Given a Default theory* (W, D), *a candidate generating default set* $C \in \mathcal{CGD}$, *the evaluation of* C *is defined by* $eval: \mathcal{CGD} \rightarrow \mathbb{Z} \cup \{\top, \bot\}$
$$if \ f_0(C) = 1$$
$$then \ eval(C) = \top$$
$$else \ \ if \ f_1(C) = 0 \ and \ f_3(C) = 0$$
$$then \ eval(C) = \bot$$
$$else \ \ eval(C) = f_1(C) - f_2(C)$$

Theorem 2. *A solution of an ECP is a set* $C \in \mathcal{CGD}$ *such that* $eval(C) = \bot$.

We now describe the different methods that we propose to solve an ECP.

3   Genetic Algorithms

Genetic Algorithms [8,6] are based on the principle of natural selection. We first consider a *population* of individuals represented by their *chromosomes*. Each chromosome represents a potential solution to an ECP. Applying a genetic algorithm consists in generating better and better individuals by evaluating, selecting, mating (crossing and mutating) them.

A representation scheme consists of the two following elements: a chromosome language $\mathcal{G}$ defined by a chosen size and an interpretation mapping to translate chromosomes in term of generating default sets, which provides the semantics of the chromosomes. In our context, for each default $\frac{\alpha \, : \, \beta_1, ..., \beta_n}{\gamma}$ we encode in the chromosome the prerequisite α with one bit, and all justifications $\beta_1, ..., \beta_n$ conjointly with one other bit. Therefore, given a set of defaults $D = \{\delta_1, \cdots, \delta_n\}$ the size of the chromosome will be $2n$ and the chromosome language $\mathcal{G}$ is the regular language $(0 + 1)^{2n}$ (i.e. strings of $2n$ bits). Given a chromosome $G \in \mathcal{G}$, $G|_i$ denotes the value of G at occurrence i, $1 \le i \le 2n$. The interpretation mapping, defining the semantics of the chromosomes (also called its phenotype), can be formally described as :

Definition 5. *Given a set of default* D *and chromosome language* $\mathcal{G}$, *an interpretation mapping is defined as*

$$\phi: \mathcal{G} \times D \rightarrow \{true, false\} \ such \ that :$$
$$\forall \delta_i \in D, \phi(G, \delta_i) = \begin{cases} true \ if \ G|_{2i-1} = 1 \ and \ G|_{2i} = 0 \\ false \ in \ other \ cases \end{cases}$$

Therefore, the chromosomes encode the candidate generating default sets as :

Definition 6. *Given a default set D, a chromosome $G \in \mathcal{G}$, the candidate generating default set associated to G is :*

$$CGD(D, G) = \{\delta_i \in D \mid \phi(G, \delta_i) = true\}$$

According to the definition 3, every chromosome G induces a candidate extension $CE(W, D, CGD(D, G))$ denoted $CE(G)$ when it is clear from the context. Intuitively, for a default δ_i, if $G|_{2i-1} = 1$ then its prerequisite is considered to be in $CE(G)$ and if $G|_{2i} = 0$ no negation of its justifications is assumed to belong to $CE(G)$.

Example 1. Let $(W, D) = (\{a\}, \{\frac{a:b}{c}, \frac{a:\neg c}{\neg b}, \frac{d:e}{f}\})$ be a default theory. We get : $CGD(100011) = \{\frac{a:b}{c}\}$ and $CE(100011) = Th(\{a, c\})$ which is really an extension but also $CGD(101011) = \{\frac{a:b}{c}, \frac{a:\neg c}{\neg b}\}$ and $CE(101011) = Th(\{a, c, \neg b\})$ which is not an extension.

The GA we use deals with some intermediate populations as it can be summarized by figure 2.

$$\longrightarrow P \longrightarrow P_{\prec} \longrightarrow P_{sel} \longrightarrow P_{parents} \longrightarrow P_{children}$$

Fig. 2. Main steps of the GA

Generation of the initial population P is crucial to the efficiency of GA. The most simple way is a random generation but this does not take into account the default theory of interest. A more efficient way consists in building chromosomes whose phenotypes are grounded (consistent) subsets of D. We introduce a *probability of insertion* of a default in the candidate generating default set p_i to randomly create a candidate and we randomly associate to each default δ of D a number $p_\delta \in [0, 1]$. The induction definition below gives by fixpoint the candidate generating default set Δ_∞.

- $\Delta_0 = \emptyset, D_0 = D,$
- $\forall j > 0, \forall \delta \in D_{j-1}, W \cup cons(\Delta_{j-1}) \vdash pre(\delta),$
  $\Delta_j = \Delta_{j-1} \cup \{\delta\}$ *if* $p_\delta < p_i$ *and*
    $W \cup cons(\Delta_{j-1} \cup \{\delta\})) \not\vdash \bot$
    $= \Delta_{j-1}$ *otherwise*
  $D_j = D_{j-1} \setminus \{\delta\}$

Then a chromosome G_∞ can be chosen randomly from $\{G | CGD(D, G) = \Delta_\infty\}$. We also guarantee that all the chromosomes of the initial population are different. If we add the condition

$$\forall \beta \in jus(\delta), W \cup cons(\Delta_{j-1} \cup \{\delta\}) \not\vdash \neg\beta$$

to the inductive part of the construction we are able to generate an initial population of incrementally non-conflicting grounded phenotypes [9]. However, we never completely check that all defaults are not conflicting because our goal is not to directly build a generating default set. As mentioned in the introduction, we think that this task is too difficult for a classical algorithm and we just search good starting points for our algorithm. Note, that for a technical reason explained below S_P, the size of the population, is such that $\exists N_P, S_P = \frac{N_P(N_P+1)}{2}$.

Then, we build $P_\prec$ where chromosomes of P are ordered w.r.t. their evaluation and where two identical chromosomes are represented only once. The ordering $\prec$ of the individuals is the natural extension of the usual ordering of $\mathbb{Z}$ extended with: $\forall x \in \mathbb{Z}, x \prec \top$ and $\forall x \in \mathbb{Z}, \bot \prec x$.

After that, the purpose of the selection stage is to generate a selected population P_{sel} containing chromosomes with the best rates according to the evaluation function. Furthermore, we try to keep a large diversity of selected chromosomes by introducing a Hamming distance Hd (Hamming distance is the number of differing bits between two chromosomes). P_{sel} is defined as the N_P-first chromosomes of $P_\prec$ respecting the Hamming distance.

We choose the ranking selection to generate the parent population $P_{parents}$. The best chromosome in P_{sel} is duplicated k times, the second one $k-1$ times, ..., and the kth one 1 time in $P_{parents}$.

Genetic operators are now applied on $P_{parents}$ in order to generate the offspring $P_{children}$. They are controlled by a crossover probability p_c and a mutation probability p_m. The crossover is performed as :

- select randomly two chromosomes $A = (a_1, ..., a_{2n})$ and $B = (b_1, ..., b_{2n})$ in $P_{parents}$
- generate randomly a number $r \in [0,1]$
- if $r < p_c$ then the crossover is possible;
  - select a random position $p \in \{1, \ldots, 2n-1\}$
  - the chromosomes $(a_1, ..., a_p, a_{p+1}, ..., a_{2n})$ and $(b_1, ..., b_p, b_{p+1}, ..., b_{2n})$ generate the two new chromosomes $(a_1, ..., a_p, b_{p+1}, ..., b_{2n})$ and $(b_1, ..., b_p, a_{p+1}, ..., a_{2n})$ that are put in $P_{children}$.
- else A and B are put in $P_{children}$ without crossover

Mutation is defined as :

- for each chromosome $G \in P_{children}$ and for each bit b_j in G, generate a random number $r \in [0,1]$,
- if $r < p_m$ then mutate the bit b_j (i.e. flip the bit).

The population obtained after these operations becomes the current population and will be the new input of the whole process described previously. This full process is repeated to generate successive populations in which the best chromosome w.r.t. the evaluation function represents the current best solution to the ECP. If a chromosome G such that $eval(CGD(D,G)) = \bot$ appears in a population then the method stops and $CE(G)$ is an extension for the given default theory. Otherwise, it stops when a maximal number of populations to be explored is reached.

4   Ant Colony Optimization

Ant Colony Optimization (ACO) metaheuristics [4,3] have been inspired by the observation of the collective behaviour of ants when they are seeking food. Let us suppose that there are many ants in a nest and that we deposit food in a place linked to the nest by two different paths P_1 and P_2, such that P_1 is shorter than P_2. At the beginning of their exploration approximatively the same number of ants will choose one path or the other. But, after few minutes, most of the ants will use the shortest path P_1. The emergence of this shortest preferred path is explained by the following points :

- every ant puts a little bit of *pheromone* all along its walk
- every ant directs itself by doing a probabilistic choice biased by the amount of pheromone that it finds on each possible path
- the pheromone evaporates

Thus, the amount of pheromone on $P1$ increases faster than on $P2$ since in a same duration a greater number of ants choose this path. As a consequence, a greater number of ants choose $P1$ since its attractivity becomes higher. By reinforcement, the amount of pheromone on $P2$ decreases and this on $P1$ increases directing almost all ants on the shortest path.

This collective behavior based on a kind of shared memory (the pheromone) can be used for the resolution of combinatorial problems that can be encoded as the search of an optimal path in a graph. For the ECP in Default Logic we propose the following encoding.

Definition 7. *The default graph of a default theory (W, D) is*

$$G(W, D) = (D \cup \{in, out\}, A)$$

where each default becomes a vertex and in and out are two particular vertices added to the default set. A is the arc set defined by

$$A = \{(in, \delta), \forall \delta \in D | W \vdash pre(\delta) \text{ and } \forall \beta \in jus(\delta) W \cup cons(\delta) \nvdash \neg \beta\}$$
$$\cup \{(\delta, \delta') \in D^2, \delta \neq \delta'\} \cup \{(\delta, out), \forall \delta \in D\} \cup \{(in, out)\}$$

In addition, each arc $(i, j) \in A$ is weighted by an artificial pheromone $\varphi_{i,j}$ that is a positive real number.

Definition 8. *Given a default theory (W, D), a path P from in to out in $G(W, D)$, the candidate generating default set associated to P is: $CGD(D, P) = P \cap D$.*

In the sequel, we identify vertices and defaults and we indifferently use P as a path in the graph or as a candidate generating default set by discarding *in* and *out* if necessary. Thus, the goal of ACO is to find a path from *in* to *out* that corresponds to a true generating default set.

We do not systematically put an arc from *in* to every default in D, since we want to start the search by defaults that can be applied in W. In addition, after the building phase, we remove from A the arcs

$$(\delta, \_) \ and \ (\_, \delta) \ if \ \exists \beta \in jus(\delta), \ W \cup cons(\delta) \vdash \neg\beta$$

because such a default δ (like $\frac{:a}{\neg a}$) can never be applied so it is useless to build path including δ.

$$(\delta, \delta') \ if \ W \cup cons(\delta) \cup cons(\delta') \vdash \bot$$

since δ and δ' are incompatible together. It does not forbid these two defaults to appear in the same path but it reduces the search space. Obviously, many other efforts could be done to prune the graph by a deep analysis of the default theory but this could become very expensive.

At the beginning, the pheromone on every arc of the graph is initialized to 1 in order to give equal chance to all paths. During the process this pheromone globally evaporates and increases on arcs that are on good paths in order to concentrate a great number of ants on the better parts of the graph.

In order to guide each ant during its journey from *in* to *out* we also use a local evaluation based on the function *loc*.

Definition 9. *Let P a path in the graph and δ a default. We say that:*

- δ *is* grounded *in P, if $W \cup cons(P) \vdash pre(\delta)$*
- δ *is* compatible *with P, if $\forall \beta \in jus(\delta), W \cup cons(P) \cup \beta$ is consistent*

and we define

$$loc(P, \delta) = \begin{cases} 1 \ if \ \delta \ is \ grounded \ in \ P \\ \quad and \ compatible \ with \ P \\ 0 \ otherwise \end{cases}$$

This local function combined with the recorded pheromone leads to the definition of the attractivity of a vertex δ for an ant staying on the last vertex of a partial path P between *in* and *out*.

Definition 10. *Let $G(W, D) = (V, A)$ a default graph, P a path from vertex in to vertex v_i. We define $\mathcal{R}(v_i, P) = \{v_j \in V \backslash P \ s.t. \ (v_i, v_j) \in A\}$ the set of vertices reachable from v_i and the attractivity of each vertex $v_j \in \mathcal{R}(v_i, P)$*

$$A(v_i, v_j, P) = \frac{\varphi_{i,j} * loc(P, v_j)}{\sum_{v_k \in \mathcal{R}(v_i, P)} \varphi_{i,k} * loc(P, v_k)}$$

On each vertex v_i during its travel from *in* to *out*, an ant chooses the next vertex by a random choice between all reachable vertices v_j and this choice is biased by the values $A(v_i, v_j, P)$. By definition of the function *loc* the only paths that can be explored correspond to sets of defaults that are grounded (in sense of def. 2) and maximal. By this way we discard candidate generating default sets that have obviously no chance to be a solution of the ECP and the search process focused on "better" candidates.

So, the main iteration of the whole algorithm is :

- release N ants at vertex in
- evaluate their paths P_i, $i = 1 \ldots n$, from in to out by $eval(CGD(D, P_i))$
- increase the pheromone on better paths : $\varphi(i, j) \leftarrow \varphi(i, j) + 0.9^{k-1}, \forall arc(i, j)$ in the best k paths
- decrease (1%) the pheromone on every arc (evaporation)
- if the evaluation of the best path is $\perp$ then the algorithm stops and the best path P gives an extension $CE(CGD(D, P))$, otherwise a next iteration starts until the maximum number of iterations is reached

5   Local Search

Local Search (LS) is a class of powerful methods to tackle difficult optimization problems. The development of modern metaheuristics such as Tabu Search or Simulated Annealing [1] has greatly increased their use and their efficiency.

In this work, LS will not be used as search heuristic alone but combined with GA and ACO to get better results. For an ECP, a chosen number of the best individuals (in the population or in the set of paths) are improved by a number of LS iterations. After this improvements, they are put back in the population (or set of paths) for the next GA or ACO iteration. This acts as an improve/repair stage. Therefore results depend on the number of individuals to submit to LS and on the number of iterations to perform.

The LS framework can be described as follows : given a finite set of configurations $\mathcal{S}$ and a cost function f, the purpose of the method is to determine an optimal s^* such that $\forall s \in \mathcal{S}, f(s^*) \leq f(s)$.

Local search mainly relies on the notion of neighborhood, which allows the search algorithm to move from a configuration to another one, in order to reach an optimum. Therefore, given a neighborhood function $\mathcal{N}: \mathcal{S} \to 2^{\mathcal{S}}$ and an initial configuration s_0, a LS algorithm produces a series of configurations $(s_i)_{i \in [0..n]}$ such that $\forall i, s_{i+1} \in \mathcal{N}(s_i)$.

Here, the search space is the previously defined candidate generating defaults set $\mathcal{CGD}$. We keep the previous evaluation function $eval$ (def. 4) as cost function. We just focus here on the definition of the neighborhood.

Concerning the moves in this search space, according to the definition of candidate extensions associated to individuals, they will be defined w.r.t. the notion of applied default. We impose that two neighbor candidate generating default sets differ only by one of their defaults. The neighborhood can be defined as a function : $\mathcal{N}: \mathcal{CGD} \to 2^{\mathcal{CGD}}$ such that $\mathcal{N}(C) = \{C' \in \mathcal{CGD} \mid C' = C \cup \{\delta\}, \delta \notin C \vee C' = C - \{\delta\}, \delta \in C\}$.

In order to experiment local search techniques and their combination with the previously described methods, two methods are used to explore the benefits of two different and representative managements of the moves: Descent with Random Walk (DRW) and Tabu Search (TS).

The DRW consists in choosing at each iteration the best neighbor which replaces the current configuration only if it is better. Using this approach, a local optimum is always reached. A random walk principle is added to escape from local optimum by moving from a current configuration to another having a worst evaluation with a certain probability.

TS consists in moving from a configuration to its best allowed neighbor which is not necessarily better than this current configuration. The allowed neighbors are configurations that are not forbidden by the tabu list and each current configuration is recorded in this list. Therefore, possible cycles are avoided thanks to this tabu list. A so-called aspiration condition insures that, if the neighborhood contains a better configuration than the current one, then it will be accepted as the new current configuration even if it is in the tabu list.

Of course, there exists many variants and extensions of these basic principles.

6   Experimental Results and Conclusion

We report here some experimental results on GA, ACO and GA+LS systems that we have implemented in Sicstus Prolog 3.8.3 (we have also implemented ACO+LS but due to a lack of space we only point out here some of our results).

Diversification : Table 1 refers to the influence of the Hamming distance for the problem ham_6_2 that encodes, with 45 defaults, a Hamiltonian cycle problem as in [2].

Tests have been done by 30 runs per Hamming distance hd with parameters $S_P = 465$, $p_c = 0.8$, $p_m = 0.1$, $p_i = 0.9$, an initial incrementally non-conflicting grounded population and a maximum number of iterations equals to 200. $\%s$ is the number of successful runs, ani the average number of iterations, at the average time in seconds for a run, ati the average time in seconds for one iteration, $anis$ the average number of iterations for the successful runs and ats the average time in seconds for one successful run. It shows the importance of population diversity to increase the stability of the method (in number of iterations) and to speed up each iteration by decreasing the size of the population. It demonstrates also that a too high selective pressure ($Hd \geq 13$) strongly reduces the chances to have a successful run by decreasing too much the size of the selected population (and then the offspring).

LS tuning : In order to get good performance improvements from the combination of LS and GA, we have to adjust the parameters of the two LS algorithms. Concerning DRW the tuning consists in determining the best value for the random walk parameter. Experiments provide us a value around 0.05 (the aim is to

Table 1. Influence of Hamming distance

hd	$\%s$	ani	at	ati	$anis$	ats
6	50	124.0	481.0	3.9	48.1	194.1
8	57	116.2	355.5	3.1	52.1	164.3
10	73	108.9	263.3	2.4	75.8	185.7
12	57	139.7	227.5	1.6	93.6	156.7
14	27	173.0	183.1	1.1	98.9	108.7

avoid too stochastic moves). Concerning TS, we have to adjust the length of the tabu list (the tabu tenure). In fact the more important parameters are the depth of the LS used and the number of candidates given to LS after each GA (or ACO) iteration. For both LS algorithms, it appears that 5 LS iterations on the 5 best candidates are a good compromise to get interesting results. Results obtained with GA+DRW and GA+TS are given in table 2. Due to the small number of iterations, it appears that the tabu tenure does not really affect the results. Due to this specific use, DRW and TS can be considered as a way to reach quickly a local optimum from a good configuration. Their respective performances depend on the two different heuristics they used to explore neighborhood. Moreover, parameters can be finely tuned according to each problem.

Results : Table 2 provides us information on the performances of our methods (with the notations of table 1). We report our best ACO experiments in which we use $N = 100$ ants and the $k = 7$ best paths for reinforcement. We can remark the great impact of LS on the number of iterations of GA while only 5 individuals of the whole population are improved at each GA iteration. This also allows us to compare the performance in time of GA w.r.t. ACO and to compare our systems with DeRes [2].

Forthcoming works : Our methodology can be easily adapted to other variants of default logic provided that we adapt the function *eval* to the definition of extension in the targeted default logic. Moreover, our systems are able to do query answering in full Reiter's Default logic and this will be described in a next paper.

We have to mention that, on logic programs with stable model semantics (a subcase of default logic), the system Smodels [12] has best performances. We think that it is because the benefit of our approaches has no effect on this kind of problem whose complexity (NP-complete) is less than $\Sigma_2^p - complete$. But, previous people example can only be encoded in full Reiter's default logic that is beyond the scope of Smodels. Another interesting feature of our approach is its ability to do a kind of anytime reasoning since when the method stops without giving an extension, we get some approximate solution that can be useful.

An interesting way to explore is to investigate how we could derive benefits from the blocking set and supporting set structures introduced in [7]. It can be useful to define a more suitable neighborhood in the LS or to introduce a

Table 2. Results on Hamilton Problem

problem	Algo	%s	ani	at	anis	ats
ham_5	ACO	100	6.5	14.9	6.5	14.9
ham_6	ACO	96	32.6	117.2	26.8	93.7
ham_5	GA	100	44.1	53.6	44.1	53.6
ham_6	GA	73	108.9	263.3	75.8	185.7
ham_6	GA + DRW	100	16.1	155.7	16.1	155.7
ham_6	GA + TS	100	8.3	91.9	8.3	91.9
ham_6	DeRes	100	−	8868.1	−	8868.1

reparation mechanism in GA or to forbid some partial paths in ACO. Another question to deal with is the non existence of extension problem. Actually, if a default theory has no extension our systems stop after having done their maximal number of iterations and we can not attest that there is an extension or not. But, the only way to assert that a general default theory (W, D) has no extension is to explore the whole set $\mathcal{CGD} = 2^D$ and this is not practicable for non trivial cases. Nevertheless, [7] gives some sufficient conditions of non existence that can be helpful in our work.

References

1. E. Aarts and J. K. Lenstra, editors. *Local Search in Combinatorial Optimization*. John Wiley and Sons, 1997. 318
2. P. Cholewiński, V. Marek, A. Mikitiuk, and M. Truszczyński. Computing with default logic. *Artificial Intelligence*, 112:105–146, 1999. 309, 319, 320
3. D. Corne, M. Dorigo, and F. Glover. *New Ideas in Optimization*. Mac Graw Hill, 1999. 316
4. M. Dorigo, E. Bonabeau, and G. Theraulaz. Ant algorithms and stimergy. *Future Generation Computer Systems*, 16:851–871, 2000. 316
5. G. Gottlob. Complexity results for nonmonotonic logics. *Journal of Logic and Computation*, 2(3):397–425, June 1992. 309
6. J. H. Holland. *Adaptation in Natural and Artificial Systemes*. University of Michigan Press, 1975. 313
7. T. Linke and T. Schaub. Alternative foundations for Reiter's default logic. *Artificial Intelligence*, 124:31–86, 2000. 320, 321
8. Z. Michalewicz. *Genetic Algorithms + Data Structures = Evolution Programs*. Springer Verlag, 1996. 313
9. P. Nicolas, F. Saubion, and I. Stephan. Combining heuristics for default logic reasoning systems. In *Proceedings of the 12th IEEE International Conference on Tools with Artificial Intelligence (ICTAI2000)*, 2000. 315
10. P. Nicolas, F. Saubion, and I. Stephan. Gadel : a genetic algorithm to compute default logic extensions. In *Proceedings of the European Conference on Artificial Intelligence*, pages 484–488, 2000. 310
11. I. Niemelä. Towards efficient default reasoning. In C. Mellish, editor, *Proceedings of the International Joint Conference on Artificial Intelligence*, pages 312–318. Morgan Kaufmann Publishers, 1995. 309
12. I. Niemelä and P. Simons. Smodels - an implementation of the stable model and well-founded semantics for normal logic programs. In *Proceedings of LPNMR*, volume 1265 of *Lecture Notes in Artificial Intelligence*, pages 420–429, 1997. 320
13. A. Provetti and L. Tari. In *Int. Genetic Evolutionary Computation GECCO'00*, pages 303–308, 2000. 310
14. R. Reiter. A logic for default reasoning. *Artificial Intelligence*, 13(1-2):81–132, 1980. 309, 311
15. V. Risch. Analytic tableaux for default logics. *Journal of Applied Non-Classical Logics*, 6(1):71–88, 1996. 311
16. C. Schwind. A tableaux-based theorem prover for a decidable subset of default logic. In M. Stickel, editor, *Proceedings of the Conference on Automated Deduction*. Springer Verlag, 1990. 311

Algorithms for Computing X-Minimal Models

Chen Avin and Rachel Ben-Eliyahu – Zohary

Communication Systems Engineering Department,
Ben-Gurion University of the Negev
Beer-Sheva 84105, Israel
{avin,rachel}@bgumail.bgu.ac.il

Abstract The problem of computing X-minimal models, that is, models minimal with respect to a subset X of all the atoms in a theory, is very relevant for computing circumscriptions and diagnosis. Unfortunately, the problem is NP-hard. In this paper we present two novel algorithms for computing X-minimal models. The advantage of these new algorithms is that, unlike existing ones, they are capable of generating the models one by one. There is no need to compute a superset of all minimal models before finding the first X-minimal one. Our procedures may use local serach techniques, or, alternatively, complete methods. We have implemented and tested the algorithms and the preliminary experimental results are encouraging.

1   Introduction

Minimal model computation is a crucial task in many reasoning systems in Artificial Intelligence, including Logic Programming, Nonmonotonic Reasoning, and Diagnosis [Re87,Mc80,dKW87]. Indeed, a considerable effort has been made to analyze the complexity of this task and to build efficient algorithms and systems that solve it [e.g. BD96,KL99,.JNS00].

In this paper, we consider a more general computational problem- the problem of computing X-minimal models. When we look for X-minimal models, we search for models that are minimal with respect to a subset X of all the atoms in the theory. The task of computing minimal models is a special case of generating X-minimal models, taking X to be all the atoms in the theory. X-minimal models are particularly relevant in Diagnosis and Circumscription [Re87,Mc80,Li85]. In the logical approach to Diagnosis, the artifact to be diagnosed and the behavior of the system are encoded as a set of logical sentences called the system description and the observations, respectively. The components of the system are represented by constants, and their status – whether or not they are functioning well - is indicated by a special predicate called an abnormality predicate and denoted $ab(.)$. Normally, we assume that all the abnormality predicates are **false**, that is, that components in the system well behave. Once there is a fault, the theory composed of the system description and the observations becomes logically inconsistent if we assume that none of the components is abnormal. To resume consistency, we must assume that some components are malfunctioning. We prefer to explain the inconsistency with a

T. Eiter, W. Faber, and M. Truszczyński (Eds.): LPNMR 2001, LNAI 2173, pp. 322-335, 2001.

minimal subset of abnormalities. It does not make sense to assume that a set of components are broken when the assumption that only a subset of this set is malfunctioning can explain the faulty behavior of the system. This is called "The Principle of Parsimony". By this principle, we assume that only minimal subsets of components are faulty, or in other words, we look for models that are minimal with respect to the abnormality predicates.

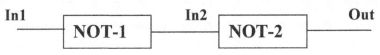

Fig. 1. An example circuit

The systems descriptions and observations are usually represented in first order logic. For the sake of simplicity, we will use propositional logic in this paper. The algorithms presented here can be used for function-free first-order minimal model computation by first grounding the theories involved. Alternatively, the algorithms shown here can serve as a basis for developing algorithms tailored for first-order logic.

As an example for model-based diagnosis using minimal models, consider the simple circuit shown in Figure 1. Assuming *AB1* and *AB2* mean that gate "not-1" and "not-2", respectively, are malfunctioning, the system description (*SD*) for this gate is:

$$\neg AB1 \rightarrow [In1 \leftrightarrow \neg In2]$$
$$\neg AB2 \rightarrow [In2 \leftrightarrow \neg Out]$$

Now, assume that In1 is 0 and Out is 1, indicating that the circuit is faulty. The observations (*OBS*) in this case are $\{\neg In1, Out\}$. If we assume that both gates are normal and take the theory that is the union of *SD*, *OBS*, and the literals $\{\neg AB1, \neg AB2\}$, - we get an inconsistent theory. However, if we consider the theory consisting of the union of *SD* and *OBS* alone, and we look at the *X*-minimal models of this theory taking *X* to be $\{AB1, AB2\}$, we obtain two such models, in each of which only one gate is abnormal. Hence the diagnosis for the above system and observations is that either the first or the second (but not both) circuit is faulty.

The circuit example also illustrates why a demand-driven computation of the *X*-minimal models is advantageous. Each *X*-minimal model explains the faulty behavior of the system by suggesting a minimal set of components that may be abnormal. If we are given the models one by one, we can test the suspect components while the next model is being computed.

The paper is organized as follows. After presenting some basic definitions and known results in Section 2, we present two demand-driven algorithms for *X*-minimal model computation in Section 3. Both algorithms may be implemented either using local search methods or complete methods. *X*-minimal models are also very relevant in computing Circumscription. We elaborate on that in Section 4. In Section 5 we report on experiments done on the algorithms developed and in Sections 6 and 7 we present related work and concluding remarks.

2   Preliminary Definitions

In this section we provide some basic terminology used throughout the paper.

- *Literal* – propositional symbol (atom) (positive literal) or its negation. (negative literal).
- *Clause* – disjunction of literals.
- *CNF theory* – conjunctive normal form, a conjunction of clauses. All the theories in this paper are assumed to be in CNF. Hence by *theory* we mean a set of clauses. A theory is *Horn* if and only if each clause in the theory contains at most one positive literal.
- *Positive graph of a theory* - Let T be a theory. The positive graph of T is an undirected graph (V, E) defined as follows: $V = \{ P |\ P$ is a positive literal in some clause in $T\}$, E$= \{(P, Q)|\ P$ and Q appear positive in the same clause$\}$.
- *Vertex cover* - Let $G = (V, E)$ be a graph. A vertex cover of G is a set $V' \subseteq V$ such that for each $e \in E$ there is some $v \in V'$ such that $v \in e$.
- *Vertex cover of a theory* – Vertex cover of the poistive graph of the theory. Note that if all the atoms of a vertex cover of a theory are instantiated, the theory becomes Horn.
- *Model* – a truth assignment to all the atoms in the theory that makes the theory true.
- *Pos (M)* – the set of the atoms assigned **true** in a model M.
- *Lit(v)* – A representation of a truth assignment v as a set of literals. For example, if $v=\{P=$**true**$, Q=$**false**$, R=$**false**$\}$, then $Lit(v)=\{P, \neg Q,, \neg R\}$.
- *Unit clause* – clause that contains only one literal.
- *Unit propagation* - the process where given a theory T, you do the following until there is no change in the theory (no new clauses are generated and no clause is deleted): you pick a unit clause C from T, delete the negation of C from each clause and delete each clause that contains C.
- $T \otimes S$ – is the result of unit propagation on $T \cup$ S.
- $\{$**true** (**false**)$\}$– set of atoms that are assigned with **true** (**false**).
- $Int_x (M)$ – the value (integer) of a model M over a given ordered set of variables $X=\{P_r,...,P_0\}$, seen as a binary number where P_r is the most significant bit (MSB or MSV - most significant variable) and P_0 is the least significant bit (LSB or LSV - least significant variable). So, for example, if $M=\{P=$**true**$, Q=$**false**$, R=$**false**$\}$ then $Int_{\{P,Q\}} (M)=(10$ in binary code$) = 2; Int_{\{P,Q,R\}} (M)=(100$ in binary code$) = 4.$
- *X-Largest (Smallest) model* – the model with the largest (smallest) value ($Int_x(M)$) with respect to a given ordered set of variables $X=\{P_r,...,P_0\}$.

X-minimal model

Let T be a theory over a set of atoms L, $X \subseteq L$, and M a model for T. M is an *X-Super* of another model M' if and only if pos(M')$\cap X$ is a proper subset of pos(M) $\cap X$.

M is an *X-minimal model* for T if and only if there is no other model M' for T such that M is an *X-Super* of M'. If M is an X-minimal model for $X = L$, it will be called simply a minimal model. It has been shown that a Horn theory has a unique minimal model that can be found in linear time [DG84].

Find-X-minimal (T,X,M)

Input: A theory T, an ordered set $X=\{P_r,...P_l\}$ which is a subset of the atoms in T.

Output: true if T is satisfiable, false otherwise. In case T is satisfiable, the output variable M is a smallest X–minimal model of T w.r.t. the ordering $\{P_r,...P_l\}$.

1. If $\neg$sat(T,M) return false;

2. For i : = r downto 1 do

   a. If isHorn(T) then M=HornMinimalModel(T), Goto 4.

   b. If sat $(T \cup \{\neg P_i\}$, M) then $T: =T \otimes \{\neg P_i\}$
      else $T: =T \otimes \{P_i\}$

3. sat(T,M)

4. Return true;

Fig. 2. Algorithm Find-X-minimal

Example 2.1 Suppose a theory T_0 has variables $P_6...P_0$, and $X=\{P_6,...P_3\}$. Assume further that T_0 has exactly four models (ordered from the X-smallest to the X-largest): $M_1=0010110$, $M_2=0011000$, $M_3= 0100111$, and $M_4=1100000$. M_1 and M_3 are the only X-minimal models of T_0.

Throughout this paper, unless stated otherwise, models that agree on the truth assignments given to all the variables in X are considered identical.

The following theorem is quite interesting. Its proof is based on results from Combinatorics [Bo86]. We provide in the appendix a proof suggested by Lomonosov [Lo00].

Theorem 2.2: Let T be a theory and let X be a subset of the atoms that are used in T. The number of X-minimal models of T is at most $\binom{n}{\lfloor \frac{n}{2} \rfloor}$, where $|X|=n$.

S-X-Min (T, X)

Input: A theory T. An ordered set $X=\{P_r, ... P_1\}$ which is subset of the variables in T.

Output: **true** if T is satisfiable, **false** otherwise. If T is satisfiable, output one by one all X-minimal models of T from the smallest to the largest w.r.t the order $\{P_r, ... P_1\}$.

1. If $\neg$Sat(T,M) return **false**.

2. *ModelsTable* $= \varnothing$.

3. For $i := 0$ to 2^r-1 do:

    a. v: = instantiation of X that equal i. (P_1 least significant, P_r most significant).

    b. If v is not an X-super of a model in *ModelsTable* then

        if Sat$(T \cup Lit(v), M)$
        Output (M);
        Add M to *ModelsTable;*

Fig. 3. Algorithm S-X-Min

Find X-Minimal

In Figure 2 we show an algorithm for computing one X-minimal model for a theory. The algorithm takes $O(|X|)$ steps and uses $O(|X|)$ calls to a satisfiability testing procedure. A similar algorithm was shown in [BD96]. Find-X-minimal tries to assign as many **false** as possible and calls a Horn satisfiability checker once there are enough instantiations so that the theory becomes Horn.

Notes on *Find-X-Minimal* (for future use):

Note 1: if the theory T is not satisfiable then M is returned with the value it was initialized with.

Note 2: The algorithm uses a procedure *sat(T,M)* that returns **true** iff T is satisfiable. In case T is satisfiable, M is a model of T. Each model M is an array of booleans, $M[i]$ being the truth value assigned to P_i. It might be the case that M has entries for variables not appearing in T. These variables will be assigned **false** by *sat(T,M)*. We do not always use the model that *sat* returns. In implementations, we can use a version of *sat* that does not return a model when we do not need it.

Note 3: If *sat(T,M)* is complete then Find-X-Minimal is also complete, otherwise Find-X-Minimal is not complete.

3   New Algorithms

In this section we will present two algorithms for computing X-minimal models.
The correctness of these algorithms can be proved only if a complete SAT procedure
is assumed. Otherwise the algorithm is not complete and may generate a model which
is not X-*minimal.*

The first algorithm, called S-X-*min,* goes over all possible instantiations to X, using
an ordering having the property that whenever a model is not X-minimal, then it must
be an X-super of an X-minimal model already generated. S-X-min is shown in
Figure 3.

J-X-min (T, X)

> **Input**: A theory T, a subset X of all the variables in T. We assume
> that $|X| = r$.

> **Output**: **true** if T is satisfiable, **false** otherwise. In case T is
> satisfiable, output one by one all X-minimal models of T from
> the smallest to the largest. Each model is an array of booleans
> M, M[i] is the truth value assigned to P_i.

1. Let $P_{n-1}, ..., P_{n-r}, ...P_0$ be an ordering on the variables in T such that
   the first r variables are all the variables from X. Variable P_0 will be
   considered the least significant and the variable P_{n-1} *will be*
   considered the most significant.

2. If Find-X-minimal(T, {$P_{n-1}, ..., P_{n-r}$}, M) == **false** return **false**;

3. *ModelsTable* = $\varnothing$.

4. Output (M); Add M to *ModelsTable*.

5. Let i be the index of the least significant variable that satisfies:

   1. $P_i \in X$

   2. M[i]= **false**

   3. P_i is more significant than another variable P_j such that $P_j \in$
      X and M[j]=**true**;.

   if there is no such variable return **true**.

6. M[i]= **true**;

7. If Find-X-minimal (T $\otimes$ Lit(M[n-1,...i]), {$P_{n-1},...P_{n-r}$}, M)=**false** then
   goto 5.

8. If M is not an X-super of a model in *ModelsTable* then goto 4. Else
   goto 5.

Fig. 4. Algorithm J-X-Min

Lemma 3.1: Algorithm S-*X*-Min is correct.

The proof is omitted due to space constraints. The basic argument is that a model which is not *X*-minimal must be an *X*-super of a model that is *X*-smaller. Since the models are generated in an increasing integer (Int_x) order, all and only the *X*-minimal models will be generated.

The second algorithm that we present is algorithm *J-X-min* shown in Figure 4. For each theory *T* there is a (possibly empty) set • of all the *X*-minimal models of T. You can order the *n* *X*-minimal models in • in order $\{M_1, \ldots, M_n\}$ where M_1 is the smallest *X*-minimal model and M_n is the largest. The algorithm is based on the following observation:

Lemma 3.2: Algorithm Find-*X*-minimal (Figure 2) will always return the smallest *X*-minimal model for some variable ordering. (If exists).

The proof is omitted due to space constraints. Intuitively, the Lemma is true because Find-*X*-minimal tries to assign as many **false** as possible and backtracks on this choice at as less significant bit as possible.

Once we find the first, smallest, *X*-minimal model, we serach for the next one. Suppose that $|X|=4$ and the smallest model is 0100.... There is no point in checking if truth assignmnets starting with 0101 or 0110 are models because it is obvious that they are *X*-super of the first model. Hence the algorithm will "jump" to check whether truth assignmnets starting with 1000 may be models. Hence the "J" in the algorithm name.

Theorem 3.3: Algorithm J-*X-Min* is correct.

Proof(*sketch*): Let *T* be a theory and let *X* be a subset of its variables. If *T* is inconsistent, the algorithm is clearly correct. Assume *T* is consistent. First, observe that models generated in Step 7 are always generated from the *X*-smallest to the *X*-largest. Let $M_0, \ldots M_k$ be all the *X*-minimal models of *T*, ordered from the *X*-smallest to the *X*-largest according to an ordering $\{P_{n-1}, \ldots P_{n-r}\}$ of *X*. We will show by induction on $0 \le t \le k$ that the *t*th model that J-*X*-min outputs is M_t.

Base case: Follows from Lemma 3.2.

Case *t>0*: Assume by contradiction that $M' \neq M_t$ is the *t*'th model that the algorithm outputs. By the induction hypothesis, it must be the case that $Int_x(M_{t-1}) < Int_x(M') < Int_x(M_t)$.

Let us look at the last time that Step 5 of the algorithm is exacuted just before model *M'* is sent to output.

Let *i* is the index that the algorithm finds at this last step.

Let $M*$ be an instantiation of the variables in *T* defined as follows: $M*[n-1, \ldots, i+1] = M_{t-1}[n-1, \ldots, i+1]$, $M*[i] = true$, $M*[i-1, \ldots, n-r] = \{$**false**$\}$. It is clear that $Int_x(M_{t-1}) < Int_x(M*) \le Int_x(M_t)$. There are 2 cases:

1. $Int_x(M_{t-1}) < Int_x(M') < Int_x(M*)$, then there is contradiction because in this case *M'* must be an *X*-super of M_{t-1} (Some of the variables $(P_{i-1}, \ldots, P_{n-r})$ that were **false** become **true** instead), hence the algorithm will not output it.
2. $Int_x(M*) \le Int_x(M') < Int_x(M_t)$. Then the following must be true:
   2.1 $M'[n-1, \ldots, i] = M_t[n-1, \ldots, i]$
   2.2 $Int(M'[i-1, \ldots, n-r]) < Int(M_t[i-1, \ldots, n-r])$.

But by Lemma 3.1 when we execute *Find-X-minimal* with $X=\{P_{i-1},..., P_{n-1}\}$ it returns the smallest possible value of $\{P_{i-1},..., P_{n-1}\}$ and therefore M' cannot be a minimal model that satisfies 2.1 & 2.2, a contradiction.

It is left to show that M_k is the last model sent to output. This is obvious because all the models generated after M_k are not X-minimal and hence must be X-super of at least one of all the X-minimal models that are already in *ModelsTable*.   □

Example 3.4 Consider again theory T_0 from Example 2.1, and suppose J-X-min is called with $X=\{P_0...P_3\}$. The first (and smallest) X-minimal model returned by Find-X-minimal is $M_1=0010110$. After that, at Step 5, we choose $i=5$ and call Find-X-minimal $(T_0 \otimes \{ \neg P_0, P_5\}, X, M)$. Find-X-minimal will return model $M_3= 0100111$, which is the 2nd and last minimal model of T_0. At Step 5 after that we choose $i=6$ and call Find-X-minimal $(T_0 \otimes \{P_6\}, X, M)$. Find-X-minimal will return model $M_4= 1100000$. M_4 is an X-super of M_3, and therefore will not be sent to output. In the next iteration, no i will be found, and the algorithm will terminate. You can see that out of 16 possible assignments to X, only 3 models were considered by J-X-min.

4   Computing Circumscription

In this section we will show how our algorithms can be used for computing circumscription. First, we will formulate deduction in circumscription in model-theoretic terminology. We will use propositional logic version of definitions from [GPP89,Li85,Mc80]. In this section we assume that T is some propositional theory and that there is a partition of all the atoms in T into three disjoint sets of atoms: P,Z, and Q.

Definition 4.1 [GPP89]. For any two models M and N of T we write $M \bullet N$ mod (P,Z) if models M and N differ only on how they interpret predicates from P and Z and if $pos(M) \bullet P$ is a subset of $pos(N) \bullet P$. We say that a model M is (P,Z)-minimal• if there is no model N such that $N<M$ mod (P,Z) (i.e. such that $N \bullet M$ but not $M \bullet N$).

That is, in order for M to be (P,Z)-minimal, the following must hold: for every model N such that M and N grant the same truth value to all the atoms in Q, the set of all atoms in P to which M assigns **true** must be a subset of the set of all atoms in P to which N assigns **true**; and we don't care about the truth assignment these models give to atoms in Z.

Theorem 4.2 [GPP89]. For any clause c, we say that c *follows from (T,P,Z) by circumscription* if and only if c is true in every (P,Z)-minimal model of T.

Example 4.3 Assume T is the following theory, having the intuitive meaning that children normally like McDonald's, and Itamar is a child:

    Child $\wedge \neg Ab \rightarrow LikesMD$.

    Child.

Suppose we want to know whether Itamar likes McDonald's. The intuition is that the answer is *yes*. Using classical logic, *LikesMD* does not follow from this theory. However, taking $P=\{Ab\}$ and $Z=\{likesMD\}$ we get that *LikesMD* follows from (T,P,Z) by circumscription . To see this, note that T has exactly three models:

$M_1=\{Child,Ab,LikesMD\}, M_2=\{Child,Ab,\neg LikesMD\},$ and $M_3=\{Child,\neg Ab,LikesMD\}.$ M_3 is the only (P,Z)-minimal model of T.

The algorithms developed here can be used for a demand-driven computation of (P,Z)-minimal models of T, in the following way:

1. Use some backtracking algorithm to find all consistent (with T) truth assignments for the variables in Q
2. For each assignment v found in step 1, compute one by one the P-minimal models of $T \cup Lit(v)$. Each model generated is a (P,Z)-minimal model of T.

A demand-driven computation is useful here because it may help us refute conclusions before all the models are generated (if a fact does not follow from some model it certainly does not follow from all of the models).

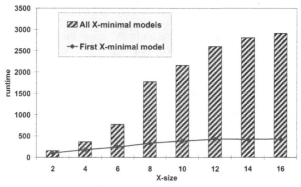

Fig. 6. Growing X size

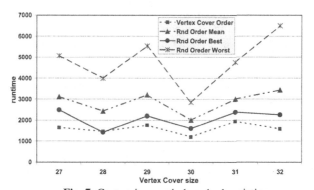

Fig. 7. Comparing symbols order heuristics

5   Experiments

We have tested algorithm *J-X-min* algorithm on a suite including hard randomly generated CNF problems (theories). The problems are 3CNF difficult random problems as describe in [SKC94] and [SK96]. The Algorithm was tested on theories

of size 50/218 (50 symbols, 218 clauses). The theories were taken from the SATLIB [SAT00]. The algorithms were implemented in JAVA on a PC having Pentium 3 600 MH processor and 128 MB memory. We have chosen JAVA because we had the intention of building an object-oriented library of tools for computing minimal models. We used a JAVA code of *walksat* [SKC94] as a (incomplete) SAT procedure. Since JAVA is a relatively ineffcient language in terms of running time, we did not pay much attention to the absolute running time of the algorithms in these experiments. However, we do believe that running time is an important factor and we plan to implement the algorithms in C in order to improve their time performance.
We have ran three experiments:

1. Compute all the minimal model of the theories and compare the results to results of a complete procedure (the dlv system [KL99]).
2. Check the growth in run-time as a function of an increasing size of X.
3. Compute all the minimal models using different symbols order heuristics.

The first experiment has shown that inspite of using incomplete *sat* algorithms, we have succeeded in computing *all* and *only* the minimal models of the theories. The set of minimal models computed by our algorithm was exactly the same set of minimal models computed by dlv. We expect though that on much larger theories an incomplete algorithm will be less accurate.

Results of the 2nd experiment are shown in Figure 6. As expected, the run-time of the algorithm (given in seconds) is growing as X grows. It is encouraging to see that the first X-minimal model is generated in about 25% of the time it takes to compute all the models, since one of the goals of this project was to output the models on a demand-driven basis.

The ordering of theory variables before calling algorithm J-X-min might be crucial. Once enough instantiations are made so that the theory is Horn, a linear algorithm can be called upon to finish the minimal model computation. In the 3rd experiment we have computed X-minimal models where X is the set of all variables in the theory. On each theory, we have tested the *J-X-min* five times, four times with random symbol order, and one time with symbol order where the vertex cover of the theory is first in the ordering. In general, the problem of finding a minimum-cardinality vertex cover of a graph is NP-hard. A greedy heuristic procedure that we used for finding a vertex cover simply removes the node with maximum degree from the graph and continues with the reduced graph until all nodes are disconnected. The set of all nodes removed is a vertex cover.

We have compared the run-time results of *J-X-min* in vertex cover order, and in random order. For the random order, we took the best,worst, and mean run time. We have divided the results according to the vertex cover of the theory. The results of this experiment are summarized in Figure 7 (run time is in seconds). We can see that in general the run time of *J-X-min* does not grow as the size of the vertex cover grows. We explain this findings by the fact that we use the *walksat* algorithm. When the *walksat a*lgorithm is checking the satisfiability of an inconsistent theory, it stops after a time-out (measured by number of flips and restarts). This time-out is almost constant and hence the run time of *J-X-min* is more or less constant on theory size with different vertex cover size. We can see that the vertex cover heuristics is quite good, always better than the worst and mean run-time of the *J-X-min* with random order, and usually even better than the best.

6   Related Work

During the last few years there have been several studies regarding the problem of minimal model computation. Ben-Eliyahu and Dechter   [BD96] have presented several algorithms for computing minimal models, all of them different from the ones proposeded here. One limitation of the algorithms presented there is that they produce a *superset* of all minimal models while we produce the minimal models one by one. Ben-Eliyahu and Palopoli [BP97] have presented a polynomial algorithm for finding a minimal model, but it works only for a subclass of all CNF theories and it finds only one minimal model.

The systems *dlv*   [KL99] and *smodels* [JNS00] compute stable models of disjunctive logic programs. If integrity constraints are allowed in the programs, every knowledge base can be represented as a disjunctive logic program such that the set of all minimal models of the first coincide with the set of all stable models of the second. An advatage of our approach compares to theirs is that our algorithms compute X-minimal models one at a time while using their approach we have to compute first all minimal models and then select the set of X-minimal ones. Another difference is that our implementaion uses local search techniques.

7   Conclusions

The task of computing X-minimal models is very relevant in many knowledge representation systems, and particularly in Diagnosis and Circumscription. We have presented two new algorithms to perform this task. The algorithms are demand driven, and can be implemented either by using incomplete local search procedures or by using complete procedures. In the future we plan to combine the algorithms presented here with the algorithm developed by [Be00] in order to produce a distributed algorithm for computing X-minimal models.

Acknowledgement

Many thanks to Professor Michael Lomonosov of the Department of Mathematics in Ben-Gurion University, Israel, for helping us with the proof of Theorem 2.2.

Reference

[Be00]   Ben-Eliyahu, R. 2000. A demand-driven algorithm for generating minimal models. In *AAAI-2000: the 17th National Conference on Artificial Intelligence,* pages 101-106.

[BD96]   Ben-Eliyahu, R., and Dechter, R. 1996. On computing minimal models. *Annals of Mathematics and Artificial Intelligence* 18:3-27. A short version in AAAI-93: Proceedings of the 11th national conference on artificial intelligence.

[BP97]   Ben-Eliyahu, R., and Palopoli, L. 1997. Reasoning with minimal models: Efficient algorithms and applications. *Artificial Intelligence* 96:421-449.

[Bo86]   Bollobas, B.; Combinatorics. Cambridge University Press, 1986.

[DG84]   William F. Dowling and Jean H. Gallier. Linear time algorithms for testing the satisfiability of propositional Horn formulae. *Journal of Logic Programming*, 3:267-284, 1984.

[dKW87]   de Kleer, J., and Williams, B. 1987. Diagnosis multiple faults. *Artificial Intelligence* 32:97-130.

[dKMR92] de Kleer, J.; Mackworth, A.; and Reiter, R. 1992. Characterizing diagnosis and systems. *Artificial Intelligence* 56:197-222.

[GPP89]   Gelfond, M.; Przymusinska, H.; and Przymusinski, T. 1989. On the relationship between Circumscription and Negation as Failure, *Artificial Intelligence* 38 75-94.

[JNS00]   Janhunen, T.; Niemella, I; Simons, P. and J. You, 2000.Unfolding partiality and disjunctions in stable model semantics. In *KR-2000: Proceedings of the Seventh International Conference on Principles of Knowledge Representation and Reasoning*.

[KL99]   Koch, C. and Leone, N. 1999. Stable Model Checking Made Easy. In IJCAI-99: Proceedings of the 16th international joint conference on Artificial Intelligence, 70-75.

[Li85]   Lifshitz, V. 1985. Computing circumscription. In *IJCAI-85: Proceedings of the international joint conference on AI* 121-127.

[Lo00]   Lomonosov, M.; Personal communication., 2000.

[Mc80]   McCarthy, J.1980. Circumscription - a form of non-monotonic reasoning. *Artificial Intelligence* 13:27-39.

[Re87]   Reiter, R.1987. A theory of diagnosis from first principles. *Artificial Intelligence* 32:57-95.

[SAT00]   SATLIB - The Satisfiability Library - http://aida.intellektik.informatik.tu-darmstadt.de/SATLIB/

[SK96]   Selman, B. and Kirkpatrick, S. 1996. Critical behavior in the computational cost of satisfiability testing. *Artificial Intelligence*, 81:273-296.

[SKC94]   Selman, B. Kautz, H. Cohen, B. Local Search Strategies for Satisfiability Testing. Proceedings of 2nd DIMACS Challenge on Cliques, Coloring and Satisfiability, 1994.

Appendix

In the following text, unless otherwise is stated, we assume some fixed theory T and some fixed subset X of all atoms in T, where $|X|=x$.

We take two truth assignmnets to be different only if they disagree on the set of atoms X.

The question we want to raise is: What is the maximum number of different X-minimal models that such a theory T may have?

Definition 1: An *assignments* (truth assignments) *X-chain* (or *X*-chain in short) is an ordered set of assignments where each assignment is an *X-super* of the next assignment.

Definition 2: an *X*-chain *Set* is a set of *X*-chains such that each possible truth assignment to X appears in exactly one *X-chain*. So there are exactly 2^x assignments in all the *X*-chains all together.

We define C_r as *chains set* that contains exactly r *assignments chains*.

Lemma 1: For any Theory T and set of atoms in T, X, such that T has a total of j different X-minimal models, and for any X-chain set C_r for T, $r \geq j$.

Proof: We will prove by contradiction that j can't be larger than r. It is obvious that two different X-minimal models of T must belong to a different X-chain of C_r (one X-minimal model can't be a *Super* of another X-minimal model by definition and therefore can't be in the same X-chain). If $j > r$ then there must be two different X-minimal models that belong to the same X-chain in C_r. A contradiction.

Lemma 2: If there is a theory T having exactly j X- minimal models and an X-chain set C_r where $r=j$ then for any theory T' and for any set of atoms X' in T' such that $|X'|=|X|$, T' may have at most j X'-minimal models.

Proof: It is easy to see that since T has an X-chain set of size r, T' must also have an X'-chain of size r. Assume that T' has j' X'-minimal models with $j'>j$. By Lemma 1, $r \geq j'$. But we also know that $r=j$, so we get that $j \geq j'$. A contradiction.

Theorem: The maximum number of X-minimal models of a theory *is* $\binom{n}{\left\lfloor \frac{n}{2} \right\rfloor}$, where $|X|=n$.

Proof: First, we will show that there is some theory T having exactly $\binom{n}{\left\lfloor \frac{n}{2} \right\rfloor}$ X-minimal models for some subset X of all the atoms in T with $|X|=n$. We will define T to be the theory that has exactly $\binom{n}{\left\lfloor \frac{n}{2} \right\rfloor}$ models where each model has a different set of $\left\lfloor \frac{n}{2} \right\rfloor$ true atoms that belong to some fixed set X of atoms with $|X|=n$, while all the other atoms in the model are assign with **false.** In this case each model is also an x-minimal model.

Next we will show that there is an X-chain set of size $\binom{n}{\left\lfloor \frac{n}{2} \right\rfloor}$. This will complete the proof because it means (according to Lemma 2) that this is the maximum number of X-minimal models that a theory may have. We will divide the 2^n different assignments to X into the following sets which reflect the number of atoms in X assign true by the assignment:

$$\binom{n}{1}, \binom{n}{2} \cdots \binom{n}{r}, \binom{n}{r+1}, \ldots, \binom{n}{\left\lfloor \frac{n}{2} \right\rfloor}, \ldots, \binom{n}{n-1}, \binom{n}{n}.$$

We will build the chains in the set as follows. We start with $\binom{n}{1}$ chains, each having one assignment that belongs to the set $\binom{n}{1}$. We then add the assignments in the set $\binom{n}{2}$ to the existing chains, possibly starting a new chain , and so on. The X-chains are growing by creating *complete matching* in bipartite graphs where the set of vertices V is the union of the assignments from $\begin{pmatrix} n \\ r \end{pmatrix}$ and the assignments from $\begin{pmatrix} n \\ r+1 \end{pmatrix}$. The edges connecting vertices in this graph reflect the X-super relation and we can show that in this case we can find a complete matching.

Fixpoint Characterizations for Many-Valued Disjunctive Logic Programs with Probabilistic Semantics

Thomas Lukasiewicz

Institut und Ludwig Wittgenstein Labor für Informationssysteme, TU Wien
Favoritenstraße 9-11, A-1040 Vienna, Austria
lukasiewicz@kr.tuwien.ac.at

Abstract. In this paper, we continue to explore many-valued disjunctive logic programs with probabilistic semantics. In particular, we newly introduce the least model state semantics for such programs. We show that many-valued disjunctive logic programs under the semantics of minimal models, perfect models, stable models, and least model states can be unfolded to equivalent classical disjunctive logic programs under the respective semantics. Thus, existing technology for classical disjunctive logic programming can be used to implement many-valued disjunctive logic programming. Using these results on unfolding many-valuedness, we then give many-valued fixpoint characterizations for the set of all minimal models and the least model state. We also describe an iterative fixpoint characterization for the perfect model semantics under finite local stratification.

1 Introduction

In a previous paper [5], we introduced many-valued disjunctive logic programs with probabilistic semantics. In particular, we defined minimal, perfect, and stable models for such programs, and showed that they have the same properties like their classical counterparts. For example, perfect and stable models are always minimal models. Under local stratification, the perfect model semantics coincides with the stable model semantics. Moreover, we also showed that some special cases of propositional many-valued disjunctive logic programming under minimal, perfect, and stable model semantics have the same complexity as their classical counterparts.

In this paper, we continue this line of research on many-valued disjunctive logic programming with probabilistic semantics. The central topic of the present paper is to elaborate algorithms for many-valued disjunctive logic programming. One way of obtaining such algorithms is to translate many-valued disjunctive logic programs into classical formalisms, and to work with existing algorithms for the classical formalisms. Another way is to simply develop completely new algorithms.

In this paper, we follow both directions. We first show that many-valued disjunctive logic programs under minimal models, perfect models, stable models,

T. Eiter, W. Faber, and M. Truszczyński (Eds.): LPNMR 2001, LNAI 2173, pp. 336–350, 2001.
© Springer-Verlag Berlin Heidelberg 2001

and least model states can be unfolded to equivalent classical disjunctive logic programs under the respective semantics. Thus, existing technology for classical disjunctive logic programming can be used to implement many-valued disjunctive logic programming.

Using these results on unfolding many-valuedness, we then develop new many-valued fixpoint characterizations for the semantics of minimal models, least model states, and perfect models under finite local stratification.

It is important to point out that our many-valued disjunctive logic programs have a probabilistic semantics in probabilities over possible worlds. Furthermore, the truth values of all clauses are truth-functionally defined on the truth values of atoms. This gives our many-valued disjunctive logic programs both nice computational properties (compared to purely probabilistic approaches) and a nice probabilistic semantics. The latter is expressed in the fact that our many-valued disjunctive logic programming under the minimal model and the least model state semantics is an approximation of purely probabilistic disjunctive logic programming.

We showed in [6,7] that many-valued *definite* logic programming with this probabilistic semantics has a model and fixpoint characterization and a proof theory similar to classical definite logic programming. Moreover, special cases of many-valued logic programming with this semantics were shown to have the same computational complexity as their classical counterparts. Interestingly, our approach in [6,7] is closely related to van Emden's quantitative deduction [19], which interprets the implication connective as conditional probability, while our work uses the material implication.

The main contributions of this paper can be summarized as follows.

- We introduce the least model state semantics for positive many-valued disjunctive logic programs with probabilistic semantics.
- We show that many-valued disjunctive logic programs under minimal model, perfect model, stable model, and least model state semantics can be unfolded to equivalent classical disjunctive logic programs under the respective semantics.
- We provide fixpoint characterizations for the set of all minimal models and the least model state of positive many-valued disjunctive logic programs.
- We describe an iterative fixpoint characterization for the perfect model of many-valued disjunctive logic programs that have a finite local stratification.

Note that proofs of all results are given in the extended paper [8].

2   Preliminaries

In this section, we recall some necessary definitions and results from [5].

2.1   Probabilistic Background

Let Φ be a first-order vocabulary that contains a set of function symbols and a set of predicate symbols (as usual, *constant symbols* are function symbols of arity zero). Let $\mathcal{X}$ be a set of variables. We define *terms* by induction as follows. A term is a variable from $\mathcal{X}$ or an expression of the form $f(t_1, \ldots, t_k)$, where f is a function symbol of arity $k \geq 0$ from Φ and $t_1, \ldots, t_k$ are terms. We define *classical formulas* by induction as follows. If p is a predicate symbol of arity $k \geq 0$ from Φ and $t_1, \ldots, t_k$ are terms, then $p(t_1, \ldots, t_k)$ is a classical formula (called *atom*). If F and G are classical formulas, then also $\neg F$ and $(F \wedge G)$. Literals, positive literals, and negative literals are defined as usual. We define *probabilistic formulas* inductively as follows. If F is a classical formula and c is a real number from $[0, 1]$, then $\mathsf{prob}(F) \geq c$ is a probabilistic formula (called *atomic probabilistic formula*). If F and G are probabilistic formulas, then also $\neg F$ and $(F \wedge G)$. We use $(F \vee G)$ and $(F \leftarrow G)$ to abbreviate $\neg(\neg F \wedge \neg G)$ and $\neg(\neg F \wedge G)$, respectively, and adopt the usual conventions to eliminate parentheses. Terms and formulas are *ground* iff they do not contain any variables. Substitutions, ground substitutions, and ground instances of formulas are defined as usual.

A *classical interpretation* I is a subset of the Herbrand base HB_Φ over Φ. A *variable assignment* σ assigns to each $x \in \mathcal{X}$ an element from the Herbrand universe HU_Φ over Φ. It is by induction extended to terms by $\sigma(f(t_1, \ldots, t_k)) = f(\sigma(t_1), \ldots, \sigma(t_k))$ for all terms $f(t_1, \ldots, t_k)$. The *truth* of classical formulas F in I under σ, denoted $I \models_\sigma F$, is inductively defined as follows (we write $I \models F$ when F is ground):

- $I \models_\sigma p(t_1, \ldots, t_k)$ iff $p(\sigma(t_1), \ldots, \sigma(t_k)) \in I$.
- $I \models_\sigma \neg F$ iff not $I \models_\sigma F$, and $I \models_\sigma (F \wedge G)$ iff $I \models_\sigma F$ and $I \models_\sigma G$.

A *probabilistic interpretation* (or *p-interpretation*) $\boldsymbol{p} = (\mathcal{I}, \mu)$ consists of a set $\mathcal{I}$ of classical interpretations (called *possible worlds*) and a discrete probability function μ on $\mathcal{I}$ (that is, a mapping μ from $\mathcal{I}$ to the real interval $[0, 1]$ such that all $\mu(I)$ with $I \in \mathcal{I}$ sum up to 1 and that the number of all $I \in \mathcal{I}$ with $\mu(I) > 0$ is countable). The *truth value* of a formula F in a p-interpretation $\boldsymbol{p}$ under a variable assignment σ, denoted $\boldsymbol{p}_\sigma(F)$, is defined as the sum of all $\mu(I)$ such that $I \in \mathcal{I}$ and $I \models_\sigma F$ (we write $\boldsymbol{p}(F)$ when F is ground). The *truth* of probabilistic formulas F in $\boldsymbol{p}$ under σ, denoted $\boldsymbol{p} \models_\sigma F$, is defined as follows (we write $\boldsymbol{p} \models F$ when F is ground):

- $\boldsymbol{p} \models_\sigma \mathsf{prob}(F) \geq c$ iff $\boldsymbol{p}_\sigma(F) \geq c$.
- $\boldsymbol{p} \models_\sigma \neg F$ iff not $\boldsymbol{p} \models_\sigma F$, and $\boldsymbol{p} \models_\sigma (F \wedge G)$ iff $\boldsymbol{p} \models_\sigma F$ and $\boldsymbol{p} \models_\sigma G$.

The probabilistic formula F *is true* in $\boldsymbol{p}$, or $\boldsymbol{p}$ is a *model* of F, denoted $\boldsymbol{p} \models F$, iff F is true in $\boldsymbol{p}$ under all variable assignments σ. The p-interpretation $\boldsymbol{p}$ is a *model* of a set of probabilistic formulas $\mathcal{F}$, denoted $\boldsymbol{p} \models \mathcal{F}$, iff $\boldsymbol{p}$ is a model of all $F \in \mathcal{F}$. A set of p-interpretations $\boldsymbol{P}$ is a *model* of F (resp., $\mathcal{F}$), denoted $\boldsymbol{P} \models F$ (resp., $\boldsymbol{P} \models \mathcal{F}$), iff every member of $\boldsymbol{P}$ is a model of F (resp., $\mathcal{F}$).

2.2   Positively Correlated Probabilistic Interpretations

We restrict our attention to the following kind of p-interpretations (that is, we assume another axiom besides the axioms of probability). A *positively correlated probabilistic interpretation* (or *pcp-interpretation*) is a p-interpretation $\boldsymbol{p}$ such that

$$\boldsymbol{p}(A \wedge B) = \min(\boldsymbol{p}(A), \boldsymbol{p}(B)) \text{ for all } A, B \in HB_{\Phi}. \tag{1}$$

Note that the condition $\boldsymbol{p}(A \wedge B) = \min(\boldsymbol{p}(A), \boldsymbol{p}(B))$ is just assumed for ground atoms A and B. It brings probabilistic logics over possible worlds closer to truth-functional logics. We do not assume that (1) always holds in the part of the real world that we want to model. The axiom (1) is simply a *technical assumption* that carries us to a form of many-valued logic programming that *approximates* probabilistic logic programming. It makes a global probabilistic semantics over possible worlds match with the truth-functionality behind logic programming techniques. Differently from many other axioms, the axiom (1) is compatible with logical implication. Note that pcp-interpretations are uniquely determined by the truth values they give to all ground atoms [5], and thus they can be identified with mappings from HB_{Φ} to $[0, 1]$.

A probabilistic formula F is a *pc-consequence* of a set of probabilistic formulas $\mathcal{F}$, denoted $\mathcal{F} \models^{pc} F$, iff each pcp-interpretation that is a model of $\mathcal{F}$ is also a model of F.

2.3 Many-Valued Disjunctive Logic Programs

We are now ready to define many-valued disjunctive logic programs. We start by defining many-valued disjunctive logic program clauses, which are special atomic probabilistic formulas that are interpreted under pcp-interpretations. A *many-valued disjunctive logic program clause* (or *mvd-clause*) is a probabilistic formula of the kind

$$\mathsf{prob}(A_1 \vee \cdots \vee A_l \leftarrow B_1 \wedge \cdots \wedge B_m \wedge \neg C_1 \wedge \cdots \wedge \neg C_n) \geq c,$$

where $A_1, \ldots, A_l, B_1, \ldots, B_m, C_1, \ldots, C_n$ are atoms, $l, m, n \geq 0$, and $c \in [0, 1]$ is rational. It is abbreviated by $(A_1 \vee \cdots \vee A_l \leftarrow B_1, \ldots, B_m, not\, C_1, \ldots, not\, C_n)[c, 1]$. We call $A_1 \vee \cdots \vee A_l$ its *head*, $B_1, \ldots, B_m, not\, C_1, \ldots, not\, C_n$ its *body*, and c its *truth value*. It is *positive* (resp., *definite*) iff $n = 0$ (resp., $l = 1$ and $n = 0$). It is called an *integrity clause* iff $l = 0$, a *fact* iff $l > 0$ and $m + n = 0$, and a *rule* iff $l > 0$ and $m + n > 0$. A *many-valued disjunctive logic program* (or *mvd-program*) P is a finite set of mvd-clauses. A *positive* (resp., *definite*) mvd-program is a finite set of positive (resp., definite) mvd-clauses. Given an mvd-program P, we identify Φ with the vocabulary $\Phi(P)$ of all function and predicate symbols in P. Denote by HB_P the Herbrand base over $\Phi(P)$, and by $ground(P)$ the set of all ground instances of members of P w.r.t. $\Phi(P)$. The *set of truth values* of P, denoted $TV(P)$, is the least set of rational numbers $\{\frac{0}{n-1}, \frac{1}{n-1}, \ldots, \frac{n-1}{n-1}\}$ that contains all the rational numbers in P, where $n \geq 2$ is a natural number. Denote by $\boldsymbol{I}_P$ the set of all pcp-interpretations over HB_P into $TV(P)$.

The following result shows that the truth of a ground mvd-clause under a pcp-interpretation is a function of the truth values of the contained ground atoms.

Theorem 2.1. *Let* $C = (A_1 \vee \cdots \vee A_l \leftarrow B_1, \ldots, B_m, not\, C_1, \ldots, not\, C_n)[c, 1]$ *be a ground mvd-clause, and let* $\boldsymbol{p}$ *be a pcp-interpretation. Then,* $\boldsymbol{p}$ *is a model of* C *iff*

$$\max(\max_{1 \leq i \leq l} \boldsymbol{p}(A_i), \max_{1 \leq i \leq n} \boldsymbol{p}(C_i)) \geq c - 1 + \min_{1 \leq i \leq m} \boldsymbol{p}(B_i).$$

We finally define queries and their correct and tight answers. A *many-valued query* (or simply *query*) is an expression $\exists(F)[t, 1]$, where F is a ground classical formula and t is a variable or a rational number from $[0, 1]$. Given the queries $\exists(F)[c, 1]$ and $\exists(F)[x, 1]$ to an mvd-program P, where $c \in [0, 1]$ and $x \in \mathcal{X}$, we define their desired semantics in terms of correct and tight answers with respect to a set $\boldsymbol{M}(P)$ of models of P as follows. The *correct answer* for $\exists(F)[c, 1]$ to P *under* $\boldsymbol{M}(P)$ is Yes if $c \leq \inf\{\boldsymbol{p}(F) \mid \boldsymbol{p} \in \boldsymbol{M}(P)\}$ and No otherwise. The *tight answer* for $\exists(F)[x, 1]$ to P *under* $\boldsymbol{M}(P)$ is the substitution $\theta = \{x/d\}$, where $d = \inf\{\boldsymbol{p}(F) \mid \boldsymbol{p} \in \boldsymbol{M}(P)\}$.

In the rest of this subsection, we recall minimal, perfect, and stable models from [5] as some ways of describing the meaning of an mvd-program.

Minimal Models. For pcp-interpretations $\boldsymbol{p}$ and $\boldsymbol{q}$, we say $\boldsymbol{p}$ is a *subset* of $\boldsymbol{q}$, denoted $\boldsymbol{p} \subseteq \boldsymbol{q}$, iff $\boldsymbol{p}(A) \leq \boldsymbol{q}(A)$ for all $A \in HB_\Phi$. We use $\boldsymbol{p} \subset \boldsymbol{q}$ as an abbreviation for $\boldsymbol{p} \subseteq \boldsymbol{q}$ and $\boldsymbol{p} \neq \boldsymbol{q}$. A model $\boldsymbol{p}$ of an mvd-program P is a *minimal model* of P iff no model of P is a proper subset of $\boldsymbol{p}$. Denote by $\boldsymbol{MM}(P)$ the set of all minimal models of P.

Perfect Models. We first define the two relations $\prec$ and $\preceq$ on ground atoms. For an mvd-program P, the priority relation $\prec$ and the auxiliary relation $\preceq$ are the least binary relations on HB_P with the following properties. If $ground(P)$ contains an mvd-clause with the atom A in the head and the negative literal $not\, C$ in the body, then $A \prec C$. If $ground(P)$ contains an mvd-clause with the atom A in the head and the positive literal B in the body, then $A \preceq B$. If $ground(P)$ contains an mvd-clause with the atoms A and A' in the head, then $A \preceq A'$. If $A \prec B$, then $A \preceq B$. If $A \preceq B$ and $B \preceq C$, then $A \preceq C$. If $A \preceq B$ and $B \prec C$, then $A \prec C$. If $A \prec B$ and $B \preceq C$, then $A \prec C$. We say that the ground atom B *has higher priority than* the ground atom A iff $A \prec B$.

We next define the preference relation $\ll$ on pcp-interpretations as follows. For pcp-interpretations $\boldsymbol{p}$ and $\boldsymbol{q}$, we say $\boldsymbol{p}$ is *preferable* to $\boldsymbol{q}$, denoted $\boldsymbol{p} \ll \boldsymbol{q}$, iff $\boldsymbol{p} \neq \boldsymbol{q}$ and for each $A \in HB_P$ with $\boldsymbol{p}(A) > \boldsymbol{q}(A)$ there is some $B \in HB_P$ with $\boldsymbol{q}(B) > \boldsymbol{p}(B)$ and $A \prec B$. We write $\boldsymbol{p} \lessapprox \boldsymbol{q}$ iff $\boldsymbol{p} \ll \boldsymbol{q}$ or $\boldsymbol{p} = \boldsymbol{q}$.

A model $\boldsymbol{q}$ of an mvd-program P is a *perfect model* of P iff no model of P is preferable to $\boldsymbol{q}$. We use $\boldsymbol{PM}(P)$ to denote the set of all perfect models of P.

Not every mvd-program has a perfect model. We next define locally stratified mvd-programs without integrity clauses, which always have a perfect model.

An mvd-program P without integrity clauses is *locally stratified* iff HB_P can be partitioned into sets $H_1, H_2, \ldots$ (called *strata*) such that for each mvd-clause

$$(A_1 \vee \cdots \vee A_l \leftarrow B_1, \ldots, B_m, not\, C_1, \ldots, not\, C_n)[c, 1] \in ground(P),$$

there exists an $i \geq 1$ such that all $A_1, \ldots, A_l$ belong to H_i, all $B_1, \ldots, B_m$ belong to $H_1 \cup \cdots \cup H_i$, and all $C_1, \ldots, C_n$ belong to $H_1 \cup \cdots \cup H_{i-1}$. For such a partition $H_1, H_2, \ldots$ of HB_P (called a *local stratification* of P) and every $i \geq 1$, we use P_i to denote the set of all mvd-clauses from $ground(P)$ whose heads belong to H_i.

Stable Models. An *extended many-valued disjunctive logic program clause* (or *emvd-clause*) is an expression $(A_1 \vee \cdots \vee A_l ; d \leftarrow B_1, \ldots, B_m, not\, C_1, \ldots, not\, C_n)[c, 1]$, where $A_1, \ldots, A_l, B_1, \ldots, B_m, C_1, \ldots, C_n$ are atoms, $l, m, n \geq 0$, $c \in [0, 1]$ is rational, and $d \in [0, 1]$. It *is true* in a pcp-interpretation $\boldsymbol{p}$ under a variable assignment σ iff

$$\max(\max_{1 \leq i \leq l} \boldsymbol{p}_\sigma(A_i), \max_{1 \leq i \leq n} \boldsymbol{p}_\sigma(C_i), d) \geq c - 1 + \min_{1 \leq i \leq m} \boldsymbol{p}_\sigma(B_i).$$

Thus, emvd-clauses may also contain truth-value constants in their heads.

For an mvd-program P and a pcp-interpretation $\boldsymbol{q}$, the expression $P/\boldsymbol{q}$ denotes the set of emvd-clauses that is obtained from $ground(P)$ by replacing every mvd-clause $(A_1 \vee \cdots \vee A_l \leftarrow B_1, \ldots, B_m, not\, C_1, \ldots, not\, C_n)[c, 1]$ by the emvd-clause

$$(A_1 \vee \cdots \vee A_l ; \max_{1 \leq i \leq n} \boldsymbol{q}(C_i) \leftarrow B_1, \ldots, B_m)[c, 1].$$

A pcp-interpretation $\boldsymbol{q}$ is a *stable model* of an mvd-program P iff $\boldsymbol{q}$ is a minimal model of $P/\boldsymbol{q}$. We use $\boldsymbol{SM}(P)$ to denote the set of all stable models of P.

2.4   Example

We now give an illustrative example. The following mvd-program P is taken from [5] (r, s, a, b, and c are constant symbols, and R, X, Y, and Z are variables):

$$P = \{(closed(r) \vee closed(s) \leftarrow)[.5, 1], (road(r, a, b) \leftarrow)[.8, 1], (road(s, b, c) \leftarrow)[.7, 1],$$
$$(reach(X, Y) \leftarrow road(R, X, Y), not\, closed(R))[.9, 1],$$
$$(reach(X, Z) \leftarrow reach(X, Y), reach(Y, Z))[.9, 1]\}.$$

The set of truth values of P is given by $TV(P) = \{0, 0.1, \ldots, 1\}$.

A query to P may be given by $\exists(reach(a, c))[U, 1]$, where U is a variable. To determine its tight answer, we must specify a set of models of P. Some models $\boldsymbol{p}_1, \boldsymbol{p}_2, \boldsymbol{p}_3$, and $\boldsymbol{p}_4$ of P are shown in Table 1 (we assume $\boldsymbol{p}_i(A) = 0$ for all unmentioned $A \in HB_P$). More precisely, the models $\boldsymbol{p}_1, \boldsymbol{p}_2, \boldsymbol{p}_3$, and $\boldsymbol{p}_4$ are some minimal models of P, whereas the models $\boldsymbol{p}_1$ and $\boldsymbol{p}_2$ are the only perfect and stable models of the locally stratified mvd-program P. The tight answer for $\exists(reach(a, c))[U, 1]$ to P under $\{\boldsymbol{p}_1, \boldsymbol{p}_2, \boldsymbol{p}_3, \boldsymbol{p}_4\}$ and $\{\boldsymbol{p}_1, \boldsymbol{p}_2\}$ is given by $\{U/0\}$ and $\{U/0.5\}$, respectively.

Table 1. Some models of the mvd-program P

	$closed(r)$	$closed(s)$	$road(r,a,b)$	$road(s,b,c)$	$reach(a,b)$	$reach(b,c)$	$reach(a,c)$
p_1	0.5	0	0.8	0.7	0.7	0.6	0.5
p_2	0	0.5	0.8	0.7	0.7	0.6	0.5
p_3	0	0.6	0.8	0.7	0.7	0	0
p_4	0	0.7	0.8	0.7	0	0	0

3   Least Model States

We now define least model states for positive mvd-programs, which are a generalization of their classical counterparts by Minker and Rajasekar [12,4].

In the sequel, we use A^α to abbreviate atomic probabilistic formulas of the form $\mathsf{prob}(A) \geq \alpha$. Given an mvd-program P, the *disjunctive Herbrand base* for P, denoted DHB_P, is the set of all disjunctions of atomic probabilistic formulas $A_1^{\alpha_1} \vee \cdots \vee A_k^{\alpha_k}$ with pairwise distinct ground atoms $A_1, \ldots, A_k \in HB_P$, $\alpha_1, \ldots, \alpha_k \in TV(P) \backslash \{0\}$, and $k \geq 1$. A *disjunctive Herbrand state* (or *state*) S is a subset of DHB_P. A state S is a *model state* of a positive mvd-program P iff

$$\{D \in DHB_P \mid S \cup P \models^{pc} D\} \subseteq S.$$

A model p of a state S is a *minimal model* of S iff no model of S is a proper subset of p. We use $MM(S)$ to denote the set of all minimal models of S. The *canonical form* (resp., *expansion*) of a state S, denoted $can(S)$ (resp., $exp(S)$), is defined by:

$$can(S) = \{D \in S \mid \forall D' \in S, \, D' \neq D \colon \{D'\} \not\models^{pc} D\},$$
$$exp(S) = \{D \in DHB_P \mid \exists D' \in S \colon \{D'\} \models^{pc} D\}.$$

A state S is *in canonical form* (resp., *expanded*) iff $S = can(S)$ (resp., $S = exp(S)$).

The following theorem shows that the intersection of a set of model states of a positive mvd-program P is also a model state of P.

Theorem 3.1. *Let P be a positive mvd-program, and let $\mathcal{S}$ be a set of model states of P. Then, the intersection of all $S \in \mathcal{S}$ is a model state of P.*

Clearly, each positive mvd-program P has the model state DHB_P. Thus, there exist model states of P, and the intersection of all of them is the least model state of P.

Definition 3.2. Denote by MS_P the least model state of a positive mvd-program P.

The following result shows that MS_P is the set of all disjunctions $D \in DHB_P$ that are pc-consequences of P. Moreover, it shows that this set coincides with the set of all disjunctions $D \in DHB_P$ that are true in all minimal models of P.

Theorem 3.3. *Let P be a positive mvd-program. Then,*

(a) $MS_P = \{D \in DHB_P \mid P \models^{pc} D\}$.
(b) $MS_P = \{D \in DHB_P \mid \boldsymbol{MM}(P) \models D\}$.

As shown in [6,7], definite mvd-programs P have a unique least model M_P. The next theorem shows that for such P, the model M_P corresponds to $can(MS_P)$.

Theorem 3.4. *Let P be a definite mvd-program, and let M_P be the least model of P. Then, $can(MS_P) = S_P$ where $S_P = \{A^\alpha \in DHB_P \mid \alpha = M_P(A)\}$.*

We give an illustrative example.

Example 3.5. Consider the following positive mvd-program P:

$$P = \{(closed(r) \vee closed(s) \leftarrow)[.5, 1], (road(r, a, b) \leftarrow)[.8, 1], (road(s, b, c) \leftarrow)[.7, 1],$$
$$(reach(X, Y) \vee closed(R) \leftarrow road(R, X, Y))[.9, 1],$$
$$(reach(X, Z) \leftarrow reach(X, Y), reach(Y, Z))[.9, 1]\}.$$

The set of truth values of P is given by $TV(P) = \{0, 0.1, \ldots, 1\}$. The canonical form of the least model state MS_P of P is given as follows:

$$can(MS_P) = \{closed^{0.5}(r) \vee closed^{0.5}(s), road^{0.8}(r, a, b), road^{0.7}(s, b, c),$$
$$reach^{0.7}(a, b) \vee closed^{0.7}(r), reach^{0.6}(b, c) \vee closed^{0.6}(s),$$
$$reach^{0.5}(a, c) \vee closed^{0.7}(r) \vee closed^{0.6}(s)\}.$$

4   Unfolding Many-Valuedness

In this section, we give translations of mvd-programs under the semantics of minimal models, perfect models, stable models, and least model states into classical disjunctive logic programs under the respective classical semantics.

4.1   Program Translations

We now formally define translations of mvd-programs and pcp-interpretations into classical disjunctive logic programs and classical interpretations, respectively.

Given an mvd-program P, the *many-valued alphabet for P*, denoted $\Phi^m(P)$, is obtained from $\Phi(P)$ by replacing each predicate symbol p by the new predicate symbols p^α with $\alpha \in TV(P) \backslash \{0\}$. The *many-valued Herbrand base* for P, denoted HB_P^m, is the Herbrand base over $\Phi^m(P)$. For atoms $A = p(t_1, \ldots, t_k)$ and $\alpha \in TV(P)$, the atom A^α over $\Phi^m(P)$ is defined as $p^\alpha(t_1, \ldots, t_k)$.

Every mvd-program P is translated into the following classical disjunctive logic program $Tr(P) = Tr_1(P) \cup Tr_2(P)$ over $\Phi^m(P)$ (based on Theorem 2.1):

$$Tr_1(P) = \{A_1^\alpha \vee \cdots \vee A_l^\alpha \leftarrow B_1^{\beta_1}, \ldots, B_m^{\beta_m}, not\, C_1^\alpha, \ldots, not\, C_n^\alpha \mid$$
$$(A_1 \vee \cdots \vee A_l \leftarrow B_1, \ldots, B_m, not\, C_1, \ldots, not\, C_n)[c, 1] \in P,$$
$$\beta_1, \ldots, \beta_m \in TV(P),\ \alpha = c - 1 + \min(\beta_1, \ldots, \beta_m) > 0\},$$
$$Tr_2(P) = \{A^\alpha \leftarrow A^\beta \mid A^\alpha,\ A^\beta \in HB_P^m,\ \alpha < \beta\}.$$

Every pcp-interpretation $\boldsymbol{p}$ is translated into the following classical interpretation:

$$\mathrm{Tr}(\boldsymbol{p}) = \{A^\alpha \in HB_P^m \mid \boldsymbol{p}(A) \geq \alpha\}.$$

The following example illustrates the above program translation.

Example 4.1. The mvd-program P given in Section 2.4 is translated into the classical disjunctive logic program $\mathrm{Tr}(P) = \mathrm{Tr}_1(P) \cup \mathrm{Tr}_2(P)$, where $\mathrm{Tr}_1(P)$ is given by:

$$
\begin{aligned}
\mathrm{Tr}_1(P) = \{\, &closed^{0.5}(r) \vee closed^{0.5}(s) \leftarrow \;\; ; road^{0.8}(r,a,b) \leftarrow \;\; ; road^{0.7}(s,b,c) \leftarrow; \\
&reach^{0.1}(X,Y) \leftarrow road^{0.2}(R,X,Y), not\ closed^{0.1}(R); \\
&reach^{0.2}(X,Y) \leftarrow road^{0.3}(R,X,Y), not\ closed^{0.2}(R); \dots; \\
&reach^{0.9}(X,Y) \leftarrow road^{1}(R,X,Y), not\ closed^{0.9}(R); \\
&reach^{0.1}(X,Z) \leftarrow reach^{0.2}(X,Y), reach^{0.2}(Y,Z); \\
&reach^{0.1}(X,Z) \leftarrow reach^{0.2}(X,Y), reach^{0.3}(Y,Z); \\
&reach^{0.1}(X,Z) \leftarrow reach^{0.3}(X,Y), reach^{0.2}(Y,Z); \\
&reach^{0.2}(X,Z) \leftarrow reach^{0.3}(X,Y), reach^{0.3}(Y,Z); \dots; \\
&reach^{0.9}(X,Z) \leftarrow reach^{1}(X,Y), reach^{1}(Y,Z)\,\}.
\end{aligned}
$$

Note that $\mathrm{Tr}_1(P)$ may be quite large. It generally has a manageable size when there are few truth values in $TV(P)$ and few positive literals in the bodies of clauses in P.

4.2   Unfolding Results

Minimal Models. The following lemma shows that every mvd-program P is equivalent to its translation $\mathrm{Tr}(P)$, under all pcp-interpretations into $TV(P)$.

Lemma 4.2. *Let P be an mvd-program, and let $\boldsymbol{p}$ be a pcp-interpretation into $TV(P)$. Then, $\boldsymbol{p}$ is a model of P iff $\boldsymbol{p}$ is a model of $\mathrm{Tr}(P)$.*

The next lemma shows that pcp-interpretations $\boldsymbol{p}$ into $TV(P)$ can be identified with their translation $\mathrm{Tr}(\boldsymbol{p})$, concerning classical disjunctive logic programs over HB_P^m.

Lemma 4.3. *Let P be an mvd-program. Let L be a classical disjunctive logic program over the alphabet $\Phi^m(P)$, and let $\boldsymbol{p}$ be a pcp-interpretation into $TV(P)$. Then, $\boldsymbol{p}$ is a model of L iff $\mathrm{Tr}(\boldsymbol{p})$ is a model of L.*

The following theorem shows that Tr translates mvd-programs under the minimal model semantics into equivalent classical disjunctive logic programs under the minimal model semantics. It can be proved using the two lemmata above.

Theorem 4.4. *Let P be an mvd-program, and let $\boldsymbol{p}$ be a pcp-interpretation. Then, $\boldsymbol{p}$ is a minimal model of P iff $\mathrm{Tr}(\boldsymbol{p})$ is a minimal model of $\mathrm{Tr}(P)$.*

Perfect Models. The alphabet $\Phi_0^m(P)$ is obtained from $\Phi(P)$ by replacing each predicate symbol p by the new predicate symbols p^α with $\alpha \in TV(P)$.

We slightly modify the translation of mvd-programs and pcp-interpretations as follows. Every mvd-program P is translated into the following classical disjunctive logic program $\mathrm{Tr}^\star(P) = \mathrm{Tr}(P) \cup \mathrm{Tr}_3(P)$ over $\Phi_0^m(P)$:

$$\mathrm{Tr}_3(P) \ = \ \{A^0 \vee A^1 \vee A^{n-1} \leftarrow \ \ | \ A \in HB_P\} \cup \{A^0 \leftarrow \ \ | \ A \in HB_P\}\,.$$

Every pcp-interpretation p is translated into the following classical interpretation:

$$\mathrm{Tr}^\star(p) = \mathrm{Tr}(p) \cup \{A^0 \ | \ A \in HB_P\}\,.$$

Roughly speaking, the next lemma shows that pcp-interpretations p into $TV(P)$ can be identified with their translation $\mathrm{Tr}^\star(p)$.

Lemma 4.5. *Let P be an mvd-program. Let L be a classical disjunctive logic program over the alphabet $\Phi_0^m(P)$, and let p be a pcp-interpretation into $TV(P)$. Then, p is a model of L iff $\mathrm{Tr}^\star(p)$ is a model of $L \cup \mathrm{Tr}_3(P)$.*

The following theorem shows that $\mathrm{Tr}^\star$ translates mvd-programs under the perfect model semantics into equivalent classical counterparts.

Theorem 4.6. *Let P be an mvd-program, and let p be a pcp-interpretation. Then, p is a perfect model of P iff $\mathrm{Tr}^\star(p)$ is a perfect model of $\mathrm{Tr}^\star(P)$.*

The following theorem shows that the translation $\mathrm{Tr}(P)$ of a locally stratified mvd-program P is also locally stratified.

Theorem 4.7. *Let P be an mvd-program. If P is locally stratified, then also $\mathrm{Tr}(P)$.*

The next theorem shows that Tr translates locally stratified mvd-programs under the perfect model semantics into equivalent classical counterparts.

Theorem 4.8. *Let P be a locally stratified mvd-program, and let p be a pcp-interpretation. Then, p is a perfect model of P iff $\mathrm{Tr}(p)$ is a perfect model of $\mathrm{Tr}(P)$.*

Stable Models. For classical disjunctive logic programs L and classical interpretations I, denote by L/I the classical Gelfond-Lifschitz transform of L w.r.t. I.

The next lemma shows that for mvd-programs P and pcp-interpretations q, the transform P/q is equivalent to $\mathrm{Tr}(P)/\mathrm{Tr}(q)$, under all pcp-interpretations into $TV(P)$.

Lemma 4.9. *Let P be an mvd-program, and let p and q be two pcp-interpretations into $TV(P)$. Then, p is a model of P/q iff p is a model of $\mathrm{Tr}(P)/\mathrm{Tr}(q)$.*

The next theorem shows that Tr translates mvd-programs under the stable model semantics into equivalent classical counterparts.

Theorem 4.10. *Let P be an mvd-program, and let p be a pcp-interpretation. Then, p is a stable model of P iff $\mathrm{Tr}(p)$ is a stable model of $\mathrm{Tr}(P)$.*

Least Model States. The following lemma shows that every mvd-program P is equivalent to its translation $\mathrm{Tr}(P)$, concerning disjunctive Herbrand states.

Lemma 4.11. *Let P be an mvd-program, and let S be a state. Then, S is a model state of P iff S is a model state of $\mathrm{Tr}(P)$.*

The following theorem shows that Tr translates an mvd-program into a classical counterpart that has the same least model state.

Theorem 4.12. *Let P be an mvd-program, and let S be a state. Then, S is the least model state of P iff S is the least model state of $\mathrm{Tr}(P)$.*

5   Fixpoint Characterizations

In this section, we provide many-valued fixpoint characterizations for the semantics of minimal models, least model states, and perfect models under finite local stratification.

5.1   Minimal Models for Positive Programs

We now give a fixpoint characterization for the set of all minimal models of a positive mvd-program, which is a generalization of the classical counterpart given in [3,18].

In the sequel, let P be a positive mvd-program. The *canonical form* (resp., *expansion*) of a set of pcp-interpretations $\boldsymbol{P}$, denoted $can(\boldsymbol{P})$ (resp., $exp(\boldsymbol{P})$), is defined by:

$$can(\boldsymbol{P}) = \{\boldsymbol{p} \in \boldsymbol{P} \mid \neg\exists \boldsymbol{q} \in \boldsymbol{P}\colon \boldsymbol{q} \subset \boldsymbol{p}\}\,,$$
$$exp(\boldsymbol{P}) = \{\boldsymbol{p} \in \boldsymbol{I_P} \mid \exists \boldsymbol{q} \in \boldsymbol{P}\colon \boldsymbol{q} \subseteq \boldsymbol{p}\}\,.$$

We say $\boldsymbol{P}$ is *in canonical form* (resp., *expanded*) iff $\boldsymbol{P} = can(\boldsymbol{P})$ (resp., $\boldsymbol{P} = exp(\boldsymbol{P})$).

The fixpoint operator is defined on the complete lattice $(\mathcal{E}, \sqsubseteq)$, where $\mathcal{E}$ is the set of all expanded sets of pcp-interpretations, and $\boldsymbol{P} \sqsubseteq \boldsymbol{Q}$ iff $\boldsymbol{Q} \supseteq \boldsymbol{P}$ for all $\boldsymbol{P}, \boldsymbol{Q} \in \mathcal{E}$. The bottom element $\bot$ is the set of all pcp-interpretations, and the top element $\top$ is the empty set. The greatest lower bound of any subset of elements is the union of the elements in the set, and the least upper bound is the intersection of the elements.

The operator T_P^M on expanded sets of pcp-interpretations $\boldsymbol{P}$ is defined by:

$$T_P^M(\boldsymbol{P}) \;=\; \bigcup\{models_{\boldsymbol{p}}(state_P(\boldsymbol{p})) \mid \boldsymbol{p} \in \boldsymbol{P}\},$$

where $state_P$ and $models_{\boldsymbol{p}}$ are given as follows:

$$state_P(\boldsymbol{p}) \;=\; \{A_1^\alpha \vee \cdots \vee A_l^\alpha \mid (A_1 \vee \cdots \vee A_l \leftarrow B_1, \ldots, B_m)[c,1] \in ground(P),$$
$$\alpha = c - 1 + \min(\boldsymbol{p}(B_1), \ldots, \boldsymbol{p}(B_m)) > 0\}\,,$$
$$models_{\boldsymbol{p}}(S) \;=\; \{\boldsymbol{q} \in \boldsymbol{I_P} \mid \boldsymbol{q} \models S,\, \boldsymbol{q} \supseteq \boldsymbol{p}\}\,.$$

The next lemma shows the immediate result that T_P^M is monotonic.

Lemma 5.1. T_P^M *is monotonic.*

We now define the powers of T_P^M. For every expanded set of pcp-interpretations P:

$$T_P^M \uparrow \alpha(P) = \begin{cases} P & \text{if } \alpha = 0; \\ T_P^M(T_P^M \uparrow (\alpha-1)(P)) & \text{if } \alpha > 0 \text{ is a successor ordinal}; \\ \bigcap\{T_P^M \uparrow \beta(P) \mid \beta < \alpha\} & \text{if } \alpha > 0 \text{ is a limit ordinal}. \end{cases}$$

As usual, we use $T_P^M \uparrow \alpha$ to abbreviate $T_P^M \uparrow \alpha(\bot)$.

The following lemma shows that the operator T_P^M is not continuous. This result is immediate by the fact that the classical counterpart of T_P^M is not continuous [18].

Lemma 5.2. T_P^M *is not continuous.*

Even though the operator T_P^M is not continuous, its least fixpoint is attained at the first limit ordinal. This is shown by the following theorem, which follows from a similar result for classical disjunctive logic programs [18].

Theorem 5.3. $lfp(T_P^M) = T_P^M \uparrow \omega$.

The next theorem shows that the set of minimal models of P is given by the canonical form of the least fixpoint of T_P^M.

Theorem 5.4. $MM(P) = can(lfp(T_P^M))$.

5.2   Least Model States for Positive Programs

We now give a fixpoint characterization for the least model state of a positive mvd-program, which is a generalization of the classical counterpart given in [12,4].

In the sequel, let P be a positive mvd-program. We now identify every disjunction $D \in DHB_P$ with the set of all contained atoms $A^\alpha \in HB_P^m$.

The operator T_P^s on expanded disjunctive Herbrand states S is defined by:

$$T_P^s(S) = exp(\{A_1^\alpha \vee \cdots \vee A_l^\alpha \vee D_1 \vee \cdots \vee D_m \mid D_1, \ldots, D_m \in DHB_P, \\ (A_1 \vee \cdots \vee A_l \leftarrow B_1 \wedge \cdots \wedge B_m)[c, 1] \in ground(P), \\ B_1^{\beta_1} \vee D_1, \ldots, B_m^{\beta_m} \vee D_m \in S, \alpha = c - 1 + \min(\beta_1, \ldots, \beta_m) > 0\}).$$

The following lemma shows that the model states of P correspond exactly to the pre-fixpoints of the operator T_P^s.

Lemma 5.5. *Let S be an expanded state. Then, S is a model state of P iff $T_P^s(S) \subseteq S$.*

The next lemma shows that the operator T_P^s is continuous. This result follows immediately from the continuity of the classical counterpart of T_P^s [12].

Lemma 5.6. T_P^s *is continuous.*

The powers of T_P^s are defined as usual: For all Herbrand states S, define $T_P^s \uparrow \omega(S)$ as the union of all $T_P^s \uparrow n(S)$ with $n < \omega$, where $T_P^s \uparrow 0(S) = S$ and $T_P^s \uparrow (n+1)(S) = T_P^s(T_P^s \uparrow n(S))$ for all $n < \omega$. We use $T_P^s \uparrow \omega$ to abbreviate $T_P^s \uparrow \omega(\emptyset)$.

The following theorem shows that the least model state of P coincides with the least fixpoint of T_P^s, and that the least fixpoint is attained at the first limit ordinal. This result follows immediately from Lemmata 5.5 and 5.6.

Theorem 5.7. $MS_P = lfp(T_P^s) = T_P^s \uparrow \omega$.

We give an illustrative example.

Example 5.8. Consider again the positive mvd-program P given in Example 3.5. Its least model state MS_P is given by $T_P^s \uparrow \omega = T_P^s \uparrow 3$:

$$can(T_P^s \uparrow 1) = S_1 = \{closed^{0.5}(r) \vee closed^{0.5}(s),\ road^{0.8}(r,a,b),\ road^{0.7}(s,b,c)\},$$
$$can(T_P^s \uparrow 2) = S_2 = S_1 \cup \{reach^{0.7}(a,b) \vee closed^{0.7}(r),\ reach^{0.6}(b,c) \vee closed^{0.6}(s)\},$$
$$can(T_P^s \uparrow 3) = S_3 = S_2 \cup \{reach^{0.5}(a,c) \vee closed^{0.7}(r) \vee closed^{0.6}(s)\}.$$

5.3 Perfect Models under Finite Local Stratification

We now give an iterative fixpoint characterization of perfect models of mvd-programs with finite local stratification. It generalizes the classical counterpart in [18].

For sets of emvd-clauses P and sets of expanded interpretations $\boldsymbol{P}$, we define:

$$\overline{T}_P^M(\boldsymbol{P}) = \bigcup \{models_{\boldsymbol{p}}(\overline{state}_P(\boldsymbol{p})) \mid \boldsymbol{p} \in \boldsymbol{P}\},$$

where $models_{\boldsymbol{p}}$ is defined as in Section 5.1 and $\overline{state}_P$ is given by:

$$\overline{state}_P(\boldsymbol{p}) = \{A_1^\alpha \vee \cdots \vee A_l^\alpha \mid (A_1 \vee \cdots \vee A_l; d \leftarrow B_1, \ldots, B_m)[c,1] \in ground(P),$$
$$\alpha = c - 1 + \min(\boldsymbol{p}(B_1), \ldots, \boldsymbol{p}(B_m)) > d\}.$$

The following theorem formulates the iterative fixpoint characterization.

Theorem 5.9. Let P be an mvd-program and let $H_1, H_2, \ldots, H_n$ be a finite local stratification of P. For pcp-interpretations $\boldsymbol{p}$, we define:

$$P_i(\boldsymbol{p}) = P_i/\boldsymbol{p} \cup \{A^\alpha \leftarrow \mid A^\alpha \in HB_P^m,\ \boldsymbol{p}(A) \geq \alpha\}.$$

Then, the set of perfect models of P is given as $\boldsymbol{P}_n$, where

$$\boldsymbol{P}_1 = can(T_{P_1}^M \uparrow \omega),$$
$$\boldsymbol{P}_i = \bigcup \{can(\overline{T}_{P_i(\boldsymbol{p})}^M \uparrow \omega) \mid \boldsymbol{p} \in \boldsymbol{P}_{i-1}\} \text{ for all } i \in \{2, \ldots, n\}.$$

6 Summary and Outlook

We introduced least model states for many-valued disjunctive logic programs. We then showed how to unfold many-valuedness under the semantics of minimal models, perfect models, stable models, and least model states. Thus, existing technology for classical disjunctive logic programming can be used to implement many-valued disjunctive logic programming. Using these results, we gave many-valued fixpoint characterizations for the set of all minimal models and the least model state. We also gave an iterative fixpoint characterization for the perfect model semantics under finite local stratification.

An interesting topic of future research is to elaborate other semantics for many-valued disjunctive logic programs, for example, to define partial stable models. Moreover, it would be very interesting to work out fixpoint characterizations for stable (and partial stable) models. This may be done by generalizing the evidential transformation in [2] or the 3-S transformation in [17]. Finally, another topic of future research is to elaborate proof theories for the various semantics.

Acknowledgments

This work has been supported by the Austrian Science Fund Project N Z29-INF and a DFG grant. Many thanks to the reviewers for their useful comments.

References

1. A. Dekhtyar and V. S. Subrahmanian. Hybrid probabilistic programs. In *Proceedings ICLP-97*, pp. 391–405. MIT Press, 1997.
2. J. A. Fernández, J. Lobo, J. Minker, and V. S. Subrahmanian. Disjunctive LP + integrity constraints = stable model semantics. *Ann. Math. Artif. Intell.*, 8(3–4):449–474, 1993. 349
3. J. A. Fernández and J. Minker. Bottom-up computation of perfect models for disjunctive theories. *J. Logic Program.*, 25(1):33–51, 1995. 346
4. J. Lobo, J. Minker, and A. Rajasekar. *Foundations of Disjunctive Logic Programming.* MIT Press, Cambridge, MA, 1992. 342, 347
5. T. Lukasiewicz. Many-valued disjunctive logic programs with probabilistic semantics. In *Proceedings LPNMR-99*, LNCS 1730, pp. 277–289. Springer, 1999. 336, 337, 339, 340, 341
6. T. Lukasiewicz. Many-valued first-order logics with probabilistic semantics. In *Proceedings CSL-98*, LNCS 1584, pp. 415–429. Springer, 1999. 337, 343
7. T. Lukasiewicz. Probabilistic and truth-functional many-valued logic programming. In *Proceedings ISMVL-99*, pp. 236–241. IEEE Computer Society, 1999. 337, 343
8. T. Lukasiewicz. Fixpoint characterizations for many-valued disjunctive logic programs with probabilistic semantics. Technical Report INFSYS RR-1843-01-06, Institut für Informationssysteme, TU Wien, 2001. 337
9. T. Lukasiewicz. Probabilistic logic programming with conditional constraints. *ACM Trans. Computat. Logic*, 2(3):289–337, 2001.

10. C. Mateis. *A Quantitative Extension of Disjunctive Logic Programming.* Doctoral Dissertation, Technische Universität Wien, 1998.
11. J. Minker. Overview of disjunctive logic programming. *Ann. Math. Artif. Intell.*, 12:1–24, 1994.
12. J. Minker and A. Rajasekar. A fixpoint semantics for disjunctive logic programs. *J. Logic Program.*, 9(1):45–74, 1990. 342, 347
13. R. T. Ng and V. S. Subrahmanian. Stable semantics for probabilistic deductive databases. *Inf. Comput.*, 110:42–83, 1994.
14. L. Ngo. Probabilistic disjunctive logic programming. In *Proceedings UAI-96*, pp. 397–404. Morgan Kaufmann, 1996.
15. T. C. Przymusinski. On the declarative semantics of stratified deductive databases and logic programs. In J. Minker, editor, *Foundations of Deductive Databases and Logic Programming*, pp. 193–216. Morgan Kaufmann, 1988.
16. T. C. Przymusinski. Stable semantics for disjunctive programs. *New Generation Comput.*, 9:401–424, 1991.
17. C. Ruiz and J. Minker. Computing stable and partial stable models of extended disjunctive logic programs. In *Nonmonotonic Extensions of Logic Programming*, LNCS 927, pp. 205–229. Springer, 1995. 349
18. D. Seipel, J. Minker, and C. Ruiz. Model generation and state generation for disjunctive logic programs. *J. Logic Program.*, 32(1):49–69, 1997. 346, 347, 348
19. M. H. van Emden. Quantitative deduction and its fixpoint theory. *J. Logic Program.*, 3(1):37–53, 1986. 337

Multi-adjoint Logic Programming with Continuous Semantics

Jesús Medina[1] *, Manuel Ojeda-Aciego[1] **, and Peter Vojtáš[2]***

[1] Dept. Matemática Aplicada. Universidad de Málaga
{jmedina,aciego}@ctima.uma.es
[2] Inst. Computer Science. Academy of Science of Czech Republic
vojtas@cs.cas.cz

Abstract. Considering different implication operators, such as Łukasie-wicz, Gödel or product implication in the same logic program, naturally leads to the allowance of several adjoint pairs in the lattice of truth-values. In this paper we apply this idea to introduce multi-adjoint logic programs as an extension of monotonic logic programs. The continuity of the immediate consequences operators is proved and the assumptions required to get continuity are further analysed.

1 Introduction

One can find several papers in the literature on applications of definite fuzzy logic programming which are based either on Łukasiewicz, or product, or Gödel implications on the unit real interval (an overview can be seen in [9]); for more complex systems it is reasonable to allow room for several different implications. In [2] an extension was presented in which the set of truth-values is generalised to a residuated lattice (in order to embed hybrid probabilistic logic programs). Another generalisation of the set of truth-values is that given by the structure of bilattice, which has been used to handle negation in logic programming [5].

The purpose of this work is to provide a further generalisation of the frame-work given in [2,3] so that: (1) it is possible to use a number of different implica-tions in the rules of our programs, (2) the algebraic requirements on residuated lattices are weaken and (3) we focus on the continuity of the immediate conse-quences operator by providing sufficient conditions for continuity.

A general theory of logic programming which allows the simultaneous use of different implications in the rules and rather general connectives in the bod-ies is presented. Models of these programs are post-fixpoints of the immediate consequences operator, which is proved to be monotonic under very general hy-potheses.

---

* Partially supported by Spanish DGI project BFM2000-1054-C02-02 and Junta de Andalucía project TIC-115.

** Partially supported by Spanish DGI project BFM2000-1054-C02-02 and Junta de Andalucía project TIC-115.

*** Supported by Grant GAČR 201/00/1489

T. Eiter, W. Faber, and M. Truszczyński (Eds.): LPNMR 2001, LNAI 2173, pp. 351–364, 2001.
© Springer-Verlag Berlin Heidelberg 2001

The final part of the paper deals with the continuity of the immediate consequences operator, which is proved under the assumption of continuity of all the
operators in the program (but, possibly, the implications). This theorem is also
re-stated in terms of lower-semicontinuity of the operators.

2   Preliminary Definitions

We will make extensive use of the constructions and terminology of universal
algebra, in order to define formally the syntax and the semantics of the languages
we will deal with. A minimal set of concepts from universal algebra, which will
be used in the sequel in the style of [2], are introduced below.

2.1   Some Definitions from Universal Algebra

Definition 1 (Graded set). *A* graded set *is a set Ω with a function which
assigns to each element $\omega \in \Omega$ a number $n \geq 0$, called the arity of ω.*

Definition 2 (Ω-Algebra). *Given a graded set Ω, an Ω-algebra $\mathfrak{A}$ is a pair
$\langle A, I \rangle$ where A is a nonempty set called the carrier, and I is a function which
assigns maps to the elements of Ω as follows:*

1. *Each element $\omega \in \Omega_n$, $n > 0$, is interpreted as a map $I(\omega): A^n \to A$, denoted
   by $\omega_{\mathfrak{A}}$.*
2. *Each element $c \in \Omega_0$ (i.e., c is a constant) is interpreted as an element $I(c)$
   in A, denoted by $c_{\mathfrak{A}}$.*

Finally, the last definition needed will be that of *subalgebra* of an Ω-algebra,
which generalises the concept of substructure of an algebraic structure. The
definition is straightforward.

Definition 3 (Subalgebra of an Ω-algebra). *Given an Ω-algebra $\mathfrak{A} = \langle A, I \rangle$,
an Ω-subalgebra $\mathfrak{B}$, is a pair $\langle B, J \rangle$, such that $B \subset A$ and*

1. *$J(c) = I(c)$ for all $c \in \Omega_0$.*
2. *Given $\omega \in \Omega_n$, then $J(\omega): B^n \to B$ is the restriction of $I(\omega): A^n \to A$.*

2.2   Multi-adjoint Semilattices and Multi-adjoint Algebras

The main concept we will need in this section is that of *adjoint pair*, firstly
introduced in a logical context by Pavelka [8], who interpreted the poset structure
of the set of truth-values as a category, and the relation between the connectives
of implication and conjunction as functors in this category. The result turned
out to be another example of the well-known concept of adjunction, introduced
by Kan in the general setting of category theory in 1950.

Definition 4 (Adjoint pair). *Let $\langle P, \preceq \rangle$ be a partially ordered set and $(\leftarrow, \&)$
a pair of binary operations in P such that:*

(a1) Operation & is increasing in both arguments, i.e. if $x_1, x_2, y \in P$ such that $x_1 \preceq x_2$ then $(x_1 \& y) \preceq (x_2 \& y)$ and $(y \& x_1) \preceq (y \& x_2)$;

(a2) Operation $\leftarrow$ is increasing in the first argument (the consequent) and decreasing in the second argument (the antecedent), i.e. if $x_1, x_2, y \in P$ such that $x_1 \preceq x_2$ then $(x_1 \leftarrow y) \preceq (x_2 \leftarrow y)$ and $(y \leftarrow x_2) \preceq (y \leftarrow x_1)$;

(a3) For any $x, y, z \in P$, we have that $x \preceq (y \leftarrow z)$ holds if and only if $(x \& z) \preceq y$ holds.

Then we say that $(\leftarrow, \&)$ forms an adjoint pair in $\langle P, \preceq \rangle$.

The need of the monotonicity of operators $\leftarrow$ and $\&$ is clear, if they are to be interpreted as generalised implications and conjunctions. The third property in the definition, which corresponds to the categorical adjointness; but can be adequately interpreted in terms of multiple-valued inference as asserting that the truth-value of $y \leftarrow z$ is the maximal x satisfying $x \& z \preceq_P y$, and also the validity of the following generalised modus ponens rule [6]:

If x is a lower bound of $\psi \leftarrow \varphi$, and z is a lower bound of φ then a lower bound y of ψ is $x \& z$.

In addition to $(a1)$-$(a3)$ it will be necessary to assume the existence of bottom and top elements in the poset of truth-values (the zero and one elements), and the existence of joins (suprema) for every directed subset; that is, we will assume a structure of complete upper-semilattice (cus-lattice, for short) but nothing about associativity, commutativity and general boundary conditions of $\&$. In particular, the requirement that $(L, \&, \top)$ has to be a commutative monoid in a residuated lattice is too restrictive, in that commutativity needn't be required in the proofs of soundness and correctness [9]. Here in this generality we are able to work with approximations of t-norms and/or conjunctions learnt from data by a neural net like in [7].

Extending the results in [2,3,9] to a more general setting, in which different implications (Łukasiewicz, Gödel, product) and thus, several modus ponens-like inference rules are used, naturally leads to considering several *adjoint pairs* in the lattice. More formally,

Definition 5 (Multi-Adjoint Semilattice). *Let $\langle L, \preceq \rangle$ be a cus-lattice. A multi-adjoint semilattice $\mathcal{L}$ is a tuple $(L, \preceq, \leftarrow_1, \&_1, \ldots, \leftarrow_n, \&_n)$ satisfying the following items:*

(l1) $\langle L, \preceq \rangle$ is bounded, i.e. it has bottom ($\bot$) and top ($\top$) elements;

(l2) $(\leftarrow_i, \&_i)$ is an adjoint pair in $\langle L, \preceq \rangle$ for $i = 1, \ldots, n$;

(l3) $\top \&_i \vartheta = \vartheta \&_i \top = \vartheta$ for all $\vartheta \in L$ for $i = 1, \ldots, n$.

Remark 1. Note that residuated lattices are a special case of multi-adjoint semilattice, in which the underlying poset has a cus-lattice structure, has monoidal structure wrt $\otimes$ and $\top$, and only one adjoint pair is present.

From the point of view of expressiveness, it is interesting to allow extra operators to be involved with the operators in the multi-adjoint semilattice. The structure which captures this possibility is that of a multi-adjoint algebra.

Definition 6 (Multi-Adjoint Ω-Algebra). *Let Ω be a graded set containing operators $\leftarrow_i$ and $\&_i$ for $i = 1, \ldots, n$ and possibly some extra operators, and let $\mathfrak{L} = (L, I)$ be an Ω-algebra whose carrier set L is a cus-lattice under $\preceq$.*

We say that $\mathfrak{L}$ is a multi-adjoint Ω-algebra *with respect to the pairs $(\leftarrow_i, \&_i)$ for $i = 1, \ldots, n$ if $\mathcal{L} = (L, \preceq, I(\leftarrow_1), I(\&_1), \ldots, I(\leftarrow_n), I(\&_n))$ is a multi-adjoint semilattice.*

In practice, we will usually have to assume some properties on the extra operators considered. These extra operators will be assumed to be either conjunctors or disjunctors or aggregators.

Example 1. Consider $\Omega = \{\leftarrow_P, \&_P, \leftarrow_G, \&_G, \wedge_L, @\}$, the real unit interval $U = [0, 1]$ with its lattice structure, and the interpretation function I defined as:

$$I(\leftarrow_P)(x, y) = \min(1, x/y) \qquad I(\&_P)(x, y) = x \cdot y$$

$$I(\leftarrow_G)(x, y) = \begin{cases} 1 & \text{if } x \leq y \\ 0 & \text{otherwise} \end{cases} \qquad I(\&_G)(x, y) = \min(x, y)$$

$$I(@)(x, y, z) = \tfrac{1}{6}(x + 2y + 3z) \qquad I(\wedge_L)(x, y) = \max(0, x + y - 1)$$

that is, connectives are interpreted as product and Gödel connectives, a weighted sum and Łukasiewicz implication; then $\langle U, I \rangle$ is a multi-adjoint Ω-algebra with one aggregator and one additional conjunctor (denoted $\wedge_L$ to make explicit that its adjoint implicator is not in the language).

Note that the use of aggregators as weighted sums somehow covers the approach taken in [1] when considering the evidential support logic rules of combination.

$\square$

2.3   General Approach to the Syntax of Propositional Languages

The syntax of the propositional languages we will work with will be defined by using the concept of Ω-algebra. To begin with, the concept of alphabet of the language is introduced below.

Definition 7 (Alphabet). *Let Ω be a graded set, and Π a countably infinite set. The* alphabet $A_{\Omega,\Pi}$ *associated to Ω and Π is defined to be the disjoint union $\Omega \cup \Pi \cup S$, where S is the set of auxiliary symbols "(", ")" and ",".*

In the following, we will use only A_Ω to designate an alphabet, for deleting the reference to Π cannot lead to confusion.

Definition 8 (Expressions). *Given a graded set Ω and alphabet A_Ω. The Ω-algebra $\mathfrak{E} = \langle A_\Omega^*, I \rangle$ of* expressions *is defined as follows:*

1. The carrier A_Ω^* is the set of strings over A_Ω.

2. *The interpretation function I satisfies the following conditions for strings $a_1, \ldots, a_n$ in A_Ω^*:*
   - *$c_{\mathfrak{E}} = c$, where c is a constant operation ($c \in \Omega_0$).*
   - *$\omega_{\mathfrak{E}}(a_1) = \omega\, a_1$, where ω is an unary operation ($\omega \in \Omega_1$).*
   - *$\omega_{\mathfrak{E}}(a_1, a_2) = (a_1 \omega\, a_2)$, where ω is a binary operation ($\omega \in \Omega_2$).*
   - *$\omega_{\mathfrak{E}}(a_1, \ldots, a_n) = \omega(a_1, \ldots, a_n)$, where ω is a n-ary operation ($\omega \in \Omega_n$) and $n > 2$.*

Note that an expression is only a string of letters of the alphabet, that is, it needn't be a well-formed formula. Actually, the well-formed formulas is the subset of the set of expressions defined as follows:

Definition 9 (Well-formed formulas). *Let Ω be a graded set, Π a countable set of propositional symbols and $\mathfrak{E}$ the algebra of expressions corresponding to the alphabet $A_{\Omega,\Pi}$. The* well-formed formulas *(in short, formulas) generated by Ω over Π is the least subalgebra $\mathfrak{F}$ of the algebra of expressions $\mathfrak{E}$ containing Π.*

The set of formulas, that is the carrier of $\mathfrak{F}$, will be denoted F_Ω. It is well-known that least subalgebras can be defined as an inductive closure, and it is not difficult to check that it is freely generated, therefore it satisfies the *unique homomorphic extension theorem* stated below:

Theorem 1. *Let Ω be a graded set, Π a set of propositional symbols, $\mathfrak{F}$ the corresponding Ω-algebra of formulas. Let $\mathfrak{L}$ be an arbitrary Ω-algebra with carrier L. Then, for every function $J: \Pi \to L$ there is a unique homomorphism $\hat{J}: F_\Omega \to L$ such that:*

1. *For all $p \in \Pi$, $\hat{J}(p) = J(p)$;*
2. *For each constant $c \in \Omega_0$, $\hat{J}(c_{\mathfrak{F}}) = c_{\mathfrak{L}}$;*
3. *For every $\omega \in \Omega_n$ with $n > 0$ and for all $F_i \in F_\Omega$ with $i = 1, \ldots, n$*

$$\hat{J}(\omega_{\mathfrak{F}}(F_1, \ldots, F_n)) = \omega_{\mathfrak{L}}(\hat{J}(F_1), \ldots, \hat{J}(F_n)).$$

3 Syntax and Semantics of Multi-adjoint Logic Programs

Multi-adjoint logic programs will be constructed from the abstract syntax induced by a multi-adjoint algebra on a set of propositional symbols. Specifically, we will consider a multi-adjoint Ω-algebra $\mathfrak{L}$ whose extra operators are either conjunctors, denoted $\wedge_1, \ldots, \wedge_k$, or disjunctors, denoted $\vee_1, \ldots, \vee_l$, or aggregators, denoted $@_1, \ldots, @_m$. (This algebra will host the manipulation the truth-values of the formulas in our programs.)

In addition, let Π be a set of propositional symbols and the corresponding algebra of formulas $\mathfrak{F}$ freely generated from Π by the operators in Ω. (This algebra will be used to define the syntax of a propositional language.)

Remark 2. As we are working with two Ω-algebras, and to discharge the notation, we introduce a special notation to clarify which algebra an operator belongs to, instead of continuously using either $\omega_{\mathfrak{L}}$ or $\omega_{\mathfrak{F}}$. Let ω be an operator symbol in Ω, its interpretation under $\mathfrak{L}$ is denoted $\dot{\omega}$ (a dot on the operator), whereas ω itself will denote $\omega_{\mathfrak{F}}$ when there is no risk of confusion.

3.1 Syntax of Multi-adjoint Logic Programs

The definition of multi-adjoint logic program is given, as usual, as a set of rules and facts. The particular syntax of these rules and facts is given below:

Definition 10 (Multi-Adjoint Logic Programs). *A* multi-adjoint logic program *is a set* $\mathbb{P}$ *of rules of the form* $\langle (A \leftarrow_i B), \vartheta \rangle$ *such that:*

1. *The* rule $(A \leftarrow_i B)$ *is a formula of* $\mathfrak{F}$;
2. *The* confidence factor ϑ *is an element (a truth-value) of* L;
3. *The* head *of the rule* A *is a propositional symbol of* Π.
4. *The* body *formula* B *is a formula of* $\mathfrak{F}$ *built from propositional symbols* $B_1, \ldots, B_n$ *(*$n \geq 0$*) by the use of conjunctors* $\&_1, \ldots, \&_n$ *and* $\wedge_1, \ldots, \wedge_k$, *disjunctors* $\vee_1, \ldots, \vee_l$ *and aggregators* $@_1, \ldots, @_m$.
5. Facts *are rules with body* $\top$.
6. *A* query *(or* goal*) is a propositional symbol intended as a question* ?A *prompting the system.*

Note that an arbitrary composition of conjunctors, disjunctors and aggregators is also an aggregator.

Sometimes, we will represent the above pair as $A \xleftarrow{\vartheta}_i @[B_1, \ldots, B_n]$, where[1] $B_1, \ldots, B_n$ are the propositional variables occurring in the body and $@$ is the aggregator obtained as a composition.

3.2 Semantics of Multi-adjoint Logic Programs

Definition 11 (Interpretation). *An* interpretation *is a mapping* $I : \Pi \to L$. *The set of all interpretations of the formulas defined by the* Ω-algebra $\mathfrak{F}$ *in the* Ω-algebra $\mathfrak{L}$ *is denoted* $\mathcal{I}_{\mathfrak{L}}$.

Note that by the unique homomorphic extension theorem, each of these interpretations can be uniquely extended to the whole set of formulas F_Ω.

The ordering $\preceq$ of the truth-values L can be easily extended to the set of interpretations as usual:

Definition 12 (Semilattice of interpretations). *Consider two interpretations* $I_1, I_2 \in \mathcal{I}_{\mathfrak{L}}$. *Then,* $\langle \mathcal{I}_{\mathfrak{L}}, \sqsubseteq \rangle$ *is a cus-lattice where* $I_1 \sqsubseteq I_2$ *iff* $I_1(p) \preceq I_2(p)$ *for all* $p \in \Pi$. *The least interpretation* $\triangle$ *maps every propositional symbol to the least element* $\bot$ *of* L.

A rule of a multi-adjoint logic program is satisfied whenever the truth-value of the rule is greater or equal than the confidence factor associated with the rule. Formally:

Definition 13 (Satisfaction, Model). *Given an interpretation* $I \in \mathcal{I}_{\mathfrak{L}}$, *a* weighted rule $\langle A \leftarrow_i B, \vartheta \rangle$ *is* satisfied *by* I *iff* $\vartheta \preceq \hat{I}(A \leftarrow_i B)$. *An interpretation* $I \in \mathcal{I}_{\mathfrak{L}}$ *is a* model *of a multi-adjoint logic program* $\mathbb{P}$ *iff all weighted rules in* $\mathbb{P}$ *are satisfied by* I.

---

[1] Note the use of square brackets in this context.

Note the following equalities

$$\hat{I}(A \leftarrow_i \mathcal{B}) = \hat{I}(A) \dot{\leftarrow}_i \hat{I}(\mathcal{B}) = I(A) \dot{\leftarrow}_i \hat{I}(\mathcal{B})$$

and the evaluation of $\hat{I}(\mathcal{B})$ proceeds inductively as usual, till all propositional symbols in $\mathcal{B}$ are reached and evaluated under I. For the particular case of a fact (a rule with $\top$ in the body) satisfaction of $\langle A \leftarrow_i \top, \vartheta \rangle$ means

$$\vartheta \preceq \hat{I}(A \leftarrow_i \top) = I(A) \dot{\leftarrow}_i \top$$

by property *(a3)* of adjoint pairs this is equivalent to $\vartheta \mathbin{\dot{\&}}_i \top \preceq I(A)$ and this by assumption *(l3)* of multi-adjoint semilattices gives $\vartheta \preceq I(A)$.

Definition 14. *An element $\lambda \in L$ is a* correct answer *for a program $\mathbb{P}$ and a query ?A if for an arbitrary interpretation $I \colon \Pi \to L$ which is a model of $\mathbb{P}$ we have $\lambda \preceq I(A)$.*

4   Fix-Point Semantics

It is possible to generalise the immediate consequences operator, given by van Emden and Kowalski in [4], to the framework of multi-adjoint logic programs as follows:

Definition 15. *Let $\mathbb{P}$ be a multi-adjoint logic program. The* immediate consequences operator $T_{\mathbb{P}}^{\mathcal{L}} \colon \mathcal{I}_{\mathcal{L}} \to \mathcal{I}_{\mathcal{L}}$, *mapping interpretations to interpretations, is defined by considering*

$$T_{\mathbb{P}}^{\mathcal{L}}(I)(A) = \sup \left\{ \vartheta \mathbin{\dot{\&}}_i \hat{I}(\mathcal{B}) \mid A \xleftarrow{\vartheta}_i \mathcal{B} \in \mathbb{P} \right\}$$

Note that all the suprema involved in the definition do exist because L is assumed to be a cus-lattice.

As it is usual in the logic programming framework, the semantics of a multi-adjoint logic program is characterised by the post-fixpoints of $T_{\mathbb{P}}^{\mathcal{L}}$.

Theorem 2. *An interpretation I of $\mathcal{I}_{\mathcal{L}}$ is a model of a multi-adjoint logic program $\mathbb{P}$ iff $T_{\mathbb{P}}^{\mathcal{L}}(I) \sqsubseteq I$.*

Proof: Assume we have an interpretation I for the program $\mathbb{P}$, then we have the following chain of equivalent statements for all rule $A \xleftarrow{\vartheta}_i \mathcal{B}$ in $\mathbb{P}$

$$\vartheta \preceq \hat{I}(A \leftarrow_i \mathcal{B})$$
$$\vartheta \preceq \hat{I}(A) \dot{\leftarrow}_i \hat{I}(\mathcal{B})$$
$$\vartheta \mathbin{\dot{\&}}_i \hat{I}(\mathcal{B}) \preceq \hat{I}(A) = I(A)$$
$$\sup\{\vartheta \mathbin{\dot{\&}}_i \hat{I}(\mathcal{B}) \mid A \xleftarrow{\vartheta}_i \mathcal{B} \in \mathbb{P}\} \preceq I(A)$$
$$T_{\mathbb{P}}^{\mathcal{L}}(I)(A) \preceq I(A)$$

Thus, if I is a model of $\mathbb{P}$, then for every A occurring in the head of a rule we have $T_{\mathbb{P}}^{\mathcal{L}}(I)(A) \preceq I(A)$. If A is not the head of any rule, we have $T_{\mathbb{P}}^{\mathcal{L}}(I)(A) = \sup \varnothing = \bot \leq I(A)$ and, therefore, I is a post-fixpoint for $T_{\mathbb{P}}^{\mathcal{L}}$.

Reciprocally, assume that I is a post-fixpoint for $T_{\mathbb{P}}^{\mathcal{L}}$, then any rule $A \xleftarrow{\vartheta}_i \mathcal{B}$ is fulfilled.

$\square$

Note that the fixpoint theorem works even without any further assumptions on conjunctors (definitely they need not be commutative and associative).

The monotonicity of the operator $T_{\mathbb{P}}^{\mathcal{L}}$, for the case of only one adjoint pair, has been shown in [3]. The proof for the general case is similar.

Theorem 3 (Monotonicity of $T_{\mathbb{P}}^{\mathcal{L}}$). *The operator $T_{\mathbb{P}}^{\mathcal{L}}$ is monotonic.*

Proof: Consider I and J two elements of $\mathcal{I}_{\mathfrak{L}}$ such that $I \sqsubseteq J$. We have to show that

$$T_{\mathbb{P}}^{\mathcal{L}}(I) \sqsubseteq T_{\mathbb{P}}^{\mathcal{L}}(J)$$

Let A be a propositional symbol in Π,

$$T_{\mathbb{P}}^{\mathcal{L}}(I)(A) = \sup \left\{ \vartheta \mathbin{\dot{\&}}_i \hat{I}(\mathcal{B}) \mid A \xleftarrow{\vartheta}_i \mathcal{B} \in \mathbb{P} \right\}$$

If we had $\hat{I}(\mathcal{B}) \leq \hat{J}(\mathcal{B})$ for all $\mathcal{B}$, then we would also have $\vartheta \mathbin{\dot{\&}}_i \hat{I}(\mathcal{B}) \preceq \vartheta \mathbin{\dot{\&}}_i \hat{J}(\mathcal{B})$ for all i, since operators $\dot{\&}_i$ are increasing. Now, by taking suprema

$$T_{\mathbb{P}}^{\mathcal{L}}(I)(A) \preceq T_{\mathbb{P}}^{\mathcal{L}}(J)(A) \quad \text{for all } A$$

Therefore, it is sufficient to prove that $\hat{I}(\mathcal{B}) \preceq \hat{J}(\mathcal{B})$ for all $\mathcal{B}$. We will use structural induction:

If $\mathcal{B}$ is an atomic formula, then it is obvious, ie

$$\hat{I}(\mathcal{B}) = I(\mathcal{B}) \preceq J(\mathcal{B}) = \hat{J}(\mathcal{B})$$

For the inductive case, consider $\mathcal{B} = @[\mathcal{B}_1, \ldots, \mathcal{B}_n]$ and assume that $\hat{I}(\mathcal{B}_i) \preceq \hat{J}(\mathcal{B}_i)$ for all $i = 1, \ldots, n$. By definition of the rules, we know that $@$ behaves as an aggregator, and therefore, using the induction hypothesis

$$
\begin{aligned}
\hat{I}(\mathcal{B}) &= \dot{@}[\hat{I}(\mathcal{B}_1), \ldots, \hat{I}(\mathcal{B}_n)] \\
&\preceq \dot{@}[\hat{J}(\mathcal{B}_1), \ldots, \hat{J}(\mathcal{B}_n)] \\
&= \hat{J}(\mathcal{B})
\end{aligned}
$$

$\square$

Due to the monotonicity of the immediate consequences operator, the semantics of $\mathbb{P}$ is given by its least model which, as shown by Knaster-Tarski's theorem, is exactly the least fixpoint of $T_{\mathbb{P}}^{\mathcal{L}}$, which can be obtained by transfinitely iterating $T_{\mathbb{P}}^{\mathcal{L}}$ from the least interpretation $\triangle$.

The proof of the monotonicity of the $T_{\mathbb{P}}^{\mathfrak{L}}$ operator in [2] is accompanied by the following statement, surely due to their wanting to stress the embedding of different logic programming paradigms:

> The major difference to classical logic programming is that our $T_{\mathbb{P}}^{\mathfrak{L}}$ may not be continuous, and therefore more than countably many iterations may be necessary to reach the least fixpoint.

In the line of the previous quotation, we would like to study sufficient conditions for the continuity of the $T_{\mathbb{P}}^{\mathfrak{L}}$ operator.

5   On the Continuity of the $T_{\mathbb{P}}^{\mathfrak{L}}$ Operator

A first result in this approach is that whenever every operator in Ω turns out to be continuous in the lattice, then $T_{\mathbb{P}}$ is also continuous and, consequently, its least fixpoint can be obtained by a countably infinite iteration from the least interpretation.

Let us state the definition of continuous function which will be used.

Definition 16. *Let L be a complete upper semilattice and let $f: L \to L$ be a mapping. We say that f is* continuous *if it preserves suprema of directed sets, that is, given a directed set X one has*

$$f(\sup X) = \sup\{f(x) \mid x \in X\}$$

A mapping $g: L^n \to L$ is said to be continuous *provided that it is continuous in each argument separately.*

Definition 17. *Let $\mathfrak{F}$ be a language interpreted on a multi-adjoint Ω-algebra $\mathfrak{L}$, and let ω be any operator symbol in the language. We say that ω is* continuous *if its interpretation under $\mathfrak{L}$, that is $\dot{\omega}$, is continuous in L.*

Now we state and prove a technical lemma which will allow us to prove the continuity of the immediate consequences operator.

Lemma 1. *Let $\mathbb{P}$ be a program interpreted on a multi-adjoint Ω-algebra $\mathfrak{L}$, and let $\mathcal{B}$ be any body formula in $\mathbb{P}$. Assume that all the operators @ in $\mathcal{B}$ are continuous, let X be a directed set of interpretations, and write $S = \sup X$; then*

$$\hat{S}(\mathcal{B}) = \sup\{\hat{J}(\mathcal{B}) \mid J \in X\}$$

Proof: Follows by induction.   □

Theorem 4. *If all the operators occurring in the bodies of the rules of a program $\mathbb{P}$ are continuous, and the adjoint conjunctions are continuous in their second argument, then $T_{\mathbb{P}}^{\mathfrak{L}}$ is continuous.*

Proof: We have to check that for each directed subset of interpretations X and each atomic formula A

$$T_{\mathbb{P}}^{\mathfrak{L}}(\sup X)(A) = \sup\{T_{\mathbb{P}}^{\mathfrak{L}}(J)(A) \mid J \in X\}$$

Let us write $S = \sup X$, and consider the following chain of equalities:

$$
\begin{aligned}
T_{\mathbb{P}}^{\mathfrak{L}}(\sup X)(A) &= \sup\{\vartheta \mathbin{\dot{\&}_i} \hat{S}(\mathcal{B}) \mid A \xleftarrow{\vartheta}_i \mathcal{B} \in \mathbb{P}\} \\
&\overset{(1)}{=} \sup\{\vartheta \mathbin{\dot{\&}_i} \sup\{\hat{J}(\mathcal{B}) \mid J \in X\} \mid A \xleftarrow{\vartheta}_i \mathcal{B} \in \mathbb{P}\} \\
&\overset{(2)}{=} \sup\{\vartheta \mathbin{\dot{\&}_i} \hat{J}(\mathcal{B}) \mid J \in X, \text{ and } A \xleftarrow{\vartheta}_i \mathcal{B} \in \mathbb{P}\} \\
&= \sup\{\sup\{\vartheta \mathbin{\dot{\&}_i} \hat{J}(\mathcal{B}) \mid A \xleftarrow{\vartheta}_i \mathcal{B} \in \mathbb{P}\} \mid J \in X\} \\
&= \sup\{T_{\mathbb{P}}^{\mathfrak{L}}(J)(A) \mid J \in X\}
\end{aligned}
$$

where equality (1) follows from Lemma 1 and equality (2) follows from the continuity of the operators $\dot{\&}_i$. □

In some sense, it is possible to reverse the implication in the theorem above.

Theorem 5. *If the operator $T_{\mathbb{P}}^{\mathfrak{L}}$ is continuous for all program $\mathbb{P}$ on $\mathfrak{L}$, then any operator in the body of the rules is continuous.*

Proof: Let @ be an n-ary connective. Assume an ordering on L^n defined on components. Denoting a tuple $(y_1, \ldots, y_n) \in L^n$ as $\bar{y}$, the ordering in L^n is: $\bar{y} \leq \bar{z}$ iff $y_i \preceq z_i$ for $i = 1, \ldots, n$.

Let Y be a directed set in L^n, and let us check that

$$\dot{@}(\sup Y) = \sup\{\dot{@}(y_1, \ldots, y_n) \mid (y_1, \ldots, y_n) \in Y)\}$$

The inequality

$$\sup\{\dot{@}(y_1, \ldots, y_n) \mid (y_1, \ldots, y_n) \in Y\} \preceq \dot{@}(\sup Y) \tag{1}$$

follows directly by monotonicity of @ and the definition of supremum.

For the other inequality, given n propositional symbols $A_1, \ldots, A_n \in \Pi$ and a tuple $\bar{y} = (y_1, \ldots, y_n) \in L^n$, consider the interpretation $I_{\bar{y}}$ defined as $I(A_i) = y_i$ for $i = 1, \ldots, n$ and $\perp$ otherwise. This way we have $I_{\bar{y}} \sqsubseteq I_{\bar{z}}$ if and only if $\bar{y} \leq \bar{z}$.

Consider, now, the set X_Y of interpretations $I_{\bar{y}}$ for all $\bar{y} \in Y$, and also consider its supremum, $S_Y = \sup X_Y$. By the ordering in L^n we have, for all $\bar{y} \in Y$

$$(y_1, \ldots, y_n) = \big(I_{\bar{y}}(A_1), \ldots, I_{\bar{y}}(A_n)\big) \leq \big(S_Y(A_1), \ldots, S_Y(A_n)\big)$$

therefore we have

$$\sup Y \leq \big(S_Y(A_1), \ldots, S_Y(A_n)\big)$$

now, by the monotonicity of $\dot{@}$ we have

$$\dot{@}(\sup Y) \preceq \dot{@}\left(S_Y(A_1), \ldots, S_Y(A_n)\right) = \widehat{S_Y}(@(A_1, \ldots, A_n)) \qquad (2)$$

On the other hand, consider the program $\mathbb{P}$ below consisting of only a rule

$$\mathbb{P} = \{A \xleftarrow{\top}_i @(A_1, \ldots, A_n)\}$$

by the assumption of monotonicity of $T_{\mathbb{P}}^{\mathcal{L}}$ we have the following chain of equalities

$$
\begin{aligned}
\widehat{S_Y}(@(A_1, \ldots, A_n)) &= \top \,\dot{\&}_i\, \widehat{S_Y}(@(A_1, \ldots, A_n)) \\
&= \sup\{\vartheta \,\dot{\&}_i\, \widehat{S_Y}(\mathcal{B}) \mid A \xleftarrow{\vartheta}_i \mathcal{B} \in \mathbb{P}\} \\
&= T_{\mathbb{P}}^{\mathcal{L}}(S_Y)(A) \\
&= \sup\{T_{\mathbb{P}}^{\mathcal{L}}(J_{\bar{y}})(A) \mid J_{\bar{y}} \in X_Y\} \\
&= \sup\{\sup\{\vartheta \,\dot{\&}_i\, J_{\bar{y}}(\mathcal{B}) \mid A \xleftarrow{\vartheta}_i \mathcal{B} \in \mathbb{P}\} \mid J_{\bar{y}} \in X_Y\} \\
&= \sup\{\top \,\dot{\&}_i\, \hat{J}_{\bar{y}}(@(A_1, \ldots, A_n)) \mid J_{\bar{y}} \in X_Y\} \\
&= \sup\{\dot{@}(J_{\bar{y}}(A_1), \ldots, J_{\bar{y}}(A_n)) \mid J_{\bar{y}} \in X_Y\} \\
&= \sup\{\dot{@}(y_1, \ldots, y_n) \mid (y_1, \ldots, y_n) \in Y\}
\end{aligned}
$$

Finally, by Eqns. (2) and (1) and this result we have

$$\sup\{\dot{@}(y_1, \ldots, y_n)\} \preceq \dot{@}(\sup Y) \preceq \widehat{S_Y}(@(A_1, \ldots, A_n)) = \sup\{\dot{@}(y_1, \ldots, y_n)\}$$

$$\square$$

Another Approach to the Continuity of $T_{\mathbb{P}}^{\mathcal{L}}$

It is possible to generalise the previous theorem by requiring weaker continuity conditions on the operators but, at the same time, restricting the structure of the set of truth-values.

Definition 18. *Let L be a poset and $f: L^n \to L$ a function. We say that f is* lower-semicontinuous, *for short LSC, in $(\vartheta_1, \ldots, \vartheta_n) \in L^n$ if for all $\varepsilon < f(\vartheta_1, \ldots, \vartheta_n)$ there exist δ_i for $i = 1, \ldots, n$ such that whenever $(\mu_1 \ldots, \mu_n)$ satisfies $\delta_i < \mu_i \leq \vartheta_i$ then $\varepsilon < f(\mu_1, \ldots, \mu_n) \leq f(\vartheta_1, \ldots, \vartheta_n)$.*
A function f is said to be lower-semicontinuous *(or LSC) if it is lower-semicontinuous in every point in its domain.*

It is obvious that the composition of two lower-semicontinuous functions is also lower-semicontinuous.

Definition 19. *A cpo L is said to satisfy the* supremum property *if for all set $X \subset L$ and for all ε we have that if $\varepsilon < \sup X$ then there exists $\delta \in X$ such that $\varepsilon < \delta \leq \sup X$.*

Lemma 1 also holds assuming LSC and the supremum property and, therefore, the continuity of the $T_{\mathbb{P}}^{\mathfrak{L}}$ operator is obtained from the combined hypotheses of LSC of the operators and the supremum property of the lattice of truth-values.

Lemma 2. *Let $\mathbb{P}$ be a program interpreted on a multi-adjoint Ω-algebra $\mathfrak{L}$ whose carrier has the supremum property for directed sets. Let $\mathcal{B}$ be any body formula in $\mathbb{P}$, and a assume that all the operators in $\mathcal{B}$ are LSC. Let X be a directed set of interpretations, and write $S = \sup X$; then*

$$\hat{S}(\mathcal{B}) = \sup\{\hat{J}(\mathcal{B}) \mid J \in X\}$$

Proof sketch: The following inequality is straightforward.

$$\sup\{\hat{J}(\mathcal{B}) \mid J \in X\} \preceq \hat{S}(\mathcal{B})$$

Now, assume the strict inequality and get a contradiction, using LSC and the supremum property separately on each argument to obtain elements $J_i(\mathcal{B})$, then apply directedness to get an uniform interpretation $J_0(\mathcal{B})$, finally use once again LSC to get a contradiction. □

Theorem 6. *If L satisfies the supremum property, and all the operators in the body are LSC and $\dot{\&}_i$ are LSC in their second argument, then the operator $T_{\mathbb{P}}^{\mathfrak{L}}$ is continuous.*

Proof: Let us prove that for a directed set X and $S = \sup X$ we have that

$$T_{\mathbb{P}}^{\mathfrak{L}}(S)(A) = \sup\{T_{\mathbb{P}}^{\mathfrak{L}}(J)(A) \mid J \in X\}$$

by showing that $T_{\mathbb{P}}^{\mathfrak{L}}(S)(A)$ fulfils the properties of a supremum for the set $\{T_{\mathbb{P}}^{\mathfrak{L}}(J)(A) \mid J \in X\}$.

1. Clearly, by monotonicity of the operator $T_{\mathbb{P}}^{\mathfrak{L}}$ and the fact that $S = \sup X$, we have that $T_{\mathbb{P}}^{\mathfrak{L}}(S)(A)$ is an upper bound for all the $T_{\mathbb{P}}^{\mathfrak{L}}(J)(A)$ with $J \in X$ and, therefore
$$\sup\{T_{\mathbb{P}}^{\mathfrak{L}}(J)(A) \mid J \in X\} \preceq T_{\mathbb{P}}^{\mathfrak{L}}(S)(A)$$

2. Reasoning by contradiction, assume the strict inequality
$$\sup\{T_{\mathbb{P}}^{\mathfrak{L}}(J)(A) \mid J \in X\} \prec T_{\mathbb{P}}^{\mathfrak{L}}(S)(A)$$

As $T_{\mathbb{P}}^{\mathfrak{L}}(S)(A) = \sup\{\vartheta \dot{\&}_i \hat{S}(\mathcal{B}) \mid A \xleftarrow{\vartheta}_i \mathcal{B} \in \mathbb{P}\}$ by the supremum property taking $\varepsilon = \sup\{T_{\mathbb{P}}^{\mathfrak{L}}(J)(A) \mid J \in X\}$ we have that there exist a rule $A \xleftarrow{\vartheta}_i \mathcal{B} \in \mathbb{P}$ such that

$$\sup\{T_{\mathbb{P}}^{\mathfrak{L}}(J)(A) \mid J \in X\} = \varepsilon \prec \vartheta \dot{\&}_i \hat{S}(\mathcal{B}) \preceq T_{\mathbb{P}}^{\mathfrak{L}}(S)(A)$$

By using lower-semicontinuity of $\vartheta \dot{\&}_i \_$ on the strict inequality, we have that there exists $\delta \prec \hat{S}(\mathcal{B})$ such that whenever $\delta \prec \lambda \preceq \hat{S}(\mathcal{B})$ then $\varepsilon \prec \vartheta \dot{\&}_i \lambda \preceq \vartheta \dot{\&}_i \hat{S}(\mathcal{B})$.

Now, by Lemma 2, we have that $\hat{S}(\mathcal{B}) = \sup\{\hat{J}(\mathcal{B}) \mid J \in X\}$, we can apply once again the supremum property and select an element $J_0 \in X$ such that $\delta \prec \hat{J}_0(\mathcal{B}) \preceq \hat{S}(\mathcal{B})$. For this element, by LSC of $\vartheta \mathbin{\dot{\&}_i}{}_-$ we have that

$$\varepsilon \prec \vartheta \mathbin{\dot{\&}_i} \hat{J}_0(\mathcal{B}) \preceq \vartheta \mathbin{\dot{\&}_i} \hat{S}(\mathcal{B})$$

But this is contradictory with the fact that $\varepsilon = \sup\{T_{\mathbb{P}}^{\mathcal{L}}(J)(A) \mid J \in X\} = \sup\{\vartheta \mathbin{\dot{\&}_i} \hat{J}(\mathcal{B}) \mid A \xleftarrow{\vartheta}_i \mathcal{B} \in \mathbb{P} \text{ and } J \in X\}$.

$\square$

6   Conclusions and Future Work

We have presented a general theory of logic programming which allows the simultaneous use of different implications in the rules and rather general connectives in the bodies.

We have shown that models of our programs are post-fixpoints of the immediate consequences operator $T_{\mathbb{P}}^{\mathcal{L}}$, and the it is monotonic under very general hypotheses. In addition we have proved the continuity of $T_{\mathbb{P}}^{\mathcal{L}}$ under the assumption of continuity of the operators in the language (but, possibly, the implications). This hypothesis of continuity of the operators can be relaxed to lower-semicontinuity, whenever we are working with a cus-lattice with the supremum property. As future work we are planning to develop a complete procedural semantics for multi-adjoint programs and further investigate lattice with the supremum property.

Acknowledgements

We thank C. Damásio and L. Moniz Pereira for communicating the existence of first drafts of their papers, on which this research began.

References

1. J. F. Baldwin, T. P. Martin, and B. W. Pilsworth. *FRIL-Fuzzy and Evidential Reasoning in AI*. Research Studies Press (John Wiley), 1995. 354
2. C. V. Damásio and L. Moniz Pereira. Hybrid probabilistic logic programs as residuated logic programs. In *Logics in Artificial Intelligence, JELIA'00*, pages 57–73. Lect. Notes in AI, 1919, Springer-Verlag, 2000. 351, 352, 353, 359
3. C. V. Damásio and L. Moniz Pereira. Monotonic and residuated logic programs. In *Sixth European Conference on Symbolic and Quantitative Approaches to Reasoning with Uncertainty, ECSQARU'01*. Lect. Notes in Comp. Sci., Springer-Verlag, 2001. 351, 353, 358
4. M. van Emden and R. Kowalski. The semantics of predicate logic as a programming language. *Journal of the ACM*, 23(4):733–742, 1976. 357

5. M. C. Fitting. Bilattices and the semantics of logic programming. *Journal of Logic Programming*, 11:91–116, 1991. 351

6. P. Hájek. *Metamathematics of Fuzzy Logic.* Trends in Logic. Studia Logica Library. Kluwer Academic Publishers, 1998. 353

7. E. Naito, J. Ozawa, I. Hayashi, and N. Wakami. A proposal of a fuzzy connective with learning function. In P. Bosc and J. Kaczprzyk, editors, *Fuzziness Database Management Systems*, pages 345–364. Physica Verlag, 1995. 353

8. J. Pavelka. On fuzzy logic I, II, III. *Zeitschr. f. Math. Logik und Grundl. der Math.*, 25, 1979. 352

9. P. Vojtáš. Fuzzy logic programming. *Fuzzy sets and systems*, 2001. Accepted. 351, 353

Multi-dimensional Dynamic Knowledge Representation

João Alexandre Leite, José Júlio Alferes, and Luís Moniz Pereira

Centro de Inteligência Artificial - CENTRIA, Universidade Nova de Lisboa
2829-516 Caparica, Portugal
{jleite,jja,lmp}@di.fct.unl.pt

Abstract. According to *Dynamic Logic Programming (DLP)*, knowledge may be given by a sequence of theories (encoded as logic programs) representing different states of knowledge. These may represent time (e.g. in updates), specificity (e.g. in taxonomies), strength of updating instance (e.g. in the legislative domain), hierarchical position of knowledge source (e.g. in organizations), etc. The mutual relationships extant among states are used to determine the semantics of the combined theory composed of all the individual theories. Although suitable to encode a single dimension (e.g. time, hierarchies...), *DLP* cannot deal with more than one simultaneously because it is defined only for a linear sequence of states. To overcome this limitation, we introduce the notion of *Multi-dimensional Dynamic Logic Programming ($\mathcal{MDLP}$)*, which generalizes *DLP* to collections of states organized in arbitrary acyclic digraphs representing precedence. In this setting, $\mathcal{MDLP}$ assigns semantics to sets and subsets of such logic programs. By dint of this natural generalization, $\mathcal{MDLP}$ affords extra expressiveness, in effect enlarging the latitude of logic programming applications unifiable under a single framework. The generality and flexibility provided by the acyclic digraphs ensures a wide scope and variety of application possibilities.

1 Introduction and Motivation

In [1], the paradigm of *Dynamic Logic Programming (DLP)* was introduced, following the eschewing of performing updates on a model basis, as in [8,15,16,19], but rather as a process of logic programming rule updates [13].

According to *Dynamic Logic Programming* (*DLP*), itself a generalization of the notion of the update of a logic program P by another one U, knowledge is given by a series of theories (encoded as generalized logic programs) representing distinct supervenient states of the world. Different states, sequentially ordered, can represent different time periods [1], different agents [9], different hierarchical instances [17], or even different domains of knowledge [12]. Consequently, individual theories may comprise mutually contradictory as well as overlapping information. The role of *DLP* is to employ the mutual relationships extant among different states to precisely determine the declarative as well as the procedural semantics for the combined theory comprised of all individual theories at each

T. Eiter, W. Faber, and M. Truszczyński (Eds.): LPNMR 2001, LNAI 2173, pp. 365–378, 2001.
© Springer-Verlag Berlin Heidelberg 2001

state. Intuitively, one can add, at the end of the sequence, newer or more specific rules (arising from new, renewly acquired, or more specific knowledge) leaving to *DLP* the task of ensuring that these added rules are in force, and that previous or less specific rules are still valid (by inertia) only so far as possible, i.e. that they are kept for as long as they are not in conflict with newly added ones, these always prevailing. The common feature among the applications of *DLP* is that the states associated with the given set of theories encode only one of several possible representational dimensions (e.g. time, hierarchies, domains,...).

For example, *DLP* can be used to model the relationship of a group of agents related according to a linear hierarchy, and *DLP* can be used to model the evolution of a single agent over time. But *DLP*, as it stands, cannot deal with both settings at once, and model the evolution of one such group of agents over time, inasmuch *DLP* is defined for linear sequences of states alone. Nor can it model hierarchical relations amongst agents that have more than one superior (and multiple inheritance). An instance of a multi-dimensional scenario is legal reasoning, where legislative agency is divided conforming to a hierarchy of power, governed by the principle *Lex Superior (Lex Superior Derogat Legi Inferiori)* by which the rule issued by a higher hierarchical authority overrides the one issued by a lower one, and the evolution of law in time is governed by the principle *Lex Posterior (Lex Posterior Derogat Legi Priori)* by which the rule enacted at a later point in time overrides the earlier one. *DLP* can be used to model each of these principles separately, by using the sequence of states to represent either the hierarchy or time, but is unable to cope with both at once when they interact.

In effect, knowledge updating is not to be simply envisaged as taking place in the time dimension alone. Several updating dimensions may combine simultaneously, with or without the temporal one, such as specificity (as in taxonomies), strength of the updating instance (as in the legislative domain), hierarchical position of the knowledge source (as in organizations), credibility of the source (as in uncertain, mined, or learnt knowledge), or opinion precedence (as in a society of agents). For this combination to be possible, *DLP* needs to be extended to allow for a more general structuring of states.

In this paper we introduce the notion of *Multi-dimensional Dynamic Logic Programming (MDLP)* which generalizes *DLP* to cater for collections of states represented by arbitrary directed acyclic graphs. In this setting, *MDLP* assigns semantics to sets and subsets of logic programs, depending on how they stand in relation to one another, this relation being defined by the acyclic digraph (DAG) that configures the states. By dint of such a natural generalization, *MDLP* affords extra expressiveness, thereby enlarging the latitude of logic programming applications unifiable under a single framework. The generality and flexibility provided by DAGs ensures a wide scope and variety of possibilities.

The remainder of this paper is structured as follows: in Section 2 we introduce some background definitions; in Section 3 we introduce *MDLP* and proffer a declarative semantics; in Section 4 some illustrative examples are presented; in Section 5 an equivalent semantics based on a syntactical transformation is provided, proven sound and complete wrt. the declarative semantics; in Section

6 we set forth some basic properties; in Section 7 we conclude and open the doors of future developments.

2   Background

Generalized Logic Programs and Their Stable Models To represent *negative* information in logic programs and in their updates, since we need to allow default negation *not A* not only in premises of their clauses but also in their heads, we use *generalized logic programs* as defined in [1][1].

By a *generalized logic program* P in a language $\mathcal{L}$ we mean a finite or infinite set of propositional clauses of the form $L_0 \leftarrow L_1, \ldots, L_n$ where each L_i is a literal (i.e. an atom A or the default negation of an atom *not A*). If r is a clause (or rule), by $H(r)$ we mean L, and by $B(r)$ we mean $L_1, \ldots, L_n$. If $H(r) = A$ (resp. $H(r) = not\,A$) then $not\,H(r) = not\,A$ (resp. $not\,H(r) = A$). By a (2-valued) *interpretation* M of $\mathcal{L}$ we mean any set of literals from $\mathcal{L}$ that satisfies the condition that for any A, *precisely one* of the literals A or *not A* belongs to M. Given an interpretation M we define $M^+ = \{A : A \text{ is an atom}, A \in M\}$ and $M^- = \{not\,A : A \text{ is an atom}, \ not\,A \in M\}$. Following established tradition, wherever convenient we omit the default (negative) atoms when describing interpretations and models. We say that a (2-valued) interpretation M of $\mathcal{L}$ is a stable model of a generalized logic program P if $\rho(M) = least\,(\rho(P) \cup \rho(M^-))$, where $\rho(.)$ univocally renames every default literal *not A* in a program or model into new atoms, say *not_A*. The class of generalized logic programs can be viewed as a special case of yet broader classes of programs, introduced earlier in [7] and in [14], and, for the special case of normal programs, their semantics coincides with the stable models one [6].

Graphs A *directed graph*, or *digraph*, $D = (V, E)$ is a pair of two finite or infinite sets $V = V_D$ of *vertices* and $E = E_D$ of pairs of vertices or (*directed*) *edges*. A *directed edge sequence from* v_0 *to* v_n in a digraph is a sequence of edges $e_1, e_2, \ldots, e_n \in E_D$ such that $e_i = (v_{i-1}, v_i)$ for $i = 1, \ldots, n$. A *directed path* is a directed edge sequence in which all the edges are distinct. A *directed acyclic graph*, or *acyclic digraph (DAG)*, is a digraph D such that there are no directed edge sequences from v to v, for all vertices v of D. A *source* is a vertex with in-valency 0 (number of edges for which it is a final vertex) and a *sink* is a vertex with out-valency 0 (number of edges for which it is an initial vertex). We say that $v < w$ if there is a directed path from v to w and that $v \leq w$ if $v < w$ or $v = w$. The *transitive closure* of a graph D is a graph $D^+ = (V, E^+)$ such that for all $v, w \in V$ there is an edge (v, w) in E^+ if and only if $v < w$ in D. The relevancy DAG of a DAG D wrt a vertex v of D is $D_v = (V_v, E_v)$ where $V_v = \{v_i : v_i \in V \text{ and } v_i \leq v\}$ and $E_v = \{(v_i, v_j) : (v_i, v_j) \in E \text{ and } v_i, v_j \in V_v \}$. The relevancy DAG of a DAG D wrt a set of vertices S of D is $D_S = (V_S, E_S)$

---

[1] In [2] the reader can find the motivation for the usage of generalized logic programs, instead of using simple denials by freely moving the head *not*s into the body.

where $V_S = \bigcup_{v \in S} V_v$ and $E_S = \bigcup_{v \in S} E_v$, where $D_v = (V_v, E_v)$ is the relevancy DAG of D wrt v.

3   Multi-dimensional Dynamic Logic Programming

As noted in the introduction, allowing the individual theories of a dynamic program update to relate via a linear sequence of states only, delimits DLP to represent and reason about a single aspect of a system (e.g. time, hierarchy,...). In this section we generalize DLP to allow for states represented by the vertices of a DAG, and their precedence relations by the corresponding edges, thus enabling concurrent representation, depending on the choice of a particular DAG, of several dimensions of an updatable system. In particular, the DAG can stand not only for a system of n independent dimensions, but also for inter-dimensional precedence. In this setting, $\mathcal{MDLP}$ assigns semantics to sets and subsets of logic programs, depending on how they so relate to one another.

We start by defining the framework consisting of the generalized logic programs indexed by a DAG. Throughout this paper, we will restrict ourselves to $DAGs$ such that, for every vertex v of the DAG, any path ending in v is finite.

Definition 1 (Multi-dimensional Dynamic Logic Program). *Let $\mathcal{L}$ be a propositional language. A* Multi-dimensional Dynamic Logic Program (MDLP), *$\mathcal{P}$, is a pair $(\mathcal{P}_D, D)$ where $D = (V, E)$ is a DAG and $\mathcal{P}_D = \{P_v : v \in V\}$ is a set of generalized logic programs in the language $\mathcal{L}$, indexed by the vertices $v \in V$ of D. We call* states *such vertices of D. For simplicity, we often leave $\mathcal{L}$ implicit.*

3.1   Declarative Semantics

To characterize the models of $\mathcal{P}$ at any given state we will keep to the basic intuition of logic program updates, whereby an interpretation is a stable model of the update of a program P by a program U iff it is a stable model of a program consisting of the rules of U together with a subset of the rules of P, comprised by all those that are not rejected due to their being overridden by program U i.e. that do not carry over by inertia. With the introduction of a DAG to index programs, a program may have more than a single ancestor. This has to be dealt with, the desired intuition being that a program $P_v \in \mathcal{P}_D$ can be used to reject rules of any program $P_u \in \mathcal{P}_D$ if there is a directed path from u to v. Moreover, if some atom is not defined in the update nor in any of its ancestor, its negation is assumed by default. Formally, the stable models of the $MDLP$ are:

Definition 2 (Stable Models at state s). *Let $\mathcal{P} = (\mathcal{P}_D, D)$ be a MDLP, where $\mathcal{P}_D = \{P_v : v \in V\}$ and $D = (V, E)$. An interpretation M_s is a stable model of $\mathcal{P}$ at state $s \in V$, iff*

$M_s = least\left(\left[\mathcal{P}_s - Reject(s, M_s)\right] \cup Default\left(\mathcal{P}_s, M_s\right)\right)$ where A is an atom and:

$\mathcal{P}_s = \bigcup_{i \leq s} P_i$

$Reject(s, M_s) = \{r \in P_i \mid \exists r' \in P_j, i < j \leq s, H(r) = not\ H(r') \wedge M_s \vDash B(r')\}$

$Default\left(\mathcal{P}_s, M_s\right) = \{not\ A \mid \nexists r \in \mathcal{P}_s : (H(r) = A) \wedge M_s \vDash B(r)\}$

Intuitively, the set $Reject(s, M_s)$ contains those rules belonging to a program indexed by a state i that are overridden by the head of another rule with true body in state j along a path to state s. $\mathcal{P}_s$ contains all rules of all programs that are indexed by a state along all paths to state s, i.e. all rules that are potentially relevant to determine the semantics at state s. The set $Default\left(\mathcal{P}_s, M_s\right)$ contains default negations $not\ A$ of all unsupported atoms A, i.e., those atoms A for which there is no rule in $\mathcal{P}_s$ whose body is true in M_s.

Example 1. Consider the diamond shaped *MDLP* $\mathcal{P} = (\mathcal{P}_D, D)$ such that $\mathcal{P}_D = \{P_t, P_u, P_v, P_w\}$ and $D = (\{t, u, v, w\}, \{(t, u), (t, v), (u, w), (v, w)\})$ where

$$P_t = \{d \leftarrow\}\ \ P_u = \{a \leftarrow not\ e\}\ \ P_v = \{not\ a \leftarrow d\}$$
$$P_w = \{not\ a \leftarrow b; b \leftarrow not\ c; c \leftarrow not\ b\}$$

The only stable model at state w is $M_w = \{not\ a, b, not\ c, d, not\ e\}$. In fact, we have that $Reject(w, M_w) = \{a \leftarrow not\ e\}$ and $Default\left(\mathcal{P}_w, M_w\right) = \{not\ c, not\ e\}$ and, finally,

$$[\mathcal{P}_w - Reject(s, M_w)] \cup Default\left(\mathcal{P}_w, M_w\right) =$$
$$= \{d \leftarrow; not\ a \leftarrow d; not\ a \leftarrow b; b \leftarrow not\ c; c \leftarrow not\ b\} \cup \{not\ c, not\ e\}$$

whose least model is M_w. M_w is *the only* stable model at state w.

The next proposition establishes that to determine the models of a *MDLP* at state s, we need only consider the part of the *MDLP* corresponding to the relevancy graph wrt state s.

Proposition 1. *Let* $\mathcal{P} = (\mathcal{P}_D, D)$ *be a* MDLP, *where* $\mathcal{P}_D = \{P_v : v \in V\}$ *and* $D = (V, E)$. *Let* s *be a state in* V. *Let* $\mathcal{P}' = (\mathcal{P}_{D_s}, D_s)$ *be a* MDLP *where* $D_s = (V_s, E_s)$ *is the relevancy DAG of* D *wrt* s, *and* $\mathcal{P}_{D_s} = \{P_v : v \in V_s\}$. M *is a stable model of* $\mathcal{P}$ *at state* s *iff* M *is a stable model of* $\mathcal{P}'$ *at state* s.

We might have a situation where we desire to determine the semantics jointly at more than one state. If all these states belong to the relevancy graph of one of them, we simply determine the models at that state (Prop. 1). But this might not be the case. Formally, the semantics of a *MDLP* at an arbitrary set of its states is determined by the definition:

Definition 3 (Stable Models at a set of states S). *Let* $\mathcal{P} = (\mathcal{P}_D, D)$ *be a* MDLP, *where* $\mathcal{P}_D = \{P_v : v \in V\}$ *and* $D = (V, E)$. *Let* S *be a set of states such*

that $S \subseteq V$. *An interpretation* M_S *is a* stable model *of* $\mathcal{P}$ *at the set of states* S
iff $M_S = least\,([\mathcal{P}_S - Reject(S, M_S)] \cup Default\,(\mathcal{P}_S, M_S))$ *where:*

$$\mathcal{P}_S = \bigcup_{s \in S}\left(\bigcup_{i \leq s}P_i\right)$$

$$Reject(S, M_S) = \left\{ \begin{array}{l} r \in P_i \mid \exists s \in S, \exists r' \in P_j, i < j \leq s, \\ H(r) = not\, H(r') \wedge M_S \vDash B(r') \end{array} \right\}$$

$$Default\,(\mathcal{P}_S, M_S) = \{not\, A \mid \nexists r \in \mathcal{P}_S : (H(r) = A) \wedge M_S \vDash B(r)\}$$

This is equivalent to the addition of a new vertex α to the DAG, and connecting to α, by addition of edges, all states we wish to consider. Furthermore,
the program indexed by α is empty. We then determine the stable models of this
new *MDLP* at state α. In Section 6, we provide semantics preserving simplifica-
tions of these definitions, according to which only a subset of these newly added
edges is needed. Note the addition of state α does not affect the stable models
at other states. Indeed, α and the newly introduced edges do not belong to the
relevancy DAG wrt. any other state. A particular case of the above definition is
when $S = V$, corresponding to the semantics of the whole *MDLP*.

4   Illustrative Examples

By its very motivation and design, $\mathcal{MDLP}$ is well suited for combining knowledge arising from various sources, specially when some of these sources have
priority over the others. More precisely, when rules from some sources are used
to reject rules of other, less prior, sources. In particular, $\mathcal{MDLP}$ is well suited
for combining knowledge originating within hierarchically organized sources, as
the following schematic example illustrates, which combines knowledge coming
from diverse sectors of such an organization.

Example 2. Consider a company with a president, a board of directors and (at
least) two departments: the quality management and financial ones.
    To improve the quality of the products produced by the company, the quality
management department has decided not to buy any product whose reliability
is less than guaranteed. In other words, it has adopted the rule[2]:

$$not\, buy(X) \leftarrow not\, reliable(X)$$

On the other hand, to save money, the financial department has decided to
buy products of a type in need if they are cheap, viz.

$$buy(X) \leftarrow type(X, T), needed(T), cheap(X)$$

The board of directors, in order to keep production going, has decided that
whenever there is still a need for a type of product, exactly one product of that
type must be bought. This can be coded by the following logic programming
rules, stating that if X is a product of a needed type, and if the need for that

---

[2] Rules with variables stand for the set of all their ground instances.

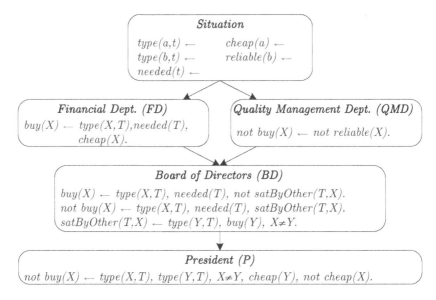

Fig. 1.

type of product has not been already satisfied by buying some other product of that type, then X must be bought; if the need is satisfied by buying some other product of that type, then X should not be bought:

$$buy(X) \leftarrow type(X, T), needed(T), not\, satByOther(T, X)$$
$$not\, buy(X) \leftarrow type(X, T), needed(T), satByOther(T, X)$$
$$satByOther(T, X) \leftarrow type(Y, T), buy(Y), X \neq Y$$

Finally, the president decided for the company never to buy products that have a cheap alternative. I.e. if two products are of the same type, and only one of them is cheap, the company should not buy the other:

$$not\, buy(X) \leftarrow type(X, T), type(Y, T), X \neq Y, cheap(Y), not\, cheap(X)$$

Suppose further that there are two products, a and b, the first being cheap and the latter reliable, both of type t and both of needed type t.

According to the company's organizational chart, the rules of the president can overrule those of all other sectors, and those established by the board can overrule those decided by the departments. No department has precedence over any other. This situation can easily be modeled by the MDLP of Figure 1.

To know what would be the decision of each of the sectors about which products to buy, not taking under consideration the deliberation of its superiors, all needs to be done is to determine the stable models at the state corresponding to that sector. For example, the reader can check that at state QMD there is a single stable model in which both $not\, buy(a)$ and $not\, buy(b)$ are true. At the state BD there are two stable models: one in which $buy(a)$ and $not\,buy(b)$ are true; another where $not\,buy(a)$ and $buy(b)$ are true instead.

More interesting would be to know what is the decision of the company as a whole, when taking into account the rules of all sectors and their hierarchical organization. This is reflected by the stable models of the whole *MDLP*, i.e. the stable models at the set of all states of the *MDLP*. The reader can check that, in this instance, there is a single stable model in which $buy(a)$ and $not\,buy(b)$ are true. It coincides with the single stable model at state *president* because all other states belong to its relevancy graph.   □

The next example describes how $\mathcal{MDLP}$ can deal with collision principles, e.g. found in legal reasoning, such as *Lex Superior (Lex Superior Derogat Legi Inferiori)* according to which the rule issued by a higher hierarchical authority overrides the one issued by a lower one, and *Lex Posterior (Lex Posterior Derogat Legi Priori)* according to which the rule enacted at a later point in time overrides the earlier one, i.e how the combination of a temporal and an hierarchical dimensions can be combined into a single *MDLP*.

Example 3. In February 97, the President of Brazil (PB) passed a law determining that, in order to guarantee the safety aboard public transportation airplanes, all weapons were forbidden. Furthermore, all exceptional situations that, due to public interest, require an armed law enforcement or military agent are to be the subject of specific regulation by the Military and Justice Ministries. We will refer to this as rule 1. At the time of this event, there was in force an internal norm of the Department of Civil Aviation (DCA) stating that "Armed Forces Officials and Police Officers can board with their weapons if their destination is a national airport". We will refer to this as rule 2. Restricting ourselves to the essential parts of these regulations, they can be encoded by the generalized logic program clauses:

$$rule1 : not\,carry\_weapon \leftarrow not\,exception$$
$$rule2 : carry\_weapon \leftarrow armed\_officer$$

Let us consider a lattice with two distinct dimensions, corresponding to the two principles governing this situation: *Lex Superior (d_1)* and *Lex Posterior (d_2)*. Besides the two agencies involved in this situation (PB and DCA), we will consider two time points representing the time when the two regulations were enacted. We have then a graph whose vertices are $\{(PB,1),(PB,2),(DCA,1),(DCA,2)\}$ (in the form (agency,time)) as portrayed in Fig.2. We have that $P_{DCA,1}$ contains rule 2, $P_{PB,2}$ contains rule 1 and the other two programs are empty. Let us further assume that there is an armed_officer represented by a fact in $P_{DCA,1}$. Applying Def.2, for $M_{PB,2} = \{not\,carry\_weapon,\ not\,exception,\ armed\_officer\}$ at state $(PB,2)$ we have that:

$$Reject((PB,2), M_{PB,2}) = \{carry\_weapon \leftarrow armed\_officer\}$$
$$Default\,(\mathcal{P}_{PB,2}, M_{PB,2}) = \{not\,exception\}$$

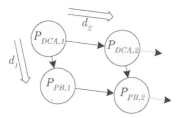

Fig. 2.

it is trivial to see that

$$M_{PB,2} = least\left([\mathcal{P}_{PB,2} - Reject((PB,2), M_{PB,2})] \cup Default\left(\mathcal{P}_{PB,2}, M_{PB,2}\right)\right)$$

which means that in spite of rule 2, since the exceptions have not been regulated yet, rule 1 prevails for all situations, and no one can carry a weapon aboard an airplane. This would correspond to the only stable model at state $(PB, 2)$.   □

The applicability of $\mathcal{MDLP}$ in a multi-agent context is not limited to the assignment of a single semantics to the overall system, i.e., the multi-agent system does not have to be described by a single DAG. Instead, we could determine each agent's view of the world by associating a DAG with each agent, representing its own view of its relationships to other agents and of these amongst themselves. The stable models over a set of states from $DAGs$ of different agents can provide us with interagent views.

Example 4. Consider a society of agents representing a hierarchically structured research group. We have the Senior Researcher (A_{sr}), two Researchers $(A_{r1}$ and $A_{r2})$ and two students $(A_{s1}$ and $A_{s2})$ supervised by the two Researchers. The hierarchy is deployed in Fig.3 a), which also represents the view of the Senior Researcher. Typically, students think they are always right and do not like hierarchies, so their view of the community is quite different. Fig.3 b) manifests one possible view by A_{s1}. In this scenario, we could use $\mathcal{MDLP}$ to determine and eventually compare A_{sr}'s view, given by the stable models at state sr in Fig.3 a), with A_{s1}'s view, given by the stable models at state $s1$ in Fig.3 b). If we assign the following simple logic programs to the five agents:

$$P_{sr} = \{a \leftarrow b\} \ P_{s1} = \{not\ a \leftarrow c\} \ P_{s2} = \{\} \ P_{r1} = \{b\} \ P_{r2} = \{c\}$$

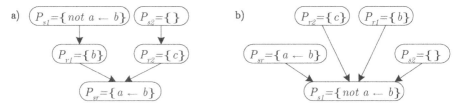

Fig. 3.

we have that state sr in Fig.3 a) has $M_{sr} = \{a, b, c\}$ as the only stable model, and state $s1$ in Fig.3 b) has $M_{s1} = \{not\, a, b, c\}$ as its only stable model. That is, according to student A_{s1}'s view of the world a is false, while according to the senior researcher A_{sr}'s view of the world a is true. $\square$

This example suggests $\mathcal{MDLP}$ to be a useful practical framework to study changes in behaviour of such multi-agent systems and how they hinge on the relationships amongst the agents, i.e. on the current DAG that represents them. $\mathcal{MDLP}$ offers a staple basic tool for the formal study of the social behaviour in multi-agent communities [10].

5   Transformational Semantics for MDLP

Definition 2 above establishes the semantics of $\mathcal{MDLP}$ by characterizing its stable models at each state. Next we present an alternative definition, based on a purely syntactical transformation that, given a $MDLP$, produces a generalized logic program whose stable models are in a one-to-one equivalence relation with the stable models of the $MDLP$ previously characterized. The computation of the stable models at some state s reduces to the computation of the transformation followed by the computation of the stable models of the transformed program. This directly provides for an implementation of $\mathcal{MDLP}$ (publicly available at centria.di.fct.unl.pt/~jja/updates) and a means to study its complexity.

Without loss of generality, we extend the DAG D with an initial state (s_0) and a set of directed edges (s_0, s') connecting the initial state to all the sources of D. Similarly, if we wish to query a set of states, all needs doing is extending the $MDLP$ with a new state α, as mentioned before, prior to the transformation. By $\overline{\mathcal{L}}$ we denote the language obtained from language $\mathcal{L}$ such that $\overline{\mathcal{L}} = \mathcal{L} \cup \{A^-, A_s, \ A_s^-, A_{P_s}, \ A_{P_s}^-, reject(A_s), reject(A_s^-) : A \in \mathcal{L}, s \in V \cup \{s_0\}\}$.

Definition 4 (Multi-dimensional Dynamic Program Update). *Let $\mathcal{P}$ be a MDLP, where $\mathcal{P} = (\mathcal{P}_D, D)$, $\mathcal{P}_D = \{P_v : v \in V\}$ and $D = (V, E)$. Given a fixed state $s \in V$, the multi-dimensional dynamic program update over $\mathcal{P}$ at state **s** is the generalized logic program $\boxplus_s \mathcal{P}$, which consists of the clauses below in the extended language $\overline{\mathcal{L}}$, where $D_s = (V_s, E_s)$ is relevancy DAG of D wrt s:*
  (RP) Rewritten program clauses:

$$A_{P_v} \leftarrow B_1, \ldots, B_m, C_1^-, \ldots, C_n^- \qquad\qquad A_{P_v}^- \leftarrow B_1, \ldots, B_m, C_1^-, \ldots, C_n^-$$

for any clause:

$$A \ \leftarrow B_1, \ \ldots, \ B_m, \ not\, C_1, \ \ldots, \ not\, C_n$$

respectively, for any clause:

$$not\, A \ \leftarrow B_1, \ \ldots, \ B_m, \ not\, C_1, \ \ldots, \ not\, C_n$$

in the program P_v, where $v \in V_s$.

(IR) Inheritance rules:

$$A_v \leftarrow A_u, not\ reject(A_u) \qquad\qquad A_v^- \leftarrow A_u^-, not\ reject(A_u^-)$$

for all atoms $A \in \mathcal{L}$ and all $(u, v) \in E_s$. The inheritance rules say that an atom A is true (resp. false) at state $v \in V_s$ if it is true (resp. false) at any ancestor state u and it is not rejected.

(RR) Rejection Rules:

$$reject(A_u^-) \leftarrow A_{P_v} \qquad\qquad reject(A_u) \leftarrow A_{P_v}^-$$

for all atoms $A \in \mathcal{L}$ and all $u, v \in V_s$ where $u < v$. The rejection rules say that if an atom A is true (resp. false) in the program P_v, then it rejects inheritance of any false (resp. true) atoms of any ancestor.

(UR) Update rules:

$$A_v \leftarrow A_{P_v} \qquad\qquad A_v^- \leftarrow A_{P_v}^-$$

for all atoms $A \in \mathcal{L}$ and all $v \in V_s$. Update rules state that atom A must be true (resp. false) at state $v \in V_s$ if it is made true (resp. false) in the program P_v.

(DR) Default Rules:

$$A_{s_0}^-$$

for all atoms $A \in \mathcal{L}$. Default rules describe the initial state s_0 by making all atoms false at that state.

(CS_s) Current State Rules:

$$A \leftarrow A_s \qquad\qquad A^- \leftarrow A_s^- \qquad\qquad not\ A \leftarrow A_s^-$$

for all atoms $A \in \mathcal{L}$. Current state rules specify the state s at which the program is being evaluated and determine the values of the atoms A, A^- and not A.

This transformation depends on the prior determination of the relevancy graph wrt. the given state. This choice was based on criteria of clarity and readability. Nevertheless this need not be so: one can instead specify declaratively, by means of a logic program, the notion of relevancy graph. As already mentioned, the stable models of the program obtained by the aforesaid transformation coincide with those characterized in Def.2, as expressed by the theorem:

Theorem 1. *Given a MDLP $\mathcal{P} = (\mathcal{P}_D, D)$, the generalized stable models of $\boxplus_s \mathcal{P}$, restricted to $\mathcal{L}$, coincide with the generalized stable models of $\mathcal{P}$ at state s according to Def.2.*

For lack of space, we do not present the proofs of the Theorems. In [11], the reader can find an extended version of this paper containing them.

6   Properties of MDLP

In this section we study some basic properties of $\mathcal{MDLP}$.

The next theorem states that adding or removing edges from a *DAG* of a *MDLP* preserves the semantics if the transitive closure of the two *DAGs* is the same DAG. In particular, it allows the use of a transitive reduction of the original graph to determine the stable models.

Theorem 2 (DAG Simplification). *Let* $\mathcal{P} = (\mathcal{P}_D, D)$ *be a* MDLP, *where* $\mathcal{P}_D = \{P_v : v \in V\}$ *and* $D = (V, E)$. *Let* $\mathcal{P}_1 = (\mathcal{P}_D, D_1)$ *be a* MDLP, *where* $D_1 = (V, E_1)$ *and* $D^+ = D_1^+$. *For any state* $s \in V$, M *is a* stable model of $\mathcal{P}$ *at state* s *iff* M *is a* stable model of $\mathcal{P}_1$ *at state* s.

One consequence of this theorem is that in order to determine the stable models at a set of states we only need to connect to the new node α the sinks of the relevancy DAG wrt. that set of states.

The following proposition relates the stable models of normal logic programs with those of *MDLPs* whose set of programs just contains normal logic programs.

Proposition 2. *Let* $\mathcal{P} = (\mathcal{P}_D, D)$ *be a* MDLP, *where* $\mathcal{P}_D = \{P_v : v \in V\}$ *and* $D = (V, E)$. *Let* $S \subseteq V$ *be a set of states and* $D_S = (V_S, E_S)$ *the relevancy DAG of* D *wrt.* S. *If all* $P_v : v \in V_S$ *are normal logic programs, then* M *is a* stable model of $\mathcal{P}$ *at states* S *iff* M *is a* stable model of the (normal) logic program $\bigcup_{v \in V_S} P_v$

The next theorem shows that $\mathcal{MDLP}$ generalizes its predecessor *DLP* [1].

Theorem 3 (Generalization of DLP). *Let* $\mathcal{P}_D = \{P_s : s \in S\}$ *be a* DLP, *i.e. a finite or infinite sequence of generalized logic programs, indexed by set of natural numbers* $S = \{1, 2, 3, \ldots, n, \ldots\}$. *Let* $\mathcal{P} = (\mathcal{P}_D, D)$ *be the* MDLP, *where* $D = (S, E)$ *is the acyclic digraph such that* $E = \{(1, 2), (2, 3), \ldots, (n-1, n), \ldots\}$. *Then, an interpretation* M *is a* stable model of the dynamic program update (DLP) at state s, $\bigoplus_s \mathcal{P}_D$, *if and only if* M *is a* stable model of $\mathcal{P}$ *at state* s.

Since *DLP* generalizes *Interpretation Updates*, originally introduced as *"Revision Programs"* by Marek and Truszczyński [15], then so does $\mathcal{MDLP}$. In [1], *DLP* was defined by means of a transformational semantics only. Theorems 1 and 3 establish Def. 2 as an alternative, declarative, characterization of *DLP*.

7   Conclusions and Future Work

We have introduced $\mathcal{MDLP}$ as a generalization of *DLP* in allowing for collections of states organized by arbitrary acyclic digraphs, and not just sequences of states. And therefore assigning semantics to sets and subsets of logic programs, on the basis of how they stand in relation amongst themselves, as defined by one acyclic digraph. Such a natural generalization imparts added expressiveness to updating, thereby amplifying the coverage of its application domains, as we've tried to illustrate via some examples. The flexibility afforded by a *DAG* accrues to the scope and variety of possibilities. The new characteristics of multiplicity and composition of $\mathcal{MDLP}$ may be used to lend a "societal" viewpoint to *Logic Programming*. Application areas such as legal reasoning, software development, organizational decision making, multi-strategy learning, abductive planning, model-based diagnosis, agent architectures, and others, have already being successfully pursued by utilizing $\mathcal{MDLP}$.

Other frameworks exist for updates [20,18], and for combining logic programs via a partial order, developed for purposes other than updating. Namely, Disjunctive Ordered Logic ($\mathcal{DOL}$) [4], itself an extension of Ordered Logic, and $DLV^<$ [3], a language that extends LP with inheritance. Lack of space prevents us from elaborating on the comparison with these frameworks, so we defer to [5], where some considerations are made to that effect.

Some of the more immediate themes of ongoing work regarding the further development of $\mathcal{MDLP}$ comprise: allowing for the *DAG* itself to evolve by updating it with new nodes and edges; enhancing the *LUPS* language to adumbrate update commands over *DAG*s; studying the conditions for and the uses of dropping the acyclicity condition; establishing a paraconsistent $\mathcal{MDLP}$ semantics and defining contradiction removal over *DAG*s.

References

1. J. J. Alferes, J. A. Leite, L. M. Pereira, H. Przymusinska, and T. Przymusinski. Dynamic updates of non-monotonic knowledge bases. *Journal of Logic Programming*, 45(1-3):43–70, 2000. Abstract titled *Dynamic Logic Programming* appeared in Procs. of KR-98. 365, 367, 376
2. J. J. Alferes, L. M. Pereira, H. Przymusinska, and T. Przymusinski. LUPS : A language for updating logic programs. *Artificial Intelligence*. To appear. 367
3. F. Buccafurri, W. Faber, and N. Leone. Disjunctive logic programs with inheritance. In *Procs. of ICLP-99*. MIT Press, 1999. 377
4. F. Buccafurri, N. Leone, , and P. Rullo. Semantics and expressiveness of disjunctive ordered logic. *Annals of Math. and Artificial Intelligence*, 25(3-4):311–337, 1999. 377
5. T. Eiter, M. Fink, G. Sabbatini, and H. Tompits. Considerations on updates of logic programs. In *Procs. of JELIA-00*, LNAI-1919. Springer, 2000. 377
6. M. Gelfond and V. Lifschitz. The stable semantics for logic programs. In *Procs. of ICLP-88*. MIT Press, 1988. 367
7. K. Inoue and C. Sakama. Negation as failure in the head. *Journal of Logic Programming*, 35:39–78, 1998. 367
8. H. Katsuno and A. Mendelzon. On the difference between updating a knowledge base and revising it. In *Procs. of KR-91*. Morgan Kaufmann, 1991. 365
9. E. Lamma, F. Riguzzi, and L. M. Pereira. Strategies in combined learning via logic programs. *Machine Learning*, 38(1/2):63–87, 2000. 365
10. J. A. Leite, J. J. Alferes, and L. M. Pereira. Minerva - a dynamic logic programming agent architecture. In *Procs. of ATAL'01*, 2001. 374
11. J. A. Leite, J. J. Alferes, and L. M. Pereira. Multi-dimensional logic programming. Technical report, Dept. Informatica, Universidade Nova de Lisboa, 2001. 375

12. J. A. Leite, F. C. Pereira, A. Cardoso, and L. M. Pereira. Metaphorical mapping consistency via dynamic logic programming. In *Procs. of AISB'00*. AISB, 2000. 365

13. J. A. Leite and L. M. Pereira. Generalizing updates: From models to programs. In *Procs of. LPKR-97*, volume 1471 of *LNAI*. Springer, 1997. 365

14. V. Lifschitz and T. Woo. Answer sets in general non-monotonic reasoning (preliminary report). In *Procs. of KR-92*. Morgan-Kaufmann, 1992. 367

15. V. W. Marek and M. Truszczyński. Revision specifications by means of programs. In *Procs. of JELIA-94*, volume 838 of *LNAI*. Springer, 1994. 365, 376

16. Teodor C. Przymusinski and Hudson Turner. Update by means of inference rules. *Journal of Logic Programming*, 30(2):125–143, 1997. 365

17. P. Quaresma and I. P. Rodrigues. A collaborative legal information retrieval system using dynamic logic programming. In *Procs. of ICAIL-99*. ACM Press, 1999. 365

18. C. Sakama and K. Inoue. Updating extended logic programs through abduction. In *Procs. of LPNMR-99*. Springer, 1999. 377

19. Marianne Winslett. Reasoning about action using a possible models approach. In *Procs. of NCAI-88*. AAAI Press, 1988. 365

20. Y. Zhang and N. Foo. Updating logic programs. In *Procs. of ECAI'98*. Morgan Kaufmann, 1998. 377

Antitonic Logic Programs

Carlos Viegas Damásio and Luís Moniz Pereira

Centro de Inteligência Artificial (CENTRIA), Departamento de Informática,
Universidade Nova de Lisboa
2829-516 Caparica, Portugal
{cd,lmp}@di.fct.unl.pt

Abstract. In a previous work we have defined Monotonic Logic Programs which extend definite logic programming to arbitrary complete lattices of truth-values with an appropriate notion of implication. We have shown elsewhere that this framework is general enough to capture Generalized Annotated Logic Programs, Probabilistic Deductive Databases, Possibilistic Logic Programming, Hybrid Probabilistic Logic Programs and Fuzzy Logic Programming [3,4]. However, none of these semantics define a form of non-monotonic negation, which is fundamental for several knowledge representation applications. In the spirit of our previous work, we generalise our framework of Monotonic Logic Programs to allow for rules with arbitrary antitonic bodies over general complete lattices, of which normal programs are a special case. We then show that all the standard logic programming theoretical results carry over to Antitonic Logic Programs, defining Stable Model and Well-founded Model alike semantics. We also apply and illustrate our theory to logic programs with costs, extending the original presentation of [17] with a class of negations.

1 Introduction

The generalization of standard logic programming to many-valued logics has been foreseen for a quite long time [20,8,9,14]. Substantial work and results have been attained in the field. In particular, Logic programming literature is prodigal in languages and semantics proposals for extensions of definite logic programs (e.g. [7,24,23,5,14]), i.e. those without non-monotonic or default negation. Usually, the authors characterize their programs with a model theoretic semantics, where a minimum model is guaranteed to exist, and a corresponding monotonic fixpoint operator (continuous or not).

In a previous work [4], which we recap here, we abstracted out all the details and defined a rather general framework of Monotonic Logic Programs that captures the core of logic programming. In the present paper we generalise the framework to allow for rules with arbitrary antitonic bodies over general complete lattices, of which normal programs are a special case, and show that all the standard logic programming theoretical results carry over to such Antitonic Logic Programs, defining for them Stable and Well-founded Model semantics alike. We also apply and illustrate our theory to logic programs with costs, extending the original presentation of [17] with a class of negations. For this purpose we follow

T. Eiter, W. Faber, and M. Truszczyński (Eds.): LPNMR 2001, LNAI 2173, pp. 379–393, 2001.
© Springer-Verlag Berlin Heidelberg 2001

an algebraic approach to the language and the semantics of logic programs, in the same spirit of [6].

Our paper proceeds as follows. First we appeal, for motivation and examples, to the logic programs with costs of [17], where associated with each rule there is a weight or cost factor. In Section 3 we recap Monotonic Logic Programs and supply its theoretical results relevant here. In Section 4, we introduce Antitonic Logic Programs, by means of a transformation into Monotonic programs, and define their semantics, showing they enjoy the properties consonant with a logic programming approach. We end by pointing to future work.

2   Logic Programming with Costs

In [17], rules of definite logic programs are assigned non-negative real numbers, ascribing to every rule in the program the cost of applying it. The authors define three interpretations of cost. The non-reusability approach, which we will discuss in this work, assumes that each individual conclusion about an atom in the program involves a cost. In the reusability approach, we only pay once for concluding about an atom, the first time around. Costs can also be interpreted as time and in this case the semantics proposed is isomorphic to van Emden's quantitative logic programs [22]. Let us illustrate the several approaches with an example:

Example 1. Consider the weighted logic program:

$$a \overset{4}{\leftarrow} b, c, c, d \quad b \overset{5}{\leftarrow} \quad b \overset{1}{\leftarrow} c \quad c \overset{3}{\leftarrow} \quad c \overset{0}{\leftarrow} b \quad d \overset{6}{\leftarrow}$$

In the non-reusability approach, we spend a minimum of 3 units to conclude c and 4 to conclude b. The minimum cost for a is therefore $4 + 4 + 3 + 3 + 6 = 20$.

If we adopt the reusability interpretation, we don't need to pay at all for the use of c at the rule for a, since the cost for c has been paid to conclude b with cost 4. Thus, the cost of atom a is $4 + 4 + 6 = 14$.

Now, for the time interpretation, we assume that the atoms in the body can be proved in parallel. Therefore the cost of applying the rule is the weight of the rule plus the maximum time to derive either atom in the body and there is no reusability. So, the derivation of a takes $4 + \max(4, 3, 3, 6) = 10$.

In [17] the authors define a model and fixpoint theory for logic programs with costs. We will employ them to illustrate the power of monotonic logic programs, and attain the same results. In the rest of the work we shall focus on much more general logic programs with costs under the non-reusability approach.

3   Monotonic Logic Programs

The theoretical foundations of logic programming were clearly established in [15,21] for definite logic programs (see also [16]), i.e. programs made up of rules of the form $A_0 \subset A_1 \wedge \ldots \wedge A_n (n \geq 0)$ where each $A_i (0 \leq i \leq n)$ is a propositional symbol (an atom), $\subset$ is classical implication, and $\wedge$ the usual Boolean conjunction.

In this section we generalize the language of definite logic programs in order to encompass more complex bodies and heads and, evidently, many-valued logics. For simplicity, we consider only the propositional (ground) case. Furthermore, we define a model and a fixpoint theory for Monotonic Logic Programs, and extend to them the classical results of logic programming. The important point to realize is that all the fundamental results of logic programming depend only on the monotonicity of the body of the rule and on the fact that it is possible to determine the truth-value of the proposition in the head from the truth-value of the rule body. Our underlying set of truth-values will form a complete lattice and the main idea is that every implication should evaluate to $\top$, the top element in the lattice.

When defining a (new) logic it is necessary to address the two distinct but related aspects: the syntax and the corresponding interpretation of the logical symbols in the language. In this paper we adopt an algebraic characterization of both the language and interpretation of operators. This is a very general and powerful framework, allowing for a simple relation between the two. For lack of space, we reduce the presentation to the essentials. For more details consult for instance [10].

The main assumptions of the paper are collected in the next two definitions.

Definition 1 (Implication Algebra). *Let $\mathfrak{T} = \; <T, \preceq>$ be a complete lattice and consider an algebra $\mathfrak{A}$ on the carrier set T. We say that $\mathfrak{A}$ is an implication algebra with respect to $\mathfrak{T}$ iff it has defined an operator $\leftarrow_{\mathfrak{A}}$ on $\mathfrak{A}$ such that*

$$\forall_{a_1, a_2 \in \mathfrak{T}} \; (a_1 \leftarrow_{\mathfrak{A}} a_2) = \top \; \text{iff} \; a_2 \preceq a_1 \tag{1}$$

where $\top$ is the top element of $\mathfrak{T}$.

Example 2. For logic programs with costs we use as set of truth-values the interval of reals greater or equal than 0, extended with infinity ($[0, \infty]$), ordered by the "greater or equal than" relation. Thus, our bottom element is ∞ and the top element is of course 0. Thus the least upper bound in this complete lattice is the infimum. We designate the complete lattice $< [\infty, 0], \geq >$ by[1] $\mathcal{R}^+$. The implication symbol is defined thus:

$$r_1 \leftarrow_{\mathfrak{C}} r_2 = \begin{cases} 0 & \text{if } r_2 \geq r_1, \text{i.e. } r_1 \leq r_2 \\ \infty & \text{otherwise} \end{cases}$$

This defines an implication algebra $\mathfrak{C} = ([\infty, 0], \leftarrow_{\mathfrak{C}})$.

Notice that some many-valued logics have implication connectives which do not comply with property (1). We refer the reader to [4] for more details.

---

[1] Note that ∞ in $[\infty, 0]$ is $+\infty$ and not $-\infty$.

Our Monotonic Logic Programs will be constructed from the abstract syntax induced by an implication algebra and a set of propositional symbols. The way syntax and semantics relate in such an algebraic setting is well-known and we defer again to [10] for more details.

Definition 2 (Monotonic Logic Programs). *Let $\mathfrak{A}$ be an implication algebra with respect to a complete lattice $\mathfrak{T}$. Let Π be a set of propositional symbols and $FORM_{\mathfrak{A}}(\Pi)$ the corresponding algebra of formulae freely generated from Π and the "symbols" of operators in $\mathfrak{A}$. A monotonic logic program is a set of rules[2] of the form $A \leftarrow \Psi$ such that:*

1. *The rule $(A \leftarrow \Psi)$ is a formula of $FORM_{\mathfrak{A}}(\Pi)$;*
2. *The head of the rule A is a propositional symbol of Π.*
3. *The body formula Ψ with propositional symbols $B_1, \ldots, B_n$ $(n \geq 0)$ corresponds to an isotonic function having those symbols as arguments.*

As usual, we shall represent binary connectives in infix notation.

A rule of a monotonic logic program expresses a (monotonic) computation method of the truth-value of the head propositional symbol from the truth-values of the symbols in the body. The monotonicity of the rule is guaranteed by the isotonicity of the function corresponding to formula Ψ: if an argument of Ψ is monotonically increased then the truth-value of Ψ also monotonically increases. Notice that the bodies of rules can be formed from any operators in the implication algebra, besides the implication connective.

Example 3. Every rule $A \overset{s}{\leftarrow} B_1, \ldots B_m$ of a weighted logic program is translated to the Monotonic Logic Program rule $A \leftarrow s + B_1 + \ldots + B_m$ over the implication algebra $\mathfrak{C}$ extended with the addition operation[3] and with constant symbols for every element of $\mathcal{R}^+$. The program of Example 1 is translated to:

$$a \leftarrow 4 + b + c + c + d \qquad b \leftarrow 5 \qquad b \leftarrow 1 + c \qquad c \leftarrow b \qquad c \leftarrow 3 \qquad d \leftarrow 6$$

Notice that if we decrease (under the ordinary ordering of real numbers) the value of a propositional symbol then the value of the sum also decreases; thus the bodies of the above rules are isotonic with respect to $\mathcal{R}^+$.

An interpretation is simply an assignment of truth-value to each propositional symbol in the language. We assume in the rest of this section an implication algebra $\mathfrak{A}$ with respect to a complete lattice $\mathfrak{T} = < \mathcal{T}, \preceq >$. The operator and implication symbol is denoted by $\leftarrow$. Consider also that a set Π of propositional symbols is given as well as the corresponding algebra $FORM_{\mathfrak{A}}(\Pi)$ of formulae over Π. Then the notion of interpretation is straightforward:

---

[2] We represent the implication operator $\leftarrow_{\mathfrak{A}}$ at the syntactic level by $\leftarrow$. The same convention applies to any other operator defined in the implication algebra $\mathfrak{A}$.

[3] The sum of ∞ with any other element of $\mathfrak{R}$ renders ∞.

Definition 3 (Interpretation). *An interpretation is a mapping $I : \Pi \to \mathcal{T}$. By the unique homomorphic extension theorem, the interpretation extends uniquely to a valuation function $\hat{I} : FORM_{\mathfrak{A}}(\Pi) \to \mathcal{T}$. The set of all interpretations with respect to the implication algebra $\mathfrak{A}$ is denoted by $\mathcal{I}_{\mathfrak{A}}$.*

The unique homomorphic extension theorem guarantees that for every interpretation of propositional symbols there is an unique associated valuation function. The ordering $\preceq$ on the truth-values in $\mathcal{T}$ is extended to the set of interpretations as follows:

Definition 4 (Lattice of interpretations). *Consider $\mathcal{I}_{\mathfrak{A}}$ the set of all interpretations with respect to implication algebra $\mathfrak{A}$, and two interpretations $I_1, I_2 \in \mathcal{I}_{\mathfrak{A}}$. Then, $< \mathcal{I}_{\mathfrak{A}}, \sqsubseteq >$ is a complete lattice where $I_1 \sqsubseteq I_2$ iff $\forall_{p \in \Pi}\ I_1(p) \preceq I_2(p)$. The least interpretation $\triangle$ maps every propositional symbol to the least element of $\mathcal{T}$, and the greatest interpretation $\triangledown$ maps every propositional symbol to the top element of the complete lattice of truth-values $\mathcal{T}$.*

A rule of a monotonic logic program is satisfied whenever the truth-value of the rule is $\top$. A model is an interpretation which satisfies every rule in the program. Formally:

Definition 5 (Satisfaction and Model). *Consider an interpretation $I \in \mathcal{I}_{\mathfrak{A}}$. A monotonic logic program rule $A \leftarrow \Psi$ is satisfied by I iff $\hat{I}((A \leftarrow \Psi)) = \top$.*

An interpretation $I \in \mathcal{I}_{\mathfrak{A}}$ is a model of a monotonic logic program P iff all rules in P are satisfied by I.

We proceed by showing that every monotonic logic program has a least model which is the least fixpoint of a monotonic operator, along with other standard logic programming results. One such result is the immediate consequences operator, extending the results of van Emden and Kowalski [21] to the general theoretical setting of implication algebras:

Definition 6 (Immediate consequences operator). *Let P be a monotonic logic program. Define the immediate consequences operator $T_P^{\mathfrak{A}} : \mathcal{I}_{\mathfrak{A}} \to \mathcal{I}_{\mathfrak{A}}$, mapping interpretations to interpretations, where A is a propositional symbol:*

$$T_P^{\mathfrak{A}}(I)(A) = lub\left\{\hat{I}(\Psi) \text{ such that } A \leftarrow \Psi \in P\right\}$$

The immediate consequences operator evaluates the body of every rule for a propositional symbol A. The truth-value of A is simply the least upper bound of the truth-values of all the bodies of the rules for it.

Example 4. For weighted logic programs the immediate consequences operator reduces to:

$$\begin{aligned}
T_P^{\mathcal{C}}(I)(A) &= lub_{\geq}\ \{s + I(B_1) + \ldots + I(B_m) \mid A \leftarrow s + B_1 + \ldots + B_m \in P\} \\
&= \inf\ \{s + I(B_1) + \ldots + I(B_m) \mid A \leftarrow s + B_1 + \ldots + B_m \in P\}
\end{aligned}$$

This is very similar to the U_P operator of [17].

A fundamental property of operator $T_P^{\mathfrak{A}}$ is:

Theorem 1 (Monotonicity of the immediate consequences operator).
Let I_1 and I_2 be two interpretations in $\mathcal{I}_{\mathfrak{A}}$, and P a monotonic logic program. Operator $T_P^{\mathfrak{A}}$ is monotonic, i.e. if $I_1 \sqsubseteq I_2$ then $T_P^{\mathfrak{A}}(I_1) \sqsubseteq T_P^{\mathfrak{A}}(I_2)$.

As usual, the set of models of P is characterized by the post-fixpoints of $T_P^{\mathfrak{R}}$:

Theorem 2. *An interpretation I of $\mathcal{I}_{\mathfrak{A}}$ is a model of a monotonic logic program P iff $T_P^{\mathfrak{A}}(I) \sqsubseteq I$. Thus, the least fixpoint of $T_P^{\mathfrak{A}}$ is the least model of P.*

Therefore, the semantics of a monotonic logic program is given by M_P, the least model of P. One can obtain the least model of a program by transfinite iteration of the immediate consequences operator, as stated in the next theorem:

Theorem 3 (Fixpoint Semantics). *Let P be a monotonic logic program, and consider the transfinite sequence of interpretations of $\mathcal{I}_{\mathfrak{A}}$:*

$$T_P^{\mathfrak{A}}{\uparrow}0 = \triangle$$
$$T_P^{\mathfrak{A}}{\uparrow}{n+1} = T_P^{\mathfrak{A}}(T_P^{\mathfrak{A}}{\uparrow}n), \text{ if } n+1 \text{ is a successor ordinal}$$
$$T_P^{\mathfrak{A}}{\uparrow}\alpha = \bigsqcup\nolimits_{\beta < \alpha} T_P^{\mathfrak{A}}{\uparrow}\beta, \text{ if } \alpha \text{ is a limit ordinal}$$

Then, there is an ordinal λ such that $T_P^{\mathfrak{A}} {\uparrow}{\lambda+1} = T_P^{\mathfrak{A}} {\uparrow}\lambda$, and the least model of P is $M_P = T_P^{\mathfrak{A}} {\uparrow}\lambda$.

The major difference from standard classical logic programming is that our $T_P^{\mathfrak{A}}$ operator might not be continuous, and therefore more than ω iterations may be necessary to "reach" the least fixpoint. All the other important results carry over to our general framework. This possibility is unavoidable if one wants to retain generality. For the study of sufficient conditions to guarantee the continuity of the $T_P^{\mathfrak{A}}$, see [18]. We now determine the least model of the weighted logic program of Example 1:

Example 5. The least interpretation over $\mathfrak{R}$ maps every literal to ∞. Continuing with Example 4, the computation proceeds as follows:

	a	b	c	d
$T_P^{\mathfrak{C}}{\uparrow}0 =$	∞	∞	∞	∞
$T_P^{\mathfrak{C}}{\uparrow}1 =$	∞	5	3	6
$T_P^{\mathfrak{C}}{\uparrow}2 =$	21	4	3	6
$T_P^{\mathfrak{C}}{\uparrow}3 =$	20	4	3	6
$T_P^{\mathfrak{C}}{\uparrow}4 =$	20	4	3	6

4   Antitonic Logic Programs

In the preceding section we reviewed the framework of Monotonic Logic Programs. Now we extend the syntax of programs allowing for rules with antitonic bodies using the techniques which have been developed in logic programming theory. Our attained aim is to define well-founded [11] and stable model semantics [12] for logic programming over arbitrary implication algebras. Thus, we can easily extend all the semantics for which we have an embedding into Monotonic Logic Programs with non-monotonic "negations." We apply these new results to logic programs with costs, answering some of the questions raised in [17].

Let us start with the language of Antitonic Logic Programs:

Definition 7 (Antitonic Logic Programs). *Let $\mathfrak{A}$ be an implication algebra with respect to a complete lattice $\mathfrak{T}$. Let Π be a set of propositional symbols and $FORM_{\mathfrak{A}}(\Pi)$ the corresponding algebra of formulae freely generated from Π and the "symbols" of operators in $\mathfrak{A}$. An antitonic logic program is a pair $< P^+, P^- >$ where P^+ and P^- are sets of rules of the form $A \leftarrow \Psi$ such that:*

1. *The rule $(A \leftarrow \Psi)$ is a formula of $FORM_{\mathfrak{A}}(\Pi)$;*
2. *The head of the rule A is a propositional symbol of Π.*
3. *If $A \leftarrow \Psi$ belongs to P^+, then the body formula Ψ with propositional symbols $B_1, \ldots, B_n$ ($n \geq 0$) corresponds to an isotonic function having those symbols as arguments.*
4. *If $A \leftarrow \Psi$ belongs to P^-, then the body formula Ψ with propositional symbols $B_1, \ldots, B_n$ ($n \geq 0$) corresponds to an antitonic function having those symbols as arguments.*

We denote a rule of P^+ by $A \stackrel{+}{\leftarrow} \Psi$, and a rule of P^- by $A \stackrel{-}{\leftarrow} \Psi$.

We recall that a function is isotonic (antitonic) iff the value of the function increases (decreases) when we increase an argument while the other remaining arguments are kept fixed. Note that we do not introduce explicitly a negation symbol in the language. A negation can be obtained by associating an antitonic function with an ordinary propositional symbol, as shown in the next Example.

Example 6. For weighted logic programs we can define a natural class of negations by considering the cost function $\vartheta - x$, onto $\mathcal{R}^+$, which returns 0 if $x \geq \vartheta$, otherwise its value is $\vartheta - x$. The special case of $\infty - x$ returns 0 whenever $x = \infty$, else it evaluates to ∞. The interpretation of this last case is immediate: if an atom cannot be concluded from the program its cost is ∞ and therefore its negation has cost 0. Otherwise, the negation does not hold and therefore the cost of $\infty - x$ is ∞. An example of an antitonic logic program is:

$$a \stackrel{+}{\leftarrow} 3 + b + not\_d. \qquad b \stackrel{+}{\leftarrow} 2. \qquad d \stackrel{+}{\leftarrow} 4 + e. \qquad e \stackrel{+}{\leftarrow} 1 + not\_a.$$
$$not\_a \stackrel{-}{\leftarrow} 7 - a \qquad\qquad\qquad not\_d \stackrel{-}{\leftarrow} 5 - d$$

The symbols 'not_a' and 'not_d' are new propositional symbols.

We proceed by first defining a well-founded like semantics for antitonic logic programs, guaranteeing the existence of a model for every program. Afterwards, we deal with stable models, which are simpler to introduce. Again, we assume an implication algebra $\mathfrak{A}$ with respect to a complete lattice $\mathfrak{T} = < \mathcal{T}, \preceq >$. Consider too that a set Π of propositional symbols is given as well as the corresponding algebra $FORM_{\mathfrak{A}}(\Pi)$ of formulae over Π. To start with a new notion of interpretation is required:

Definition 8 (Partial Intepretations). *A partial interpretation is a pair of interpretations* $< I^t, I^{tu} >$. *The set of all partial interpretations is* $\mathcal{I}^p_{\mathfrak{A}}$.

The I^t component contains what is "true" in the interpretation, while I^{tu} what is "non-false", i.e. true or undefined. It is important to mark that we do not impose consistency of the interpretation (i.e. $I^t \sqsubseteq I^{tu}$) and thus allow for paraconsistency. Two orders among partial interpretations are useful:

Definition 9 (Truth and knowledge ordering). *Let* I_1 *and* I_2 *be two partial interpretations. The truth and knowledge orders among partial interpretations are defined by:*

Truth ordering: $I_1 \sqsubseteq_t I_2$ *iff* $I^t_1 \sqsubseteq I^t_2$ *and* $I^{tu}_1 \sqsubseteq I^{tu}_2$.
Knowledge ordering: $I_1 \sqsubseteq_k I_2$ *iff* $I^t_1 \sqsubseteq I^t_2$ *and* $I^{tu}_2 \sqsubseteq I^{tu}_1$.

The set of partial interpretations ordered by $\sqsubseteq_t$ *or* $\sqsubseteq_k$ *is a complete lattice. Clearly, the bottom and top elements of these lattices are* $\perp_t =<\triangle, \triangle>$, $\top_t =< \triangledown, \triangledown >$, $\perp_k =<\triangle, \triangledown >$ *and* $\top_k =< \triangledown, \triangle>$.

Given a partial interpretation, we can define the model of an antitonic logic program:

Definition 10. *Let* $P =< P^+, P^- >$ *be an antitonic logic program. A partial interpretation* $I =< I^t, I^{tu} >$ *satisfies a rule* $A \leftarrow \Psi$ *of* P *iff:*

- $I^t(A) \leftarrow_{\mathfrak{A}} \hat{I}^t(\Psi) = \top$, *if the rule belongs to* P^+.
- $I^t(A) \leftarrow_{\mathfrak{A}} \hat{I}^{tu}(\Psi) = \top$, *if the rule belongs to* P^-.

We say that I *is a model of* P *iff the interpretation satisfies all the rules of* P.

Notice that the heads of rules are always evaluated with respect to I^t while the truth-values of bodies are determined from I^t (I^{tu}) for isotonic (antitonic) rules. The attentive reader will have noticed that with the above definition our programs define only positive information from the bodies. Because of the antitonic character of rules in P^-, the greater the body arguments the lesser is $\hat{I}^{tu}(\Psi)$ and the lesser is $I^t(A)$. Clearly, our framework captures normal logic programs: every rule of the form $A \leftarrow B_1, \ldots, B_m, \mathrm{not} C_1, \ldots, \mathrm{not} C_n$ is translated into $A \leftarrow B_1 \wedge \ldots \wedge B_m \wedge \mathrm{not\_} C_1 \wedge \ldots \wedge \mathrm{not\_} C_n$ and a further rule exists for each new atom $\mathrm{not\_} C_i$ of the form $\mathrm{not\_} C_i \leftarrow 1 - C_i$. The underlying lattice of truth-values is $\{0, 1\}$ with $0 < 1$.

A natural generalization is to include rules which declare directly the truth-values of I^{tu}. Here we enter the arena of extending logic programming and general logic programming, where rules with explicit and default negation in their heads are permitted, which we will deal with in subsequent work.

In order to define the semantics of Antitonic Logic Programs we will resort to a Gelfond-Lifschitz like division operator [12], which transforms an Antitonic Logic Program into a Monotonic one, for which we know how to compute the corresponding least model. This is the usual technique for defining well-founded and stable model semantics for normal logic programs. Our definition and results orbit around this notion.

Definition 11 (Program Division). *Consider an antitonic logic program P and an interpretation*[4] I^{tu}. *The division of program P by I^{tu} is the monotonic logic program:*

$$\frac{P}{I^{tu}} = P^+ \cup \left\{ A \leftarrow \vartheta \text{ such that } A \leftarrow \Psi \in P^- \text{ and } \vartheta = \hat{I}^{tu}(\Psi) \right\}$$

We assume that every truth-value in $\mathfrak{T}$ has a corresponding constant operator in $\mathfrak{A}$ which returns its value.

Example 7. Consider the program of Example 6 and interpretation I mapping a, not_a, b, d, not_d and f to ∞, 0, 2, 3, 0 and 1, respectively. The division of that program by I is:

$$a \leftarrow 3 + b + not\_d \qquad b \leftarrow 2 \qquad d \leftarrow 4 + e \qquad e \leftarrow 1 + not\_a$$
$$not\_a \leftarrow 0 \qquad\qquad\qquad\qquad not\_d \leftarrow 2$$

Thus, the program division operation substitutes the bodies of antitonic rules by their truth-value in the given interpretation. The result is a monotonic logic program. Now we can define an auxiliary operator mapping partial interpretations into interpretations, which will be extensively used:

Definition 12. *Consider an antitonic logic program P and a partial interpretation $I = < I^t, I^{tu} >$. Then, $C_P^{\mathfrak{A}}(I) = T^{\mathfrak{A}}_{\frac{P}{I^{tu}}}(I^t)$.*

The $C_P^{\mathfrak{A}}(I)$ operator determines what follows immediately from the program given the partial interpretation. We have the following important results:

Proposition 1. *A partial interpretation I is a model of an antitonic logic program P iff $C_P^{\mathfrak{A}}(I) \sqsubseteq I^t$. Furthermore, let J be another partial interpretation such that $I \sqsubseteq_k J$ then $C_P^{\mathfrak{A}}(I) \sqsubseteq C_P^{\mathfrak{A}}(J)$.*

The last proposition is simply assuring that if we have more knowledge (less undefined values in the interpretation) then we can extract more information from our programs.

Operator $C_P^{\mathfrak{A}}$ maps partial interpretations to interpretations. We now define a new operator which maps partial interpretations to partial interpretations, given what is known to be true and to be false, in the same spirit of Przymusinski's Θ operator [19]:

Definition 13 (Partial Consequences Operator). *Let P be an antitonic logic program, and the two partial interpretations I and J. The partial consequences operator is given by the equation:*

$$\Theta_P^{\mathfrak{A}}(I, J) = \left\langle C_P^{\mathfrak{A}}\left(< I^t, J^{tu} >\right), C_P^{\mathfrak{A}}\left(< I^{tu}, J^t >\right) \right\rangle$$

We usually omit the subscript $\mathfrak{A}$ and denote $\Theta_P^{\mathfrak{A}}(I, J)$ by $\Theta_P^J(I)$.

---

[4] Mark well this is an interpretation, not a partial interpretation!

Interpretation J represents safe knowledge. On the one hand, from J^{tu} one can conclude what definitely doesn't hold, and thus we use this interpretation for deriving what holds surely. On the other hand, from J^t one knows what is true, and so we use it for deriving what may possibly hold.

Proposition 2. *Let I, J and K be partial interpretations. If $I \sqsubseteq_t J$ then $\Theta_P^K(I) \sqsubseteq_t \Theta_P^K(J)$.*

Basically we have shown in the previous proposition that Θ_P^J is a monotonic operator on the lattice of partial interpretations according to the truth-ordering. Its least fixpoint is guaranteed to exist and is important for our objectives:

Definition 14 (Full Consequences Operator). *Let P be an antitonic logic program and J a partial interpretation. Define $\Omega_P^{\mathfrak{A}}(J) = \text{lfp } \Theta_P^J$. Alternatively, $\Omega_P^{\mathfrak{A}}(J)$ is given by $\Theta_P^J{\uparrow}^\lambda$ where λ is the least ordinal for which $\Theta_P^J{\uparrow}^{\lambda+1} = \Theta_P^J{\uparrow}^\lambda$ with*

$$\Theta_P^J{\uparrow}^0 = <\triangle, \triangle>$$
$$\Theta_P^J{\uparrow}^{n+1} = \Theta_P^J(\Theta_P^J{\uparrow}^n), \text{ if } n+1 \text{ is a successor ordinal}$$
$$\Theta_P^J{\uparrow}^\alpha = \bigsqcup_t \left\{ \Theta_P^J{\uparrow}^\beta \text{ such that } \beta < \alpha \right\}, \text{ if } \alpha \text{ is a limit ordinal}$$

By an easy transfinite induction proof one concludes:

Proposition 3. *Let P be an antitonic logic program and J an arbitrary partial interpretation then:*

$$\Theta_P^J{\uparrow}^\alpha = \left\langle T_{\frac{P}{J^{tu}}}^{\mathfrak{A}}{\uparrow}^\alpha, T_{\frac{P}{J^t}}^{\mathfrak{A}}{\uparrow}^\alpha \right\rangle$$

So, the least fixpoint of Θ_P^J is in fact obtained from the least model of monotonic logic programs $\frac{P}{J^{tu}}$ and $\frac{P}{J^t}$. This deserves a definition and a theorem:

Definition 15 (Gamma operator). *Let P be an antitonic logic program and J an interpretation. Define*

$$\Gamma_P^{\mathfrak{A}}(J) = M_{\frac{P}{J}} = \text{lfp } T_{\frac{P}{J}}^{\mathfrak{A}} = T_{\frac{P}{J}}^{\mathfrak{A}}{\uparrow}^\lambda, \text{ for some ordinal } \lambda$$

Theorem 4. *Let P be an antitonic logic program and J a partial interpretation. Then,*

$$\Omega_P^{\mathfrak{A}}(J) = \left\langle \Gamma_P^{\mathfrak{A}}(J^{tu}), \Gamma_P^{\mathfrak{A}}(J^t) \right\rangle$$

Thus, we have defined the full consequences operator in terms of the least model of two monotonic logic programs. Basically, Theorem 4 states that the least model of $\frac{P}{J^{tu}}$ gives what is true given the safe knowledge J, and that the least model of $\frac{P}{J^t}$ provides what is non-false.

A well-known result of logic programming theory is that operator Γ is anti-monotonic. The same happens with antitonic logic programs:

Proposition 4. *Consider the antitonic logic program P. Let I and J be two interpretations such that $I \sqsubseteq J$, then $\Gamma_P^{\mathfrak{A}}(J) \sqsubseteq \Gamma_P^{\mathfrak{A}}(I)$.*

From this there follows a fundamental result:

Theorem 5 (Monotonicity of the full consequences operator). *Let P be an antitonic logic program, and $I \sqsubseteq_k J$ two partial interpretations. Then, $\Omega_P^{\mathfrak{A}}(I) \sqsubseteq_k \Omega_P^{\mathfrak{A}}(J)$.*

We conclude immediately, again by the Knaster-Tarski fixpoint theorem, that $\Omega_P^{\mathfrak{A}}$ has a least fixpoint under the knowledge ordering of partial interpretations.

Definition 16 (Well-founded Semantics). *Consider an antitonic logic program P. The partial stable models of P are the fixpoints of operator $\Omega_P^{\mathfrak{A}}$. The least one under the knowledge ordering of partial interpretations is the well-founded model WFM_P, and can be obtained by transfinitely iterating the $\Omega_P^{\mathfrak{A}}$ operator from the least partial interpretation $\perp_k = <\triangle, \triangledown >$.*
Given a partial stable model M we say that an atom A is:

- **true** *with degree ϑ wrt. M if $\vartheta \preceq M^t(A)$ and $\vartheta \preceq M^{tu}(A)$.*
- **undefined** *with degree ϑ wrt. M if $\vartheta \not\preceq M^t(A)$ and $\vartheta \preceq M^{tu}(A)$.*
- **false** *with degree ϑ wrt. M if $\vartheta \not\preceq M^t(A)$ and $\vartheta \not\preceq M^{tu}(A)$.*
- **inconsistent** *with degree ϑ wrt. M if $\vartheta \preceq M^t(A)$ and $\vartheta \not\preceq M^{tu}(A)$.*

By resorting to the definition of $\Omega_P^{\mathfrak{A}}$ in terms of $\Gamma_P^{\mathfrak{A}}$ we can present an alternating fixpoint definition [1] of the well-founded semantics for antitonic logic programs:

Theorem 6. *Consider an antitonic logic program P. The partial interpretation I is a fixpoint of $\Omega_P^{\mathfrak{A}}$ iff $\Gamma_P^{\mathfrak{A}}(\Gamma_P^{\mathfrak{A}}(I^t)) = I^t$ and $I^{tu} = \Gamma_P^{\mathfrak{A}}(I^t)$.*

Example 8. The well-founded model in Example 6 is determined as follows:

	a	not_a	b	d	not_d	e
$I_0 = \infty$	∞	∞	∞	∞	∞	
$\Gamma_P^{\mathfrak{C}}(I_0) = 5$	0	2	5	0	1	
$I_1 = \Gamma_P^{\mathfrak{C}}(\Gamma_P^{\mathfrak{C}}(I_0)) = 5$	2	2	7	0	3	
$\Gamma_P^{\mathfrak{C}}(I_1) = 5$	2	2	7	0	3	

The well-founded model of P is $< I_1, \Gamma_P^{\mathfrak{C}}(I_1) > = < I_1, I_1 >$, and thus we conclude a with cost 5. The example illustrates a possible interpretation of negation in logic programs with costs: what costs more to prove true costs less to show false, and vice-versa.

Thus, the well-founded model of P is given by the least fixpoint of the $\left(\Gamma_P^{\mathfrak{A}}\right)^2$ operator, a well-known result in the theory of logic programming [1]. We have the next reassuring result:

Theorem 7. *The partial stable models of an antitonic logic program P are models of P.*

A partial stable model is said consistent whenever there is no propositional symbol A which is inconsistent to any degree ϑ. It is said fully defined whenever there is no propositional symbol with undefined truth-value to any degree ϑ. Clearly, the following is expected:

Proposition 5. *A partial stable model $\mathcal{M}$ of antitonic logic program P is consistent iff $\mathcal{M}^t \sqsubseteq \mathcal{M}^{tu}$. It is fully defined whenever $\mathcal{M}^{tu} \sqsubseteq \mathcal{M}^t$.*

The consistent and fully-defined partial stable models of P are the stable models of P:

Definition 17 (Stable Models). *Let P be an antitonic logic program. We say that M is a stable model of P iff it is a consistent and fully defined partial stable model of P. Furthermore, $M^t = M^{tu}$ and M is a stable model iff it is a fixpoint of $\Gamma_P^{\mathfrak{A}}$, i.e. $M = \Gamma_P^{\mathfrak{A}}(M)$.*

The program of Example 6 has a single stable model which coincides with its well-founded model.

Example 9. The program containing the rules $a \xleftarrow{-} \vartheta_1 - not\_a.$ and $not\_a \xleftarrow{-} \vartheta_2 - a.$ has a single stable model when $\vartheta_1 = 0$ or $\vartheta_2 = 0$. Suppose now that both are finite non-zero real numbers. In this case if $\vartheta_1 \neq \vartheta_2$ then the program has no stable models. Assume that $\vartheta_1 = \vartheta_2 > 0$. All interpretations such that $a + not\_a = \vartheta_1$ are stable models of the program, therefore there exist an infinite number of them. Finally, if both $\vartheta_1 = \vartheta_2 = \infty$ then there are two stable models of the program. If $\vartheta_1 = \infty$ and $\vartheta_2 \neq \infty$ we have a single stable model.

The analysis of the program comprising the single rule $a \xleftarrow{-} \vartheta - a$ is easier. If $\vartheta = \infty$ then there are no stable models. Otherwise, the single stable model assigns the truth-value $\frac{\vartheta}{2}$ to a.

Example 10. Consider this variant of Example 6:

$$a \xleftarrow{+} 3 + b + not\_d. \qquad b \xleftarrow{+} 2. \qquad d \xleftarrow{+} 4 + e. \qquad e \xleftarrow{+} 1 + not\_a.$$
$$not\_a \xleftarrow{-} \infty - a \qquad\qquad\qquad not\_d \xleftarrow{-} \infty - d$$

The well-founded model and its two stable models are shown below :

	a	not_a	b	d	not_d	e
$WFM^t =$	∞	∞	2	∞	∞	∞
$WFM^{tu} =$	5	0	2	5	0	1

	a	not_a	b	d	not_d	e
$M_1 =$	∞	0	2	5	∞	1
$M_2 =$	5	∞	2	∞	0	∞

The positive part of the well-founded model is not very informative, except that we can conclude b with cost 2. However, the non-false part provides the joint limits of the stable models. In general, $WFM^t \sqsubseteq \sqcap_i M_i$ and $\sqcup_i M_i \sqsubseteq WFM^{tu}$.

The interpretation of the negation $\infty - A$ in stable model semantics should now be clear. Given an atom that we can prove then its negation is not provable and it therefore costs ∞ to prove. Also, by simply looking at the model, one can see what does not hold, and therefore know instantly that its negation holds without any extra effort, justifying its zero cost. We believe this is in accordance with the ideas advanced in the conclusions section of [17], as a possible interpretation for negation in logic programs with costs. Obviously, any other antitonic negation can be easily encoded in our framework.

5   Conclusions and Future Work

In a single sentence, this paper shows how to (logically) program with arbitrary monotonic and anti-monotonic (antitonic) operators over a complete lattice. This is a simple and powerful idea with an enormous range of applications. In particular, the present work paves the way to combine and integrate several forms of reasoning into a single framework, namely fuzzy, probabilistic, uncertain, and paraconsistent ones.

This paper is the natural extension of the seminal works by Subrahmanian [20,14] and Fitting [8,9]. However, these authors stick to a logic programming syntax instead of considering arbitrary monotonic and antitonic functions in the bodies. This is a major contribution of our work. To be absolutely fair, the article [9] introduces the notions of *attenuation operators* which can be viewed as arbitrary monotonic functions over bilattices.

Quite recently, there appeared in the literature a profound work [6] entitled "Approximations, Stable Operators, Well-founded Fixpoints and Applications in Nonmonotonic Reasoning". The stance there is to depart from either a monotone or antitonic operator and define approximations to it, via a *stable operator* which corresponds to an abstract version of the well-founded semantics. The interesting case is when O is antitonic. In this situation, most of the results in [6] are obtained in our scheme by considering the single rule program $A \xleftarrow{-} O(A)$. It is also true that our results follow immediately from [6]. So, both frameworks are capable of expressing each other. However, we show how multiple operators should be combined in order to extend the widely accepted well-founded and stable model semantics for normal logic programs, a point not addressed in [6].

Regarding future work, we expect to show the embeddings of other cost functions introduced in [17], as well as those of [22]. Extension of our antitonic results to residuated lattices (c.f. [2,13]), where a generalized modus ponens rule is defined, is also foreseen. We also aim to provide a proof theory for (instances) of our framework.

Acknowledgements

Work partially supported by PRAXIS projects FLUX and RACIO. We thank the anonymous referees for their comments and references to related work. Special thanks to Manuel Ojeda-Aciego for his insightful remarks.

References

1. C. Baral and V. S. Subrahmanian. Duality between alternative semantics of logic programs and nonmonotonic formalisms. *Journal of Automated Reasoning*, 10:399–420, 1993. 389
2. L. Bolc and P. Borowik. *Many-Valued Logics. Theoretical Foundations.* Springer–Verlag, 1992. 391

3. C. V. Damásio and L. M. Pereira. Hybrid probabilistic logic programs as residuated logic programs. In M. O. Aciego, I. P. de Guzmán, G. Brewka, and L. M. Pereira, editors, *Proc. of JELIA'00*, pages 57–72. LNAI 1919, Springer–Verlag, 2000. 379

4. C. V. Damásio and L. M. Pereira. Monotonic and residuated logic programs, 2001. Accepted in ECSQARU-2001. 379, 381

5. A. Dekhtyar and V. S. Subrahmanian. Hybrid probabilistic programs. In *International Conference on Logic Programming 1997*, pages 391–495. MIT Press, 1997. 379

6. M. Denecker, V. Marek, and M. Truszczyński. Approximations, stable operators, well-founded fixpoints and applications in nonmonotonic reasoning. In J. Minker, editor, *Logic-Based Artifical Intelligence*, pages 127–144. Kluwer Academic Publishers, 2000. 380, 391

7. D. Dubois, J. Lang, and H. Prade. Towards possibilistic logic programming. In *International Conference on Logic Programming 1991*, pages 581–598. MIT Press, 1991. 379

8. M. Fitting. Bilattices and the semantics of logic programs. *Journal of Logic Programming*, 11:91–116, 1991. 379, 391

9. M. Fitting. The family of stable models. *Journal of Logic Programming*, 17:197–225, 1993. 379, 391

10. J. H. Gallier. *Logic for Computer Science*. John Wiley & Sons, 1987. 381, 382

11. A. Van Gelder, K. A. Ross, and J. S. Schlipf. The well-founded semantics for general logic programs. *Journal of the ACM*, 38(3):620–650, 1991. 385

12. M. Gelfond and V. Lifschitz. The stable model semantics for logic programming. In R. Kowalski and K. A. Bowen, editors, *5th International Conference on Logic Programming*, pages 1070–1080. MIT Press, 1988. 385, 386

13. P. Hájek. *Metamathematics of Fuzzy Logic*. Trends in Logic. Studia Logica Library. Kluwer Academic Publishers, 1998. 391

14. M. Kifer and V. S. Subrahmanian. Theory of generalized annotated logic programming and its applications. *J. of Logic Programming*, 12:335–367, 1992. 379, 391

15. R. Kowalski. Predicate logic as a programming language. In *Proceedings of IFIP'74*, pages 569–574. North Holland Publishing Company, 1974. 380

16. J. W. Lloyd. *Foundations of Logic Programming*. Springer–Verlag, 1987. 380

17. V. W. Marek and M. Truszczyński. Logic programming with costs. Technical report, 2000. Available at ftp://al.cs.engr.uky.edu/cs/manuscripts/lp-costs.ps. 379, 380, 383, 385, 390, 391

18. J. Medina, M. Ojeda-Aciego, and P. Vojtas. Multi-adjoint logic programming with continuous semantics. In *Proc. of LPNMR'01*, September 2001. This issue. 384

19. H. Przymusinska and T. C. Przymusinski. Semantic issues in deductive databases and logic programs. In R. Banerji, editor, *Formal Techniques in Artificial Intelligence, a Sourcebook*, pages 321–367. North Holland, 1990. 387

20. V. S. Subrahmanian. Algebraic properties of the space of multivalued and paraconsistent logic programs. In *9th Int. Conf. on Foundations of Software Technology and Theoretical Computer Science*, pages 56–67. LNCS 405, Springer–Verlag, 1989. 379, 391

21. M. van Emden and R. Kowalski. The semantics of predicate logic as a programming language. *Journal of ACM*, 4(23):733–742, 1976. 380, 383

22. M. H. van Emden. Quantitative deduction and its fixpoint theory. *Journal of Logic Programming*, 4:37–53, 1986. 380, 391

23. P. Vojtás. Fuzzy logic programming. *Fuzzy Sets and Systems*, 2001. Accepted. 379

24. P. Vojtás and L. Paulík. Soundness and completeness of non-classical extended SLD-resolution. In *Proc. of the Ws. on Extensions of Logic Programming (ELP'96)*, pages 289–301. LNCS 1050, Springer–Verlag., 1996. 379

$\mathcal{A}$-system: Declarative Programming with Abduction*

Bert Van Nuffelen[1] and Antonis Kakas[2]

[1] Dept. Computer Science, K.U.Leuven
Celestijnenlaan 200A, Leuven, Belgium
bertv@cs.kuleuven.ac.be
[2] Dept. of Computer Science, University of Cyprus
75 Kallipoleos St. Nicosia, Cyprus
antonis@ucy.ac.cy

1 General Information

The $\mathcal{A}$-system [4] is a new system for performing abductive reasoning within the framework of Abductive Logic Programming (ALP). The principles behind the system are founded by work on two earlier systems ACLP [2,3] and SLD-NFA(C) [1,6]. The basic inference mechanism of the system combines abductive logic programming and constraint logic programming. In its computation it reduces the high level specification of the problem and goal at hand to a lower level constraint store. This constraint store is managed by an efficient constraint solver returning information to the abductive reduction process in order to help this in its search for a solution.

In the development of the $\mathcal{A}$-system particular attention was put into general purpose control and search strategies in order to enhance the computational behaviour of the system. The main idea is to suspend each commitment to a choice up to the moment where no other information can be derived in a deterministic way. This improves it over its ancestors.

The $\mathcal{A}$-system is implemented as a meta interpreter on top of Sicstus Prolog where at least version 3.8.5 is needed. The system is therefore available on each platform on which Sicstus is available.

2 Description of the System

The $\mathcal{A}$-system is a declarative problem solving environment. It allows us to specify the problem domain in a well structured way in terms of an abductive logic program (ALP). A problem specification consists of two parts of information: definitional knowledge and assertional knowledge or integrity constraints. In the definitional part predicates are defined in a (constraint) logic program by specifying the rules embodying all the information known of these predicates.

In a planning domain example the predicate holds_at(P,T) is defined as:

---

* http://www.cs.kuleuven.ac.be/~dtai/kt

T. Eiter, W. Faber, and M. Truszczyński (Eds.): LPNMR 2001, LNAI 2173, pp. 393–397, 2001.

```
holds_at(P,T):- initially(P), not(init_clipped(P,T)).
holds_at(P,T):- initiates(P,A), act(A,E), E<T,not(clipped(E,P,T)).
```

The predicates which are not defined like `act(A,E)` are called *open or abducible*.

Integrity constraints are universal quantified statements which express a property of the theory (application domain) that must remain true whenever this theory is extended with a (partial) definition of the open predicates. In practice, this means that the integrity constraints encode at a declarative level properties of the abductive solutions to the goals of our problem domain. In the $\mathcal{A}$-system they have to be specified as denials with as head `ic`. For example the two constraints below ensure that the second argument of `act(A,T)` is within the valid time interval; and that the preconditions of each action is satisfied.

```
ic:- act(A,T),not(time(T)).
ic:- act(A,T),not(pre_conditions_hold(A,T)).
```

Given a query Q the $\mathcal{A}$-system computes an extension of the open predicates such that this set entails Q and the integrity constraints. Semantically this solution is formalised as an abductive explanation of Q. Computationally this is found through a reduction process where the system goes through a cycle of selecting a choice point, making this choice and propagating deterministicaly this choice as much as possible. In general, the $\mathcal{A}$-system postpones choices as long as possible and tries to evaluate the choice points in an informed way. This is mainly done by interacting with the constraint solver.

3   Applying the System

A simple preprocessor accepts the ALP problem representation and compiles it into a readable format for the system. The preprocessor will load automatically the compiled specification. The $\mathcal{A}$-system can then be queried by the call *asystem_solve(query(Args))*. The system returns as answer a table of atoms of the open predicates whose addition to the program will entail the query.

3.1   Methodology

The $\mathcal{A}$-system has been applied on a number of applications. Although most of them are not of "industrial scale" some general guidelines have emerged from these experiments, which can be followed to build an application.

The main advantage of the $\mathcal{A}$-system is the modular development of the problem representation that it allows. This stems from the fact that this representation can be a direct mapping of the declarative high-level specification of the problem. The $\mathcal{A}$-system thus allows us to build up the problem representation incrementally. Typically, this starts with a choice of the alphabet. The alphabet will determine the way the specification will look and will potentially influence the reasoning efficiency of the system. For example, in the block world planning, in the simplest case, it is sufficient to capture the movement of a block from one place to another in one action move(X,Y,T). This specification cannot represent a state in which the robot is holding a block. If that becomes important the move action can be split into pick(X,T) and put(X,Y,T). This refinement is done locally affecting only part of the specification. In general, such refinements allow the user to solve first a more abstract problem whose solutions can then be further reduced to give concrete actual solution of the problem e.g. as in the process of hierarchical planning.

Another way of refining the declarative problem representation in ALP is to add extra integrity constraints. Due to this extra knowledge the 𝒜-system will (in most cases) be able to prune unwanted branches earlier or eliminate uninteresting solutions from the more general specification. The compactness of the ALP representations also means that the framework is well suited for problems in which the specification is subject to (regular) changes. The adaptation to changes can be done easily without disturbing the whole specification.

3.2 Users and Useability

A user familiar with logic programming or first order logic will be able to use the 𝒜-system with little extra help. A good knowledge about the problem domain will result in better and more informed specifications and thus in better performance. The 𝒜-system also allows the user to influence its behaviour using some parameters on how this would interact with the underlying constraint solver. For this reason it is useful to be familiar with some details of CLP.

The modeling language poses very few restrictions on the problem domains on which it can be applied. However, the current implemented prototype has some. At this moment only problems which can be modeled inside the finite domains framework can be solved efficiently. This is because only the finite domain CLP solver is integrated in the system. In principle there are no limitations to integrating CLP solvers over other domains. Furthermore, we are extending the system with aggregates (e.g. cardinality, sum, and average) so that a wider range of problem domains can be solved. This extension will allow the 𝒜-system to solve for example problems of planning with resources.

4 Evaluating the System

The 𝒜-system has been tested on constraint satisfaction problems (CSP) (e.g. N-Queens, Graph Coloring and Scheduling problems), examples of diagnosis and standard planning problems taken from the AI Planning Systems Competition 2000. Most extensively it has been tested on planning as in this domain the problems cannot be reduced in a deterministic way to a constraint store but the system must search for a solution. In simple CSP problems like the n-queens or graph coloring and scheduling problems the whole specification can be reduced to a CLP-constraint store. The real problem solving is then left to CLP solver. However in the planning domain, the search for a solution is an interleaved process of making a choice by the high level procedure of the $\mathcal{A}$-system and utilizing the information about the impact of this choice on the constraint store.

As mentioned above, currently only a finite domain solver is incorporated in the system, and thus the problem size is limited by the efficiency of the constraint solver as this size increases. As the problem size increases the system, due to non optimal data structures that it uses, may slow down on large problem instantiations. It has been successfully tested in the blocks world domain (using the move operator) up to 100 blocks. On other planning domains like logistics the scaling was not as good. In general, the problem size which can be handled depends on the generated constraint store. If this store becomes too complex for the constraint solver, the derivation process might get stuck in a local satisfiability check of this.

4.1 Benchmarks and Comparison

Currently very few benchmarks are available for testing the full capabilities of the $\mathcal{A}$-system with the AIPS planning competition test set being the best example. The $\mathcal{A}$-system has been evaluated in [4] with some of the problems from this set.

A comparison of the $\mathcal{A}$-system with other systems can be separated in two classes: to other general purpose systems like Smodels and DLV or more specialized systems like AI planners. At this moment no extensive study has been made to compare the $\mathcal{A}$-system with the second class of systems. In the first class, the $\mathcal{A}$-system is capable to solve the same type of applications. However, Smodels and DLV which work on propositional theories are more robust on some problems making extensive use of heuristics in their bottom up computation. Currently, we are experimenting with different general heuristics that would allow the $\mathcal{A}$-system to avoid infinitely growing search branches and thus make it more robust. A number of recent comparison experiments [5] indicate that the top down reducing process of the $\mathcal{A}$-system performs, on some classes of problems, better than Smodels. A characteristic for such a class is that the high-level specification can be deterministically reduced into a constraint store.

References

1. Marc Denecker and Danny De Schreye. SLDNFA: an abductive procedure for normal abductive programs. *J. Logic Programming*, 34(2):111–167, 1998. 393
2. A. C. Kakas and C. Mourlas. ACLP: Flexible solutions to complex problems. In *Proceedings of LPNMR-97*, pages 387–398, 1997. 393
3. A. C. Kakas, A. Michael, and C. Mourlas. ACLP: Abductive constraint logic programming. *Journal of Logic Programming*, 44(1-3):129–177, July,August 2000. 393
4. A.C Kakas, Bert Van Nuffelen, and Marc Denecker. A-system : Problem solving through abduction. In *Proceedings of IJCAI'01*, 2001. to appear. 393, 396
5. Nikolay Pelov, Emmanuel De Mot, and Maurice Bruynooghe. A comparison of logic programming approaches for representation and solving of constraint satisfaction problems. In *Proceedings of NMR'2000*, pages 1–15, 2000. 396

6. Bert Van Nuffelen and Marc Denecker. Problem solving in ID-logic with aggregates. In *Proceedings of NMR'2000, special track on Abductive Reasoning*, pages 1–9, 2000. 393

An Update Front-End
for Extended Logic Programs

Thomas Eiter, Michael Fink, Giuliana Sabbatini, and Hans Tompits

Institut für Informationssysteme, Abt.Wissensbasierte Systeme 184/3,
Technische Universität Wien, Favoritenstrasse 9-11, A-1040 Vienna, Austria
{eiter,michael,giuliana,tompits}@kr.tuwien.ac.at

Abstract. In recent years, several approaches for dealing with updates
of logic programs have been proposed. In this paper, we describe the system **upd**, an implementation of the update formalism due to Eiter *et al.*
This method is based on a compilation technique to standard answer set
semantics, in which update sequences are translated into single logic programs, and which allows the use of existing logic programming systems
as underlying reasoning engine. In the present case, **upd** is conceived as
a front-end to the state-of-the-art solver **DLV**. Besides the basic update
semantics of Eiter *et al.*, the implementation handles also refinements of
the semantics involving certain minimality-of-change criteria.

1 Background

The problem of updating nonmonotonic knowledge bases has gained increasing
interest in recent years. In particular, several update approaches have been proposed in which knowledge bases are represented as logic programs [1,2,3,6,7]. In
this paper, we present the system **upd**, which is an implementation of the method
for updating logic programs due to Eiter *et al.* [2,3].This approach is based on
the answer set semantics for extended logic programs, and, like related update
formalisms, it incorporates new information into the current knowledge base according to a *causal rejection principle*. This principle enforces that, in case of
conflicts between rules, more recent rules have precedence over older rules. The
general approach can be described as follows.

Given a sequence $(P_1, \ldots, P_n)$ of extended logic programs, each P_i is assumed
to update the information expressed by the initial sequence $(P_1, \ldots, P_{i-1})$. The
sequence $(P_1, \ldots, P_n)$ is then translated into a single logic program P', respecting
the successive update information, such that the answer sets of P' represent the
"update answer sets" of $(P_1, \ldots, P_n)$. The translation is realized by introducing
new atoms which control the applicability of rules with respect to the given
update information. Informally, if two rules, $r \in P_i$ and $r' \in P_j$, assert conflicting
information, where $i < j$, then the more recent rule, r', is applied, whilst r is
"rejected". From a technical point of view, this rejection principle is expressed
in terms of the so-called *rejection set*, $rej(S, \boldsymbol{P})$, which consists of all rules of the
given update sequence $\boldsymbol{P} = (P_1, \ldots, P_n)$ which are rejected on the basis of an
update answer set S.

T. Eiter, W. Faber, and M. Truszczyński (Eds.): LPNMR 2001, LNAI 2173, pp. 397–401, 2001.
© Springer-Verlag Berlin Heidelberg 2001

A property which this basic update semantics intuitively does not respect is *minimality of change*. In general, however, it is desirable to incorporate a new set of rules into an existing program with as little change as possible. This is realized by the notions of *minimal* and *strictly minimal update answer sets*, as introduced in [2,3]. Intuitively, an update answer set S is minimal iff there is no update answer set S' of the update sequence $\boldsymbol{P} = (P_1, \ldots, P_n)$ yielding a smaller rejection set, i.e., such that $rej(S', \boldsymbol{P}) \subset rej(S, \boldsymbol{P})$ holds. Strict minimality is a somewhat stronger notion taking also the rules rejected at specific levels into account. More specifically, let $rej_i(S, \boldsymbol{P})$ be the rejected rules contained in P_i ($1 \leq i \leq n$), then the update answer set S is strictly minimal iff there is no update answer set S' of the update sequence $\boldsymbol{P}$ such that $rej_i(S', \boldsymbol{P}) \subset rej_i(S, \boldsymbol{P})$ and $rej_j(S', \boldsymbol{P}) = rej_j(S, \boldsymbol{P})$ for $i + 1 \leq j \leq n$.

Generally speaking, the implementation upd handles the following reasoning tasks: (i) checking the existence of an update answer set for a given update sequence, (ii) brave reasoning, and (iii) skeptical reasoning. Each of these tasks is realized for the basic update semantics, as well as for minimal and strictly minimal update answer sets. Furthermore, the tasks are defined for function-free (datalog) programs, utilizing the advanced grounding mechanism of DLV.

2   System Specifics

2.1   General Information

Since the above update approach is based on a compilation technique to standard answer set semantics, it is possible to build an implementation using an existing logic programming system as underlying reasoning engine. In the present case, upd is realized as a front-end to the logic programming tool DLV [4,5], which is a state-of-the-art solver for disjunctive logic programs under the answer set semantics. Of course, smodels [8], a state-of-the-art system for normal logic programs, could also be employed as underlying reasoning engine.

Given a sequence of update programs as input, upd first translates this sequence into a single extended logic program, $\boldsymbol{P}_\lhd$, and then invokes DLV to calculate the answer sets of $\boldsymbol{P}_\lhd$. In order to obtain update answer sets of the given input sequence, the special-purpose atoms introduced by the translation are filtered from the answer sets of $\boldsymbol{P}_\lhd$.

For dealing with minimal and strictly minimal update answer sets, upd employs a two-phase evaluation approach. The overall algorithm for calculating minimal update answer sets is depicted in Figure 1. Roughly speaking, the algorithm proceeds as follows: First, the answer sets of the update program $\boldsymbol{P}_\lhd$ are calculated. As soon as an answer set S is produced (denoted by $Next\_Answer\_Set(\boldsymbol{P}_\lhd)$), it is tested for being minimal by calculating the answer sets of a particular test program, $\boldsymbol{P}_S^{min}$, consisting of the rules of $\boldsymbol{P}_\lhd$ together with a set of additional rules. S is minimal iff the test program $\boldsymbol{P}_S^{min}$ has no answer set. The algorithm for strictly minimal update answer sets is analogous, the only difference is that the test program $\boldsymbol{P}_S^{min}$ is replaced by a suitable test program $\boldsymbol{P}_S^{strict}$.

Algorithm Compute_Minimal_Models(P)

Input: A sequence of ELPs $P = (P_1, \ldots, P_n)$.

Output: All minimal answer sets of P.

var S : *AnswerSet*;
var *MinModels* : *Set_Of_AnswerSets*;
$S := Next\_Answer\_Set(P_{\lhd})$;
while $S \neq$ nil **do**
      var *Counter* : *Set_Of_AnswerSets*;
      Counter := *Compute_Answer_Sets*(P_S^{min});
      if (*Counter* $= \emptyset$) **then**
            MinModels := *MinModels* $\cup \{S\}$;
      fi
      $S := Next\_Answer\_Set(P_{\lhd})$;
od
return *MinModels*;

Fig. 1. Algorithm to calculate minimal update answer sets

2.2 Applying the System

The general syntax of **upd** coincides with the syntax of DLV. Update sequences are represented by grouping rules using the braces "{" and "}", as illustrated by the following example:

```
{sleep :- night, not tv_on.
 watch_tv :- tv_on.
 night.
 tv_on.}
{-tv_on :- power_failure.
 power_failure.}
```

This input represents an update sequence (P_1, P_2), where the first group of rules constitutes the initial knowledge base, P_1, and the second group corresponds to the update information P_2.

Intuitively, the above example expresses the following situation: The initial program specifies that someone sleeps at night unless the TV is on, in which case the person is watching TV. This knowledge is updated by the information that the TV is not on providing there is a power failure, and there is actually a power failure.

The program **upd** processes inputs either in the form of files or as immediate input via a command shell. Supposing the above sequence of programs has been saved in a file named `tv.lps`, the computation of the corresponding update answer sets can be engaged by the command "**upd**", producing the following output:

```
> upd -p=~/bin/dlv  tv.lps
upd [build BEN/Nov 15 2000    gcc 2.95.2 19991024 (release)]

dlv [build BEN/Jun 11 2001    gcc 2.95.2 19991024 (release)]
```

{night, power_failure, sleep, -tv_on}

Observe that upd requires the explicit specification which particular prover should be invoked during the computation process. This choice is determined by the option -p, which allows for selecting alternate evaluation tools besides DLV.

It is also possible to feed upd with multiple inputs. For instance, suppose we have another file, say tv_cont.lps, containing the following sequence of programs:

```
{-power_failure.}
{switched_off :- not tv_on, not power_failure.
 tv_on :- not switched_off, not power_failure.
 -tv_on :- switched_off.}
```

If these programs are assumed to update the information given by file tv.lps, the update answer sets of the overall sequence (comprised of four programs) can be computed as follows:

```
> upd -silent -p=~/bin/dlv -o=-silent tv.lps tv_cont.lps
{-tv_on, night, switched_off, -power_failure, sleep}
{tv_on, watch_tv, night, -power_failure}
```

Here, options -silent and -o=-silent have been invoked to suppress any additional upd and DLV messages, where -o allows to pass options to the employed evaluation program (DLV in the present case).

Further options of upd are -min and -strict, which specify whether minimal or strictly minimal update answer sets should be computed, respectively. For instance, if we are interested in computing the minimal update answer sets of the sequence given by the files tv.lps and tv_cont.lps, we may call upd as follows:

```
> upd -min -silent -p=~/bin/dlv -o=-silent tv.lps tv_cont.lps
{tv_on, watch_tv, night, -power_failure}
```

Finally, upd can be downloaded from the Web at

http://www.kr.tuwien.ac.at/staff/giuliana/project.html.

Acknowledgments

This work was supported by the Austrian Science Fund (FWF) under grants P13871-INF and N Z29-INF.

References

1. Alferes, J. J., Leite, J. A., Pereira, L. M., Przymusinska, H., & Przymusinski, T. C.: Dynamic Updates of Non-Monotonic Knowledge Bases. *Journal of Logic Programming*, 45(1-2):43-70, 2000. 397
2. Eiter, T., Fink, M., Sabbatini, G., & Tompits, H.: Considerations on Updates of Logic Programs. In *Proc. JELIA 2000*. Lecture Notes in AI (LNAI), vol. 1919. Springer. 397, 398
3. Eiter, T., Fink, M., Sabbatini, G., & Tompits, H.: On Updates of Logic Programs: Semantics and Properties. Technical Report INFSYS 1843-00-08, TU Wien, 2000. 397, 398
4. Eiter, T., Leone, N., Mateis, C., Pfeifer, G., & Scarecello, F.: A Deductive System for Nonmonotonic Reasoning. *Pages 363–374 of: Proc. LPNMR'97*, 1997. Lecture Notes in AI (LNAI), vol. 1265. 398
5. Eiter, T., Faber, W., Leone, N., & Pfeifer, G.: Declarative Problem-Solving Using the dlv System. *Pages 79–103 of: Logic-Based Artificial Intelligence*, 2000. Kluwer Academic Publishers. 398
6. N. Foo, N., & Zhang, Y.: Updating Logic Programs. *Pages 403–407 of: Proc. ECAI'98*,1998. John Wiley and Sons. 397
7. Inoue, K., & Sakama, C.: Updating Extended Logic Programs through Abduction. *Pages 147–161 of: Proc. LPNMR'99*,1999 Lecture Notes in AI (LNAI), vol. 1730. Springer. 397
8. Niemelä, I., & Simons, P.: Efficient Implementation of the Well-founded and Stable Model Semantics. *Pages 289–303 of: Proc. Joint International Conference and Symposium on Logic Programming*, 1996. 398

aspps – An Implementation of Answer-Set Programming with Propositional Schemata

Deborah East and Mirosław Truszczyński

Department of Computer Science, University of Kentucky
Lexington KY 40506-0046, USA

Abstract. We present an implementation of an answer-set programming paradigm, called *aspps* (short for answer-set programming with propositional schemata). The system *aspps* is designed to process PS^+-theories. It consists of two basic modules. The first module, *psgrnd*, grounds an PS^+-theory. The second module, referred to as *aspps*, is a solver. It computes models of ground PS^+-theories.

1 Introduction

The most advanced answer-set programming systems are, at present, *smodels* [NS00] and *dlv* [ELM+98]. They are based on the formalisms of logic programming with stable-model semantics and disjunctive logic programming with answer-set semantics, respectively. We present an implementation of an answer-set programming system, *aspps* (short for answer-set programming with propositional schemata). It is based on the *extended logic of propositional schemata with closed world assumption* that we denote by PS^+. We introduced this logic in [ET01].

A theory in the logic PS^+ is a pair (D, P), where D is a collection of ground atoms representing a *problem instance* (input data), and P is a *program* — a collection of PS^+-clauses (encoding of a problem to solve). The meaning of a PS^+-theory $T = (D, P)$ is given by a *family* of PS^+-models [ET01]. Each model in this family represents a solution to a problem encoded by P for data instance D.

The system *aspps* is designed to process PS^+-theories. It consists of two basic programs. The first of them, *psgrnd*, grounds a PS^+-theory. That is, it produces a ground (propositional) theory extended by a number of special constructs. These constructs help model cardinality constraints on sets. The second program, referred to as *aspps*, is a solver. It computes models of grounded PS^+-theories. It is designed along the lines of a standard Davis-Putnam algorithm for satisfiability checking. Both *psgrnd* and *aspps*, examples of PS^+-programs and the corresponding performance results are available at
http://www.cs.uky.edu/ai/aspps/.

T. Eiter, W. Faber, and M. Truszczyński (Eds.): LPNMR 2001, LNAI 2173, pp. 402–405, 2001.

2 PS^+-Theories

A PS^+-*theory* is a pair (D, P), where D is a collection of ground atoms and P is a collection of PS^+-clauses. Atoms in D represent input data (an instance of a problem). In our implementation these atoms may be stored in one or more *data* files. The set of PS^+-clauses models the constraints (specification) of the problem. In our implementation, all the PS^+-clauses in P are stored in a single *rule* file.

All statements in data and rule files must end with a period (.). Clauses may be split across several lines. Blank lines can be used in data and rule files to improve readability. Comments may be used too. They begin with '%' and continue to the end of the line.

Data files. Each ground atom in a data file must be given on a single line. Constant symbols may be used as arguments of ground atoms. In such cases, these constant symbols must be specified at the command line (see Section 3). Examples of ground atoms are given below:

$vtx(2)$.
$vtx(3)$.
$size(k)$.

A set of ground atoms of the form $\{p(m), p(m + 1), \ldots, p(n)\}$, where m and n are non-negative integers or integer constants specified at the command line, can be represented in a data file as '$p[m..n]$.'. Thus, the two ground atoms $vtx(2)$ and $vtx(3)$ can be specified as '$vtx[1..3]$.'.

Predicates used by ground atoms in data files are called *data predicates*.

Rule files. The rule file of a PS^+-theory consists of two parts. In the first one, the *preamble*, we declare all *program* predicates, that is, predicates that are not used in data files. We also declare types of all variables that will be used in the rule files. Typing of variables simplifies the implementation of the grounding program *psgrnd* and facilitates error checking.

Arguments of each program predicate are typed by unary *data* predicates (the idea is that when grounding, each argument can only be replaced by an element of an extension of the corresponding unary data predicate as specified by the data files). A program predicate q with n arguments of types $dp_1, \ldots, dp_n$, where all dp_i are data predicates, is declared in one of the following two ways:

$pred\ q(dp_1, \ldots, dp_n)$.
$pred\ q(dp_1, \ldots, dp_n) : dp_m$.

In the second statement, the n-ary data predicate dp_m further restricts the extension of q — it must be a subset of the extension of dp_m (as specified by the data files).

Variable declarations begin with the keyword *var*. It is followed by the *unary* data predicate name and a list of alpha-numeric strings serving as variable names (they must start with a letter). Thus, to declare two variables X and Y of type dp, where dp is a unary data predicate we write:

$var\ dp\ X, Y$.

The implementation allows for *predefined* predicates and function symbols such as the equality operator ==, arithmetic comparators <=, >=, < and >, and arithmetic operations +, −, ∗ ,/, $abs()$ (absolute value), $mod(N, b)$, $max(X, Y)$ and $min(X, Y)$. We assign to these symbols their standard interpretation. However, we emphasize that the domains are restricted only to those constants that appear in a theory.

The second part of the rule file contains the program itself, that is, a collection of clauses describing constraints of the problem to be solved.

By a *term tuple* we mean a tuple whose each component is a variable or a constant symbol, or an arithmetic expression. An atom is an expression of one of the following four forms.

1. $p(t)$, where p is a predicate (possibly a predefined predicate) and t is a tuple of variables, constants and arithmetic expressions.
2. $p(t, Y) : dp(Y)$, where p is a program predicate, t is a term tuple, and dp is a unary data predicate
3. $m\{p(t) : d_1(t_1) : \ldots : d_k(t_k)\}n$, where p is a program predicate, each d_i is a data or a predefined predicate, and t and all t_i are term tuples
4. $m\{p_1(t), \ldots, p_k(t)\}n$, where all p_i are program predicates and t is a term tuple

Atoms of the second type are called *e-atoms* and atoms of types 3 and 4 are called *c-atoms*. Intuitively, an e-atom '$p(t, Y) : dp(Y)$' stands for 'there exists Y in the extension of the data predicate dp such that $p(t, Y)$ is true'. An intuitive meaning of a c-atom '$m\{p(t) : d_1(t_1) : \ldots : d_k(t_k)\}n$' is: from the set of all atoms $p(t)$ such that for every i, $1 \leq i \leq k$, $d_i(t^{p,i})$ is true ($t^{p,i}$ is a projection of t onto attributes of d_i), at least m and no more than n are true. The meaning of a c-atom '$m\{p_1(t), \ldots, p_k(t)\}n$' is similar: at least m and no more than n atoms in the set $\{p_1(t), \ldots, p_k(t)\}$ are true.

We are now ready to define clauses. They are expressions of the form

$$A_1, \ldots, A_m \rightarrow B_1 | \ldots | B_n.$$

where A_i's and B_j's are atoms, ',' stands for the conjunction operator and '|' stands for the disjunction operator.

3   Processing PS^+-Theories

To compute models of a PS^+-theory (D, P) we first ground it. To this end, we use the program *psgrnd*. Next, we compute models of the ground theory produced by *psgrnd*. To accomplish this task, we use the program *aspps*. For the detailed description of the grounding process and, especially, for the treatment of e-atoms and c-atoms, and for a discussion of the design of the *aspps* program, we refer the reader to [ET01].

The required input to execute *psgrnd* is a single program file, one or more data files and optional constants. If no errors are found while reading the files and during grounding, an output file is constructed. The output file is a machine readable file whose name is a catenation of the constants and file names with the extension .tdc.

psgrnd **-r** rfile **-d** dfile1 dfile2 ... [**-c** c1=v1 c2=v2 ...]

Required arguments

-r **rfile** is the file describing the problem (rule file). There must be exactly one rule file.

-d **datafilelist** is one or more files containing data that will be used to instantiate the theory.

Optional arguments

-c **name**=**value** This option allows the use of constants in both the data and rule files. When **name** is found while reading input files it is replaced by **value**; **value** can be any string that is valid for the data type. If **name** is to be used in a range specification, then **value** must be an integer.

The program *aspps* is used to solve the grounded theory constructed by *psgrnd*. The name of the file containing the theory is input on the command line. After executing the *aspps* program, a file named aspps.stat is created or appended with statistics concerning this run of *aspps*.

aspps **-f** filename [**-A**] [**-P**] [**-C** [**x**]] [**-S** name]

Required arguments

-f **filename** is the name of the file containing a theory produced by *psgrnd*.

Optional arguments

-A Prints the positive atoms for solved theories in readable form.

-P Prints the input theory and then exits.

-C [**x**] Counts the number of solutions. This information is recorded in the statistics file. If **x** is specified it must be a positive integer; *aspps* stops after finding **x** solutions or exhausting the whole search space, whichever comes first.

-S **name** Show positive atoms with predicate name.

References

ELM+98. T. Eiter, N. Leone, C. Mateis, G. Pfeifer, and F. Scarcello. A KR system dlv: Progress report, comparisons and benchmarks. In *Proceeding of the Sixth International Conference on Knowledge Representation and Reasoning (KR '98)*, pages 406–417. Morgan Kaufmann, 1998. 402

ET01. D. East and M. Truszczyński. Propositional satisfiability in answer-set programming. In *Proceedings of Joint German/Austrian Conference on Artificial Intelligence, KI'2001*. Lecture Notes in Artificial Intelligence, Springer Verlag, 2001. 402, 404

NS00. I. Niemelä and P. Simons. Extending the smodels system with cardinality and weight constraints. In J. Minker, editor, *Logic-Based Artificial Intelligence*, pages 491–521. Kluwer Academic Publishers, 2000. 402

NoMoRe: A System for Non-Monotonic Reasoning under Answer Set Semantics

Christian Anger, Kathrin Konczak, and Thomas Linke

Universität Potsdam, Institut für Informatik,
{canger,konczak,linke}@cs.uni-potsdam.de

1 Introduction

NoMoRe implements answer set semantics for normal logic programs. It realizes a novel paradigm to compute answer sets by computing *a-colorings* (non-standard graph colorings with two colors) of the *block graph* (a labeled digraph) associated with a given program P (see [5] for details). Intuitively, an a-coloring reflects the set of generating rules for an answer set, which means that noMoRe is rule-based and not atom-based like most of the other known systems. Since the core system was designed for propositional programs only, we have integrated lparse [8] as a grounder in order to deal with variables. Furthermore, we have included an interface to the graph drawing tool DaVinci [6] for visualization of block graphs. This allows for a structural analysis of programs.

The noMoRe-system is implemented in the programming language Prolog; it has been developed under the ECLiPSe Constraint Logic Programming System [1] and it was also successfully tested with SWI-Prolog [9]. The system is available at http://www.cs.uni-potsdam.de/~linke/nomore. In order to use the system, ECLiPSe- or SWI-Prolog is needed [1,9][1].

2 Theoretical Background

The current prototype of the noMoRe system implements nonmonotonic reasoning with normal logic programs under answer set semantics [4]. We consider rules r of the form $p \leftarrow q_1, \ldots, q_n, not\ s_1, \ldots, not\ s_k$ where p, q_i ($0 \leq i \leq n$) and s_j ($0 \leq j \leq k$) are atoms, $head(r) = p$, $body^+(r) = \{q_1, \ldots, q_n\}$, $body^-(r) = \{s_1, \ldots, s_k\}$ and $body(r) = body^+(r) \cup body^-(r)$.

Look at the following normal logic program

$$P = \{a \leftarrow b, not\ e. \quad b \leftarrow d. \quad c \leftarrow b. \quad d \leftarrow . \quad e \leftarrow d, not\ f. \quad f \leftarrow a.\} \quad (1)$$

Let us call the rules of program (1) r_a, r_b, r_c, r_d, r_e, and r_f, respectively. P has the answer sets $A_1 = \{d, b, c, a, f\}$ and $A_2 = \{d, b, c, e\}$. It is easy to see that the application of r_f blocks the application of r_e wrt A_1, because if r_f contributes to A_1, then $f \in A_1$ and thus r_e cannot be applied. Analogously, r_e blocks r_a wrt answer set A_2. This observation leads us to a strictly blockage-based approach.

The block graph of program P is a directed graph on the rules of P:

---

[1] Both Prolog systems are freely available for scientific use.

T. Eiter, W. Faber, and M. Truszczyński (Eds.): LPNMR 2001, LNAI 2173, pp. 406–410, 2001.
© Springer-Verlag Berlin Heidelberg 2001

Definition 1. *([5]) Let P be a logic program and let $P' \subseteq P$ be maximal grounded[2]. The block graph $\Gamma_P = (V_P, A_P^0 \cup A_P^1)$ of P is a directed graph with vertices $V_P = P$ and two different kinds of arcs*

$$A_P^0 = \{(r',r) \mid r',r \in P' \text{ and } head(r') \in body^+(r)\}$$
$$A_P^1 = \{(r',r) \mid r',r \in P' \text{ and } head(r') \in body^-(r)\}.$$

Figure 1 shows the block graph of program (1). Since groundedness (by definition) ignores negative bodies, there exists a unique maximal grounded set $P' \subseteq P$ for each program P, that is, Γ_P is well-defined. Definition 1 captures the conditions under which a rule r' blocks another rule r (i.e. $(r',r) \in A^1$). We also gather all groundedness information in Γ_P, due to the restriction to rules in the maximal grounded part of P. This is essential because a block relation between two rules r' and r becomes effective only if r' is groundable through other rules. Therefore Γ_P captures all information necessary for computing the answer sets of program P.

Answer sets then are characterized as special non-standard graph colorings of block graphs. We denote 0-predecessors, 0-successors, 1-predecessors and 1-successors of Γ_P by $\gamma_0^-(v)$, $\gamma_0^+(v)$, $\gamma_1^-(v)$ and $\gamma_1^+(v)$ for $v \in V$, respectively.

Definition 2. *([5]) Let P be a logic program, s.t. $|body^+(r)| \leq 1$ for each $r \in P$, let $\Gamma_P = (P, A_P^0 \cup A_P^1)$ be the corresponding block graph and let $c : P \mapsto \{\ominus, \oplus\}$ be a mapping. Then c is an a-coloring (application-coloring) of Γ_P iff the following conditions hold for each $r \in P$[3]*

A1 $c(r) = \ominus$ *iff one of the following conditions holds*
   a. $\gamma_0^-(r) \neq \emptyset$ *and for each $r' \in \gamma_0^-(r)$ we have $c(r') = \ominus$*
   b. *there is some $r'' \in \gamma_1^-(r)$ s.t. $c(r'') = \oplus$.*
A2 $c(r) = \oplus$ *iff both of the following conditions hold*
   a. $\gamma_0^-(r) = \emptyset$ *or it exists grounded 0-path G_r s.t. $c(G_r) = \oplus$*
   b. *for each $r'' \in \gamma_1^-(r)$ we have $c(r'') = \ominus$.*

Observe, that there are programs (e.g. $P = \{p \leftarrow not\ p\}$) s.t. no a-coloring exists for Γ_P. Intuitively, each node of the block graph (corresponding to some rule) is colored with one of two colors, representing application ($\oplus$) or non-application ($\ominus$) of the corresponding rule. The coloring presented in Figure 1 corresponds to answer set A_1 of P. Node (rule) r_e has to be colored $\ominus$ (not applied), because there is some 1-predecessor of r_e colored $\oplus$ (applied). In other words, r_f blocks r_e.

---

[2] A set of rules S is *grounded* iff there exists an enumeration $\langle r_i \rangle_{i \in I}$ of S such that for all $i \in I$ we have that $body^+(r_i) \subseteq head(\{r_1, \cdots, r_{i-1}\})$. A maximal grounded set P' is a grounded set that is maximal wrt set inclusion. We generalize the definition of the head of a rule to sets of rules in the usual way.

[3] A subset of rules $G_r \subseteq P$ is a *grounded 0-path* for $r \in P$ if G_r is a 0-path from some fact to r in Γ_P. For a set of rules $S \subseteq P$ we write $c(S) = \oplus$ or $c(S) = \ominus$ if for each $r \in S$ we have $c(r) = \oplus$ or $c(r) = \ominus$, respectively. For the generalization of condition $|body^+(r)| \leq 1$ see [5]. There you can also find further details on a-colorings and the algorithm to compute them.

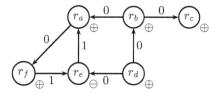

Fig. 1. Block graph of program (1 with a-coloring corresponding to answer set A_1)

3   Description of the System

NoMoRe uses a compilation technique to compute answer sets of a logic program P in three steps (see Figure 2). At first, the block graph Γ_P is computed. Secondly, Γ_P is compiled into Prolog code in order to obtain an efficient coloring procedure. The compiled Prolog code is then used to actually compute the answer sets. To read logic programs we use a parser (eventually after running lparse) and there is a separate part for interpretation of a-colorings into answer sets. For information purpose there is yet another part for visualizing block graphs using the graph drawing tool DaVinci [6]. The noMoRe system is used for purposes

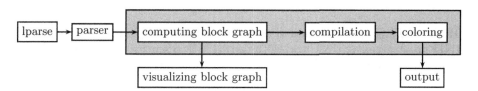

Fig. 2. The architecture of noMoRe

of research on the underlying paradigm. But even in this early state, usability for anybody familiar with the logic programming paradigm is given. The syntax accepted by noMoRe is Prolog-like. For example, the first rule of program (1) is represented through a :- b, not e.

4   Evaluating the System

As a first benchmark, we used two NP-complete problems proposed in [2]: the problem of finding a Hamiltonian path in a graph (**Ham**) and the independent set problem (**Ind**). In terms of time used for computing answer sets, our first prolog implementation is not comparable with state of the art C/C++ implementations, e.g. smodels [7] and dlv [3]. Therefore we compare the number of used choice points, because it reflects how an algorithm deals with the exponential part of a problem. Unfortunately, only smodels gives information about its

Table 1. Number of choice points for **HAM**-problems of complete graphs with n nodes

	all solutions for **Ham** of K_n				one solution for **Ham** of K_n							
$n =$	7	8	9	10	5	6	7	8	9	10	11	12
smodels	4800	86364	1864470	45168575	3	4	30	8	48	1107	18118	398306
noMoRe	14335	115826	1160533	7864853	16	20	31	34	58	69	79	108

choice points. For this reason, we have concentrated on comparing our approach with smodels.

Results are given for finding all solutions of different instances of **Ham** and **Ind**. Table 1 shows results for some **Ham**-encodings of complete graphs K_n where n is the number of nodes[4]. Surprisingly, it turns out that noMoRe performs very good on this problem class. That is, with growing problem size we need less choice points (and less time) than smodels. This can also be seen in Table 2 which shows the corresponding time measurements. To be fair, for **Ind**-problems of graphs Cir_n[5] we need more choice points (and much more time) smodels needs. However, even with the same number of choice points smodels is faster than noMoRe, because noMoRe uses general backtracking of prolog, whereas smodels backtracking is highly specialized for computing answer sets. The same applies to dlv. Even so, it is clear that our approach is a very promising one.

Table 2. Time measurements in seconds with ECLiPSe Prolog for **HAM**- and **IND**-problems on a SUN Ultra2 with two 300MHz Sparc processors (compilation time not included)

	Ham of K_n											**Ind** of Cir_n		
	all solutions			one solution								all solutions		
$n =$	8	9	10	5	6	7	8	9	10	11	12	40	50	60
smodels	54	1334	38550	0.01	0.02	0.04	0.04	0.11	1.61	24	526	8	219	4052
dlv	4	50	493	0.02	0.03	0.03	0.05	0.06	0.07	0.09	0.15	13	259	4594
noMoRe	208	2556	21586	0.01	0.02	0.06	0.12	0.25	0.40	0.53	1.02	39	706	12767

References

1. A. Aggoun, D. Chan, P. Dufresne, and other. Eclipse user manual release 5.0. Available at http://www.icparc.ic.ac.uk/eclipse, 2000. 406
2. P. Cholewiński, V. Marek, A. Mikitiuk, and M. Truszczyński. Experimenting with nonmonotonic reasoning. In *Proceedings of the International Conference on Logic Programming*, pages 267–281. MIT Press, 1995. 408

---

[4] In a complete graph each node is connected to each other node.
[5] A so-called circle graph Cir_n has n nodes $\{v_1, \cdots, v_n\}$ and arcs $A = \{(v_i, v_{i+1}) \mid 1 \le i < n\} \cup \{(v_n, v_1)\}$.

3. T. Eiter, N. Leone, C. Mateis, G. Pfeifer, and F. Scarcello. A deductive system for nonmonotonic reasoning. In J. Dix, U. Furbach, and A. Nerode, editors, *Proceedings of the Fourth International Conference on Logic Programming and Non-Monotonic Reasoning*, volume 1265 of *Lecture Notes in Artificial Intelligence*, pages 363–374. Springer Verlag, 1997. 408

4. M. Gelfond and V. Lifschitz. Classical negation in logic programs and deductive databases. *New Generation Computing*, 9:365–385, 1991. 406

5. Th. Linke. Graph theoretical characterization and computation of answer sets. In *Proceedings of the International Joint Conference on Artificial Intelligence*, 2001. to appear. 406, 407

6. M.Werner. davinci v2.1.x online documentation. daVinci is available at http://www.tzi.de/ davinci/doc_V2.1/, University of Bremen, 1998. 406, 408

7. I. Niemelä and P. Simons. Smodels: An implementation of the stable model and well-founded semantics for normal logic programs. In J. Dix, U. Furbach, and A. Nerode, editors, *Proc. of the Fourth International Conference on Logic Programming and Nonmonotonic Reasoning*, pages 420–429. Springer, 1997. 408

8. T. Syrjänen. Lparse 1.0 user's manual. Available at http://saturn.tcs.hut.fi/Software/smodels/, 2000. 406

9. Jan Wielemaker. Swi-prolog 3.4.3 reference manual. SWI-Prolog is available at http://www.swi.psy.uva.nl/projects/SWI-Prolog/Manual/, 1990–2000. 406

plp: A Generic Compiler for Ordered Logic Programs

James P. Delgrande[1], Torsten Schaub[2]*, and Hans Tompits[3]

[1] School of Computing Science, Simon Fraser University
Burnaby, B.C., Canada V5A 1S6
jim@cs.sfu.ca
[2] Institut für Informatik, Universität Potsdam
Postfach 60 15 53, D–14415 Potsdam, Germany
torsten@cs.uni-potsdam.de
[3] Institut für Informationssysteme, Abt. Wissensbasierte Systeme 184/3,
Technische Universität Wien, Favoritenstraße 9–11, A–1040 Vienna, Austria
tompits@kr.tuwien.ac.at

Abstract. This paper describes a generic compiler, called plp, for translating ordered logic programs into standard logic programs under the answer set semantics. In an ordered logic program, preference information is expressed at the object level by atoms of the form $s \prec t$, where s and t are names of rules. An ordered logic program is transformed into a second, regular, extended logic program wherein the preferences are respected, in that the answer sets obtained in the transformed theory correspond with the preferred answer sets of the original theory. Currently, plp treats three different types of preference strategies, viz. those proposed by (i) Brewka and Eiter, (ii) Delgrande, Schaub, and Tompits, and (iii) Wang, Zhou, and Lin. Since the result of the translation is an extended logic program, existing logic programming systems can be used as underlying reasoning engine. In particular, plp is conceived as a front-end to the logic programming systems dlv and smodels.

1 General Information

Several approaches have been introduced in recent years for expressing preference information within declarative knowledge representation formalisms [7,11,1,10]. However, most of these methods treat preferences at the meta-level and require a change of the underlying semantics. As a result, implementations need in general fresh algorithms and cannot rely on existing systems computing the regular (unordered) formalisms.

In this paper, we describe the system plp, which avoids the need of new algorithms, while computing preferred answer sets of an ordered logic program. plp is based on an approach for expressing preference information *within* the framework of standard answer set semantics [6], and is conceived as a front-end

---

* Affiliated with the School of Computing Science at Simon Fraser University, Burnaby, Canada.

T. Eiter, W. Faber, and M. Truszczyński (Eds.): LPNMR 2001, LNAI 2173, pp. 411–415, 2001.
© Springer-Verlag Berlin Heidelberg 2001

Table 1. The syntax of plp input files

Meaning	Symbols	Internal
$\bot, \top$	false/0, true/0	
$\neg$	neg/1, -/1 (prefix)	neg_L, $L \in \mathcal{L}$
not	not/1, $\sim$/1 (prefix)	
$\wedge$	,/1 (infix; in body)	
$\vee$	;/1, v/2, |/2 (infix; in head)	
$\leftarrow$	:-/1 (infix; in rule)	
$\prec$	</2 (infix)	prec/2
$n_r : \langle head(r) \rangle \leftarrow \langle body(r) \rangle$	$\langle head(r) \rangle$:- name$(n_r), \langle body(r) \rangle$	
	$\langle head(r) \rangle$:- $[n_r], \langle body(r) \rangle$	
ok, rdy		ok/1, rdy/2
ap, bl		ap/1, bl/1

to the logic programming systems dlv [5] and smodels [8]. The general technique is described in [4] and derives from a methodology for addressing preferences in default logic first proposed in [2].

We begin with an *ordered logic program*, which is an extended logic program in which rules are named by unique terms and in which preferences among rules are given by a new set of atoms of the form $s \prec t$, where s and t are names. Such an ordered logic program is then transformed into a second, regular, extended logic program wherein the preferences are respected, in the sense that the answer sets obtained in the transformed theory correspond to the preferred answer sets of the original theory. The transformation is realized by adding sufficient control elements to the rules of the given ordered logic program which guarantee that successive rule applications are in accord with the intended order. More specifically, the transformed program contains control atoms ap($\cdot$) and bl($\cdot$), which detect when a rule has been applied or blocked, respectively, as well as auxiliary atoms ok($\cdot$) and rdy($\cdot, \cdot$) which control the applicability of rules based on antecedent conditions reflecting the given order information.

The approach is sufficiently general to allow the specification of preferences among preferences, preferences holding in a particular context, and preferences holding by default. Moreover, the approach permits a generic compilation methodology, making it possible to express differing preference strategies. Basically, this is achieved by varying the specific antecedent conditions for the control atoms ok($\cdot$) and rdy($\cdot, \cdot$). Currently, plp treats three kinds of preference strategies, viz. those proposed by Brewka and Eiter [1], Delgrande, Schaub, and Tompits [2,4], and Wang, Zhou, and Lin [10].

2 Applying the System

The syntax of plp is summarised in Table 1. An example file comprising an ordered logic program is the following:

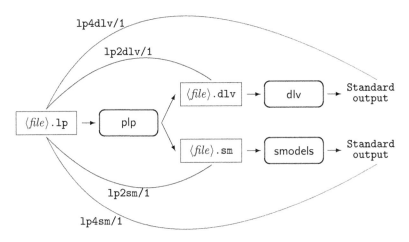

Fig. 1. Compilation with plp: external view

```
neg a .
    b :- name(n2), neg a, not c.
    c :- name(n3), not b.
(n3 < n2) :- not d.
```

Here, `name(n2)` and `name(n3)` serve as names for the rules in which these terms occur, and the last rule expresses that the rule named `n2` is preferred over the rule named `n3`, in case atom `d` cannot be inferred.

Once this file, say `example.lp`, is read into plp, it is subject to multiple transformations. Most of these transformations are rule-centered in the sense that they apply in turn to each single rule. The first phase of the compilation is system-independent and corresponds to the transformations given in [4]. While the original file is supposed to have the extension `lp`, the result of the system-independent compilation phase is kept in an intermediate file with extension `pl` (e.g., `example.pl`).

While this compilation phase can be engaged explicitly by the command `lp2pl/1`, one is usually interested in producing system-specific code that is directly usable by either dlv or smodels. This can be done by means of the commands `lp2dlv/1` and `lp2sm/1`,[1] which then produce system-specific code resulting in files having extensions `dlv` and `sm`, respectively. These files can then be fed into the respective system by a standard command interpreter, such as a UNIX shell, or from within the Prolog system through commands `dlv/1` or `smodels/1`. For example, after compiling our example by `lp2dlv`, we may proceed as follows:

```
| ?- dlv('Examples/example').
Calling :dlv  Examples/example.dlv
dlv [build BEN/Jun 11 2001   gcc 2.95.2 19991024 (release)]
```

---

[1] These files are themselves obtainable from the intermediate pl-files via commands `pl2dlv/1` and `pl2sm/1`, respectively.

```
{true, name(n2), name(n3), neg_a, ok(n2), rdy(n2,n2),
 rdy(n2,n3), rdy(n3,n3), prec(n3,n2), neg_prec(n2,n3),
 ap(n2), b, rdy(n3,n2), ok(n3), bl(n3)}
```

Both commands can be furnished with the option `nice` (as an additional argument) in order to strip off the auxiliary predicates:

```
| ?- dlv('Examples/example',nice).
Calling :dlv  -filter=a [...] -filter=neg_d Examples/example.dlv
dlv [build BEN/Jun 11 2001    gcc 2.95.2 19991024 (release)]
```

```
{neg_a, b}
```

The above series of commands can be engaged within a single one by means of `lp4dlv/1` and `lp4sm/1`, respectively. Moreover, for changing the underlying preference strategy, a simple patch is executed, which redefines certain predicates. The overall (external) comportment of plp is illustrated in Figure 1.

For treating variables, some additional preprocessing is necessary for instantiating the rules before they are compiled. The presence of variables is indicated by file extension `vlp`. The content of such a file is first instantiated by systematically replacing variables by constants and then freed from function symbols by replacing terms by constants, e.g., `f(a)` is replaced by `f_a`. This is clearly a rather pragmatic approach. A more elaborated compilation would be obtained by proceeding right from the start in a system-specific way.

Finally, the current prototype is available at
`http://www.cs.uni-potsdam.de/~torsten/plp/`.

Acknowledgements

The first author received partial support from the Natural Sciences and Engineering Research Council of Canada; the second author was partially supported by the German Science Foundation (DFG) under grant FOR 375/1-1, TP C; the third author was partially supported by the Austrian Science Fund (FWF) under grant P13871-INF.

References

1. G. Brewka and T. Eiter. Preferred answer sets for extended logic programs. *Artificial Intelligence*, 109(1-2):297–356, 1999. 411, 412
2. J. Delgrande and T. Schaub. Compiling reasoning with and about preferences into default logic. In *Proc. IJCAI-97*, pages 168–174. Morgan Kaufmann Publishers, 1997. 412
3. J. Delgrande, T. Schaub, and H. Tompits. A compilation of Brewka and Eiter's approach to prioritization. In *Proc. JELIA-00*, pages 376–390. Springer Verlag, 2000.
4. J. Delgrande, T. Schaub, and H. Tompits. Logic programs with compiled preferences. In *Proc. ECAI-00*, pages 392–398. IOS Press, 2000. 412, 413

5. T. Eiter, N. Leone, C. Mateis, G. Pfeifer, and F. Scarcello. A deductive system for nonmonotonic reasoning. In *Proc. LPNMR-97*, pages 363–374. Springer Verlag, 1997. 412

6. M. Gelfond and V. Lifschitz. Classical negation in logic programs and deductive databases. *New Generation Computing*, 9:365–385, 1991. 411

7. M. Gelfond and T. Son. Reasoning with prioritized defaults. In *Third International Workshop on Logic Programming and Knowledge Representation*, pages 164–223. Springer Verlag, 1997. 411

8. I. Niemelä and P. Simons. Smodels: An implementation of the stable model and well-founded semantics for normal logic programs. In *Proc. LPNMR-97*, pages 420–429. Springer Verlag, 1997. 412

9. T. Schaub and K. Wang. A comparative study of logic programs with preference: Preliminary report. In *Proc. AAAI Spring Symposium on Answer Set Programming*, pages 151–157. AAAI Press, 2001.

10. K. Wang, L. Zhou, and F. Lin. Alternating fixpoint theory for logic programs with priority. In *Proc. First International Conference on Computational Logic*, pages 164–178. Springer Verlag, 2000. 411, 412

11. Y. Zhang and N. Foo. Answer sets for prioritized logic programs. In *Proc. ILPS-97*, pages 69–84. MIT Press, 1997. 411

Prototypes for Reasoning with Infinite Stable Models and Function Symbols

Piero A. Bonatti

Dipartimento di Tecnologie dell'Informazione, Università di Milano
bonatti@dti.unimi.it

1 Introduction

A recent paper [1] laid out the theoretical basis for effective reasoning with infinite stable models and normal programs with function symbols. For the class of *finitary programs* introduced there, ground queries are decidable and nonground queries are semi-decidable under both credulous and skeptical stable model semantics. Finitary programs are expressive enough to simulate any given Turing machine. In order to exploit the potential expressiveness of finitary programs, a family of tools is needed, including:

1. Tools for automatic recognition of finitary programs. This task can only be approximated, as the class of finitary programs is not decidable. For this purpose, we use techniques related to abstract interpretations and automated program analysis.
2. Front ends that given a finitary program P and a query Q construct the finite fragment of Ground(P) needed to answer Q. The fragment (whose existence is proved in [1]) is meant to be fed to credulous engines such as SMODELS [4].

In this note we introduce prototypes of the above tools implemented in XSB (http://xsb.sourceforge.net), and illustrate their relationships with SMODELS and the resolution-based skeptical reasoner illustrated in [2]. The prototypes are meant to demonstrate the feasibility of these techniques as a preliminary step toward more advanced implementations.

2 Theoretical Preliminaries

The *dependency graph* of a program P is a labelled directed graph whose vertices are the ground atoms of P's language. Moreover, *i)* there exists an edge from B to A iff there is a rule $r \in Ground(P)$ with A in the head and an occurrence of B in the body; *ii)* such edge is labelled "negative" if B occurs in the scope of $\neg$, and "positive" otherwise. An atom A depends positively (resp. negatively) on B if there is a directed path from B to A in the dependency graph with an even (resp. odd) number of negative edges. By *odd-cycle* we mean a cycle in the dependency graph with an odd number of negative edges.

We say a program P is *finitary* if the following conditions hold:

T. Eiter, W. Faber, and M. Truszczyński (Eds.): LPNMR 2001, LNAI 2173, pp. 416–419, 2001.

Condition 1 For each node A of the dependency graph of P, the set of all nodes B such that A depends (either positively or negatively) on B is finite.

Condition 2 Only a finite number of nodes of the dependency graph of P occurs in an odd-cycle.

The *relevant universe* for a ground formula F (w.r.t. program P), denoted by $U(P, F)$, is the set of all ground atoms A such that the dependency graph of P contains a path from A to an atom occurring either in F or in some odd-cycle of the graph.

The *relevant subprogram* for a ground formula F (w.r.t program P), denoted by $R(P, F)$, is the set of all rules in $Ground(P)$ whose head belongs to $U(P, F)$. The important properties of relevant subprograms are the following. If P is finitary, then for all ground goals G:

1. $R(P, G)$ is finite;
2. P credulously entails G iff $R(P, G)$ does.
3. P skeptically entails G iff $R(P, G)$ does.

3   Recognizing Finitary Programs

Establishing whether a given program is finitary is an undecidable problem. We approximate this decision problem using program analysis techniques. In particular, Condition 1 is checked by analyzing the recursion patterns of the input program, looking for arguments whose *norm* (a measure of term size) does not increase indefinitely. The finitary program recognizer consists in four stages:

1. **Interargument analysis.** During this phase, the mutual relationships between the size of each predicate's arguments is evaluated. For example, for each call `append(A,B,C)` the analysis would discover that $|A| < |C|$ and $|B| < |C|$. Interargument information yields bounds on the size of local variables—this is essential for proving Condition 1.

2. **Recursion analysis.** At this stage, the recognizer looks for cyclic atom dependencies, then refines them by identifying suitable *recursion patterns*, i.e., sets of predicate arguments that either strictly decrease or almost never get larger at each recursion. After this analysis each predicate is labelled as *acyclic* or *potentially cyclic*. The underlying data structure is a graph whose size is linear in the input (nonground) program. Among other predicates, this recursion analysis verifies Condition 1 for all the main standard predicates on lists, including `list`, `member`, `append`, `reverse`, and `merge`.

3. **Recursive domain predicate identification.** During this phase, the analyzer identifies acyclic predicates that can be evaluated at program instantiation time to instantiate all local variables in finitely many ways (thereby avoiding infinite branching in the dependency graph). These predicates play the same role as Lparse's domain predicates [5]. One important difference is that recursive domain predicates can be locally stratified, while Lparse's domain predicates can only be stratified.

4. **Cycle analysis.** Condition 2 is checked at this stage. The recognizer looks for odd-cycles (i.e. cycles through an odd number of negations). Cycle identification takes into account recursion information (derived during the second stage) so that the analysis is sharper than a simple inspection of the predicate dependency graph. For instance, the following program would be accepted and recognized as acyclic:

```
even(0)
even(s(X)) :- not even(X).
```

If a (potential) odd cycle is identified, then it is required to be ground. A sharper analysis—to be included in future versions—is discussed in the last section.

4   Credulous Reasoning

To use the existing credulous reasoning engines, a suitable front-end is needed whose function is computing the (ground) relevant subprogram $R(P, G)$. The relevant subprogram can be fed to the existing engines, including SMODELS, to answer the given goal G. Part of the construction of $R(P, G)$ is common to all G and can be factorized. In particular the part of the program on which the odd cycles depend is always contained in $R(P, G)$ and can be pre-computed once and for all. This part of the computation needs the results of the recognizer's analysis to identify the odd-cycles. Recursive domain predicates are evaluated at instantiation time. Currently, instantiation proceeds top-down, starting from the input goal G. Since P is finitary, the procedure is guaranteed to terminate.

5   Skeptical Reasoning

A prototype skeptical reasoner based on the skeptical resolution calculus [2] has been implemented in XSB. The prototype is a semi-naive meta-interpreter. A brief description can be found in the journal version of [2]. The credulous resolution calculus is sound for all programs [2] and complete for all finitary programs [1]. In other words, the prototype can be used to find the (nonground, existentially quantified) skeptical consequences of finitary programs with no modification to the existing code (although it had been designed for function-free programs). The relevant subprogram has only a theoretical role, in proving completeness. The instantiation tool is of no use for skeptical reasoning, as resolution instantiates program rules as needed, without necessarily grounding them. The program recognizer is still needed to accept admissible programs. As a by-product, the recognizer (approximately) identifies cyclic and odd-cyclic atoms; such information is needed by—and can be fed to—the *restricted split strategy* implemented by the metainterpreter (see [2] for a definition). In the first version of the meta-interpreter, cycle information was calculated with much less precision, affecting the effectiveness of the strategy.

6   Future Enhancements

Currently the recognizer computes only relative estimates of term size. For a sharper analysis, we are planning to replace the interargument analysis predicates with a module based on abstract interpretation, currently being developed at the University of Parma. The abstract domain consists of polyhedra and describes interargument size relations as linear equations. In order to use such information, the recognizer should be extended with symbolic calculation capabilities. The term norms used in the current prototype are not the only possible norms. Existing work on automatic norm selection will be considered in future implementations. A second enhancement consists in recognizing ω-stratified [5] subprograms, that are guaranteed to be finitary. ω-stratification poses more restrictions on domain predicates and clause variables, but then all cycles are guaranteed to be finite, including some that otherwise would not be accepted by the 4th stage of the recognizer.

References

1. P. A. Bonatti. Reasoning with infinite stable models. In Proc. of *IJCAI'01*, 2001. 416, 418
2. P. A. Bonatti. Resolution for skeptical stable model semantics. *Journal of Automated Reasoning*, to appear. Preliminary version in Proc. of LPNMR'97, Springer, 1997. 416, 418
3. S. Decorte, D. de Schreye, M. Fabris. Exploiting the Power of Typed Norms in Automatic Inference of Interargument Relations. Technical report, Department of Computer Science, K. U.Leuven, Belgium, 1994.
4. I. Niemelä, P. Simons. Smodels - an implementation of the stable model and well-founded semantics for normal LP. In Proc. of *LPNMR'97*, LNAI 1265, Springer Verlag, Berlin, 1997. 416
5. Tommi Syrjänen. Omega-Restricted Logic Programs. This book. 417, 419

psmodels: Stable Models Based on Pertinence

Ramón P. Otero

AI Lab. - Dept. of Computer Science, University of Corunna
15071 Corunna, Galicia, Spain
otero@dc.fi.udc.es

Abstract. The characterization of stable models using the monotonic logic of pertinence helps identifying program transformations leading to a new normal form of programs. This provides an alternative view on automated reasoning for stable models from which improvements on existing systems, e.g. *smodels*, can be identified.

1 Introduction

In [2] a logic program is characterized as a *pertinence logic* theory, such that for each rule of the program there is a formula in pertinence logic in the form,

$$A_0 \leftarrow A_1, \ldots, A_m, not\ A_{m+1}, \ldots, not\ A_n \tag{1}$$

where $n \geq m \geq 0$, and each A_i is an atom[1].

The stable models of the program correspond to the *p-stable causal* models of the pertinence theory. Causal models are minimal models defining a non-monotonic pertinence logic; and p-stable models are those models that verify an structural condition.

Pertinence logic is a monotonic logic, thus a semantic characterization of strongly equivalent programs is presented. Two programs are strongly equivalent if the (monotonic) models of the corresponding pertinence theories are the same.

These results can be used in automated reasoning for stable logic programs. In the next section we identify program transformations leading to a new normal form where automated inference can be applied. This constitutes an alternative view on inference for stable models that includes, e.g. program reduction based on strong equivalence (section 3), and computation of stable models (section 4).

2 Normal Form

For every formula in the form (1) in pertinence logic, the following two constraint formulas are equivalent to it.

$$\leftarrow not\ A_0, A_1, \ldots, A_m, not\ A_{m+1}, \ldots, not\ A_n \tag{2}$$

$$\leftarrow nop\ A_0, A_1, \ldots, A_m, not\ A_{m+1}, \ldots, not\ A_n \tag{3}$$

---

[1] In that work the operator for negation in truth and in pertinence was denoted *notp*. To clarify this description here we denote it by the usual LP operator *not* to which it corresponds.

T. Eiter, W. Faber, and M. Truszczyński (Eds.): LPNMR 2001, LNAI 2173, pp. 420–423, 2001.
© Springer-Verlag Berlin Heidelberg 2001

The head A_0 is 'moved' to the body with negation in truth and in pertinence—corresponding to negation as failure—in rule (2) and with negation in pertinence—a new negation not defined in LP—in rule (3).

To get an intuitive idea of this transformation we recall from [2] that pertinence logic gives to each atom *two* truth values simultaneously, one from the set {T,F} corresponding to true and false, and another from the set {P,N} corresponding to *pertinent* and *nonpertinent*.

Atoms TP (true and pertinent) will correspond to true atoms in the 2-valued semantics of stable models; and atoms FN (false and nonpertinent) will correspond to false atoms. The other remaining valuations—TN and FP—do not have a correspondence in the 2-valued semantics. For instance, the structural condition that defines *p-stable* models among all the pertinence models is that all the atoms in the model have valuation TP or FN.

The first constraint (2) can be read as: "there is a contradiction if the body is true and pertinent and the head is false and nonpertinent"; and the second constraint (3) as: "there is a contradiction if the body is true and pertinent and the head is true and nonpertinent". (In fact, we would need a third constraint for FP value in order to prove equivalence, but see [2]; in any case the two constraints are implied by the rule and, as far as stable models, this will be enough for this work.)

In summary, the introduction of the *nop* operator in the syntax provides a way to represent any normal logic program as a set of constraint rules.

Example 1. Consider the following program and the corresponding constraint form

$$q \leftarrow p \qquad \begin{cases} \leftarrow not\, q, p \\ \leftarrow nop\, q, p \end{cases}$$

$$q \leftarrow not\, p \qquad \begin{cases} \leftarrow not\, q, not\, p \\ \leftarrow nop\, q, not\, p \end{cases}$$

$$p \leftarrow not\, p, not\, q \begin{cases} \leftarrow not\, p, not\, q \\ \leftarrow nop\, p, not\, p, not\, q \end{cases}$$

Note that the constraint $\leftarrow not\, p, not\, q$ is included twice, and the constraint $\leftarrow nop\, p, not\, p, not\, q$ is a tautology and can be deleted from the program.   □

3   Program Transformations

Let us define three transformations in constraint form.

- *Tautology* Delete a constraint if an atom appears in two different literals. Note that in constraint form we have three types of literals, e.g. p, $not\, p$, and $nop\, p$.
- *Subsumption* Delete a constraint if it is a superset of another constraint in the program. Consider constraints denoted by the set of its literals.
- *Literal Reduction* If there are three constraints that only differ in one literal, and this different literal appears in the three possible forms for the same

atom, then replace the three constraints by a constraint corresponding to its intersection.

These three transformations preserve the semantics of the program, the deleted constraints are (monotonically) entailed by the remaining ones.

In Example 1 the two constraints of rule $p \leftarrow not\,p, not\,q$ will be deleted (the rule is entailed by $q \leftarrow not\,p$), thus this rule can be deleted from the program.

When the program in Example 1 is run in system *smodels* [1] the three rules are not simplified by *lparse*. It is worth noting that the program $\{q \leftarrow p \quad q \leftarrow not\,p\}$—the program in the example is strongly equivalent to it—is simplified by lparse to $\{q \leftarrow\}$.

We compared several programs strongly equivalent by simple application of subsumption, i.e. the program is translated to constraint form and subsumption is applied, then back to LP form. The speed up seems to follow the relation on the number of rules in the original program wrt the number of rules that remain.

An extended lparse (or alternatively an additional simplifier run between lparse and smodels) performing these reductions makes more efficient system smodels.

4   Computing the Stable Models

In constraint form the program represents more directly the interpretations that are not models of the rules. Developing on this idea, we provide an alternative view on automated reasoning for stable models.

Let us represent the collection of all the possible models with a common subset by (P, N), where P is the set of positive atoms common and N is the set of negative atoms common, i.e. not present in the models. Then for a constraint of the form (2), the collection that includes all the non-models of it is

$$(\{A_1, \ldots, A_m\}, \{A_0, A_{m+1}, \ldots, A_n\}).$$

All these are not monotonic models of the rule thus they are not stable of the program. We do not need to try these models for stability.

Consider now the constraints of the form (3), we will call them nop-constraints. This constraint also has a collection of non-models associated, but actually the constraint in the form (2)—not-constraint—from the same rule also includes all these as non-models. The nop-constraints have one *nop* A_0 literal. Thus they delete some interpretations that do not correspond to 2-valued interpretations.

Recalling the monotonic characterization in [2], stable models of a program are minimal models (causal models) of the pertinence theory. A model is minimal iff there is no other model for the same truth with a subset of pertinent atoms. Intuitively a (p-stable) model would be stable iff all the other models that minimize it, are not models of the theory. Lets us call minimizers the models that minimize a p-stable.

The nop-constraints have minimizers as counter-models. Every stable model (unless {}) has at least one minimizer. Thus every stable needs at least a nop-constraint. Furthermore we can identify the collection of (possible) stable to which a nop-constraint deletes minimizers, thus contributing to its stability,

$$(\{A_0, A_1, \ldots, A_m\}, \{A_{m+1}, \ldots, A_n\}).$$

Then from the nop-constraints we get the collections of all possible stable of the program.

Example 2. Consider the following program and the corresponding collections.

		not-collection	nop-collection
$a \leftarrow c, not\, b$	$\leftarrow not\, a, not\, b, c$	$(\{c\}, \{a, b\})$	
	$\leftarrow nop\, a, not\, b, c$		$(\{c, a\}, \{b\})$
$b \leftarrow c, not\, a$	$\leftarrow not\, b, not\, a, c$	$(\{c\}, \{a, b\})$	
	$\leftarrow nop\, b, not\, a, c$		$(\{c, b\}, \{a\})$
$c \leftarrow not\, a$	$\leftarrow not\, c, not\, a$	$(\{\}, \{a, c\})$	
	$\leftarrow nop\, c, not\, a$		$(\{c\}, \{a\})$

We only need to search on the collections associated to the nop-constraints, and that do not appear in the collections of the not-constraints. □

Comparing with the characterization in which system smodels is based, the search is performed on the set of the negative antecedents of the rules. Note that there is no atom in the N component of the nop-collections that is not a negative antecedent of a rule. But in the nop-collections there is additional information on the positive atoms associated to a particular subset of the negative antecedents. Furthermore, some of the combinations of negative antecedents could belong to a not-collection, thus no need to try them. This information is introduced in system smodels and compared with its strategy.

Acknowledgements

This research is partially supported by Government of Spain grant PB97-0228.

References

1. Ilkka Niemelä and Patrick Simons. Smodels - an implementation of the stable model and well-founded semantics for normal logic programs. In *Proc. of the 4th International Conference on Logic Programming and Nonmonotonic Reasoning, LPNMR 97, LNAI 1265*, pages 420–429, 1997. 422
2. Ramón P. Otero. A pertinence logic characterization of stable models (preliminary report). In A. Provetti and T. C. Son, editors, *Answer Set Programming – AAAI Spring 2001 Symposium*, pages 153–159, Stanford, CA, 2001. 420, 421, 422

System Description: DLV [*]

Tina Dell'Armi[1], Wolfgang Faber[2], Giuseppe Ielpa[1], Christoph Koch[2],
Nicola Leone[3], Simona Perri[3], and Gerald Pfeifer[2]

[1] D.E.I.S., University of Calabria
87030 Rende (CS), Italy
{dellarmi,ielpa}@si.deis.unical.it
[2] Institut für Informationssysteme, TU Wien
A-1040 Wien, Austria
faber@kr.tuwien.ac.at
{pfeifer,koch}@dbai.tuwien.ac.at
[3] Department of Mathematics, University of Calabria
87030 Rende (CS), Italy
leone@unical.it
sperri@si.deis.unical.it

1 General Information

DLV is an efficient Answer Set Programming (ASP) system implementing the consistent answer set semantics [5] with various language enhancements like support for logic programming with inheritance and queries, integer arithmetics, and various other built-in predicates.

DLV is being developed using GNU tools (GCC, flex, and bison) and is therefore portable to most Unix-like platforms as well as Microsoft Windows. For up-to-date information on the system and a full manual please refer to the URL http://www.dbai.tuwien.ac.at/proj/dlv/, where you can also download binaries and various examples.

2 DLV Language

The kernel language of **DLV** is disjunctive datalog extended with strong negation under the consistent answer set semantics [5].

Let $a_1, \cdots, a_n, b_1, \cdots, b_m$ be classical literals (atoms possibly preceded by the classical negation symbol $-$) and $n \geq 0$, $m \geq k \geq 0$. A *(disjunctive) rule* r is a formula
$$a_1 \text{ v } \cdots \text{ v } a_n :\text{- } b_1, \cdots, b_k, \text{ not } b_{k+1}, \cdots, \text{ not } b_m.$$
A *strong constraint* is a rule with empty head ($n = 0$). A *weak constraint* is
$$:\sim b_1, \cdots, b_k, \text{ not } b_{k+1}, \cdots, \text{ not } b_m. \; [Weight : Level]$$
where both Weight and Level are positive integers. A *disjunctive datalog program* $\mathcal{P}$ is a finite set of rules and constraints.

---

[*] This work was supported by FWF (Austrian Science Funds) under the projects Z29-INF and P14781 and MURST under project COFIN-2000 "From Data to Information (D2I)".

T. Eiter, W. Faber, and M. Truszczyński (Eds.): LPNMR 2001, LNAI 2173, pp. 424–428, 2001.
© Springer-Verlag Berlin Heidelberg 2001

The semantics of these programs is provided in [1] as an extension of the classical answer set semantics given in [5].

In addition to its kernel language, **DLV** provides a number of application frontends that show the suitability of our formalism for solving various problems from the areas of Artificial Intelligence, Knowledge Representation and (Deductive) Databases. In particular, the following frontends are currently available: *Brave and Cautious Reasoning Frontend*, *Diagnosis Frontend*, *SQL3 Frontend*, *Inheritance Frontend*, and *Planning Frontend*.

3   Representing Problems in DLV

The core language of **DLV** can be used to encode problems in a highly declarative fashion. We will next show a number of sample **DLV** encodings. We will see that several problems, also problems of high computational complexity, can be solved naturally in **DLV** by using a declarative style of programming.

3-Colorability (3COL) Given a graph, represented by facts of the form node(_) and edge(_,_), assign each node one of three colors such that no two adjacent nodes have the same color. 3-Colorability is a classical NP-complete problem. In **DLV**, the problem can be encoded in a very easy and natural way by means of disjunction and constraints:

$$col(X, red) \text{ v } col(X, green) \text{ v } col(X, blue) :\!\!- node(X).$$
$$:\!\!- edge(X, Y), col(X, C), col(Y, C).$$

The disjunctive rule nondeterministically chooses a color for each node X in the graph; the constraint enforces that the choices are legal.

Hamiltonian Path (HAMPATH) is another classical NP-complete problem from the area of graph theory:

Given an undirected graph $G = (V, E)$, where V is the set of vertices of G and E is the set of edges, and a node $a \in V$ of this graph, does there exist a path of G starting at a and passing through each node in V exactly once?

Suppose that the graph G is specified by using two predicates $node(X)$ and $arc(X, Y)$, and the starting node is specified by the predicate $start(X)$ which contains only a single tuple. Then, the following program solves the problem HAMPATH.

$$inPath(X, Y) \text{ v } outPath(X, Y) :\!\!- reached(X), arc(X, Y).$$
$$:\!\!-node(X), \text{not } reached(X).$$
$$reached(X) :\!\!- start(X).$$
$$reached(X) :\!\!- inPath(Y, X).$$
$$:\!\!- inPath(X, Y), inPath(X, Y1), Y <> Y1.$$
$$:\!\!- inPath(X, Y), inPath(X1, Y), X <> X1.$$

Timetabling The problem consists of assigning course exams to time slots in such a way that no two exams are assigned the same time slot if they are "incompatible", i.e the respective courses have a student in common. Assuming that there are three time slots available, namely, s_1, s_2 and s_3, we express the problem as follows:

$$assign(X, s1) \text{ v } assign(X, s2) \text{ v } assign(X, s3) \text{ :- } course(X).$$
$$\text{:-}assign(X, S), assign(Y, S), incompatible(X, Y).$$

Clearly, it may happen that there is no way to assign courses to time slots without having some overlapping between incompatible courses. Then, an approximate solution where constraints are satisfied as much as possible is desirable. In this light, the problem at hand can be restated as follows: assign courses to time slots trying to minimize the overlapping of incompatible courses. To solve this problem we resort to the notion of *weak* constraints, as shown below:

$$assign(X, s1) \text{ v } assign(X, s2) \text{ v } assign(X, s3)\text{:-}course(X).$$
$$\text{:}\sim assign(X, S), assign(Y, S), incompatible(X, Y).$$

Intuitively, of the weak constraint above states: "Preferably, do not assign the courses X and Y to the same slot S if they are incompatible".

Strategic Companies (STRATCOMP) finally, is a Σ_2^P-complete problem[2]: A holding owns companies $C(1), \ldots, C(c)$, each of which produces some goods. Some of these companies may jointly control another one. This is modelled by means of predicates $produced\_by(P, C1, C2)$ — product P is produced by companies $C1$ and $C2$ — and $controlled\_by(C, C1, C2, C3)$ — company C is jointly controlled by $C1$, $C2$ and $C3$. Now, some companies should be sold, under the constraint that all goods can be still produced, and that no company is sold which would still be controlled by the holding afterwards. A company is strategic, if it belongs to a *strategic set*, which is a minimal set of companies satisfying these constraints. Checking whether any given company C is strategic is done by brave reasoning: "Is there *any* answer set containing C?"

$$strategic(C1) \text{ v } strategic(C2) \text{ :- } produced\_by(P, C1, C2).$$
$$strategic(C)\text{:-}controlled\_by(C, C1, C2, C3),$$
$$strategic(C1), strategic(C2), strategic(C3).$$

We assume that each product is produced by at most two companies and each company is jointly controlled by at most three companies to allow for an easier representation.

4   System Architecture

An outline of the general architecture of our system is depicted in Fig.1.

The heart of the system is the **DLV** *core*. Wrapped around this basic block are frontend preprocessors and output filters (which also do some post-processing for frontends). The system takes input data from the user via the command line and from the file system and/or database systems.

Upon startup, input is possibly translated by a frontend. Together with relational database tables, provided by an Oracle database, an Objectivity database, or ASCII text files, the *Intelligent Grounding Module* efficiently generates a subset of the grounded input program that has exactly the answer sets as the full program, but is much smaller in general.

After that, the Model Generator is started. It generates one answer set candidate at a time and verifies it using the Model Checker. Upon success, filtered output is generated for the answer set. This process is iterated until either no more answer sets exist or an explicitly specified number of answer sets has been computed.

Not shown in Fig.1 are various additional data structures, such as dependency graphs.

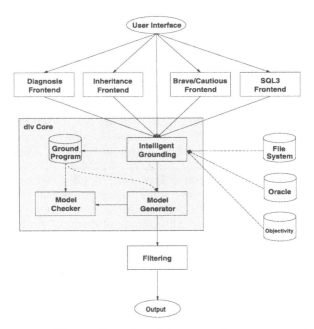

Fig. 1. Overall architecture of **DLV**

5   Current Applications

Currently, the **DLV** system is used for educational purposes in courses on Databases and on AI, both in European and American universities. It is also used by several researchers for knowledge representation, for verifying theoretical work, and for performance comparisons, in which **DLV** compares favorably to similar systems [4,3]. For the development of some deductive database applications **DLV** can compete with database systems. Indeed, **DLV** is being considered by CERN for such an application which could not be handled by other systems. One of the latest applications of **DLV**, issued by the Italian national statistics institute (ISTAT), concerns the automatic correction of census data.

References

1. F. Buccafurri, N. Leone, and P. Rullo. Enhancing disjunctive datalog by constraints. *TKDE*, 12(5), 2000. 425
2. M. Cadoli, T. Eiter, and G. Gottlob. Default Logic as a Query Language, *TKDE*, 9(3):448–463, 1997. 426
3. U. Egly, T. Eiter, H. Tompits, and S. Woltran. Solving Advanced Reasoning Tasks using Quantified Boolean Formulas. In *Proc. of AAAI'00*, pp. 417–422. 427
4. T. Eiter, N. Leone, C. Mateis, G. Pfeifer, and F. Scarcello. The KR System **dlv**: Progress Report, Comparisons and Benchmarks. in *Proc. of KR-98*, pp. 406–417. 427
5. M. Gelfond and V. Lifschitz. Classical Negation in Logic Programs and Disjunctive Databases. *New Generation Computing*, 9:365–385, 1991. 424, 425

System Description: The DLV$^\mathcal{K}$ Planning System[*]

Thomas Eiter[1], Wolfgang Faber[1], Nicola Leone[2],
Gerald Pfeifer[1], and Axel Polleres[1]

[1] Institut für Informationssysteme, TU Wien
A-1040 Wien, Austria
{eiter,faber,axel}@kr.tuwien.ac.at
pfeifer@dbai.tuwien.ac.at
[2] Department of Mathematics, University of Calabria
87030 Rende, Italy
leone@unical.it

1 Introduction

DLV$^\mathcal{K}$ is a knowledge based planning system. It is based on the declarative language $\mathcal{K}$ [2], which is similar in spirit to the logic-based language $\mathcal{C}$ [5], but includes some logic-programming features (e.g., default negation and strong negation). $\mathcal{K}$ offers the following distinguishing features:

- **handling of incomplete knowledge:** for a fluent f, in a state neither f nor its opposite $\neg f$ may be known.
- **nondeterministic effects:** actions may have multiple possible outcomes.
- **optimistic and secure (conformant) planning:** construction of a "credulous" plan or a "sceptical" plan, which works in all cases.
- **parallel actions:** More than one action may be executed simultaneously.

A fully operational prototype of DLV$^\mathcal{K}$, built as frontend on top of the DLV system [1], is available on the Web at

<URL:http://www.dbai.tuwien.ac.at/proj/dlv/>.

2 The DLV$^\mathcal{K}$ System by Example: Blocks World

We assume that the reader is familiar with action languages and the notion of actions, fluents, goals, and plans; see e.g. [4] for a background. To give a flavor of DLV$^\mathcal{K}$, we refer here to well-known planning problems in the blocks world, which require to turn given configurations of blocks into other ones (see Figure 1).

In DLV$^\mathcal{K}$, problem domains are defined in two parts: (i) a normal (disjunction-free) stratified logic program representing the **static background knowledge** of the domain, and (ii) a $\mathcal{K}$ **domain description**.

The static background knowledge of the blocks world consists of the following logic program:

---

[*] This work was supported by FWF (Austrian Science Funds) under the projects Z29-INF and P14781 and MURST under project COFIN-2000.

T. Eiter, W. Faber, and M. Truszczyński (Eds.): LPNMR 2001, LNAI 2173, pp. 429–433, 2001.
© Springer-Verlag Berlin Heidelberg 2001

Fig. 1. A blocks world example

```
block(a). block(b). block(c). location(table).
location(B) :- block(B).
```

Referring to Figure 1, we want to turn the initial configuration of blocks into the goal state[1] in three steps, where only one block may be moved in each step (i.e., concurrent moves are not permitted).

The $\mathcal{K}$ domain description uses an action move and two fluents on and occupied. We shall consider different scenarios. In a basic one, we assume that the knowledge in the initial state is complete (i.e., the locations of all blocks are known) and correctly specified. We will then show how to deal with incorrect and incomplete initial state specifications.

Basic version of blocks world. The domain description is in this case as follows:

```
fluents:    on(B,L) requires block(B), location(L).
            occupied(B) requires location(B).
actions:    move(B,L) requires block(B), location(L).
always:     executable move(B,L) if not occupied(B), not occupied(L),B <> L.
            inertial on(B,L).

            caused occupied(B) if on(B1,B), block(B).
            caused on(B,L) after move(B,L).
            caused -on(B,L1) after move(B,L), on(B,L1), L <> L1.
initially:  on(a,table). on(b,table). on(c,a).

            noConcurrency.
goal:       on(c,b),on(b,a),on(a,table)? (3)
```

First, each fluent and action has to be declared using a **type declaration**, which specifies the ranges of its arguments. The literals to the right of "requires" (block(B) and location(L)) must not involve default-negation "not" and must be defined in the static background knowledge.

The next part of our domain description consists of executability conditions and causation rules describing the possible states and transitions. Intuitively, the executable statement for action move(B,L) says that a block B can be moved on location L $\neq$ B if both B and L are clear (the table is always clear). in $\mathcal{K}$, multiple executable statements for the same action are allowed. An

---

[1] This is an implementation of the well-known Sussman Anomaly, similar to one in [3].

executable statement with empty body **executable A.** says that the action **A** is always executable. Execution of an action **A** under condition **B** is forbidden by **nonexecutable A if B.** In case of conflicting specifications, **nonexecutable A** overrides **executable A.**

The causation rules for **on** and **-on** specify the dynamic effects of a move. Informally, a causation rule **caused f if C1 after A, C2.** means that **f** is known to be true if **C1** holds in the state and actions in **A** have (not) been executed, and condition **C2** was true in the previous state. It is worthwhile noting that the totality of the fluenton is not enforced. Both **on(X,Y)** and **-on(X,Y)** may happen to be unknown at a given instant of time. Actually, the rule for **-on** could be replaced by "**caused -on(B,L1) if on(B,L), L <> L1.**" stating: wherever a block is, it is not anywhere else. This rule would give us a sharper description of the state making fluent **on** total at every instant of time. However, using the more general rule would cause a computational overhead (as more inferences are to be done during the computation) without providing relevant benefits.

The statement **inertial on(X,Y).** is a shortcut equivalent to the rule

> **caused on(X,Y) if not -on(X,Y) after on(X,Y).**

and encodes the principle of inertia for positive knowledge about **on.**
Static rules (i.e. rules with an empty **after** part) like

> **caused occupied(B) if on(B1,B), block(B).**

model a static causation. This can be used to model indirect effects of actions.

The **initially:** section of the domain description consists of facts/constraints which must be satisfied only in the initial state. Static rules are also allowed here.

Simultaneous execution of several actions is normally allowed in $\mathcal{K}$. This can be prohibited by the statement **noConcurrency.** which enforces the execution of at most one action at a time.

Finally, the **goal:** section defines the goal to be reached and the maximum plan length given as a positive integer.

The execution of the above DLV$^\mathcal{K}$ program computes the following result:

> **PLAN: move(c,table,0), move(b,a,1), move(c,b,2)**

Here, the additional argument in a **move** atom represents the instant of time when the action is executed. Thus, according to the above plan, first **c** is moved onto the table, then **b** is moved on top of **a**, and, finally, **c** is moved onto **b** which obviously leads to the desired goal.

Dealing with incomplete knowledge. To show the advanced capabilities of DLV$^\mathcal{K}$, we will extend our example now to deal with partial knowledge. Here we have to verify that every block: (i) is on top of a unique location, (ii) does not have more than one block on top of it, and (iii) is supported by the table (i.e., it is either on the table or on a stack of blocks which is on the table) [6]. To this end, we add a new fluent declaration

```
supported(B) requires block(B).
```

and the following rules in the initially section:

```
caused false if on(B,L), on(B,L1), L<>L1.
caused false if on(B1,B), on(B2,B), block(B), B1<>B2.
caused supported(B) if on(B,table).
caused supported(B) if on(B,B1), supported(B1).
caused false if not supported(B).
```

Note that, under noConcurrency, the action move preserves the properties (i), (ii), (iii) above; thus, we do not need to check these properties in all states, if concurrent actions are forbidden.

A further block Suppose now that we have another block d in Figure 1. The exact location of d is unknown, but we know that it is not on top of c.

We are interested in a plan that works on every possible initial state (i.e., no matter if on(d,b) or on(d,table) holds), and reaches the goal on(a,c), on(c,d), on(d,b), on(b,table) in four steps. We modify the domain description by adding (i) -on(d,c) and total on(X,Y) in the initially section, and (ii) the command securePlan. In $\mathcal{K}$, we can "totalize" the knowledge of a fluent f by declaring total f. which means that, unless a truth value for f is derivable, the cases where f resp. -f is true will be both considered. By securePlan. we ask the system to compute only *secure* plans (alias *conformant* plans in the literature). Informally, a plan is secure, if it works on every legal initial state, i.e., never gets stuck by nonexecutable actions or a non-existing next state, and always enforces the goal.

The execution of this program on DLV$^{\mathcal{K}}$ computes the following result:

```
PLAN: move(d,table,0), move(d,b,1), move(c,d,2), move(a,c,3)
```

The plan clearly works on the two legal initial states, and leads always to the desired result. Thus, the plan is secure. On the other hand, the 2-step plan move(c,d,0), move(a,c,1) it not secure. It works for the initial state in which d is on b, but if d is on the table, the goal state is not reached after its execution.

Further examples and detailed information on the planning system can be found on our website (<URL:http://www.dbai.tuwien.ac.at/proj/dlv/>).

References

1. T. Eiter, W. Faber, N. Leone, and G. Pfeifer. Declarative problem-solving using the DLV system. In: J. Minker (ed.), *Logic-Based Artificial Intelligence*, pp. 79–103. Kluwer, 2000. 429

2. T. Eiter, W. Faber, N. Leone, G. Pfeifer, and A. Polleres. Planning under incomplete knowledge. *Proc. CL 2000*, pp. 807–821, LNAI 1861, Springer, 2000. 429

3. E. Erdem. Applications of logic programming to planning: computational experiments. Draft, http://www.cs.utexas.edu/users/esra/papers.html, 1999. 430

4. M. Gelfond and V. Lifschitz. Action languages. *Electronic Transactions on Artificial Intelligence*, 3(16):193–210, 1998. 429
5. E. Giunchiglia and V. Lifschitz. An action language based on causal explanation: preliminary report. In *Proc. AAAI '98*, pp. 623–630, 1998. 429
6. V. Lifschitz. Answer set planning. *Proc. ICLP '99*, pp. 23–37. The MIT Press. 431

The Smodels System[*]

Tommi Syrjänen and Ilkka Niemelä

Helsinki University of Technology, Dept. of Computer Science and Eng., Laboratory
for Theoretical Computer Science,
P.O.Box 5400, FIN-02015 HUT, Finland
{Tommi.Syrjanen,Ilkka.Niemela}.@hut.fi

1 Introduction

The Smodels system is an Answer Set Programming (ASP) implementation
based on the stable model semantics of normal logic programs. The basic idea
of ASP is to encode the constraints of a problem as a logic program such that
the answer sets (stable models) of the program correspond to the solutions of
the problem. Then we can solve the problem by letting a logic program engine
to find the answer sets of the program.

The Smodels system provides such an engine for computing answer sets. It
extends the class of normal logic programs with cardinality and weight constraints as well as arithmetic built-in functions. Additionally, function symbols
are also supported. However, the input programs have to be *domain-restricted*
in a sense that will be explained in Section 2. The Smodels system is available
for download at http://www.tcs.hut.fi/Software/smodels.

For a practical Smodels example, consider the following logical puzzle: *On the
Island of Knights and Knaves there are two types of persons: knights, who always
tell the truth, and knaves, who always lie. A visiting logician met two natives, A
and B. When asked about their types, A answered: "We are both knaves." What
are their types?* We can solve the puzzle with the following Smodels program:

```
person(a; b). type(knight; knave).
1 { is_type(P, T) : type(T) } 1 :- person(P).
true_statement :- is_type(a, knave), is_type(b, knave).
    :- is_type(a, knight), not true_statement.
    :- is_type(a, knave), true_statement.
```

Here the first line defines facts for the persons and types, and the second line
assigns a unique type for all persons. The third line tells that A's answer is true
if both of them are knaves and the last two rules enforce the condition that
knights never lie and knaves never tell the truth. The constructs of the form
L { $l_1, l_2, \ldots, l_n$ } U are *cardinality constraints* that are satisfied whenever the
number of satisfied literals l_i is between the integral bounds L and U, inclusive. A
cardinality constraint in a rule head imposes a non-deterministic *choice* over the

[*] This work has been funded by Academy of Finland (project no. 43963). The work
of the first author has been supported by HeCSE and Tekniikan edistämissäätiö.

T. Eiter, W. Faber, and M. Truszczyński (Eds.): LPNMR 2001, LNAI 2173, pp. 434–438, 2001.

literals in it when the rule body is satisfied. The construct $a(X) : b(X)$ denotes the set of atoms $a(X)$ for which $b(X)$ also holds. For example, $is\_type(P,T) :$ $type(T)$ denotes the set $\{is\_type(P, knight), is\_type(P, knave)\}$.

The Smodels system itself consists of two parts, smodels, which is the actual inference engine, and lparse, a front-end that instantiates and simplifies user programs. If we have stored the above program in a file puzzle.lp, we can find its answer sets by invocating Smodels as follows:

```
% lparse -d none puzzle.lp | smodels 0
smodels version 2.26. Reading...done
Answer: 1
Stable Model: is_type(a,knave) is_type(b,knight)
False
```

We see that in the unique solution A is a knave and B is a knight. The lparse argument '-d none' discards the domain predicates *person* and *type* from the output, and the argument '0' asks smodels to compute all stable models.

2   Theoretical Background

The Smodels system has a declarative formal semantics that extends the stable model semantics of normal logic programs with cardinality and weight constraints. Intuitively, a set of atoms is a stable model of if it satisfies all rules of the program and each atom in the model occurs as a head of a rule with a satisfied body. A program may have none, one, or many stable models. The details of the semantics are explained in Niemelä and Simons [8].

The predicate symbols of a Smodels program P are automatically divided into two classes, *domain* and *non-domain predicates*. The domain predicates of P are the predicates that are not defined in terms of negative recursion or using choice rules, and they form a stratified hierarchy where complex domains are defined in terms of simple ones. The intuition of domain predicates is that they are used to define the set of terms over which the variables range in each rule of the program. All rules in a program have to be *domain-restricted* in the sense that each variable in a rule has to occur also in a positive domain predicate in the rule body. In a rule defining a domain predicate this *domain literal* has to belong to a strictly lower stratum than the head of the rule. This syntactic restriction is strong enough to guarantee that the problem of finding an answer set stays decidable even when function symbols are allowed since it ensures that only a finite number of ground atoms can be derived using a single rule [11]. Consider the following program:

```
number(0..n). even(0).
even(X+1) :- number(X), odd(X).
odd(X+1) :- number(X), even(X).
interesting(X) :- odd(X), not dull(X).
dull(X) :- odd(X), not interesting(X).
```

The predicate *number* is trivially a domain predicate since it does not depend on any other predicates. Here n is a numeric constant that can be defined from the command line. Predicates *even* and *odd* are also domain predicates since they depend only on each other and on *number* that gives the domain for X in the two recursive rules. If we left the atom $number(X)$ out of the rule bodies, the stable models of the program would be infinite. The predicates *interesting* and *dull* are not domain predicates since they depend negatively on each other.

The computational complexity of determining whether there exists an answer set of a propositional Smodels program is NP-complete. For function-free programs with variables, it is EXP-complete and when function symbols are used, it is 2-EXP-complete [11]. Thus, the high expressive power has a significant computational cost.

3 Implementation

The Smodels system is composed of two independent components, smodels and lparse, that are both implemented in C++. The smodels finds answer sets of variable-free primitive logic programs using a Davis-Putnam like backtracking search procedure [9]. It also uses inherent properties of the stable model semantics to infer and propagate truth values to prune the search space. The lparse is a front-end that translates user programs into the smodels internal format by instantiating non-ground rules and simplifying complex constructs.The lparse first creates the dependency graph of the program and identifies the domain predicates by computing strongly connected components of the graph. Next, the extensions of the domain predicates are computed and they are used to instantiate the rest of the rules.

4 Applications

The Smodels system is actively used in dozens of research groups all over the world. Next we briefly review some interesting application areas already studied.

Planning is a potential application area for ASP and Smodels has been used in a number of approaches, see e.g. [4,10]. An interesting example of an advanced project is research at Texas Tech University on developing a decision support system for the flight controllers of space shuttles using the ASP approach [3].

General methodology for product configuration using ASP techniques has been developed and interesting application projects have been started, see

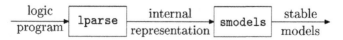

Fig. 1. System Architecture

e.g. the WeCoTin project (http://www.soberit.hut.fi/WeCoTin/). Research on software configuration using ASP has lead to a prototype configurator for the Debian Linux system distribution (http://www.tcs.hut.fi/~tssyrjan/configuration/). Smodels has been used for a variety of key inference tasks in computer aided verification. An analysis method for Petri nets based on finite complete prefixes has been built on top of Smodels, see the mcsmodels and unfsmodels tools (http://www.tcs.hut.fi/~kepa/tools/). Similarly, it has been used in a stubborn set reduction method for Petri net reachability analysis, see the prod tool (http://www.tcs.hut.fi/Software/prod/). Recently, a symbolic model checking method for asynchronous systems based on bounded model checking techniques and ASP has been developed [5].

There are a number other interesting areas where Smodels has been employed including logical cryptanalysis [6], security protocol analysis [1], network inhibition analysis [2], and computation of (total and partial) stable models for disjunctive programs [7].

References

1. L. C. Aiello and F. Massacci. An executable specification language for planning attacks to security protocols. In *Proc. of the IEEE Computer Security Foundations Workshop*, pages 88–102, Cambridge, UK, 2000. IEEE Computer Society Press. 437
2. T. Aura, M. Bishop, and D. Sniegowski. Analyzing single-server network inhibition. In *Proc. of the IEEE Computer Security Foundations Workshop*, pages 108–117, Cambridge, UK, July 2000. IEEE Computer Society Press. 437
3. M. Balduccini, M. Barry, M. Gelfond, M. Nogueira, and R. Watson. An A-Prolog decision support system for the space shuttle. In *Proc. of the Third International Symposium on Practical Aspects of Declarative Languages*. Springer-Verlag, 2001. 436
4. Y. Dimopoulos, B. Nebel, and J. Koehler. Encoding planning problems in non-monotonic logic programs. In *Proceedings of the Fourth European Conference on Planning*, pages 169–181, Toulouse, France, September 1997. Springer-Verlag. 436
5. K. Heljanko and I. Niemelä. Bounded LTL model checking with stable models. In *Proceedings of the 6th International Conference on Logic Programming and Non-monotonic Reasoning*, Vienna, Austria, September 2001. Springer-Verlag. 437
6. M. Hietalahti, F. Massacci, and I. Niemelä. DES: a challenge problem for non-monotonic reasoning systems. In *Proc. of the 8th International Workshop on Non-Monotonic Reasoning*, Breckenridge, Colorado, USA, April 2000. cs.AI/0003039. 437
7. T. Janhunen, I. Niemelä, P. Simons, and J. You. Unfolding partiality and disjunctions in stable model semantics. In *Proceedings of the Seventh International Conference on Principles of Knowledge Representation and Reasoning*, pages 411–419, Breckenridge, Colorado, USA, April 2000. Morgan Kaufmann Publishers. 437
8. I. Niemelä and P. Simons. Extending the Smodels system with cardinality and weight constraints. In Jack Minker, editor, *Logic-Based Artificial Intelligence*, chapter 21, pages 491–521. Kluwer Academic Publishers, 2000. 435

9. P. Simons. Extending and implementing the stable model semantics. Research Report 58, Helsinki University of Technology, Helsinki, Finland, 2000. 436
10. T. C. Son, C. Baral, and S. McIlraith. Extending answer set planning with sequence, conditional, loop, non-deterministic choice, and procedure constructs. In *Proceedings of the AAAI Spring 2001 Symposium on Answer Set Programming*, pages 202–209, Stanford, USA, March 2001. AAAI Press. 436
11. T. Syrjänen. Omega-restricted logic programs. In *Proc. of the 6th Intl. Conference on Logic Programming and Nonmonotonic Reasoning*. Springer-Verlag, 2001. 435, 436

The USA-Advisor:
A Case Study in Answer Set Planning

Marcello Balduccini, Michael Gelfond, R. Watson, and M. Nogueira

[1] Department of Computer Science, Texas Tech University
Lubbock, TX 79409, USA
{balduccini,mgelfond,rwatson}@cs.ttu.edu
[2] Department of Computer Science, The University of Texas at El Paso
El Paso, TX 79968, USA
monica@cs.utep.edu

Abstract. In this work we show how control knowledge was used to improve planning in the USA-Advisor decision support system for the Space Shuttle. The USA-Advisor is a medium size, real-world planning application for use by NASA flight controllers and contains over a dozen domain dependent and domain independent heuristics. Experimental results are presented here, illustrating how this control knowledge helps improve both the quality of plans as well as overall system performance.

1 Introduction

This paper is a report on the development of a medium size, real-world application, the USA-Advisor[1] - a decision support system for the Space Shuttle flight controllers. While the methods used in this work are general enough to model any of the subsystems of the shuttle, our initial prototype models the Reaction Control System (RCS) [1]. This system maneuvers the Space Shuttle while it is in orbit. In order for the Space Shuttle to perform a given maneuver, a set of jets, belonging to one or more of the three RCS's subsystems, and pointing in the correct directions, must be prepared to fire. Preparing a jet to fire involves providing an open, non-leaking path for the fuel to flow from fuel tanks to the jet. Fuel flow is controlled by opening and closing valves through either having an astronaut flip a switch or by instructing the computer to issue special commands. Switches are connected to valves through fairly complex electrical circuits.

Plans can been created for simple, single failure situations, but it is impossible to create in advance plans for every possible combination of failures. The USA-Advisor was designed to help verify and generate plans for operation in such situations. More details on the design of the system can be found in [2].

---

[1] The USA-Advisor was created with the support of, United Space Alliance under Research Grant 26-3502-21 and Contract COC6771311. The authors thank Matt Barry of the USA Advanced Technology Development Group for his technical support.

T. Eiter, W. Faber, and M. Truszczyński (Eds.): LPNMR 2001, LNAI 2173, pp. 439–442, 2001.
© Springer-Verlag Berlin Heidelberg 2001

2 The USA-Advisor

The USA-Advisor consists of a collection of largely independent modules and a graphical Java interface. The interface gives a simple way for the user to enter information about the history of the RCS, its faults, and the task to be performed. There are two possible types of tasks: checking if a sequence of occurrences of actions satisfies a goal, G, and finding a plan for G of a length not exceeding some number of steps, N. Based on this information, the interface verifies if the input is complete, selects an appropriate combination of modules, assembles them into an A-Prolog[2] program, Π, and passes Π as an input to SMODELS[3] - a reasoning system for computing stable models. In this approach, the task of checking a plan P is reduced to checking if there exists a stable model of the program $\Pi \cup P$. A planning module is used to generate a set of possible plans and a correctness theorem guarantees that there is a one-to-one correspondence between the plans and the set of stable models of the program. Planning is reduced to finding such models. Finally, the Java interface extracts the appropriate answer from the SMODELS output and displays it in a user-friendly format.

3 The Planners

To investigate the role of heuristics on the efficiency of the USA-Advisor, we ran experiments using two different planning modules. The structure of the Basic Planner, a planning module that contains no control information, follows the generate and test approach from [3,4]. Since the RCS contains more than 200 actions, with rather complex effects, and may require long plans, this standard approach needed to be improved. This was done by adding various forms of heuristic, domain-dependent information. We refer to the Basic Planner expanded by such heuristics as the Smart Planner. The modular design of the USA-Advisor allows for the creation of a variety of such modules. Coding the control knowledge information in A-Prolog is straightforward and does not require any additional language features. We do not present here examples of such heuristics because of space limitations.

One interesting characteristic of the RCS domain is that the goal can be *decomposed* in independent subgoals which can be solved in *parallel*. Parallel subgoals can easily be coded in A-Prolog and were used in both planners.

4 Experiments

In this section we give an overview of our experiments with the two planners used by the USA-Advisor. We used a 933 Mhz Pentium III computer with 128 MB of RAM, running the NetBSD 1.5 Operating System; SMODELS version 2.26 with input from Lparse version 1.0.2 were used to find the plans.

---

[2] The language of logic programs under the answer set semantics.

[3] http://www.tcs.hut.fi/Software/smodels

By a *test instance* we mean a collection of system faults together with a maneuver to be performed by the shuttle. There are two possible types of faults: *mechanical* faults which render valves, switches or jets non-functional; and *electrical* faults which affect electrical circuits by having a value of 0 or 1 permanently present on the input or output wire(s) of a component.

In the first series of experiments, we: randomly generated a collection of test instances with a given number of mechanical and electrical faults; run the basic and the smart planners in a loop with *lasttime* ranging from 3 to 10. The duration of each iteration of the loop was limited to 10 minutes.

Overall, about 500 test instances were generated in this manner. Here we discuss the performance of both planners for 60 instances containing three mechanical and two electrical faults (the most interesting situation from the standpoint of the USA experts). In all 60 cases, the Smart Planner was able to find the plans or discover their absence in less than 22 seconds. The Basic Planner required substantially more time. In some cases the difference exceeded 2 orders of magnitude. On average the Smart Planner was about 10 times faster. The plans generated by both planners did not exceed 15 actions performed in 5 steps. Other random experiments run on tests with numbers of faults between 3 and 8 did not produce any new insights. The plans produced by the Smart Planner were of good quality. They were minimal in the number of steps and satisfied the requirements of the USA experts. The Basic Planner did substantially worse, finding only one plan of good quality.

The second series of experiments dealt with our deliberate attempt to crash the system. We selected a number of test instances which correspond to especially difficult situations. Even though the size of the grounded programs (up to 156,500 rules), length of plans (7 to 8 time steps), and number of actions involved (up to 24) are substantially larger than those in the initial experiments, the time is still quite acceptable. Each test run took less than 90 seconds while the USA's requirement set the limit at 15 minutes. In contrast, the Basic Planner was not able to find solutions to any of these problems - in each instance we stopped the planner after 24 hours of CPU work. It is interesting to note that to achieve this performance we need all of the Smart Planner heuristics. Even though removal of some of them gave us small improvements on a few test instances, on others the performance was worsened by more than an order of magnitude.

5 Conclusion

In this paper we described experiments with two planners used by a medium size decision support system[4] written in A-Prolog. The domain of the planners and their construction can be of interest to the reader from several different standpoints.

---

[4] The code for the USA-Advisor and details on experiment results are available on request from the authors.

- Since a single action of an astronaut changes the values of many inter-related fluents of the RCS the description of effects of this action becomes a non-trivial task. We solved this problem by using the techniques developed in theory of actions and change and the power of A-Prolog rules. It is not clear to us how these effects could be accurately represented by more traditional STRIPS like action languages.
- A-Prolog proved to be a language capable of specifying the initial situation, causal and other relations of the domain, as well as the heuristic information limiting the search space and improving quality of plans. This contrasts with some of the other representational approaches which require separate languages for each of these classes of statements.
- Answer set planning proved to be a good tool for our purpose. Partly this is due to non-numerical nature of the problem. But the planner's ability to mix parallel and sequential plans and to efficiently search for them are the key ingredients in the success of the project.
- The heuristics used in the Smart Planner were easy to encode and to use. Our experiments show that they significantly improve both, quality of plans and efficiency of search.
- It was interesting to notice that many fluents of the RCS domain had natural recursive definitions, easily expressible in A-Prolog. This simplified the representation but precluded the immediate use of CCALC[5] style planning with satisfiability solvers. It will be interesting to see if such solvers could be used after some modifications of the representation. It is probably also worth mentioning that non-monotonicity of A-Prolog played an important role in the formalization of the domain, e.g. in specifying the inertia axiom, closed world assumptions used for describing the initial situation, and other typical default knowledge.
- The complexity of representing indirect effects of actions and the seemingly essential presence of recursion make a question of building the USA-Advisor, not based on A-Prolog, an interesting (possibly not trivial) open question.

References

1. Balduccini, M., Gelfond, M., and Nogueira, M.: A-Prolog as a tool for declarative programming. In *Procs of SEKE'00*, (2000), 63–72 439
2. Balduccini, M., Barry, M., Gelfond, M., Nogueira, M., and Watson, R.: An A-Prolog decision support system for the Space Shuttle. *LNCS Procs of PADL'01*, (2001), 1990:169–183 439
3. Dimopoulos, Y., Nebel, B., and Koehler, J.: Encoding planning problems in non-monotonic logic programs. *LNAI Proceedings of ECP'97*, (1997), 1348:169–18 440
4. Lifschitz, V.: Action languages, Answer Sets, and Planning. In *The Logic Programming Paradigm: a 25-Year Perspective*, Spring-Verlag, (1999), 357–373 440

---

[5] http://www.cs.utexas.edu/users/tag/cc

Author Index

Lecture Notes in Artificial Intelligence (LNAI)

Lecture Notes in Computer Science